France

Vintage	Red Bordeaux		White Bordeaux		Alsace
	Médoc/Graves	Pom/St-Ém	Sauternes & sw	Graves & dry	
2023	7–8	6–8	7–8	7–8	7–8
2022	7–8	7–8	7–9	6–7	6–7
2021	5–7	5–7	7–8	7–9	6–8
2020	7–8	7–9	7–8	7–8	8–9
2019	7–9	6–9	7–8	7–9	6–8
2018	8–9	8–9	7–9	7–8	7–8
2017	6–8	6–7	8–9	7–8	9–10
2016	8–9	8–9	8–10	7–9	7–8
2015	7–9	8–10	8–10	7–9	7–9
2014	7–8	6–8	8–9	8–9	7–8
2013	4–7	4–7	8–9	7–8	8–9
2012	6–8	6–8	5–6	7–9	8–9
2011	7–8	7–8	8–10	7–8	5–7
2010	8–10	7–10	7–8	7–9	8–9
2009	7–10	7–10	8–10	7–9	8–9
2008	6–8	6–9	6–7	7–8	7–8
2007	5–7	6–7	8–9	8–9	6–8
2006	7–8	7–8	7–8	8–9	6–8
2005	9–10	8–9	7–9	8–10	8–9

France, continued

Vintage	Burgundy			Rhône	
	Côte d'Or red	Côte d'Or white	Chablis	North	South
2023	7–9	6–8	7–8	6–8	6–8
2022	7–9	7–9	7–8	7–8	6–8
2021	6–8	7–8	7–8	6–8	6–8
2020	6–8	7–9	6–8	7–8	6–8
2019	7–9	7–10	7–9	8–9	7–9
2018	6–9	7–8	7–8	7–9	6–8
2017	6–9	8–9	8–9	7–9	7–9
2016	7–8	6–8	5–7	7–9	8–9
2015	7–9	6–8	7–8	8–9	8–9
2014	6–8	8–9	7–9	7–8	6–8
2013	5–7	6–7	6–8	7–9	7–8
2012	8–9	7–8	7–8	7–9	7–9
2011	7–8	7–8	7–8	7–8	6–8
2010	8–10	8–10	8–10	8–10	8–9

Beaujolais 23 22 21 20 19 18 17 15 14, crus will keep. **Mâcon-Villages** white 23 22 21 20 19 18 17 15. **Loire** sweet Anjou, Touraine 23 22 21 20 19 18 15 10 09 07 05 02 97 96 93 90; Bourgueil, Chinon, Saumur-Champigny 23 22 21 20 19 18 17 15 14 10 09 06 05 04; Sancerre, Pouilly-Fumé 23 22 21 20 19 18 17 15 14; Muscadet 23 22 21 20 19 18 17 16 15 14.

HUGH
JOHNSON'S
POCKET
WINE BOOK
2025

Hugh Johnson's Pocket Wine Book 2025

First published in Great Britain in 2024 by Mitchell Beazley,
an imprint of Octopus Publishing Group Limited,
Carmelite House, 50 Victoria Embankment,
London EC4Y 0DZ
www.octopusbooks.co.uk

An Hachette UK Company
www.hachette.co.uk

First edition published 1977

Revised editions published 1978, 1979, 1980, 1981, 1982,
1983, 1984, 1985, 1986, 1987, 1988, 1989, 1990, 1991, 1992,
1993, 1994, 1995, 1996, 1997, 1998, 1999, 2000, 2001, 2002
(twice), 2003, 2004, 2005, 2006 (twice), 2007, 2008, 2009,
2010, 2011, 2012, 2013, 2014, 2015, 2016, 2017, 2018, 2019,
2020, 2021, 2022, 2023, 2024

Distributed in the US by Hachette Book Group
1290 Avenue of the Americas, 4th and 5th Floors,
New York, NY 10104

Distributed in Canada by Canadian Manda Group
664 Annette St., Toronto, Ontario, Canada M6S 2C8

ISBN (UK): 978-1-78472-870-0
ISBN (US): 978-1-78472-959-2

General Editor **Margaret Rand**
Commissioning Editor **Hilary Lumsden**
Senior Developmental Editor **Pauline Bache**
Proofreader **David Tombesi-Walton**
Art Director **Yasia Williams-Leedham**
Designer **Jeremy Tilston**
Picture Researchers **Giulia Hetherington and Jennifer Veall**
Senior Production Manager **Katherine Hockley**

Printed and bound in China

Mitchell Beazley would like to acknowledge and thank the following
for supplying photographs for use in this book:

Alamy Stock Photo: B.A.E. Inc. 24; Bouchard Pere & Fils 333; **Cephas
Picture Library Ltd.:** © Kevin Judd 327; **Dreamstime.com:** Michal Oska 336,
Rostislav Sedlacek 7; **Getty Images:** Imagno/brandstaetter images/Hulton
Archive 323; **iStock:** FiledIMAGE 321, Giovanni Magda-linos 6, Gregory_
DUBUS 10; Margaret Rand 331; **Pexels:** Pixabay 12, Vics 1; Weinhaus Heger
OHG/Peter Bender 328–29; Wiston Estate 334–35.

HUGH
JOHNSON'S
POCKET
WINE BOOK
2025

GENERAL EDITOR
MARGARET RAND

Contributors

To demonstrate that no one person can be up-to-date with the vinous affairs of every wine-producing country in the world, this is the book's team of contributors:

Key: ❶ Facebook; ❷ Instagram; ❸ X; ❹ website; ❺ book/press; ❻ blog/other media

Helena Baker DipWSET, Czechia, Slovakia: ❶ helena.baker.73; ❷ @bakerwine837; ❸ @HelenaB62554469; ❹ bakerwine.cz

Kristel Balcaen DipWSET, Belgium: ❶ kristel.balcaen.1; ❷ @kristel_balcaen; ❹ wineandwords.be; ❺ *Wijnboek voor Foodies*

Amanda Barnes, S America: ❶ SouthAmericaWineGuide; ❷ @southamericawineguide; ❸ @amanda_tweeter; ❺ *South America Wine Guide*

Raymond Blake, Burgundy: ❷+❸ @blakeonwine; blakeonwine.com; ❺ *Wine Talk*

Juliet Bruce Jones MW, Midi, Provence, Corsica: ❶ latasque; ❷ @domainelatasque; ❹ domainelatasque.com

Ch'ng Poh Tiong, Asia: ❶+❷ @Chngpohtiong, 100TopChineseRestaurants; chngpohtiong.com, wineguru.com.sg, 100chineserestaurants.com

Samantha Cole-Johnson, Oregon: ❷ @samanthacolejohnson; ❹ jancisrobinson.com

Michael Cooper ONZM, NZ: ❶ MichaelCooperNZWine; ❹ michaelcooper.co.nz; ❺ *New Zealand Wines: Michael Cooper's Buyer's Guide; Wine Atlas of New Zealand*

Ian D'Agata, Alsace, Italy, Malta: ❷ @ian_dagata; ❹ iandagata.com, terroirsense.com; ❺ *Italy's Native Wine Grape Terroirs; Native Wine Grapes of Italy*

Sarah Jane Evans MW, Spain: ❶ Sarah Jane Evans MW; ❷+❸ @sjevansmw; ❹ sarahjaneevans.com; ❺ *The Wines of Northern Spain*

Jane Faulkner, Australia: ❶+❷+❸ @winematters; ❺ *Halliday Wine Companion*

Simon Field MW, Champagne: ❺ *The World of Fine Wine*

Caroline Gilby MW, E Europe, Cyprus: ❶ Caroline Gilby; ❷ @Caroline Gilby; ❺ *The Wines of Bulgaria, Romania and Moldova*

Susan H Gordon PhD MFA, US E States: ❷ @susanhillaryg; ❺ *ForbesLife; Gastronomica; The Story of Prosecco Superiore*

Michael Karam, Lebanon: ❺ *Wines of Lebanon; Arak and Mezze; Tears of Bacchus; Lebanese Wine: A Complete Guide*); ❻ *Wine and War* (Amazon Prime)

Chris Kissack, Loire ❶ drchriskissack; ❷+❸ @chriswinedoctor; ❹ thewinedoctor.com

James Lawther MW, Bordeaux: ❹ jancisrobinson.com; ❺ *The Finest Wines of Bordeaux; On Bordeaux*

Konstantinos Lazarakis MW, Greece: ❶ Konstantinos Lazarakis II; ❷ @Konstantinos Lazarakis MW; ❸ @Lazarakis; ❹ wspc.gr, aioloswines.gr; ❺ *The Wines of Greece*

John Livingstone-Learmonth, Rhône: ❸ @drinkrhone; ❹ drinkrhone.com; ❺ *The Wines of the Northern Rhône*

Michele Longo, Italy: ❷ @michele_nebbiolo; ❹ iandagata.com; ❺ *The Grapes and Wines of Italy; Barolo Terroir: Grapes Crus People Places; Barolo & Co*

Wink Lorch, Bugey, Jura, Savoie: ❶+❷+❸ @WinkLorch; ❹ winetravelmedia.com; ❺ *Jura Wine; Wines of the French Alps* ❻ jurawine.co.uk

Adam Sebag Montefiore, Israel, Turkey, N Africa: ❹ adammontefiore.com, wines-israel.com; ❺ *Jerusalem Post; The Wine Route of Israel; Wines of Israel*

Marcel Orford Williams, SW France: ❸ @owmarcel

Rod Phillips, Canada ❸ @rodphillipswine; ❹ rodphillipsonwine.com; ❺ *The Wines of Canada; French Wine: A History; 9000 Years of Wine*

Margaret Rand, General Editor, England: *see back flap of book*

André Ribeirinho, Portugal: ❶+❷+❸ @andrerib; ❹ andrerib.co

Ulrich Sautter, Germany, Switzerland, Luxembourg: ❹ falstaff.com, weinverstand.com

Luzia Schrampf, Austria: ❶+❷ @Luzia Schrampf; ❺ *111 Austrian Wines You Must Not Miss; 111 Sparkling Wines Worldwide You Must Not Miss* (both with D Dejnega)

Eleonora Scholes, Black Sea & Caucasus: ❷ @spaziovino; ❹ spaziovino.com

Sean P Sullivan, Washington State & Idaho: ❶+❷ @northwestwinereport; ❸ @nwwinereport; ❹ northwestwinereport.com; ❺ *Seattle Metropolitan*

Tim Teichgraeber, California: ❷ @timskyscraper; ❻ modernwine.blogspot.com

James Tidwell MS, US SW&SE States, Wisconsin, Mexico: ❶ JamesTidwellMS; ❷+❸ @winejames; ❹ texsom.com

Philip van Zyl, S Africa: ❺ *Platter's by Diners Club South African Wine Guide*

Contents

The top line of most entries consists of the following information:

1. Aglianico del Vulture Bas

2. ★★★

3. 15' 16 17 18 19' 20 (21)

1. Aglianico del Vulture Bas

Wine name and region. Abbreviations of regions are listed in each section.

2. ★★★

Indication of quality – a necessarily rough-and-ready guide:

★	plain, everyday quality
★★	above average
★★★	excellent
★★★★	outstanding, compelling
★ etc.	Stars are coloured for any wine that, in our experience, is usually especially good within its price range. There are good everyday wines, as well as good luxury wines. This system helps you find them.

We try to be objective, but no wine rating can ever be wholly objective.

3. 15' 16 17 18 19' 20 (21)

Vintage information: those recent vintages that are outstanding, and of these, which are ready to drink this year, and which will probably improve with keeping. Your choice for current drinking should be one of the vintage years printed in **bold** type.

Buy light-type years for further maturing.

21 etc.	recommended years that may be currently available
20' etc.	vintage regarded as particularly successful for the property in question
17 etc.	years in bold should be ready for drinking (those not in bold will benefit from keeping)
19 etc.	vintages in colour are those recommended as first choice for drinking in 2025. (*See also* Bordeaux introduction, p.101)
(22) etc.	provisional rating

How to use this book

The German vintages work on a different principle again: *see* p.170.

Abbreviations

Style references appear in brackets where required:

r	red
w	white
dr	dry
sw	sweet
s/sw	semi-sweet
sp	sparkling

DYA	drink the youngest available
NV	Non Vintage; in Champagne this means a blend of several vintages for continuity
CHABLIS	properties, areas or terms cross-referred within the section; all grapes cross-ref to Grape Varieties chapter on pp.12–22
Foradori	entries styled this way indicate wine especially enjoyed by Margaret Rand and/or the author of that section (mid-2023–24)

For help in sourcing wines in this book we recommend winesearcher.com

If you have any feedback, please contact us on pocketwine@octopusbooks.co.uk

How much should one pay for a bottle of wine? Even as I write that, I'm conscious that it's the wrong question: we all know how much we should pay. What is interesting is another question: how much is it reasonable for a wine to cost?

In this year's *Pocket Wine Book* we talk about wines at a great many price points. We don't talk much about the very cheapest, because they are sold on price alone and rarely have much else to recommend them. If you are interested enough in wine to buy this book, you probably already know that by paying more than the absolute minimum you get a big uptick in quality, simply because a larger proportion of the price is for the wine rather than the tax.

But once you start going up in price, there seems to be no limit to what wine can cost. It's easy, once you get into the luxury market, to find wines at £600–700 ($750–850) a bottle. Top California Cabs, top red Bordeaux will cost that. Top burgundy? At the time of writing, a bottle of Domaine Leflaive Montrachet Grand Cru 2015 could be had for around £1400 ($1750) a bottle. If you wanted a bottle of Domaine Leroy, you could have a bottle of Bourgogne Rouge for £240 ($300) or a bottle of Musigny for a price in five or six figures. Yes, a bottle.

What dictates such prices? Rarity, and demand. Most proprietors – all, probably – would say that the art of setting a price is finding the precise point at which demand intersects with supply. Price a wine too high, and you're stuck with it.

There are examples of this in Bordeaux, which has the biggest secondary market of any wine. New proprietors sometimes set an en primeur price that they think the market ought to pay for their wine; this is normally, funnily enough, considerably more than it has paid up to that point. The results can become clear embarrassingly quickly: on the Bordeaux internal market, the Place, the price will soon drop to what the market considers the proper price. This happened to Yquem some years ago; the market might understand the extraordinary costs involved in making Sauternes (possibly the highest of any wine), but it still wasn't prepared to pay the price the owner of Yquem thought it should.

The cost of making a bottle of top wine in the leading vineyards of the world is probably seldom more than €25. Sauternes is higher because of its enormous vintage variation: in a bad year, production costs here might be as high as €60. These figures do not take into account the price of land, if you have to buy it. On the Côte d'Or, top Grand Cru vineyard is now so expensive that not only can families not afford to inherit it (because of the tax), but those who buy it – usually billionaires or their multi-national companies – cannot expect to make a profit for several generations.

How much do consumers think about the cost price of wine? Probably not much, is the answer. If you were about to pay €800 for a bottle of burgundy, would you base your decision on what profit the grower was making on that bottle? No: you would buy it because you wanted it and reckoned that it was an acceptable price. Because nobody's making you buy it. It costs that much because enough people want it. They may want it for reasons you consider spurious: prestige or investment, as opposed to your pure, unsullied wish to enjoy the taste. And if your view is that no wine should cost that much, because the cost price cannot be more than x, then maybe I could point you towards the only thing I can think of where price does not rocket with quality or demand: books.

But back to wine. What does a wine have to taste like to be worth £1000 ($1250) or more a bottle?

Certainly, one that costs £1000 will not be twice as good as one that costs £500 ($650). And a £500 bottle will not be twice as good as a £250 ($300) one. But a £50 ($65) bottle might well be twice as good as a £25 ($30) one – though please don't ask me how one might measure that. And yes, a £25 bottle should be twice as good as a £12.50 ($16) bottle, which in turn might well be more than twice as good as a £6.25 ($8) bottle. At the bottom end, quality rises faster than price. Then at the top (though there never seems to be an absolute top), every minute increase in quality can produce a startling increase in price.

Providing, that is, that it comes from a fashionable region, probably Burgundy. For those of us who are not in the market for such wines, it means that there are many, many other wines that don't cost as much, because for the moment the market won't accept astonishing prices. The Rhône, for example. Rosés from outside Provence. Garnacha from Spain's Gredos. Carricante from Italy's Etna. Sherry. German Riesling.

This last is one of the great wines of the world, is it not? Yes, Germany has its VDP auctions, glitzy events at which rare bottlings are sold, hopefully for remarkable prices that alert drinkers and collectors to the glories they might be missing. But those headline wines have a vast hinterland of reasonably priced wines of fascination, of intriguing, layered, coiled flavours; wines to lay down and return to a few years later; of young growers branching out in all directions.

Our supplement this year is on Pinot Noir, but that doesn't have to mean Grand Cru burgundy. There are great Pinots from Germany, from Australia, from Chile – look for the unexpected. And be aware of that shifting sweet spot where price and quality are just where you need them to be.

Ten wines to try in 2025

Four whites and six reds this year, not least because I've tasted so many incredible Pinot Noirs and had to include two, plus a Grenache that Pinot-lovers should note. All startled me with their quality.

White wines

Vinho de Talha Branco, Cartuxa, Alentejo, Portugal

A *talha* is a clay amphora, as used in Portugal's Alentejo for centuries, and now fashionable again. This is a supple, fluid wine with enough skin tannins to give it texture – like the brush of a bird's feather. The fruit has notes of herbs, orange pith and fresh Victoria plum, and it's fresh, alive and would be extremely useful with food.

Misco Riserva, Tenuta di Tavignano, Verdicchio di Castelli di Jesi, Marches, Italy

Verdicchio is hugely underrated: resolutely non-aromatic and slightly tannic, it's a white wine masquerading as a red, for food-matching purposes. This is energetic, sappy and grippy, with flavours of almonds and tarragon. After eight years or so, deep, rich flavours of apricot emerge as if from nowhere, and it gets silkier and fatter. To drink it too young is to miss most of what it can offer.

Archineri, Pietrodolce, Etna, Sicily, Italy

Etna is a charismatic wine region; and this is made by one of its leading names, from 130-year-old Carricante vines grown, like all Etna wines, in lava that over the centuries and millennia has weathered into powdery, black, mineral-rich soil. Think of honey and fennel and a fine, tense structure with lovely acidity and a long finish; it's very concentrated and wears it lightly, but it will age happily, and become more honeyed, for 10–20 years.

Rotsbank, The Sadie Family Wines, Swartland, S Africa

Everything Eben Sadie makes is wonderful, but this wine has tension and a sense of effortlessness. It's pure Chenin Blanc, bright, deep, subtle, sleek and pure, grown on shallow topsoil on a rock shelf. The vineyard, bought in 2021, is clearly outstanding: the wine is leaner than Skurfberg Chenin, with knife-edge precision, perfect focus. There is fine acidity and depth, salt and silk, earth and power and great length. Given the price of fine wine today, it's also rather good value.

Red wines

Centgrafenberg Spätburgunder Grosse Lage, Weingut Fürst, Franken, Germany

Pinot Noir is now a star grape in Germany, and Germany is a star producer of Pinot. It's fascinating: tense, brisk and ripe, subtle and focused, with sweet-cherry fruit and a strong sense of terroir. Lots of aroma, lots of spice. The Centgrafenberg vineyard is iron-rich red sandstone; in the cellar they use whole-cluster fermentation, ambient yeasts, wooden and concrete tanks, no fining, no filtration. It adds up to wines of focus, energy and elegance.

One Man Band by Iona, Rozy Gunn, Elgin, S Africa

Rozy Gunn and her husband had one plot of vines – and when he was killed in a car crash, she decided to go it alone. This is made with Iona; the Syrah is Rozy's, from that plot. It's agriculture that fascinates her, and it's the land she wants to express – via bio farming, and via a blend, in this, of Syrah plus Petit Verdot, Mourvèdre, and 3% Viognier to bring perfume and a touch of creaminess to the *garrigue* red fruit, pepper and earth. The texture is beautiful: silk over a firm structure.

Santa Rita Hills Pinot Noir, Tyler Winery, California, US

You start tasting a wine; you start writing a note. Just occasionally, when you've written "layered, precise, very pretty fruit, beautiful balance, compelling", words fail you, and you abandon any attempt at describing the flavour. You settle for "terrific" or "superb". I should be able to do better, I know. But this is Tyler Winery's entry-level Pinot – the others can be two or three times the price – and it is good value. To get burgundy of this quality, you'd be looking at a top grower.

Baracija Refošk, Clai, Istria, Croatia

"Clai" rhymes with "sky"; a useful aide-memoire. These are natural wines of a very high order: we're talking about natural yeasts and ageing in old Slavonian oak, with no fining or filtration, from local varieties grown on limestone flysch, which is sandstone, sand and marl. But it's the flavour that matters most, and this is a wine that feels at ease with itself. It has depth and tension, great detail and precision, and it glides across the palate like a supermodel on a catwalk.

Rebellie Grenache, Van Niekerk Vintners, Walker Bay, S Africa

Beautiful Grenache that combines new-wave delicacy with a firm core and good concentration: Grenache is wonderful when it's light, but that shouldn't mean weedy. This has a beautiful lavender nose with great purity on the palate, and depth hidden under freshness and aromatic fruit. Pinot-lovers should adore it; and it's remarkably good value too.

Caballo Loco, Valdivieso, Curicó, Chile

Unconventional: a blend of several vintages and even more grapes and regions; No.20 (most recent iteration at the time of writing), has nine varieties from cool and less cool regions, some picked early for acidity, some picked later for richness. It's alive and supple, with great length and lift – a revelation to anyone who thinks they know Chilean reds. It's wonderful with steak, even tuna: the secret is the fluid texture. Extremely good value.

Grape varieties

This is where the most fundamental changes in wine are appearing. No longer are half a dozen international grape varieties worshipped around the globe to the exclusion of all else: now it's all about old indigenous varieties. Everybody wants a point of difference. In Europe, there are hundreds of varieties that were once grown but fell from favour. Grapes that wouldn't ripen in the cooler past but ripened in the warmer further-past might be promising in a warmer future – and they might not present the problems of ever-higher alcohol and ever-lower acidity with which growers are currently grappling. Even different clones of popular vines can be interesting: centenarian vineyards across the world are being studied to see if individual vines might ripen later, keep their acidity better; everybody is scrabbling to see what we might still have. And then there are PIWI varieties. The name (a brand) stands for Pilzwiderstandsfähig. They are crossings, often over several generations, of *Vitis vinifera*, the European wine vine, with American fungus- and disease-resistant *Vitis* species. They require less spraying and make organic and bio viticulture more possible in awkward climates. You might come across Solaris or Souvignier Gris; there are many others. And then there are the familiar international grapes. They're not going away. They have forged superb reputations in many countries, and they give many of the greatest wines in the world. But now they're not the only choice.

All grapes and synonyms are cross-referenced in SMALL CAPITALS throughout every section of this book.

Grapes for red wine

Agiorgitiko Greek; the grape of Nemea, now planted all over Greece. Versatile and delicious, from soft and charming to dense and age-worthy. A must-try.

Aglianico S Italy's best red, the grape of Taurasi; dark, deep and fashionable.

Alfrocheiro Portuguese; A Preto same grape. Lovely aromas: blackberry, strawberry, plus freshness, dark colour, fine tannins. Can be v.gd, esp in Dão.

Alicante Bouschet Used to be shunned, now stylish (Alentejo, Chile), esp old vines.

Aragonêz *See* TEMPRANILLO.

Auxerrois *See* MALBEC, if red. White Auxerrois has its own entry in White Grapes.

Băbească Neagră Moldovan trad "black grandmother grape"; light body and ruby-red colour.

Babić Dark grape from Dalmatia, grown in stony seaside vyds around Šibenik. Exceptional quality potential.

Baga Portugal. Bairrada grape. Dark, tannic, fashionable. Needs a gd grower.

Barbera Widely grown in Italy, best in Piedmont: high acidity, low tannin, cherry fruit. Ranges from serious and age-worthy to semi-sweet and frothy. Fashionable in California and Australia; promising in Argentina.

Bastardo Iberian TROUSSEAU.

Blauburger Austrian cross of BLAUER PORTUGIESER, BLAUFRÄNKISCH. Simple wines.

Blauburgunder *See* PINOT N.

Blauer Portugieser Central European, esp Germany (Rheinhessen, Pfalz, mostly for rosé), Austria, Hungary. Light, fruity reds: drink young, slightly chilled.

Blaufränkisch (Kékfrankos, Lemberger, Modra Frankinja) Widely planted in Austria's Mittelburgenland: medium-bodied, peppery acidity, fresh, berry aromas, eucalyptus. Can be top quality: Austria's star red. Often blended with CAB SAUV or ZWEIGELT. Lemberger in Germany (esp Württemberg), Kékfrankos in Hungary, Modra Frankinja in Slovenia.

Bobal Spain. Can be rustic; best at high altitude; gd acidity.

Boğaskere Tannic and Turkish. Produces full-bodied wines.

Bonarda Ambiguous name. In Oltrepò Pavese, an alias for Croatina, soft fresh *frizzante* and still red. In Lombardy and Emilia-Romagna, an alias for Uva Rara. Different in Piedmont. Argentina's Bonarda can be any of these, or something else. None is great.

Bouchet St-Émilion alias for CAB FR.

Brunello SANGIOVESE, splendid at Montalcino.

Cabernet Franc [Cab Fr] In Bx: more important than CAB SAUV in St-Émilion. Outperforms Cab Sauv in Loire (Chinon, Saumur-Champigny, rosé), in Hungary (depth, complexity in Villány, Szekszárd) and often in Italy. Much of NE Italy's Cab Fr turned out to be CARMENÈRE. Used in Bx blends of Cab Sauv/MERLOT across the world.

Cabernet Sauvignon [Cab Sauv] Characterful: slow-ripening, spicy, herby, tannic, with blackcurrant aroma. Main grape of the Médoc; also makes some of the best California, S American, E European reds. Vies with SHIRAZ in Australia. Grown almost everywhere, but few places make great varietal Cab Sauv: usually benefits from blending with eg. MERLOT, CAB FR, SYRAH, TEMPRANILLO, SANGIOVESE, etc. Makes aromatic rosé. Top wines need ageing.

Cannonau GRENACHE in its Sardinian manifestation; can be v. fine, potent.

Carignan (Carignane, Carignano, Cariñena) Low-yielding old vines now fashionable everywhere from S France to Chile, via S Africa. Lots of depth, vibrancy, but must never be overcropped. Found esp in California, Israel, N Africa, Spain (as Cariñena).

Carignano *See* CARIGNAN.

Cariñena *See* CARIGNAN.

Carmenère An old Bx variety now a star, rich and deep, in Chile (where it's pronounced "carmeneary"); Bx is looking at it again.

Castelão *See* PERIQUITA.

Cencibel *See* TEMPRANILLO.

Chiavennasca *See* NEBBIOLO.

Cinsault (Cinsaut) A staple of S France, v.gd if low-yielding, hopeless if not. Makes gd rosé. One of parents of PINOTAGE.

Cornalin du Valais Swiss speciality with high potential, esp in Valais.

Corvina Dark and spicy; one of best grapes in Valpolicella blend. Corvinone, even darker, is a separate variety.

Côt *See* MALBEC.

Dolcetto Source of relatively light red in Piedmont. Now high fashion.

Dornfelder Gives deliciously light reds, straightforward, often rustic, and well coloured in Germany, parts of the US, even England.

Duras Spicy, peppery and structured; exclusive to Gaillac and parts of Tarn V in SW France.

Fer Servadou Exclusive to SW France, aka Mansois in Marcillac, Braucol in Gaillac and Pinenc in St-Mont. Redolent of red summer fruits and spice.

Fetească Neagră Romania: "black maiden grape" with potential as showpiece variety; can give deep, full-bodied wines with character.

Freisa Old Piedmontese vine, related to NEBBIOLO. Acidic, tannic, strawberry fruit, quite aromatic. Can be sparkling or semi-sparkling; gd, can be acquired taste.

Frühburgunder An ancient German mutation of PINOT N, mostly in Ahr but also in Franken and Württemberg, where it is confusingly known as Clevner. Lower acidity than Pinot N.

Gamay The Beaujolais grape: light, fragrant wines, best young, except in Beaujolais crus (*see* France) where quality can be high, wines for 2–10 yrs. Grown in Loire Valley, Central France, Switzerland, Savoie, Canada. California's Napa Gamay is Valdiguié.

Gamza *See* KADARKA.

Garnacha (Cannonau, Garnatxa, Grenache) Important pale, potent grape for warm climates, fashionable with *terroiristes* because it expresses its site. Usually quite high alc, but much more delicate than of yore, even in Priorat. The base of Châteauneuf-du-Pape. Rosé and *vin doux naturel* in S France, Spain, California. Old-vine versions prized in S Australia. Often blended. Cannonau in Sardinia, Grenache in France.

Garnatxa *See* GARNACHA.

Graciano Spanish; part of Rioja blend. Aroma of violets, tannic, lean structure, a bit like PETIT VERDOT. Difficult to grow but increasingly fashionable.

Grenache *See* GARNACHA. **GSM**: GRENACHE/SHIRAZ/MOURVÈDRE blend.

Grignolino Italy: gd everyday table wine in Piedmont.

Kadarka (Gamza) Spicy, light reds in E Europe. In Hungary revived, esp for Bikavér.

Kalecik Karasi Turkish: sour-cherry fruit, fresh, supple. Bit like GAMAY. Drink young.

Kékfrankos Hungarian BLAUFRÄNKISCH.

Lagrein N Italian, dark, bitter finish, rich, plummy. DOC in Alto Adige (*see* Italy).

Lambrusco Productive grape of lower Po Valley; cheerful, sweet, fizzy, can be v.gd.

Lefkada In Cyprus, higher quality than MAVRO. Usually blended, as tannins can be aggressive. Called Vertzami in its Greek homeland.

Lemberger *See* BLAUFRÄNKISCH.

Malbec (Auxerrois, Côt) Minor in Bx, major in Cahors (alias Auxerrois) and the star in Argentina. Dark, dense, tannic but fleshy wine capable of real quality. High-altitude versions in Argentina best.

Manseng Noir SW Fr Basque origin. Deep colour, tannic; interesting for lowish alc.

Maratheftiko Deep-coloured Cypriot grape with quality potential.

Marselan CAB SAUV X GRENACHE, 1961; gd colour, structure, supple tannins, ages well. A success in China.

Mataro *See* MOURVÈDRE.

Mavro Most planted black grape of Cyprus but only moderate quality. Best for rosé.

Mavrodaphne Greek; means "black laurel". Sweet fortifieds, speciality of Patras, also in Cephalonia. Dry versions too, great promise.

Mavrotragano Greek, almost extinct; now revived; found on Santorini. Top quality.

Mavrud Probably Bulgaria's best. Spicy, dark, plummy late-ripener native to Thrace. Ages well.

Melnik Bulgarian; from region of same name. There are two Melniks: Shiroka (Broadleafed) M and its offspring, Early M. Both have dark colour, nice dense, tart-cherry character and age well.

Mencía Making waves in Bierzo, N Spain. Aromatic, steely tannins, lots of acidity.

Merlot The grape behind the great fragrant and plummy wines of Pomerol and (with CAB FR) St-Émilion, a vital element in the Médoc, soft and strong in California, Washington, Chile, Australia. Lighter, often gd in N Italy (can be world-class in Tuscany), Italian Switzerland, Slovenia, Argentina, S Africa, NZ, etc. More often dull than great. Much planted in E Europe, esp Romania.

Meunier *See* PINOT M.

Modra Frankinja *See* BLAUFRÄNKISCH.

Modri Pinot *See* PINOT N.

Monastrell *See* MOURVÈDRE.

Mondeuse In Savoie; the skier's red; deep-coloured, gd acidity. Related to SYRAH.

Montepulciano Deep-coloured, dominant in Italy's Abruzzo and important along Adriatic coast from Marches to S Puglia. Also name of a Tuscan town, unrelated.

Morellino SANGIOVESE in Maremma, S Tuscany. Esp Scansano.

Mourvèdre (Mataro, Monastrell) A star of S France (eg. Bandol, growing influence Châteauneuf), Australia (aka Mataro) and Spain (aka Monastrell). Excellent dark, aromatic, tannic; gd for blending. Also S Australia, California, S Africa.

Napa Gamay Identical to Valdiguié (S France). Nothing to get excited about.

Nebbiolo (Chiavennasca, Spanna) One of Italy's best; makes Barolo, Barbaresco, Gattinara and Valtellina. Intense, nobly fruity, perfumed wine; tannins now better managed, still improves for yrs.

Négrette SW France; Fronton. Blends with SYRAH: purply black, fruity, sappy wines.

Negroamaro Puglian "black bitter" red grape with potential for either high quality or high volume.

Nerello Mascalese Sicilian red grape, esp Etna; characterful, best v. elegant, fine.

Nero d'Avola Dark-red grape of Sicily, quality levels from sublime to industrial.

Nielluccio Corsican; plenty of acidity and tannin, gd for rosé.

Öküzgözü Soft, fruity Turkish grape, usually blended with BOĞASKERE, rather as MERLOT in Bx is blended with CAB SAUV.

País (Listán Prieto, Mission) Trendy/trad in Chile, rustic. Listán Prieto in Canaries, Mission in CA.

Pamid Bulgarian: light, soft, everyday red.

Periquita (Castelão) Common in Portugal, esp around Setúbal. Originally nicknamed Periquita after Fonseca's popular (trademarked) brand. Firm-flavoured, raspberryish reds develop a figgish, tar-like quality.

Petite Sirah Nothing to do with SYRAH; gives rustic, tannic, dark wine. Brilliant blended with ZIN in California; also found in S America, Mexico, Australia.

Petit Verdot Excellent but awkward Médoc grape, now increasingly planted in CAB areas worldwide for extra fragrance. Mostly blended but some gd varietals, esp in Virginia (US).

Pinotage Singular S African cross (PINOT N X CINSAULT). Has had a rocky ride; getting better from top producers. Rosé gd too. "Coffee Pinotage" is espresso-flavoured, sweetish, aimed at youth.

Pinot Crni *See* PINOT N.

Pinot Meunier (Schwarzriesling) [Pinot M] The 3rd grape of Champagne, better known as Meunier, great for blending but occasionally fine in its own right. Best on chalky sites (Damery, Leuvigny, Festigny) nr Épernay.

Pinot Noir (Blaublurgunder, Modri Pinot, Pinot Crni, Spätburgunder) [Pinot N] On a roll; Burgundy no longer has monopoly of great wines. Modri Pinot in Slovenia; probably country's best red. In Italy, best in ne, gets worse as you go s. PINOTS BL/GR mutations of Pinot N. Important in fizz.

Plavac Mali (Crljenak) Croatian, and offspring of ZIN, aka PRIMITIVO, Crljenak, Kratosija. Lots of quality potential, can be alcoholic, dull.

Primitivo S Italian grape, originally from Croatia, making big, dark, rustic wines, now fashionable because genetically identical to ZIN. Early ripening, hence the name. The original name for both seems to be Tribidrag.

Refosco (Refošk) Various DOCs in Italy, esp Colli Orientali. Deep, flavoursome, age-worthy, esp in warmer climates. Dark, high acidity. Refošk in Slovenia and points e, genetically different, tastes similar. On limestone karst in Slovenia takes PDO of Teran, which otherwise is a grape. Got it?

Rubin Bulgarian cross, NEBBIOLO X SYRAH. Peppery, full-bodied.

Sagrantino Italian grape grown in Umbria for powerful, cherry-flavoured wines.

St-Laurent Dark, smooth, full-flavoured Austrian speciality, tricky to grow and make. Can be light and juicy or deep and structured. Also in Pfalz.

Sangiovese (Brunello, Morellino, Sangioveto) Principal red grape of Tuscany and central Italy. At best, sublime and long-lasting; richness balances tea-scented astringency. Dominant in Chianti, Vino Nobile, Brunello di Montalcino, Morellino di Scansano and various fine IGT offerings. Also in Umbria (eg. Montefalco and Torgiano) and across the Apennines in Romagna and Marches. Not so clever in the warmer, lower-altitude vyds of the Tuscan coast, nor in other parts of Italy despite its nr-ubiquity. Interesting in Australia.

Sangioveto *See* SANGIOVESE.

Saperavi The main red of Georgia, Ukraine, etc. Blends well with CAB SAUV (eg. in Moldova). Huge potential, some gd winemaking.

Schiava *See* TROLLINGER.

Schioppettino NE Italian, high acidity, high quality. Elegant, refined, can age.

Schwarzriesling PINOT M in Württemberg.

Sciacarello Corsican, herby and peppery. Not v. tannic.

Shiraz *See* SYRAH.

Spanna *See* NEBBIOLO.

Spätburgunder German for PINOT N.

Syrah (Shiraz) The great Rhône red grape: tannic, purple, peppery, matures superbly. Important as Shiraz in Australia. Widely grown and a gd traveller.

Tannat Raspberry-perfumed, highly tannic force behind Madiran, Tursan and other firm reds from SW France. Also rosé. The star of Uruguay.

Tempranillo (Aragonêz, Cencibel, Tinto Fino, Tinta del País, Tinta Roriz, Ull de Llebre) Aromatic, fine Rioja grape, called Ull de Llebre in Catalonia, Cencibel in La Mancha, Tinto Fino in Ribera del Duero, Tinta Roriz in Douro, Tinta del País in Castile, Aragonêz in S Portugal. Now Australia too. It's v. fashionable; elegant in cool climates, beefy in warm. Early ripening, long maturing.

Teran (Terrano) Close cousin of REFOSCO.

Teroldego Rotaliano Trentino's best indigenous variety; serious, full-flavoured, esp on the flat Campo Rotaliano.

Tinta Amarela *See* TRINCADEIRA.

Tinta del País *See* TEMPRANILLO.

Tinta Negra (Negramoll) Used to be Tinta Negra Mole. Madeira's most planted, mainstay of cheaper Madeira. Now too in Colheita wines (*see* Portugal).

Tinta Roriz *See* TEMPRANILLO.

Tinto Fino *See* TEMPRANILLO.

Touriga Nacional [Touriga N] The top Port grape, now widely used in the Douro for floral, stylish table wines. Australian Touriga is usually this; California's Touriga can be either this or Touriga Franca.

Trincadeira (Tinta Amarela) Portuguese; v.gd in Alentejo for spicy wines. Tinta Amarela in the Douro.

Trollinger (Schiava, Vernatsch) Popular pale red in Württemberg; aka Schiava, Vernatsch. Covers group of vines, not necessarily related. In Italy, snappy, brisk.

Trousseau (Bastardo) Jura. Robust, age-worthy. Bastardo in Iberia. Also found in California, Oregon.

Ull de Llebre *See* TEMPRANILLO.

Vernatsch *See* TROLLINGER.

Vranac W Balkans, old and varied. Related to ZINFANDEL – they're all connected around there. Soft, high tannin, colour, alc, can age.

Xinomavro Greece's answer to NEBBIOLO. "Sharp-black"; the basis for Naoussa, Rapsani, Goumenissa, Amindeo. Some rosé, still or sparkling. Top quality, can age for decades. Being tried in China.

Zinfandel [Zin] California. Blackberry-like, sometimes metallic flavour. Love it or hate it. Can be serious, structured, long-ageing, or simple. Pink too. Same as S Italian PRIMITIVO.

Zweigelt (Blauer Zweigelt) BLAUFRÄNKISCH X ST-LAURENT, popular in Austria for aromatic, dark, supple wines. Underrated. Also in Hungary, Germany.

Grapes for white wine

Airén Bland workhorse of La Mancha, Spain: fresh if made well. Old-vine versions can surprise.

Albariño (Alvarinho) Fashionable, expensive in Spain: apricot-scented, gd acidity. Superb in Rías Baixas; shaping up elsewhere, but not all live up to the hype. Alvarinho in Portugal just as gd: aromatic Vinho Verde, esp in Monção, Melgaço.

Aligoté Burgundy's 2nd white grape, now trendy and often serious. Widely planted in E Europe, Russia.

Alvarinho *See* ALBARIÑO.

Amigne One of Switzerland's speciality grapes, trad in Valais, esp Vétroz. Full-bodied, tasty, often sweet but also bone-dry.

Ansonica *See* INSOLIA.

Arinto Portuguese, rather gd; mainstay of aromatic, citrus Bucelas; also adds welcome zip to blends, esp in Alentejo.

Arneis Fine, aromatic, appley-peachy, high-priced NW Italian grape, DOCG in Roero, DOC in Langhe, Piedmont.

Arvine Rare but excellent Swiss *spécialité*, from Valais. Also Petite Arvine. Dry or sweet, fresh, long-lasting wines with salty finish.

Assyrtiko From Santorini; one of the best grapes of the Mediterranean, balancing power, minerality, extract and high acid. Built to age. Could conquer the world...

Auxerrois Red Auxerrois is a synonym for MALBEC, but white Auxerrois is like a fatter, spicier PINOT BL. Found in Alsace; much used in Crémant; also Germany.

Bacchus German-bred crossing, England's answer to NZ SAUV BL; v. aromatic, can be shrill.

Beli Pinot *See* PINOT BL.

Blanc Fumé *See* SAUV BL.

Boal *See* BUAL.

Bourboulenc This and the rare Rolle make some of the Midi's best wines.

Bouvier Indigenous aromatic Austrian grape, esp gd for BA, TBA, rarely dry.

Bual (Boal) Makes top-quality sweet Madeira wines, not quite so rich as MALMSEY.

Cabernet Blanc [Cab Bl] German PIWI (*see* p.12) with SAUV BL-like flavours.

Camaralet Jurançon. Aromatic; adds complexity to GROS MANSENG-led dry wines.

Carricante Superb grape of Etna Bianco; lemon and herbs, acidity, ages 20 yrs.

Catarratto Prolific white grape found all over Sicily, esp in w in DOC Alcamo.

Cerceal *See* SERCIAL.

Chardonnay (Morillon) [Chard] Grape of Burgundy and Champagne, ubiquitous worldwide, easy to grow and vinify. Reflects terroir but also winemaker's intentions: often a fashion victim. Can be steely or fat. Also the name of a Mâcon-Villages commune. Morillon in Styria, Austria.

Chasselas (Fendant, Gutedel) Swiss. Neutral, can be elegant (Geneva); refined, full (Vaud); exotic, racy (Valais). Fendant in Valais. Also in France, esp Savoie. Gutedel in Germany, esp S Baden. Elsewhere usually a table grape.

Chenin Blanc [Chenin Bl] Wonderful white grape of the middle Loire (Vouvray, Layon, etc). Wine can be dry or sweet (or v. sweet), but with plenty of acidity. Superb old-vine versions in S Africa, esp Swartland.

Cirfandl *See* ZIERFANDLER.

Clairette Important Rhône/Midi grape, white and rosé versions, gives freshness, restrained degree, part of many blends, incl Tavel rosé.

Colombard Slightly fruity, nicely sharp grape, makes everyday wine in S Africa, California and SW France. Often blended.

Cortese Italian; grape of Gavi. Fairly neutral, pleasant, fresh.

Dimiat Perfumed Bulgarian grape, made dry or off-dry, or distilled. Far more synonyms than any grape needs.

Encruzado Portuguese, serious; fresh, versatile, ages well; esp gd in Dão.

Ermitage Swiss for MARSANNE.

Esgana Cão *See* Sercial.

Ezerjó Hungarian, with sharp acidity. Name means "thousand blessings".

Falanghina Ancient grape of Campanian hills (Italy); gd dense, aromatic dry whites.

Fendant *See* CHASSELAS.

Fernão Pires *See* MARIA GOMES.

Fetească Albă / Regală (Királyleanyka, Leanyka) Romania has two Fetească grapes, both with slight MUSCAT aroma. F Regală is a cross of F Albă and Frâncușă; more finesse, gd for late-harvest wines. F NEAGRĂ (unrelated) is dark-skinned.

Fiano High quality, giving peachy, spicy wine in Campania, S Italy.

Folle Blanche (Gros Plant) High acid/little flavour make this ideal for brandy. Gros Plant in Brittany, Picpoul in Armagnac, but unrelated to true PICPOUL. Also respectable in California.

Friulano (Sauvignonasse, Sauvignon Vert) N Italian: fresh, pungent, subtly floral. Best in Collio, Isonzo, Colli Orientali. Found in nearby Slovenia as Sauvignonasse; also in Chile.

Fumé Blanc *See* SAUV BL.

Furmint (Šipon) Superb, characterful. Trademark of Hungary: both principal grape in Tokaji and vivid, vigorous dry wine, mineral, apricot-flavoured. Šipon in Slovenia. Some grown in Rust (Austria) for sweet and dry.

Garganega Best grape in Soave blend; also in Gambellara. Top, esp sweet, age well.

Garnacha Blanca (Grenache Blanc) White version of GARNACHA/Grenache, much used in Spain and S France. Low acidity. Can be innocuous or surprisingly gd.

Gewurztraminer (Traminac, Traminec, Traminer, Tramini) [Gewurz] One of the most pungent grapes, spicy with aromas of rose petals, face cream, lychees, grapefruit. Often rich and soft, even when fully dry. Best in Alsace; gd elsewhere. Can be relatively unaromatic if just labelled Traminer (or variants). Italy uses the name Traminer Aromatico for its (dr) "Gewurz" versions. (Name takes umlaut in German.) Non-aromatic version is SAVAGNIN.

Glera Uncharismatic new name for Prosecco vine: Prosecco is now wine only in the EU but still a grape name in Australia.

Godello Top quality (intense, mineral) in nw Spain. Called Verdelho in Dão, Portugal, but unrelated to true VERDELHO.

Grasă (Kövérszőlő) Romanian; name means "fat". Prone to botrytis; important in Cotnari, potentially superb sweet wines. Kövérszőlő in Hungary's Tokaj region.

Graševina *See* WELSCHRIESLING.

Grauburgunder *See* PINOT GR.

Grechetto Ancient grape of central/S Italy: vitality, style. Blended or solo in Orvieto.

Greco S Italian: there are various Grecos, probably unrelated, perhaps of Greek origin. Brisk, peachy flavour, most famous as Greco di Tufo. Greco di Bianco is from semi-dried grapes. Greco Nero is a black version.

Grenache Blanc *See* GARNACHA BLANCA.

Grillo Italy: main grape of Marsala. Also v.gd full-bodied dry table wine.

Gros Plant *See* FOLLE BLANCHE.

Grüner Veltliner [Grüner V] Austria's fashionable flagship white; v. diverse – from simple, peppery, everyday, to great complexity, ageing potential. Useful because gd at all levels. Found elsewhere in Central Europe and outside.

Gutedel *See* CHASSELAS.

Hárslevelű Other main grape of Tokaji, but softer, peachier than FURMINT. Name means "linden-leaved"; gd in Somló, Eger as well.

Heida Swiss for SAVAGNIN.

Humagne Swiss speciality, older than CHASSELAS. Fresh, plump, not v. aromatic. Humagne Rouge is not related but increasingly popular: same as Cornalin du Aosta. Cornalin du Valais is different. (Keep up at the back, there.)

Insolia (Ansonica, Inzolia) Sicilian; Ansonica on Tuscan coast. Fresh, racy wine at best. May be semi-dried for sweet wine.

Irsai Olivér Hungarian cross; aromatic, MUSCAT-like wine for drinking young.

Johannisberg Swiss for SILVANER.

Kéknyelű Low-yielding, flavourful grape giving one of Hungary's best whites. Has the potential for fieriness and spice. To be watched.

Kerner Quite successful German cross. Early ripening, flowery (but often too blatant) wine with gd acidity.

Királyleanyka *See* FETEASCĂ ALBĂ/REGALĂ.

Koshu More or less indigenous Japanese table-turned-wine grape, much hyped. Fresh, tannic. Orange versions gd.

Kövérszőlő *See* GRASĂ.

L'Acadie Blanc Cold-climate Canadian hybrid; some weight, honeyed; gd fizz.

Laški Rizling *See* WELSCHRIESLING.

Leányka *See* FETEASCĂ ALBĂ.

Len de l'El Gaillac; aka Loin de l'Oeuil. Versatile; usually blended; gd dessert wines.

Listán *See* PALOMINO.

Longyan (Dragon Eye) Chinese original; gd substantial, aromatic wine.

Loureiro Best Vinho Verde grape after ALVARINHO: delicate, floral. Also in Spain.

Macabeo *See* VIURA.

Maccabeu *See* VIURA.

Malagousia Rediscovered Greek grape for gloriously perfumed wines.

Malmsey *See* MALVASIA. Sweetest style of Madeira.

Malvasia (Malmsey, Malvazija, Malvoisie, Marastina) Italy, France and Iberia. Not a single variety but a whole stable, not necessarily related or even alike. Can be white or red, sparkling or still, strong or mild, sweet or dry, aromatic or neutral. Slovenia's and Croatia's version is Malvazija Istarka, crisp and light, or rich, oak-aged. Sometimes called Marastina in Croatia. Malmsey (as in the sweetest style of Madeira) is a corruption of Malvasia.

Malvoisie *See* MALVASIA. Name used for several varieties in France, incl BOURBOULENC, Torbato, VERMENTINO. Also PINOT GR in Switzerland's Valais.

Manseng, Gros / Petit Exuberantly fruity whites from SW France, esp Jurançon, Pacherenc and Irouléguy. Gros Manseng is picked earlier and tends to be made dry. Petit Manseng is picked later, often sweet.

Maria Gomes (Fernão Pires) Portuguese; aromatic, ripe-flavoured, slightly spicy whites in Barraida and Tejo.

Marsanne (Ermitage Blanc) Principal white grape (with ROUSSANNE) of N Rhône; gd in Australia, California, Valais (Ermitage Bl). Soft, full wines, age v. well.

Mauzac SW France. Aromatic, note of apples. Best known for sparkling.

Melon de Bourgogne *See* MUSCADET.

Misket, Red Bulgarian. Pink-skinned, mildly aromatic; the basis of most country whites. There are many other Miskets, all recent crosses and less planted.

Morillon CHARD in parts of Austria.

Moscatel / Moscato *See* MUSCAT.

Moschofilero Pink-skinned, rose-scented, high-quality, high-acid, low-alc Greek grape. Makes white, some pink, some sparkling.

Müller-Thurgau [Müller-T] Aromatic wines to drink young. Makes gd sweet wines but usually dull, often coarse, dry ones. In Germany, most common in Pfalz, Rheinhessen, Nahe, Baden, Franken. Has some merit in Italy's Trentino-Alto Adige, Friuli. Sometimes called RIES X SYLVANER (incorrectly) in Switzerland.

Muscadelle Adds aroma to white Bx, esp Sauternes. In Victoria used (with MUSCAT, to which it is unrelated) for Rutherglen Muscat.

Muscadet (Melon de Bourgogne) Light, refreshing, dry wines with seaside tang, to complex ones around Nantes. Also found (as Melon) in parts of Burgundy.

Muscat (Moscatel, Moscato, Muskateller) Many varieties; the best is Muscat Blanc à Petits Grains (alias Gelber Muskateller, Rumeni Muškat, Sarga Muskotály, Yellow Muscat, Tămâioasă Românească). Widely grown, easily recognized, pungent grapes, mostly made into perfumed sweet wines, often fortified, as in France's *vin doux naturel*. Superb, dark and sweet in Australia. Sweet, sometimes v.gd in Spain. Most Hungarian Muskotály is Muscat Ottonel except in Tokaj, where Sarga Muskotály rules, adding perfume (in small amounts) to blends. Occasionally (eg. Alsace, Austria, parts of S Germany) made dry. Sweet Cap Corse Muscats often superb. Light Moscato fizz in N Italy.

Muskateller *See* MUSCAT.

Narince Turkish; fresh and fruity wines.

Neuburger Austrian, rather neglected; mainly in the Wachau (elegant, flowery), Thermenregion (mellow, ample-bodied) and n Burgenland (strong, full).

Olaszrizling *See* WELSCHRIESLING.

Païen *See* SAVAGNIN.

Pálava Czech, rather gd. Pink-skinned, rose aromas, gd freshness.

Palomino (Listán) Great grape of Sherry; little intrinsic character, gains all from production method. Now table wine too. As Listán, makes dry white in Canaries.

Pansa Blanca *See* XAREL·LO.

Pecorino Italian: not a cheese but alluring dry white from a revived variety.

Pedro Ximénez [PX] Makes sweet brown Sherry under its own name, and used in Montilla, Málaga. Also in Argentina, Australia, California, Canaries, S Africa.

Petit Courbu SW France. Age-worthy, some distinction.

Picolit NE Italian, used for late-harvest (sw); grapes dried on mats or left on vine, with botrytis or not. Delicate wine, should be v.gd, sometimes is.

Picpoul (Piquepoul) S French, best known in Picpoul de Pinet. Should have high acidity. Picpoul N is black-skinned.

Pinela Local to Slovenia. Subtle, lowish acidity; drink young.

Pinot Bianco *See* PINOT BL.

Pinot Blanc (Beli Pinot, Pinot Bianco, Weissburgunder) [Pinot Bl] Mutation of PINOT N, similar to but milder than CHARD. Light, fresh, fruity, not aromatic, to drink young; gd for Italian *spumante*, and potentially excellent in the ne, esp high sites in Alto Adige. Widely grown. Weissburgunder in Germany and best in s: often racier than Chard.

Pinot Gris (Pinot Grigio, Grauburgunder, Ruländer, Sivi Pinot, Szürkebarát) [Pinot Gr] Popular as Pinot Grigio in N Italy, even for rosé, but top, characterful versions can be excellent (Alto Adige, Friuli); trad *ramato* is skin-contact. Cheap versions are just that. Terrific in Alsace for full-bodied, spicy whites. Once important in Champagne. In Germany can be alias Ruländer (sw) or Grauburgunder (dr): best in Baden (esp Kaiserstuhl) and S Pfalz. Szürkebarát in Hungary, Sivi P in Slovenia (characterful, aromatic).

Pošip Croatian; mostly on Korčula. Quite characterful and citrus; high-yielding.

Prosecco Old name for grape that makes Prosecco. Now you have to call it GLERA.

Renski Rizling Rhine RIES.

Rèze Super-rare ancestral Valais grape used for *vin de glacier*.

Ribolla Gialla / Rebula Acidic but characterful. In Italy, best in Collio. In Slovenia, trad in Brda. Can be v.gd. Favourite of amphora users.

Rieslaner Rare German cross (SILVANER X RIES); fine Auslesen in Franken and Pfalz.

Riesling (Renski Rizling, Rhine Riesling) [Ries] The greatest, most versatile white grape, diametrically opposite in style to CHARD. From steely to voluptuous, always perfumed, far more ageing potential than Chard. Great in all styles in Germany; forceful and steely in Austria; lime cordial fruit and toast in S Australia; rich and spicy in Alsace; often v.gd elsewhere.

Riesling Italico *See* WELSCHRIESLING.

Rkatsiteli Found widely in E Europe, Russia and Georgia. Can stand cold winters and has high acidity; protects to a degree from poor winemaking. Also grown in NE US.

Robola In Greece (Cephalonia) a top-quality, floral grape, unrelated to RIBOLLA GIALLA but related to Rebula.

Roditis Pink grape, all over Greece, usually making whites. Gd when yields low.

Roter Veltliner Austrian; unrelated to GRÜNER V. There is also a Frühroter and an (unrelated) Brauner Veltliner.

Rotgipfler Austrian; indigenous to Thermenregion. With ZIERFANDLER, makes lively, lush, aromatic blends.

Roussanne (Bergeron) Rhône grape of real finesse, called Bergeron in Savoie. Now popping up in California and Australia. Can age many yrs.

Ruländer *See* PINOT GR.

Sauvignonasse *See* FRIULANO.

Sauvignon Blanc [Sauv Bl] Distinctive aromatic, grassy to tropical wines. Grassy, pungent NZ style taken over world; trad blackcurrant-leaf Sancerre-style more rewarding. Blended with SÉM in Bx. Sauv Gr is pink-skinned, less aromatic version with untapped potential.

Sauvignon Vert *See* FRIULANO.

Savagnin (Heida, Païen) Grape for VIN JAUNE from Jura: aromatic form is GEWURZ. In Switzerland known as Heida, Païen or Traminer. Full-bodied, high acidity.

Scheurebe (Sämling) Grapefruit-scented German RIES X SILVANER (possibly), esp successful in Pfalz (Auslese and up). Can be weedy: must be v. ripe to be gd.

Sémillon [Sém] Contributes lusciousness to Sauternes but decreasingly important for Graves and other dry white Bx. Grassy if not fully ripe, but can make soft dry wine of great ageing potential. Superb in Australia.

Sercial (Cerceal, Esgana Cão) Portuguese: makes the driest Madeira. Cerceal, also Portuguese, seems to be this plus any of several others.

Seyval Blanc [Seyval Bl] French hybrid of French and American vines; v. hardy, attractively fruity. Popular and reasonably successful in E US and England.

Silvaner (Johannisberg, Sylvaner) Can be excellent in Germany's Rheinhessen, Pfalz, esp Franken, plant/earth flavours and mineral notes. As Johannisberg in Valais (Switzerland) v.gd (and powerful). Lightest of Alsace grapes.

Šipon *See* FURMINT.

Sivi Pinot *See* PINOT GR.

Spätrot *See* ZIERFANDLER.

Sylvaner *See* SILVANER.

Tămâioasă Românească *See* MUSCAT.

Torrontés Name given to a number of grapes, mostly with an aromatic, floral character, sometimes soapy. A speciality of Argentina; also in Spain. DYA.

Traminac Or Traminec. *See* GEWURZ.

Traminer Or Tramini (Hungary). *See* GEWURZ.

Trebbiano (Ugni Blanc) Principal white grape of Tuscany, but all over Italy in many guises. Rarely rises above the plebeian except in Tuscany's Vin Santo. Some gd dry whites under DOCs Romagna or Abruzzo. Trebbiano di Soave, aka VERDICCHIO, only distantly related; T di Lugana now called Turbiana. Grown in S France as Ugni Bl, and Cognac as St-Émilion. Mostly thin, bland wine; needs blending (and better growing).

Ugni Blanc [Ugni Bl] *See* TREBBIANO.

Verdejo The grape of Rueda in Castile, potentially fine and long-lived.

Verdelho Great quality in Australia (pungent, full-bodied); rare but gd (and medium-sweet) in Madeira.

Verdicchio Potentially v.gd, muscular, dry; central-E Italy. Wine of same name.

Vermentino Italian, sprightly with satisfying texture; ageing capacity.

Vernaccia Name given to many unrelated grapes in Italy. Vernaccia di San Gimignano is crisp, lively; Vernaccia di Oristano is Sherry-like.

Vidal French hybrid much grown in Canada for Icewine.

Vidiano Cretan producers love this. Powerful, stylish. Lime/apricot, gd acidity; gd fizz too.

Viognier Ultra-fashionable Rhône grape, finest in Condrieu, less fine but still aromatic in the Midi. Often gd to v.gd elsewhere.

Viura (Macabeo, Maccabéo, Maccabeu) Workhorse white grape of N Spain, widespread in Rioja, Cava country, over border in SW France; gd quality potential.

Weissburgunder PINOT BL in Germany.

Welschriesling (Graševina, Laški Rizling, Olaszrizling, Riesling Italico) Not related to RIES. Light and fresh to sweet and rich in Austria; ubiquitous in Central Europe, where it can be remarkably gd for dry and sweet wines.

Xarel·lo (Pansa Blanca) A trad Catalan grape, for Cava (with Parellada, MACABEO). Tannic, can age, can be superb. Lime-cordial character in Alella, as Pansa Blanca.

Xynisteri Cyprus's most planted white grape. Can be simple and is usually DYA, but when grown at altitude makes appealing, mineral whites.

Zéta Hungarian; BOUVIER X FURMINT used by some in Tokaji Aszú production.

Zierfandler (Spätrot, Cirfandl) Found in Austria's Thermenregion; often blended with ROTGIPFLER for aromatic, orange-peel-scented, weighty wines.

Wine & food

Matching wine and food is nothing if not subjective. Don't think of any of these pairings as instructions, or rules, or anything other than ideas of the sort of flavours and weights that might go together – and then adapt them. And by the way, when we suggest, eg., "white burgundy" or "Sancerre", don't take that too prescriptively. We mean it as an indication of style. So, eg., Chardonnay, yes, but Chardonnay in a burgundian idiom rather than something louder. And thinking of that as a style might lead you to other alternatives: Sémillon, perhaps, or even aged Assyrtiko. It's about having fun, not making rules.

On p.35 you'll find a box of can't-go-wrong favourites with food; the entries below give lots of specific matches enjoyed over the years.

Before the meal – apéritifs
Don't be tempted by quantity over quality here. The best value is Fino Sherry, the most expensive is gd fizz – but if you're going for fizz, make sure it's gd. Or how about a magnum of rosé?

First courses
Aïoli Chances are you're on holiday, and cold Provence rosé is ideal. Or anything cold, fresh and neutral.

Antipasti / tapas / mezze You can be in Italy, Spain, Greece or Edinburgh: a selection of savoury, salty, meaty, cheesy, fishy, veggie bits and pieces works perfectly with Fino Sherry, XYNISTERI, orange wines. Roasted peppers, aubergines suit young fruity reds: CAB FR, KADARKA. Gd Prosecco in emergencies.

Burrata Richness in excelsis. Worth top Italian white: FIANO or Cusumano's GRILLO. Or mature SÉM.

Carpaccio, beef or fish Beef version works well with most wines, incl reds. Tuscan is appropriate, but fine CHARDS are gd. So are pink and Vintage Champagnes. Give Amontillado a try. **Salmon** Chard or Champagne. **Tuna** VIOGNIER, California Chard, Sancerre. Or sake.

Charcuterie / prosciutto / salami High-acid, unoaked red works better than white. Simple Beaujolais, BARBERA, Etna, REFOSCO, SCHIOPPETTINO, TEROLDEGO, Valpolicella. If you must have white, it needs acidity. Chorizo makes wines taste metallic. Prosciutto with melon or figs needs full dry or medium white: CHENIN BL, FIANO, MUSCAT, VIOGNIER.

Dim sum Classically, China tea. Alsace PINOT GR or German dry RIES; light PINOT N. For reds, soft tannins, freshness are key. Bardolino, GARNACHA, Rioja; Côtes du Rhône. Also NV Champagne or English fizz.

Eggs *See also* SOUFFLÉS. Not easy: eggs have a way of coating your palate. Omelettes: follow the other ingredients; mushrooms suggest red; Côtes du Rhone is a safe bet. With a truffle omelette, Vintage Champagne, or perhaps Volnay. Florentine, with spinach, is not a winey dish.

   gulls' eggs Push the luxury: mature white burgundy or Vintage Champagne.

   oeufs en meurette Burgundian genius: eggs in red wine with glass of the same.

   quails' eggs Blanc de Blancs Champagne; VIOGNIER.

Mozzarella with tomatoes, basil Fresh Italian white, eg. Soave, Alto Adige. VERMENTINO from Liguria or Rolle from the Midi. *See also* VEGETABLE/AVOCADO.

Oysters, raw NV Champagne, Chablis, MUSCADET, white Graves, Sancerre, or Guinness. Experiment with Sauternes. Manzanilla is gd. Flat oysters worth gd wine; Pacific ones drown it in brine.

stewed, grilled or otherwise cooked Puligny-Montrachet or gd NZ CHARD. Champagne is gd with either.

Pasta Red or white according to the sauce:

creamy sauce (eg. carbonara) Orvieto, GRECO di Tufo. Young SANGIOVESE.

meat sauce MONTEPULCIANO d'Abruzzo, Salice Salentino, MALBEC.

pesto (basil) sauce BARBERA, VERMENTINO, NZ SAUV BL, Hungarian FURMINT.

seafood sauce (eg. vongole) VERDICCHIO, Lugana, Soave, GRILLO, unoaked CHARD.

tomato sauce Chianti, Barbera, Sicilian red, ZIN, S Australian GRENACHE.

Pâté Chicken liver calls for pungent white (Alsace PINOT GR, or MARSANNE), smooth red, eg. light GARNACHA or PINOT N. More strongly flavoured (duck, venison) needs Chianti Classico, Gigondas, or gd white Graves. Amontillado can be marvellous match.

foie gras Sweet white: Sauternes, Tokaji Aszú 5 Puttonyos, late-harvest RIES or PINOT GR, Vouvray, Jurançon *moelleux*, GEWURZ. Old dry Amontillado. NB: hot fresh foie gras (not pâté) needs mature Vintage Champagne.

Risotto Follow the flavour:

funghi porcini Finest mature Barolo or Barbaresco.

nero A rich dry white: VIOGNIER or even Corton-Charlemagne.

seafood A favourite dry white.

vegetables (eg. Primavera) PINOT GR from Friuli, Gavi, youngish SÉM, DOLCETTO or BARBERA d'Alba.

Soufflés As show dishes, these deserve ★★★ wines:

cheese Mature red burgundy or Bx, CAB SAUV, etc. Or fine mature white burgundy, Hunter SEM or Rioja.

fish (esp smoked haddock with chive cream sauce) Dry white, ★★★ burgundy, Bx, Alsace, CHARD, etc.

spinach (tough on wine) Mâcon-Villages, St-Véran or Valpolicella. Champagne (esp Vintage) can also spark things with the texture of a soufflé.

Fish

Abalone Dry or medium white: SAUV BL, unoaked CHARD. A touch of oak works with soy sauce, oyster sauce, etc. In Hong Kong: Dom Pérignon (at least).

Anchovies Fino, obviously. Or try orange wine.

bocquerones VERDEJO, unoaked SÉM.

salade niçoise Provence rosé.

Bacalão Salt cod needs acidity: young Portuguese red or white. Or Italian ditto. Orange can be good.

Bass, sea Fine white, eg. Clare RIES, Chablis, white Châteauneuf, ALBARIÑO, VERMENTINO, WEISSBURGUNDER. Rev up the wine for more seasoning, eg. ginger, spring onions; more powerful Ries, not necessarily dry.

Beurre blanc, fish with Deserves gd unoaked white with maturity: Hunter SEM, Premier Cru Chablis, CHENIN BL, RIES, Swartland white blend, gd Austrian, Etna CARRICANTE. Applies to most veg with beurre blanc too.

Caviar Iced vodka (and) full-bodied Champagne (eg. Bollinger, Krug). Don't (ever) add raw onion.

Ceviche Can be applied to anything now, but here, it's fish. Australian RIES or GRÜNER V, TORRONTÉS, VERDELHO. Manzanilla.

Crab (esp Dungeness) and RIES together are part of the Creator's plan. But He also created Champagne.

Chinese, with ginger & onion German RIES Kabinett or Spätlese Halbtrocken. Tokaji FURMINT, GEWURZ.

cioppino SAUV BL; but West Coast friends say ZIN. Also California sparkling.

cold, dressed Top Ries (Alsace, Australian, Austrian or Mosel) or ASSYRTIKO.

crab cakes Any of the above.

softshell Unoaked CHARD, ALBARIÑO or top-quality German Ries Spätlese.

Cured fish Salmon can have a whisky cure, a beetroot cure; all have sweetness and pungency. With gravadlax, sweet mustard sauce is a complication. SERCIAL Madeira (eg. 10-yr-old Henriques), Amontillado, Tokaji Szamarodni, orange wine. Or NV Champagne.

Curry A vague term for a vast range of flavours. S African CHENIN BL, Alsace PINOT BL, Franciacorta, fruity rosé, not too pale and anodyne; look at other flavours. Prawn and mango need more sweetness, tomato needs acidity. Fino can handle heat. So can IPA or Pilsner.

Fish pie (with creamy sauce) Can be homely or fancier. ALBARIÑO, Soave Classico, RIES Erstes Gewächs, Mâcon Bl, Spanish GODELLO.

Grilled, roast or fried fish Also applies to **fish & chips, tempura, fritto misto, baked... cod, haddock** CHARD, PINOT BL, MALVAZIJA.

Dover sole Perfect with fine wines: white burgundy or equivalent.

halibut, turbot, brill Best rich, dry white; top Chard, mature RIES Spätlese.

monkfish Meaty but neutral; full-flavoured white or red, according to sauce.

mullet, grey VERDICCHIO, unoaked Chard, rosé.

oily fish like herrings, mackerel, sardines More acidity, weight: ASSYRTIKO, VERDELHO, FURMINT, orange, rosé.

perch, sandre Top white burgundy, Mosel, Grand Cru Alsace, mature top fizz.

plaice, flounder Light, fresh whites.

red fish like salmon, red mullet PINOT N. For salmon, also best Chard, Grand Cru Chablis, top Ries.

skate, ray Delicate, but brown butter, capers need oomph: Alsace, ROUSSANNE, CHENIN BL.

swordfish Full-bodied dry white (or why not red?) of the country. Nothing grand.

trout Gd Chard, Furmint, Ries, Malvazija, Pinot N.

tuna Best served rare (or raw) with light red: young Loire CAB FR or red burgundy. Young Rioja is a possibility.

whitebait Crisp dry whites, eg. Furmint, Greek, Touraine SAUV BL, Verdicchio, white Dão, Fino Sherry, rosé. Or beer.

Kedgeree Full white, still or sparkling: Mâcon-Villages, S African CHARD, GRÜNER V, German Grosses Gewächs or (at breakfast) Champagne.

Lobster with a rich sauce Eg. Thermidor: Vintage Champagne, fine white burgundy, Cru Classé Graves, ROUSSANNE, top CHARD. Alternatively, for its inherent sweetness, Sauternes, Pfalz Spätlese, even Auslese.

plain grilled, or cold with mayonnaise NV Champagne, Alsace RIES, Premier Cru Chablis, Condrieu, Mosel Spätlese, GRÜNER V, Hunter SEM, white Rioja or local fizz.

Mussels marinière MUSCADET sur lie, unoaked CHARD, ASSYRTIKO. Or try light, brisk English red.

curried Alsace RIES or PINOT BL.

Paella, shellfish Full-bodied white or rosé, unoaked CHARD, ALBARIÑO, or GODELLO. Or local Spanish red.

Prawns, crayfish with garlic Keep the wine light, white, or rosé, and dry.

with mayonnaise English CHARD or rosé.

with spices Up to and incl chilli, go for a bit more body, but not oak: dry RIES or Italian, eg. FIANO, GRILLO. *See also* CURRY.

Sardines in saor Local neutral, fresh white with acidity.

Sashimi KOSHU comes into its own here, either as orange or white, and can deal with wasabi and soy, within reason. Otherwise, try white with body (Chablis Premier Cru, Alsace RIES) with white fish, PINOT N with red. Both need acidity.

Simple Chablis can be too thin. If soy is involved, then low-tannin red (again, Pinot). Remember sake (or Fino).

Scallops An inherently slightly sweet dish, best with medium-dry whites.

cream sauces German Spätlese, Montrachets or top Australian CHARD.

grilled or seared Hermitage Bl, GRÜNER V, Pessac-Léognan Bl, Vintage Champagne or PINOT N.

Asian seasoning CHENIN BL, GEWURZ, GODELLO, Grüner V.

Scandi fish dishes Scandinavian dishes often have flavours of dill, caraway and cardamom and combine sweet and sharp notes. Go for acidity and some weight: FALANGHINA, GODELLO, VERDELHO, Australian, Alsace or Austrian RIES.

Shellfish Dry white with plain boiled shellfish, richer wines with richer sauces. RIES is the grape.

plateaux de fruits de mer Etna white, MUSCADET de Sèvre et Maine, PICPOUL de Pinet, Alto Adige PINOT BL.

Smoked fish All need freshness and some pungency; Fino Sherry works with all.

eel Often with beetroot, crème fraîche: Fino again, or Mosel RIES.

haddock Quality Chablis, MARSANNE, GRÜNER V. *See also* SOUFFLÉS.

kippers Try Oloroso Sherry or Speyside malt.

mackerel Not wine-friendly. Try Fino.

salmon Condrieu, Alsace PINOT GR, Grand Cru Chablis, German Ries Spätlese, Vintage Champagne, vodka, schnapps, or akvavit.

trout More delicate: Mosel Ries.

Squid / octopus Fresh white: ALBARIÑO, MUSCADET, Greek, sparkling, esp with salt-and-pepper squid. Squid ink (risotto, pasta) needs Soave.

Sushi Hot wasabi is usually hidden in every piece. KOSHU is 1st choice. Failing that, German Trocken, Greek white, ALVARINHO, GRÜNER V or NV Brut Champagne. Obvious fruit doesn't work. Or, of course, sake or beer.

Tagine N African flavours need substantial whites to balance – Austrian, Rhône – or crisp, neutral whites that won't compete. Go easy on the oak. VIOGNIER or ALBARIÑO can work well. So can Amontillado Sherry.

Taramasalata A Med white with personality, Greek if possible. Fino Sherry works well. Try Rhône MARSANNE.

Teriyaki A way of cooking, and a sauce, used for meat, as well as fish. Germans favour off-dry RIES with weight: Kabinett can be too light.

Meat / poultry / game

Barbecues The local wine: Australian, Argentine, Chilean, S African, are right in spirit. Reds need tannin, vigour, freshness; don't have to be grand.

Beef *See also* STEAK. **boiled** Red: Light Douro red, BLAUFRÄNKISCH, PINOT N or SYRAH. Medium-ranking white burgundy is gd, eg. Auxey-Duresses. In Austria you may be offered skin-fermented TRAMINER. Mustard softens tannic reds, horseradish kills your taste; can be worth the sacrifice.

roast An ideal partner for fine red, esp PINOT N. *See* above for mustard. The silkier the texture of the beef (wagyu, Galician, eg.), the silkier the wine. Wagyu, remember, is about texture; has v. delicate flavour.

stew, daube Sturdy red: Pomerol or St-Émilion, Cornas, Hermitage, Napa CAB SAUV, Ribera del Duero, BARBERA, SHIRAZ, or Douro red.

stroganoff Dramatic red: Amarone, Barolo, Hermitage, Priorat, late-harvest ZIN. Georgian SAPERAVI or Moldovan Negru de Purkar.

Boudin blanc CHENIN BL, esp when served with apples: dry Vouvray, Saumur, Savennières, S African; mature red PINOT N if without.

Boudin noir / morcilla Local SAUV BL or CHENIN BL (esp in Loire). Or Beaujolais cru, esp Morgon. Or light TEMPRANILLO. Or Fino.

Brazilian dishes Pungent flavours that blend several culinary traditions. Rhônish grapes work for red, or white with weight: VERDICCHIO, California CHARD. Or a Caipirinha (better not have two).

Cajun food Gutsy reds, preferably New World: ZIN, CARMENÈRE, SHIRAZ. Fish or white meat: off-dry RIES, MARSANNE, ROUSSANNE. Or, of course, cold beer.

Cassoulet Fresh red from SW France – Corbières, Fitou, Gaillac, Minervois, St-Chinian – or BAGA, SHIRAZ, TEMPRANILLO.

Chicken / turkey / guinea fowl, roast Virtually any wine, incl v. best bottles of dry to medium white and finest old reds (esp burgundy). Sauces can make it match almost any fine wine (eg. coq au vin: r or w burgundy, or *vin jaune* for that matter).
chicken Kyiv Alsace RIES, Collio, CHARD, Bergerac rouge.
fried Sparkling works well.

Chilli con carne Young red: Beaujolais, TEMPRANILLO, ZIN, Argentine MALBEC, Chilean CARMENÈRE. Or beer.

Chinese dishes Food in China is regional – like Italian, only more confusing. It's easiest to have both white and red; no one wine goes with all. Peking duck is pretty forgiving. Champagne becomes a thirst-quencher. Beer too.
Cantonese Big, slightly sweet flavours work with slightly oaky CHARD, PINOT N, off-dry RIES. GEWURZ is often suggested but rarely works; GRÜNER V is a better bet. You need wine with acidity. Dry sparkling (esp Cava) works with textures.
Shanghai Richer and oilier than Cantonese, not one of wine's natural partners. Shanghai tends to be low on chilli but high on vinegar of various sorts. German and Alsace whites can be a bit sweeter than for Cantonese. For reds, try MERLOT – goes with the salt. Or mature Pinot N, but a bit of a waste.
Szechuan VERDICCHIO, Alsace PINOT BL, or v. cold beer. Mature Pinot N can also work; but *see* above. The Creator intended tea.
Taiwanese LAMBRUSCO works with trad Taiwan dishes if you're tired of beer.

Choucroute garni Alsace PINOT BL, PINOT GR, RIES, or lager.

Cold roast meat Generally better with full-flavoured white than red. German or Austrian RIES, lightish CHARD are v.gd, as is light GARNACHA. Leftover Champagne too.

Confit d'oie / de canard Young, brisk CAB FR, California CAB SAUV or MERLOT, Priorat cuts richness. Alsace PINOT GR or GEWURZ match it.

Coq au vin Red burgundy. Ideal: one bottle of Chambertin in the dish, two on the table. *See also* CHICKEN.

Dirty (Creole) rice Rich, supple red: NZ PINOT N, Bairrada, GARNACHA, MALBEC.

Duck / goose PINOT N is tops. Also other red in the Pinot idiom, like GARNACHA; also BLAUFRÄNKISCH. Or rich white, esp for goose: Pfalz Spätlese or off-dry Grand Cru Alsace. With oranges or peaches, the Sauternais propose drinking Sauternes, others Monbazillac or RIES Auslese. Mature and weighty Vintage Champagne handles accompanying red cabbage surprisingly well. So does decent Chianti.
Peking See CHINESE DISHES.
roast breast & confit leg with Puy lentils Madiran (best), St-Émilion, Fronsac, Maremma.
wild duck Worth opening gd Pinot N. Austrian, Tuscan red (easy on oak) also gd.
with olives Top-notch Chianti or other Tuscans.

Filipino dishes Spanish-influenced flavours, lots of garlic, bell peppers, adobo, not always super-spicy. Straightforward unoaked white with acidity (adobo can have a burst of vinegar) or fizz, Côtes de Gascogne, Rueda, RIES, rosé, even light red.

Game birds, young, roast The best red wine you can afford, but not too heavy. Partridge is more delicate than pheasant, which is more delicate than grouse. Up the weight of wine accordingly, starting with youngish PINOT N, BLAUFRÄNKISCH, SYRAH, GARNACHA, and moving up.

cold game Best German RIES or mature Vintage Champagne.

older birds in casseroles Gevrey-Chambertin, Pommard, Châteauneuf, Dão, or Grand Cru Classé St-Émilion, Rhône.

well-hung game Vega-Sicilia, great red Rhône or NZ Syrah, Ch Musar.

Game pie, hot Red: Oregon PINOT N, St-Émilion Grand Cru Classé.

cold Quality white burgundy or German Erstes Gewächs, Etna red, Champagne.

Goat (hopefully kid) As for lamb.

Jamaican curry goat See INDIAN DISHES. And don't forget MALBEC.

Goulash Flavoursome young red: Hungarian Kékoportó, ZIN, Uruguayan TANNAT, Douro, MENCÍA, young Australian SHIRAZ, SAPERAVI; or dry Tokaji Szamarodni.

Haggis Fruity red, eg. young claret, young Portuguese or Spanish red, CAB SAUV, MALBEC or Rhône blend. Or, of course, malt whisky.

Ham, cooked A gift to wine. Softish PINOT N (Côte de Beaune, Martinborough); Loire red or BLAUFRÄNKISCH; sweetish German white (RIES Spätlese); lightish CAB SAUV (eg. Chilean), or New World Pinot N. And don't forget the heaven-made match of ham and Amontillado.

Hare Jugged hare calls for flavourful red: not-too-old burgundy or Bx, Rhône (eg. Gigondas), Bandol, Barbaresco, Ribera del Duero, Rioja Res. The same for saddle or for hare sauce with pappardelle.

Indian dishes Various options: dry Sherry is brilliant. Choose a fairly weighty Fino with fish, and Palo Cortado, Amontillado, or Oloroso with meat, according to weight of dish; heat's not a problem. The texture works too. Otherwise, medium-sweet white, v. cold, no oak: Orvieto *abboccato*, S African CHENIN BL, Alsace PINOT BL, TORRONTÉS, Indian sparkling, Cava or NV Champagne. Rosé is gd all-rounder. For tannic impact Barolo or Barbaresco, or deep-flavoured reds, eg. Châteauneuf, Cornas, Australian GRENACHE or MOURVÈDRE, or Valpolicella Amarone – will emphasize the heat. Hot-and-sour flavours need acidity.

Sri Lankan More extreme flavours, coconut. Sherry, rich red, rosé, mild white.

Japanese dishes A different set of senses come into play. Texture and balance are key; flavours are subtle. A gd mature fizz works well, as does mature dry RIES; you need acidity, a bit of body, and complexity. Dry FURMINT can work well. Umami-filled meat dishes favour light, supple, bright reds: Beaujolais perhaps, or mature PINOT N. Full-flavoured yakitori needs lively, fruity, younger versions of the same reds. KOSHU with raw fish – but why not sake? Orange Koshu with wagyu beef. *See also* FISH/SASHIMI, SUSHI, TERIYAKI.

Korean dishes Fruit-forward wines seem to work best with strong, pungent Korean flavours. PINOT N, Beaujolais, Valpolicella can all work: acidity is needed. Non-aromatic whites: GRÜNER V, SILVANER, VERNACCIA. Beer too.

Lamb, roast One of trad and best partners for v.gd red Bx, or equivalents from elsewhere. In Spain, finest old Rioja and Ribera del Duero Res, or Priorat, in Italy ditto SANGIOVESE. Fresh mint is gd, but mint sauce should be banned.

milk-fed Is delicate: deserves top, delicate GARNACHA, even white Rueda, Rhône.

slow-cooked roast Flatters top reds but needs less tannin than pink lamb. *See also* TAGINES.

Liver, incl venison Young red: Bairrada, BLAUFRÄNKISCH, Breganze CAB SAUV, Italian MERLOT, Médoc, Priorat, St-Joseph, ZIN.

calf's Red Rioja Crianza, Fleurie. Or a big Pfalz RIES Spätlese.

Mexican food Californians favour RIES, esp German. Or beer.

Moussaka Red or rosé: Ajaccio, Corbières, Côtes de Provence, Greek red, SANGIOVESE, TEMPRANILLO, young ZIN.

Mutton A stronger flavour than lamb, and not usually served pink. Needs a strong sauce. Robust red; top-notch, mature CAB SAUV, SYRAH. Sweetness of fruit (eg. Barossa) suits it.

'**Nduja** Calabria's spicy, fiery spreadable salumi needs a big, juicy red: young Rioja, Valpolicella, CAB FR, AGLIANICO, CARIGNAN, NERELLO MASCALESE.

Osso bucco Low-tannin, supple red such as DOLCETTO d'Alba or PINOT N. Or dry Italian white such as Soave.

Ox cheek, braised Superbly tender and flavoursome, this flatters the best reds: Vega-Sicilia, St-Émilion. Best with substantial wines.

Oxtail Rather rich red: St-Émilion, Pomerol, Pommard, Nuits-St-Georges, Barolo, or Rioja Res, Priorat or Ribera del Duero, California or Coonawarra CAB SAUV, Châteauneuf, mid-weight SHIRAZ, Barolo, Amarone.

Paella Young Spanish wines: red, dry white, or rosé: Penedès, Somontano, Navarra, or Rioja.

Pastrami Alsace RIES, young SANGIOVESE, or St-Émilion.

Pigeon or squab PINOT N is perfect; or young Rhône, Argentine MALBEC, young SANGIOVESE. Try Franken SILVANER Spätlese. With luxurious squab, top quite tannic red.

   pastilla Depends on sweetness of dish. As above, or if authentically sweet, try RIES Spätlese, Alsace PINOT GR with some sweetness.

Pork A perfect rich background to a fairly light red or rich white.

   belly Slow-cooked and meltingly tender, needs red with some tannin or acidity. Italian would be gd: Barolo, DOLCETTO, or BARBERA. Or Loire red, or lightish Argentine MALBEC. With Chinese spices, VIOGNIER, CHENIN BL.

   Mangalica pork Fashionable, fatty. KÉKFRANKOS or other brisk red.

   pulled Often with spicy sauce: juicy New World reds.

   roast Deserves ★★★ treatment: Médoc is fine. Portugal's suckling pig is eaten with Bairrada; S America's with CARIGNAN; Chinese is gd with PINOT N.

   with prunes or apricots Something sweeter: eg. Vouvray.

Pot au feu, bollito misto, cocido Rustic red wines from region of origin; SANGIOVESE di Romagna, Chusclan, Lirac, Rasteau, Portuguese Alentejo or Spain's Yecla or Jumilla.

Quail Succulent, delicate: try red or white. Rioja Res, mature claret, PINOT N. Or mellow white: Vouvray, Hunter SEM.

Quiche Egg and bacon are not great wine matches, but one must drink something. Alsace RIES or PINOT GR, even GEWURZ, is classical. Beaujolais could be gd too.

Rabbit Lively, medium-bodied young Italian red, eg. AGLIANICO del Vulture, REFOSCO; MALBEC, Chiroubles, Chinon or Rhône rosé.

   as ragu Medium-bodied red with acidity: Aglianico, NEBBIOLO.

   with mustard Cahors.

   with prunes Bigger, richer, fruitier red.

Satay SHIRAZ, Alsace or NZ GEWURZ. Peanut sauce: problem for wine. Orange?

Sauerkraut (German) German RIES, lager or Pils. (But *see also* CHOUCROUTE GARNI.)

Singaporean dishes Part Indian, part Malay and part Chinese, Singaporean food has big, bold flavours that don't match easily with wine – not that that bothers the country's many wine-lovers. Off-dry RIES is as gd as anything. With meat dishes, ripe, supple reds: Valpolicella, PINOT N, DORNFELDER, unoaked MERLOT, or CARMENÈRE.

Steak Rare steak needs brisker, more tannic reds; well done needs juicy, fruity reds, eg. young Argentine MALBEC. Fattier cuts need acidity, tannin.

   au poivre A fairly young Rhône red or CAB SAUV. Nothing too sweetly fruity.

   fillet Silky red: Pomerol or PINOT N.

   fiorentina (bistecca) Chianti Classico Riserva or BRUNELLO.

   from older cattle Has deep, rich savouriness. Top Italian, Spanish red.

   Korean yuk whe (world's best steak tartare) Sake.

   ribeye, tomahawk, tournedos Big, pungent red: Barolo, Cahors, SHIRAZ, Rioja.

sirloin Suits most gd reds. Bx blends, Tuscans.

tartare Vodka or light young red: Beaujolais, Bergerac, Valpolicella. Aussies drink GAMAY with kangaroo tartare, charred plums, Szechuan pepper.

T-bone Reds of similar bone structure: Barolo, Hermitage, Australian CAB SAUV or Shiraz, Chilean SYRAH, Douro.

wagyu Delicate, silky red, or orange wine.

Steak-&-kidney pie or pudding Red Rioja Res or mature Bx. Pudding (with suet) wants vigorous young wine. Madiran with its tannin is gd. Or Greek.

Stews & casseroles Village burgundy or equivalent if fairly simple; otherwise lusty and full-flavoured red, eg. young Côtes du Rhône, Corbières, BARBERA, BLAUFRÄNKISCH, SHIRAZ, ZIN, etc.

Sweetbreads A rich dish, so grand white wine: Rheingau RIES or Franken SILVANER Spätlese, Grand Cru Alsace PINOT GR, or Condrieu, depending on sauce.

Tagines Depends on what's under the lid, but fruity young reds are a gd bet: Valpolicella, MERLOT, SANGIOVESE, SHIRAZ, TEMPRANILLO. Amontillado is great. Amarone is fashionable.

chicken with preserved lemon, olives VIOGNIER.

Tandoori chicken RIES or SAUV BL, young red Bx or light N Italian red served cool. Also Cava, NV Champagne or, of course, Palo Cortado or Amontillado Sherry.

Thai dishes Ginger and lemongrass call for pungent SAUV BL (Loire, Australia, NZ, S Africa) or RIES (Spätlese or Australian). Most curries suit aromatic whites with a touch of sweetness: GEWURZ also gd.

Tongue Any red or white of abundant character. Alsace GEWURZ or PINOT GR, gd GRÜNER V. Also Loire reds, BLAUFRÄNKISCH, TEMPRANILLO and full, dry rosés.

Veal A friend of fine wine. Rioja Res, CAB blends, PINOT N, NEBBIOLO, German or Austrian RIES, Vouvray, Alsace PINOT GR, Italian GRECO di Tufo.

Venison Big-scale reds, incl MOURVÈDRE solo or blended. Rhône, Languedoc, Barolo, Bx, top mature NZ or California CAB SAUV; or rather rich white (Pfalz Spätlese or Alsace PINOT GR).

with sweet & sharp berry sauce Try a German Grosses Gewächs RIES, or Chilean CARMENÈRE, or SYRAH.

Vietnamese food RIES, dry or up to Spätlese, German, Austrian, NZ, also GRÜNER V, SÉM. For reds, BLAUFRÄNKISCH, CAB FR, PINOT N.

Vitello tonnato Full-bodied whites: CHARD. Light reds (Langhe Nebbiolo, TEMPRANILLO) served cool. Or a southern rosé.

Wild boar Serious red: top Tuscan or Priorat. NZ SYRAH. I've even drunk Port; Amarone would be a compromise.

Vegetable dishes

With few tannins to help or hinder, matching wine to veg is about sweetness, acidity, weight and texture. *See also* FIRST COURSES.

Agrodolce Italian sweet-and-sour, with pine kernels, sultanas, capers, vinegar and perhaps anchovies. Go to fresh white: VERDICCHIO, unoaked CHARD. Etna rosato. Or orange.

Artichokes Not great for wine. Incisive dry white: NZ SAUV BL; Côtes de Gascogne or Greek (precisely, 4-yr-old MALAGOUSIA, but easy on the vinaigrette); VERMENTINO. Orange wine, yes; red, no. Better no wine than red.

Asparagus Is lightly bitter and needs acidity, if it needs wine at all. Asparagus solo: skip the wine. With other ingredients: go by those.

Aubergine Comes in a multitude of guises, usually strongly flavoured. Sturdy reds with acidity are a gd bet: SHIRAZ, Greek, Lebanese, Bulgarian, Hungarian, Turkish. Structured white, eg. VERDICCHIO, or go further and have orange wine.

Avocado Not a wine natural. Dry to slightly sweet RIES Kabinett will suit the dressing. Otherwise, light and fresh: ALIGOTÉ, TREBBIANO, PINOT GRIGIO.

Beetroot Mimics a flavour found in red burgundy. You could return the compliment. New-wave (ie. light) GARNACHA/Grenache is gd, as well, as is GAMAY.

Bitter leaves: radicchio etc. Bone-dry, aged Palo Cortado. But easy on the dressing. Fab combo. Or NEBBIOLO, LAGREIN, white VERMENTINO, orange.

   roast radicchio, chicory etc. Valpolicella, SANGIOVESE, BLAUFRÄNKISCH, Etna red.

Cauliflower roast, etc. Go by the other (usually bold) flavours. Try Austrian GRÜNER V, Valpolicella, NZ PINOT N.

   cauliflower cheese Crisp, aromatic white: Sancerre, RIES Spätlese, MUSCAT, ALBARIÑO, GODELLO. CHARD too, and Beaujolais-Villages.

   with caviar – yes, really. Vintage Champagne.

Celeriac, slow-roast or purée Won't interfere with rest of dish. Acidity works well, so classic CAB blends, SANGIOVESE, PINOT N, according to dish.

   remoulade with smoked ham Needs bright red: DOLCETTO, simple GAMAY, Valpolicella. Or white GRÜNER V.

Chestnuts Earthy, rich red: Tuscan or S Rhône.

Chickpeas Look at other flavours in dish. Casserole works with TEMPRANILLO or S French reds.

   hummus Any simple red, pink or white, or, of course, Fino.

Chilli Some like it hot, but not with your best bottles. Tannic wines become more tannic; if you like that, go for it. Light, fruity reds and whites are refreshing: TEMPRANILLO, Chilean MERLOT, Argentinian MALBEC, NZ SAUV BL. Same for harissa. *See also* MEAT/CHILLI CON CARNE, CHINESE DISHES, INDIAN DISHES.

Couscous with vegetables Young red with a bite: SHIRAZ, Corbières, Minervois; rosé, esp Etna; orange wine; Italian REFOSCO or SCHIOPPETTINO.

Dhal Comes with many variations, but all share aromatic earthiness. Simple, warm-climate reds work best: CARMENÈRE, Dão, S Italian.

Fennel-based dishes SAUV BL: Pouilly-Fumé or NZ; SYLVANER or English SEYVAL BL; or young TEMPRANILLO. **Deep-flavoured braised fennel** Light GAMAY, PINOT N.

Fermented foods *See also* CHOUCROUTE GARNI, KOREAN DISHES, SAUERKRAUT. Kimchi and miso are being worked into many dishes. Fruit and acidity are generally needed. If in sweetish veg dishes, try Alsace.

Grilled Mediterranean vegetables Italian whites, or for reds Brouilly, BARBERA, TEMPRANILLO or SHIRAZ.

Lentil dishes Sturdy reds such as Corbières, ZIN or SHIRAZ. *See also* DHAL.

Mac 'n' cheese As for CAULIFLOWER CHEESE.

Mushrooms (in most contexts) A boon to most reds and some whites. Context matters as much as species. Pomerol, California MERLOT, Rioja Res, top burgundy or Vega-Sicilia.

   button or Paris with cream Fine whites, even Vintage Champagne.

   ceps / porcini Ribera del Duero, Barolo, Chianti Rufina, Pauillac or St-Estèphe, NZ Gimblett Gravels.

   on toast Best claret, even Port.

Onion / leek tart / flamiche Fruity, off-dry or dry white: Alsace PINOT GR or GEWURZ is classic; Canadian, Australian or NZ RIES; Jurançon. Or Loire CAB FR.

Peppers, cooked Mid-weight Rhône grapes, CARMENÈRE, Rioja; or ripe SAUV BL (esp with green Hungarian wax peppers).

   stuffed Full-flavoured red, white, or pink: Languedoc, Greek, Spanish, Etna. Or orange.

Pickled foods & vinegar Vinegar and wine don't go, it's true, but pickled foods are everywhere. Try Alsace, German RIES with CHOUCROUTE/SAUERKRAUT (*see* MEAT). With pickled veg as part of a dish, just downgrade the wine a bit (no point in opening best bottles) and make sure it has some acidity. (Or have beer.) In dressings, experiment with vinegars: Sherry vinegar can work with Amontillado, etc., big reds; Austrian apricot vinegar is delicate; balsamic can work with rich Italian reds. Wine just has to work harder than it used to.

Pumpkin / squash ravioli or risotto Full-bodied, fruity dry or off-dry white: VIOGNIER or MARSANNE, demi-sec Vouvray, Gavi or S African CHENIN. If you want red, MERLOT, ZIN.

Ratatouille (or piperade) Vigorous young red: Chianti, Languedoc, NZ CAB SAUV, MALBEC, MERLOT, TEMPRANILLO. A gd rosé can be best of all.

Roasted veg Can be root veg or more Mediterranean, but all have plenty of sweetness. Rosé, esp with some weight, or orange wine. Lightish reds with acidity to match the dressing. Pesto will tilt it towards white with weight.

Saffron Found in sweet and savoury dishes, and wine-friendly. Rich white: ROUSSANNE, VIOGNIER, PINOT GR. Orange wines can be gd too. With desserts, Sauternes or Tokaji. *See also* MEAT/TAGINES.

Salsa verde Whatever it's with, it points to more acidity, less lushness in the wine.

Seaweed (nori) Depends on the context. *See also* FISH/SUSHI. Iodine notes go well with Austrian GRÜNER V, RIES.

Sweetcorn fritters Often served with a hot, spicy sauce. Rosé, orange, or neutral white all safe.

Tahini Doesn't really affect wine choice. Go by rest of dish.

Tapenade Manzanilla or Fino Sherry, or any sharpish dry white or rosé. Definitely not Champagne.

Tomatoes Generally call for acidity in wine: think of Italian reds like BARBERA, Etna, Valpolicella, etc. for deep-flavoured cooked tomatoes. White with acidity for raw.

Truffles Black truffles are a match for finest Right Bank Bx or Volnay, but even better with mature white Hermitage or Châteauneuf. White truffles call for best Barolo or Barbaresco of their native Piedmont. With buttery pasta, Lugana. Or at breakfast, on fried eggs, BARBERA.

Watercress, raw Makes every wine on earth taste revolting.

Wild garlic leaves, wilted Tricky: a fairly neutral white with acidity will cope best.

Desserts

Apples: Cox's Orange Pippins with Cheddar cheese Vintage Port.
    Russets with Caerphilly Old Tawny, or Amontillado.
    Pie, etc. Sweet Vouvray or similar.

Bread-&-butter pudding Fine 10-yr-old Barsac, Tokaji Aszú, or an Australian botrytized SEM.

Cakes *See also* CHOCOLATE, COFFEE, RUM. BUAL or MALMSEY Madeira, Oloroso or Cream Sherry. Asti, sweet Prosecco.

Cheesecake Sweet white: Vouvray, Anjou, or Vin Santo – nothing too special.

Chocolate Don't try to be too clever. Texture matters. BUAL, California Orange MUSCAT, Tokaji Aszú, Australian Liqueur Muscat, 10-yr-old Tawny or even young Vintage Port; Asti for light, fluffy mousses. Or *vins doux naturels* (VDN) Banyuls, Maury, or Rivesaltes. Some like Médoc with bitter black chocolate, though it's a bit of a waste of both. A trial of SYRAH with bitter chocolate showed that you shouldn't, ever. Armagnac, or a tot of gd rum.

Christmas pudding, mince pies Tawny Port, Cream Sherry or that liquid Christmas pudding itself, PEDRO XIMÉNEZ Sherry. Tokaji Aszú. Asti, or Banyuls.

Coffee desserts Sweet MUSCAT, Australia Liqueur Muscats, or Tokaji Aszú.

Creams, custards, fools, syllabubs *See also* CHOCOLATE, COFFEE, RUM. Sauternes, Loupiac, Ste-Croix-du-Mont or Monbazillac.

Crème brûlée Sauternes or Rhine Beerenauslese, best Madeira, or Tokaji Aszú.

Ice cream & sorbets PX with vanilla, or Australian Liqueur MUSCAT. Sorbets: give wine a break.

Lemon flavours For dishes like tarte au citron, try sweet RIES from Germany or Austria or Tokaji Aszú; v. sweet if lemon is v. tart.

Meringues (eg. Eton mess) Recioto di Soave, Asti, mature Vintage Champagne.

Nuts (incl praline) Finest Oloroso Sherry, Madeira, Vintage or Tawny Port (nature's match for walnuts), Tokaji Aszú, Vin Santo, or Setúbal MOSCATEL. Cashews and Champagne. Pistachios with Fino.

Salted nut parfait Tokaji Aszú, Vin Santo.

Orange flavours Experiment with old Sauternes, Tokaji Aszú, or California Orange MUSCAT.

Panettone Vin Santo. Jurançon *moelleux*, late-harvest RIES, Barsac, Tokaji Aszú.

Pears in red wine Rivesaltes, Banyuls, or RIES Beerenauslese.

Pecan pie Orange MUSCAT or Liqueur Muscat.

Raspberries (no cream, little sugar) Excellent with fine reds that themselves taste of raspberries: young Juliénas, Regnié. Even better with cream and something in the Sauternes spectrum.

Rum flavours (baba, mousses) MUSCAT – from Asti to Australian Liqueur, according to weight of dish.

Strawberries, wild, no cream With red Bx (most exquisitely Margaux) poured over. **with cream** Sauternes or similar sweet Bx, Vouvray *moelleux*, or Vendange Tardive Jurançon.

Summer pudding Fairly young Sauternes of a gd vintage.

Sweet soufflés Sauternes or Vouvray *moelleux*. Sweet (or rich) Champagne.

Tiramisù Vin Santo, young Tawny Port, MUSCAT de Beaumes-de-Venise, Sauternes, or Australian Liqueur Muscat. Better idea: skip the wine.

Trifle Should be sufficiently vibrant with its internal Sherry (Oloroso for choice).

Zabaglione Light-gold Marsala or Australian botrytized SEM, or Asti.

Wine & cheese

Counterintuitively, white is a safer option than red. Fine red wines are slaughtered by strong cheeses. Principles to remember (despite exceptions): 1st, the harder the cheese, the more tannin the wine can have; 2nd, the creamier the cheese, the more acidity is needed in the wine – and don't be shy of sweetness. Cheese is classified by its texture and the nature of its rind, so its appearance is a guide to the type of wine to match it.

Bloomy-rind soft cheeses: Brie, Camembert, Chaource Full, dry white burgundy or Rhône. Not tannic red.

Blue cheeses The extreme saltiness of Roquefort or most blue cheeses needs sweetness: Sauternes, Tokaji, youngish Vintage or Tawny Port, esp with Stilton. Intensely flavoured old Oloroso, Amontillado, Madeira, Marsala and other fortifieds go with most blues. Dry red does not. Trust me.

Cooked cheese dishes: fondue Trendy again. Light, fresh white as below.

frico Cheese baked or fried with potatoes or onions, trad in Friuli; high-acid local REFOSCO (r), or RIBOLLA GIALLA (w).

macaroni or cauliflower cheese *See* VEGETABLE DISHES/CAULIFLOWER.

Mont d'Or Delicious baked, and served with potatoes. Fairly neutral white with freshness: GRÜNER V, Jura Savagnin.

Fresh cream cheese, fromage frais, mozzarella Light crisp white: Bergerac, Jura, Loire; juicy rosé can work too.

Hard cheeses: Gruyère, Manchego, Parmesan, Cantal, Comté, old Gouda, Cheddar Hard to generalize, relatively easy to match. Gouda, Gruyère, some Spanish, and a few English cheeses complement fine claret or CAB SAUV and great SHIRAZ/ SYRAH. But strong cheeses need less refined wines, preferably local ones. Granular old Dutch red Mimolette, Comté, or Beaufort gd for finest mature Bx. Also for Tokaji Aszú. But try tasty whites too: Jura, Vin Jaune.

Natural rind (mostly goats' cheese): St-Marcellin Sancerre, light SAUV BL, Jurançon, Savoie, Soave, Italian CHARD; or young Vintage Port.

Semi-soft cheeses: Livarot, Pont l'Evêque, Reblochon, St-Nectaire, Tomme de Savoie Powerful white Bx, even Sauternes, CHARD, Alsace PINOT GR, dryish RIES, S Italian and Sicilian whites, aged white Rioja, dry Oloroso Sherry. The strongest of these cheeses kill almost any wines. Try marc or Calvados.

Washed-rind soft cheeses: Carré de l'Est, mature Époisses, Langres, Maroilles, Milleens, Münster Local reds, esp for Burgundian cheeses; vigorous Languedoc, Cahors, Côtes du Frontonnais, Corsican, S Italian, Sicilian, Bairrada. Also powerful whites, esp Alsace GEWURZ, MUSCAT. Gewurz with Münster, always.

Food & your finest wines

With v. special bottles, the wine guides the choice of food rather than vice versa. The following is based largely on gastronomic conventions, some bold experiments and much diligent and on-going research.

Red wines

Amarone Classically, in Verona, risotto all'Amarone or pastissada. But if your butcher doesn't run to horse, then shin of beef, slow-cooked in more Amarone.

Barolo, Barbaresco Risotto with white truffles; pasta with game sauce (eg. pappardelle alla lepre); porcini mushrooms; Parmesan.

Great Syrahs: Hermitage, Côte-Rôtie, Grange, Vega-Sicilia Beef, venison, well-hung game; bone marrow on toast; English cheese (Lincolnshire Poacher) but also hard goats'-milk and ewes'-milk cheeses such as England's Lord of the Hundreds. I treat Côte-Rôtie like top red burgundy.

Great Vintage Port or Madeira Walnuts or pecans. A Cox's Orange Pippin and a digestive biscuit is a classic English accompaniment.

Red Bordeaux, v. old, light, delicate wines (eg. pre-82) Leg or rack of young lamb, roast with a hint of herbs (not garlic); entrecôte; simply roasted partridge; roast chicken never fails.

  fully mature great vintages (eg. 85 89 90) Shoulder or saddle of lamb, roast with a touch of garlic; roast ribs or grilled rump of beef.

  mature but still vigorous (eg. 00 05) Shoulder or saddle of lamb (incl kidneys) with rich sauce. Fillet of beef marchand de vin (with wine and bone marrow). Grouse. Avoid beef Wellington: pastry dulls the palate.

  Merlot-based Beef (fillet is richest) or well-hung venison. In St-Émilion, lampreys.

Red burgundy Consider the weight and texture, which grow lighter/more velvety with age. Also the character of the wine: Nuits is earthy, Musigny flowery, great Romanées can be exotic, Pommard relatively sturdy. Roast chicken or (better) capon is a safe standard with red burgundy; guinea fowl for slightly stronger wines, then partridge, grouse, or woodcock for those progressively richer and more pungent. Hare and venison are alternatives.

  great old burgundy The Burgundian formula is cheese: Époisses (unfermented); a fine cheese but a terrible waste of fine old wines. *See* above.

  vigorous younger burgundy Duck or goose roasted to minimize fat. Or faisinjan (pheasant cooked in pomegranate juice). Coq au vin, or lightly smoked gammon.

Rioja Gran Reserva, top Duero reds Richly flavoured roasts: wild boar, mutton, venison, saddle of hare, whole suckling pig.

White wines

Beerenauslese / Trockenbeerenauslese Biscuits, peaches, greengages. But TBAs don't need or want food.

Condrieu, Ch-Grillet, Hermitage Bl Pasta, v. light, scented with herbs and tiny peas or broad beans. Or v. mild tender ham. Old white Hermitage loves truffles.

Grand Cru Alsace Gewurz Cheese soufflé (Münster cheese).

Pinot Gr Roast or grilled veal. Or truffle sandwich. (Slice a whole truffle, make a sandwich with salted butter and gd country bread – not sourdough or rye – wrap and refrigerate overnight. Then toast it in the oven. Thanks, Dom Weinbach.)

Ries Truite au bleu, smoked salmon, or choucroute garni.

Vendange Tardive Foie gras or tarte tatin.

Old Vintage Champagne (not Blanc de Blancs) As an apéritif, or with cold partridge, grouse, or woodcock. The evolved flavours of old Champagne make it far easier to match with food than the tightness of young wine. Hot foie gras can be sensational. Don't be afraid of garlic or even Indian spices, but omit the chilli.

late-disgorged old wines These have extra freshness plus tertiary flavours. Try with truffles, lobster, scallops, crab, sweetbreads, pork belly, roast veal, chicken. Saffron is flattering to old Champagne.

old Vintage Rosé Pigeon, veal.

Sauternes Simple crisp buttery biscuits (eg. langues de chat), white peaches, nectarines, strawberries (without cream). Not tropical fruit. Pan-seared foie gras. Lobster or chicken with Sauternes sauce. Yquem recommends oysters (and indeed lobster). Experiment with blue cheeses. Rocquefort is classic but needs one of the big Sauternes. Savoury food, apart from cheese, seldom works. Cantonese dishes can be gd. A chilled glass as an apéritif can be even better.

Sherry VOS or VORS Just some almonds or walnuts, or gd cheese. And time to appreciate them.

Tokaji Aszú (5–6 Puttonyos) Foie gras recommended. Fruit desserts, cream desserts, even chocolate can be wonderful. Roquefort. It even works with some Chinese, though not with chilli – the spice has to be adjusted to meet the sweetness. Szechuan pepper is gd. Havana cigars are splendid. So is the naked sip.

Top Chablis White fish simply grilled or *meunière*. Dover sole, turbot, halibut are best; brill, drenched in butter, can be excellent. (Sea bass is too delicate; salmon passes but does little for the finest wine.)

Top white burgundy, top Graves, top aged Ries Roast veal, farm chicken stuffed with truffles or herbs under the skin, or sweetbreads; richly sauced white fish (turbot for choice) or scallops, white fish as above. Lobster, wild salmon.

Vouvray moelleux, etc. Buttery biscuits, apples, apple tart.

Fail-safe face-savers

Some wines are more useful than others – more versatile, more forgiving. If you're choosing restaurant wine to please several people, or just stocking the cellar with basics, these are the wines: **Red** BARBERA d'Asti/d'Alba, BLAUFRÄNKISCH, Beaujolais, Chianti, GARNACHA/Grenache, young MALBEC (easy on the oak), PINOT N, SYRAH (more versatile than Shiraz), Valpolicella. **White** Alsace PINOT BL, ASSYRTIKO, cool-climate CHARD, CHENIN BL from the Loire or S Africa, Fino Sherry, GRÜNER V, dry RIES, Sancerre, gd Soave, VERDICCHIO. And the greatest of these is Ries. Always go for the best producer you can afford, and don't get too hung up on appellations or even vintages, within reason. If you can't afford gd Chablis, buy Assyrtiko, not cheap Chablis.

France

More heavily shaded areas are
the wine-growing regions.

Abbreviations used in the text:

Al	Alsace
Beauj	Beaujolais
Burg	Burgundy
Bx	Bordeaux
Cas	Castillon-Côtes de Bordeaux
Chab	Chablis
Champ	Champagne
Cors	Corsica
C d'O	Côte d'Or
Ldoc	Languedoc
Lo	Loire
Mass C	Massif Central
Prov	Provence
N/S Rh	Northern/Southern Rhône
Rouss	Roussillon
Sav	Savoie
SW	Southwest
AC	appellation contrôlée
ch, chx	château(x)
dom, doms	domaine(s)

Le Havre
Caen
Brest
LOIRE
Loire
Nantes
Muscadet
Anjou-Saumur
La Rochelle
BORDEAUX
Médoc
Pomerol
St-Emilic
Bordeaux
Entre-Deux-
Graves
Sauternes
Côtes du
Marmanda
Buzet
Tursan
Côtes d
St-Mon
Biarritz
Madira
Jurançon

There is (and I say this fully aware of the implications) reason to be pleased with the effects of climate change so far in France. Simply, grapes get riper, and wines taste nicer. France has almost entirely recovered from its fling with overripeness, overextraction and overoaking, and most French regions – temperature-wise – are comfortably within their comfort zone. The exception might be Burgundy, because Pinot Noir is a tetchy plant and extremely inelastic in climate terms, and in Chablis now it's really easy to get wines that taste like Puligny, but more difficult to get wines that taste like Chablis as we used to know it. But look at the Northern Rhône; look at the Loire. Glorious wines, full of freshness and complexity and life. I cannot remember these wines ever being so good. Frost is a problem; hail is a problem; extreme weather events are a nightmare. But for those of us who don't have to do the hard work, there is some good news. And the best way we can support growers is – of course – by buying their wines.

France entries also cross-refer to Châteaux of Bordeaux

Recent vintages of the French classics

Red Bordeaux

Médoc / Red Graves For many wines, bottle-age is optional; for these it is indispensable. Minor chx from light vintages may need only 1 or 2 yrs these days, but even modest wines of gd yrs can improve for 10 or so, and the great chx of these yrs can profit from double that time.

2023 Big crop (when mildew contained). Powerful but balanced Cab Sauv. Potential to age.

2022 Hot, dry. Cab Sauv dense but supple tannins; gd ageing potential.

2021 Complicated: frost, rain, mildew. Cab Sauv variable but classic. Be choosy.

2020 Cab Sauv rich, dark, expressive. High alc but elegant. Low yields.

2019 Great balance; concentration plus freshness. Cab Sauv-led blends. Will age.

2018 Pure, aromatically intense Cab Sauv. Rich, powerful (alc high), balanced. Long-term potential.

2017 Attractive wines: gd balance, fairly early drinking. Volumes often small.

2016 Cab Sauv with colour, depth, structure. Vintage to look forward to.

2015 Excellent Cab Sauv yr, but not structure of 05 10. Some variation. Keep.

2014 Cab Sauv bright, resonant: gd to v.gd; classic style. Ready for drinking.

Earlier fine vintages: 10 09 08 06 05 00 98 96 95 90 89 88 86 85 82 75 70 66 62 61 59 55 53 49 48 47 45 29 28.

St-Émilion / Pomerol

2023 Merlot hit hardest by mildew. Yields variable. Gd in top terroirs.

2022 As Méd. Young vines suffered. Merlot excellent on limestone, clay soils.

2021 Merlot hit by frost, mildew. Low yields, variable quality. Cab Fr did better.

2020 Merlot rich and gourmand. Cabs Fr/Sauv also v.gd. Great potential.

2019 Drought. Merlot excellent on limestone, clay soils. Sandier areas suffered.

2018 Powerful but pure. Best from limestone, clay soils. Mildew affected yields.

2017 Balanced, classic fruit-cake flavours. Will be quite early drinking.

2016 As Méd. Some young vines suffered in drought but overall v.gd.

2015 Great yr for Merlot. Perfect conditions. Colour, concentration, balance.

2014 More rain than the Méd so Merlot variable; v.gd Cab Fr. Drinking now.

Earlier fine vintages: 10 09 05 01 00 98 95 90 89 88 85 82 71 70 67 66 64 61 59 53 52 49 47 45.

Red Burgundy

Côte d'Or Côte de Beaune reds generally mature sooner than grander wines of Côte de Nuits. Earliest drinking dates are for lighter commune wines, eg. Volnay, Beaune; latest for GCs, eg. Chambertin, Richebourg. Even the best burgundies are more attractive young than equivalent red Bx. But great red burgundy is more age-worthy, and rewarding, than is generally supposed.

2023 Sunny harvest after variable summer. Careful sorting = quality, quantity.

2022 Shaping up beautifully. Lovely balance, delicious length. Watch.

2021 Wicked weather in growing season. Much reduced harvest, yet some lovely wines. Choose carefully.

2020 Concentrated: some superb, some too robust. Avoid later-picked wines.

2019 June/July heat gave lavish wines, many great, a few too high-octane. Keep.

2018 Sumptuous reds, gd young or old. Some overripe or flawed.

2017 Attractive, mostly ripe enough, stylish, enjoyable already. Don't overlook.

2016 Some spectacular reds with great energy, fresh acidity. Will keep.

2015 Already a storied yr. Dense, concentrated, as 05 but juiciness of 10. Patience needed. Greatness beckons.

2014 Overshadowed by 15. Attractive fresh reds, some lack depth. Drinking now.

2013 Light yr, though not as weak as Bx. Some charming; only best have time.

Earlier fine vintages: (drink or keep) 10 09 08 05 02 99 96 93 (mature) 90 89 85 78 76 71 69 66 64 62 59.

White Burgundy

Côte d'Or White wines are now rarely (sadly) made for long ageing, but top wines should still improve for 10 yrs or more. Most Mâconnais and Chalonnais (St-Véran, Mâcon-Villages, Montagny) usually best drunk early (2–3 yrs). Note the scourge of premox still hangs over wines post-1995 and 5 yrs old+.

2023 Abundant harvest, fully ripe. Harnessing opulence will be key.

2022 Summer heat after early rain; large crop, leaning to lavish flavour register.

2021 Trounced by frost but survivors are promising. Will be rare jewels.

2020 Crop gd, unlike reds. Powerful, surprising freshness; v. v. promising.
2019 Rich wines after summer heat. Best retained delicious acidity. Some stellar wines.
2018 More potential than 1st thought. Delicious from start, but power to age.
2017 Magnificent. Poised, elegant, lingering intensity. Even humblest are excellent. Rivals 14.
2016 Small, frosted crops, inconsistent results. Most ready now.
2015 Lush wines. Early pickers gd, later wines may be too heavy. Similar to 09 but more successes. Keep the winners.
Earlier fine vintages (ready): 14 12 10 09 08 07 05 02 99 96 93 92 90.

Chablis has suffered disproportionately from the twin terrors of frost and hail in recent yrs. GCs of top vintages need at least 5 yrs, can age superbly for 15+; PCs proportionately less, but give them 3 yrs at least. Then serve at cellar temp, not iced, and decant. Yes, really.
2023 Summer oscillated between heat/rain. Challenge, but results generally gd.
2022 Well-balanced wines in gd volumes, despite drought and heat.
2021 Frost calamity. Survivors should be fine.
2020 Hot and dry, but wines have turned out well, esp at higher end.
2019 Small crop of concentrated wine: typical marine Chab, exotic notes.
2018 Vintage of century (volume): attractive quality, ready soon. 17 even better.
Earlier fine vintages: 12 10 08 02 00.

Beaujolais

23 Variable summer, but looks promising. 22 Small harvest, gd quality. Plenty of future drinking pleasure here. 21 Frost and dreadfully wet summer. 20 A v. early harvest, but promising quality. 19 Hot dry summer, gorgeously juicy and satisfying wines.

Languedoc-Roussillon

2023 Dry, esp Rouss. Low yields. Intense, fresh reds, esp Carignan, Mourvèdre.
2022 Drought lowered some yields, overall gd quality. Carignan, Grenache top.
2021 Frost, drought, pre-harvest rain in Ldoc, variable. Rouss fared better, v.gd.
2020 Lovely balance, gd acidity, freshness. Rouss gd.
2019 Hot dry summer; some sunburn; gd to v.gd, but small vintage.

SW France

2023 Mixed, but generally low yields. Mildew, hail, heat left mark. Pick carefully.
2021 Relentless frost, rain, mildew, more rain. Keep to older vintages for reds.
2022 Crop size reduced by frost, then drought and heat. Quality likely to be gd.
2020 Summer heat, drought. A little uneven but gd, occasionally exceptional.
2019 Spring storms, heatwave summer. Small crop, fine quality.
2018 Big yr. Some fabulous wines in all styles.

Northern Rhône

Hillside plots, manual work, precise, often granite terroirs, top reds (Cornas, Côte-Rôtie, Hermitage) can live 30 yrs+. White Hermitage can age as red.
2023 Weather setbacks, mixed, Côte-Rôtie gd, also n of St-Joseph. Fruit-forward, some lack true richness. V.gd Condrieu, whites pretty gd.
2022 Prominent fruit, brio at Côte-Rôtie, Cornas, reds gd, some v.gd. Best terroirs handled drought best. Appealing, rounded whites. Sound yields.
2021 Aromatic reds, purity over power. Hermitage, Cornas (depth, gd) fuller than Côte-Rôtie. Not esp long-keeping. Beautiful whites, top Condrieu.

2020 Stylish reds. Côte-Rôtie aromatic, outstanding Hermitage (r/w).
Top whites, esp if Marsanne-based, v.gd.

2019 Tremendous reds, flair at Côte-Rôtie; like 16 with more stuffing.
No hurry. Whites concentrated. Note Hermitage, St-Joseph.

2018 Scaled-up reds, v.gd; Hermitage (r), similar Côte-Rôtie. Crozes variable.
Whites: depth, surprising freshness; Condrieu, Hermitage, St-Péray.

2017 V.gd, esp Côte-Rôtie. Full reds, deeper than 16, show sunshine, firm
tannins, benefit from time. Whites for hearty food, Condrieu variable.

2016 Reds lucid, harmonious, classic at Côte-Rôtie, gd to v.gd. Stylish Cornas.
Marvellous Hermitage whites, other white gd, precise.

2015 Excellent, concentrated full-tannin reds; long-lived Côte-Rôtie, Hermitage.
Time still essential. Full whites, can be heady.

2014 Juicy reds, humming now. Excellent whites: style, freshness.

Southern Rhône

2023 Grenache handled heat, drought. Gigondas did well, Châteauneuf mixed,
purity in top wines. Variable Côtes-du-Rh (r). Whites gd, balanced.

2022 Concentration, heat; dense reds, forward aromas, some tannin issues,
best balanced. Châteauneuf gd. Firm, full whites, geared to *la table*.

2021 Select with care: v. drinkable, aromatic reds from best names, bright fruit,
elegance. Whites can be exceptional, best-ever Châteauneuf (w).

2020 Can be variable at modest price. Top: rich, splendid, gd acidity. Whites
tricky from less gd zones, stick to best.

2019 Flamboyant, deep reds, character. Intense Grenache. Châteauneuf back
on form, Gigondas excellent. Top names demand patience. Whites v.gd.

2018 Mixed, can be gd. Early signs of advance in reds already. Note Valréas,
Visan, Vinsobres: higher, later vyds. Also Lirac, Rasteau. Whites v. full.

2017 Drought, can be variable. Full, bold reds, tannins just easing. Top doms
best, stylish. Rasteau, Visan gd. Full whites.

2016 Excellent for all. Sensuous reds. Sun-filled whites; keep some to age.

2015 Rich, dark, body, firm tannins, often enticing flair; v.gd. Full whites v.gd.

2014 Aromatic finesse returns to Châteauneuf. Stick to best names. Note
Gigondas, Rasteau, Cairanne. Fresh, v.gd whites.

Champagne

2023 Large yield, enormous berries. Overall promising, esp Chard.

2022 Relief at big, gd yr; hot in vein of 18, but long growing season.

2021 Cold spring, April frost, mildew = v. low yields. Sad in Marne V.

2020 Miraculous trio: 18 19 20. Beautiful ripe wines.

2019 Excellent quality. Pure fruit, tension, better acidity than much-lauded 18.

2018 Best in Pinot GCs of N Montagne. Chard more mixed: heat stress.

2017 Athletic wines of grace, energy.

2016 Underrated. Gently expressive Pinot Ns give much pleasure.

Earlier fine vintages: 12 10 09 08 07 06 04 02 00 98 96 95 92 90.

The Loire

2023 Warm summer, tempered by pre-harvest rain. Yields gd, quality
potentially gd.

2022 Despite heat/drought, v.gd to exceptional: early, perfect fruit; gd yields.

2021 Difficult, complicated yr: frost, mildew, hail in places. Small crop saved by
fine autumn. Fresher style than recently.

2020 Incredible 7th successive v.gd yr; gd quality, quantity. Some high alc.

2019 Well-balanced wines but volume down, esp Muscadet, Anjou (April frost).

Alsace

2023 Sunny, dry but cool; v.gd Pinot N, Ries. No noble rot, so little if any memorable late harvest.

2022 Scorching heat; then rain; gd, lowish acid, clay-limestone soils best.

2021 Tumultuous rain, disease. Pinots suffered, but sunny Sept gave fine Ries.

2020 Refined, elegant, scented across board, as growers master climate change.

2019 Hot; e-facing hills, esp GCs, may be v.gd, ripe, dry (Ries, Pinot Gr, Gewurz). Wines from plains could be a problem.

2018 Warm, but fresh wines. Gewurz, Pinot Gr, Ries tops in high-altitude GCs.

2017 One of best since World War Two, but small crop. Recalls 71 08.

Earlier fine vintages: 16 12 10 08 07 04 02 96 95 92 90.

Abymes Sav On limestone rubble of Mont Granier by APREMONT. DYA. Vin de SAV AOP cru. Jacquère grape. Try ★ 13 Lunes, ★★ A&M QUENARD, Giachino, Labbé, P&S Ravier.

Agrapart Champ ★★★ 13' 16' 17 18 Pascal A makes precise CHAMP from scrupulously tended vyds in AVIZE. Impressive quartet; Mineral, *Venus*, L'Avizoise, Experience.

Ajaccio Cors ★★→★★★ AOP W Corsica. Lots of granite. SCIACCARELLU shines here, classy VERMENTINO too.

Alary, Dom S Rh ★★★ Leading CAIRANNE family estate, stylish reds encouraged by son Jean-Etienne's Burg education. Top terroirs, mature vines = quality. Compelling Cairanne Jean de Verde (r, gd w), genuine, rich Brunote (r), gd VDF L'Exclus (Counoise).

Albert de Conti, Dom SW Fr Other branch of the Conti family (*see* CH TOUR DES GENDRES). Chez Paul CAB SAUV; more unusually, pure dry MUSCADELLE Conti-ne Périgourdine. Pét-nat too.

Allemand, Thierry N Rh ★★★★ 01' 05' 06' 07' 08' 09' 10' 12' 13' 15' 16' 17' 18' 19' 20' 21' 22' 23 High-profile wine, low-profile person, v. accomplished vigneron, started from zero; son Théo now present. Magisterial CORNAS from organic DOM, low sulphur. Two v. deep, smoky, lingering wines, hot prices. Top is Reynard (mineral, intricate, 20 yrs+); Chaillot (bursting fruit, floral) drinks earlier.

Alliet, Philippe Lo ★★★★ Superb CHINON DOM, run by Philippe and son Pierre. Top CUVÉES *Coteau de Noiré*, *L'Huisserie* 09 10' 15' 16 17 18' 19 20 (22) (23). Drink VIEILLES VIGNES and white younger.

Aloxe-Corton Burg ★★→★★★ 05' 09' 10' 12' 15' 17 18' 19' 20' 21 22' The n end of CÔTE DE BEAUNE, famous for GC CORTON, CORTON-CHARLEMAGNE. Others don't set pulse racing. Tasty reds improved by recent warm yrs. Reasonable value. Best: Capitain-Gagnerot, Follin-Arbelet, Rapet, Senard, TOLLOT-BEAUT.

Alsace ★★ →★★★★ Vosges rain-shadow effect means driest French wine region: aromatic, fruity, full whites, increasingly gd PINOT N. Varietal-labelling rules, so wines easy to grasp. Sec (dry), demi-sec (medium-dry), *moelleux* (medium-sweet), *doux* (sweet) clearly indicated on front or back label, or use of numerical scale, means you know what you're getting.

Alsace Grand Cru ★★★ →★★★★ 08' 10' 12 13 14 (esp RIES) 15 17' 18 19 20' Only 51 GC, incl some of the world's greatest vyds (Brand, HENGST, RANGEN, Sporen). Since 22 vintage, Hengst and Kirchberg de Barr PINOT N can also be GC-labelled. Huge geological diversity means terroir-lovers' bonanza; but some GCs are too large. PC in gd sites coming soon. Some of world's most age-worthy wines (40 yrs+), esp 61 67 71 83 90 08 10.

Alzipratu Cors ★★★ Pierre Acquaviva, nr Calvi, makes gd-value Fiumeseccu (r/w/ rosé). Iniziu (r), pale herby expression of NIELLUCCIU.

Amadieu, Pierre S Rh Quality, long-est producer, with gd vyds at GIGONDAS, notably Grand Romane (top fruit) and Romane Machotte (50S GRENACHE).

Also owns CAIRANNE DOM Hautes Cances (stylish). Gigondas white (CLAIRETTE) is gd. Merchant range is VACQUEYRAS.

Amirault, Yannick Lo ★★★→★★★★ Brilliant BOURGUEIL, splendid ST NICOLAS DE BOURGUEIL. Top (limestone): Les Malgagnes, La Petite Cave, Le Grand Clos, Les Quartiers 09 10' 15' **16 17** 18' 19 20 22 (23). Drink others younger. Also new CHENIN BL Bâtard-Princesse.

Ampeau C d'O ★★★ Step back in time at MEURSAULT DOM specializing in long-aged cellar releases (c.25 yrs old). Properly mature, lush, succulent whites: reminder of what was lost through premature oxidation. Reds impressive, less sumptuous.

Angerville, Marquis d' C d'O ★★★★ VOLNAY bio superstar. Great range of PCS topped by legendary CLOS des DUCS (MONOPOLE). Elegant, balanced, harmonious; *vrai* Volnay, hard to fault. *See also* DOM DU PÉLICAN for Jura.

Anjou Lo ★→★★★★ Region and AOP: Anjou. CHENIN BL is king; exciting dr ANJOU BL and SAVENNIÈRES; sweet BONNEZEAUX, COTEAUX DU LAYON, QUARTS DE CHAUME. Reds more varied; fruity GAMAY; Anjou Rouge (CAB FR), age-worthy ANJOU-VILLAGES (CABS FR/SAUV). Underrated CABERNET D'ANJOU rosé (dr/s/sw) still a thing. Plenty of fizz (esp CRÉMANT). Some top natural wines.

Anjou Blanc Lo ★→★★★★ 14' 15 16' 17' 18 **19 20** 21 22 (23) Revitalized AOP now laser-sharp, acid-framed CHENIN BL. Early picked, barrel-fermented, now challenging SAUMUR/VOUVRAY on quality. Best age well. Look for Bablut, BAUDOUIN, *Belargus*, Bergerie, CADY, Juchepie, Le Clos Galerne, OGEREAU, PIERRE-BISE, *Pierre Ménard*, *Plaisance*, *Richard Leroy* (VDF), Sansonnière (VDF), Terra Vita Vinum.

Anjou-Villages Lo ★→★★★ 09' 10' 11' 15' **16 17** 18' 19 20 (22) AOP for age-worthy CABS FR/SAUV blends, a few 100% Cab Sauv (esp warm schist soils). More tannic than SAUMUR/TOURAINE reds. Best: *Bergerie*, Brancherau, CH PIERRE-BISE, *Ogereau*. Associated enclave Anjou Brissac (previously Anjou-Villages-Brissac) covers same area as COTEAUX DE L'AUBANCE; try *Bablut*, Montgilet, *Rochelles*, Varière.

Anne Gros & Jean-Paul Tollot, Dom Ldoc ★★★★ Burg winemakers apply know-how to high-altitude MINERVOIS terroir with stunning results. Les Carretals from 100-yr-old CARIGNAN/GRENACHE. La Cinso (r) floral, delicate.

Antech, Maison Ldoc ★★★ Françoise Antech-Gazeau is queen of all styles of Limoux fizz. Brut Nature MAUZAC, ripe apples, yeasty. CRÉMANT Eugénie shines. Méthode Ancestrale sweetly fruity.

AOP / AC or AOC (appellation contrôlée) Government control of origin and production (but not quality) of most French wines; around 45% of total. AOP (appellation d'origine protégée) is new term.

Aphillanthes, Dom Les S Rh ★★→★★★ 20' 22' 23 Organic, bio DOM in hot PLAN DE DIEU. Deep, terroir wines, value. Two CUVÉES: des Galets, VIEILLES VIGNES (50S GRENACHE). CÔTES DU RH (r); GIGONDAS PROMESSE; RASTEAU 1921.

Apremont Sav Largest cru of SAV, thus quality varies. Steely, light Jacquère on limestone rubble. Keep up to 4 yrs. Try ★ 13 Lunes, Apffel, ★ Blard, Chevillard, ★ Dupraz, ★★ Giachino, ★★ *Masson*, Perrier, Richel.

Arbin Sav ★★ A SAV cru. Dark, spicy MONDEUSE on steep slopes. Drink to 8 yrs+. Try ★ A&M QUENARD, ★ Genoux, ★ Jacquet, ★ F Trosset, ★★ *Magnin*.

Arbois Jura AOP of N Jura, and Jura wine tourism capital. CHARD and/or SAVAGNIN whites, VIN JAUNE, reds from Poulsard/Ploussard, TROUSSEAU or PINOT N.

The newbie Jurassiens
Jura boasts an impressive number of exciting, recently est wineries, and those galvanized by a new generation. Seek out for true Jura flavours with a modern twist: Cellier Saint-Benoit, Désiré Petit, Fumey-Chatelain, Mouillard. And for natural innovation: Les Bottes Rouges, Les Pieds sur Terre, Novice, or Villet. *See also* ARBOIS, CÔTES DU JURA.

Try terroir-true ★★★ Stéphane TISSOT; sheer class from ★★★ *Pélican* and ★★ Rijckaert, sulphur-free from ★★ MAISON OVERNOY, ★ St-Pierre and ★★ *Tournelle*, plus all-rounders ★★ Aviet, ★ Borde, Fruitière (Co-op) Arbois/Béthanie, ★ Pinte, ★ Renardière, Rolet, J-L Tissot and ★ Touraize.

Ardèche S Rh ★ →★★ 22' 23 IGP Rocky granite hills, valleys w of S Rh, often use looser VDF. Also HQ for Rhône Vin Nature, all VdF (A Calek, Les Deux Terres, Mazel). Quality up, often gd value. Direct, clear reds; MARSANNE, VIOGNIER (CHAPOUTIER). Best from SYRAH, also GAMAY (often old vines), CAB SAUV (Serret). Restrained, burg-style Ardèche CHARD by LOUIS LATOUR (Grand Ardèche much oak). CH de la Selve; DOMS de Vigier, du Grangeon, JF Jacouton; Mas d'Intras (organic).

Ardoisières, Dom des Sav IGP Vin des Allobroges organic estate with vyds outside AOP. Superb, eclectic ★★★ range, incl Améthyste (r) blend, Quartz Altesse, Schist (w) blend, plus ★ Argile blends (r/w).

Aristide Larrieu, Les Vins d' Ldoc ★★★ Armelle Dubois takes grandfather's name for brand-new CORBIÈRES DOM. Cracking Carignan Bl C1617, perfect with oysters, being snapped up by Michelin-star restos. One to watch.

Arlaud C d'O ★★★ →★★★★ Leading MOREY-ST-DENIS estate energized by Cyprien A, new heights with 19. Older vintages could be hearty, now beautifully poised, from exceptional BOURGOGNE Roncevie up to GCS. Fine Morey PCS (Ruchots).

Arlot, Dom de l' C d'O ★★→★★★ AXA-owned estate; stylish, fragrant across range from HAUTES-CÔTES to GC ROMANÉE-ST-VIVANT. Star buy is NUITS CLOS des Forêts St-Georges. Reds fully destemmed since 2021. Interesting whites too.

Armand, Comte C d'O ★★★★ MONOPOLE CLOS des Epeneaux may be POMMARD's most graceful, effortless, ageless, GC quality; gd value from AUXEY, VOLNAY too.

Arnoux-Lachaux C d'O ★★★★ VOSNE superstar. All change under Charles Lachaux: no-till, high-trellised, unhedged vines, v.-light-hand vinification with whole bunches, much reduced oak. Sublime. Breathtaking prices. PCS Grand Suchots, Reignots and GC ROMANÉE-ST-VIVANT.

Arretxea SW Fr Tiny Basque estate producing ★★★ IROULÉGUY. The real thing.

Aube Champ (aka Côte des Bar) CHAMP's southerly vyds; v.gd PINOT N by great Reims houses, eg. KRUG, VEUVE CLICQUOT. Aube 11' excels, less lauded elsewhere. Torrential rain, heat spikes in 21; v. warm but promising 22. Capacious 23.

Aubert et Matthieu Ldoc ★★★ Dynamic duo making offbeat, modern wines from best terroirs. CUVÉE Milo in La Livinière, Pablo Maria CORBIÈRES, TERRASSES DU LARZAC. Hors Piste IGP. CHARD, PINOT N from cooler areas.

Aubuisières, Dom des Lo ★★→★★★ VOUVRAY stalwart, now in hands of Charles Lesaffre. Historically leading source of *moelleux* 89 90 96 97 02 03 08 09 10 14 18 20, now focus on SEC, DEMI-SEC. Look for CUVÉE de Silex, Le Bouchet, Le Petit Clos, Les Girardières, Le Marigny. Also gd fizz.

Aupilhac, Dom d' Ldoc ★★★ Sylvain Fadat, pioneer of MONTPEYROUX, cultivates bio s-facing old-vine CARIGNAN, MOURVÈDRE. Les Cocalières (r/w) from high-altitude VYDS on Mt Baudile shine.

Auxey-Duresses C d'O ★★ →★★★ (r) 15' 16 17 18' 19' 20' (w) 14' 15' 17' 18 19' 20' 21 22' MEURSAULT neighbour enjoying climate change. Whites are "junior Meursault", can be excellent, look for Les Hautés vyd. Reds now ripen properly. Best: (r) COCHE-DURY, COMTE ARMAND, d'Auvenay (Boutonniers), Gras, Jessiaume, Paquet, Prunier; (w) Diconne, Lafouge, LEROUX, Paquet, Vincent.

Avize Champ ★★★★ Côte des Blancs GC CHARD, home to finest growers AGRAPART, Bonville, SELOSSE, Thienot. Huge co-op Union CHAMP provides base wines to biggest houses.

Aÿ Champ ★★★→★★★★ Revered PINOT N village, home of BOLLINGER and DEUTZ. Mix of merchants and growers, more oak than elsewhere (eg. Sébastien Giraud). Aÿ Rouge (AOP COTEAUX CHAMPENOIS) now excellent in riper yrs: 15' 18' 19' 20 22.

Ayala Champ ★★★ 13 **14** 19 20' Revitalized AŸ house, owned by BOLLINGER. Excellent BLANC DE BLANCS, BRUT NATURE and N° 7 13, *La Perle 14.*

Ayze Sav ★★ Cru closest to Mont Blanc, sometimes spelt Ayse. Rare Gringet grape: fruity fizz, mineral (dr) whites. Belluard winery now re-baptized Gringet with new owners.

Bachelet Burg ★★★ →★★★★ Well-regarded CÔTE DE BEAUNE family. *B-Monnot* for superb village wines and BÂTARD-M, Bernard B (MARANGES), Jean-Claude B for similar quality in ST-AUBIN and CHASSAGNE (PC Boudriotte). No relation to Denis B (great GEVREY-CHAMBERTIN).

Balthazar, Franck N Rh ★★★ 18 19 20' 21 22' 23' Handmade, fruit purity; organic CORNAS, incl delightful zero-added-sulphur Chaillot. Pretty ST-PÉRAY (w).

Bandol Prov ★★★→★★★★ AOP on slopes by Med, nr Toulon, renowned for noble reds for ageing, majority MOURVÈDRE, plus GRENACHE, CINSAULT. Rosé now main production; can be v. pale, Prov-style, or gutsier, gastronomic from Mourvèdre, often excellent, age well. White (5%): CLAIRETTE, UGNI BL, occasionally SAUV BL. Top: DOMS DE LA BÉGUDE, du Gros'Noré, de la Ribotte, Guilhem Tournier, La Bastide Blanche, Lafran Veyrolles, La Suffrène, Mas de la Rouvière, Pibarnon, Pradeaux, Ray-Jane, Roche Redonne, TEMPIER, Terrebrune, des Trois Filles, Val d'Arenc, Vannières.

Banyuls Rouss ★★★ Undervalued, sometimes brilliant VDN from steep vyds, by Med, nr Spanish border. COLLIOURE same area. From GRENACHE of all colours. Young, fresh style is *rimage*, but stars are RANCIOS, long-aged, pungent, intense. Wood-aged GC, 30 mths min. Try with chocolate. Best: DOMS de la Rectorie, du Mas Blanc, la Tour Vieille, Madeloc, Piétri Géraud, Vial Magnères; Bila-Haut, CLOS ST SÉBASTIEN, Coume del Mas, Les Clos de Paulilles. *See also* MAURY.

Barmes-Buècher, Dom Al ★★→★★★ Wettolsheim estate making gd CRÉMANT and SGNS, bevy of GCs; lieu-dit CLOS Sand RIES, GC Steingrubler GEWURZ best buys.

Barrique 225-litre oak barrel. Now more subtle use, or none. Cost: €800+/barrel.

Barsac Saut ★★→★★★★ 09' 11' 13 **14** 15' 16' 18 **19 20** 22 (23) Neighbour of SAUT with similar botrytized wines from lower-lying limestone; fresher, less powerful; 23 potential quality, quantity. Top: *Climens*, COUTET, DOISY-DAËNE, *Doisy-Védrines*. Value: Cantegril, Closiot, La Clotte Cazalis, Liot.

Barthod, Ghislaine C d'O ★★★→★★★★ A reason to fall in love with CHAMBOLLE-MUSIGNY. Son Clément in charge (2019), further refining style. Perfume, delicacy yet depth, concentration. Unbeatable range of 11 different PCs, incl Baudes, Beaux Bruns, Cras, Fuées. BOURGOGNE rouge can age 10 yrs.

Bâtard-Montrachet C d'O ★★★★ 08' 09' 10 12 **14**' 15 **17**' 18 19' 20' 21 22' A 12-ha GC, downslope from LE MONTRACHET. Full, usually impressive wines that need time; more power than neighbours Bienvenues-B-M (more graceful) and CRIOTS B-M. Seek out: BACHELET-Monnot, BOILLOT (both H and J-M), FAIVELEY, GAGNARD, LATOUR, LEFLAIVE, LEROUX, MOREY, OLIVIER LEFLAIVE, PERNOT, RAMONET, SAUZET, VOUGERAIE. Also J-C BACHELET, J CARILLON for Bienvenues version.

Baudouin, Patrick Lo ★★→★★★ ANJOU figurehead; fine CHENIN BL (dr/sw). Dry *Effusion* 16 18 19 **20** and *Le Cornillard* esp worthy. Benchmark COTEAUX DU LAYON and QUARTS DE CHAUME.

Baudry, Dom Bernard Lo ★★★ →★★★★ Leading CHINON DOM. Top limestone CUVÉES La Croix Boissée, Le CLOS Guillot 05' 09 10' **15' 16** 17 18' 19 20 21 (22) (23). Les Grézeaux (gravel) also ages well. New cuvée Les Mollières (limestone). Drink Les Granges (sand) young. Fine white, rosé.

Baumard, Dom des Lo ★★ ANJOU "old guard". Famed for long-lived dry SAVENNIÈRES CLOS du Papillon 02' 05 08 10' **14 18** 19 20 and CLOS Saint Yves. Also sweet QUARTS DE CHAUME 03 05 07' 09 **10** 16 18.

Baux-de-Provence, Les Prov ★★→★★★ Stunning, touristy village. Almost all organic/

bio. Mostly red: CAB SAUV, GRENACHE, SYRAH. White: CLAIRETTE, GRENACHE BL, Rolle, ROUSSANNE. TRÉVALLON best, prefers IGP Alpilles. Others: Dalmeran, d'Estoublon, DOM Hauvette, Gourgonnier, Lauzieres, Mas de Carita, Mas de la Dame, Mas Ste Berthe, ROMANIN, Terres Blanches, Valdition; atypical Milan.

Béarn SW Fr ★→★★ AOP DYA Reds from ★ JURANÇON co-op, DOMS Guilhémas, Lapeyre. Same grapes as MADIRAN and Jurançon.

Beaucastel, Ch de S Rh ★★★★ 05' 06' 07' 09' **10'** 12' **13' 15'** 16' 17' **18'** 19' 20 21 22' 23 Long-time organic CHÂTEAUNEUF estate, piles of large galet-stone soils: noted for old MOURVÈDRE, 100-yr-old ROUSSANNE; drink latter at 5–25 yrs. Only 30% GRENACHE in dark-fruited, upfront, suave, elegant red, drink at 2 yrs or from 7–8. Top-quality, v. long-lived 60% Mourvèdre Hommage à Jacques Perrin (r). Much style in own-vines CÔTES DU RH Coudoulet de Beaucastel (r), lives 10 yrs+. Famille Perrin GIGONDAS (three wines, v.gd), RASTEAU, VINSOBRES (best) all gd, authentic. Note organic Perrin Nature Côtes du Rh (r/w). Growing N Rh merchant-vyds venture, Maison Les Alexandrins (elegant). Diversifying: gin, grape-scented oils, Miraval Provence rosé. (*See also* Tablas Creek, California.)

Beaujolais ★→★★ Besmirched but now resurgent name. Time to fall in love again with the simple fresh fruit, and more from growers in the hills. Avoid industrial examples. Also sold as COTEAUX BOURGUIGNONS. Serve cool.

Beaujolais Primeur / Nouveau Raised the image, destroyed the reputation: BEAUJ of the new vintage, hurriedly made for release at midnight on the 3rd Wednesday in Nov. Enjoy juicy fruit, but don't let it put you off real thing.

Beaujolais-Villages ★★ 17 18' **19' 20'** 21 22' Challenger vyds to the ten named crus, eg. MOULIN-À-VENT. May specify best village, eg. Lantigné. Try CH de Basty, Ch des Vergers, F Berne, F Forest, JM BURGAUD, N Chemarin.

There's a River Rhone in N Ireland; c.100 Newcastles (Châteauneuf) around world.

Beaumes-de-Venise S Rh ★★ (r) 16' 17' 18 **19' 20'** 22' 23 Village nr GIGONDAS, best high ochre-stony Trias for red, with flatland vyds, noted for VDN MUSCAT apéritif/ dessert. Serve v. cold: musky-grapey, honeyed, ages well, eg. DOMS Beaumalric, Bernardins (character, complex), Coyeux, Durban (rich, long life, 20 yrs), Fenouillet (brisk), Fontavin, JABOULET, Perséphone (stylish), Pigeade (racy, v.gd), VIDAL-FLEURY, co-op Rhonéa. Also robust, herbal, grainy reds, can be powerful: CH Redortier; Doms Bouïssière, de Fenouillet, Durban, la Ferme St-Martin (organic), Les Baies Gouts, Martinelle, Mathiflo, Piéblanc (organic), St-Amant (also gd w). Leave for 2–3 yrs. Simple whites (some dry Muscat, VIOGNIER).

Beaune C d'O ★★→★★★ 05' 09' 10' **12 15'** 16 17 18' 19' 20 21 22' Wine capital of Burg, more reliable than exciting. Classic merchants: BOUCHARD, CHANSON, DROUHIN, JADOT, LATOUR; and more recent contenders Bernstein, Lemoine, LEROUX, Pacalet. Top DOMS: Bellène, Besancenot, Croix, DE MONTILLE, Dominique LAFON, Morot, plus iconic HOSPICES DE BEAUNE. Graceful, perfumed PC reds offer value, eg. Bressandes, Cras, VIGNES Franches; more power from Grèves. Try Aigrots, CLOS St-Landry and esp *Clos des Mouches (Drouhin)* for whites.

Beauregard, Ch de Burg ★★→★★★ Unmissable POUILLY-FUISSÉ from Frédéric Burrier: Les Reisses, Ménétrières, Vers Cras. Fine BEAUJ: FLEURIE, MOULIN-À-VENT.

Beaurenard, Dom de S Rh ★★★ 19' 20 21' 22' 23' Classy organic/bio CHÂTEAUNEUF estate. Sleek red, table-friendly, beautiful white. Boisrenard older-vine, deeper, more oaked (r/w). Two high-grade RASTEAU reds (Argiles Bleus old vines).

Begude, Dom Ldoc ★★★ AOP LIMOUX, 300m (984ft) altitude gives freshness, pristine fruit to top-class CHARD, PINOT N. Fun pét-nat, GEWURZ orange too.

Bégude, Dom de la Prov ★★★★ Guillaume Tari makes astonishing, long-lived BANDOL. La Brulade (r), powerful, complex. Irréductible rosé, packed with flavour, rewards ageing.

Belargus, Dom Lo ★★★★ Relatively new ANJOU project. Huge investment. Dry, mineral, new-style ANJOU BL (Bonnes Blanches, *Treilles*, Quarts, Rouères, etc.), SAVENNIÈRES (Gaudrets, Ruchères) 18 **19** 20 21 (22) (23). Top QUARTS DE CHAUME.

Bellivière, Dom de Lo ★★★ →★★★★ Top JASNIÈRES, COTEAUX DU LOIR. Superb CHENIN BL Calligramme, VIEILLES VIGNES Éparses (can vary dr to sw) 10 14' 15' **16'** 18' 19 20' (22) (23). Drink others younger. Reds gd (Pineau d'Aunis).

Bergerac SW Fr ★ →★★★ (w) 19 20 22 (23) AOP, more continental climate produces fuller-bodied wines. Côtes de Bergerac for sweet white or fuller red from lower yields. Huge variations in styles, quality. Best: ★★★ *Tour des Gendres*, ALBERT DE CONTI, DOM de l'Ancienne Cure, ★★ CH de la Jaubertie, Malfourat, Moulin Caresse (also Montravel AOP), Thénac, Tirecul La Gravière, CAVE de Sigoules (reliable co-op). *See* sub-AOPs: MONBAZILLAC, PÉCHARMANT, SAUSSIGNAC.

Berthet-Bondet, Dom Jura ★★ Biggest producer (still small) of CH-CHALON VIN JAUNE but reliably covers all bases for CÔTES DU JURA (r/w/CRÉMANT); gd-value organic.

Beyer, Léon Al ★★★★ Comtes d'Eguisheim GEWURZ (GC Pfersigberg) one of AL's best, just-as-gd R de Beyer showcases different GC terroir (Eichberg). Dry, food-friendly, virtually ageless (40 yrs+); SGNS grand.

Bichot, Maison Albert Burg ★★ →★★★★ Major BEAUNE merchant/grower with bio DOMS in BEAUJ (Rochegrès), CHAB (LONG-DEPAQUIT), MERCUREY (Adélie), NUITS (CLOS Frantin), POMMARD (Pavillon). Previously so-so, impressive recent improvement across all labels. Major buyer at HOSPICES auction.

Billaud Chab ★★★ →★★★★ Difficult CHAB choice between DOM Billaud-Simon back on form under FAIVELEY ownership and Samuel B's sensational wine under his own label. Both brilliant: characterful, authentic, age-worthy.

Phylloxera spreading in Bollinger's ungrafted Vieilles Vignes Françaises. RIP soon.

Billecart-Salmon Champ ★★★★ Revered family house, 7th generation. Supremely reliable Rosé CUVÉE; Cuvée Louis BLANC DE BLANCS **07'** 08; single-plot CLOS St-Hilaire 02 **04' 05' 06**; NF Billecart 02 08; excellent *Elisabeth Salmon Rosé* 02 **06' 09**. New Les Rendez-vous series: N° 4 CHARD, N° 5 PINOT N.

Bize, Simon C d'O ★★★ Chisa B makes delicious bio whole-bunch-style reds, from BOURGOGNE to GC LATRICIÈRES-CHAMBERTIN. Also SAVIGNY Grands Liards, PCS Guettes, Vergelesses and tasty whites too. Once dependable, now exemplary.

Blagny C d'O ★★ →★★★★ 05' **09'** 10' 12 15' **16'** 17 18' 19' 20' 21 22' Remote hamlet on hillside above MEURSAULT and PULIGNY. Offers value. Own AOP for austere yet fragrant reds. Whites sold as Meursault-Blagny PC. Home to evocative vyd names: La Jeunelotte, Pièce Sous le Bois, Sous le Dos d'Ane. Best growers: (r) Lamy-Pillot, LEROUX, MATROT; (w) de Cherisey, JOBARD, LATOUR, LEFLAIVE.

Blanc de Blancs Any white made from white grapes only, esp CHAMP. Description of style, not quality.

Blanc de Noirs White (or slightly pink or "blush", or "gris") wine from red grapes, esp CHAMP: much more elegant now.

Blanck, Paul & Fils Al ★★★ →★★★★ GEWURZ, PINOT GR, RIES v.gd: GC SCHLOSSBERG Ries best **17' 18' 19'**. SYLVANER 22 v.gd.

Blanquette de Limoux Ldoc ★★ Lively, appley fizz; 90% MAUZAC plus CHARD, CHENIN BL. AOP CRÉMANT de LIMOUX, more classic with Chard, Chenin Bl, PINOT N, and less Mauzac. Sieur d'Arques co-op is biggest. Try Delmas, Jo Riu, La Coume-Lumet, LAURENS, MAISON ANTECH, Robert, Les Hautes Terres, Monsieur S.

Blaye Bx ★ →★★ 15 16 17 19 **20** 22 Designation for better reds (lower yields, higher vyd density, longer maturation) from AOP BLAYE-CÔTES DE BX.

Blaye-Côtes de Bordeaux Bx ★ →★★ 16' 19 20 **22** Mainly (90%) MERLOT-led red AOP on right bank of Gironde. A little dry white (mainly SAUV BL). Best CHX: Bel-Air la Royère, Bourdieu, Cantinot, des Tourtes, Gigault (CUVÉE Viva), Haut-Bertinerie,

Haut-Grelot, Jonqueyres, Les Bertrands, Monconseil-Gazin, Mondésir-Gazin, Montfollet, Peybonhomme Les Tours, Roland la Garde. Go-ahead VIGNERONS de Tutiac co-op (r/w) too.

Boeckel, Dom Al ★★★ Mittelbergheim organic winery; rich but refined, outstanding SYLVANER (GC ZOTZENBERG); RIES Wibbelsberg 17' fine, CLOS Eugénie 18 19' rich.

Boillot C d'O Leading Burg family. ★★★ Jean-Marc (POMMARD), esp fine, long-lived (w); ★★★→★★★★ Henri (MEURSAULT), potent, stylish (r/w); ★★★ Louis (CHAMBOLLE) great reds, both Côtes, brother Pierre (DOM Lucien B) ★★→★★★ (GEVREY). Marthe Henry B (Meursault), no close relation, interesting post-modern wines. Seek them all out, esp Henri B.

Boisset, J-C Burg Ultra-successful merchant/grower group created over past 60 yrs. Boisset label, once humdrum, now exciting, from magnificent new winery in NUITS. Check *Dom de la Vougeraie*. Recent additions: (Burg) Alex Gambal, VINCENT GIRARDIN. Also high-end JCB CRÉMANTS labelled as "Brut Burgundy". Projects in BEAUJ, Jura, California (Gallo connection), Canada, Chile, Uruguay.

Boizel Champ ★★★ Family-run; value. BLANC DE BLANCS NV, esp on base of 13' 17' 18. CUVÉE Sous Bois, wood well handled. Prestige Cuvée Joyau de France 08, also Rosé 12. *Collection Trésor* 90 96.

Bollinger Champ ★★★★ Great classic house, power and glory. BRUT Special NV singing since 2012, RD 02 04' 05' 07 08, Grande Année 08 12 14, Vintage Rosé 12 14. New CUVÉE showing new faces of eponymous PINOT N villages, thus far Verzenay (VZ 15 16), Tauxières 17, AŸ 13. Sublime *Vieilles Vignes Françaises* 12; La Côte aux Enfants (still) 16 and new sparkling 13.

Bonnaud, Ch Henri Prov ★★★→★★★★ Top DOM in tiny AOP PALETTE, nr Aix. Silky red, elegant rosé. Quintessence (CLAIRETTE) v. fine.

Bonneau du Martray, Dom C d'O (r) ★★★ (w) ★★★→★★★★ Famed producer for CORTON-CHARLEMAGNE, owned by Stanley Kroenke, owner of Screaming Eagle (California); 3 ha leased to DRC. Intense, for long ageing, glorious vibrant fruit, underlying minerality. Older vintages variable. Small amount of red CORTON.

Bonnes-Mares C d'O ★★★★ 90' 93 96' 99' 02' 05' 09' 10' 12' 15' 16' 18 19 20 21 22' The GC between CHAMBOLLE-MUSIGNY and MOREY-ST-DENIS with some of latter's robust, *sauvage* character. Structured, long-lived, less fragrant than MUSIGNY. Best: ARLAUD, d'Auvenay, Bart, BRUNO CLAIR, DE VOGÜÉ, Drouhin-Laroze, DUJAC, GROFFIER, H BOILLOT, JADOT, MORTET, ROUMIER, VOUGERAIE.

Bonnet, Alexandre Champ ★★★ Fascinating producer in Les Riceys, nearer to CHABLIS than Épernay. Beguiling range: Côteaux Champenois (w) 18 20, La Fôret Rosé de Saignée 16 18 19, Les Contrées (incl 7 Cépages 18 19). Champ at its most intriguing.

Bonnezeaux Lo ★★★ 07' 09' 10' 11' 13 14 15 16 17 18' 19 20 (22) AOP for sweet CHENIN BL; three slopes (schist) in COTEAUX DU LAYON. Best: Deux Arcs, *Fesles*, Fontaines, Mihoudy, *Petit Val*, Petite Croix, Varière.

Bordeaux ★ →★★ 19 20 22 Catch-all AOP for generic Bx (c. half region's production). Most brands (*Dourthe*, MOUTON CADET, *Sichel*) in this category. Up to 10% new grapes (MARSELAN, TOURIGA N, etc.) now permitted. Wildly varying yields in 23 (mildew). Try CHX Bauduc, BONNET, Lamothe-Vincent, Reignac.

Bordeaux Supérieur ★ →★★ 18 19 20 22 Higher min alc, lower yield, age longer than BX. Mainly bottled at property. Consistent CHX: Argadens, Bolaire, Camarsac, de Seguin, Grand Village, Landereau, Le Grand Verdus, Méaume, *Parenchère* (CUVÉE Raphaël), Penin, *Pey la Tour* (Rés), Pierrail, Reignac, *Thieuley*, Turcaud.

Borgeot C d'O ★★★ No need to move beyond excellent BOURGOGNE C D'O CHARD from Remigny-based DOM, but if you wish to, aim for PULIGNY-MONTRACHET Le Meix.

Borie-Manoux Bx Admirable BX shipper. Part of Group BCAP: BATAILLEY, BEAU-SITE, TROTTEVIEILLE and NÉGOCIANT Mähler-Besse.

Bouchard Père & Fils Burg ★★→★★★★ Owned by Artemis Domaines (CLOS DE TART, EUGÉNIE). Major BEAUNE merchant with impressive, visitor-friendly, town-centre cellars. All-round, robust style. Whites best in MEURSAULT and GC, esp CHEVALIER-MONTRACHET. Flagship reds: Beaune VIGNE de L'Enfant Jésus, CORTON. (No longer connected with HENRIOT, WILLIAM FEVRE.)

Boudignon, Thibaud Lo ★★★★ High-quality SAVENNIÈRES DOM. Astonishingly gd; from replanted historic vyds. *Clos de la Hutte, Clos de Fremine*, La Vigne Cendrée, super-rare Franc de Pied 14' 15 16 18' **19 20** 21 22 (23). Don't overlook ANJOU BL.

Boulay, Gérard Lo ★★★★ Thrilling white SANCERRE (Chavignol). CUVÉES CLOS de Beaujeu, Comtesse (Monts Damnés), La Côte: 12' 14' 16 17 **19 20** 21 (22) (23). Drink DOM cuvée younger. Also gd red Oriane.

Bouley Burg ★★★ Developing stars in VOLNAY, at van of cutting-edge higher-trained viticulture. Smart reds, esp Volnay PCS, from cousins Thomas and Pierrick at their respective DOMS. Insistent but never overbearing flavours.

Bourgeois, Henri Lo ★→★★★★ Major SANCERRE DOM/NÉGOCIANT: broad range (outside Sancerre too); reliable. Top CUVÉES Bourgeoisie, *d'Antan, Etienne Henri*, Jadis: 12' 14' 15' 16 **17 18** 19 20 22. Exciting single-vyd Le Cotelin, Le Graveron (r), Les Côtes aux Valets, Les Ruchons.

Bourgogne Burg ★→★★★ (r) 15' **17** 18' **19**' 20' 21 22 (w) 14' 17' **18** 19' 20' 21 22' Basic Burg AOP. Seek brilliant egs from top DOMS. Sometimes with subregion attached, eg. CÔTE CHALONNAISE, HAUTES-CÔTES and now, C D'O. Whites from CHARD unless B ALIGOTÉ. Reds from PINOT N unless declassified BEAUJ crus (sold as B GAMAY) or B Passetoutgrains (Pinot/Gamay mix, must have 30%+ of former). Value.

Bourgueil Lo ★★ →★★★ 09' 10' 15' 16 **17 18**' **19 20** 21 (22) (23) AOP CAB FR; from drink-now to age-worthy. Look for *Yannick Amirault*, Bel Air, *Chevalerie*, Cotelleraie, *La Butte*, Lamé Delisle Boucard, Minière, Nau Frères, Omasson, L'Oubliée, Ouches, Petit Bondieu, Seb David, Revillot, Rochouard.

Bouscassé, Dom SW Fr ★★★ 15' **18** 19 20 21 22 MADIRAN palace. BRUMONT's Napa V-style home. Reds a shade quicker to mature than tighter flagship Montus. VIEILLES VIGNES (100% TANNAT) is star.

Bouvet-Ladubay Lo ★★→★★★ Big name in sparkling SAUMUR, CRÉMANT DE LOIRE. Try Brut Zéro, Instinct, Trésor. Rare *Ogmius* is excellent.

Bouzereau C d'O ★★→★★★ Extended family, MEURSAULT to core. DOM Michel B is leader (marvellous BOURGOGNE C D'O), but try also Jean-Marie B, Philippe B (CH de Cîteaux), Vincent B or B-Gruère & Filles for gd-value whites.

Bouzeron Burg ★★→★★★ 17' 18 19 20' 21 22' CÔTE CHALONNAISE village with unique AOP for ALIGOTÉ, esp golden version. Stricter rules and greater potential than straight BOURGOGNE Aligoté. Chanzy and esp *de Villaine* outstanding (put Bouz on map). Also gd CHARD, PINOT N as Bourgogne Côte Chalonnaise.

Bouzy Rouge Champ ★★★ **09** 12 15' 18' 19' Still red of famous PINOT N village. Formerly like v. light burg, now with more intensity (climate change, better viticulture), also refinement. Best: COLIN, Paul Bara, VEUVE CLICQUOT.

Boxler, Albert Al ★★★★ Complex, dry wines. Jean B one of AL greats. Not just GC but GC subzones too: RIES Brand Vanne new in 21, also outstanding Ries Sommerberg Mittelberg Adele VT 21. Rare PINOT BL truly 100% Pinot Bl (no AUXERROIS): 21' a gem. Great buy, hard-to-find SYLVANER.

Brana, Dom SW Fr Illustrious Basque family helped regenerate ★★★ IROULÉGUY. Red/white. CAB FR shares star role with TANNAT. Micro-cuvées worth tracking down incl rare pre-phylloxera red.

Briday Burg ★★→★★★ Catastrophic start in 1976, when 95% lost to hail, did not deter Michel B, now succeeded by son Stéphane. All wines punch above weight, esp creamy-fruited RULLY MONOPOLE CLOS de Remenot (w), from 45-yr-old vines.

Brocard, J-M Chab ★★→★★★ Quality and commercial acumen under one roof:

CHAB Ste Claire and fine range of PC, GC. Son Julien B has impressive bio range under 7 Lieux label. Always reliable.

Brochet, Emmanuel Champ ★★★ Bijou producer from steep Mont Bernard. Extra BRUT pure, exhilarating, organic, in barrel 9 mths. Excelled in sumptuous 18' 19'. *Haut Chardonnay Extra Brut* 09 12 14' 15. Le Mont Benoît PC excellent.

Brouilly Beauj ★★ 17 18' 19' 20' 21 22' Largest and most s of ten BEAUJ crus: solid, rounded, with some depth of fruit, approachable early but can age 3–5 yrs. Top growers: CHX de la Chaize, des Tours; DOMS Chermette, J-C Lapalu, L&R Dufaitre, Piron. Even better is adjacent Côte de Brouilly, esp CH THIVIN.

Brumont, Alain SW Fr ★★★★ MADIRAN's pioneer and living icon, creator of BOUSCASSÉ, LA TYRE, MONTUS, but also quaffing Gascogne. PACHERENCS (dr/sw) outstanding, named after mth of picking, using revolutionary calender: Vendemiaire = October, Frimaire = December.

Brut Champ Term for dry classic wines of CHAMP. Dosage usually less than of yore. Under 6g residual sugar = Extra Brut, increasingly modish.

Brut Ultra / Zéro Term for bone-dry wines (no dosage) in CHAMP (aka Brut NATURE); fashionable, esp with sommeliers, quality better with warmer summers: needs ripe yr, old vines, max care, eg. *Pol Roger Pure*, ROEDERER Brut Nature Philippe Starck 09' 12' 14' 15 VEUVE FOURNY Nature.

Bugey ★★ Small AOP w of SAV. Light, fresh sparkling and all colours of still. Crus incl Cerdon (pink GAMAY/Poulsard *méthode ancestrale*), Manicle (CHARD, PINOT N), Montagnieu (Altesse, MONDEUSE, sp). Whites mainly Altesse (Roussette du B AOP), CHARD. Red/rosé: GAMAY, Mondeuse, Pinot N. Try Balivet P (Cerdon), ★ Bonnard, Cortis, ★★ Dentelle (Cerdon), ★ D'Ici Là, ★ Lingot-Martin (Cerdon), ★ Grangeons de l'Albarine, ★★ Renardat-Fache (Cerdon), ★★ Peillot, Tissot.

Burgaud Beauj ★★★ Jean-Marc B from MORGON, top bottlings of Charmes, Côte du Py, Grands Cras, etc, best with age, when precocious flavours of youth have settled. Nephew Alexandre promising too.

Burn, Ernest / Clos Saint-Imer Al ★★→★★★★ Late harvesting makes some of AL's richest but balanced, often off-dry. Incredibly rich MUSCAT, SYLVANER SGN (Al best?) from MONOPOLE CLOS Saint-Imer in GC GOLDERT 10 13 15 16 17 18 19 21 22'. PINOT GR v.gd: 10 12 15' 18 20'.

Bursin, Agathe Al ★★★→★★★★ 17' 18' 19' 20' Classy, often slightly off-dry wines from Bollenberg and GC Zinnkoepflé; outstanding SYLVANER (Lutzental and esp Eminence) from v. old vines. Also v.gd GEWURZ, PINOT N.

Buxy, Caves de Burg ★→★★ Leading CÔTE CHALONNAISE co-op for decent CHARD, PINOT N, source of many merchants' own-label ranges. Easily largest supplier of AOP MONTAGNY. Reliable, gd value, not to be sniffed at.

Buzet SW Fr ★★ 19 20 22 AOP Plummy cousin of BX. Dominated by exemplary co-op, incl CHX de Guèyze, Padère. Also Vigouroux-managed Ch Tournelles.

Cabardès Ldoc ★★★ AOP on s facing slopes of Black Mtns, overlooking Carcassonne. Where Med varieties GRENACHE, SYRAH meet Atlantic CAB SAUV, MERLOT. Style (r) is sleek black fruit with Med herbs. Rosé too. CHX La Bastide Rougepeyre, Pennautier, Salitis; DOMS Bancalis, CABROL; MAISON VENTENAC,

Cabernet d'Anjou Lo ★→★★ CABS FR/SAUV rosé (s/sw) Old yrs (40s–80s) from *Bablut* a revelation. For younger yrs: Bergerie, Montgilet, OGEREAU, Sauveroy.

Cabidos SW Fr ★★★ 17 18 19 20 Proper CH in BÉARN, outside JURANÇON yet similar wines: ★★ Gaston Phoebus PETIT MANSENG (dr); ★★★ St Clément, gorgeous, golden, sweet, worth seeking. L'Or de Cabidos, best yrs, is heavenly.

Cabrières Ldoc ★★→★★★★ Terroir on schist in LDOC AOP nr PÉZENAS, reputed for fine rosé, eg. Gerard Bertrand's super-premium CLOS du Temple. Characterful reds too. Top co-op CAVES d'Estabel, Mas de Valbrune.

Cabrol, Dom de Ldoc ★★★→★★★★ Star AOP CABARDÈS, 3rd-generation Nicolas

Carayol, in safe hands. SYRAH-dominant Vent d'Est, fragrant, fiercely Med style. Vent d'Ouest, more CAB SAUV, quieter, herbal. Pique de Nore (w), floral, saline GRENACHE BL/PETIT MANSENG/CHENIN BL.

Cadillac-Côtes de Bordeaux Bx ★ →★★ 19 20 22 Long, narrow, hilly zone on right bank of Garonne. Mainly MERLOT with CABS SAUV/FR. Medium-bodied, fresh reds. Cellar 2–8 yrs. Best: Alios de Ste-Marie, Biac, *Carsin*, CH Carignan, CLOS Chaumont, Clos Ste-Anne, de Fontenille, de Ricaud, Grand-Mouëys, Lamothe de Haux, Le Doyenné, Mont-Pérat, Plaisance, Réaut (Carat), *Reynon*, Suau.

Cady, Dom Lo ★★→★★★ 19' 20' 21 (22) (23) ANJOU DOM devastated by fire 2021. New cellars 2023. Historically great for COTEAUX DU LAYON *Cuvée Volupté*. Also dry CHENIN BL Cheninsolite.

Cahors SW Fr ★★★ 15' 18' 19 20 22 Historical AOP on River Lot. Now wrestling back its MALBEC birthright. All red (some IGP w). Mercifully less extraction now. Easy-drinking ★★ CH de Hauterive, CLOS Coutale. More substance from ★★★ CH DU CÈDRE, Clos d'Un Jour, *Clos Triguedina*, Clos Troteligotte, de la Bérengeraie, DOM Cosse-Maisonneuve, Haut-Monplaisir; ★★ Chx Gaudou, Hautes-Serres, La Coustarelle, Lamartine, Les Croisille, Mas La Périé, Mercuès, Ponzac.

Cailbourdin, Alain and Loïc Lo ★★→★★★ POUILLY-FUMÉ classicism from Alain, with son Loïc increasingly taking over. Top cuvée *Nanogyra* 19 20 21 (22), barrel-aged Triptyque and Triptyque Calcaire 14 15 16 18 19 worth tracking down (to cellar).

Cailhol Gautran, Dom Ldoc ★★★→★★★★ Thoughtful bio MINERVOIS DOM, 5th generation in charge. No added sulphites. La Table du Loup (r), expressive; Villa Lucia (r), opulent, rewards ageing. MUSCAT de St Jean gd.

Cailloux, Les S Rh ★★★ 09' 10' 16' 18 19' 20' 21 22' 23 Benchmark CHÂTEAUNEUF DOM, consistent, fab value; elegant, profound, handmade reds, accomplished, *garrigue* white. Special red Centenaire, oldest GRENACHE 1889, classy 16' 19'.

Cairanne S Rh ★★→★★★ 18 19' 20' 22' 23 Area noted for refinement, many options from *garrigue* soils, wines of character, dark fruits, local herbs, esp CLOS des Mourres (organic), Clos Romane; DOMS ALARY (organic), Boisson, Brusset, Cros de Romet, des Amadieu (bio), ESCARAVAILLES, Grands Bois (organic), Grosset, Hautes Cances (sleeker since 19), Jubain, *Oratoire St Martin* (bio), Rabasse-Charavin, Richaud, Roche. Food-friendly, full, multi-variety whites.

Canard-Duchêne Champ ★★→★★★ House owned by ALAIN THIÉNOT. Modernizing. CUVÉE Léonie increasingly impressive. Charles VII BLANC DE BLANCS and NOIRS NV. BRUT Vintage 09' 12, single-vyd AVIZE Gamin 12 13 17' 19'.

Canon-Fronsac Bx ★★→★★★ 16 18 19' 20' 22 Tiny enclave within FRON, otherwise same wines. Environmental action. Best: rich, full, cellar-worthy. Try Barrabaque, Canon Pécresse, Cassagne Haut-Canon la Truffière, GABY, Grand-Renouil, La Fleur Cailleau, Lamarche Canon, MOULIN PEY-LABRIE.

Carême, Vincent Lo ★★→★★★★ Brightest new star in VOUVRAY for 20–30 yrs.

Chablis

There is still no CHARD to rival the tense, "stone and savour" wines of CHAB, although its style is threatened by warmer summers. The best are delicate but intense, never blowsy. Added richness comes with age. **Top:** BILLAUD, DAUVISSAT (V), Droin, FÈVRE (W), LAROCHE, Michel (L), MOREAU (C), Pinson, RAVENEAU. **Challengers:** Bessin, BROCARD (J-M), CHABLISIENNE, Collet, Dampt (D), Davenne, Defaix (B), DROUHIN-Vaudon, Duplessis, Fèvre (N&G), Garnier, Grossot, LAROCHE, LONG-DEPAQUIT, Malandes, MOREAU-Naudet, Picq, Piuze, Pommier, Oudin, Tribut. **Up-and-coming:** Dauvissat (J & Fils), d'Henri, Gautheron, Lavantureux, Vocoret (E&E), Vrignaud. **Organic/natural:** Brocard (J), CH de Béru, de Moor, Goulley, *Pattes Loup*.

Exemplary, with single-vyd dry *Le Clos* 14 15 16 17 **18** 19 20 21 22 (23), Clos de la Roche Vouvray, Le Peu Morier highlights. Also top *moelleux*. Don't miss pét-nat *Plaisir Ancestrale*.

Carillon C d'O ★★★ Contrasting PULIGNY brothers: Jacques unchangingly classical; try PC Referts. François for exciting modern approach, lovely polish; try Combettes, Folatières, Cap au Sud (VDF CHARD). Village Puligny great from both.

Castelnau, De Champ ★★★ Co-op now merged with larger Nicolas Feuillate. Excellent BLANC DE BLANCS and Vintage 02 **08**. Innovative Prestige Collection Hors d'Age, different each yr: current release CCF2067 led by fine MEUNIER. Impressive Hors Categorie NV CT 2015 and BRUT Oenothèque in magnum **98** 02. Inspiring chef de CAVE Carine Bailleul.

Castillon-Côtes de Bordeaux Bx ★★ →★★★ 16 18 **19** 20 22 Appealing neighbour of ST-ÉM; similar, usually gd value. New "Castillon Caractères" club of 19 top names. Top: Alcée, Ampélia, Cap de FAUGÈRES, CLOS Les Lunelles, Clos Louie, *Clos Puy Arnaud*, Côte Montpezat, *d'Aiguilhe, de l'A*, de Pitray, Joanin Bécot, La Brande, *La Clarière*, l'Aurage, *Le Rey, l'Hêtre*, Montlandrie, Poupille, Veyry.

Cathiard, Dom Sylvain C d'O ★★★★ Sébastien C makes wines of astonishing quality from VOSNE, esp Malconsorts, Orveaux, Reignots, plus NUITS Aux Thorey, Murgers. New range of generic BOURGOGNES. Style is pick late and destem.

Cauhapé, Dom SW Fr ★★★ Trail-blazing JURANÇON estate, exceptional whites (dr and sw). Canopé PETIT MANSENG rivals any top white for complexity. Folie de Janvier (sw), exceptional yrs only, picked in Jan.

Cave Cellar, or any wine establishment.

Cave coopérative Growers' co-op winery; over half of all French production. Wines often well priced, probably not most exciting. Many co-ops closing down.

Cazeneuve, Ch Ldoc ★★★ Consistently gd PIC ST-LOUP. ★★★ Cynarah (r) delightfully fruity, herbal. Les Calcaires (r) v gd. Top Le Causse (SYRAH), rewards ageing.

Cazes, Dom Rouss ★★★ Biggest bio vyd in France. VDN: RIVESALTES Ambré, Tuilé, Grenat and sensational, aged Aimé Cazes. MAURY SEC. Ambre (SW GRENACHE BL), Le Canon du Maréchal (GRENACHE/SYRAH). Top red Crédo CÔTES DU ROUSS-VILLAGES with Ego, Alter. CLOS de Paulilles BANYULS, COLLIOURE.

Cébène, Dom de Ldoc ★★★★ Brigitte Chevalier makes thrilling FAUGÈRES from high-altitude, n-facing, organic vyds. Flagship Felgaria, mostly MOURVÈDRE, is elegance, power. Ages well. Les Bancels SYRAH et al earlier drinking, no less fine. Belle Lurette shows what CARIGNAN can do.

Cédre, Ch du SW Fr ★★ →★★★ 15' 18 19 20 22 Verhaeghe bros make best-known modern-style CAHORS. Delicious ★★ MALBEC IGP for everyday. Also consultant to CHX Haut Monplaisir, Ponzac (both Cahors).

Cellier aux Moines Burg ★★★ Now top DOM in GIVRY based in vyd of same name; reached new heights after investment in new winery and winemaker Guillaume Marko. Interesting options in CÔTE DE BEAUNE, but star is home vyd.

Cépage Grape variety. *See* pp.12–22 for all.

Cérons Bx ★★ 18 19 22 (23) Tiny appn. Sweet wines next to BARSAC (limestone soils), but less intense. Best: CHX de Cérons, DE CHANTEGRIVE, du Seuil, Grand Enclos.

Chablis ★★ →★★★ 14' **15** 17' **18' 19'** 20 21 22 One of most traduced names in wine world; gd Chab is a beguiling iteration of CHARD, pure-fruited yet shot through with stony savour. Warmer vintages adding succulence to trad lean framework. Also PETIT CHAB, DYA lighter version. (For top names, *see* box, p.50.)

Chablis Grand Cru ★★★ →★★★★ 10' 12' **14' 15** 17' **18'** 19' 20 21 22 Contiguous s-facing block overlooking River Serein, grandest CHAB, needs 5–15 yrs to show detail. Seven vyds: Blanchots (floral), Bougros (incl Côte Bouguerots), CLOS (usually best), Grenouilles (spicy), Preuses (cashmere), Valmur (structure), Vaudésir (plus brand La Moutonne). Many gd growers. Value versus C D'O GCS.

Chablisienne, La Chab ★★→★★★ Exemplary co-op responsible for huge slice of CHAB production, esp supermarket own-labels. Trade up to bio CUVÉES of PETIT CHAB and Chab. Top wine is GC CH Grenouilles, a winner. Value.

Chablis Premier Cru ★★★ 14′ 15 17′ 18′ 19′ 20 21 22 Well worth premium over straight CHAB: better sites on rolling hillsides can deliver great satisfaction. Mineral favourites: Montmains, Vaillons, Vaucoupin; softer-style Côte de Léchet, Fourchaume; Mont de Milieu, *Montée de Tonnerre*, Vaulorent greater opulence.

Chambertin C d'O ★★★★ 90′ 93 96′ 99′ 02′ 05′ 09′ 10′ 12′ 14 15′ 16 17 18′ 19′ 20′ 21 22′ Commanding in youth, compelling with age, most masculine burg. Meat and muscle abound, harnessed by abundant fruit in best egs. Imperious wine. Producers who match potential incl Bernstein, BOUCHARD PÈRE & FILS, CHARLOPIN, Damoy, DOM LEROY, DUGAT-Py, DROUHIN, MORTET, ROSSIGNOL-TRAPET, ROUSSEAU, TRAPET. Clos de Bèze next door is "serene and triumphant" (E Waugh), velvet texture, deeply graceful: Bart, B CLAIR, Damoy, Drouhin, Drouhin-Laroze, Duroché, FAIVELEY, GROFFIER, JADOT, Prieuré-Roch, Rousseau.

Chambolle-Musigny C d'O ★★★→★★★★ 93 99′ 02′ 05′ 09′ 10′ 12′ 15′ 16 17 19′ 20 21 22′ Even the name seduces. Silky, velvety wines, textbook purity: Charmes, Combe d'Orveau for substance, more chiselled from Cras, Fuées, bewitching from Amoureuses, plus GCS BONNES-MARES, MUSIGNY. Superstars: BARTHOD, MUGNIER, ROUMIER, VOGÜÉ. Try Amiot-Servelle, DROUHIN, Felettig, GROFFIER, HUDELOT-Baillet, Pousse d'Or, RION, Sigaut.

Champagne Sparkling wines of PINOT N, MEUNIER and CHARD: 33,805 ha, heartland c.145 km e of Paris. Sales 300m+ bottles/yr. Some PINOT BL further s in AUBE adds freshness. Other sparkling, however gd, cannot be called Champ. Thrives on chalky tension and biscuity development (autolysis).

Champagne le Mesnil Champ ★★★ Top-flight co-op, based in centre of Le Mesnil-sur-Oger; inspired leadership of Gilles Marguet; exceptional GC CHARD village. *Cuvée Sublime* 08′ 09′ 13′ 15 17′ 19 from finest site. Majestic CUVÉE Prestige 07′ 05. Value the watchword here.

Champagne Marguet Champ ★★★ Unfazed by having KRUG as neighbour in Ambonnay; 5th generation transformed estate, bio since 2009. Names reveal philosophy: Sapience Rosé 19 20; Shamen Rosé 20; Shamen BRUT 12 14′ 15.

Champalou Lo ★★→★★★ Elegant side of VOUVRAY from C family. Classic sweet, esp *La Moelleuse*, *Les Tries* 89 95 96 97 02 03 09 15 18. SEC, DEMI-SEC, fizz also gd.

Chandon de Briailles, Dom C d'O ★★★ Defined by bio farming, min sulphur, whole bunches, no new oak. Brilliantly pure perfumed reds reaching new heights, esp CORTON-Bressandes, PERNAND-VERGELESSES PC Île de Vergelesses.

Chanson Père & Fils Burg ★→★★★ Has improved, can improve. Quality whites (CLOS DES MOUCHES, CORTON-Vergennes), idiosyncratic reds (whole-cluster aromatics), esp CLOS des Fèves. Recent purchase of 50 ha in CÔTE CHALONNAISE cements transition from merchant to DOM.

Chapelle-Chambertin C d'O ★★★ 99′ 02′ 05′ 09′ 10′ 12′ 15′ 16 18′ 19′ 20′ 21 22′ Lighter neighbour of CHAMBERTIN; thin soil does better in cooler, damper yrs. Fine-boned wine, less meaty. Slightly overlooked. Top: Damoy, DROUHIN-Laroze, JADOT, PONSOT, ROSSIGNOL-TRAPET, TRAPET, TREMBLAY.

Chapoutier N Rh ★★ →★★★★ Strong opinions, overdrive grower-merchant. Stylish SYRAH: low-yield, plot-specific. CÔTE-RÔTIE La Mordorée. HERMITAGE: L'Ermite (outstanding r/w), Le Pavillon (granite, deep r), Cuvée de l'Orée (w), Le Méal (r/w). ST-JOSEPH Les Granits (r/w). *Hermitage whites*, character, complexity, all old-vine MARSANNE, Chante-Alouette a favourite. Meysonniers Crozes, Duché d'Uzès (r/w) gd value. Profound GRENACHE CHÂTEAUNEUF: Barbe Rac, Croix de Bois (r). Also vyds in CÔTES DU ROUSS-VILLAGES (gd DOM Bila-Haut), COTEAUX D'AIX-EN-PROV, RIVESALTES; owns FERRATON at Hermitage, BEAUJ house Trenel, CH des

Ferrages (Prov); has AL vyds; past Australian joint ventures, esp Doms Tournon and Terlato & Chapoutier (fragrant). Hotel, wine bars in Tain.

Charbonnière, Dom de la S Rh ★★★ 10′ **16′** 17 18 19′ 20′ 22′ 23 Maret sisters produce emphatic, local-identity CHÂTEAUNEUF. Consistent Tradition (r), deep, special: VIEILLES VIGNES (vigour, best), authentic Mourre des Perdrix, also Hautes Brusquières; v. stylish, pure white. Also peppery, grassroots VACQUEYRAS red.

Charlopin C d'O ★★★ Large DOM, 25 ha. Philippe C makes impressive range of reds. Substance now matched by style. BOURGOGNE C D'O, MARSANNAY for value; gd range GC for top of line. Son Yann C, DOM C-Tissier also exciting.

Charmes-Chambertin C d'O ★★★★ 99′ 02′ **03 05′** 09′ 10′ **12′** 15′ 16 **17** 18′ 19′ 20′ 21 22′ GEVREY GC, 31 ha, incl neighbour MAZOYÈRES-CHAMBERTIN. Raspberries and cream plus dark-cherry fruit, sumptuous texture, fragrant finish. Best: ARLAUD, BACHELET, Castagnier, Coquard-Loison-Fleurot, DUGAT, DUJAC, Duroché, LEROY, MORTET, Perrot-Minot, Roty, ROUSSEAU, Taupenot-Merme, VOUGERAIE.

Chartogne-Taillet Champ A disciple of SELOSSE, Alexandre Chartogne now celebrated in own right. Based in village of Merfy; bio inclinations. Ideal BRUT Ste Anne NV, single-vyds *Couarres Château* (BLANC DE NOIRS), Le Chemin de Reims, Les Barres (excellent 15′ 17′ 18). Superb Hors Serie BLANC DE BLANCS too.

Charvin, Dom S Rh ★★★ 09′ 10′ 12′ **15′** 16′ 17′ **18′** 19′ 20′ 21′ 22′ 23′ Magic terroir truth at underrated CHÂTEAUNEUF estate, one of best; 85% (average) 50-yr-old GRENACHE, no oak; just one handmade red, spiced, mineral, high-energy, vintage accuracy. Recent gd white. Top-value, long-lived CÔTES DU RH (r).

Chassagne-Montrachet C d'O ★★→★★★★ (w) 08′ **09′** 12′ **14′** 15 17′ 18′ 19′ 20′ 21 22′ The C D'O's most exciting commune? Great white vyds Blanchot, Cailleret, LA ROMANÉE, Ruchottes and GCS. Try COLIN, GAGNARD, MOREY, PILLOT families, plus DOMS HEITZ, MOREAU, Niellon, RAMONET. Overlooked reds can age superbly, from eg. Boudriotte, CLOS St-Jean, Morgeot.

Château (Ch) Estate, big or small, gd or indifferent, esp BX (*see* pp.101–21). Literally, castle or great house. In Burg, DOM is usual term.

Château-Chalon Jura ★★★→★★★★ **09** 10′ **14** 15 16 Not a CH but AOP and village, summit of VIN JAUNE elegance from SAVAGNIN grape; min 6 yrs barrel-age under veil of yeast, worth investing. Drink with Comté cheese (or with/in chicken dish). Ages for decades. Search out Baud, ★ BERTHET-BONDET, Chevassu-Fassenet, ★★ *Macle*, Rousset-Martin, ★ Stéphane TISSOT, or Bourdy for old vintages.

Château-Grillet N Rh ★★★★ 10′ 12′ 14′ 15′ 16′ 17′ 18 **19** 20′ 21′ 22′ 23′ France's smallest AOP, 3.7-ha picturesque terraced amphitheatre s of CONDRIEU, sandy-granite, v. precise vyd care. Owned by F Pinault of CH LATOUR, prices v. high, wine *en finesse*, more restrained these days. Can be great at 20 yrs. Scented, oily, pinpoint VIOGNIER: drink lightly chilled, decanted, with refined dishes. Condrieu La Carthery since 2017, vyd nearby; also CÔTES DU RH (w).

Châteaumeillant Lo ★→★★ 20′ 21 22 Small AOP s of REUILLY. Mostly straightforward red/rosé led by GAMAY with PINOTS N/GR. Some QUINCY vignerons have moved in. Look for Chaillot, Geoffrenet-Morval, Lanoix, Lecomte, Roux, Rouzé.

Châteauneuf-du-Pape S Rh ★★★→★★★★ 07′ 09′ **10′** 12 **15** 16′ **17** 19′ 20′ 21 22′ 23 World famous, 3200 ha+, nr Avignon. Maze of soils incl clay, sand and fossils, limestone plus up to 13 grapes (r/w), led by GRENACHE, plus SYRAH, MOURVÈDRE (increasing, important), Counoise = many different styles. Around 55 gd DOMS (other 85 fair, uneven to poor). Spiced, oily, long-lived, best to wait 8 yrs+; should be fine, pure, caressing. Phase from 90s to mid-2010s too many heavy, sip-only wines. Young generation more finesse-aware. Small, trad names often gd value. Prestige old-vine wines (top Grenache 16′ 19′). To avoid: mix of new oak, 16% abv, steep prices. Grand whites: fresh, fruity, or rich, endowed, textured, table-friendly, best can age 15 yrs+, storming 21. (For top names, *see* box, p.54.)

> **Châteauneuf: kings & queens of the castle**
> Leading producers at this enormous and maze-like (different soils,
> blends, styles) appellation: CHX DE BEAUCASTEL, Gardine, Mont-Redon,
> Nalys, Nerthe, RAYAS, Sixtine, Vaudieu; DOMS Barroche, BEAURENARD
> (bio, classy), Bosquet des Papes (full), Chante Cigale, Chante Perdrix,
> CHARBONNIÈRE, CHARVIN, CLOS DES PAPES, CLOS du Caillou (organic), Clos
> du Mont-Olivet, Clos St-Jean (scale), Cristia (also v. pure Chapelle St
> Théodoric), de la Biscarelle (fruit), de la Janasse (strength), de la Vieille
> Julienne (bio), du Banneret (trad), Fontavin, Font-de-Michelle, Galet des
> Papes, Grand Tinel, Grand Veneur (organic), Henri Bonneau (depth),
> Famille Ferrando, LES CAILLOUX (value), MARCOUX (bio, esp VIEILLES
> VIGNES), Mas du Boislauzon, Pegaü, Pères de l'Église, Pierre André
> (bio, terroir), Porte Rouge, Famille P Usseglio, R Usseglio (bio, style),
> Roger Sabon, Sénéchaux, Vieux Donjon (classic), VIEUX TÉLÉGRAPHE.
> Whites: Chx de Beaucastel (fab ROUSSANNE), Gardine, RAYAS, Vaudieu;
> Doms Beaurenard, Clos des Papes (long life), Les Cailloux (genuine),
> Marcoux (stylish), R Usseglio (v.gd Roussanne), Vieux Donjon
> (authentic, depth), Vieux Télégraphe (deep, terroir).

Chave, Dom Jean-Louis N Rh ★★★★ 05′ 07′ **09**′ 10′ 11′ 12′ 13′ 15′ 16′ 17′ 18′ 19′ 20′
21′ 22′ 23′ Outstanding 14-ha family DOM at heart of HERMITAGE, v.gd mix of
soils, so blending artful. Classy, sensuous, lingering SYRAHS, incl v. occasional,
astronomically priced Cathelin. Complex, long-lived white (mainly MARSANNE).
ST-JOSEPH reds dark, smoky, beautiful fruit, single-vyd CLOS Florentin (since 2015)
v. aromatic, classy; also zappy J-L Chave brand St-Joseph Offerus, jolly CÔTES DU
RH Mon Coeur, steady-value merchant Hermitage Farconnet (r), Blanche (w).

Chénas Beauj ★★★ **15**′ **16** 18′ 19′ 20′ 21 Smallest BEAUJ cru, between MOULIN-À-VENT
and JULIÉNAS, gd value, meaty, age-worthy, merits more interest. Thillardon is
reference DOM, but try also Janodet, LAPIERRE, Pacalet, Piron, Trichard, co-op.

Chevalier-Montrachet C d'O ★★★★ 08 09′ 10 12 **14**′ 15 17′ 18′ 19′ 20′ 21 22′ Just
above MONTRACHET on hill, barely below in quality; brilliant crystalline wines,
singing purity. Long-lived but can be accessible early. Top grower is LEFLAIVE,
special CUVÉES Les Demoiselles from JADOT, LOUIS LATOUR and La Cabotte from
BOUCHARD. Also: Chartron, COLIN (P), Dancer, DE MONTILLE, Niellon, VOUGERAIE.

Cheverny Lo ★→★★ **20 21 22** AOP: (w) SAUV BL/CHARD/Menu Pineau, (r) GAMAY/
PINOT N/CAB FR/CÔT. Easy-going wines. Try Cazin, Clos du Tue-Boeuf, *Huards*,
Montcy, Tessier. Blends with Menu Pineau from *Veilloux* are ★★★.

Chevillon, R C d'O ★★★ With GOUGES, reference DOM for NUITS, dark-fruited,
muscular but not overtannic PCS: Bousselots, Chaignots, Pruliers more
accessible; Cailles, Les St-Georges, Vaucrains for long term.

Chevrot C d'O ★★ Great source for juicy MARANGES, esp Sur les Chênes, PC Croix
Moines. Decent whites, esp ALIGOTÉ Tilleul, Maranges Fussière. CRÉMANT too.
Lively wines, fair prices.

Chidaine, François Lo ★★★→★★★★ One of saviours of MONTLOUIS. Precise, age-
worthy. Dry CLOS du Breuil, *Les Bournais* 14′ 15 16 17 **18** 19 20 (22). Les Tuffeaux
(s/sw/sw), *Clos Habert*, Moelleux age longer. Has historic *Clos Baudoin* in
VOUVRAY (VDF on label).

Chignin Sav ★→★★ AOP: Jacquère, MONDEUSE. Chignin-Bergeron is ROUSSANNE. Try
★ A Berlioz, ★★ A&M QUENARD, ★★ *Berthollier*, ★★ J-F Quenard, ★★★ Partagé.

Chinon Lo ★★→★★★★ 05′ 09′ 10′ 15′ 16 17 **18**′ **19 20** (22′) AOP, CAB FR from sand (drink
young), gravel (can age), limestone (age well). Also dry CHENIN BL. Best: *Alliet*,
Baudry, CLOS des Capucins, Couly-Dutheil, Grosbois, *Charles Joguet*, J-M Raffault,
Noblaie, Olga Raffault, Pallus, Pascal Lambert, Pierre Sourdais, Wilfrid Rousse.

Chiroubles Beauj ★★ 15' 18' 19' 20' 21 22' A BEAUJ cru in hills above FLEURIE: fresh, fruity, savoury. Growers: Berne, CH de Javernand, Cheysson, LAFARGE-Vial, Métrat, Passot, Raousset, or merchants DUBOEUF, Trenel.

Chorey-lès-Beaune C d'O ★★ 15' 17 **18** 19' 20 21 22' Village just n of BEAUNE. TOLLOT-BEAUT remains the benchmark for this reliable rather than exciting, fruit-forward AOP. Also Arnoux, DROUHIN, Gay, Guyon, JADOT, Rapet, ROUGET.

Clair, Bruno C d'O ★★★ Below-the-radar DOM; understated, never flashy. Marked by a lighter weave than some. Promising new generation; gd-value MARSANNAY, old-vine SAVIGNY La Dominode, GEVREY-CHAMBERTIN (CLOS ST-JACQUES, Cazetiers), standout CHAMBERTIN-Clos de Bèze. Best whites from CORTON-CHARLEMAGNE, MOREY-ST-DENIS.

Clairet Bx Between rosé/red. AOP BX Clairet: CHX Penin, Thieuley, Turcaud.

Clairette de Die N Rh ★★ Low-Alpine bubbly – flinty or (better) MUSCAT (s/sw), great wedding opener, gd value, low alc. Or dry CLAIRETTE, can age 3 yrs. Note Achard-Vincent (organic, bio, bright), Carod, David Bautin (organic), Jaillance (value), J-C Raspail (organic, IGP SYRAH), Poulet & Fils (terroir, Chatillon-en-Diois r). Fab apéritif, crime not to try.

Clape, Dom N Rh ★★★→★★★★ 05' 06' 07' **09**' 10' **12' 14**' 15' **16**' 17' 18' 19' 20' 21' 22' 23' Top-drawer CORNAS from many old vines, central hillside vyds, detailed granite-soil care. Smouldering, complex reds, remarkable vintage accuracy; be patient. Present for a godchild? Need 7 yrs+, live 25+. Direct fruit in younger-vines label Renaissance. Superior CÔTES DU RH, ST-PÉRAY (MARSANNE), VDF (r).

Clape, La Ldoc ★★★→★★★★ Limestone massif on Med nr Narbonne. Driest, sunniest AOP in LDOC. MOURVÈDRE hotspot with SYRAH, GRENACHE for characterful herb-scented reds with freshness from sea breezes. Salty, herbal whites from BOURBOULENC with dash of ROUSSANNE are underrated, worth seeking out. DOMS Anglès, Barbier, Camplazens, Capitoul, La Combe St-Paul, LA NÉGLY, Laquirou, l'Hospitalet, Mire l'Etang, Pech-Céleyran, Pech-Redon, Ricardelle, ROUQUETTE-SUR-MER, SARRAT DE GOUNDY.

Climat Burg Individual named vyd (almost interchangeable with lieu-dit), esp in C D'O. UNESCO World Heritage status. Say "klee-mah".

Clos Distinct (walled) vyd, often in one ownership (esp AL, Burg, CHAMP). Often prestigious. In Burg, walls on three sides, of four, suffice for "clos".

Clos Alivu Cors ★★→★★★ AOP PATRIMONIO. Stylish, fresh wines from talented Eric Poli, also owner of DOM Poli, gd-value AOP CORS (r/w/rosé), IGP Île de Beauté.

Clos Canarelli Cors ★★★ Revered bio estate in s. AOP CORS Figari. Reviving indigenous grapes plus more mainstream NIELLUCCIO, SCIACARELLO. Core range aged in and named after amphorae, worth seeking out. Excellent Tarra di Sognu (r/w), rare Tarra d'Orasi (r/w) from ungrafted vines.

Clos Cibonne Prov ★★★ Small estate nr Toulon, making red/rosé from rare local Tibouren as AOP CÔTES DU PROV. Wonderful trad labels, gastronomic, ethereal wines. Tentations range: fruitier, early drinking. Marius (old vines): a revelation.

Clos d'Alzeto Cors ★★★ Highest vyd in CORS, 500m (1640ft). AJACCIO (r) from SCIACARELLO, prestige VERMENTINO, floral, fine.

Clos de L'Écotard Lo ★★→★★★ Relatively young project from Michel and Thibaud Chevré. Top SAUMUR Bl channelling limestone. Look for *Les Pentes* 20 **21** (22) (23). Also La Haie Nardin, fine Les Quarts St-Vincent (sp).

Clos de Tart C d'O ★★★★ 02' 05' 08' 10' 13' 14 15' 16' 17 18' 19' 20' 21 22' Expensive MOREY-ST-DENIS GC. MONOPOLE of Pinault/Artemis empire (CHX GRILLET, Latour, etc.). Becoming more refined with earlier picking and rebuilt winery, while retaining natural intensity. Vines planted across the slope. La Forge de T, value.

Clos de Vougeot C d'O ★★→★★★★ 99' **02**' 03' 05' **09**' 10' 12' 13' 15' 16 17 18' 19' 20' 21 22' CÔTE DE NUITS GC with many owners; 50 ha, needs trimming. Sometimes excellent, can be ho-hum. Needs 10 yrs+ to show real class. Better in recent warm vintages. Style, quality depend on producer's philosophy, technique, position. Top: ARNOUX-LACHAUX, CH de la Tour, EUGÉNIE, *Faiveley*, GRIVOT, *Gros (Anne)*, HUDELOT-Noëllat, LEROY, LIGER-BELAIR (both), MÉO-CAMUZET, MORTET, *Vougeraie*. Also v.gd BOUCHARD, Castagnier, Clerget (Y), Coquard-Loison-Fleurot, DROUHIN, Forey, MONTILLE, MUGNERET-Gibourg.

Clos des Fées Rouss ★★★→★★★★ Hervé Bizeul's wines have playful names, but serious stuff. La Petite Siberie (r), sublime CÔTES DU ROUSS pure GRENACHE; Sorcières (r/w) gd value; Le Chat de Marquis, scented TEMPRANILLO, IGP CÔTES CATALANES. Fine PINOT N too.

Clos des Lambrays C d'O ★★★ 05' 09' 10' 15' 16' 18' 19' 20' 21 22' All-but-MONOPOLE GC vyd at MOREY-ST-DENIS, now belongs to LVMH. Big investment and new winemaker from 2019, leap in quality. Previously attractive, early picked, spicy, stemmy style. Also Puligny PCS CLOS du Cailleret, Les Folatières.

Clos des Mouches C d'O ★★★ (w) 02 05' 09' 10' 14' 15 17' 18 19' 20' 21 22' A PC vyd in several Burg AOPS. Mostly reds, but most famous for glorious BEAUNE white. *Mouches* = honeybees; see label of DROUHIN's iconic Beaune bottling. Also BICHOT, CHANSON (Beaune), MOREAU, Muzard (SANTENAY); Germain (MEURSAULT).

Clos des Papes S Rh ★★★★ 05' 07' 09' 10' 12' 13' 14' 15' 16' 17' 18' 19' 20' 21' 22' 23' Outstanding CHÂTEAUNEUF DOM of Avril family, v. small yields, burg elegance, long life, tremendous consistency; v. stylish, striking red (GRENACHE, high MOURVÈDRE, drink at 2–3 yrs or from 8+); complex white (six varieties, intricate, be patient, requires noble cuisine; 2–3 yrs, then 10–20).

Clos du Mesnil Champ ★★★★ KRUG's walled vyd in GC Le Mesnil. Dates from 1698. Richly indulgent CHARD. On-going battle between mature **95** and **96**, Cavalier vs Roundhead. Wait a little longer for similar duel between **02** and **08**. Also aristocratic **03'**. Look forward to 13' and, many yrs hence, 15 19' *et seq*.

Clos de la Roche C d'O ★★★★ 90' 93' **96' 99'** 02' 05' 08 09' 10' 15' 16' 17 18' 19' 20' 21 22' Overlooked though not underpriced: finest GC of MOREY-ST-DENIS, as much grace as power, more savoury than sumptuous. Glorious with time. ARLAUD, **Dujac**, H LIGNIER, PONSOT references, but try Amiot, Bernstein, Castagnier, Coquard, LEROY, LIGNIER-Michelot, Pousse d'Or, Remy, ROUSSEAU.

Clos du Roi C d'O ★★→★★★ Frequent Burg vyd name, sometimes as Clos du Roy. Best vyd in GC CORTON (DE MONTILLE, Pousse d'Or, VOUGERAIE); top PC vyd in MERCUREY, future PC (still waiting) in MARSANNAY. Less classy in BEAUNE.

Clos Naudin, Dom du Lo ★★★★ Reference DOM in VOUVRAY. Philippe and Vincent Foreau currently in charge. Stunning *Moelleux (and Rés)* 89 90 97 02 03 05 09 10 15 16 18 19 20. Vouvray's best sparkling, *Brut Rés*. SEC, DEMI-SEC also v.gd.

Clos Rougeard Lo ★★★★ 05' 09 10' 14 15' **16** 17 18' 19 20 21 (22) (23) World-famous SAUMUR-CHAMPIGNY. Prices reflect renown. Huge recent investments by Bouygues family. White also much admired.

Clos St-Denis C d'O ★★★ 90' 93' **96' 99'** 02' 05' 09' 10' 12' 15' 16' 17 18' 19' 20' 21 22' MOREY-ST-DENIS GC. Sumptuous in youth, silky with age. Outstanding from DUJAC, PONSOT (Laurent P from 2016). Try also Amiot-Servelle, ARLAUD, Bertagna, Castagnier, Coquard-Loison-Fleurot, Heresztyn-Mazzini, JADOT, Jouan, LEROUX.

Clos Ste-Hune Al ★★★★ Legendary TRIMBACH single site from GC Rosacker. World's greatest dry RIES. Super 71' 75' 13' 15' 16' 17' 18 19' 20' need 10 yrs; 22' nr perfection.

Clos St-Jacques C d'O ★★★★ 90' 93 **96' 99'** 02' 05' **09'** 10' 12' 15' 16 17 18' 19' 20' 21 22' Hillside PC in GEVREY with perfect SE exposure. Shared by five excellent producers: CLAIR, ESMONIN, FOURRIER, JADOT, ROUSSEAU. (Each holding runs top to bottom.) Power, poise; GC in all but name. Sublime with age.

Clos St Sebastien Rouss ★★★ Joint venture, shipbuilder and winemaker, prime vyds in COLLIOURE. Top: Celeste (GRENACHE/SYRAH), Inspiration Marine (MOURVÈDRE). Empreintes (r/w) gd-value.

Clusel-Roch, Dom N Rh ★★★ 05' 09' 10' 11 12' 13' 14 15' 16' 17' 18' 19' 20' 21' 22' 23' Organic CÔTE-RÔTIE DOM (higher costs, rare), gd range vyds, mostly Serine (pre-clone SYRAH). Tight, smoky, patience rewarded. Les Schistes gd entry point, high-quality La Viallière (floral), Les Grandes Places (schist, iron, v. long lived). Son Guillaume C makes v.gd Coteaux du Lyonnais (GAMAY, incl 1896 vines; w).

Coche-Dury C d'O ★★★★ Top MEURSAULT DOM led by Raphaël C in succession to legend Jean-François. Exceptional, palate-dazzling whites from ALIGOTÉ to CORTON-CHARLEMAGNE; pretty reds too. Stratospheric prices. Cousin Coche-Bizouard (eg. Meursault Goutte d'Or) sound, gd value, different style.

Colin C d'O ★★★→★★★★ Extended family of CHASSAGNE and ST-AUBIN vinous nobility, all noted for superlative whites; current generation turning heads, esp Pierre-Yves C-MOREY, DOM Marc C, Joseph C and their cousins Bruno C, Philippe C, Simon C.

Colin-Morey Burg ★★★→★★★★ Pierre-Yves C-M has made his name with vibrant tingling whites, esp from *St-Aubin* and CHASSAGNE PC, with their characteristic gunflint bouquets. Bland labels give no hint of the complex glories within. Exemplary wines at all levels, incl NÉGOCIANT CUVÉES.

Collin, Ulysse Champ ★★★→★★★★ Cerebral grower on Côteaux du Petit Morin, sw of Vertus. Single-vyds only, all subtly oaked, low dosage. Les Pierrières and Les Enfers, both BLANC DE BLANCS, Les Maillons Rosé de Saignée, Le Jardin d'Ulysse. Value (relative) BLANC DE NOIRS. A CHAMP odyssey, not lacking drama, tension.

Is there such a thing as good-value Grand Cru Burgundy? Yes, Chablis.

Collines Rhodaniennes N Rh ★★ IGP great value, character, racy quality, incl v.gd Seyssuel (nr Vienne, schist, steep), granite hillside, plateau reds, often from top names. ("Rhodanienne" = "of the Rhône".) Mostly SYRAH (best), plus GAMAY, mini-CONDRIEU VIOGNIER (best). Reds: A Chatagnier, A Paret, A PERRET, Bonnefond, CLOS de la Bonnette (organic), E Barou (organic), Hameau Touche Boeuf, *Jamet*, Jasmin, J-M GÉRIN, L Chèze, Monier-Pérréol (bio), N Champagneux, S Pichat, ROSTAING, Y CUILLERON. Whites: Alexandrins, Amphores, A Perret (v.gd), Barou, F Merlin, *G Vernay*, P-J Villa, P Marthouret, X Gérard, Y Cuilleron.

Collioure Rouss ★★★ Same vyds as BANYULS, dry wines (r/w/rosé), poised, elegant, among best in ROUSS. Mainly GRENACHE of all colours. Top: DOMS Augustin, Bila-Haut, de la Rectorie, du Mas Blanc, du Traginer, La Tour Vieille, Madeloc, Vial-Magnères; Coume del Mas, CLOS ST SEBASTIEN, Les CLOS de Paulilles. Co-ops Cellier des Templiers, l'Étoile.

Comps, Dom Ldoc ★★ Pierre-François C makes delightful, *garrigue*-scented ST-CHINIAN from characterful cellar in Puisserguier, nr Beziers. CUVÉE Juliette, Le Soleiller classy; easy-drinking Les Gleizettes.

Comte Abbatucci Cors ★★★ Prominent bio DOM in S CORS, saviour of indigenous varieties. Humble but top-quality VDF. CUVÉE Fustine, Valle de Nero (both r/rosé). Collection range recalls military connections of ancestor, pal of Napoleon.

Condrieu N Rh ★★★→★★★★ 21' 22' 23' Beating heart of VIOGNIER; acacia, musky, perfumed, pear, apricot flavours from sand-granite terraces, slopes. Best: mystical, mineral; avoid heavy oak, sweetness, alc. Growers, and vines, adapting to v. hot yrs; 80 producers, not all gd. Rare white friend of asparagus. Best: A Paret, *A Perret*, Boissonnet, CHAPOUTIER, CLOS de la Bonnette (organic), C Pichon, DELAS, L Faury (esp La Berne), F Merlin, F Villard (lighter recently), GANGLOFF (rich), GUIGAL, *G Vernay* (Coteau de Vernon), Monteillet, Mouton, Niéro, ROSTAING, ST COSME, Semaska, X Gérard (value), Y CUILLERON.

Corbières Ldoc ★→★★★ Huge AOP, varied but some excellent, characterful reds, styles reflect contrasts of terroir from coastal lagoons to windswept foothills of Pyrénées and inland to cooler Carcassonne. Plenty of CARIGNAN, can be fabulous in Cru Boutenac. Some v.gd white. Try CHX Aiguilloux, Aussières, Borde-Rouge, CARAGUILHES, de Sérame, Grand Moulin, La Baronne, Lastours, La Voulte-Gasparets, Les Palais, OLLIEUX ROMANIS, Pech-Latt, Vaugelas; DOMS de Fontsainte, de la Cendrillon, de Villemajou, DES DEUX CLÉS, du Grand Crès, du Vieux Parc, PY, Trillol; CLOS de l'Anhel, Famille Fabre, Grand Arc, Les Clos Perdus, MAXIME MAGNON, Sainte-Croix, Serres Mazard. Castelmaure co-op.

Cornas N Rh ★★★ 01′ 05′ 09′ **10′ 12′** 15′ **16′** 17′ 18′ 19′ 20′ 21′ 22′ 23′ Long underestimated and now acclaimed granite-slope SYRAH from ARDÈCHE, v. fashionable, justifiably. Dark, deep, always iron-clad, gd and spinal. Some made for early fruit, really need 5 yrs+. Top: A&E Verset (organic), *Allemand* (top two), BALTHAZAR (trad, incl zero sulphur), *Clape* (benchmark), Colombo (modern), Courbis (modern), DELAS, DOM DU TUNNEL, Dumien Serrette (deep), G GILLES (stylish), J&E Durand (racy fruit), Lemenicier, Lionnet (character, organic), M Barret (bio), M Bourg (character), P&V Jaboulet, Tardieu-Laurent (stylish, oak), Voge (swish, oak), V Paris (esp La Geynale).

Corsica / Corse ★★→★★★ "Île de Beauté" aptly named IGP for whole island. Plenty of variety; altitude, sea winds give freshness. Reds elegant, spicy from SCIACARELLO, structured from rarer NIELLUCCIO aka SANGIOVESE; gd rosés; tangy VERMENTINO whites. VDN sweet MUSCATS. Local varieties championed by top producers CLOS CANARELLI, COMTE ABBATUCCI et al. Nine AOPS incl crus PATRIMONIO in n, AJACCIO to w. AOP Corse plus villages Calvi, Coteaux du Cap Corse, Sartène. Top: Antoine Arena, ALZIPRATU, CLOS ALIVU, Clos Canereccia, Clos Calviani, Clos Capitoro, Clos Columbo, CLOS D'ALZETO, Clos Nicrosi, Clos Poggiale, Clos Venturi; DOMS de Grenajolo, Fiumicicoli, Giacometti, Maestracci, Orsucci, Peraldi, PIERETTI, PINELLI, Poli, Saperale, Torraccia, YVES LECCIA, U STILICCIONU, Vaccelli.

Corton C d'O ★★→★★★★★ 02′ 03′ 05′ 09′ 10′ **12′** 15′ **17** 18′ 19′ 20′ 21 22′ Largely overpromoted GC, can be stellar, often dull. Too much vyd classified as GC. Needs trimming. Choose carefully. Best vyds: CLOS DU ROI, Bressandes, Renardes, Rognet. References: BOUCHARD, CHANDON DE BRIAILLES, DRC, Dubreuil-Fontaine, FAIVELEY (CLOS des Cortons), Follin-Arbelet, MÉO-CAMUZET, Rapet, TOLLOT-BEAUT. Under the radar and can be gd value: Bichot, Camille Giroud, Capitain-Gagnerot, Clavelier, DOM des Croix, H&G Buisson, Mallard, Pousse d'Or, Terregelesses. Best whites from Vergennes vyd, eg. CH de MEURSAULT, CHANSON, HOSPICES DE BEAUNE.

Corton-Charlemagne C d'O ★★★ →★★★★ 05′ 09′ 10′ 14′ **15′ 17′** 18 19′ 20′ 21 22′ Potentially scintillating GC, invites mineral descriptors, should age well; sw- and w-facing limestone slopes, plus band around top of hill. Top: BIZE, Bonneau du Martray, BOUCHARD, CLAIR, *Coche-Dury*, FAIVELEY, HOSPICES DE BEAUNE, JADOT, Javillier, LATOUR, Mallard, MONTILLE, Rapet, Rollin. Magnificent DRC from 19. *Dom Vougeraie* uses rarely seen sister AOP, Charlemagne.

Costières de Nîmes S Rh ★→★★ Located n of Rhône delta, sw of CHÂTEAUNEUF; comparable v. stony soils, Mistral wind, maritime influences; gd quality, value. Red (GRENACHE, SYRAH) deep, spiced, up to 10 yrs. Best: CHX de Grande Cassagne, de Montfrin (organic), de Nages (gd w), d'Or et de Gueules (full), La Tour de Beraud, L'Ermitage, Mourgues-du-Grès (organic), Roubaud, Vessière (w); DOMS de la Patience (organic), du Vieux Relais, du Petit Romain, Galus, Gassier, M KREYDENWEISS (bio); CHAPOUTIER, CLOS des Boutes (organic, bio), Mas Carlot (zappy fruit), Mas des Bressades (ace fruit), Mas Neuf, Terre des Chardons (bio). Uptempo, table-friendly rosés; some stylish whites (esp ROUSSANNE).

Cotat, François Lo ★★→★★★★ Fabulously age-worthy SANCERRE from top Chavignol vyds. *Les Monts Damnés*, *Les Culs de Beaujeu*. Often superb at 10 yrs+. Cousin Pascal C also doing gd things.

Coteaux Bourguignons Burg ★ DYA Mostly reds, GAMAY, PINOT N. AOP est in 2011 to replace BOURGOGNE Grand Ordinaire and to sex up basic BEAUJ. Market accepting the change. Rare whites ALIGOTÉ, CHARD, MELON, PINOTS BL/GR.

Coteaux Champenois Champ ★★★ AOP for still wines of CHAMP, eg. BOUZY. Vintages as for Champ. Better reds with climate change (12'). Impressive range of Coteaux Champenois Grands Blancs based on 17' by CHARLES HEIDSIECK, burgundian by inclination. Also worth a look: Tarlant, Drappier, Etienne Calsac. Not to forget BOLLINGER's La Côte aux Enfants.

Coteaux d'Aix-en-Provence Prov ★★ Mostly pale, fruity rosé from AOP centred on Aix. GRENACHE, CINSAULT. Some reds: CAB SAUV in cooler n (Pigoudet, Revelette, VIGNELAURE); Med grapes often more interesting in warmer spots: CHX Calissanne, de Beaupré, La Realtière, Les Bastides, Les Béates, Paradis; DOM d'Eole (on Alpilles). *See also* LES BAUX-DE-PROV.

Coteaux d'Ancenis Lo ★→★★ 20' 21 22 (23) Small AOP overlying MUSCADET Coteaux de la Loire e of Nantes. Age-worthy sweet MALVOISIE; straightforward white, light red, rosé. Look for Galloires, Guindon, Landron-Chartier, Paonnerie, Sedes.

Coteaux de l'Aubance Lo ★★→★★★ 10' 15 18' 19 20 (22) (23) Small AOP. Little brother to COTEAUX DU LAYON. Sweet CHENIN BL from schist, more nervous style. Try *Bablut*, Bois Brinçon, Dittière, *Montgilet*, *Rochelles*, Terra Vita Vinum, Varière.

Coteaux du Giennois Lo ★→★★ 20' 22 (23) AOP just n of POUILLY-FUMÉ; SAUV BL often gd value; GAMAY/PINOT N (r blends). Try Balland, *Berthier*, Coste, L'Épineau, Langlois, Terres Blanches, Treuillet, *Villargeau*.

Wild vines, *Vitis sylvestris*, are an endangered species in France; protected by law.

Coteaux du Layon Lo ★★→★★★★ 07' 09 10 11' 13 14 15 **16 17** 18' 19 20 (22) (23) Iconic AOP for exciting sweet CHENIN BL, incl six villages and PC Chaume; BAUDOUIN, BAUMARD, BELARGUS, Bergerie, Breuil, *Cady*, Ch Pierre-Bise, Deux Vallées, Forges, Juchepie, PIERRE MÉNARD, *Ogereau*, Soucherie.

Coteaux du Loir Lo ★→★★★ Super-cool (climate and image) AOP in N TOURAINE, on Loir (tributary of Loire). Taut CHENIN BL 10 14' 15' **16' 18'** 19 20' (22). Red/rosé blends led by Pineau d'Aunis. Best: *Bellivière* (★★★★), Briseau, Cézin, Gigou, Janvier, Maisons Rouges, Percheron, Roche Bleue, Rycke.

Coteaux du Quercy SW Fr ★ DYA AOP between CAHORS and GAILLAC. Hearty country wines based on CAB FR plus TANNAT or MALBEC. Active co-op challenged by independents: ★★ DOMS du Guillau, Lacoste, Revel.

Coteaux du Vendômois Lo ★→★★ Minor AOP on upper Loir. Whites principally CHENIN BL 21 **22**. Peppery red blends led by Pineau d'Aunis. Try Brazilier, CAVE du Vendômois, Patrice Colin, Montrieux.

Coteaux Varois-en-Provence Prov ★★ High, cooler AOP, on chalky soils; mostly appealing fresh, pale rosé. GRENACHE, CINSAULT, SYRAH, VIOGNIER in cooler n. Tiny-production red gd, fruity with lift. Try CHX des Annibals, la Calisse, Carpe Diem, de l'Escarelle, Lafoux, Miraval (Brad Pitt), St Julien, Trians; DOMS des Aspras, du Deffends, du Loou, La Grand'vigne, La Rose des Vents, Les Terres Promises, Routas, St Mitre.

Côte Chalonnaise Burg ★★→★★★ Lunatic prices for top C D'O wines may finally deliver deserved recognition for this overshadowed region. Lighter wines. BOUZERON for ALIGOTÉ; *Rully* for accessible, juicy wines in both colours; *Mercurey* and GIVRY, more structure, can age; MONTAGNY for leaner, often impressive CHARD.

Côte d'Or Burg Golden or e-facing slope. Département name applied to central and principal Burg vyds: CÔTE DE BEAUNE and CÔTE DE NUITS.

Côte de Beaune C d'O ★★→★★★★ The s half of C D'O. Also a little-seen AOP applying to top of hill above BEAUNE itself. DROUHIN's versions (r/w) also incl declassified Beaune PC. Try DOM VOUGERAIE too. Confusingly, C de B-Villages is different – often a blend from lesser villages of s half of C d'O. Read label carefully.

Côte de Brouilly Beauj ★★ 15' 17 18' **19**' 20' 21 22' Range of styles: soils vary around Mt Brouilly. Merits a premium over straight BROUILLY. Reference is CH THIVIN, but try also Brun, Dufaitre, LAFARGE-Vial, Le Grappin, Martray, Pacalet.

Côte de Nuits C d'O ★★→★★★★ The n half of C D'O. Nearly all red, from CHAMBOLLE-MUSIGNY, MARSANNAY, FIXIN, GEVREY-CHAMBERTIN, MOREY-ST DENIS, NUITS, VOSNE, VOUGEOT. Wine doesn't get more patrician than best CdN.

Côte de Nuits-Villages C d'O ★★ 12' **15**' **16** 17 18' 19' 20' 21 22' A jnr AOP for extreme n/s ends of CÔTE DE NUITS; can be bargains. Specialists: Chopin, Gachot-Monot, Jourdan. Top single-vyds CLOS du Chapeau (Arlot), Croix Violette (FOURNIER, Pernot), Faulques (Millot), Leurey (J-J Confuron), Meix Fringuet (TRAPET), Montagne (many), Robignotte (Jourdan), Vaucrains (JADOT). Monts de Boncourt best for whites.

Côte Roannaise Lo, Mass C ★★→★★★ 18' 19 20' **21 22**' (23) Delicious GAMAY. Granite and basalt soils. Best easily outclass BEAUJ: Bonneton, Giraudon, Pothiers, Sérol. Also check out curious IGP Urfé whites.

Côte-Rôtie N Rh ★★★→★★★★ 05' 09' **10**' 12' **15**' **16**' **17**' 18' 19' 20' 21 22' 23' Most fine, scented Rh red, mainly SYRAH, touch of VIOGNIER, granite, schist soils, style links to burg. Violet airs, pure, complex, allow 5–10 yrs+. Exceptional, v. long-lived 10 15 19, silken 20, pure 21, jolly-fruited 22. Top: *Barge*, B Chambeyron, Billon (energy), Bonnefond (oak), Bonserine (esp La Garde), Burgaud, CHAPOUTIER, *Clusel-Roch* (organic), DELAS, DOM de Rosiers, Duclaux, Gaillard (oak), Garon, GUIGAL (long oaking), *Jamet*, Jean-Luc Jamet, Jasmin, J-M GÉRIN, J-M Stéphan (organic), Lafoy, Levet (trad), *Rostaing* (fine), Semaska, S OGIER (racy), S Pichat (Grandes Places), VIDAL-FLEURY (La Chatillonne), Xavier Gérard, Y CUILLERON.

Côtes Catalanes Rouss ★★★ Arguably most thrilling IGP in France. From fruity gd value from big Vignerons Catalans co-op to serious age-worthy wines from some of ROUSS's finest growers. CLOS DES FÉES, DANJOU-BANESSY, GAUBY, Ch de l'Ou, Paetzold among others use for top wines. Covers most of Rouss except BANYULS, COLLIOURE, which are IGP Côte Vermeille.

Côtes d'Auvergne Lo, Mass C ★★→★★★ 21' 22' High altitude (for Lo) AOP around Clermont-Ferrand (w of Lyon). Burgundian varieties: GAMAY, PINOT N, CHARD. Also SYRAH in IGP Puy de Dôme. Try Cave St-Verny, Les Chemins de l'Arkose, Miolanne, Montel, Pelissier, Sauvat.

Côtes de Bordeaux ★ AOP for reds. For cross-blending between CAS, FRANCS, BLAYE, CADILLAC and Ste-Foy. If Cas, Cadillac, etc. comes before Côtes de Bx, expect

---

Village goings-on: best of Côtes du Rhône-Villages
Too many, but try Gadagne (hearty, spiced), MASSIF D'UCHAUX, Ste-Cécile (medium weight), Signargues (punchy), VISAN. CHX Bois de la Garde, Fontségune, Signac; DOMS Aure, Bastide, Bastide St Dominique (organic), Bois de St Jean (full), Buissonnade (organic), Cabotte (bio), Coste Chaude (organic), Crève Coeur (bio), Echevin (gd w), Florane (bio), Grand Veneur, Grands Bois (organic), Gravennes (smooth), Janasse (top class), Jérôme, *Les Aphillanthes* (bio), Montbayon, Montmartel (organic), Mourchon, Pascal Chalon (bio), Pasquiers (organic), Pique-Basse (organic, gd w), *Rabasse-Charavin*, Réméjeanne (v.gd), Renjarde, Romarins, Saladin (organic), St-Siffrein, STE-ANNE, Valériane; CAVE de RASTEAU Ortas, Les VIGNERONS d'Estézargues (GRENACHE range best, incl Doms Génestas, Pierredon).

single terroir, stiffer controls. BLAYE-CÔTES DE BX, FRANCS-CÔTES DE BX, Ste-Foy Côtes de Bx: some dry white too. CHX Crabitan-Bellevue, Dudon, Malagar.

Côtes de Bourg Bx ★→★★ 18 19 **20** 22 Solid, savoury reds, a little white from e bank of Gironde; 10% MALBEC planted in AC. Top CHX: Brûlesécaille, Bujan, *Falfas*, Fougas-Maldoror, Grand-Maison, Haut-Guiraud, Haut-Macô, Haut-Mondésir, La Grolet (Tête de Cuvée), Le Clos du Notaire, Macay, Mercier, Nodoz, *Roc de Cambes*, Rousset, Sociondo.

Côtes de Duras SW Fr ★→★★ 19 20 22 (23) Affordable AOP s of BERGERAC; Bergerac lookalike. Best known for crisp dry white. Berticot co-op is sound. ★★ DOMS de Laulan, Grand Mayne.

Côtes de Gascogne / Comté Tolosan SW Fr Usually DYA. Two catch-all IGPS covering most of sw. Kaleidoscope of styles, mostly entry level. ★★ Joy, Menard Pellehaut, Plaimont, Tariquet for Gascony. DOM de Ribonnet stands out for Tolosan. Unbeatable value, infinite possibilities, wide selection of grapes.

Côtes de Millau SW Fr ★ DYA IGP. Foster's Millau viaduct celebrated in wines from popular co-op. ★ DOMS du Vieux Noyer, La Tour-St-Martin best of independents.

Côtes de Provence ★→★★★ DYA Huge amounts of fashionably pale-pink rosé, AOP from swathe of vyds from Marseilles to Cannes and inland. Together with COTEAUX D'AIX, COTEAUX VAROIS accounts for 90% of Prov rosé. Whites (increasingly 100% Rolle) and reds (GRENACHE, SYRAH; MOURVÈDRE nearer coast) can be more interesting. Five subzones: La Londe, STE-VICTOIRE best, plus Fréjus, Notre Dame des Anges, Pierrefeu. Top: CLOS CIBONNE (primarily Tibouren), DOMS Gavoty, Ott (Ch de Selle, Clos Mireille), CHX D'ESCLANS, de l'Ille, Gasqui (bio), La Gordonne, LA MASCARONNE, Léoube; Estandon, MIRABEAU, Rimauresq.

Côtes du Brulhois SW Fr ★ 19 20 (22) Small AOP nr Agen, softer version of TANNAT (obligatory) and CAB SAUV, MALBEC, MERLOT in support. Local co-op unusually supportive of a few independents. Best for quaffing reds, pinks.

Côtes du Forez Lo, Mass C ★→★★ 20' 21 22 (23) Super AOP for GAMAY; more juicy, early/easy-drinking than CÔTE ROANNAISE. Try *Bonnefoy*, CLOS de Chozieux, Guillot, Mondon et Demeure, Poyet, *Verdier-Logel*. Growers experimenting with whites use IGP Urfé.

Côtes du Jura AOP covering all Jura, but mainly s. Organic, natural encouraged exports and can be pricey. Whites dominate from mineral CHARD to deliberately oxidative SAVAGNIN (incl VIN JAUNE). Light earthy reds from PINOT N, Poulsard, TROUSSEAU. Great food wines. Try classic Badoz, ★ Baud, Grand, Pêcheur, or CH d'Arlay; organic bankers from ★★ BERTHET-BONDET, ★ Buronfosse, ★★ *Labet*, ★ Marnes Blanches and ★★ *Pignier*, and natural names ★★ Dolomies, ★★★ GANEVAT, or Miroirs. *See also* ARBOIS, CH-CHALON, L'ÉTOILE AOPs.

Côtes du Marmandais SW Fr ★→★★ (r) 18 19 20 22 AOP, neighbour of BX, increasingly eccentric in style thanks to local Abouriou grape and SYRAH. ★★★ Cult winemaker Elian da Ros. Old yrs of CH Beaulieu worth seeking out until 2013; ★★ DOMS Beyssac, Bonnet, Cavenac and Ch Lassolle blend with usual Bx grapes. Co-ops (95% total production) still dull.

Côtes du Rhône S Rh ★→★★ 22' The base of S Rh, 170 communes, incl gd SYRAH of Brézème, St-Julien-en-St-Alban (N Rh). Ranges between enjoyable, high quality (esp CHÂTEAUNEUF estates, top value) and a hard-to-sell dull, mass-volume, high-degree lake. Expect spice, live fruit. Mainly GRENACHE, also Syrah, often old CARIGNAN. Most best drunk young. Vaucluse best, then Gard (Syrah). Dom whites improving fast, rocking value recent vintages.

Côtes du Rhône-Villages S Rh ★→★★★ 22' 23 Spiced reds from 7700 ha, incl 22 named S Rh villages (Nyons, new 2020), numbers rising, some ghost-like. Best are generous, gd value. Red heart is GRENACHE, plus SYRAH, MOURVÈDRE. Improving whites, often incl VIOGNIER, ROUSSANNE added to rich base CLAIRETTE,

GRENACHE BL, gd with food. Top three: PLAN DE DIEU (gd range), SÉGURET (quality, choice), VISAN (improving, many organic). *See* LAUDUN (esp w), SABLET (style, gd w), VALRÉAS; St-Gervais (DOM Sainte-Anne). (*See* box, p.60, for best growers.)

Côtes du Roussillon (Villages) Rouss ★→★★★ AOP for ROUSS, varied styles, often v.gd: lots of CARIGNAN, also old-vine GRENACHES BL/Gr, MACCABEO for whites. AOP Côtes du Rouss-Villages smaller area, just reds, some excellent. 32 villages: Caramany, Latour de France, Les Aspres, Lesquerde, Tautavel singled out on label. Brial co-op gd, plus v.gd individual estates: Boucabeille, CAZES, Charles Perez, CLOS DES FÉES, Clot de l'Oum, des Chênes, GAUBY, Les vignes de Bila-Haut (CHAPOUTIER), Mas Becha, MAS DE LA DEVÈZE, Mas Crémat, Modat, Piquemal, Rancy, ROC DES ANGES, Thunevin-Calvet, Venus. *See also* CÔTES CATALANES.

Coudoulet, Dom Ldoc ★★★ Ournac family-owend, 8th generation. Innovative. Fine La Livinière, CH de Cesseras, alongside IGP from non-LDOC varieties: ASSYRTIKO, PINOT GR, PETIT VERDOT, PINOT N.

Coulée de Serrant Lo ★★ 16 18 19 20 21 Historic CHENIN BL AOP; wonderful 7-ha site on schist in SAVENNIÈRES. Home to bio guru and non-interventionist Nicolas Joly. Wines feature botrytis and high alc; could be better.

Courcel, Dom de C d'O ★★★ Idiosyncratic POMMARD estate. Late-picking, whole bunches. Pommard structure without undue heft. Top: age-worthy PCS Rugiens and Épenots, plus interesting Croix Noires.

Cour-Cheverny Lo ★★→★★★ 14 16 18 19 20 22 Little-known AOP for rare Romorantin grape. Distinctive whites, can age. Look for *Cazin*, Huards.

Crémant AOP for quality classic-method sp from AL, BX, BOURGOGNE, Die, Jura, LIMOUX, Lo, Luxembourg, SAV. Many gd egs.

Crémant de Loire Lo ★★→★★★ AOP for potentially high-quality fizz. Best feature CHENIN BL, CHARD. Wide range from big houses: Bouvet-Ladubay, De Chanceny, Langlois-Château and small DOMS: *Arnaud Lambert*, Aulée, *Plaisance*.

Criots-Bâtard-Montrachet C d'O ★★★ 09 10 12 14' 15 17' 18 19' 21 22' Tiny and much-morcellated MONTRACHET satellite, 1.57 ha. D'Auvenay for lottery winners. More accessible from Blain- or Fontaine-GAGNARD, LAMY and now Caroline MOREY. Hangs on Montrachet's coat-tails. Doesn't burnish the term GC.

Cros, Dom du SW Fr Philippe Teulier was pioneer of MARCILLAC: started with 1 ha, today probably largest producer. Le Sang del Païs is flagship red, from FER SERVADOU, locally known as Mansois.

Cros Parantoux Burg ★★★→★★★★ Cult PC in VOSNE, made famous by Henri Jayer. Now made to great acclaim and greater price by DOMS ROUGET and MÉO-CAMUZET. If fairy godmother is paying, don't refuse.

Crozes-Hermitage N Rh ★★→★★★ 22' 23 Said to be France's most profitable AOP. SYRAH from mostly flat vyds: costs low, demand high, quality now variable. Black fruits, oiliness, black-olive flavours. Most early drinking (2–5 yrs). Tight, cooler (more interesting) Syrah from granite hills n of HERMITAGE: red-fruited, iron, take time. Best (simple CUVÉES) ideal for parties. Oaked, older-vine wines cost more, age nicely. Top: *A Graillot* (fab La Guiraude), Aléofane (r/w), Belle (organic), CHAPOUTIER, *Dard & Ribo* (low sulphur, high character), DELAS (Le CLOS v.gd, DOM des Grands Chemins), G Robin; Doms Combier (organic), de Thalabert of JABOULET, des Entrefaux, des Hauts-Châssis, des Lises (fine), *du Colombier* (*Gaby* great), Dumaine (organic), Habrard (organic), *Laurent Fayolle* (v. stylish, ace Clos Cornirets), Les Bruyères (bio, grand fruit), Machon, Martinelles (trad), Melody, Michelas St Jemms, Mucyn (fine), Remizières (oak), Rousset (top Picaudières), Ville Rouge (bio), Vins de Vienne, Y Chave. Drink *white* (mostly MARSANNE) early, v.gd vintages recently, 21 22. Value.

Cuilleron, Yves N Rh ★★★ Important name at CONDRIEU, always skilful with stylish whites. Top: Les Chaillets. Note old-vine ST-JOSEPH (r) Les Serines. CÔTE-RÔTIE okay, oaked, best La Viallière. COLLINES RHODANIENNES Ripa Sinistra (SYRAH, Seyssuel), MARSANNE, VIOGNIER gd. Much recent vyd-merchant expansion.

Cuve close Quicker method of making fizz in tank. Bubbles die away in glass much faster than with *méthode traditionnelle*.

Cuvée Usually indicates a blend. In CHAMP, means 1st and best juice off the press.

Dagueneau, Louis-Benjamin Lo ★★★→★★★★ The biggest name in SAUV BL, now all VDF rather than POUILLY-FUMÉ/SANCERRE. Complex, age-worthy wines. Top cuvées; Buisson Renard, *Pur Sang*, Le Mont Damné, *Silex* 12′ 14′ 16′ 17 18′ 19 20 21 (22′) (23). Also Les Jardins de Babylone (JURANÇON).

Danjou-Banessy, Dom Rouss ★★★★ Extraordinarily complex, fresh, bio wines in Agly V. IGP CÔTES CATALANES; v.gd La Truffière (r/w), Les Myrs (100% CARIGNAN).

Dard & Ribo N Rh ★★★ Quirky duo, deservedly loved by natural-wine amateurs. Old-vine CROZES-HERMITAGE, ST-JOSEPH, relaxed approach, no new oak; character, charm. Note whites (ROUSSANNE); Crozes Les Bâties, St-Joseph Pitrou (both r/w).

Dauvissat, Vincent Chab ★★★★ Supreme bio CHAB using old barrels and local 132-litre *feuillettes*. Grand, age-worthy, similar to RAVENEAU cousins. Best: La Forest, Les CLOS, Preuses, Séchet. Try also DOM Jean D & Fils (no relation).

Deiss, Dom Marcel Al ★★★ Famous Bergheim estate favouring field blends. Altenberg de Bergheim 16, Engelgarten 18, Schoenenbourg 13′ 17′ outstanding; 20 delicious.

Delamotte Champ ★★★ Fine, small, CHARD-dominated house. Managed with SALON by LAURENT-PERRIER. BRUT, fascinating Rosé, BLANC DE BLANCS 07 08 13′ 14′; 18 19′ 20 trilogy promises much; 19 *primus inter pares*, I wager.

Delas Frères N Rh ★★★ Owner-merchant in N Rh, with CONDRIEU, CROZES-HERMITAGE, CÔTE-RÔTIE, HERMITAGE vyds. Sleek reds, steady quality, high prices. Best: Côte-Rôtie Landonne, Hermitage DOM des Tourettes (r/w), *Les Bessards* (r, strong granite, sublime finesse 15 yrs+, smoky), Ligne de Crête (subtle), ST-JOSEPH Ste-Épine (r, intricate); S Rh CÔTES DU RH St-Esprit (r), Grignan-les-Adhémar (r, value). Whites less engaging, lighter recently. Owned by ROEDERER.

Delaunay, Edouard C d'O ★★★ Old Burg name revived in NUITS and l'Étang-Vergy by Laurent D; wide range NÉGOCIANT CUVÉES all price points. Gaining widespread plaudits. Name to watch. Check Septembre Bourgogne CHARD, PINOT N.

Demi-sec Half-dry – but in practice more like half-sweet (eg. CHAMP typically 45g/l dosage).

Derenoncourt, Stéphane Bx International winemaker. Own property, *Dom de l'A* in CAS. President of Castillon Caractères club.

Deutz Champ ★★★★ One of best medium-sized houses, owned by ROEDERER family. CEO Fabrice Rosset has handed over to Marc Hoellinger after a mere 26 yrs at (v.) top. Winemaker Caroline Latrive was at AYALA. Supreme CHARD *Cuvée Amour de Deutz* 08 10 13 15′; AdD Rosé 12 13 15; superb CUVÉE William Deutz 08 12 13; BLANC DE BLANCS 13 14 16′ 17′.

Deux Clés, Dom des Ldoc ★★★ Burgundian Gaëlle, Florian Richter bring light touch to terroir-driven wines (r/w) from old vines in deepest CORBIÈRES. IGP Vallée du Paradis terrific CARIGNAN.

Devaux Champ ★★→★★★ In Côte des Bars, reliable CUVÉE D; project with far-from-predictable Michel CHAPOUTIER Sténopé 08 09 10 11′ 12. So far so v.gd.

Dirler-Cadé, Dom Al ★★★→★★★★ Top old-vines MUSCAT GC Saering and Spiegel and SYLVANER VIEILLES VIGNES 16 17′ 18′ 19 20 22; v.gd Saering and Kitterlé RIES 10 14′ 16 17′ 18 19 20 22. Amazing GEWURZ Spiegel VT 19.

Domaine (Dom) Property, except next entry. *See* under name, eg. TEMPIER, DOM.

Dom Pérignon Champ ★★★★ Vincent Chaperon, chef de CAVE, now firmly into his stride at luxury CUVÉE of MOËT & CHANDON. Consistently excellent quality, huge quantities. Reductive style but assumes seductive creamy allure, esp after

10–15 yrs. Plénitude releases: long bottle-age, recent disgorgement, huge price, at 7, 16, 30 yrs+ (P1, P2, P3); superb P2 98 99 00 02 04'; still-vibrant P3 70 82 85 90 93'. More PINOT N focus in DP since 2000, 06 07 08 10 12 13'. Superb, ultra-expensive Rosé too.

Dopff au Moulin Al ★★★→★★★★ Pioneer of AL CRÉMANT in pretty Riquewihr; some wines dilute but GEWURZ GCS Brand, Sporen 12 16 18' 20', RIES SCHOENENBOURG 13 17', SYLVANER de Riquewihr 19' v.gd.

Dourthe Bx Sizeable merchant-grower, nine properties (incl CHX BELGRAVE, Grand Barrail Lamarzelle Figeac, LA GARDE, LE BOSCQ). *Dourthe Nº 1* (esp w) well-made generic BX. Also Essence de Dourthe blend from best parcels.

Drappier, Michel Champ ★★★ Family-run AUBE house, children of Michel D now in charge. Fine PINOT N, 60 ha+, bio; Pinot-led NV, BRUT ZÉRO, Brut *sans souffre*, Millésime d'Exception 12 14' 16 18 Prestige CUVÉE Grande Sendrée 08' 09 12, plus GS Rosé 08 09 10' CUVÉE Quatuor (four CÉPAGES). Superb 95' 82 (magnums). Constant research into early C17 vines resistant to climate change. More use of large oak *foudres*.

DRC (Dom de la Romanée-Conti) C d'O ★★★★ Grandest estate in Burg (or world). MONOPOLES ROMANÉE-CONTI and LA TÂCHE, major parts of ÉCHÉZEAUX, GRANDS-ÉCHÉZEAUX, RICHEBOURG, ROMANÉE-ST-VIVANT and a tiny part of MONTRACHET. Also CORTON from 09, superb CORTON-CHARLEMAGNE. Crown-jewel prices. Scintillating 22, esp La Tâche.

Drouhin, Joseph & Cie Burg ★★★→★★★★ Grower-NÉGOCIANT in BEAUNE; vyds (bio) incl (w) Beaune *Clos des Mouches*, MONTRACHET (Marquis de LAGUICHE) and large CHAB holdings. Great range of stylish reds: CHOREY-LÈS-BEAUNE, Beaune, CHAMBOLLE, VOSNE (Petits Monts) and now GEVREY. Recent purchase of Rapet (ST-ROMAIN) and CH de Chasselas (ST-VÉRAN), adds 20 ha. Avoids négociant trap of all wines tasting much the same. Also Dom Drouhin Oregon (US).

Duboeuf, Georges Beauj ★★→★★★ From hero (saviour of BEAUJ) to less so (too much BEAUJ NOUVEAU), always major player. Sound source for Beauj crus that age well, Mâcon bottlings. Georges D RIP 2020; son Franck continues gd work.

Dugat C d'O ★★★→★★★★ Cousins Claude and Bernard (Dugat-Py) made excellent, deep-coloured GEVREY-CHAMBERTIN, respective labels. Both flourishing with new generation. Tiny volumes, esp GCS, huge prices. Collector territory. Almost ageless. Try D-P's excellent BOURGOGNE rouge to gain hint of GC quality above.

Dujac, Dom C d'O ★★★→★★★★ MOREY-ST-DENIS grower originally noted for sensual reds that aged into delicate intensity, from village Morey to outstanding GCS, esp CLOS DE LA ROCHE, CLOS ST-DENIS, ÉCHÉZEAUX. Slightly more mainstream these days; gd *whites* from Morey and PULIGNY. Lighter merchant wines as D Fils & Père and DOM Triennes in COTEAUX VAROIS.

Dureuil-Janthial Burg ★★ Vincent D-J runs outstanding DOM in RULLY, with *fresh, punchy whites* and cheerful, juicy reds. All recommended but esp Maizières (r/w) or PC Meix Cadot (w).

Duval-Leroy Champ ★★★ Family-owned, over 200 ha mainly fine CHARD crus. Excellent sites. Fleur de CHAMP GC 96 00 02. CLOS des Bouveries 05 06'.

Échézeaux C d'O ★★★ 99' 02' 05' 09' 10' 12' 15' 16 17 18' 19' 20' 21 22' A GC next to CLOS DE VOUGEOT, but totally different style: lacy, ethereal, scintillating. Can vary depending on exact location. Outstanding quality, price: ARNOUX-LACHAUX, Bizot, Coquard-Loison-Fleurot, DRC, DUJAC, EUGÉNIE, G NOËLLAT, GRIVOT, GROS, LIGER-BELAIR, MÉO-CAMUZET, *Mugneret-Gibourg*, ROUGET, TREMBLAY. Other fine choices: Berthaut-Gerbet, *Guyon*, Lamarche, Millot, MUGNERET, Naudin-Ferrand, Tardy.

Edelzwicker Al ★ DYA Blended, entry-level fresh white: HUGEL Gentil, Meyer-Fonné.

Egly-Ouriet Champ ★★★→★★★★ Family affair in GC Ambonnay, 4th generation. Outstandng VIEILLES VIGNES CUVÉES: Les Crayères BLANC DE NOIRS and VP. Also

NV PC Les Prémices. Fashionable (and brilliant) Coteaux Champenois; CUVÉE des Grands Côtés 16 19 20.

Entraygues & du Fel and Estaing SW Fr ★→★★ DYA Two tiny AOP neighbours in almost vertical terraces above Lot V. Bone-dry CHENIN BL for white, esp ★★ DOMS Laurent Mousset (gd r, esp La Pauca, excellent rosé), Méjanassère. ★★ Nicolas Carmarans makes wines in and out of AOP.

Entre-Deux-Mers Bx ★→★★ DYA Often gd-value dry white BX from between rivers Garonne and Dordogne. New red from 2023. Best: CHX Beauregard Ducourt, BONNET, Fontenille, Haut-Rian, La Freynelle, Landereau, La Mothe du Barry (French Kiss), Lauduc, Les Arromans, Marjosse, Nardique-la-Gravière, Sainte-Marie, *Tour de Mirambeau*, Turcaud, Vignol.

Escaravailles, Dom des S Rh ★★→★★★ Versatile range. Flair in reds: CAIRANNE, top Roaix Village (SYRAH) too. Daughter Madeline achieving lovely fruit. Note Ad Argillam, Cairanne Scarabée Libérée (no sulphur), Rasteau Héritage 1924, VDN.

Esclans, Ch D' Prov ★→★★★ Sacha Lichine, self-styled architect of "Rosé Renaissance", has built six high-profile rosé brands, most for export. Part-owned by LVMH. Whispering Angel hugely successful everywhere. Garrus GRENACHE/ROLLE, oaked, is top-notch, expensive, will age. Les Clans, partially oaked v. stylish.

Esmonin, Dom Sylvie C d'O ★★★ Rich, dark wines from fully ripe grapes, whole-bunch vinification and new oak. Best: CLOS ST-JACQUES, GEVREY-CHAMBERTIN VIEILLES VIGNES. Slightly below radar, hence appealing quality/value combination.

Etoile, L' Jura AOP for stony CHARD, SAVAGNIN on limestone and marl, usually oxidative. VIN JAUNE, VIN DE PAILLE also allowed but not reds (sold as AOP CÔTES DU JURA). Try ★★ *Montbourgeau*, ★ Mouillard, P Vandelle, Rolet.

Eugénie, Dom C d'O ★★★→★★★★ Artemis Estates' 1st foray into burg. Intense, dark wines now enlivened by more whole-bunch vinification. CLOS VOUGEOT, GRANDS-ÉCHÉZEAUX outstanding, but try village CLOS d'Eugénie too.

Faiveley, Dom Burg ★★→★★★★ Has transitioned from NÉGOCIANT to DOM, revitalized by Erwan F since 2005, incl great new vat room, inspired by railway station architecture. Once serviceable, now exciting. Leading light in CÔTE CHALONNAISE, but save up for top wines from CHAMBERTIN-CLOS de Bèze, CHAMBOLLE-MUSIGNY, CORTON *Clos des Cortons*, NUITS. Also owns classy DOM Billaud-Simon (CHAB).

Faugères Ldoc ★★★ Exciting AOP on foothills of Cevennes. Altitude, schist soil = unique terroir, fragrant *garrigue*-scented, poised reds. Will age. Elegant whites from GRENACHE BL, MARSANNE, ROUSSANNE, VERMENTINO. Drink CH de Ciffre, DE LA LIQUIÈRE. DOMS Ancienne Mercerie, Bardi-Alquier, CÉBÈNE, Chenaie, DES TRINITÉS, Estanilles, Grézan, LA SARABANDE, Léon Barral, Mas d'Alezon, Mas Gabinèle, Méteore, Ollier-Taillefer, St Antonin.

Ferraton Père & Fils N Rh ★★★ Grower-merchant, CHAPOUTIER-owned, bio. Broad selection, gd to v.gd, esp CROZES-HERMITAGE Grand Courtil (r/w 50/50% MARSANNE/ROUSSANNE), HERMITAGE Le Méal (r, 60s SYRAH), Le Reverdy (w, solid, elegant), Les Dionnières (r, finesse), ST-JOSEPH Bonneveau (r, terroir).

Fèvre, William Chab ★★★→★★★★ Biggest owner of CHAB GCs; Bougros Côte Bougerots and Les CLOS outstanding. Small yields, no expense spared, priced accordingly; GCs can be splendid, humbler wines a little safe in style. Visitor-friendly. Look also for cousins N&G Fèvre, esp PC Vaulorent and GC Preuses. Now owned by DBR Lafite.

Fiefs Vendéens Lo ★→★★★ 19' 20' 21 (22) Fascinating Atlantic AOP marrying Lo fruit with saline, oceanic influences. Whites led by CHENIN BL, reds a melting pot incl CAB FR, GAMAY, NÉGRETTE and more. Best: *Dom Saint Nicolas* (VDF), Mourat, Prieuré-la-Chaume.

Fitou Ldoc ★★→★★★ AOP Lots of CARIGNAN gives rugged richness, taste of the sun. Two parts: schist on inland hills s of Narbonne; and chalk, limestone nr coast. Seek out: CHX de Nouvelles, Grand Guilhem, Champs des Soeurs; DOMS Bertrand-Bergé, de la Rochelierre, JONES, Lérys, MAS DES CAPRICES.

Fixin C d'O ★★→★★★ 05' 09' 10' 12' 14 **15'** 16 17 18' 19' 20' 21 22' When GEVREY goes beyond budget, switch to Fixin. Watch. Structured reds, previously hearty but enjoying warmer vintages. Best vyds: Arvelets, CLOS de la Perrière, Clos du Chapitre, Clos Napoléon. Top locals: Berthaut-Gerbet, Gelin, Joliet, Naddef. Also Bart, CLAIR, FAIVELEY, MORTET.

Fleurie Beauj ★★→★★★ 15' 18' 19' **20'** 21 22' Top BEAUJ cru for perfumed, strawberry fruit, immediate appeal. Potential PCS applied for, likely to be yrs. Classic: CHX BEAUREGARD, Chatelard, de Poncié; DOMS Brun, Chignard; CLOS de la Roilette, Depardon, DUBOEUF, Métrat, co-op. Naturalists: Balagny, Dutraive, Métras, Pacalet, Sunier. New: Chapel, Clos de Mez, Dom de Fa, Hoppenot, Lafarge-Vial.

Fourrier, Dom C d'O ★★★★ GEVREY DOM producing sensual vibrant reds with magical fruit flavours, from ancient vines. Age beautifully. Best: CLOS ST-JACQUES, Combe aux Moines (complete with monk sculpture in vyd), GRIOTTE-CHAMBERTIN. Cult prices. Also Bass Phillip (Australia).

Francs-Côtes de Bordeaux Bx ★★ 16 18 19 **20** 22 Tiny CÔTES AOP next to CAS. Fief of Thienpont (PAVIE MACQUIN family). Mainly red; MERLOT-led (60%). Some gd white (Charmes-Godard, Puyanché). Try Ad Francos, Cru Godard, Francs (Les Cerisiers), La Prade, Marsau, *Puygueraud*.

Fronsac Bx ★★→★★★ 16 18 **19'** 20' 22 Great-value, hilly AOP w of POM. MERLOT-led on clay-limestone; some ageing potential. Top CHX: Arnauton, DALEM, Fontenil, George 7, Haut-Carles, *La Dauphine*, La Grave, La Rivière, LA VIEILLE CURE, LES TROIS CROIX, Mayne-Vieil (CUVÉE Alienor), *Moulin Haut-Laroque*, Tour du Moulin, Villars. *See also* CANON-FRON.

Sign of Rhône whites progress: Gigondas AOP white (mainly Clairette) from 2023.

Fronton SW Fr ★★ 19 20 22 AOP n of Toulouse. Rare (sometimes unblended) NÉGRETTE grape (violets, cherries, licorice flavours). Often blended with SYRAH. Vibrant, fruity, purple-hued ★★★ CHX Baudare, Bouissel, Caze, ★★ *du Roc*, Laurou, Plaisance. ★★ CH BELLEVUE-LA-FORÊT best known. Also ★ Boujac, Clamens, La Colombière, Viguerie de Belaygues. No AOP for whites as yet.

Fuchs, Henri Al ★★→★★★ Founded 1922, 4th generation, organic Ribeauvillé winery. Outstanding, deep SYLVANER VIEILLE VIGNE 19 20 21, from old vines in late-ripening, top Weinbaum site. Also v.gd RIES GC Kirchberg de Ribeauvillé.

Fuissé, Ch Burg ★★→★★★ Smart operation in POUILLY-FUISSÉ with long track record. Concentrated oaky (too oaky?) whites. Top terroirs Le CLOS, Combettes. Also BEAUJ crus, eg. JULIÉNAS.

Gagnard C d'O ★★★ Respected clan in CHASSAGNE. Long-lasting wines, esp BÂTARD, Caillerets from Jean-Noël G; while Blain-G, Fontaine-G have full range, incl rare CRIOTS-BÂTARD, MONTRACHET itself; gd value all round. Tasty Chassagne reds too. Reliable name in all its iterations; seek out.

Gaillac SW Fr ★→★★ Mostly DYA Ramshackle vyds ne of Toulouse. Cornucopia of grapes, incl Braucol (Fer), Duras, SYRAH (r), LEN DE L'EL, MAUZAC (w). Prunelard gaining ground for red, while Ondenc (w) has legendary status at *Plageoles*. Quality variable but also look for ★★★ CHX Lastours, *L'Enclos des Roses*; DOMS Brin, Causse-Marines, d'Escausses, La Ramaye, La Vignereuse, Le Champ d'Orphée, Peyres-Roses, Rotier. Perlé is refreshing, summery white with slight prickle; can be delicious. Co-ops do it well and cheaply.

Ganevat Jura ★★★→★★★★ CÔTES du JURA bio superstar with single-vyd CHARD (eg. Chalasses, Grands Teppes), SAVAGNIN Vignes de Mon Père (topped up 10 yrs). Expressive reds. Cult pricing. Anne & Jean-François G NÉGOCE business too.

Gangloff, Yves N Rh ★★★ Rock-star (literally) CONDRIEU producer, cult following;

luscious, rich style. Also two CÔTE-RÔTIES: Barbarine, younger vines, dark fruit; Sereine Noire, deep, complex. Correct ST-JOSEPH (r/w).

Garrabou, Dom Ldoc ★★★ Frèderic G now in charge. Smart AOP LIMOUX CHARD, IGP Le Salsous PINOT N. Intense MALBEC Le Gouffre de Diable, needs time.

Gauby, Dom Gérard Rouss ★★★★ Iconic DOM nr village of Calce. Bio, agroforestry, IGP CÔTES CATALANES; son Lionel taking over. High-altitude vyds up to 550m (1804ft), chalk for fresh acidity. Try Les Calcinaires, VIEILLES VIGNES (r/w), Muntada, 100-yr-old GRENACHE, stupendous.

GC (Grand Cru) Official term meaning different things in different areas. One of top Burg vyds with its own AOP. In AL, one of 51 top vyds, each now with own rules. In ST-ÉM, 60% of production is St-Ém GC, often run of the mill. In MÉD, five tiers of GC CLASSÉS. In CHAMP, top 17 villages are GCs. Since 2011 in Lo for QUARTS DE CHAUME; emerging system in LDOC. Take with pinch of salt in Prov.

Gérin, Jean-Michel N Rh ★★★ 19' 20' 21' 22' 23' Progressive 15-ha CÔTE-RÔTIE estate, gd spread schist-granite vyds, racy wines, led by Les Grandes Places (brooding depth), Côte Brune (7% VIOGNIER, complex), also La Landonne (rich), La Viallière (stylish). Some oak. Two sound CONDRIEU.

Gevrey-Chambertin C d'O ★★→★★★★ 05' 09' 10' 12' **15' 16** 17 18' 19' 20' 21 22' Major AOP for reds of substance and structure, from serviceable to supreme, up to great CHAMBERTIN and GC cousins. Some trade on name, but best brilliant. Top PCS Cazetiers, Combe aux Moines, Combottes, CLOS ST-JACQUES. Value single-vyd village wines (En Champs, La Justice), VIEILLES VIGNES bottlings. Top: BACHELET, BOILLOT, *Burguet*, Damoy, Drouhin-Laroze, DUGAT, Dugat-Py, Duroché, ESMONIN, FAIVELEY, FOURRIER, Guillon, Harmand-Geoffroy, Hereztyn-Mazzini, LEROY, Magnien (H), Marchand-Grillot, MORTET, Rebourseau, ROSSIGNOL-TRAPET, Roty, ROUSSEAU, Roy, SÉRAFIN, TRAPET, and all gd merchants.

Gigondas S Rh ★★→★★★ 05' 06' 09' 10' 12' 13' **15'** 16' 17' 18 19' 20 21 22' 23 Top red; from 2023 white (mainly CLAIRETTE) too. Beautiful vyds on stony clay-sand *garrigue* plain rise to alpine limestone hills e of Avignon; GRENACHE, plus SYRAH, MOURVÈDRE. A gd area for walking holidays. Spiced, menthol-fresh wines; best give cool, fine dark-red fruit, true terroir reflection. Top 10 15 16 19. Try Boissan, Bosquets (modern, oak), Bouïssière (punchy), Brusset, Cayron (character), CH de Montmirail, CH DE ST COSME (flair, oak), *Clos des Cazaux* (value), CLOS du Joncuas (organic), DOM *Famille Perrin*, Goubert, Gour de Chaulé (fine), Grapillon d'Or, Les Pallières, Longue Toque, Moulin de la Gardette (organic), Notre Dame des Pallières, P AMADIEU (consistent), Pesquier (authentic), Piéblanc (organic), Pourra (robust), *Raspail-Ay* (ages), Roubine (hearty), *St Gayan* (ages), Santa Duc (stylish), Semelles de Vent, Teyssonières. Powerful rosés.

Gilbert, Philippe Lo ★★→★★★ Leading DOM in AOP MENETOU-SALON; bio. Top CUVÉES *Clos des Treilles* (r/w), 35/44 Rangs 19 20 **21 22** (23).

Gilles, Guillaume N Rh ★★★ 19' 20' 21' 22' 23' Classic CORNAS; 3 ha; detailed, structured wines, evolve well, notably Chaillot. CÔTES DU RH, GAMAY gd.

Gimonnet, Pierre Champ ★★★★ Didier G makes beautifully consistent CHARD on N Côte des Blancs, 28 GCS, PCS. Great-value Le Perlé de Gimonnet 12 **13** 16 18'. Special Club is complex expression of great Chard 13 **14** 15 17' 19 20 for long ageing. Oger GC a (glorious) departure from philosophy of assemblage 15'. Ditto Chouilly 12 16 and Cramant GC **12** 16'.

Girardin, Vincent C d'O ★★★ MEURSAULT-based NÉGOCIANT, part of BOISSET group. Excellent whites, esp CORTON-CHARLEMAGNE. Pierre-Vincent G, son of the original, is installed afresh in impressive new winery in Meursault; real promise.

Givry Burg ★★→★★★ 15' 17 18' **19'** 20' 21 22' Top tip in CÔTE CHALONNAISE for tasty, age-worthy reds, esp when C D'O reds beyond budget. Rare whites, nutty. Best (r): CELLIER AUX MOINES, CLOS Salomon, *Faiveley*, F Lumpp, Joblot, Masse, Thénard.

Goisot Burg ★★★ Guilhem and J-H G, outstanding bio producers of single-vyd ST-BRIS (SAUV BL) and Côtes d'Auxerre for CHARD, PINOT N. Racy, mineral, perky. Deserve to be better known.

Goldert Al Exceptional AL marl-limestone GC; v. aromatic wines. Some of Al's best GEWURZ, MUSCAT, SYLVANER. Try ERNEST BURN, ZIND HUMBRECHT.

Gonon, Dom N Rh ★★★ 10' 13' 14 15' 16' 17 18' 19' 20' 21' 22' 23' Major family estate at ST-JOSEPH, loved by hipsters, prices hot; bros Pierre and Jean work organically, hand-graft cuttings on 10-ha prime, terraced vyds. Mainly whole-bunch, old 600-litre casks, aromatic, peppered, iron-toned red, SYRAH delight; smoothly rich 50–80-yr-old vines *Les Oliviers* (w, great *à table*), both live 20 yrs.

Gosset Champ ★★★★ Oldest house, based in AŸ, owned by Cointreau. Chef de CAVE Odilon de Varine passionate about terroir. Grand Blanc de MEUNIER a 1st for house; mainly 07, elegant, aged on CHARD lees. Prestige *Celebris Extra Brut* outstanding 04 07' 08. Rosé just as gd 08. Sublime Les Célébrissimes 95' in same spirit; long-aged 12 Ans de Cave a Minima (Rosé now added). Outstanding double act with BLANC DE BLANCS and Millésime 12'. Let's not forget triumphant Grand Millésime 15'. A house to celebrate.

Gouges, Henri C d'O ★★★ Days of forbidding concentration and structure at Gouges are over. Grégory and Antoine G now making wine in a lighter iteration, though no less compelling. Great PCS: CLOS des Porrets, Vaucrains and esp Les St-Georges. Also excellent *white Nuits*, from PINOT BL.

Graillot, Dom Alain N Rh ★★★ 17 18' 19' 20' 21' 22' 23 Leading-edge CROZES-HERMITAGE, organic vyds, whole-bunch ferments. Dashing, dark fruited red: La Guiraude special selection, deep, long life. Crozes (w, suave, tuneful), ST-JOSEPH (r). RIP Alain 2022. Son Maxime: Crozes DOM des Lises fruit, early drinking, gd merchant wines, old vines, Equis (CORNAS, St-Joseph).

Burgundy prices? Consumers (not investors) want a collapse. Unlikely, though.

Gramenon, Dom S Rh ★★→★★★ 20' 22' 23' Trendsetter; organic since 70s, *garrigue* vyds, bio since 2007. Compelling fruit purity, v. low sulphur, gd range. Son Maxime-François now the boss. CÔTES DU RH: La Papesse (30s GRENACHE), La Sagesse (Grenache), Poignée des Raisins (glug glug), Sierra du Sud (SYRAH).

Grande Rue, La C d'O ★★★ 05' 06 09' 10' 12' 15' 16 17 18' 19' 20' 21 22' MONOPOLE of DOM Lamarche, GC between LA TÂCHE, LA ROMANÉE-CONTI. Quality, consistency improved under Nicole Lamarche. Fascinating blood-orange hallmark across vintages. Also special bottling dubbed 1959 – not better, just different.

Grands-Échézeaux C d'O ★★★★ 90' 93 96' 99' 02' 05' 09' 10' 12' 15' 17 18' 19' 20' 21 22' Superlative GC next to CLOS DE VOUGEOT, but with a MUSIGNY silkiness. More weight than most ÉCHÉZEAUX. Top: BICHOT (CLOS Frantin), Coquard-Loison-Fleurot, DRC, DROUHIN, EUGÉNIE, Millot, NOËLLAT G.

Gratien & Meyer / Alfred Gratien Champ ★★★ (BRUT) 93 12 13 15' 18' Small but wonderfully idiosyncratic CHAMP house, owned by Henkell Freixenet. Brut NV. Well-named CHARD-led Prestige *Cuvée Paradis Brut* 02 04 12 13' 15. Fine, v. dry, lasting, oak-fermented wines. Also Gratien & Meyer in SAUMUR.

Graves Bx ★→★★ 18 19 20 22 Appetizing grainy reds from MERLOT, CAB SAUV, fresh SAUV/SÉM (dr w); Grav Supérieures denotes *moelleux*. "Ambassadeur des Graves" selected CHX. Some of best value in BX today. Top Chx: ARCHAMBEAU, Brondelle, CHANTEGRIVE, CLOS Bourgelat, *Clos Floridène*, CRABITEY, de Cérons, Ferrande, Fougères, Grand Enclos du Ch de Cérons, Haura, Liber Pater, Pont de Brion, Portets, RAHOUL, *Respide Medeville*, Roquetaillade La Grange, Seuil, Torteau Chollet, *Vieux Ch Gaubert*, Villa Bel-Air.

Graves de Vayres Bx ★ DYA Tiny AOP within E-2-M zone. Red, white, *moelleux*.

Grés de Montpellier Ldoc ★★★ Terroir in LDOC AOC, stone's throw from Montpellier, hotspot for reds. Nearby St-Georges d'Orques similar quality. DOMS Bas d'Aumelas, de Blanville, de L'Engarran, de Roquemale, de Saumarez, Henry, La Magdelaine, La Marfée; CLOS des Nines, MAS DU NOVI, Mas de Lunés.

Grignan-les-Adhémar S Rh ★→★★ AOP, stony lands, on e of S Rh fringe; best reds dark, spiced, herbal, drink within 4–5 yrs. Best: DELAS (value); CHX Bizard, La Décelle (incl CÔTES DU RH w); DOMS de Bonetto-Fabrol, de Montine (stylish r, gd w/rosé, also Côtes du Rh r), Grangeneuve best (esp VIEILLES VIGNES), St-Luc.

Griotte-Chambertin C d'O ★★★★ 96' 99' 02' 05' **09'** 10' 12' 15' 16 17 18' 19' 20' 21 22' Small GC next to CHAMBERTIN; nobody has much volume. Brisk red fruit, depth and ageing potential: DROUHIN, DUGAT, Duroché, FOURRIER, Ponsot (L).

Gripa, Dom Bernard N Rh ★★★ 15' 16' 17' **18'** 19' 20' 21' 22' 23' Top ST-JOSEPH, best ST-PÉRAY DOM, v. refined whites. St-Joseph Le Berceau (w) 100% 60-yr+ MARSANNE; *St-Péray Les Figuiers*, mainly ROUSSANNE, classy. Both St-Joseph reds gd, top Le Berceau tracks vintage: deep 15, pure-fruit 16, dense 17, bold 18, rich 19, stylish 20, clear 21, bright 22.

Grivot, Jean C d'O ★★★→★★★★ VOSNE DOM that may improve even further as Mathilde G takes over. Superb range of PCS (note Beaux Monts, NUITS Boudots) topped by GCS CLOS DE VOUGEOT, ÉCHÉZEAUX, RICHEBOURG. Beautiful wines. Days of heft over beauty are gone.

Groffier C d'O ★★★ Sizzling 22, incl two versions of GC LES AMOUREUSES. Bewitching flavours capture, and hold, the tastebuds' attention. Raid the piggybank.

Gros, Doms C d'O ★★★→★★★★ Family of vignerons in VOSNE, with stylish wines from Anne (RICHEBOURG), succulent reds from Michel (CLOS de Réas), Anne-Françoise (now in BEAUNE) and Gros Frère & Soeur (CLOS VOUGEOT En Musigni). Marvellous view across Vosne GCS from new tasting room at Gros F&S. Not just GC; try value HAUTES-CÔTES DE NUITS. Also Anne's DOM Gros-Tollot in MINERVOIS. From 2022, some vyds changing hands within family.

Gros Plant du Pays Nantais Lo ★→★★ 22 (23) Atlantic AOP for Gros Plant (FOLLE BLANCHE). Taut and bracing foil for oysters; gd-value alternative to MUSCADET. Best: Chéreau-Carré, Famille Lieubeau, LUNEAU-PAPIN.

Guigal, Ets E N Rh ★★→★★★★ Best-known Rh name: justly celebrated, constantly enlarging grower-merchant. CÔTE-RÔTIE mainly, plus CONDRIEU, CROZES-HERMITAGE, HERMITAGE, ST-JOSEPH, 52-ha CHÂTEAUNEUF CH de Nalys (improving), plus two lots of 7-ha and 18-ha vyds there, top TAVEL Ch d'Aquéria (elegant). Merchant: Condrieu, Côte-Rôtie, Crozes-Hermitage, Hermitage, S Rh. Owns DOM de Bonserine (Côte-Rôtie), VIDAL-FLEURY. Top, v. expensive Côte-Rôties La Mouline, La Landonne, La Turque (mega-rich, dense, 42 mths new oak, so atypical), also v.gd Hermitage, St-Joseph VIGNES de l'Hospice. Standard also gd: *brilliant-value Côtes du Rh* (r/w/rosé). Best whites: Condrieu, Condrieu La Doriane (oak), Hermitage, St-Joseph Lieu-dit St-Joseph (fine, detail).

Hautes-Côtes de Beaune / Nuits C d'O ★★ (r) 15' 18' 19' 20' 21 22' (w) **17'** 18 19' 20' 21 22' Generic BOURGOGNE AOP for villages in hills behind main C D'O vyds. Climate change means both colours gaining style and elegance, losing rusticity. Sweet spots are villages of Arcenant, Meloisey, Nantoux and plateau above CÔTES DE NUITS. Look for Carré, Champy (Boris), CHEVROT, Devevey, DOM de la Douaix, Faure, Hoffmann-Jayer, Jacob, Naudin (Claire), Parigot, Vantey.

Haut-Médoc Bx ★★→★★★★ 15 16' 18 **19'** 20 22 Prime source of dry, digestible CAB/MERLOT reds. Usually gd value. Plenty of CRUS BOURGEOIS. Wines usually sturdier in n; finer in s. Five Classed Growths (BELGRAVE, CAMENSAC, *Cantemerle*, *La Lagune*, LA TOUR-CARNET). Eight Crus Bourgeois Exceptionnels (Arnauld, BELLE-VUE, CAMBON LA PELOUSE, Charmail, D'AGASSAC, de Malleret, du Taillan, *Malescasse*). Try also BEAUMONT, BERNADOTTE, CISSAC, CITRAN, COUFRAN, *de Lamarque*, LANESSAN, Madame de Beaucaillou, SÉNÉJAC, *Sociando-Mallet*.

Haut-Poitou Lo ★→★★ 20 21 22 Small AOP n of Poitiers, early drinking: white SAUVS BL/Gr, juicy red blends CAB FR-led. Few of note. La Tour Beaumont, Villemont.

Heidsieck, Charles Champ ★★★★ Iconic house, small but beautiful, wines perennially exquisite. Shock departure of winemaker Cyril Brun to Italy (Ferrari). Replaced by Elise Losfeld, ex-MOËT. NV Brut all purity, subtle yet ripe complexity, a beguiling paradox. Peerless **Blanc des Millénaires** 04 06 07. Great Vintage 12'. Older La Collection Crayères 83 81. Returning CHAMP Charlie multi-vintage prestige CUVÉE, icon if ever there was one. BLANC DE BLANCS NV nicely priced, delicious. Ditto Vintage Rosé 04 06' 07 08.

Heitz C d'O ★★★ Armand H is in Chaudenay, off the main drag of the C D'O. Gentle purity marks the reds, deliciously appealing even from barrel. Classy whites too.

Hengst Al Marl-limestone-sandstone GC, powerful wines: GEWURZ (ZIND H); AUXERROIS, PINOT GR (JOSMEYER). Now one of two AL PINOT N GC sites (A MANN).

Henriot Champ ★★★ Two changes in ownership in past 2 yrs; 1st Artemis and now co-op Terroirs et Vignes de Champagne (TEVC). Newish winemaker Alice Tétienne continues to impress. BLANC DE BLANCS de CHARD NV; BRUT 98' 02' 08; Brut Rosé 09. Exceptional prestige CUVÉE *Hemera* 05 06 08. New (and well named) from AVIZE: L'Inattendu 16. Unexpected style, but gd. Will next vintage have to change its name?

Herbert, Didier Champ ★★★ PINOT N specialist from Montagne de Reims. PN DH2 EB NV tastes a lot better than it sounds. *À suivre*.

Hermitage N Rh ★★★ →★★★★ 05' 06' 07' 09' 10' 11' 12' **13'** 15' **16'** 17' 18' 19' 20' 21' 22' 23' (10 15 20 brilliant). Home of a mighty hill and majestic wine (r/w). Granite, Alpine soils, complex terroir gives grandest, deepest SYRAH and nutty/white-fruited, stirring, v.long-lived white (MARSANNE, some ROUSSANNE) best left for 7 yrs+. Best: Alexandrins, Belle (organic), *Chapoutier (bio, magic w)*, Colombier (value), Darnaud, DELAS, Faurie (pure, last vintage 20), GUIGAL, Habrard (w), *J-L Chave* (much style), PAUL JABOULET AÎNÉ (sleek), Philippe & Vincent Jaboulet (r/w), SORREL (mighty Le Gréal r, deep, true Les Rocoules w), Tardieu-Laurent (oak). TAIN co-op gd (esp Gambert de Loche r, super VIN DE PAILLE w).

Hertz, Albert Al ★★ →★★★★ 15' **17'** 18' 19' Father/son team Albert and Frédéric of Eguisheim bio estate. GEWURZ (Eichberg GC 18, VT 15), PINOT GR (Zinnkopflé GC 18), RIES (Eichberg), SYLVANER (Eguisheim 18), v.gd, but can be uneven. Unforgettable SGNS.

Horizon, Dom de l' Rouss ★★★ Pure expression of rugged ROUSS terroir under IGP CÔTES CATALANES from old vines nr Calce. Mar y Muntanya gd-value SYRAH; gd, minerally, gastronomic rosé.

Hortus, Dom de l' Ldoc ★★★ Pioneering, family-run PIC ST-LOUP estate. Fine SYRAH-based reds: elegant Bergerie, oak-aged Grande CUVÉE (r). New Le Dit d'Hortus 100% SYRAH. Intriguing Bergerie IGP Val de Montferrand (w) with seven grapes.

Hospices de Beaune C d'O Massive hype and razzmatazz surround the annual charity auction of CUVÉES from the Hospices' 61 ha for Beaune's hospital. Once a triumph of spectacle over substance. Now much improved. Individuals can buy as well as trade. Winemaker Ludivine Griveau doing a great job. Quality high, prices too; charity is the point. Try BEAUNE cuvées, VOLNAYS or expensive GCS, (r) CORTON, ÉCHÉZEAUX, MAZIS-CHAMBERTIN, (w) BÂTARD-MONTRACHET.

Hudelot C d'O ★★★ VIGNERON family in CÔTE DE NUITS. H-Noëllat (VOUGEOT) is top class, esp harmonious, elegant GCS ROMANÉE-ST-VIVANT, RICHEBOURG, while H-Baillet (CHAMBOLLE) is challenging with punchy reds.

Huet, Dom Lo ★★★★ Reference DOM for CHENIN BL, VOUVRAY; bio. Top vyds: CLOS du Bourg, Le Mont (limestone), Le Haut Lieu (more clay). SEC to *moelleux*, all age magnificently 89' 90' 93 96 97' 02' 03 10 14' **16 17 18' 19 20'** 21 (22'). Also v.gd Pétillant.

Hugel & Fils Al ★★★→★★★★ Wines better than ever; famed late harvest, esp GEWURZ
RIES VT, SGN. Superb Ries Schoelhammer 10 13 17 from GC SCHOENENBOURG.
Don't miss 15' Grossi Laue ("great growth") wines.

IGP (indication géographique protegée) Potentially most dynamic category in
France (150+ regions), scope for experimentation. Replacing VdP, but new
terminology still not accepted by every area. Zonal names most individual, eg.
CÔTES DE GASCOGNE, Côtes de Thongue, Pays des Cévennes, Haute Vallée de
l'Orb, among others. Enormous variety in taste, quality, never ceases to surprise.

Irancy Burg ★★ 16 17 18' 19 21 22' Structured red nr CHAB made from PINOT N and
more rustic local César. Beware hot, dry vintages. Best vyds: Mazelots, Palotte.
Best: Cantin, Ferrari, GOISOT, Maison Chapelle, Renaud and Richoux.

Irouléguy SW Fr ★→★★★ 15' 18' 19 20 22 From green Basque Country hillsides.
Reds based on Axéria (CAB FR), TANNAT. Look out for rediscovered vines like
Arrouya (MANSENG N), Erremaxaoua. Best: ★★★ ARRETXEA, Bordaxuria, *Brana*,
Ilarria. Fruity white based on PETIT COURBU and both MANSENGS.

Jaboulet Aîné, Paul N Rh Formerly top grower-merchant. Organic vyds at
HERMITAGE, CONDRIEU, CORNAS, CROZES-HERMITAGE, CÔTE-RÔTIE, ST-JOSEPH. Reds
sleek, polished, spotless, would love more local identity. Best red is Hermitage
★★★★ La Chapelle (legendary 61 78 90), quality varied since 90s, some revival
since 2010 on reds. Also CORNAS St-Pierre, Crozes Thalabert (can be stylish),
Roure (decent). Merchant of other Rh, notably robust VACQUEYRAS, VENTOUX
(r, quality/value). Whites: neat, bit short on true Rh body, drink most young,
range incl new v. expensive La Chapelle (not every yr).

Jacquart Champ ★★★ Simplified range from co-op-turned-brand, concentrating
on what it does best: PC Côte des Blancs CHARD from member growers. Fine
range of Vintage BLANC DE BLANCS 13' 17 19'. Vintage Rosé 12 impresses. As does
CUVÉE Mosaïque 08. Villers-Marméry Blanc de Blancs captures the esence of an
underrated village 16'.

Jacquart, André Champ ★★★→★★★★ Marie Doyard has 24 ha incl 18 ha in GC LE
MESNIL. Flagship is Mesnil Experience 12 13. Magic Vintage trio 18 19 20. BLANC
DE BLANCS specialist, best special indeed.

Jacquesson Champ ★★★★ Superlative Dizy house for precise, v. dry wines. Chiquet
brothers have sold to Artemis Group. Outstanding single-vyd Avize CHAMP Caïn
09 12' 13. Corne Bautray, all CHARD. Dizy 09 10' 12 13'. Terres Rouges 09 12 13.
Innovative *numbered NV cuvées* 730° *et seq*... 744 745' 746. Focus on intrinsic
character of each base-wine harvest rather than notional consistency yr on yr.
Pioneers thus, and oft imitated. 746, eg., based on 18.

Jadot, Louis Burg ★★→★★★★ BEAUNE merchant, powerful whites, wide range of reds.
Significant vyd holdings in BEAUJ, C D'O, Mâcon incl POUILLY-FUISSÉ (Dom Ferret),
MOULIN-À-VENT (CH des Jacques); GCS could be more exciting. Long-standing
CEO, P-H Gagey, now succeeded by Thomas Seiter, ex-BOUCHARD PÈRE & FILS.

Jamet N Rh ★★★★ 05' 09' 10' 12 13' 14 15' 16' 17' 18' 19' 20' 21 22' 23' Jean-
Paul and Corinne J make must-buy, stirring, iron-filled CÔTE-RÔTIE, v. long-lived,
complex *vins de terroir* from multiple sites, mainly schist. Classic red intricate,
dashing fruit, Côte Brune (r) is mighty, smoky, mysterious, 30 yrs+. High-
quality CÔTES DU RH (r/w), COLLINES RHODANIENNES (r), also live well.

Jasnières Lo ★→★★★ Tiny but historical AOP in N TOURAINE, on tributary Loir. Taut
CHENIN BL 10 14' 15' 16' 18' 19 20' (22) (23). Best: *Bellivière* (★★★★), Cézin,
Gauletteries, Gigou, Janvier, Maisons Rouges, Raderie, Roche Bleue, Rycke.

Jobard C d'O ★★★ Vigneron family in MEURSAULT. Antoine J for esp long-lived
CHARMES, Genevrières, Poruzots; compelling whites, incl superb BOURGOGNE Bl,
plus reds from former DOM Mussy (POMMARD). Rémi J for immediately classy
Meursaults, esp Poruzots. Valentin J impressing too.

Joguet, Charles Lo ★★→★★★★ AOP CHINON superstar, essential for your cellar. Currently on the up under Anne-Charlotte Genet. Top CUVÉES *Clos du Chêne Vert*, *Clos de la Dioterie* 89 03 05 09 10 15 16 18 19 20 (22) (23). Entry-level/mid-range also worth investigating.

Jones, Dom Rouss ★★★ Englishwoman Katie J; characterful CÔTES CATALANES, CÔTES DU ROUSS, fragrant, gd-value FITOU. Perle Rare VDF (w) v.gd. Engaging virtual vyd rambles, adopt-an-old-vine scheme.

Josmeyer Al ★★★→★★★★ Siblings Isabelle and Celine Meyer run Wintzenheim bio-viticulture AL pioneer. Top 10 Al RIES, PINOT GR GCS Brand, Hengst 13 14 16 17' 18' 19 (but PG Hengst now macerated), AL's best AUXERROIS "H" 21'.

Juliénas Beauj ★★★ 15' 18' 19' 20' 21 22' Source of dark-fruited wines – for those who believe BEAUJ cannot age, esp CLIMATS Beauvernay, Capitans, etc. Try Audras (CLOS de Haute Combe), Aufranc, Besson, Burrier, CH BEAUREGARD, CH FUISSÉ, DOM Granit Doré, Perrachon.

Jurançon SW Fr ★→★★★ (sw) 18 19 20 (dr) 18' 19 20 22 Separate AOPS (dr/sw w). Balance of richness, acidity is key to quality. ★★★ DOMS *Cauhapé*, Guirardel, *Lapeyre*, Larrédya, Larrouyat. ★★ CH Jolys; Doms Bellegarde, Bordenave, Castéra, CLOS Benguères, Nigri, Uroulat. ★ Gan co-op gd value. *See also* CABIDOS.

Kientzler, Andre Al ★★→★★★★ High-acid, pure, mineral RIES, SYLVANER; sensual GEWURZ GC Kirchberg 16 17' 18' 19 20; v.gd VT wines.

Kreydenweiss, Marc Al ★★★→★★★★ Age-worthy limestone GC Moenchberg PINOT GR and black-schist Kastelberg RIES 10 17' ★★★★ 18' 19. Bio for decades. Also in COSTIÈRES DE NÎMES.

Krug Champ ★★★★ Supremely prestigious deluxe house. Grande CUVÉE, Edition 168, based on superb 12; E 169 on 13 etc.; latest E 171 on 15. Vintage 98 02 04 06' 08; Rosé; CLOS D'AMBONNAY 95' 96 98' 00 02 06'; *Clos du Mesnil* 98 02 03' 04 06' 08; Krug Collection 69 76' 81 85 88 89 90 95 00 08. Rich, nutty wines, oak-fermented; highest quality, ditto price. For the desert island.

Kuentz-Bas Al ★★→★★★★ Organic/bio outstanding SYLVANER 13 15 17' 20. GEWURZ VT CUVÉE Caroline winery's most balanced 09 12 17, though SGN CUVÉE Jeremy richer, more famous.

Labet, Dom Jura ★★ Long-admired CÔTES DU JURA organic estate in Rotalier. Best known for vibrant single-vyd CHARD whites, eg. En Chalasse, La Bardette, Les Varrons; natural PINOT N, Poulsard and classic VIN JAUNE.

Ladoix C d'O ★★ (r) 15' 17 18' 19' 20' 21 22' (w) 14' 15 17' 18 19' 20' 21 22' Exuberant whites (PC Grechons): Chevalier, FAIVELEY, Loichet. Juicy reds (PC Joyeuses): Capitain-Gagnerot, CH DE MEURSAULT, *Mallard*, Naudin-Ferrand, Ravaut.

Lafage, Dom Rouss ★★→★★★ Jean-Marc L, 7th-generation VIGNERON and gd winemaker, marketeer. Impressive, consistent range from ROUSS. AOP and IGP. Centenaire (w), Fundació (r), Miraflors (rosé) stand out.

Lafarge, Michel C d'O ★★★ VOLNAY bio estate run by Frédéric L. PCS Clos des Chênes, CLOS du CH des Ducs. Also fine BEAUNE, esp Grèves (r) and Clos des Aigrots (w). Plus FLEURIE project, Lafarge-Vial. Wines delightful in youth, then close down, time needed.

Lafon, Dom des Comtes Burg ★★★→★★★★ Celebrated bio MEURSAULT DOM, has emerged from shadow of premox. PCS Perrières, Genevrières; GC MONTRACHET. Superb red VOLNAY *Santenots*. Entry-level Héritiers du Comte L label from Mâconnais. Try also Dominique L's own label for BEAUNE, Volnay, Meursault.

Lafond Roc-Epine, Dom S Rh ★★★ Prominent TAVEL and LIRAC name, organic, gd drive and fruit in wines. Tavel La Relève rosé high interest, Lirac (r/w) both gd, CHÂTEAUNEUF (r) a terroir wine.

Laguiche, Marquis de C d'O ★★★→★★★★ Largest owner of LE MONTRACHET (2 ha/one-quarter) and a fine PC CHASSAGNE, both made for yrs by DROUHIN.

Lahaye, Benoit Champ ★★★ Cerebral bio producer; GC Bouzy. *Cuvée Violaine* 12 13 15 18 19; Le Jardin de La Grosse Père 09 13 15 17 18'. Quintessence of PINOT N CHAMP. Flagship BLANC DE NOIRS Extra Brut NV. Fascinating Rosé de Maceration.

Lalande de Pomerol Bx ★★→★★★ 15 16 18 19 **20** 22 Satellite neighbour of POM; similar but less depth, class; value. Largely MERLOT on clay, gravel and sandy soils. Top CHX: Ame de Musset, Annereaux, Belles-Graves, Chambrun, Garraud, Grand Ormeau, Haut-Chaigneau, Jean de Gué, La Chenade, LA FLEUR DE BOÜARD, La Sergue, Les Cruzelles, *Les Hauts Conseillants*, Pavillon Beauregard, Sabines, Samion, Siaurac, *Tournefeuille*.

Lallier Champ ★★★→★★★★ Artisan CHAMP from GC AŸ. Black Label R series 13 14'. Lovely Oger CHARD too. Interesting Parcels, Loridon and Les Sous, BLANC DE BLANCS and NOIRS, respectively. Now owned by Campari group; Dominique Demarville now chef de CAVE. On way up.

Lamy C d'O ★★★ DOM Hubert L, now run by Olivier L, for matchless ST-AUBIN. Breathtakingly fresh, concentrated whites, tense and reserved, often from higher-density plantings. Fastidious viticulture. Also Doms L-Caillat (intense w). Don't ignore L-Pillot in CHASSAGNE.

Landron, Jo Lo ★★→★★★ One of top DOMS in MUSCADET SÈVRE ET MAINE; organic. Cru communal prototype is *Fief du Breil* 12' 14' 15 16 17 **18** 20 (23). Drink others younger.

Langlois-Chateau Lo ★★→★★★ Fine source of CRÉMANT DE LO (*Quadrille*), BOLLINGER-owned. Dabbles in dry, esp SAUMUR. Owns Hubert Brochard (SANCERRE).

Not all red: 75 producers in Médoc make dry white Bordeaux.

Languedoc Biggest wine region in France, stretching from Nîmes towards Perpignan nr Spanish border, inland to Carcassonne and LIMOUX. AOP Ldoc, covers much of region with specific terroirs allowed to append name to AOP: CABRIÈRES, GRÈS DE MONTPELLIER, PÉZENAS, Quatourze, St-Saturnin, St-Georges d'Orques. Other AOPs incl FAUGÈRES, FITOU, MINERVOIS, ST-CHINIAN. CLAIRETTE du Ldoc tiny AOP for white Clairette. Top of hierarchy: crus incl CORBIÈRES-Boutenac, Minervois la Livinière, PIC ST-LOUP, LA CLAPE, TERRASSES DU LARZAC. Usual Ldoc grapes: (r) CARIGNAN, CINSAULT, GRENACHE, MOURVÈDRE, SYRAH; (w) GRENACHE BL, ROUSSANNE, VERMENTINO, but many others. IGP d'Oc covers whole region, regional IGPs too, source of quaffers and gd quality, quirky wine from producers who don't follow AOP rules.

Lanson Champ ★★★ Major house, owned by BCC. Black Label NV; Rosé NV; Le Vintage BRUT on a roll, esp 02 **08** 12 13. Prestige NV Noble CUVÉE BLANC DE BLANCS, Rosé and Vintage 98 02 04. Single-vyd Brut Vintage CLOS Lanson 06' 07 09 12. Now some malo: rounder style. Inspiring winemaker Hervé Danton.

Lapierre, Marcel Beauj ★★★ Mathieu and Camille L in vanguard of sulphur-free movement. Magnificent when on song. CUVÉES of BEAUJ, MORGON.

Laplace family SW Fr Oldest and at one time only producer of MADIRAN. Still at top. Top wine ★★★ *Ch d'Aydie*, needs time. Odie d'Aydie less so. Beautifully polished, less extracted than before; ★ Les Deux Vaches easy intro to TANNAT, lighter, rounder. Excellent ★★★ PACHERENCS (dr/sw). Sweet fortified Maydie (think BANYULS) gd with chocolate. Also gd-value IGP.

Larmandier, Guy Champ ★★★ Epitome of BLANC DE BLANCS elegance. Based in Vertus, but best wine GC Cramant. Also excellent CUVÉES Perlée, Signe François.

Larmandier-Bernier Champ ★★★★ Exemplary CHARD-dominated range from Côtes des Blancs. Longitude and Latitude magnificent BLANCS DE BLANCS. Zero-dosed Terre de Vertus 12 13 14' 15 16 great value; renamed *Vieille Vigne du Levant* (was du Cramant) 08 10 12 13 14' 15 merely great.

Laroche Chab ★★→★★★ Major player in CHAB with quality St Martin blend, Vieille

Voye special CUVÉE, Rés de l'Obédience made from exacting selection of GC Blanchots, named after historic HQ. Winemaker Grégory Viennois involved in NÉGOCIANT IRANCY project. Also Mas La Chevalière in LDOC.

Latour, Louis Burg ★★→★★★ Trad BEAUNE merchant noted for rich, age-worthy CORTON-CHARLEMAGNE, far superior to other whites. Also Mâconnais, ARDÈCHE (all CHARD). Reds improved, can improve; GCS (CORTON, ROMANÉE-ST-VIVANT) deliver occasional splendour. Also Henry Fessy in BEAUJ.

Latricières-Chambertin C d'O ★★★★ 99' 05' 09' 10' **12'** 15' 16 **17** 18' 19' 20' 21 22' A GC next to CHAMBERTIN. Deep soil, cooler site gives rich earthy wines in warm dry yrs. Best: ARNOUX-LACHAUX, BIZE, Drouhin-Laroze, Duband, Duroché, FAIVELEY, LEROY, Remy, ROSSIGNOL-TRAPET, TRAPET.

Laudun S Rh ★→★★ 22' **23** CÔTES DU RH-VILLAGE, close to being full cru, not sure about that. Brightly fruited, uplifted, superior whites, drink young. Red-fruit, spicy reds (much SYRAH), lively rosés. Immediate flavours from Maison Sinnae (old name Laudun-CHUSCLAN) co-op. DOM Pelaquié best, esp racy white. Also CHX Courac, de Bord, Saint-Maurice (VIEILLES VIGNES r); Doms Carmélisa (ex-footballer), Maravilhas (bio, character, r/w), Olibrius.

Laureau, Damien Lo ★★→★★★★ Leading light in AOP SAVENNIÈRES. *Roche-aux-Moines* 08 09 10 14' 15' 16' **18** will take your breath away. Also Chambourcier, new CUVÉE from rhyolite terroir.

Laurens, J Ldoc Specialist in LIMOUX bubbles. BLANQUETTE Le Moulin v.gd value. CLOS des Demoiselles Vintage CRÉMANT rivals many CHAMPS.

Laurent-Perrier Champ ★★★→★★★★ Important house. BRUT NV (CHARD-led) perfect apéritif; v.gd skin-contact Rosé. Fine vintages 08 12'. Grand Siècle CUVÉE multi-vintage on form, now released as a numbered "Iteration"; latest I 26 and I 24 in magnum. Peerless *Grand Siècle Alexandra Rosé* 98 04 12 14'. Also owns DELAMOTTE, SALON. Outstanding, longstanding chef de CAVE, Michel Fauconnet, has finally handed over reins to equally excellent Maximilien Bernardeau.

Lauzeta, Dom La Ldoc ★★★ Masterful bio ST-CHINIAN red with purity, minerality from schist. Super barrel-aged rosé, for the table.

Lavantureux Chab ★★→★★★ Specialist source for PETIT CHAB, CHAB, esp single-vyd Vauprin. Also PC Vau de Vey. BOURGOGNE Epineuil reds from 19 look brilliant.

Leccia, Yves Cors ★★★ Small bio DOM nr Bastia. Intense, precise fruit rather than oak. AOP PATRIMONIO El Croce, IGP Île de Beauté YL. Worth seeking out.

Leclapart, David Champ ★★★★ High priest of bio, based in Trépail, CHARD stronghold in Montagne. Barrel-fermented, oak sourced at LEFLAIVE; min sulphur, mainly zero dosage. *L'Artiste Blanc de Blancs* 12 13 **18** 19. Other inspired names (and wines): L'Aphrodisiaque, L'Apôtre, L'Astre.

Leclerc Briant Champ ★★★→★★★★ Impressive Épernay house, bio, guided by guru Hervé Jestin. Broad range, excelling at every level. Noteworthy NV BRUT Rés, deep-sea-matured Abyss 15 16 17 **18** 19', Le CLOS des Trois Clochers 15 16, intriguing oak-aged Blanc de MEUNIERS 13 16 (last three zero dosage). Finally Ch d'AVIZE, also Brut Zero.

Leflaive, Dom Burg ★★★★ PULIGNY-MONTRACHET DOM, back on form since 2017. Poise, precision hallmarks. High prices. Outstanding GCS incl MONTRACHET, CHEVALIER; *fabulous PCs* Combettes, Folatières, Pucelles, etc. Also try S Burg range, eg. Mâcon Verzé. Beware premoxed older vintages, esp in auction.

Leflaive, Olivier C d'O ★★★ White specialist NÉGOCIANT at PULIGNY-M. Outstanding BOURGOGNE Les Sétilles and all levels up to own GC vyds. Reds improving. Also La Maison d'Olivier, classy hotel, restaurant, tasting room. Real style here.

Leprince Burg ★★→★★★ Marvellous, entry-level ALIGOTÉ is Frédéric L's calling card, a perky-fruity masterclass in what can be achieved with this grape. Numerous other delights in range too.

FRANCE

Leroux, Benjamin C d'O ★★★ BEAUNE-based NÉGOCIANT equally at home in red or white; C D'O only, strengths (w) in MEURSAULT with increasing DOM and (r) BLAGNY, GEVREY, VOLNAY. Rock-solid consistency. Subtle labels signify subtle wines. Experimenting with glass globes in cellar.

Leroy, Dom C d'O ★★★★ Lalou Bize L, bio pioneer, delivers extraordinary reds, more impressive than charming, from tiny yields in VOSNE and from DOM d'Auvenay (more w). Ludicrously expensive even ex-dom, as is amazing trove of mature wines from family NÉGOCIANT Maison L.

Leroy, Richard Lo ★★★★ Cult ANJOU DOM, working in VDF since 2008. An exemplar. Both *Les Noëls de Montbenault*, *Les Rouliers* outstanding. Buy any vintage you can find; drink while grinning wildly.

Liger-Belair, Comte C d'O ★★★★ Comte Louis-Michel L-B makes brilliantly ethereal wines in VOSNE; ever-increasing stable headed by "bucket list" MONOPOLE LA ROMANÉE. Recent additions incl GCS CLOS DE VOUGEOT, ÉCHÉZEAUX, GRANDS-ÉCHÉZEAUX. New La Cuverie wine bar (eclectic selection), guest rooms.

Liger-Belair, Thibault C d'O ★★★→★★★★ Succulent bio burg from generics up to Les St-Georges (may someday be upgraded to GC) and GC RICHEBOURG. Outstanding ALIGOTÉ. Also stellar old-vine, single-vyd MOULIN-À-VENT. Thibault talks the talk, his wines walk the walk.

Lignier C d'O ★★★ Family in MOREY-ST-DENIS. Understated and stylish, from Laurent L (DOM Hubert L), esp CLOS DE LA ROCHE; v.gd PCS from Virgile L-Michelot, esp Faconnières. Fresh, bordering on austere, from Dom Georges L.

Limoux Ldoc ★★→★★★ Coolest part of Ldoc, nr Carcassonne, cradle of fizz BLANQUETTE, CRÉMANT de Limoux. Don't miss stylish still white AOP Limoux from CHARD, CHENIN BL, MAUZAC; must be barrel-aged. Red AOP: MERLOT, plus SYRAH, GRENACHE, Cabs. PINOT N in Crémant and for IGP Haute Vallée de l'Aude. Try Chx de Gaure, Rives-Blanques; DOMS de Baronarques, BEGUDE, de Fourn, de l'Aigle, de Mouscaillo, GARRABOU; J-L Denois, MAISON ANTECH, Plô Roucarels, VIGNOBLE Nicolas Therez.

Liquière, Ch de la Ldoc ★★★ AOP FAUGÈRES, family estate, never disappoints. Les Amandières (r/w/rosé) terrific value. Cistus old vines (r/w). Malpas top SYRAH. Les Racines (w) racy blend of five LDOC grapes.

Lirac S Rh ★★→★★★ 18 19' 20 22' 23 Four villages nr TAVEL, many large stones, quality terroir. Rolling, upbeat, spiced red (life 6 yrs+), gd impetus from recent CHÂTEAUNEUF owners via clearer fruit, more flair. Reds best, esp DOMS Anglore (low sulphur), Carabiniers (bio), *de la Mordorée* (organic, best w, cracking Reine des Bois r), Giraud, Joncier (bio), LAFOND ROC-EPINE (organic), La Lôyane, La Rocalière (bio, gd fruit), Maby (Fermade, gd w), Maravilhas (bio), MARCOUX (elegance), Plateau des Chênes (swish); CHX Boucarut (organic, revived), de Bouchassy (gd w), de Manissy (organic, bio), de Montfaucon (ace w, incl CÔTES DU RH), Mont-Redon, St-Roch; Clos du Mont-Olivet, Famille P Usseglio, Mas Isabelle (handmade), Rocca Maura (esp w), R Sabon. Whites always gd, convey freshness, body, go 6 yrs. Sound table rosés, note Romain le Bars (character).

Listrac-Médoc H-Méd ★★→★★★ 15 16' 18 **19** 20 22 Much-improved AOP for savoury red BX; now more fruit, depth and MERLOT due to clay soils. Also gd whites under AOP Bx (Le Blanc de Fourcas-Hosten). Best CHX: Cap Léon Veyrin, CLARKE, FONRÉAUD, FOURCAS-DUPRÉ, FOURCAS-HOSTEN, l'Ermitage, LESTAGE, Liouner, MAYNE-LALANDE, Reverdi, SARANSOT-DUPRÉ.

Long-Depaquit Chab ★★★ BICHOT-owned CHAB DOM with famous flagship brand, GC La Moutonne. Much recent improvement, well worth trying.

Lorentz, Gustave Al ★★→★★★ Bergheim grower-merchant of approachable, easy-going wines: v.gd RIES GC Altenberg de Bergheim 12 **13** 14 16 18 19. Best: VT, SGN (esp *Gewurz*).

Lorenzon Burg ★★→★★★ Bruno L (not dissimilar to George Orwell in looks) is maestro of MERCUREY. Practises meticulous viticulture based on high-trained vines, high-density planting, self-described as *un travail de haute couture*. Precision-flavoured wines, rare delicacy for CÔTE CHALONNAISE.

Loupiac Bx ★★ 16 17 18 19 22 (23) Minor SÉM-dominant *liquoreux*. Lighter, fresher than SAUT. Some can age. Top CHX: CLOS Jean, *Dauphiné-Rondillon, de Ricaud*, du Cros, Les Roques, *Loupiac-Gaudiet*, Noble.

Luberon S Rh ★→★★ 22' 23 Hilly, tourist region in e of S Rh; terroir v. dry, can be *ordinaire*. Excess of technical wines, but young incomers making gd VDF (Alexandre Dalet, DOM des Passages, Laura Aillaud). SYRAH has lead role. Whites improving. Bright star: CH de la Canorgue (organic). Also gd: Chx Clapier, Edem, Fontvert (bio, gd w), La Verrerie, Puy des Arts (w), Ravoire, St-Estève de Neri (improver); Doms de la Citadelle (organic), Fontenille (organic), La Cavale, Le Novi (terroir), Marrenon, Maslauris (organic), Val-Joanis; top-quality/value La Vieille Ferme (w/rosé) from Famille Perrin.

Luneau-Papin, Dom Lo ★★★★ No. 1 in MUSCADET SÈVRE ET MAINE? Quite possibly. Increasingly focused site-specific CUVÉES, all bio. Top: *Excelsior, L d'Or* 02' 05 07' 10 12' 14 16 19 20 (23). All worth a punt though.

Lussac-St-Émilion Bx ★★ 18 19 20 22 Most n of ST-ÉM satellites; lightest in style. Top CHX: Barbe Blanche, Bel-Air, Bellevue, Courlat, Croix de Rambeau, DE LUSSAC, La Rose-Perrière, Le Rival, LYONNAT, Mayne-Blanc.

Macle, Dom Jura ★★★ Legendary producer of CH-CHALON VIN JAUNE for long ageing. Best drunk 10 yrs+ after bottling. Also CÔTES DU JURA white.

Mâcon-Villages Burg ★★→★★★ 14' 17' 18 19' 20' 21 22' Chief appellation for Mâconnais whites. Individual villages may also use own names, eg. Mâcon-Lugny. Co-ops at Lugny, Terres Secrètes, Viré for value, plus *brilliant grower wines* from Guffens-Heynen, Guillot, Guillot-Broux, Maillet, Merlin, Paquet and C D'O based DOMS BOILLOT (J-M), LAFON, LEFLAIVE. Also major NÉGOCIANTS DROUHIN, LATOUR, etc. Worth exploring. Choose carefully for gd results.

Macvin Jura AOP, not Scottish. Grape juice fortified by oak-matured local marc to make off-dry apéritif of 16–20% abv. Usually white, can be red. Try over ice cream. Best by far are organic.

Madiran SW Fr ★★→★★★★ 12 15' 16 18 19 20 (22) Gascon AOP, France's home of TANNAT grape. Worthy reds in range of styles with many keepers. Look for ★★★ CHX BOUSCASSÉ, *Montus* (owner BRUMONT has 15% entire AOP), Laffitte-Teston, *Laplace*. Wide ranges from ★★★ Chx Arricaud-Bordès, de Gayon; DOMS Berthoumieu, Capmartin, Damiens, Dou Bernés, Labranche-Laffont, Laffont, *Pichard*; CLOS Basté. Doms ★★ Barréjat, ★★ Crampilh, Maouries not far behind. Laougue is new kid and looking gd.

Magnon, Maxime Ldoc ★★→★★★ Farms steep, high vyds in rugged CORBIÈRES; Burg native; bio. Rozeta (r), fruit-bomb with elegance, spice. Unfashionably dark, delicious Métisse rosé.

Mailly Grand Cru Champ ★★★→★★★★ Top co-op, all GC grapes. Prestige *Cuvée des Echansons* 08 09 12' for long ageing. Sumptuous Echansons Rosé 12; refined, classy L'Intemporelle 15 18 19'. Sébastien Moncuit, cellarmaster since 14, a real talent. New nicely named Poétique de la Terre BLANC DE NOIRS.

Mann, Albert Al ★★→★★★★ Barthelmé family-owned Wettolsheim bio estate: v. pure GCS HENGST, SCHLOSSBERG (esp 17' 20') and RIES Epicentre. One of AL's two best PINOT N producers (Les Stes Claires 15 18' 19).

Maranges C D'O ★★→★★★ 15' 17 18' 19' 20' 21 22' Name to watch. Robust well-priced reds from s end of CÔTE DE BEAUNE. Try PCS Boutière, Clos Roussots, Croix Moines, Fussière. Best: BACHELET-Monnot, *Charleux*, CHEVROT, Giroud, MATROT, Rouges Queues.

Marcillac SW Fr ★★ 19 20 22 Aveyron AOP based on Mansois (aka FER SERVADOU). Fruity, curranty/raspberry food wines; rustic, lowish alc. Best at 3 yrs. Try with strawberries as well as charcuterie or sausages, and of course *aligot* (mashed potato, garlic, an unhealthy amount of cheese). ★★ *Dom du Cros* largest independent grower (gd w IGPS too), also DOMS des Boissières, Laurens. Excellent co-op. Recent heatwave vintages outstanding.

Marcoux, Dom de S Rh ★★★ The 1st bio CHÂTEAUNEUF, still top; approachable fruited classic red; deep, lingering, impressive VIEILLES VIGNES (1900 GRENACHE, sand-clay). Stylish white; gd, clear LIRAC La Lorentine (r).

Margaux H-Méd ★★→★★★★ 10′ 14 15 16′ 18 19′ 20′ 22′ (23) Most S MÉD communal AOP. Famous for elegance, fragrance; reality more diverse. Top: BRANE-CANTENAC, DURFORT-VIVENS, FERRIÈRE, GISCOURS, ISSAN, KIRWAN, LASCOMBES, MALESCOT ST EXUPÉRY, MARGAUX, PALMER, PRIEURÉ-LICHINE, RAUZAN-SÉGLA. Value: ANGLUDET, Arsac, Deyrem Valentin, LABÉGORCE, Mongravey, Paveil de Luze, SIRAN.

Marionnet, Henry Lo ★★→★★★ 20′ 21 22′ (23) Important DOM in TOURAINE, noteworthy for ungrafted vyds and old-vine Romorantin (planted c.1820) *Provignage* (gd but pricey). Juicy GAMAY reds worth a punt: usually v.gd value.

Maris, Ch Ldoc ★★★ Opulent polished wines, cool eco winery in MINERVOIS La Livinière; bio. SYRAH-dominant Les Amandiers, Les Anciens CARIGNAN.

Marsannay C d'O ★★→★★★ (r) 15′ 17 18′ 19′ 20 21 22′ Most N AOP of CÔTE DE NUITS. PCS in (long) pipeline (eg. CHAMP Salomon, CLOS du Roy, Longeroies). Further village-level vyds added in 2019, eg. Le Chapitre. Satisfying, mildly rustic, fruit-laden reds, from energetic producers: Audoin, Bart, Bouvier, CHARLOPIN, CH de M, CLAIR, Derey, Fournier, *Pataille*; gd unfashionable rosé needs 1–2 yrs; whites getting better.

M 'n' M: Marsannay and Maranges for quality and value in the Côte d'Or.

Mas, Doms Paul Ldoc ★★→★★★ Jean-Claude M owns/manages 2400 ha in LDOC-ROUSS. Working on bio, low sulphur. IGP gd value, different labels for export: Arrogant Frog, Astelia, Côté Mas, La Forge, Les Tannes, Les VIGNES de Nicole. Owns Crès Ricards in TERRASSES DU LARZAC, Martinolles in LIMOUX; CHX Lauriga in ROUSS, Villegly in MINERVOIS.

Mas Amiel Rouss ★★★ Leading MAURY, Côtes du ROUSS, IGP. Look for Altaïr (w), Origine, Vers le Nord, Vol de Nuit from v. old CARIGNAN/GRENACHE, others. Plus excellent VDN from young, fruity *grenat*, to venerable RANCIO 20–40-yr-old Maury aged in 60-litre glass demijohns, intensely sweet and savoury.

Mascaronne, Ch La Prov ★★★ Same ownership as CH COS D'ESTOURNEL. CÔTES DE PROVENCE, beguiling bio rosé for the table, not by the pool.

Mas de Daumas Gassac Ldoc ★★★→★★★★ A LDOC pioneer, now 2nd-generation Samuel Guibert. Famed for CAB SAUV-based age-worthy reds. Perfumed white from CHENIN BL blend arguably better; super-CUVÉE Émile Peynaud (r); rosé Frizant; v.gd sweet Vin de Laurence (MUSCAT/SERCIAL).

Mas des Caprices Ldoc ★★★ Ex-restaurateurs from AL, Pierre and Mirelle Mann make complex yet accessible wines from bio vyds in FITOU, CORBIÈRES. Retour aux Sources, Ze Fitou (r); gd VDN RIVESALTES Grenat, RANCIO.

Mas de la Devèze Rouss ★★→★★★ Harmonious terroir-driven CÔTES DU ROUSS-VILLAGES. Pandore (w), powerful Tautavel (r), Malice (r/w) v. fine. MAURY VDN too.

Mas du Novi Ldoc ★★→★★★ Once part of Cistercian abbey, now leading light in GRÈS DE MONPELLIER; bio. Powerful Ô de Novi, Prestigi (r). Masterful SYRAH/VIOGNIER N de Novi. Stylish IGP CHARD.

Mas Jullien Ldoc ★★★★ Olivier J leader in TERRASSES DU LARZAC: outstanding Lous Rougeos (LDOC varieties at 400m/1312ft). Autour de Jonquières (MOURVÈDRE/CARIGNAN); Carlan, États d'Âme. Sublime minerally CARIGNAN BL (w).

Mas Llossanes Rouss ★★★ Highest vyds in ROUSS (700m/2297ft): fresh, elegant. Pure SYRAH, Pur CARIGNAN, super varietal expression; Au Dolmen, Dotrera gd red blends. Pur Chasan (w) perhaps most thrilling of all. IGP CÔTES CATALANES,

Mas Rouge, Dom du Ldoc ★★★ Next to Med, nr Montpellier. Seductive, fragrant MUSCAT VDN from both Frontignan and Miraval, latter elegant, fresh.

Mas Sibert Ldoc ★★★★ Tiny bio DOM, unfiltered/unfined VDF from un-LDOC grapes MERLOT, PETIT VERDOT, ALBARIÑO, PETITE ARVINE. Saramon dark rosé, SANGIOVESE-based, v.gd.

Massif d'Uchaux S Rh ★★ 22' 23 Superior CÔTES DU RH-VILLAGE, intimate pine-tree vyds, crisply fruited, spiced reds, not easy to sell, but best truthful, stylish. Note CH St-Estève (incl gd old-vine VIOGNIER), DOMS Cros de la Mûre (character, gd value), de la Guicharde, La Cabotte (bio, on great form), Renjarde (swell fruit).

Matrot Burg ★★→★★★ Since sisters Elsa and Adèle took over, quality, consistency soared at MEURSAULT DOM. Equally gd in red (BLAGNY, VOLNAY Santenots) and white (Meursault Blagny, Charmes, Les Perrières; PULIGNY PCS). Name to watch, on gd trajectory. Prices not wild, in context of C D'O.

Maury Rouss ★★→★★★ Sweet VDN from GRENACHES N/BL/Gr on island of schist. Ambré, tuilé and RANCIO styles. Don't confuse with AOP Maury SEC, dry red. MAS AMIEL leader for both styles; CH de l'Ou; DOMS de Lavail, LAFAGE, of the Bee, Pouderoux; Maury co-op.

Mazis- (or Mazy-) Chambertin C d'O ★★★★ 90' 93 96' 99' 05' 09' 10' 12' 15' 16' 17 18' 19' 20' 21 22' GEVREY-CHAMBERTIN GC, top class in upper part; intense, heavenly wines. Best: Bernstein, DUGAT-Py, FAIVELEY, HOSPICES DE BEAUNE, LEROY, MORTET, Rebourseau, ROUSSEAU, Tawse.

Mas production, or not: "mas" = Midi word for farmhouse, often v.gd artisan doms.

Mazoyères-Chambertin C d'O ★★★★ Usually sold as CHARMES-CHAMBERTIN, but style is different: less succulence, more stony structure. Try DUGAT-Py, MORTET, Perrot-Minot, Taupenot-Merme, Tawse.

Médoc Bx ★★ 16 18 19 20 22 AOP for reds in low-lying n part of Méd peninsula. Often more guts than grace. Lots of CRUS BOURGEOIS. Can be gd value; be selective. Top CHX: Castera, CLOS Manou, d'Escurac, Fleur La Mothe, GREYSAC, La Cardonne, La Tour-de-By, LES ORMES-SORBET, LOUDENNE (Le Ch), Lousteauneuf, Patache d'Aux, POITEVIN, Potensac, PREUILLAC, Ramafort, Rollan-de-By (HAUT-CONDISSAS), TOUR ST BONNET, Tour Séran, Vieux Robin.

Meffre, Gabriel S Rh ★★→★★★ Quality merchant, owns GIGONDAS DOM Longue Toque (top Hommage GM, gd VACQUEYRAS r). Improved fruit, reduced oak. Produces CHÂTEAUNEUF (incl small doms), VACQUEYRAS St-Barthélemy. Reliable-to-gd S/N Rh oaked Laurus range, esp CONDRIEU, HERMITAGE (w), ST-JOSEPH (r).

Mellot, Alphonse Lo ★★→★★★★ Leading SANCERRE bio DOM. Top white Edmond and Génération XIX 12' 14' 15 16' 17 18 19 20 21 (22) (23). Large portfolio, incl widely distributed La Moussière. High-quality, oak-aged reds, eg. En Grands Champs.

Menard, Pierre Lo ★★→★★★ Young up-and-coming ANJOU superstar. Delicious single-vyd ANJOU BL, mostly schist: Le Clos des Mailles 16 17 18 19 20 (21) (22) (23); Le Quarts des Noëls, Pluton. COTEAUX DU LAYONS Chaos, Cosmos.

Menetou-Salon Lo ★★→★★★ 14' 16 20' 21 22 AOP adjacent to SANCERRE, top wines superior to many lesser Sancerres. Try Chatenoy, Gilbert, Henry Pellé, La Tour St-Martin, Prieuré de Saint-Céols, Teiller.

Méo-Camuzet C d'O ★★★★ Noted DOM in VOSNE: icons Brûlées, CROS PARANTOUX, RICHEBOURG. Value from M-C Frère & Soeur (NÉGOCIANT branch). Full-bodied, dense-flavoured, need age. Interesting HAUTES-CÔTES white Clos St-Philibert.

Mercurey Burg ★★→★★★★ 15' 17 18' 19' 20' 21 22' Leading CÔTE CHALONNAISE village, hearty reds, aromatic whites. Try BICHOT, Champs de l'Abbaye, Ch de Chamirey *(esp Clos du Roi)*, CH Philippe Le Hardi, DOM de Suremain, FAIVELEY, Génot-Boulanger, *Juillot-Theulot*, LORENZON, M Juillot, Raquillet.

Merlin Burg ★★→★★★ Olivier M, wizard of the Mâconnais, now joined by sons. Top wines Mâcon La Roche Vineuse Les Cras, expanding POUILLY-FUISSÉ range, MOULIN-À-VENT La Rochelle. Co-owner CH des Quarts with Dominique LAFON.

Mesclances, Ch les Prov ★★★ Farmed by same family since C16, delicious rosé from La Londe, terroir of CÔTES DE PROV. Try GRENACHE DOM St Honorat; Faustine more ambitious, needs food. Silky reds too.

Mesnil-sur-Oger, Le Champ Top Côte des Blancs village, v. long-lived CHARD: ANDRÉ JACQUART, JL Vergnon, PIERRE PÉTERS, not forgetting the eponymous co-op with grape contracts to die for. Needs 10 yrs+ ageing. Top named vyd Les Chétillons.

Méthode champenoise Champ The trad method of putting bubbles into CHAMP by re-fermenting in the bottle. Outside Champ region, makers must use terms "classic method" or *méthode traditionnelle*.

Meunier, Dom Paul Rouss ★★★ Organic, horse instead of tractor, low-intervention wines vinified in old co-op in Centernach. Chorème COTES DU ROUSS: (w) haunting MACCABEO, (r) perfumed, silky. Falguayra MAURY GRENAT VDN.

Meursault C d'O ★★★ →★★★★ 09' 10' 12 14' 15 17' 18 19' 20' 21 22' Potentially great full-bodied whites from PCS: Charmes, Genevrières, Perrières, more nervy from hillside vyds Narvaux, Tesson, Tillets. Try Ballot-Millot, BOILLOT, Boisson-Vadot, BOUZEREAU, *Ch de Meursault*, COCHE-DURY, *de Montille*, Ente, Fichet, *Girardin*, Javillier, JOBARD, *Lafon*, *Latour-Giraud*, LEROUX, *Matrot*, Michelot, *Mikulski*, *P Morey*, PRIEUR, Rougeot, *Roulot*. Also de Cherisey for Meursault-BLAGNY.

Meursault, Ch de C d'O ★★★ A 61-ha bio estate, CH recently restored; once-sleepy name now buzzing with vitality. Tasty reds: BEAUNE, POMMARD, VOLNAY. Some stunning whites: MEURSAULT. BOURGOGNE Bl, PULIGNY PC v.gd. Try long-aged Marc. Also CH de MARSANNAY.

Milhau-Lacugue, Ch Ldoc ★★★ Jean L makes joyously fruity, herb-scented ST-CHINIAN from 60 ha nr Beziers. CUVÉE Magali gd value, Les Truffières savoury, autumnal. IGP VERMENTINO a bargain.

Minervois Ldoc ★★→★★★ Undulating AOP ne of Carcassonne, source of gently fruity, herbal reds from SYRAH, GRENACHE, MOURVÈDRE, CARIGNAN. Small quantity of stylish white, rosé too. Look for CHX Coupe-Roses, d'Agel, Donjon, Gourgazaud, de Homs, La Grave, La Tour Boisée, Oupia, Paumarhel, St-Jacques d'Albas, Senat, Villerambert-Julien; DOM CLOS Centeilles; Abbaye de Tholomiès, Borie-de-Mauriel, CAILHOL-GAUTRAN, Laville-Bertrou, Pierre Cros, PIERRE FIL. A GROS & J-P TOLLOT (from Burg) raising bar. La Livinière on Black Mtn slopes cru for fine, long-lived red. Clos d'Ora (Gérard Bertrand), Combe Blanche, COUDOULET, Gayda, MARIS, de l'Ostal, Piccinini, Ste Eulalie excel. St Jean de Minervois is delicious fresh MUSCAT VDN: Barroubio, Clos du Gravillas, Montahuc best.

Mirabeau, Maison Prov ★★→★★★ Stylish, well-packaged CÔTES DE PROV rosé, bought-in fruit, by Stephen and Jeany Cronk. Brands Etoile, Pure gd. DOM Res from own vyds a further step up. Focus on regenerative viticulture.

Mis en bouteille au château / domaine Bottled at CH, property, or estate. Note *dans nos caves* (in our cellars) or *dans la région de production* (in the area of production) often used but mean little.

Moët & Chandon Champ ★★★★ By far largest CHAMP house, impressive quality for such a giant. Fresher, drier BRUT Imperial NV, dosage conspicuously and successfully lowered of late. Rare prestige CUVÉE MCIII "solera" concept now superseded by *Collection Impériale Creation No. 1* (NV of seven vintages) – philosophy of "haut oenologie". Outstanding Grand Vintages Collection, showcase for urbane chef de CAVE Benoît Gouez: 02 08 09 12 13' 15. Outposts across New World. *See also* DOM PÉRIGNON.

Monbazillac SW Fr ★★→★★★ 18 19 20 21 BERGERAC sub-AOP: ★★★★ *Tirecul-la-Gravière* up there with gd SAUTERNES. ★★★ CLOS des Verdots, L'Ancienne Cure, Les Hauts de Caillavel, co-op's *Ch de Monbazillac*. ★★ CHX de Belingard-Chayne, Grande Maison, Kalian, Le Faget, Monestier la Tour, Pech La Calevie, Pécoula. Neighbouring SAUSSIGNAC makes similar wines.

Monopole A vyd in single ownership. Usually prestigious, and not common, in Burg, eg. LA ROMANÉE.

Montagne-St-Émilion Bx ★★ 18 19 20 22 Largest satellite of ST-ÉM. Solid reputation. Top CHX: Beauséjour, CLOS de Boüard, Corbin, Croix Beauséjour, Coucy, Faizeau, La Couronne, Maison Blanche, Malengin (Eve), Roudier, Simon Blanchard, Teyssier, Vieux Bonneau, Vieux Ch Palon, *Vieux Ch St-André*.

Montagny Burg ★★ 14' 17 18 19' 20' 21 22' CÔTE CHALONNAISE village with crisp whites, best of which punch well above reputation, mostly in hands of CAVES DE BUXY. Also LOUIS LATOUR, O LEFLAIVE. Top growers: Aladame, Berthenet, Cognard, Feuillat-Juillot, *Lorenzon*.

Monthélie C d'O ★★→★★★ 15' 16 17 18' 19' 20' 21 22' Crisp, juicy reds, grown uphill from VOLNAY, but less fine. Les Duresses best PC. Also *Ch de Monthélie* (de Suremain), Changarnier, Dubuet, Dujardin, Garaudet. Whites interesting (hillside sites). Value can still be found here.

Montille, de C d'O ★★★ Supple intensity in reds: BEAUNE, CÔTE DE NUITS (Malconsorts), POMMARD (Rugiens), VOLNAY (Taillepieds). Impressive whites: MEURSAULT, PULIGNY-MONTRACHET Caillerets. Glorious BOURGOGNE CHARD. Since 2017, CH de Puligny wines incl under de Montille. Abandoned confusing Deux Montille label. New projects in Sta Rita Hills (California), Hokkaido (Japan).

Montlouis sur Loire Lo ★★→★★★★ 14' 15 16 17 18 19' 20' 21 22' AOP; fine CHENIN BL (dr/sw/sp). Similar in style to much larger VOUVRAY, v. age-worthy. Top: Chanson, *Chidaine*, Delecheneau, Jousset, Merias, Pierres Ecrites, *Taille aux Loups*, Vallée Moray, *Weisskopf*.

Montpeyroux Ldoc ★★★ Cru 40 km n of Montpellier dominated by Mt Baudile. Innovative growers. DOM D'AUPILHAC, also Chabanon, Divem, Jasse-Castel, Joncas, Mas d'Amile, Villa Dondona. Serious co-op.

Montrachet (or Le Montrachet) C d'O ★★★★ 02' 04 05 08 09' 10 12 14' 15 17 18 19' 20' 21 22' A GC vyd straddling PULIGNY-CHASSAGNE boundary, hence both claimed it. *Should* be greatest white burg for intensity, richness of fruit and reverberating length. Top: BOUCHARD, COLIN, DRC, LAFON, LAGUICHE (DROUHIN), LEFLAIVE, RAMONET. Temper expectations to avoid disappointment.

Montus, Ch SW Fr ★★★★ 15' 16 17 18 19 20 22 Alain BRUMONT's flagship property, famous for long-extracted oak-aged wines. Long-lived all-TANNAT reds, much prized by lovers of old-fashioned MADIRAN. Classy (sw/dr w) barrel-raised PACHERENC-DU-VIC-BILH. La Tyre (tiny plot), Prestige equal to Classed Growths.

Mordorée, Dom de la S Rh ★★★ 16' 17' 18' 19' 20 22' 23' Leading estate at TAVEL, bio/organic, rosés with brio, depth, impetus; also LIRAC, La Reine des Bois (stunning r, gd w). CHÂTEAUNEUF La Reine des Bois (incl 1929 GRENACHE), La Dame Voyageuse (r) gd. Nifty VDF La Remise (r/w/rosé).

Moreau Chab ★★→★★★ Widespread family, esp *Dom Christian M*, noted for PC Vaillons CUVÉE Guy M and superlative GC Les CLOS des Hospices. Louis M, more commercial range; DOM M-Naudet, concentrated wines for longer keeping. Improving *J Moreau*. BOISSET-owned.

Moreau C d'O ★★★→★★★★ Outstanding CHASSAGNE PCS from DOM Bernard M, now divided between sons Alex and Benoît; fine La Cardeuse (r). Appealing range of SANTENAY, MARANGES from David M. Neither related to CHAB dynasty.

Morey, Doms C d'O ★★★→★★★★ VIGNERON family in CHASSAGNE. Exemplary wines from: Caroline M and husband Pierre-Yves COLIN-M, Marc (En Virondot),

Sylvain, Thibault M-Coffinet (LA ROMANÉE), Thomas (v. fine pure w), Vincent (plumper). Also Pierre M in MEURSAULT for Perrières and BÂTARD. All v. reliable.

Morey-St-Denis C d'O ★★★ →★★★★ 99' 02' 05' 09' 09' 10' 12' 15' 16' 17 18' 19' 20' 21 22' The Janus appellation, caught between GEVREY's grandeur and CHAMBOLLE's grace. Deserves better recognition for its own merits; GCS CLOS DE LA ROCHE, CLOS DE LAMBRAYS, CLOS DE TART, CLOS ST-DENIS. Top producers: ARLAUD, CLOS DE TART, Clos des Lambrays, *Dujac*, GROFFIER, *H Lignier*, Perrot-Minot, PONSOT, Roumier, TREMBLAY. Also Amiot, Castagnier, Coquard-Loison-Fleurot, LIGNIER-Michelot, Magnien, Remy, Taupenot-Merme. Interesting whites too, esp PC Monts Luisants.

Morgat, Eric Lo ★★→★★★ One of new stars of SAVENNIÈRES. Look out for *Fidès* 14' 15' 18 and rarely seen CLOS Sertaux. Do not overlook ANJOU BL Litus: better than many a dull Savennières.

Morgon Beauj ★★★ 15' 17 18' 19' 20' 21 22' Powerful BEAUJ cru; volcanic slate of Côte du Py makes meaty, age-worthy wine, clay of Les Charmes for earlier, smoother drinking. *Burgaud*, CH de Pizay, Chs des Lumières (JADOT), *Desvignes*, Foillard, Gaget, Godard, *Lapierre*, Piron, Sunier. It's Morgon 1st, Beauj 2nd.

Mortet C d'O ★★★→★★★★ Arnaud M on song with powerful, refined reds from BOURGOGNE Rouge to CHAMBERTIN. Key wines GEVREY-CHAMBERTIN Mes Cinq Terroirs; PCS Champeaux, Lavaut St-Jacques. Also separate Arnaud M label, equally brilliant, incl CHARMES- and MAZOYÈRES-CHAMBERTIN. Thierry M: lighter, finessed style.

Moueix, J-P & Cie Bx Respected Libourne-based NÉGOCIANT and proprietor, family-owned. CHX BELAIR-MONANGE, HOSANNA, LA FLEUR-PÉTRUS, LAGRANGE, *La Grave à Pomerol*, LATOUR-À-POMEROL, *Trotanoy*. *See also* Dominus Estate (California).

Moulin-à-Vent Beauj ★★★ 09' 11' 15' 18' 19' 20' 21 22' Grandest BEAUJ cru, transcending GAMAY grape. Weight, spiciness of Rh but matures towards gamey PINOT flavours, easily mistaken for C d'O red at 10 yrs old+. Increasing interest in single-vyd bottlings from eg. *Ch des Jacques*, *Ch de Moulin-à-Vent*, DOMS Janin, Janodet, Labruyère, *Merlin* (La Rochelle), Rottiers. *See also* C d'O producers, eg. BICHOT (Rochegrès), L BOILLOT (Brussellions), T LIGER-BELAIR (Rouchaux).

Moulin de la Gardette S Rh ★★★ 16' 17' 19' 20 21' 22' 23' Organic 10 ha GIGONDAS, made with care, genuine *garrigue* herbal expression, benefit from time. Petite Gardette top value; main red Tradition is GRENACHE with local identity, 20 yrs+ life. Oaked Ventabren substantial.

Moulis H-Méd ★★ →★★★ 15 16 18 19 20 22 Tiny inland AOP w of MARGAUX. Honest, gd-value wines; best can age. Top CHX: Anthonic, Biston-Brillette, BRANAS GRAND POUJEAUX, Caroline, *Chasse-Spleen*, Dutruch Grand Poujeaux, *Gressier Grand Poujeaux*, La Garricq, MAUCAILLOU, *Mauvesin Barton*, *Poujeaux*.

Mourgues du Grès, Ch S Rh ★★→★★★ 22' 23' Highly enjoyable, sure-bet COSTIÈRES DE NÎMES estate, organic, early drinking range: racy rosé (Dorés, Galets Rouges, Rosés). Firmer Capitelles: Terre d'Argence (SYRAH), Terre de Feu (GRENACHE).

Mugneret C d'O ★★★→★★★★ VIGNERON family in VOSNE. Sublime wines of grace and restrained vigour from Georges M-Gibourg (from BOURGOGNE to ÉCHÉZEAUX), now matched by cousins at DOM Gérard M. Also Dom Mongeard-M.

Mugnier, J-F C d'O ★★★★ Outstanding grower of CHAMBOLLE-MUSIGNY *Les Amoureuses* and *Musigny*. Do not miss PC Fuées. Finesse, and never shouty; thinkers' wines. Also MONOPOLE NUITS CLOS de la Maréchale (watch for reversed "a" in "la" on labels). No longer sells young vintages of magnificent MUSIGNY, to avoid infanticide.

Mumm, GH & Cie Champ ★★★ Revitalized house owned by Pernod Ricard. Tragic early death of chef de CAVE Laurent Fresnet. Increasingly impressive RSRV series; Mumm de Verzenay BLANC DE NOIRS 08 09 12 13, BLANC DE BLANCS (formerly Mumm de Cramant) 12' 13 15, CUVÉE Lalou 06 08. RSRV 4.5. Cordon Rouge NV much improved: PINOT-led weight with tension. Also gd in California.

Muré / Clos Saint Landelin Al ★★★→★★★★ A trad Rouffach winery, more innovative than most. AL's best PINOT N (CUVÉE V 15' 18') and CRÉMANTS. Also outstanding SYLVANER Steinstuck, Cuvée Oscar 17 18 19 22, PINOT GR 17' 18 from iron-rich CLOS St Landelin (12-ha monopole in GC Vorbourg) and up-and-coming SYRAH.

Muscadet Lo ★→★★ 20' 21 22' Resurgent seafood-friendly wines from Atlantic vyds. MUSCADET is generic AOP (20% production). Zonal AOPs better: Coteaux de la Loire (Champ Chapron), Côtes de Grandlieu (Haut-Bourg, Herbauges), SÈVRE ET MAINE.

Muscadet Crus Communaux Lo ★★→★★★ 05' 07' 08' 09 10 12' 14 16 **18 19 20** (22) (23) MUSCADET's superior cru system; complex, lees-aged, zone-specific. Seven ratified: Clisson (granite), Gorges, Mouzillon-Tillières (gabbro), Goulaine (mostly schist), Ch-Thébaud (graniodorite, gneiss), Monnières-St Fiacre (mostly gneiss), Le Pallet (mixed). Three more planned: Champtoceaux, La Haye Fouassière, Vallet. (For top names, *see* box, below.)

Muscadet Sèvre et Maine Lo ★→★★★★ 12' 14 16 19' 20' 21 22' Largest MUSCADET zone. High quality, drink well young, but top wines age well. Try Bonnet-Huteau, *Brégeon*, Chereau-Carré, Cormerais, Delhommeau, Gadais, Grand Mouton, Grenaudière, Gunther-Chereau, Haute-Fevrie, Huchet, LANDRON, Lieubeau, *Luneau-Papin*, *Pépière*, Vincent Caillé.

Musigny C d'O ★★★★ 93 **96'** 99' 02' 05' 09' 10' 12' 15' 17 18 19' 20' 21 22' Most beautiful red burg; the queen to CHAMBERTIN's king. Fragrance made flesh. Deceptive delicacy cloaks sinuous power. Never refuse – if someone else footing the bill. Best: DE VOGÜÉ, DROUHIN, FAIVELEY, JADOT, LEROY, *Mugnier*, PRIEUR, ROUMIER, VOUGERAIE.

Nature Unsweetened, esp for CHAMP: no dosage. Fine if v. ripe grapes, raw otherwise. Vin Nature = natural wine; *see* A Little Learning.

Negly, Ch la Ldoc ★★★★ Leading LA CLAPE estate, impressive range from salty Brise Marine (w), La Côte (r), and La Falaise (r) for everyday to icon La Porte du Ciel (SYRAH), MOURVÈDRE-based L'Ancely.

Négociant-éleveur Merchant who "brings up" (ie. matures) the wine.

Noblaie, Dom de la Lo ★★→★★★ Fine CHINON DOM. Top Chiens Chiens, Les Blancs Manteaux, *Pierre de Tuf* 05' 09 10' 15' **18' 19 20 21** (22') (23). Also two top CHENIN BL: Chant le Vent, *La Part des Anges*.

Noëllat C d'O ★★★ Noted VOSNE family. Maxime Cheurlin at DOM Georges N on top form: try NUITS Boudots, Vosne Petits-Monts and GC ÉCHÉZEAUX, also some gd-value lesser appellations. Cousins at *Michel N* starting to cause a stir (Vosne Les Suchots). *See also* v. stylish HUDELOT-N in VOUGEOT.

Nuits-St-Georges C d'O ★★→★★★★ 99' 02' **05' 09'** 10' **12'** 15' 16 **17** 18' 19 20 21 22'

Muscadet crus: the state of play

Oldest crus now over 10 yrs old (1st four ratified 2011, next lot 2017), but concept as exciting as ever, as are wines. Growers with parcels in delimited zones must apply for inclusion and work to quality-minded criteria in vyd and cellar, with ageing on lees for 18–24 mths(+). Serious wines, not simply for washing down oysters. Château-Thébaud: *Lieubeau*, PÉPIÈRE, Salmon. Clisson: Cognettes, Cormerais, D&V Papin, Lieubeau, Ollivier Père et Fils, *Pépière*. Gorges: *Brégeon*, Ch Elget, Cornulière, La Tour Gallus, Le Fay d'Homme, Martin-Luneau, Pépière. Goulaine: Lieubeau, *Luneau-Papin*. Le Pallet: Les Vignerons du Pallet. Monnières-St Fiacre: Julien Braud, *Le Fay d'Homme*, Les Bêtes Curieuses, Pépière, VIGNOBLES Günther-Chéreau. Mouzillon-Tillières: Michel Luneau.

FRANCE

Three parts to this major AOP: Premeaux vyds for elegance (various CLOS: de la Maréchale, des Corvées, des Forêts, St-Marc), centre for dense dark plummy wines (Cailles, Les St-Georges, Vaucrains) and n side for the headiest (Boudots, Cras, Murgers, Richemone). Hearty, heavy reputation of yore increasingly outdated, Nuits treads lighter today. Worth a close look. Top: ARLOT, ARNOUX-LACHAUX, CATHIARD, CHEVILLON, *Faiveley*, GOUGES, GRIVOT, LEROY, *Liger-Belair*, *Mugnier*, but try also Ambroise, Chauvenet, Chicotot, Confuron, Gavignet, Lechéneaut, Ledy, Machard de Gramont, Michelot, Millot, Perdrix, Rion.

Ogereau, Dom Lo ★★→★★★ Longstanding, leading ANJOU DOM; full, complex range. Control now passed from Vincent to Emmanuel. Look for 100% CAB SAUV ANJOU-VILLAGES *Côte de la Houssaye* 03 05 09 10 **15 18** 19 20 (22). Also top COTEAUX DU LAYON, QUARTS DE CHAUME.

Ogier, Stéphane N Rh ★★★ 20' 21 22' 23' Go-go CÔTE-RÔTIE DOM; upbeat fruit, oaked style, crisp tannins, several recent v. small plot-specific (Bertholon, Leyat). Top: Belle Hélène (50s SYRAH), Côte Blonde (floral depth), La Viallière (iron depth). IGP Seyssuel (r), VDF Syrah, VIOGNIER.

Ollieux Romanis, Ch Ldoc ★★★★ Pierre Bories runs tight ship at impeccable CORBIÈRES bio DOM. Tradition (r/w/rosé) gd value. Prestige (r/w) a step up, oaked, stylish. Terrific Atal Sia pure expression of Boutenac terroir.

Oratoire St Martin, Dom de l' S Rh ★★★ 19' 20' **21'** 22' 23 At CAIRANNE, top-drawer vyds, owned by CH Mont-Redon of CHÂTEAUNEUF. Excellent bio reds, deep purity, Haut Coustias (vines c.70 yrs), Les Douyes (1905 GRENACHE/MOURVÈDRE); gd table-suited whites (Haut-Coustias, Rés Seigneurs).

Ostertag, Dom Al ★★★ Top bio estate now run by Arthur O. Terroir-driven RIES Muenchberg 10 **14 18'**, trend-setting barrique-fermented, rich Muenchberg PINOT GR **15**. Excellent SYLVANER VIEILLES VIGNES 15 **18'** 19'.

Overnoy, Maison Jura AOP ARBOIS-Pupillin. Founded by natural-wine pioneer Pierre O, run by Emmanuel Houillon. Otherworldly CHARD, SAVAGNIN and ★★ Ploussard (Poulsard). Several other Jura Overnoy estates are cousins.

Pabiot, Jonathan Lo ★★★ →★★★★ 17' 19' 20' 21 (22) (23) Leading POUILLY-FUMÉ DOM, bio. Top CUVÉES brilliantly expressive, incl *Luminance* (previously Prédilection, from Kimmeridgian), Aubaine (Portlandian). Entry-level Léon (previously Florilège), Elisa (previously Prélude) great value.

Pacherenc du Vic-Bilh SW Fr ★★→★★★ White AOP contiguous with MADIRAN. Gros/Petit MANSENG (dr/sw). Made by most Madiran growers, but note ★★ CHX d'Aydie, de Mascaaras. Best: PETIT COURBU (dr w) from ALAIN BRUMONT.

Paillard, Bruno Champ ★★★ Youngest *grande marque* (1981). Top-quality BRUT Première CUVÉE NV, Rosé Première Cuvée; refined style, esp in slow-ageing Prestige *NPU* 95 **04** 02' 08. BP assemblage 08 **09** 12' 19. BLANC DE BLANCS on the up **04** 06 09 13'. Bruno P heads LANSON-BCC group of mainly family houses; daughter Alice has taken over at Paillard.

Palette Prov ★★★ Tiny AOP nr Aix. GRENACHE, MOURVÈDRE; floral, age-worthy reds, fragrant rosés; intriguing forest-scented whites, also oddities like FURMINT; trad, serious CH SIMONE, Crémade, HENRI BONNAUD.

Palmer & Co Champ ★★★→★★★★ Exemplary co-op, enviable patchwork of vyds. PINOT N-dominated. Inspired leadership by Rémi Vervier; v. reliable BRUT Rés. Unsurprisingly powerful NV Amazone; well-named Grands Terroirs **03** 12 15'.

Partagé, Dom Sav ★★ Tiny bio DOM of Gilles Berlioz in CHIGNIN, v.gd. Altesse, Jacquère, ★★ MONDEUSE and range of fun ★★★ Chignin-Bergeron (ROUSSANNE), incl Les Christine, Les Filles, Les Fripons.

Pascal C d'O ★★★ Look hard enough and value can still be found in C D'o. Pascal's BOURGOGNE C d'O CHARD offers unrivalled quality at fair price. Move up to PULIGNY village for even greater delight.

Pataille Burg ★★★ Wild-haired guru Sylvain P is MARSANNAY's standard-bearer. Cult following for single-vyd reds, white (esp site-specific ALIGOTÉ) and rosé (Fleur de PINOT), low sulphur, long-ageing. Cutting-edge and consistent quality. Value.

Paternal, Dom du Prov Santini bros make consistently elegant (w) Cassis, small AOP for mainly white; gd BANDOL too.

Patrimonio Cors AOP in N CORS with cru status, along with AJACCIO. Sumptuous reds, fresh rosé from NIELLUCCIO, VERMENTINO for white. Lots of organic.

Pauillac H-Méd ★★★→★★★★ 09' 10' **15 16'** 18' 19' 20' 22' (23) Communal AOP in N MÉD with 18 Classed Growths, incl LAFITE, LATOUR, MOUTON. Famous for long-lived wines, the acme of CAB SAUV. Other top CHX: CLERC MILON, DUHART-MILON, GRAND-PUY-LACOSTE, LYNCH-BAGES, PICHON BARON, PICHON LALANDE, PONTET-CANET. BATAILLEY, HAUT-BAGES-LIBÉRAL, HAUT-BATAILLEY also on song.

Pays d'Oc, IGP Ldoc ★→★★★ Largest French IGP, covering whole of LDOC-ROUSS. Extremes of quality from simple, quaffing varietals to innovative, exciting. At last count, 58 different grapes allowed. Big players: Fortant de France, Gérard Bertrand, Jeanjean, PAUL MAS and co-op Foncalieu.

PC (Premier Cru) First Growth in BX; 2nd rank of vyds (after GC) in Burg; 2nd rank in Lo: one so far, COTEAUX DU LAYON Chaume.

Pécharmant SW Fr ★★ 18 19 20 22 BERGERAC inner AOP on edge of town. Iron and manganese in soil generate biggest, longest-living wines of area. Veteran ★★★ CH de Tiregand, DOM du Haut-Pécharmant, l'Ancienne Cure; ★★ Chx Beauportail, Corbiac, du Rooy, Terre Vieille; Dom des Bertranoux.

Pélican, Dom du Jura ★★★ VOLNAY's MARQUIS D'ANGERVILLE venture nr ARBOIS; bio vyds incl those from retired legend Jacques Puffeney – giving pristine range.

Pellé, Dom Lo ★★→★★★ Exemplary quality from MENETOU-SALON, range of single-vyds. Look for (w) Le Carroir, *Les Blanchais* 18 19 20 **21** (22) (23), Vignes de Ratier; (r) *Les Cris* 15 **18** 19 20 (22).

Poulsard or Ploussard? Depends on the Jura village – always Ploussard in Pupillin.

Pena, Ch de Rouss ★★ Tiny co-op of 20 families making cracking, approachable wines. Try Ninet de Pena ("little stone" in Catalan), IGP CÔTES CATALANES.

Pépière, Dom de la Lo ★★→★★★★ 12' 14 18 19' 20 (23) Iconic MUSCADET DOM, mostly granite. Now run by Rémi Branger, Gwénaëlle Croix. Top source of crus, eg. *Clisson, Ch-Thébaud.* Old-vine *Briords* also top-notch. One to hunt down.

Pernand-Vergelesses C d'O ★★★ (r) 10' **12 15'** 17 18' 19' 20' (w) **14'** 15' 17' 18' 19' 20' 21 22' Village hosting w-facing part of CORTON-CHARLEMAGNE. Lacks recognition due to clumsy name. Different vyds thrive in each colour: (r) Île des Vergelesses; (w) Combottes, Sous Frétille. Local DOMS CHANDON DE BRIAILLES, Dubreuil-Fontaine, Rapet, Rollin lead way. Check RAMONET Les Belles Filles.

Perret, André N Rh ★★★ 18' 19' 20' **21 22'** 23' CONDRIEU DOM, top class. Three whites: classic, neat-fruiting; stylish, clear CLOS Chanson; rich, prolonged, intriguing Chéry. ST-JOSEPH (r/w): buzzy-fruit classic red; deep, flowing, smoky old-vine Les Grisières (r). Also gd COLLINES RHODANIENNES (r/w).

Perrier, Joseph Champ ★★★ Fine family-run CHAMP house with v.gd PINOTS N/M vyds, esp in own Cumières DOM. Prestige CUVÉE Joséphine 12'; BRUT Royale NV more focused with lower dosage. Distinctive, tangy BLANC DE BLANCS 08 **13'** 17' 19 20. Cuvée Royale 08 12 **15'** 16; older BLANC DE BLANCS vintages age well, esp 95. Owner Jean-Claude Fourmon, easing reins to son.

Perrier-Jouët Champ ★★★ The 1st (in C19) to make dry CHAMP for UK market; strong in GC CHARD, best for vintage, deluxe Belle Époque in painted bottle 08 12' **13 15** 16' BRUT NV; Blason de France NV Brut and Rosé; Belle Époque Rosé 12 **13** 14'; Belle Époque BLANC DE BLANCS **07'** 12 13 **14'**. New chef de CAVE Séverine Frerson.

Pessac-Léognan Bx ★★★→★★★★ 10′ 15 16 18 19′ 20′ 22 (23) AOP for best part of N GRAV, incl all Crus Classés: DOM DE CHEVALIER, HAUT-BAILLY, HAUT-BRION, LA MISSION HAUT-BRION, PAPE CLÉMENT, SMITH HAUT LAFITTE, etc. Aspiring unclassified: LES CARMES HAUT-BRION. Firm, full-bodied, earthy reds; BX's finest dry whites. Value from LA LOUVIÈRE, LARRIVET HAUT-BRION, OLIVIER.

Péters, Pierre Champ ★★★★ Superb Côte des Blancs estate. *Les Chétillons* probably longest-lived CHARD in CHAMP 08 09 12 13 14′ 15 16; a cooler classic. Fascinating project with CH DE BEAUCASTEL, Fleur de Miraval; ER I, II, III (Exclusivemoon Rosé, not late Queen of England). Rodolphe P one of Champ's finest winemakers.

Petit Chablis Chab ★ DYA Refreshing mini-CHAB from outlying vyds mostly not on Kimmeridgian clay. Move up when refreshed. Best: BILLAUD, BROCARD, DAUVISSAT, Defaix, LAVANTUREUX, Pommier, RAVENEAU and co-op LA CHABLISIENNE.

Pézenas Ldoc Charming medieval town, birthplace Molière. AOP LDOC, diverse soils, fun to explore. Big gun PAUL MAS and smaller estates Mas Gabriel. Also DOMS Allegria, des Aurelles, de Nizas, Les Trois Puechs, Magellan, Prieuré St Jean de Bebian, Villa Tempora.

Philipponnat Champ ★★★→★★★★ Small house based in Mareuil-sur-AŸ, distinct PINOT N style. Now owned by LANSON-BCC group, but Charles P has hand firmly on the tiller. NV BRUT, NV Rosé, CUVÉE 1522 12 13 15 16. Famous for majestic single-vyd *Clos des Goisses* 08 09 12 13 14′. And from within Goisses itself, minute production of Les Cintres 08 09 12. Also exceptional late-disgorged vintage known as CLOS des Goisses LV (Long Vieillissement) 94′ 95 96.

Picpoul de Pinet Ldoc ★→★★★ DYA AOP for PICPOUL around Pinet, increasingly popular white, vyds overlooking oyster farms by Med, cooled by sea breezes. Wines have salty tang, lemony freshness. Perfect with seafood. Best not oaked. Co-ops l'Ormarine, Pomerols do gd job, also DOMS de Belle Mare, des Lauriers, Félines-Jourdan, Font-Mars, La Croix Gratiot, Petit Roubié, Reine Juliette, St Martin de la Garrigue.

Pic St-Loup Ldoc ★★★★ AOP n of Montpellier with dramatic scenery dominated by eponymous peak. Higher, cooler, wetter; more elegance to wines; 50% min SYRAH plus GRENACHE, MOURVÈDRE. Reds for ageing, rosé gd; white potential considerable but still AOP LDOC or IGP Val de Montferrand. Growers: Chx CAZENEUVE, de Lancyre, de Lascaux, de Valflaunès, La Roque, PUECH-HAUT; CLOS de la Matane, Clos Marie; DOMS DE L'HORTUS, Pegaline; Bergerie du Capucin, Le Chemin des Rêves, Mas Bruguière, Mas Gourdou, Mas Peyrolle. Tiny co-op Hommes & Terres du Sud v.gd.

Pieretti, Dom Cors ★★→★★★ Small estate in windswept Cap CORSE, n of Bastia. Lina Pieretti-Venturi makes top rosé, also delicious red and sweet MUSCAT.

Pierre-Bise, Ch Lo ★★→★★★★ Excellent ANJOU DOM. Complex portfolio from René Papin. Leader in QUARTS DE CHAUME 07′ 09 10 11′ 13 14′ 15 16 17 18′ (22) (23), SAVENNIÈRES incl ROCHE-AUX-MOINES (all age well). Also top terroir-driven COTEAUX DU LAYON, gd ANJOU BL, fine CRÉMANT DE LO and decent reds.

Pierre Fil, Dom Ldoc ★★★ MINERVOIS; USP MOURVÈDRE with carbonic maceration. Top Dolium and CUVÉE M superb, reward ageing. Drink *garrigue*-scented Orebus while waiting.

Pillot C d'O ★★★ Ultra-reliable family in CHASSAGNE, all branches on form: F&L P (sound all round), Jean-Marc P (esp CLOS St-Marc) and Paul P (Grandes Ruchottes, LA ROMANÉE, etc.). Also red Chassagne PCS from all three.

Pinard, Vincent Lo ★★→★★★ Leading SANCERRE DOM. Exemplary single-vyd *Le Grand Chemarin*, *Le Petit Chemarin*, Le Château 16 19 20 21 (22) (23). Also top reds Charlouise, Vendanges Entières.

Pinelli, Dom Cors ★★→★★★ Marie-Charlotte P, young talent at family DOM, PATRIMONIO; Campo Vecchio (r), Impassitu MUSCAT, sweet VIN DE FRANCE.

Pinon, François et Julien Lo ★★★★ Fine complex VOUVRAY from Julien P. Moelleux eg. *Cuvée Botrytis* age brilliantly 89' 90' 96' 02 03 05' **09 10 14 18**' 19' 20 (22) (23). Dry and DEMI-SEC (speciality), incl excellent *Deronnières*, drink younger; gd fizz.

Piper-Heidsieck Champ ★★★→★★★★ On surging wave of quality. Dynamic BRUT Essentiel with more age, less sugar, floral yet vigorous. *Prestige Rare*, now made as separate brand in-house, is a jewel, precise, pure, refined texture **02 06 07 08 12**' 13. Exceptional Rare Rosé 12'. Equally rare, the Hors Serie late-disgorged range, only **71 82** released thus far.

Place, La Bx Internal BX NÉGOCIANT marketplace. Middlemen buy from brokers who buy from CHX, and sell to other merchants, or to you and me.

Plageoles, Dom SW Fr ★★★ Defenders and rebels guarding true GAILLAC style. Rare local grapes rediscovered incl Ondenc (base of ace sw ★★★ Vin d'Autan), ★★ Prunelard (r, deep, fruity), Verdanel (dr w, oak-aged) and countless sub-varieties of MAUZAC. More reds from Braucol (FER SERVADOU), Duras.

Plaisance, Ch de Lo ★★→★★★ Historical ANJOU property, revitalized by Vanessa Cherruau. Exciting, nervous, single-parcel ANJOU BL; a little sweet wine on side. Try *La Grande Pièce*, Ronceray, *Zerzilles* 19 20.

Plan de Dieu S Rh ★→★★ 18 19' 20 **22**' **23** Leading Village nr CAIRANNE with stony, wind-lashed *garrigue* plain, can need irrigation. Charged, spiced, tannic, mainly GRENACHE wines; drink with game, stews. Selection gd. Best: CH la Courançonne, CLOS St Antonin, Le Plaisir; DOMS APHILLANTHES (bio), Arnesque, Durieu (full), Espigouette, Favards (organic), Grand Retour, La Bastide St Vincent, Longue Toque, Martin (full, trad), Pasquiers (organic), St-Pierre (trad).

Pol Roger Champ ★★★★ Family-owned Épernay house, *sine qua non* of elegance. 2023 RIP Christian de Billy, great-great grandson of Pol Roger himself. BRUT Rés NV excels, dosage lowered since 2012; Brut Vintage 08 09 **12**' **13 15**' **16**; Rosé 09 15; BLANC DE BLANCS 08 09' **12 13 15**' also fine *Pure* (no dosage). Sumptuous *Cuvée Sir Winston Churchill* 02 09 **12 13 14**' 15, a serious keeper.

Pomerol Bx ★★★→★★★★ 10' **15 16**' **18**' 19' 20' 22' (23) Tiny, pricey AOP; MERLOT-led, plummy to voluptuous, but long life. Top CHX on clay, gravel plateau: CLINET, HOSANNA, L'ÉGLISE-CLINET, L'ÉVANGILE, LA CONSEILLANTE, LAFLEUR, LA FLEUR-PÉTRUS, LE PIN, PETRUS, TROTANOY, *Vieux Ch Certan*. Relative value from BOURGNEUF, CLOS du Clocher, FEYTIT-CLINET, MAZEYRES.

Pommard C d'O ★★★→★★★★ 96' 99' **03** 05' 09' 10' **12** 15' 16' 17 18' 19' 20' 21 22' Once "wine in workboots", now lighter shod. Prepare to be charmed. Best PC vyds: Epenots for grace, Rugiens for power. Try Noizons at village level. Top: BICHOT (DOM du Pavillon), *Ch de Pommard*, Clerget, Commaraine, COMTE ARMAND, DE COURCEL, DE MONTILLE, HOSPICES DE BEAUNE, J-M BOILLOT, Launay-Horiot, Lejeune, Parent, Rebourgeon-Mure, Violot-Guillemard. Relative value.

Pommery Champ ★★→★★★ Historical house with spectacular cellars; brand owned by Vranken. BRUT NV steady bet, no fireworks; Rosé NV; Brut 04 08 09 12'. Once-outstanding CUVÉE Louise slowly regaining ground 02 **04** 05 06'.

Ponsot, Dom C d'O ★★→★★★★ Idiosyncratic MOREY-ST-DENIS DOM. Rose-Marie P in charge since departure of Laurent P (2016). No significant changes in style. Key wines: *Clos de la Roche*, exceptional and age-worthy PC Monts Luisants (ALIGOTÉ).

Ponsot, Laurent C d'O ★★→★★★★ Man who made DOM PONSOT wines for 30 yrs left family business to create own haute-couture label nearby (2016). Kept sharecropping contracts, incl amazing CLOS ST-DENIS, GRIOTTE-CHAMBERTIN. Buying vines and developing whites, in new purpose-built winery (Gilly).

Pouilly-Fuissé Burg ★★→★★★★ 14' 15 17 18 **19**' 20' 21 22' Top AOP of Mâcon; potent, rounded but intense whites from around Fuissé, more mineral in Vergisson. Offers value compared to C D'O; PC classification finally in place for 2020 vintage, hurrah! Top: Barraud, Bret, Carette, *Ch de Beauregard*, CH DE FUISSÉ, CH des

Quarts, Ch des Rontets, Cornin, *Ferret*, Forest, Lassarat, *Merlin*, Paquet, Renaud, Robert-Denogent, Rollet, Saumaize, Saumaize-Michelin, VERGET.

Pouilly-Fumé Lo ★★→★★★★ 12 14 19' 20' **21** 22' (23) Famed AOP for SAUV BL next to SANCERRE. Top wines stunning, but quality variable. Best age well. Try CAILBOURDIN, Chx de Tracy, *Jonathan Pabiot*, Masson-Blondelet, Michel Redde, Pascal Jolivet, Régis Minet, Sébastien Treuillet, Serge Daguéneau & Filles. Notable VDF: Alexandre Bain, *Louis-Benjamin Dagueneau*.

Pouilly-Vinzelles Burg ★★ 14' **15** 17 **18** 19' 20' 21 22' Close to POUILLY-FUISSÉ geographically and in quality. Outstanding vyd: Les Quarts; PC on way, with two others. Best: CH de V, DROUHIN, Soufrandière (Bret), Valette. Volume from CAVE des GCS Blancs.

Premières Côtes de Bordeaux Bx ★ →★★ 19 20 22 (23) Same zone as CADILLAC-CÔTES DE BX but sweet whites only; SÉM-dominated *moelleux*. Generally early drinking. Best: CHX Crabitan-Bellevue, du Juge, Faugas, Marsan.

Prieur, Dom Jacques C d'O ★★★ Major MEURSAULT estate, wide range of GCS from MONTRACHET to MUSIGNY. Style aims at weight from late-picking and oak. More verve and excitement would be welcome. New project Labruyère-Prieur in Burg. Owner Famille Labruyère also CH ROUGET (BX), CHAMP, MOULIN-À-VENT projects.

Producteurs Plaimont SW Fr ★→★★ France's most dynamic co-op, bestriding SAINT MONT (best wines), MADIRAN and CÔTES DE GASCOGNE. Has abandoned BX varieties for grapes trad to the sw, incl some pre-phylloxera discoveries. All colours, styles, mostly ★★, all tastes, purses. Colombelle is entry level (w/rosé).

Propriétaire-récoltant Champ Owner-operator, literally owner-harvester.

Puech-Haut, Ch Ldoc ★★→★★★ AOP LDOC St Drézéry. Powerful Prestige (r/w), Tête de Belier (r/w/rosé) swish wine, packaging. IGP Argali rosé gd value. Owns ★★★ PIC ST-LOUP CH Lavabre.

Puisseguin St-Émilion Bx ★★ 18 19 20 22 Most e of four ST-ÉM satellites; MERLOT-led; meaty but firm. Top: CHX BEAUSÉJOUR, Branda, Clarisse, de l'Anglais, DES LAURETS, de Roques, Durand-Laplagne, Fongaban, Guibeau (Noé), Haut-Bernat, La Mauriane, Soleil.

Puligny-Montrachet C d'O ★★★ →★★★★ 09' 10' 12 14' **15** 17' **18** 19' 20' 21 22' Floral, fine-boned, tingling white burg. At its best, the finest of all. Elegant and assured. Curiosity red too. Outstanding PCS, esp Caillerets, Champ Canet, Combettes, Folatières, Pucelles, plus amazing MONTRACHET GCS. Producers: *Carillon*, *Chartron*, *Chavy*, *Dom Leflaive*, *Drouhin*, *Ente*, *J-M Boillot*, *O Leflaive*, *Pascal*, Pernot family, *Sauzet*, Thomas-Collardot.

Py, Dom Ldoc ★★ →★★★ Py's bio vyds on n flank of Mt Alaric, nr Carcassonne. Antoine (r/w) expressive, approachable CORBIÈRES.

Quarts de Chaume Grand Cru Lo ★★★ →★★★★ 07' 09 10 11' 13 14' **15** 16 17 **18'** (22) (23) Leading AOP for sweet CHENIN BL. Best rich in botrytis complexity. Volume down: dry sells better. Try BAUDOUIN, BAUMARD, *Belargus*, *Bergerie*, FL, Forges, *Ogereau*, *Pierre-Bise*, PLAISANCE, Suronde.

Quenard Sav Six separate Q estates in CHIGNIN incl ★★ super-reliable A&M Q; ★★ excellent J-F Q and ★★ small-but-lovely organic P&A Q. All offer top ROUSSANNE (Chignin-Bergeron), Jacquère, MONDEUSE. Try J-F Q Persan.

Quincy Lo ★★ 20' 21 22' (23) AOP for SAUV BL. Warm sandy soils give more texture than SANCERRE or POUILLY-FUMÉ. Try Tatin/Ballandors/Tremblay (all Jean Tatin), Lecomte, Adéle/Jacques Rouzé, Villalin.

Ramonet, J-C C d'O ★★★ →★★★★ Distinctive, verging on idiosyncratic, often ethereal whites. Excellent, age-worthy reds remain largely under radar, *value*.

Rancio Rouss Describes complex, evolved aromas from extended, oxidative ageing. Reminiscent of Tawny Port, or old Oloroso Sherry. Associated specifically with BANYULS, MAURY, RASTEAU, RIVESALTES. Can be a grand experience; don't miss.

Rangen Al Uniquely steep, volcanic, hot, most s GC of AL at Thann. Top: ZIND HUMBRECHT PINOT GR CLOS St Urbain 08' 10' 17' 21' (world's greatest dr Pinot Gr), SCHOFFIT RIES St-Théobald 15' 17'.

Rasteau S Rh ★★ 16' 17' 19' **20** 22' 23 Mostly GRENACHE, often robust, peppery, some suave, early reds, primarily clay soils, so best in hot yrs, v. consistent quality. Note BEAURENARD (bio, serious, ages), CAVE Ortas/Rhonéa, CH La Gardine, Ch du Trignon, Famille Perrin; DOMS Beau Mistral, Collière (handmade, style), Combe Julière (punchy), Coteaux des Travers (bio), Elodie Balme (soft), ESCARAVAILLES (style), Girasols, Gourt de Mautens (supreme character, one-off, talented, IGP from 2010), Gramiller (organic), Grand Nicolet (deep, character), Grange Blanche, M Boutin (handmade, organic), Rabasse-Charavin (full), Soumade (polished), *St Gayan*, Trapadis (bio). Grenache dessert VDN, quality rising: Doms Banquettes, Combe Julière, Coteaux des Travers, Escaravailles, Trapadis. Also gd source of CÔTES DU RH (r).

Raveneau Chab ★★★★ Topmost CHAB producer, using classic methods for *extraordinary long-lived wines*. A little more modern while still growing in stature of late. Excellent value (except in secondary market). Look for PC Butteaux, Chapelot, Vaillons and GC Blanchots, Les CLOS.

Rayas, **Ch** S Rh ★★★★ 05' 06' 07' 09' 10' 11' 12' 15' 16' 17' 19' 20' 21' 22' 23' Splendiferous, mystical, lost-in-time, one-off CHÂTEAUNEUF estate, tiny yields, sandy soils, tree-sheltered, nr-garden plots, late harvesting. Pale, sensuous, aromatic reds (100% GRENACHE) age superbly, 30 yrs+. Save up. White Rayas (CLAIRETTE, GRENACHE BL) rich, v.gd over 20 yrs+. Stylish second wine, Pignan. Supreme CH Fonsalette CÔTES DU RH, incl marvellous, pricey, long-lived SYRAH. Decant all; each an occasion. No 18 (mildew). Ch des Tours VACQUEYRAS, gd VDP.

Regnié Beauj ★★ 18' 19 **20'** 21 22' Most recent BEAUJ cru, lighter wines on sandy soil, meatier nr MORGON. Starting to get some gd growers now. Try Burgaud, Chemarin, de la Plaigne, Dupré, Rochette, Sunier (A), Sunier (J).

Réserve d'O, Dom de la Ldoc ★★★★ High altitude, bio, min sulphites, one of best DOMS in top TERRASSES DE LARZAC, with hallmark freshness, dark fruit. Try Bilbo, Hissez O (r), IGP St Guilhem le Desert (w).

Reuilly Lo ★★ →★★★ 20' **21** 22' (23) AOP for SAUV BL, but also pale rosés (*vin gris*) from PINOTS GR and/or N, and Pinot N reds. All can trump lesser SANCERRE, esp *Claude Lafond*, *Denis Jamain*. Also Cordaillat, Jacques Rouzé, Pagerie, Renaudat, Sorbe.

Riceys, Les Champ Key AOP in AUBE for notable PINOT N rosé. Producers: A Bonnet, Brice, Jacques Defrance, Morize. Excels, almost counterintuitively, in warm yrs, *viz.* 09 15' 18 19 (20).

Richebourg C d'O ★★★★ 90' 93' 96' 99' 02' 05' **09'** 10' 12' 15' 16 17 18' 19' 20' 21 22' VOSNE GC, cheek-by-jowl with ROMANÉE-CONTI. Supreme burg with extraordinary depth and endless waves of flavour. Sonorous name, sonorous wine. Growers: DRC, GRIVOT, GROS, HUDELOT-NOËLLAT, LEROY, LIGER-BELAIR (T), MÉO-CAMUZET.

Rion C d'O ★★ →★★★ Related DOMS in NUITS, VOSNE. Patrice R for excellent Nuits CLOS St-Marc, Clos des Argillières and CHAMBOLLE-MUSIGNY. Daniel R for Nuits

---

Big guns eye Provence

The BX CHX are trad on shopping list of big corps and billionaires; now Prov is a hotspot for investors. LVMH has stakes in rosé powerhouses CHX D'ESCLANS, Galoupet, Minuty (nr St Tropez). Pernod-Ricard has share of Ch Ste Marguerite, while Monaco-based Mark Dixon's Provence Rosé Group owns four DOMS, incl flagship Ch de Berne. Teetotal ex-President Sarkozy is in a consortium that snapped up Ch Beaulieu, Dom de Canterelle, La Ferme des Lices. Prov rosé is taking over the world. Or the world is taking over Prov rosé.

and Vosne PCS, now being split between family members; A&B R Vosne-based, visitor-friendly. All dependable, fairly priced.

Rivesaltes Rouss ★★→★★★ Underappreciated VDN with various styles: Ambré, RANCIO/Hors d'Age, Rosé, Tuilé. Mostly GRENACHE, except MUSCAT de Rivesaltes AOP fragrant, youthful. Look for Boucabeille, des Chênes, des Schistes, DOM CAZES, Puig-Parahy, Rancy, ROC DES ANGES, Sarda-Malet, Valmy, Vaquer. You won't be disappointed.

Roc des Anges, Le Rouss ★★★→★★★★ Stand-out DOM, terroir quartz, schist; freshness, minerality in Llum GRENACHE GR. IGP CÔTES CATALANES. Reliefs CARIGNAN (120-yr-old vines).

Roches Neuves, Dom des Lo ★★★→★★★★ Stunning SAUMUR Bl and SAUMUR-CHAMPIGNY; bio; top *Clos Romans* 12 14 16 18 19 20 (22) (23). All reds gd, led by Les Mémoires, Clos de L'Échelier 14 16 18 19 20 (22) (23).

Roederer, Louis Champ ★★★★ Family ownership par excellence, courtesy Fréderic Rouzaud. Enviable vyds, largest bio holdings. Brilliant chef de CAVE Jean-Baptiste Lecaillon. BRUT Premier NV phased out in favour of MV Collection; 242 243 244 (245). BLANC DE BLANCS 13 14' 15 16. Far-from-disagreeable Cristal 08 09 12 13 14 15; superb *Cristal Vinothèque Bl and Rosé* 95; Brut NATURE Philippe Starck (all Cumières 09 12 15'). *Late Release Vintage* 90 95 96 97 99. Also CH PICHON LALANDE, DEUTZ and *see* California.

Rolland, Michel Bx Veteran international consultant, MERLOT specialist. New Pangaea from five countries.

Rolly Gassmann Al ★★★ Outstanding now bio DOM, of mostly off-dry, rich, luscious wines; maybe too sweet for some. Outstanding SGNS. Mineral RIES and rich SYLVANER 13 16 17' 18 19'.

Romanée, La C d'O ★★★★ 09' 10' 12' 15' 16' 17 18' 19' 20 21 22' Tiniest GC in VOSNE, MONOPOLE of COMTE LIGER-BELAIR. Contiguous with, and upslope of, ROMANÉE-CONTI. Exceptionally fine, perfumed and intense. Superlative burg; superlative price.

Romanée-Conti, La C d'O ★★★★ 90' 93' 96' 99' 00 02' 05' 09' 10' 12' 14' 15' 16' 17 18' 19' 20' 21 22' GC in VOSNE, MONOPOLE of DRC. Grandest name in all Burg (and the world), needs long ageing before it unfolds into magnificence. When on song, no superlative can capture its haunting delight.

Romanée-St-Vivant C d'O ★★★★ 90' 99' 02' 05' 09' 10' 12' 15' 16' 17 18' 19' 20' 21 22' GC in VOSNE, downslope from LA ROMANÉE-CONTI. Seductive perfume, delicate but intense. Less magisterial, perhaps more beautiful, than famous neighbours. Growers: if you can't afford ARNOUX-LACHAUX, DRC or LEROY, or indeed CATHIARD or HUDELOT-NOËLLAT now, try ARLOT, Follin-Arbelet, J-J Confuron, LATOUR, Poisot. Nobody letting side down.

Romanin, Ch Prov ★★★ Leading bio DOM in BAUX-EN-PROV, worth visiting for magnificent cathedral cellar. Grand vin (r/w), equally majestic.

Rosé d'Anjou Lo ★→★★ DYA Historically significant, cash-generating AOP for off-dry to sweet rosé. Grolleau usually dominates blend. Unfashionable. Few interesting examples these days.

Rosé de Loire Lo ★→★★ Multi-regional Lo AOP; dry alternative to sweeter ROSÉ D'ANJOU and CABERNET D'ANJOU. Grolleau-led blend, but (almost) anything goes. Try Bablut, CADY, Passavant.

Rossignol-Trapet C d'O ★★★ Well removed from hearty GEVREY stereotype, yet not lacking in penetrating, memorable flavours. Healthy holdings of GCS, esp CHAMBERTIN; gd value across range from GEVREY VIEILLES VIGNES up. Also some BEAUNE vyds from Rossignol side.

Rostaing, Dom N Rh ★★★→★★★★ 09' 10' 12' 13' 15' 16' 17' 18' 19' 20' 21' 22' 23' High-level CÔTE-RÔTIE DOM: five tightly knit wines from top plots, all v. fine, clear, low-key oak, wait 6 yrs+, decant. Ampodium for value, complex, top-class Côte Blonde (5% VIOGNIER), Côte Brune (iron, no 21), also La Landonne (dark fruits, 20–25 yrs), occasional Viallière (pure). Mineral, tight CONDRIEU, also IGP COLLINES RHODANIENNES (r/w), LDOC Puech Noble (r/w).

Rouget, Dom C d'O ★★★★ Renamed as DOM R rather than Emmanuel R with new generation refreshing dom famed for Henri Jayer connection and CROS PARANTOUX vyd. Late picking means turbocharged wines in recent vintages.

Roulot, Dom C d'O ★★★→★★★★ Outstanding MEURSAULT DOM. Poised, precise wines, never flashy. Sign on chai, in gold: "I pick when I want." Great PCS, esp CLOS des Bouchères, Perrières; value from top village sites Luchets, Meix Chavaux, esp Clos du Haut Tesson. Excellent BOURGOGNE Bl.

Roumier, Georges C d'O ★★★★ Reference DOM for BONNES-MARES and other *brilliant Chambolle* wines (incl Amoureuses, Cras) from Christophe R. Long-lived but still attractive early. Tiny amount of MUSIGNY attracts ridiculous prices on secondary market. Best value: MOREY CLOS de la Bussière.

Rouquette-sur-Mer, Ch Ldoc ★★★★ Impressive LA CLAPE estate, vyds, *garrigue* right by Med. *Arpège* (w), crisp, herby, terrific value. L'Esprit terroir benchmark red. Le Clos de la Tour top MOURVÈDRE.

Rousseau, Dom Armand C d'O ★★★★ Legendary GEVREY-CHAMBERTIN DOM: balanced, fragrant, majestic, age-worthy GCS; Chambertin doesn't get any better than at Rousseau; legendary PC CLOS ST-JACQUES. Village wines less commanding.

Roussette de Savoie Sav Regional AOP, same area as AOP SAV; 100% ALTESSE. Age to 5 yrs+. Try ★ Chevalier Bernard, ★ Chevillard ★ Côtes Rousses ★★ Dupasquier, ★ Lupin, ★★ *St-Germain*, ★★★ Prieuré St-Christophe.

Roussillon Often linked with LDOC, and incl in AOP Ldoc, but has distinct identity. Exciting region with different soils and topography, innovative producers, some brilliant wines. Lots of old vines, tiny yields, intense. GRENACHE key variety. Largest AOP CÔTES DU ROUSS, gd-value spicy reds. Original, sometimes stunning, trad VDN (eg. BANYULS, MAURY, RIVESALTES). Also serious age-worthy table wines (r/w). *See* COLLIOURE, CÔTES DU ROUSS (VILLAGES), MAURY (SEC). IGP excellent CATALANES, Côte Vermeille.

Ruchottes-Chambertin C d'O ★★★★ 99' 02' 05' 09' 10' 12' 15' 16 17' 18' 19' 20' 21 22' Tiny GC neighbour of CHAMBERTIN. Less weighty but ethereal, great finesse. Top: MUGNERET-Gibourg, ROUMIER, ROUSSEAU (needs time). Also CH de MARSANNAY, F Esmonin, H Magnien, Marchand-Grillot, Pacalet. Plus Lambrays from 2021.

Ruinart Champ ★★★★ Oldest sparkling CHAMP house (1729). High standards getting higher still. Rich, elegant R de Ruinart BRUT NV; Ruinart Rosé NV; R de Ruinart Brut 10' 15 16. Prestige CUVÉE Dom Ruinart BLANC de BLANCS 02 04' 06 07 09 10. No 08 made; shame. Magnificent gastronomic *DR Rosé* 90 96 98' 02 04 07 09; NV Blanc de Blancs much improved. Winemaker Fred Panaïotis at top of game; focus on ageing top wines under cork rather than crown cap.

Rully Burg ★★→★★★ (r) 15' 17 18' 19' 20' 21 22' (w) 17' 18 19' 20' 21 22 CÔTE CHALONNAISE village. Slowly gaining more recognition for tasty whites and fruity reds. Best vyds: Grésigny, Pucelle, Rabourcé. Try BRIDAY, Champs l'Abbaye, Devevey, *de Villaine*, DOM de la Folie, DROUHIN, *Dureuil-Janthial*, FAIVELEY, *Jacqueson*, Jaeger-Defaix, Jobard (C), Leflaive (O). *Picamelot* for top CRÉMANT.

Sablet S Rh ★★ 22' 23 Front rank CÔTES DU RH-VILLAGE on mostly sandy soils (hence name), some terraces nr GIGONDAS. Supple mainly GRENACHE wines, trim red-berry fruit, some darker. Note CAVE co-op Gravillas, CH Cohola (organic), du Trignon (stylish); DOMS de Boissan (organic, full), Les Goubert (r/w), Pasquiers (organic, best). Full whites gd, for apéritifs/food: Boissan (ages well), ST GAYAN.

St-Amour Beauj ★★ 18' 19' 20' 21 22' Most n BEAUJ cru, mixed soils, variable character, signs of revival: Cheveau, DOM de Fa, Patissier, *Pirolette*, Revillon. Watch.

St-Aubin C d'O ★★★ (w) 14' 15 17' **18** 19' 20' 21 22' Ever-improving source for *increasingly complex whites*; PC St-A now challenging the big three of CHASSAGNE, PULIGNY, MEURSAULT. Also juicy, easy-drinking reds. Best vyds: Chatenière, *En Remilly*, *Murgers Dents de Chien*. Best growers: BACHELET (JC), COLIN (Joseph, Marc), COLIN-MOREY, *Lamy*, Larue. Value Prudhon.

St-Bris Burg ★ DYA Unique AOP for SAUV BL in N Burg. Fresh, lively, but can age (de Moor, GOISOT). Try also Bersan, Davenne, Felix, Simonnet-Febvre, Verret.

St-Chinian Ldoc ★★→★★★ Large hilly area nr Béziers; two distinct zones. Schist in ne, fragrant, nervy reds, CRUS Berlou (mostly CARIGNAN), Roquebrun (mostly SYRAH). Limestone clay in s, broader, spicy. Usual suspects Syrah, GRENACHE, Carignan, MOURVÈDRE. Whites from ROUSSANNE, MARSANNE, VERMENTINO, GRENACHE BL. Roquebrun co-op excels; CH Castigno; DOMS Borie la Vitarèle, COMPS, des Jougla, La Dournie, LA LAUZETA, LA LINQUIÈRE, La Madura, Les Eminades, Milhau-Lacuge, Navarre, Rimbert; CLOS Bagatelle, Mas Champart, Mas de Cynanques, Quartironi de Sars, Viranel.

St Cosme, Ch de S Rh ★★★ 09' 10' 11' 12' **13'** 14' **15'** 16' 17' 18' 19' 20' 21' 22' 23 High-quality bio GIGONDAS estate; wine with flair, drive, oak. Plot-specific CÔTES DU RH Les Deux Albion (r), Gigondas Classique (genuine, value), Hominis Fides (1902 GRENACHE), Le Poste (class). Owner CH de Rouanne, VINSOBRES. Fine N Rh merchant range, esp CONDRIEU, CÔTE-RÔTIE.

Ste-Anne, Dom S Rh ★★ Exceptional CÔTES DU RH VILLAGE estate above St-Gervais; limestone, old vines, robust, character reds incl Rouvières (mainly 60s MOURVÈDRE), Mourillons (mostly SYRAH), live 15 yrs. VDF from 1977 VIOGNIER, more subtle than most, worth tracking down.

Ste-Croix-du-Mont Bx ★★ 16 18 19 **20** 22 (23) AOP for sweet white. Soils consist of fossilized oysters. Best: rich, creamy, can age. Top CHX: Crabitan-Bellevue, des Arroucats, du Mont, La Caussade, La Rame, *Loubens*.

St-Émilion Bx ★★→★★★★ 09' 10' 15' 16 **18** 19' 20' 22' Big MERLOT-led AOP on BX's Right Bank; CAB FR also strong. Many GCS, mixed quality. Environmental certificate obligatory. Top designation St-Ém PREMIER GRAND CRU CLASSÉ (14 in 2022 classification). Warm, full, rounded style, but much diversity due to terroir, winemaking and blend. Best firm, v. long-lived. Top CHX: ANGÉLUS, AUSONE, CANON, CHEVAL BLANC, FIGEAC, PAVIE.

St-Estèphe H-Méd ★★→★★★★ 09' 10' **15 16'** 18 19' 20' 22' (23) Most n communal AOP in MÉD. Gravel, but more limestone, clay. Solid, structured wines for ageing. Five Classed Growths: CALON SÉGUR, COS D'ESTOURNEL, COS LABORY, LAFON-ROCHET, MONTROSE. Top unclassified estates: CAPBERN, DE PEZ, LE BOSCQ, LE CROCK, LILIAN LADOUYS, MEYNEY, ORMES-DE-PEZ, PHÉLAN SÉGUR, TRONQUOY-LALANDE.

Ste-Victoire Prov ★★→★★★ Subzone of CÔTES DE PROV, majority rosé. Limestone slopes of Montagne Ste-Victoire: much-needed freshness in hotter vintages. DOMS de St Ser, Gassier, Mas de Cadenas, St Pancrace. IGP Dom Richeaume.

Saint Gayan, Dom S Rh ★★★ 05' 06' 07' **10' 15' 16'** 17' 18' 19' 20' 21 22' 23 High-quality GIGONDAS estate, deep, long-lived, low oak, value across range: Origine (80% GRENACHE), RASTEAU Ilex (r), SABLET L'Oratory (w), CHÂTEAUNEUF (w).

St-Georges-St-Émilion Bx ★★ 18 19 **20** 22 Smallest ST-ÉM satellite. Sturdy and

---

Adolescent Aligoté

ALIGOTÉ, the once-cantankerous wild-child grape of Burg, has grown up. Now being made to great acclaim by scores of C D'O DOMS, it presents varied faces to the world: usually racy, poised, elegant; sometimes fuller, richer. In whatever guise, it is frequently satisfying, often exceptional, seldom disappointing. Quirkily promoted by Les Aligoteurs: *see* aligoteurs.wordpress.com.

structured. Best CHX: Calon, Cap St-Georges, CLOS Albertus, Haut St-Georges, Macquin, St-André Corbin, St-Georges, Tour du Pas-St-Georges.

St-Joseph N Rh ★★→★★★ 10′ 15′ 16′ 17′ 18′ 19′ 20′ **21** 22′ 23 Mostly hand-worked terrace, hill granite vyds, 64 km n–s, along w bank of N Rh. SYRAH reds. Prime, oldest vyds nr Tournon: stylish, red-fruited wines, need a little time; further n nr Chavanay darker, peppery, younger oak. More complete, character than CROZES-HERMITAGE, esp CHAPOUTIER (Les Granits), *Gonon* (top class), *Gripa*, GUIGAL (VIGNES de l'Hospice), *J-L Chave* (high interest). Plus Alexandrins, Amphores (bio), A PERRET (Grisières), B Jolivet (coming force), Boissonnet, Chèze, Courbis (modern), Coursodon (racy, modern), E Darnaud, DELAS, Faury, FERRATON, F Villard, Gaillard (esp CLOS de Cuminaille), Iserand (handmade), J Cécillon (energy), J&E Durand (much fruit), Marsanne (trad), Monier-Perréol (bio), P-J Villa, P Marthouret, S Blachon (trad), Sept Lunes (bio), Vallet, Vins de Vienne, Y CUILLERON. Food-friendly, gd *white (mainly Marsanne)*, esp A PERRET, Barge, *Chapoutier* (Les Granits), Curtat, DOM Faury, *Gonon*, Gouye, *Gripa*, Guigal, J P Marthouret, Pilon (style), Vallet, Y Cuilleron.

St-Julien H-Méd ★★★→★★★★ 09′ **10′** 15 16′ 18 19′ 20′ 22′ (23) Epitome of harmonious, fragrant, savoury red; v. consistent mid-MÉD communal AOP; 11 classified (1855) estates own most of vyd area; incl BEYCHEVELLE, DUCRU-BEAUCAILLOU, GRUAUD-LAROSE, LAGRANGE, LÉOVILLES (x3), TALBOT.

Saint Mont SW Fr ★★ (r) 18 19 20 (22) AOP from Gascon heartlands in all colours. Red, similar to MADIRAN but often softer and less intense. PRODUCTEURS PLAIMONT's André Dubosc largely responsible for creating this AOP and PP makes most of the wine. Try ★★★ *Ch de Sabazan*. White is dry, PACHERENC-like, less intense, terrific value.

St Nicolas de Bourgueil Lo ★→★★★ 10′ 15′ 16 17 18′ **19** 20 (22′) (23) AOP w of BOURGUEIL, stylistically indistinguishable; CAB FR red, rosé only. Try David, Delanoue, *Frédéric Mabileau*, Jamet, Laurent Mabileau, Mortier, PIERRE MÉNARD, Taluau-Foltzenlogel, Vallée, Xavier Amirault, *Yannick Amirault*.

St-Péray N Rh ★★ 22′ 23′ Finely mineral, flinty white (MARSANNE/ROUSSANNE) from hilly granite, some lime vyds opposite Valence, lots of rapid new planting, core quality gd. Once *famous for fizz*, drunk by Wagner; classic-method bubbles worth trying: A Voge (vintaged), Pic & CHAPOUTIER (vintaged), R Nodin, TAIN co-op. Best still white: Chapoutier, Clape (pure), Colombo (stylish), *du Tunnel* (v. elegant), Gripa (best; top-notch mainly ROUSSANNE Figuiers), J&E Durand, J Michel, L Fayolle, R Nodin (ace old-vine Suchat), TAIN co-op, Vins de Vienne, Voge (esp Fleur de Crussol, oak), Y CUILLERON (esp Biousse).

St-Pourçain Lo, Mass C ★→★★★ 20′ 21 22′ (23) Little-known AOP nr Vichy. White principally CHARD/Tressalier (aka Sacy) and/or SAUV BL. Red/rosé: GAMAY/PINOT N. Try Bellevue, *Bérioles*, CLOS de Breuilly, Grosbot-Barbara, Nebout, Ray, Terres d'Ocre, Terres de Roa, VIGNERONS de St-Pourçain.

St-Romain C d'O ★★ →★★★ (w) 15 17′ 18′ 19′ 20′ 21 22′ *Crisp whites* from side valley of CÔTE DE BEAUNE. Gaining in stature, gd value by Burg standards. Best vyds Combe Bazin, Sous la Roche, Sous le CH. Specialists *Alain Gras*, de Chassorney, outstanding *H&G Buisson*; try most NÉGOCIANTS. Some fresh reds too. Watch.

St-Véran Burg ★★ 17 18′ 19 20′ 21 22′ AOP in s, either side of POUILLY-FUISSÉ. Best sites: Davayé. Try CH de Beauregard, Chagnoleau, Corsin, Deux Roches, Litaud, Merlin; gd-value DUBOEUF, Poncetys, Terres Secrètes co-op. Watch for DROUHIN.

Salon Champ ★★★★ Original BLANC DE BLANCS, from LE MESNIL in Côte des Blancs. Tiny quantities. Long-lived luxury-priced wines. On song recently, quality once again catching up with reputation, *viz.* **90** 96 **97′** 02 04′ **08** 10 12 13. *See also* DELAMOTTE. Both owned by LAURENT-PERRIER.

Sancerre Lo ★→★★★★ 19′ 20′ 21 (22) (23) AOP famed for SAUV BL, but don't ignore

PINOT N (r/rosé). Drink well young but top wines can age. Best: A Girard, A Mellot, *Boulay*, *Bourgeois*, Cotat, C Riffault, Delaporte, Dezat, D Roger, Fleuriet, Fouassier, *François Crochet*, J Mellot, J-M Roger, Jolivet, L Crochet, Natter, Neveu, P&N Reverdy, Paul Prieur, Pierre Martin, *Pinard*, Raimbault, Roblin, Thomas Labaille, VACHERON, Vatan, Vattan.

Sang des Cailloux, Dom Le S Rh ★★★ 15' 16' 17' 18' 19' 20' 21 22' 23 Best VACQUEYRAS DOM, bio, spice, *garrigue* thrust, heart-on-sleeve mainly GRENACHE reds. Classic red rotates name every 3 yrs, Floureto (22), Azalaïs (21), Doucinello (23). Top, supreme, deep, rich Lopy (r) ages well. Solid Un Sang Bl (w).

Santenay C d'O ★★→★★★ 09' 12 15' 16 17 18' 19' 20' 21 22' The s end of COTE DE BEAUNE, fine reds. Best vyds: CLOS de Tavannes, Clos Rousseau, Gravières (r/*w*); some lovely whites too. Local producers: *Bachey-Legros*, *Capuano-Ferreri*, *Ch Philippe le Hardi*, CHEVROT, Girardin (Justin), Jessiaume, MOREAU, *Muzard*, *Olivier*, VINCENT. Try also Giroud, JADOT (incl DOM Prieur-Brunet), LAMY. No longer the country cousin.

Sarabande, Dom La Ldoc ★★→★★★ Australian/Irish couple making impressive FAUGÈRES. Les Espinasses powerful SYRAH-based. ROUSSANNE/MARSANNE stylish minerality from schist.

Sarrat de Goundy Ldoc ★★→★★★ Innovative Olivier Calix makes v.gd-value LA CLAPE du Planteur (r/w/rosé). CUVÉE Sans Titre (r) scented NIELLUCCIO; (w) 100% BOURBOULENC, floral, mineral.

Saumur Lo ★→★★★★ 19' 20' 21 22' (23) Region and AOP. Latter provides fine, dry, occasionally age-worthy CHENIN BL, fresh often lighter CAB FR (r/rosé/ sp). Region also home to AOPs SAUMUR-CHAMPIGNY (top r), Saumur-Le-Puy-Notre-Dame (r), rare Coteaux du Saumur (sw). Best: Antoine Foucault, Antoine Sanzay, Arnaud Lambert, BOUVET-LADUBAY, CLOS DE L'ÉCOTARD, *Clos Rougeard*, Dittière, Guiberteau, Nerleux, Paleine, Parnay, Rocheville, ROCHES NEUVES, Targé, *Villeneuve*, Yvonne.

Wagner wrote *Parsifal* while drinking fizzy St-Péray. Seems slightly frivolous.

Saumur-Champigny Lo ★★ →★★★★ 05' 10' 15' 16 17 18' 19 20 21 22' (23) AOP for top CAB FR. Usually more structured/complex than SAUMUR. Best: *Antoine Sanzay*, Arnaud Lambert, Bonnelière, Bruno Dubois, Champs Fleuris, *Clos Rougeard*, Dittière, Filliatreau, Hureau, Nerleux, Petit St-Vincent, ROCHES NEUVES, Rocheville, St-Vincent, Seigneurie, Targé, Vadé, Val Brun, *Villeneuve*, Yvonne.

Saussignac SW Fr ★★ 18' 19 20 (22) BERGERAC sub-AOP, adjoining MONBAZILLAC, similar sweet wines perhaps a shade more acidity. Best: ★★★ DOMS de Richard, La Maurigne, *Les Miaudoux*, Lestevenie; ★★ CHX Le Chabrier, Le Payral, Le Tap.

Sauternes Bx ★★ →★★★★ 09' 11' 13 14 15' 16' 18 **19 20** 22 (23) AOP making France's best *liquoreux* from "noble rotted" grapes. Luscious, golden and age-worthy. Plenty of dry white BX also produced. Top classified (1855) CHX: GUIRAUD, *Lafaurie-Peyraguey*, LA TOUR BLANCHE, RIEUSSEC, SUDUIRAUT, YQUEM. Exceptional unclassified: *Fargues*, *Gilette*, *Raymond-Lafon*.

Sauzet, Etienne C d'O ★★★ Leading DOM in PULIGNY with superb range of PCS (Combettes, Champ Canet best) and GC BÂTARD-M. Concentrated, lively wines, certified bio, once again capable of ageing. Magnificent BOURGOGNE Bl.

Savennières Lo ★★→★★★★ 10' 14' 15 16 18 **19 20** (22') (23) AOP for complex, age-worthy wines from schist, also lighter earlier drinkers from sand. Try BAUDOUIN, BAUMARD, *Belargus*, Bergerie, *Boudignon*, Closel, DOM FL, Epiré, *Laureau*, Mahé, Mathieu-Tijou, MORGAT, OGEREAU, PIERRE-BISE, Soucherie.

Savennières Roche-aux-Moines Lo ★★★ →★★★★ 10' 14' 15 16 18 **19 20** (22') Top AOP within SAVENNIÈRES. Remarkable, must-try, age-worthy CHENIN BL: *Dom aux Moines*, FL, Forges, *Laureau*, PIERRE-BISE.

Savigny-lès-Beaune C d'O ★★→★★★ 09' 10' 15' **18' 19'** 20' 21 22' Important village next to BEAUNE; similar mid-weight wines, more dependable than exciting. Top vyds: Dominode, Guettes, Lavières, Vergelesses. Local growers: *A Guyon, Bize*, Camus-Bruchon, Chandon de Briailles, Chenu, Girard, Guillemot (w), Pavelot, Rapet, *Tollot-Beaut*. Exceptional CUVÉES from CLAIR, DROUHIN, JP Guyon, LEROY.

Savoie AOP Alpine wines, two-thirds white; 20 crus incl APREMONT, ARBIN, AYZE, Chautagne, CHIGNIN, Crépy, Jongieux and regional AOPs incl CRÉMANT de Sav, ROUSSETTE DE SAV (Altesse), SEYSSEL; 25 grapes (r) mainly GAMAY, MONDEUSE, Persan, PINOT N; (w) Altesse, CHARD, CHASSELAS, Gringet, Jacquère, ROUSSANNE. Organic stars ★ Baraterie, ★★ A Berlioz, ★ Côtes Rousses, Chevillard, ★★ Prieuré St-Christophe, *St-Germain*; safe bets L'Idylle, Perrier, P Grisard.

Schlossberg Al Famed GC at Kientzheim, since C15. Glorious compelling RIES from WEINBACH 10 and new TRIMBACH 15 20 21 22.

Schlumberger, Doms Al ★★★→★★★★ Huge quality DOM (owns c.1% all AL vyds); GCS Kessler, Kitterlé, Saering. Superb quality RIES 08 17' 18 19, but GEWURZ tops, esp VT CUVÉE Christine (unforgettable 76') and SGN Cuvée Anne (masterpiece 89').

Schoenenbourg Al Historic Riquewihr GC famous for RIES. (Voltaire owned vines here.) Top HUGEL Ries Schoelhammer; fine VT, SGN Ries DOPFF AU MOULIN.

Schoffit, Dom Al ★★★★ Rare winery situated in Colmar. Contrast RIES RANGEN CLOS St-Théobald 10' **17' 18'** 20' (volcanic soil) and Ries GC Sommerberg 13 **15 16** 17' (granite). Harth CHASSELAS VIEILLES VIGNES AL best. Superb VT/SGN and hard-to-find pure SYLVANER.

Sec Literally means dry, though CHAMP so called is medium-sweet (and can be welcome at breakfast, teatime, weddings).

Savagnin is escaping Jura and popping up in Savoie, Bugey (and California).

Séguret S Rh ★★ 21 22' **23** Picturesque hillside village nr GIGONDAS in Rh-Villages top three; vyds mix of plain heat, cool heights. Mainly GRENACHE, peppery reds; well-fruited table whites. Try CH la Courançonne (gd w), DOMS Crève Coeur (bio), de Cabasse (charm), de l'Amauve (organic, gd w), Fontaine des Fées (organic), Garancière (organic, bio), Maison Plantevin (organic), Malmont (also v.gd rosé), Mourchon (deep, best), Pourra (intense), Soleil Romain.

Selosse, Anselme Champ ★★★★ Leading grower, prophet no longer in wilderness. Vinous, oxidative style, oak-fermented. Son Guillaume adding finesse: Version Originale still vibrant after 7 yrs on lees. NV BRUT Initial and fantastically rare Substance. Well-named Contraste BLANC DE NOIRS. Côte des Blancs parcels wonderfully different: lieux-dits Les Carelles, Le Bout du Clos, *La Côte Faron* Blanc de Noirs. Much of range NV; but Millésime 02 04 06 08 09 10' 12.

Sérafin, Dom C d'O ★★★ Niece Frédérique in charge, continuing Christian S recipe: deep colour, intense flavours, new wood. Wines need age. Full-throttle GEVREY, structured and firm. Try Cazetiers (DOM's back garden), CHARMES-CHAMBERTIN, GEVREY-CHAMBERTIN VIEILLES VIGNES.

Sérol, Dom Lo ★★★ **18'** 19 20' **21** 22' (23) Leading DOM in CÔTE ROANNAISE; bio. Granite/basalt gives GAMAY Saint-Romain a drive not found in TOURAINE Gamay (nor in some BEAUJ). Single-vyds serious, age-worthy. Long-term partnership with Troisgros restaurant.

Seyssel Sav Small regional AOP with long history. Light white, sparkling; Altesse, Molette. Try ★ Caves de Seyssel (esp Royal Seyssel).

SGN (Sélection des Grains Nobles) Al Term coined by HUGEL for AL equivalent of German Beerenauslese. Today, *grains nobles* mostly made with noble rot-affected grapes, not just v. sweet grapes that meet legal SGN requirement.

Sichel & Co Bx Notable BX merchant: Sirius a top brand. Family-run. Interests in CHX ANGLUDET, Daviaud, PALMER and Trillol in CORBIÈRES.

Sigoulès, Les Vignerons de SW Fr Much-improved source for BERGERAC, incl top CLOS d'Yvigne.

Simone, Ch Prov ★★★ Historic estate outside Aix, where Churchill painted Mont STE-VICTOIRE. Rougier family for c.200 yrs. AOP PALETTE; n-facing slopes on limestone with clay, gravel give freshness. Many vines over 100 yrs old. Seek age-worthy whites; iconic rosé, elegant reds from GRENACHE, MOURVÈDRE, with rare grape varieties Castet, Manosquin (r).

Sipp, Louis Al ★★→★★★ Trades in big volumes of young wines, but also two GC: fine RIES GC Kirchberg 13 16. Luscious GEWURZ GC Osterberg VT 09 15 16 18 19.

Sipp-Mack Al ★★→★★★ Large range of lively, easy-drinking, dry, mineral wines, but not last word in concentration. RIES GC Rosacker, expansive PINOT GR best.

Sorg, Bruno Al ★★★ Small grower at Eguisheim, GCS Florimont (RIES 13 14 16' great 17') and PFERSIGBERG (MUSCAT) 18'. Immaculate eco-friendly vyds.

Sorrel, Dom N Rh ★★★→★★★★ 18' 19' 20' 21 22' 23' Small HERMITAGE grower; the genuine article. Top: Hermitage Le Gréal (r, v. deep, long life, wait), Les Rocoules (w, rich, beautiful at 10 yrs+). Also authentic old-vine CROZES-HERMITAGE (r/w).

Sousa, De Champ ★★★ Erick and daughters enter 2nd decade as bio heroes in AVIZE. CUVÉE Les Caudalies BLANC DE BLANCS 08 10 12 13'. Well-named Cuvée Umami 13 15 16'; GC Blanc de Blancs Rés consistently excellent.

Sur lie "On the lees", as in MUSCADET. Bottled straight from vat: zest, body, character.

Tâche, La C d'O ★★★★ 90' 93' 96' 99' 02' 03 05' 09' 10' 12' 15' 16' 17 18' 19' 20' 21 22' VOSNE GC, DRC MONOPOLE. Firm in its youth, but how glorious with age. More tannic than stablemates, develops extraordinary complexity and allure with time, floral and perfumed. Can age for decades – then, fairest of all DRCS?

Taille-aux-Loups, Dom de la Lo ★★★→★★★★ 14' 15 16 17' 18 19' 20' 21 (22') (23) Leading MONTLOUIS-SUR-LOIRE DOM; Jacky Blot RIP 2023; son Jean-Philippe now in charge. Brilliant MONTLOUIS, VOUVRAY (labelled VDF). All barrel-fermented, largely dry, high quality. Single-vyds **Clos Mosny**, **Clos Michet** best, also top Triple Zéro (sp).

Tain, Cave de N Rh ★★→★★★ Reliable co-op, plenty of mature vyds, incl 25% of all HERMITAGE. Sound-to-v.gd red Hermitage, esp Gambert de Loche (best, value), rich Hermitage Au Coeur des Siècles (w, value). ST-JOSEPH (r/w) gd, ST-PÉRAY, interesting Bio (organic) range (St-Joseph), others modern, mainstream, can be dull. Classy, genuine MARSANNE VIN DE PAILLE.

Taittinger Champ ★★★→★★★★ Family-run Reims house, unfailing elegance. BRUT NV, Rosé NV, Brut Vintage Collection Brut 89 95'. Epitome of apéritif style, inimitable weightlessness. Luxury **Comtes de Champagne** 95' 02 04' 08 09 12 13 14'. Opinions differ on tricky 11, but for some, wine of the vintage. Comtes Rosé also shines in 12'. English bubbly project in Kent, DOM Evremond. *See also* Dom Carneros, California.

Tasque, Dom La Ldoc Contributor Juliet Bruce Jones MW's small bio DOM. In MINERVOIS, but most IGP. Easy-drinking SYRAH-led Appia; old-vine CARIGNAN; ASSYRTIKO 1st vintage 2023.

Tavel S Rh ★★ Mainly DYA Historical, full-bodied rosé from hot *garrigue* soils, across River Rhône from CHÂTEAUNEUF. Aided by white grapes for texture, should be bright red, deep, herbal, for vivid Med, garlic dishes. Best show well 3–4 yrs. Now a few lighter, Prov-style, more for apéritif. Top: CHX Aquéria (stylish), de Manissy (organic), La Genestière (organic), Ségriès, **Trinquevedel** (fine, organic); DOMS A Hote (organic), Corne-Loup, *de la Mordorée* (top, bio), des Carabiniers (bio), LAFOND ROC-EPINE (organic), Maby, Moulin-la-Viguerie (character), Rocalière (bio, stylish); Alain Jaume, GUIGAL, L'Anglore (character, no sulphur), Tardieu-Laurent (organic, full), VIDAL-FLEURY, Vignerons de Tavel.

Tempier, Dom Prov ★★★★ Iconic BANDOL: where Lucien and Lulu Peyraud revived AOP in 30s. Tops for elegance, concentration, longevity. Single-vyds Cabassaou, La Tourtine, pure expressions of MOURVÈDRE; v.gd rosé.

Terrasses du Larzac Ldoc ★★★(★) One of Ldoc's best terroir, nw of Montpellier. High AOP on limestone with cold nights makes poised, complex reds. Attracts innovative growers, small plots of vines; 50%+ organic/bio. Try CH de Jonquières; DOMS DE LA RÉSERVE D'O, de Malavielle, de Montcalmès, du Pas de l'Escalette; La Peira, Le Clos du Serres, L'Écriture, Mas Cal Demoura, Mas Combarèla, Mas Conscience, Mas d'Agamas, Mas des Brousses, MAS JULLIEN. Neighbouring AOP LDOC St-Saturnin: DOMS Archimbaud, Virgile Joly.

Thénard, Dom Burg ★★→★★★★ Historical; large holding of MONTRACHET, mostly sold on to NÉGOCIANTS. Look out for v.gd reds from home base in GIVRY.

Thévenet, Jean Burg ★★★ Top MÂCONNAIS purveyor of rich, some semi-botrytized CHARD, eg. CUVÉE Levroutée at *Dom de la Bongran*. Also DOMS de Roally, Emilian Gillet. Distinctive style divides opinion.

Thiénot, Alain Champ ★★★ Young house, new generation Stan and Garance now in charge. Ever-improving quality; one to watch. BRUT NV; Rosé NV Brut; Vintage Stanislas 02 04 06 08'. Voluminous VIGNE aux Gamins (single-vyd AVIZE 06' 08 09 10). CUVÉE Garance CHARD 07 08. Interesting Garance Blanc des Rouges 08 10 12. Also owns CANARD-DUCHÊNE, JOSEPH PERRIER and CH Ricaud in LOUPIAC.

Thivin, Ch Beauj ★★→★★★ Eight generations of Geoffray family make great Côte de Brouilly. Single-vyd bottlings cover soil types. Sept VIGNES blend also a winner.

Are big glass globes the new barrels? Now seen everywhere. No oak flavours.

Tissot Jura Dominant family around ARBOIS. ★ Jacques T (volume); ★★ Jean-Louis T (value). ★★★ Stéphane T (also as A&M Tissot), bio with top single-vyd CHARD, VIN JAUNE, brooding reds and classy CRÉMANT du Jura, Indigène.

Tollot-Beaut C d'O ★★★ Utterly dependable CÔTE DE BEAUNE grower with 20 ha in BEAUNE (Grèves, CLOS du Roi), CORTON (Bressandes), SAVIGNY (esp MONOPOLE PC Champ Chevrey) and at CHOREY-LÈS-BEAUNE base (note Pièce du Chapitre). Immediately appealing gd-value wines that can age. CORTON-CHARLEMAGNE gd.

Touraine Lo ★→★★★ Region and AOP. Latter a source of easy-going white/red. Some more serious, even age-worthy, esp from sub-AOPs: AMBOISE, Azay-le-Rideaux, Chenonceaux, Mesland, Noble Joué (rosé), Oisly. Best: Bessons, Biet, Clos du Porteau, Corbillières, Desroches-Manois, Echardières, Fontenay, Garrelière, Gosseaume, Grosbois, J-F Mérieau, Joël Delaunay, Lacour, *La Grange Tiphaine*, Mandard, Marionnet, Montdomaine, Morantin, Plou, Presle, Ricard, Rousseau, *Roussely*, Sauvète, Tue-Boeuf, T/X Frissant, Villebois.

Tour des Gendres, Ch SW Fr BERGERAC estate; ALBERT DE CONTI other part of same family; new grape varieties in response to climate change, eg. SAVAGNIN. Also craft beer and spirits.

Tour Saint-Martin, La Lo ★★→★★★ Home to Bertrand Minchin, leading light in MENETOU-SALON. Top whites *Fumet*, *Honorine* 19 20 21 (22) (23). Reds also worthwhile, age surprisingly well. VALENÇAY Le Claux Delorme v.gd value.

Trapet C d'O ★★★ Long-est GEVREY DOM. Sensual bio wines: eye-catching COTEAUX BOURGUIGNONS up to majestic GC CHAMBERTIN plus AL whites by marriage. Sons Pierre and Louis T pushing boundaries: glass globes, steel barrels.

Tremblay, Dom Cecile C d'O ★★★→★★★★ Wines of elegance, harmony, persistence; DOM doubled in size 2022, adding 4 ha, incl 1.8-ha VOSNE PC, Les Beaux Monts.

Trévallon, Dom de Prov ★★★ Famous DOM at LES BAUX; daughter Ostiane now in charge. No GRENACHE, so must be IGP Alpilles. Huge reputation fully justified: meticulous viticulture, age-worthy wines. Intense CAB SAUV/SYRAH. Barrique-aged MARSANNE/ROUSSANNE, drop of CHARD and now GRENACHE BL. Terrific.

FRANCE

Trimbach, FE Al ★★★★ Top, refined, ageless wines: RIES CLOS STE-HUNE without peers, 71' 75' 89' still great, **13** 17' 18 21' 22' classic; almost-as-gd (much cheaper) *Frédéric Emile* 10 12 **13** 14 16 17' 20' 21 22'. Most improved wine Ries Schlossberg, exceptional 20 21' 22'. Underrated, fresh PINOT GR, Osterberg 15' superb; knockout RIES-like SYLVANER from Trottacker lieu-dit, ages spectacularly well.

Trinités, Dom des Ldoc ★★★ Brit Simon Coulshaw's complex FAUGÈRES: Le Portail. L'Etranger, 100% CINSAULT mere VDF.

Tunnel, Dom du N Rh ★★★ Four high-quality and elegant ST-PÉRAY, notably Prestige and Pur Blanc (30S MARSANNE). Rich CORNAS, incl Pur Noir (1900S SYRAH), ST-JOSEPH (r).

Tursan SW Fr ★★ Mostly DYA AOP in LANDES. Super-chef Michel Guérard makes ★★★ lovely wines in chapel-like cellar at CH de Bachen, but not trad Tursan. Real thing from ★★ DOM de Perchade. Lovely dry white from ★★ Dom de Cazalet (two MANSENGS plus rare local Baroque). Worthy co-op rather outclassed.

U Stiliccionu, Dom Cors ★★★ Sebastian Poly-Casabianca's 7-ha bio DOM in AJACCIO. Hardly any sulphites. Granite, finesse; Antica (r) GRENACHE, SCIACCERELLO. Emy-Lidia VERMENTINO.

Vacheron, Dom Lo ★★→★★★ Top SANCERRE DOM, led the way on single vyds. Try Chambrates, Guigne-Chèvres, Le Paradis, *Les Romains* 14' 15 16 **17** 19 (21) (23). Also Belle Dame (r).

Vacqueyras S Rh ★★ 15' 16' 17' **18** 19' **20** 22' 23 Elemental, spiced, tannic GRENACHE-fuelled neighbour of GIGONDAS, baked, flat vyds; for game, hearty dishes. Lives 10 yrs+. Note CHX de Montmirail, *des Tours* (v. fine, RAYAS stable); CLOS de Caveau (organic), *Clos des Cazaux* (top value); DOMS Amouriers (organic), Archimbaud-Vache, CHARBONNIÈRE, Couroulu (v.gd, last yr 2022), Famille Perrin, Font de Papier (organic), Fourmone (fine), Garrigue, Grapillon d'Or, LE SANG DES CAILLOUX (organic, esp Lopy), Monardière (organic, v.gd), Montirius (bio), Montvac (organic), Roucas Toumba (organic), Semelles de Vent (handmade), Verde; JABOULET, P AMADIEU. Whites substantial, dining wines (Ch des Roques, Clos des Cazaux, Fourmone, Mas des Restanques, Sang des Cailloux).

Val de Loire Lo ★→★★ Mainly DYA Regional IGP; mostly minor wines but occasional gem, eg. Bâtard-Princesse from YANNICK AMIRAULT.

Valençay Lo ★→★★ 21 22' (23) AOP e of TOURAINE. Easy-drinking SAUV BL/CHARD, CÔT/GAMAY/PINOT N. Try Gibault, Jourdain, *Lafond, Le Claux Delorme*, Preys, Sinson, Vaillant.

Valréas S Rh ★★ 22' 23 CÔTES DU RH-VILLAGE in N Vaucluse truffle and wine territory, quality ascending; large co-op. Spiced, fresh, red-fruited mainly GRENACHE (r), improving white with style. Try CH la Décelle, CLOS Bellane incl Val des Rois (organic), Mas de Ste-Croix, DOMS des Grands Devers, du Séminaire (organic, pure r), Prévosse (organic).

VdF (Vin de France) Replaces Vin de Table, but with mention of grape variety, vintage. Often blends of regions with brand name. Can be source of unexpected delights if talented winemaker uses this category to avoid bureaucractic hassle, eg. Mark Angeli, Y CUILLERON VIOGNIER, S ARDÈCHE, ANJOU hotbeds of VdF.

VDN (vin doux naturel) Rouss Sweet wine fortified with wine alc, so sweetness natural, not strength. Speciality of ROUSS based on GRENACHES BL/Gr/N. Top, esp aged RANCIOS, can finish a meal on a sublime note. MUSCAT from BEAUMES DE VENISE, FRONTIGNAN, Lunel, RIVESALTES, ROUSS, St Jean de MINERVOIS gd.

VDP (Vin de Pays) *See* IGP.

Vendange Harvest. **VT (Vendange Tardive)** Late-harvest; AL equivalent to German Auslese but usually higher alc.

Venoge, de Champ ★★★ Venerable house, precise, more elegant under LANSON-BCC ownership; articulate boss in Gilles de la Bassetière. Cordon Bleu Extra-

BRUT, Vintage BLANC DE BLANCS 12 13' 16 17. Prestige CUVÉE Louis XV 10-yr-old BLANC DE NOIRS **08** 10' 12 14'.

Ventenac, Maison Ldoc ★★★ Vines overlook Carcassonne and Pyrénées; gd-value varietal IGP d'Oc, stonking CAB FR Les Dissidents Patience. CABARDÈS also shines (CUVÉE Jules, Res de Jeanne).

Ventoux S Rh ★★ 22' **23** Widespread AOP circles much of mighty Mont Ventoux between Rh and Prov, so mixed soils, plain and altitude. Some top DOMS: v.gd-value reds, gd choice. Tangy red (GRENACHE/SYRAH, café-style to deeper, peppery, quality on the up), lucid rosé, gd white (more oak). Best: CH Unang (organic, gd w), Ch Valcombe, Chêne Bleu (oak), CLOS des Patris (organic), Gonnet, La Ferme St Pierre (w/rosé, organic), La Vieille Ferme (r, also VDF), St-Marc, Terra Ventoux, VIGNERONS Mont Ventoux; Doms Allois (organic), Anges, Berane, Brusset, Cascavel, Champ-Long, Croix de Pins (gd w), du Tix, Fondrèche (organic, fun), Grand Jacquet, Martinelle (organic, style), Murmurium, Olivier B (organic), PAUL JABOULET, Pesquié (modern), Piéblanc (organic, fresh depth), Pigeade, St-Jean du Barroux (organic, character, incl w), Terres de Solence, Tix, Verrière, VIDAL-FLEURY, Vieux Lazaret, Vignobles Brunier, co-op Bédoin.

Vernay, Dom Georges N Rh ★★★★ 21' 22' 23' Top-of-the-tree CONDRIEU: three wines, balance, refinement, purity, Terrasses de l'Empire *deluxe apéritif*. Chaillées d'Enfer, richness; Coteau de Vernon, magic, mystery, lives 20 yrs+. CÔTE-RÔTIE, ST-JOSEPH (r), lucid red fruit, restraint; classy IGP COLLINES RHODANIENNES (r/w).

Veuve Clicquot Champ ★★★★ Historical house, both trad and creative. Improving Yellow Label NV; 5% oak. Impressive DEMI-SEC NV. Vintage Rés **12** a wonder of perfect maturity. Luxe La Grande Dame (GD) **12' 15**; PINOT N takes control with aplomb. Older vintages of GD stay course, *viz.* 04' (no 02, deemed too muscular for GD), glorious in **89**. GD Rosé 06 delicious, ready. Experienced Didier Mariotti chef de CAVE since 2020. In gd hands.

Veuve Fourny Champ ★★★→★★★★ Superb archetypal Côte des Blancs specialist, delightful brothers Charles-Henri and Emmanuel. Sustainable (HVE) based in Vertus, where they also grow PINOT N. BLANC DE BLANCS PC 13 **14' 15** and NV exceptional *rapport qualité prix*.

Vézelay Burg ★→★★ Age 1–2 yrs. Lovely location (with abbey) in NW Burg. Promoted to full AOP for tasty whites from CHARD. Also try revived MELON (COTEAUX BOURGUIGNON) and light PINOT (generic BOURGOGNE). Best: DOM de la Cadette, des Faverelles, Elise Villiers, La Croix Montjoie.

Vidal-Fleury N Rh ★★ →★★★ GUIGAL-owned merchant-grower of CÔTE-RÔTIE. Top-rank, distinguished, full *La Chatillonne* (from Blonde, 12% VIOGNIER, oak, wait min 7 yrs) streets ahead of rest of range: decent CAIRANNE (r), gd CHÂTEAUNEUF (w), sound CÔTES DU RH (w/rosé), CROZES-HERMITAGE (r), MUSCAT de BEAUMES-DE-VENISE, TAVEL, VENTOUX.

Vieille Ferme, La S Rh ★→★★ Ubiquitous brand from Famille Perrin of CH DE BEAUCASTEL, v.gd value; much labelled VDF, with VENTOUX (r), LUBERON (w/rosé) in some countries (France, Japan, better than VdF). Back on song recently (r/w).

Vieilles vignes Old vines. Can give extra depth, complexity. But no rules about age and can be a tourist trap. Can a vine be old if it's younger than you are?

Vieux Télégraphe, Dom du S Rh ★★★ 05' 07' **09' 10'** 12' **14' 15'** 16' **17'** 18' 19' 20' 21 23' High-quality, renowned estate, in gd form; highly visual big-stone plateau soils, sealed, slow-burn, deep red CHÂTEAUNEUF; top two wines La Crau (long life, no 22), Piedlong et Pignan (aromatic, pure). Rich, splendid, true *garrigue* Med table white *La Crau* (v.gd 18 19 20 21 22), CLOS La Roquète (fine, top with food). Owns clear, slow-to-evolve, spiced, complex GIGONDAS DOM Les Pallières with US importer Kermit Lynch.

Vignelaure, Ch de Prov ★★★ Top estate for reds, AOP COTEAUX D'AIX EN PROVENCE.

FRANCE

CAB SAUV, SYRAH at 300m (984ft) give depth, freshness. Will age 10 yrs. Rosé up to 5 yrs; intriguing ROUSSANNE, Rolle, SÉM.

Vigne or vignoble Vineyard (vyd), vineyards (vyds). **Vigneron** Vine-grower.

Vignoble du Rêveur Al ★★★ Mathieu DEISS/Emanuelle Milan project using Mathieu's maternal family vines. Field blends in Bennwihr (bio), dry, food-friendly, pure, from uncommonly talented duo that won't make a horse faint like many "natural" wines; superb Singulier and Pierre Sauvages 17′ 18 20 21.

Vigouroux, Georges SW Fr Top name in CAHORS, instrumental in reviving the AOP. Estates incl Haute Serre and Mercues. Generations have changed; wines seem to be getting better after a slightly dull period.

Villeneuve, Ch de Lo ★★→★★★ 18′ 19′ 20′ 21 22′ (23) Well-known, excellent SAUMUR (w), SAUMUR-CHAMPIGNY (r). Top: Les Cormiers, Grand Clos. Age-worthy.

Vilmart & Cie Champ ★★★→★★★★ Exemplary biodynamic farming 11 ha of PC Montagne village Rilly. Oak fermentation and attention to detail from long-serving chef de CAVES Laurent Champs. Superb Coeur de cuvée 08 **09 12 13 15′** 16, Grand Cellier d'Or 13 **16 18** 19. Try Rubis Rosé.

Vincent C d'O ★★★ Few people devote as much thought and effort to their viticulture as Jean-Marc V. Excellent whites, v.gd reds. Check daring, multi-vintage ALIGOTÉ blend Soler-Al. Daughter Anaïs waiting in wings.

Vin de paille From grapes dried before pressing, so concentrated sweetness, acidity; esp in Jura.

Vin gris Pale pink. "Oeil de perdrix" means much the same; so does "blush".

"Downright velvet", Honoré Balzac on Vouvray, back in 1833. Still true today.

Vin jaune Jura ★★→★★★★ Speciality of Jura; inimitable not-so-"yellow" wine. SAVAGNIN, 6 yrs+ in barrel without topping up, develops flor like Sherry but no added alc. Ages for decades. Top spot, CH-CHALON has own AOC. Sold in unique 62cl clavelin bottles. S TISSOT specializes in single-vyd bottlings, Bourdy in old vintages. Grab Puffeney if you can. *See also* ARBOIS, CÔTES DU JURA, L'ÉTOILE.

Vinsobres S Rh ★★ 19′ 20 21 **22′** Low-profile AOP starting to stir, marked by quality SYRAH in blend, mix gd hillside, high-plateau vyds. Best reds are smooth flow, brightly fruited, to accompany red meats; age 10 yrs. New DOMS emerging. Leaders: CAVE la Vinsobraise (Diamant N), CH Rouanne (plot-specific wines), CLOS Volabis (organic), Doms Autrand (stylish), Chaume-Arnaud (bio, v.gd), Constant-Duquesnoy, du Tave, Famille Perrin (*Hauts de Julien* top class, Cornuds value), Jaume (modern), Moulin (trad, gd r/w), Péquélette (bio, character), Serre Besson (gd VDF), Vallot (bio, fruit).

Viré-Clessé Burg ★★ 14′ 17′ **18 19′** 20′ 21 22′ AOP, two of best white villages of MÂCON. Exuberant rich style, esp from Quintaine area, sometimes late-harvest. Try Bonhomme, Chaland, DOM de la Verpaille, Gandines, Goisot-Perrin, Guillemot-Michel, J-P Michel, THÉVENET and all gd Mâconnais NÉGOCIANTS.

Visan S Rh ★★ **22′ 23** Progressive CÔTES DU RH-VILLAGE, now top three: peppery, mostly GRENACHE reds, restrained depth, crisp fruit; some softer, gd amount of organic. Whites fair. Best: DOMS Au 7ème Clos (organic), Bastide, Coste Chaude (organic), Dieulefit (bio, low sulphur), Florane (bio), Fourmente (bio, esp Nature), Guintrandy (organic, full), Montmartel (organic), Philippe Plantevin, Roche-Audran (organic, style), VIGNOBLE Art Mas (organic).

Vogüé, Comte Georges de C d'O ★★★★ Aristo CHAMBOLLE estate with lion's share of MUSIGNY. Great from barrel, but takes many yrs in bottle to reveal glories. Unique and splendid *Musigny Bl*, a one-off. New winemaker 2021.

Volnay C d'O ★★★→★★★★ 99′ 05′ 09′ 10′ 15′ 16 **17′** 18 19 20 21 22′ Top CÔTE DE BEAUNE reds, except when it hails or gets too hot. The s echo of CHAMBOLLE, similar grace, slightly more structure. (Moving to ban weedkillers in PC vyds.)

Best vyds: Caillerets, Champans, CLOS des Chênes, Santenots (more clay), Taillepieds and MONOPOLES Clos de la Bousse d'Or, Clos de la Chapelle, Clos des Ducs, Clos du CH des Ducs. Growers: BOULEY, D'ANGERVILLE, *de Montille*, *Lafarge*, *Pousse d'Or*. Also v.gd Bitouzet-Prieur, Buffet, Clerget, Glantenay, H BOILLOT, HOSPICES DE BEAUNE, LAFON, Rossignol.

Vosne-Romanée C d'O ★★★→★★★★ 90' 93' 96' 99' 02' 05' 09' 10' 12 15' 16' 17 18' 19' 20' 21 22' Most patrician village in Burg, with celebrated GCS and outstanding PCS Beaumonts, Brûlées, Malconsorts, Suchots etc. Should always be special and regularly sublime. No excuses for anything less. Just question of price... Top: ARNOUX-LACHAUX, Bizot, CATHIARD, Coquard-Loison-Fleurot, DRC, EUGÉNIE, GRIVOT, GROS, Lamarche, LEROY, LIGER-BELAIR, MÉO-CAMUZET, MUGNERET, NOËLLAT, ROUGET. Plus Clavelier, *Confuron-Gindre*, Forey, Guyon, Tard.

Vougeot C d'O ★★★ 99' 02' 05' 09' 10' 12' 15' 16 17 18' 19' 20 21 22' Mostly GC as CLOS DE VOUGEOT (could be trimmed), but also village and PCS Les Cras, Les Petits Vougeots; MONOPOLES *Clos de la Perrière* and outstanding *Clos Blanc de V* (w). Best: *Bertagna*, Clerget, Fourrier, GROS (A), HUDELOT-NOËLLAT, LEROUX, *Vougeraie*.

Vougeraie, Dom de la C d'O ★★★ →★★★★ Unites all BOISSET's vyd holdings; bio; turned 25 in 2024. Fine-boned, perfumed wines, whole-bunch vinification, most noted for sensual GCS, esp *Bonnes-Mares*, CHARMES-CHAMBERTIN, MUSIGNY. Fine whites: superb, age-worthy *Clos Blanc de Vougeot*, four GCs incl unique Charlemagne.

Vouvray Lo ★→★★★★ (dr) 18' 19' 20' 21 22 (23) (sw) 02' 03 05 08' 09 10 11' 15' 16 17 18' 20' (22) (23) Famed AOP for CHENIN BL. All styles. Top sweet wines astonishing. DEMI-SEC classic; dry is fresh, mineral. Much fizz, not all top quality. Best: *Aubuisières*, Autran, Brunet, *Carême*, CHAMPALOU, Florent Cosme, *Foreau*, FRANÇOIS CHIDAINE (VDF), Gaudrelle, HUET, Mathieu Cosme, Meslerie, Perrault-Jadaud, PINON, *Taille-aux-Loups* (VdF), Vigneau-Chevreau.

Weinbach, Dom Al ★★★★ World's best GEWURZ (Furstentum, Mambourg), PINOT GR SGN, but all exceptionally elegant, pure gastronomic wines: MUSCAT 22', SYLVANER 19' 20, RIES GC SCHLOSSBERG, Pinot Gr Altenbourg 10' 13' 17' 18' 19' 21'. Théo Faller, Cathy's son, making superlative wines across all varieties, styles (even superb orange if you like).

Zind Humbrecht, Dom Al ★★★★ Four new wines from AL quality leader (AUXERROIS Rotenberg, RIES Hengst, Ries Sommerberg, also CHARD fizz). But estate's stars still stellar Ries, GEWURZ, PINOT GR from GCS Brand, HENGST, GOLDERT, RANGEN, plus MUSCAT GC Goldert (Al's best along with Ernest BURN's). CLOS Windsbuhl (not GC) Ries, Pinot Gr great too. Splendid 21, classic 19, sumptuous 18.

Zotzenberg Al Only GC for SYLVANER (should be many more). Different geologic-era limestone marls give full, fresh, age-worthy wines. Best: Albert Seltz, BOECKEL, Hirtz, Rieffel.

Pinot Noir in Champagne – return of the native

In the days of the Doms (PÉRIGNON and RUINART), the PINOTS (N and M) dominated CHAMP. Then came SALON and TAITTINGER's Comtes and the rise and rise of BLANC DE BLANCS; today Pinot N covers only 38% of the region's 34,000 ha. But the fight-back has started; BOLLINGER led the way in 1969 with VIEILLES VIGNES Françaises and now again with its PN series, each focusing on a great village. Soon no self-respecting Champenois will be without one. The fact that KRUG's CLOS d'Ambonnay commands twice the price of its famous CLOS DU MESNIL (CHARD) tells its own tale. Look out for BILLECART-SALMON's Clos St-Hilaire and La Côte Faron from SELOSSE. VEUVE CLICQUOT's legendary La Grande Dame seems to like it more and more; recent vintages (08 12 15) all contain more than 90% of our new best friend, Pinot N.

Châteaux of Bordeaux

Abbreviations used in the text:

Bx	Bordeaux
Bar	Barsac
Cas	Castillon-Côtes de Bordeaux
E-2-M	Entre-Deux-Mers
Fron	Fronsac
Grav	Graves
H-Méd	Haut-Médoc
L de P	Lalande de Pomerol
List	Listrac
Marg	Margaux
Méd	Médoc
Mou	Moulis
Pau	Pauillac
Pe-Lé	Pessac-Léognan
Pom	Pomerol
Saut	Sauternes
St-Ém	St-Émilion
St-Est	St-Estèphe
St-Jul	St-Julien

Bordeaux, too, has its problems. The French are drinking less wine (from 120 litres/head in 1960 to 40 litres/head today and falling), and this, plus world events, means sales and demand are flagging. Add in frost in 2021, heat and drought in 2022 and an unprecedented attack of mildew in 2023, and all is not rosy outside the comfort zone of the Grands Crus (5% of the vineyard area). Initiatives to address the situation have seen plans to grub-up 10% of the vineyard area (108,000 ha in 2022), an increase in the production of Crémant de Bordeaux (now 1.5% of total production and very much in demand) and

Châteaux of Bordeaux entries also cross-refer to France

more thought given to making wines that will appeal to a younger generation. Accessibility, fun and innovation is what is needed here so an emphasis on fruit, softer tannins (with preferably little or no oak) and variability in blends are the methods that are being applied. This does not mean the demise of classic Bordeaux, but a stepping stone to bring new consumers into the fold.

Vintage 2023, like 22, was early: picking for white and Crémant started mid-August, and Merlot the first week in September. The crop had started large, but rain and heat brought mildew – hence a disparity in yields, with Merlot the hardest hit. A hot, dry August and September gave full maturity, particularly for the Cabernets. For those who escaped the mildew, there's both quality and quantity, with reds of a solid constitution that should age. Luckily there are plenty of vintages for drinking now. The luscious 09s are tempting at whatever level. The 08s have come into their own. The 10s are opening, as are the "classic" 14s, although the Grands Crus need longer. For early drinking, try the often-charming 12s or underrated 11s, which have improved with bottle-age.

Of recent years, the softer 17s will be the first to broach. Mature vintages to look for are 96 (best Médoc), 98 (particularly Right Bank, Graves), 00 01 (Right Bank, but don't dismiss Médoc), 02 04 06. The splendid 05s are also opening, although patience is still a virtue here. Dry white Bordeaux remains consistent in quality and value, the whites in 23 seemingly balanced and fresh. Fine white Graves can age as well as white burgundy, providing there's acidity and freshness. And Sauternes continues to offer an array of remarkable years: 23 has both quantity and quality. Even moderate years like 08 14 16 offer approachability and a fresher touch, while great years – 09 11 15 17 – have the concentration and hedonistic charm that make them indestructible.

A, Dom de l' Cas ★★ 16 17 18 **19 20** 22 Leading CAS property owned by STÉPHANE DERENONCOURT and wife. Consistent quality.

Agassac, D' H-Méd ★★ 16' 18 **19 20'** 22 CRU BOURGEOIS Exceptionnel in S H-MÉD. Modern, accessible. Lots of CAB SAUV. Luxury hotel to open in 2025.

Aiguilhe, D' Cas ★★ 15 16 18 **19 20** 22 23 Large von Neipperg-owned estate. MERLOT-led *power, finesse.* Also BX white. CANON-LA-GAFFELIÈRE, LA MONDOTTE same stable.

Andron-Blanquet St-Est ★★ 15 16' 18 **19 20** Sister to COS LABORY. Can be value.

Angélus St-Ém ★★★★ 09 **10'** 11 12 14 **15'** 16' **17** 18' 19' 20 21 22' 23 Declined classification in 2022. Dark, rich, sumptuous. More finesse from 19. New *cuvier* in 23. Second label: Carillon d'Angélus. Also N°3 d'Angélus and BX red Tempo d'Angélus; all made in state-of-the-art winery.

Angludet Marg ★★ 14 15' 16' **18'** 19 20 21 23 Property owned by NÉGOCIANT SICHEL. Lots of PETIT VERDOT in blend. Bio methods. Fragrant, stylish. Often gd value.

Archambeau Grav ★★ (r) 18 19 **20** (w) 21 22 Family-owned property. 20 ha in a single block. *Fruity dry white* (60/40% SAUV BL/SÉM); fragrant reds (50/50% MERLOT/CAB); all gd value.

Arche, D' Saut ★★ 11 15 16 17 **18 20** 22 Second Growth steadily being overhauled. Also "A" (BX r/w/rosé).

Armailhac, D' Pau ★★★ 12 14 **15' 16'** 17 18 19 20 21 22' 23 (MOUTON) ROTHSCHILD-owned Fifth Growth. A step up in 22. Fair value.

Aurelius St-Ém ★★ 17 18 **19 20** Top CUVÉE from go-ahead ST-ÉM co-op; 80/20% MERLOT/CAB FR, new oak, concentrated.

Ausone St-Ém ★★★★ 04 05' 06' 08 09' 10' 12 14 15' 16' 17 18' 19' 20' 21 22 23 Tiny, illustrious CH owned by Vauthier family. Declined classification in 2022, so now just basic ST-ÉM. Only 1500 cases; vyds s- and se-facing, sheltered; lots of CAB FR (60% in 22). Long-lived wines with volume, texture, finesse. At a price. Second label: Chapelle d'Ausone (500 cases). *La Clotte*, FONBEL, MOULIN ST-GEORGES, Simard sister estates.

Balestard la Tonnelle St-Ém ★★ 14 15 16 18 19 20 22' 23 Capdemourlin-owned property on limestone plateau. MERLOT-led. More elegance in 22.

Barde-Haut St-Ém ★★→★★★ 10 14 15' 16 18 19' 20 MERLOT-led GRAND CRU CLASSÉ in St-Christophe-des-Bardes. Modern, but limestone terroir shows.

Bastor-Lamontagne Saut ★★ 11 14 15 17 18 19 21 22 23 Large Preignac estate; SÉM/SAUV BL (55% in 22); organic. Second label: Les Remparts de Bastor. Also dry whites B de B-L and Confidence.

Batailley Pau ★★★ 09' 10' 11 12 14 15 16 17 18 19' 20 21 22 23 Relatively gd value, CAB SAUV-led Fifth Growth. Borie-Manoux owned.

Beaumont H-Méd ★★ 15 16 18 19 20 Large CRU BOURGEOIS Supérieur. Easily enjoyable wines. Usually gd value. Same stable as BEYCHEVELLE.

Beauregard Pom ★★★ 12 14 15 16 18 19' 20' 21 22 23 Much improved; organic, modern winery. MERLOT-led but 6% CAB SAUV in 22. Second label: Benjamin de Beauregard.

Beauséjour St-Ém ★★★ 10' 12 14 15 16 17 18' 19' 20' 22 Tiny PREMIER GRAND CRU CLASSÉ (B). Owned by Joséphine Duffau-Lagarrosse and Courtin family (Clarins cosmetics). New label in 2022. Rich, cellar-worthy.

Beau-Séjour Bécot St-Ém ★★★ 10' 12 14 15 16 17 18 19 20' 21 22 23 Distinguished PREMIER GRAND CRU CLASSÉ (B) on plateau. New cellar 2023. More finesse these days, but still gd ageing potential. Limestone terroir comes through.

Beau-Site St-Est ★★ 15 16 18 19 20 22 Owned by BORIE-MANOUX. CAB SAUV-led (70%). Supple, fresh, accessible.

Bélair-Monange St-Ém ★★★ 09' 10' 11 12 14 15 16' 17 18 19 20 21 22 23 PREMIER GRAND CRU CLASSÉ (B) on limestone plateau and côtes. MOUEIX-owned. Huge investment in vyd and new winery (inaugurated 2022). Refined style; more intensity, precision these days. Second label: Annonce.

Belgrave H-Méd ★★ 10' 14 15 16 18 19 20 21 22 23 DOURTHE-owned Fifth Growth. Steady investment. Understated but consistent. Can be value.

Bellefont-Belcier St-Ém ★★ 14 15' 16 17 18 19' 20 21 22 23 Much-improved GRAND CRU CLASSÉ on s côtes. Former ANGÉLUS winemaker.

St-Émilion classification – 2022 edition

The 2022 classification incl a total of 85 CHX: 14 PREMIERS GRANDS CRUS CLASSÉS and 71 GRANDS CRUS CLASSÉS. FIGEAC received promotion, joining PAVIE as the only Premiers Grands Cru Classés (A), ANGÉLUS, AUSONE and CHEVAL BLANC having officially withdrawn from the classification. There were no other changes at Premier Grand Cru Classé (B) level barring the absence of LA GAFFELIÈRE, which had also withdrawn. New to status of Grand Cru Classé were Badette, Boutisse, Clos Badon Thunevin, Clos Dubreuil, Clos St-Julien, La Confession, Corbin Michotte (declassified in 2012), Croix de Labrie, La Croizille, Lassègue, MANGOT, Montlabert, Montlisse, ROL VALENTIN, Tour Baladoz and TOUR SAINT CHRISTOPHE. Among the absentees from the 2012 classification, Grand Pontet, L'Arrosée and Tertre Daugay are now all part of newly created QUINTUS. Others withdrew (LA CLOTTE, QUINAULT L'ENCLOS), and some were absorbed by a sister property (PAVIE DECESSE by PAVIE). Classification reviewed every 10 yrs.

Belle-Vue H-Méd ★★ 14 15' 16 17 **18 19 20** (22) CRU BOURGEOIS Exceptionnel in S H-MÉD. Dark, dense but firm. Lots of PETIT VERDOT.

Berliquet St-Ém ★★ 10 14 **15' 16'** 17 18 19' 20 21 22 23 Tiny GRAND CRU CLASSÉ on plateau and côtes. Same stable as CANON. On an upward curve.

Bernadotte H-Méd ★★ 14 15' 16' 17 **18' 19 20** CRU BOURGEOIS Supérieur. Hong Kong-based ownership. Environmental certification. Savoury; gd value.

Beychevelle St-Jul ★★★ 09' 10' 11 12 14 **15' 16'** 17 18 19' 20 21 22 23 Sizeable Fourth Growth owned by Castel and Suntory. Wines of consistent *elegance* rather than power. Visitor-friendly. Second label: Amiral de Beychevelle.

Yields in Bordeaux have plummeted: c.65 hl/ha in 1982, 35 hl/ha now. Perfectionism.

Biston-Brillette Mou ★★ 15 16' **18 19 20** (22) Family-owned CRU BOURGEOIS Supérieur. Attractive, early drinking and gd value. 50/50% MERLOT/CAB SAUV. Environmental certification.

Bonalgue Pom ★★ 14 15 **16 18 19 20** (22) Much-improved 90/10% MERLOT/CAB FR POM from sand, gravel, clay soils; gd value for AOP. Owned by NÉGOCIANT J-B Audy. Sisters CLOS du Clocher; CH du Courlat in LUSSAC-ST-EM.

Bonnet Bx ★★ (r) 19 20 (22) (w) DYA Forged by André Lurton; now run by son Jacques. Large producer of some best E-2-M and red (oak-aged Rés) BX. Single-variety Diane range, natural Eden. Also *Couhins-Lurton*.

Bon Pasteur, Le Pom ★★★ 11 12 14 **15' 16** 17 18 19 20 22 23 Tiny cru on ST-ÉM border. MICHEL ROLLAND makes the wine. Ripe, opulent, seductive, but ages well. Second label: L'Étoile de Bon Pasteur.

Boscq, Le St-Est ★★ 15' **16'** 17 **18' 19'** 20 (22) DOURTHE-owned, CRU BOURGEOIS Exceptionnel. Consistently great value.

Bourgneuf Pom ★★ 11 14 15' **16'** 17 18 19' 20 21 22 MERLOT-led (85%). Vayron family-owned. Subtle, savoury wine; gd value for POM.

Bouscaut Pe-Lé ★★★ (r) 14 15 **16'** 17 18 19 20 21 22 (w) 19 20 21 22 23 Classed Growth. Structured, MERLOT-based reds. Sappy, age-worthy *whites*. Organic since 2023. Gîte to rent.

Boyd-Cantenac Marg ★★★ 10' 14 **15 16** 18 19 20 Tiny Cantenac-based Third Growth. Owned by Guillemet family since 1932. CAB SAUV-dominated. Needs time. Second label: Jacques Boyd. Also POUGET.

Branaire-Ducru St-Jul ★★★ 10' 12 14 **15 16'** 17 18' 19 20 21 22 23 Consistent Fourth Growth; regularly gd value; ageing potential. New *cuvier* (75 tanks) in 2022. Second label: *Duluc*.

Branas Grand Poujeaux Mou ★★ 14 15' **16'** 17 **18 19' 20'** (22) A gd neighbour of CHASSE-SPLEEN, POUJEAUX. Investment, expansion. Rich, modern style. Second label: Les Eclats de Branas.

Brane-Cantenac Marg ★★★→★★★★ 10' 11 12 14 **15' 16'** 17 18 19' 20 22 23 Second Growth owned by Henri Lurton. CAB SAUV-led (74% in 22). Classic, fragrant MARG with structure to age. Second label: *Baron de Brane*, value, consistent.

Brillette Mou ★★ 15 16' **18 19 20** Reputable DOM on gravelly soils. Acquired by CHASSE-SPLEEN in 2023, will be integrated into that.

Cabanne, La Pom ★★ 14 15 **16'** 18 19 20 22 23 MERLOT-dominant (90%+) DOM on w slope. Firm when young; needs bottle-age.

Caillou Saut ★★ 14 15' 16 19 **20** (22) Second-Growth BAR for pure *liquoreux*. 100% SÉM. Family-owned. Second label: Les Erables.

Calon Ségur St-Est ★★★★ 09' 12 13 14 **15' 16'** 17 18' 19' 20 21 22 23 Third Growth on top form; more CAB SAUV these days (70%+). Firm but fine, complex. Second label: Le Marquis de Calon (value).

Cambon la Pelouse H-Méd ★★ 15 16' 18 **19 20** Big, reliable CRU BOURGEOIS Exceptionnel. Australian-owned (TWE).

Camensac, De H-Méd ★★ 14 15 16 18' 19 20 22 Sizeable Fifth Growth in N H-MÉD. Merlaut family-owned (CHASSE-SPLEEN, GRUAUD-LAROSE). Steady improvement; recent vintages clearly better.

Canon St-Ém ★★★★ 08' 09' 10' 12 13 14 15' 16' 17 18' 19' 20 21 22' 23 Esteemed PREMIER GRAND CRU CLASSÉ (B) with vyd on limestone plateau. Wertheimer-owned, like BERLIQUET, RAUZAN-SÉGLA, so plenty investment; CH designated a historical monument. Elegant, complex, for long ageing. Second label: Croix Canon (separate winery formerly a C12 chapel).

Canon-la-Gaffelière St-Ém ★★★ 10' 11 14 15' 16 17 18 19' 20 22 23 PREMIER GRAND CRU CLASSÉ (B) on s foot slope. Lots of CABS FR (40%) and SAUV (10%). Average age of vyd 50 yrs. Stylish, impressive. Organic. Also D'AIGUILHE, LA MONDOTTE.

Cantemerle H-Méd ★★★ 10' 12 14 15 16 18 19' 20 22 23 Large Fifth Growth in S H-MÉD. Replanted over past 40 yrs. On-going renovation of CH, *cuvier* and park: ready in 2025. On gd form and gd value too.

Cantenac-Brown Marg ★★★ 10' 14 15 16' 17 18 19' 20 21 22 23 Third Growth; vyd expanded 2020. New eco winery built entirely of raw earth. More voluptuous, refined these days. CAB SAUV-led (69% in 22). Second label: BriO de Cantenac-Brown. Also SAUV BL-led (90%) dry white AltO.

Capbern St-Est ★★ 10' 14 15' 16' 18 19 20 21 22 23 Same ownership and team as CALON SÉGUR; CAB SAUV-led; gd form and value.

Cap de Mourlin St-Ém ★★ 10 14 15 16 18 19 20 22 GRAND CRU CLASSÉ on n slopes. Same family ownership since C16. MERLOT-led (65%). Firm, tannic wines. Also BALESTARD LA TONNELLE.

Carbonnieux Pe-Lé ★★★ 10 14 15' 16' 18 19' 20 21 22 Classed-Growth GRAV, owned by Perrin family since 1956. Sterling red/white; large volumes of both. Fresh *whites*, 65% SAUV BL, eg. 20 21 22. Red can age. Visitor-friendly. Second label: La Croix de Carbonnieux.

Carles, De Fron ★★ 15 16 18 19 20 Haut-Carles is prestige CUVÉE; 90% MERLOT. Environmental certification.

Carmes Haut-Brion, Les Pe-Lé ★★★ 14 15 16' 17 18' 19' 20' 21 22' 23 Tiny, high-flying property in heart of Bordeaux city; CABS FR (40%+) and SAUV-led wines, structured but suave. Plenty of investment. Second label: Le C des Carmes Haut-Brion from vines in Martillac.

Caronne Ste Gemme H-Méd ★★ 15 16 18 19 20 CAB SAUV-led wines; fresh, structured; 21 last vintage; now integrated into LA TOUR CARNET.

Carruades de Lafite Pau ★★★ Second label of CH LAFITE; 20,000 cases/yr. Second-Growth prices. Accessible but potential to age 20-odd yrs.

Carteau Côtes-Daugay St-Ém ★★ 15 16' 18 19 20 (22) Small s-facing GRAND CRU ST-ÉM. Full-flavoured, supple, gd value.

Certan de May Pom ★★★ 11 14 15' 16' 17 18 19' 20 21 22 23 Much-improved neighbour of VIEUX CH CERTAN; POM of an elegant nature.

Until 1956 French schoolchildren were served up to 0.5 litre wine each with lunch.

Chantegrive, De Grav ★★ →★★★ 15 16 18 19 20' 21 22 Leading large estate; v.gd quality, value. MERLOT/CAB SAUV red. Henri Lévêque is special selection. CUVÉE Caroline is top, *fragrant white* 20 21 22.

Chasse-Spleen Mou ★★★ 09' 10' 14 15 16' 17 18 19' 20 21 22 Well-known CH owned by Céline Villars. Often impressive, long-maturing; classical structure, fragrance. CH BRILLETTE acquired and integrated in 2023.

Chauvin St-Ém ★★ 15 16' 18' 19' 20' 21 22' GRAND CRU CLASSÉ owned by Sylvie Cazes since 2014. Constant progression. Second label: Folie de Chauvin.

Cheval Blanc St-Ém ★★★★ 09' 10' 11 12 13 14 15' 16' 17 18' 19' 20' 21 22 23 Declined classification in 2022. Superstar, easier to love than buy. Sustainable viticulture.

High CAB FR (60%). Firm, fragrant, verging on POM. Delicious young; lasts a generation. Second label (r/w): Le Petit Cheval.

Chevalier, Dom de Pe-Lé ★★★★ 05' 08 09' **10'** 12 **14 15'** 16' **17** 18' 19' 20 21 22 23 Reliable Classed Growth managed by Olivier Bernard (40th vintage: 22). Elegant, finely textured red. Impressive, complex, long-ageing white (drink early on the fruit or later for more complexity) 17' 18 **19' 20 21** 22 23. Second label (r/w): l'Esprit de Chevalier.

Cissac H-Méd ★★ 15 16' 17 **18** 19 20 (22) Large CRU BOURGEOIS Supérieur in N H-MÉD, 5th generation Vialard family. Classic CAB SAUV-led wines; structured but more fruit than in past.

Cab Fr is very old: probably Basque. Parent of Cab Sauv, Merlot, Sauv Bl.

Citran H-Méd ★★ 15 **16 18 19** 20 22 Sizeable S H-MÉD estate owned by Merlaut family (GRUAUD-LAROSE). Medium-weight, accessible.

Clarence de Haut-Brion, Le Pe-Lé ★★★ 08 09' **10'** 11 12 **14 15** 16' **17 18** 19' 20 21 22 23 Second label of CH HAUT-BRION, known as Bahans Haut-Brion until 2007. Usually MERLOT-led, same suave texture, elegance as *grand vin*. More approachable but can age.

Clarke List ★★→★★★ 14 15 **16'** 17 **18** 19 20 21 22 23 Style change from 2016; more length and precision. Renovated chai with 50 new tanks (2022). Also dry white: Le Merle Blanc du CH Clarke.

Clerc Milon Pau ★★★ 08 09 **10'** 11 12 14 15 **16'** 17 **18'** 19' 20 21 22 23 Fifth Growth owned by (MOUTON) ROTHSCHILD since 1970. Powerful but harmonious: consistent quality but prices up. Second label: Pastourelle.

Climens Bar ★★★★ 02 05 07 09' 10' 11' 12' **13' 14 15 16'** 19 22 23 Classed Growth owned by Moitry family. Concentrated, vibrant acidity; ageing potential guaranteed; bio. No 17 18 20 21 (frost). Second label: Les Cyprès (gd value). Also dry whites Asphodèle, Lilium.

Clinet Pom ★★★ **10'** 11 12 14 15 **16' 17 18** 19 20 21 22 23 Family property, well located on plateau. MERLOT-led, 20% CAB SAUV. Sumptuous, modern, to age. Also CH Lécuyer (POM).

Clos des Jacobins St-Ém ★★→★★★ 10' 12 14 **15'** 16' **18** 19 20 22 23 Côtes GRAND CRU CLASSÉ owned by Decoster family. MERLOT-led (80%), great consistency; powerful, modern style. Sister CHX La Commanderie, Candale.

Clos du Marquis St-Jul ★★→★★★ 10' 11 14 **15'** 16' **17** 18' 19' 20 21 22 23 Owned by Domaines Delon (LÉOVILLE LAS CASES, POTENSAC); gd ST-JUL character. Second label: La Petite Marquise (young vines).

Clos de l'Oratoire St-Ém ★★ **14 15** 16' **17** 18 19 20 22 23 Supple GRAND CRU CLASSÉ in von Neipperg stable; 80% MERLOT. Organic.

Clos Floridène Grav ★★ (r) 15' 16 18' **19 20** 22 (w) 19 21 **22** Dubourdieu family-owned/run. SAUV BL/SÉM from limestone, *fine modern white*; vibrant, CAB SAUV-led red. CHX DOISY-DAËNE, Haura, REYNON same stable.

Clos Fourtet St-Ém ★★★ 10' 11 14 **15' 16'** 17 18 19 20 21 22 23 PREMIER GRAND CRU CLASSÉ (B) on limestone plateau; 20 yrs Cuvelier ownership in 2022; CH Les Grands Murailles integrated same yr. Classic, stylish ST-ÉM. Consistently gd form. Second label: La Closerie de Fourtet.

Clos Haut-Peyraguey Saut ★★★ 11' 12 13 14 15 16 17 **18 19** 20 21 22 23 First Growth in Bommes. Owned by magnate Bernard Magrez (PAPE CLÉMENT, FOMBRAUGE). Harmonious wines; majority SÉM with SAUV BL; can age. Second label: Symphonie.

Clos l'Église Pom ★★★ 09' 10 14 15' **16 18** 19 20 (22) Tiny estate on edge of plateau. 80/20% MERLOT/CAB FR on clay-gravel. Seductive wines that will age. Also Poesia in ST-ÉM.

Clos Puy Arnaud Cas ★★ 14 15 16' 17 **18** 19' 20' (22) Leading CAS estate run with passion by Thierry Valette. Vibrant wines with plenty of energy, bio. CUVÉE Pervenche is for young vines.

Clos René Pom ★★ 10 11 14 15' **16 18'** 19 20 (22) MERLOT-led with a little spicy MALBEC (10%); sand and gravel soils. Classical rather than modern; reasonable value for POM.

Clotte, La St-Ém ★★→★★★ 14 15' **16'** 17 18 19' 20 21 22' 23 Much-improved ST-ÉM under Vauthier ownership (AUSONE): 22 one of best yet.

Conseillante, La Pom ★★★★ 08 09' **10'** 11 12 **14 15' 16' 17** 18 19' 20 (22) Nicolas family-owned for over 150 yrs. Some of noblest, most fragrant POM. Organic practices. Second label: Duo de Conseillante.

Corbin St-Ém ★★ 15' 16' **18 19 20** 22 Consistent, gd-value GRAND CRU CLASSÉ. Relatively accessible; mid-term ageing.

Cos d'Estournel St-Est ★★★★ 08 09' **10'** 11 12 13 **14 15' 16' 17** 18 19' 20' 21 22 23 Big Second Growth owned by Michel Reybier (COS LABORY). Refined, suave, high-scoring. Pricey SAUV BL-dominated white; now more refined. Second label (r/w): Les Pagodes de Cos. Also Goulée in MÉD.

Cos Labory St-Est ★★→★★★ 09' 10' 11 12 **14 15 16'** 18 19 20 21 22 23 Small Fifth Growth; acquired by Michel Reybier (COS D'ESTOURNEL) in 2023. Savoury and firm, usually gd value.

Coufran H-Méd ★★ 10 14 15' **16' 18** 19 20 22 Atypical: 85% MERLOT (since 20s). Supple wine, some ageing potential. Older vintages available from property.

Couhins-Lurton Pe-Lé ★★→★★★ (r) 14 15 16 **18 19** 20 22 (w) 17 **18** 19 20 **22** *Fine white*, tense, long-lived SAUV BL (100%). MERLOT-led red. Act II (r/w) for earlier drinking.

Couspaude, La St-Ém ★★★ 09' 10' **14 15 16 18 19** 20 22 GRAND CRU CLASSÉ on limestone plateau. MERLOT-led; more refined these days.

Coutet Saut ★★★ 10' 11' 12 13 14' 16 17' 18 **19'** 20 21 22 23 Classed Growth; majority SÉM. Consistently v. fine. CUVÉE Madame: v. rich, old-vine selection 97 01 03 09. Second label: La Chartreuse de Coutet. Dry white Opalie v.gd.

Couvent des Jacobins St-Ém ★★ 10 12 14 15 **16' 18 19'** 20 22 GRAND CRU CLASSÉ in town of St-Émilion. Ample but fresh. Also micro-CUVÉE Calicem.

Crabitey Grav ★★ (r) 16 18 19 **20** (22) (w) 19 20 (22) On gravelly soils of Portets. Harmonious CAB SAUV-led reds and small volume of lively 70/30% SAUV BL/ SÉM white.

Crock, Le St-Est ★★ 10 14 15 **16' 18** 19' 20 21 22 23 CRU BOURGEOIS Exceptionnel on plateau de Marbuzet. Firm, but polished, can age. Usually gd value.

Croix, La Pom ★★ 10 14 15 **16 18 19** 20 (22) Owned by NÉGOCIANT Janoueix. Rich, MERLOT-led (60%) with CABS FR/SAUV. Also HAUT-SARPE.

Cru Bourgeois – 2025 edition
The Alliance des CRUS BOURGEOIS has now stipulated entry conditions for the 2025 edition of the three-tier classification (CB, CB Supérieur, CB Exceptionnel). All candidates will have to have environmental certification – HVE level 2 or 3 (Haute Valeur Environnementale). The five vintages to be tasted will be 17–21. Dossiers needed to be deposited in autumn 2023, the tastings and examination of dossiers running through 2024, with the results released in February 2025. Also, as of 2022 all those wishing to use the CB certificate needed to present their wines in bottles that weigh no more than 390g (a reduction of 22% on the preious max weight). The classification is now organized every 5 yrs, the present 2020 edition totalling 250 classified CHX.

Croix de Gay, La Pom ★★★ 14 15 **16** 17 **18 19** 20 22 Tiny MERLOT-dominant (95%) vyd. Rich, round wines. Sister La Fleur de Gay.

Croix du Casse, La Pom ★★ 15' 16 **18 19 20** (22) Supple, early drinking. MERLOT-based (90%+), sandy/gravel soils, gd value. Second label: Les Chemins de la Croix du Casse.

Croizet-Bages Pau ★★ 10' 14 **15 16'** 18 19 20 22 23 Striving, CAB SAUV-led (58%) Fifth Growth. More consistency, but there is still room to improve. Owned by Quié family.

Cru Bourgeois Méd Three-tier classification in 2020 (CB, CB Supérieur and CB Exceptionnel). 250 CHX all told. Next edition 2025. *See* box, p.107.

Lur Saluces family has owned de Fargues since 1472. Longest continuous ownership?

Cruzelles, Les L de P ★★ 10 14 **15' 16'** 17 18 19' 20 21 22 23 Consistent, expressive, gd-value, MERLOT-led wine. Ageing potential in top yrs. Sister La Chenade.

Dalem Fron ★★ 15 16 17 **18'** 19 20 21 22 MERLOT-dominated (85%) property. Smooth, ripe, fresh. Eric Boissenot consults.

Dassault St-Ém ★★ 10 14 15 16 **18'** 19 20 22 23 Rich, modern GRAND CRU CLASSÉ on sandy soils. Dassault-owned since 1955; 70/30% MERLOT/CABS FR/SAUV. Second label: D de Dassault. Also CH La Fleur.

Dauphine, De La Fron ★★→★★★ 10' 15 16 17 **18' 19** 20 21 22 Expansion, renovation over past 20 yrs. Organic. Now more substance, finesse. Second label: Delphis. Also BX white, rosé.

Dauzac Marg ★★→★★★★ 10' 14 **15 16'** 17 18' 19 20 (22) Busy Fifth Growth at Labarde. Sustainable approach. Dense, rich, dark wines. Second label: La Bastide Dauzac. Also D de Dauzac (r/w).

Desmirail Marg ★★→★★★★ 10' 12 14 **15 16'** 18 19 20 21 22 23 Discreet Third Growth; 30 yrs of Denis Lurton ownership in 2022 (special label). Fine, delicate style.

Destieux St-Ém ★★ 10 14 15 16 18 19 20 22 GRAND CRU CLASSÉ. MERLOT-based; firm, powerful, modern. La Clémence (POM) sister.

Doisy-Daëne Bar ★★★ 10' 11' 13' 14 15' **17' 18'** 19 20 21 22 23 *Fine, sweet* but tangy BAR. Pure SÉM. L'Extravagant **17' 18'** 19' 22 intensely rich, expensive, 100% SAUV BL CUVÉE. Also dry white Doisy-Daëne SEC.

Doisy-Védrines Bar ★★★ 10' 11' 12 13 14 15' 16' 17 **18'** 19 20 22 23 *Long-term fave*; delicious, gd value; 80/20% SÉM/SAUV BL.

Dôme, Le St-Ém ★★★ 10' 14 15 **16** 17 18 19 20 Micro-wine; rich, modern, powerful. Two-thirds old-vine CAB FR, lots of new oak. Circular, Norman Foster-designed cellar (2020). Also CH Teyssier (value).

Dominique, La St-Ém ★★★ 09' 10' 14 **15 16'** 17 **18'** 19 20 21 22 GRAND CRU CLASSÉ. Rich and juicy. MERLOT-led. Visitor-friendly (with restaurant). Environmental certification. Second label: Relais de la Dominique.

Ducru-Beaucaillou St-Jul ★★★★ 08 09' **10'** 11 12 14 **15'** 16 17 18' 19' 20' 21 22 23 Outstanding Second Growth. Large estate with C19 CH. Majors in CAB SAUV (82% in 2022). Excellent form; classic cedar-scented claret for long ageing. Also La Croix Ducru-Beaucaillou.

Duhart-Milon Rothschild Pau ★★★ 08 09' 10' **12 14 15 16'** 17 18' 19' 20 21 22 23 Fourth Growth owned by LAFITE ROTHSCHILD. CAB SAUV-dominated; v. fine quality. On up and up. Also dry white BX from 2021.

Durfort-Vivens Marg ★★★ 05 08 09' 10' 14 **15' 16'** 17 18 19' 20' 21 22 23 Much-improved Second Growth; recent yrs tiptop; 90% CAB SAUV. Organic, bio. Three CUVÉES parcellaires (Les Plantes, Le Plateau, Le Hameau); La Nature (no added sulphites).

Eglise, Dom de l' Pom ★★ 10' 14 15 **16** 18 19 20 (22) Owned by BORIE-MANOUX.

MERLOT-led (95%). Clay/gravel soils of plateau. Consistent, fleshy of late. CROIX DU CASSE, TROTTEVIEILLE same stable.

Église-Clinet, L' Pom ★★★★ 05' 06 08 09' **10'** 11' 12 13 14 15' 16' **17** 18 19' 20' 21 22 23 Tiny, top-flight. Great consistency; full, concentrated, fleshy but expensive. Needs time; long ageing. Second label: La Petite Église.

Evangile, L' Pom ★★★★ 08 09' 10' 11 12 14 **15'** 16' 17 18' 19' 20' 21 22 23 Rothschild (LAFITE)-owned since 1990. MERLOT-led but more CAB FR these days (+1% CAB SAUV) and more finesse. Second label: Blason de L'Evangile.

Fargues, De Saut ★★★ 08 09' 10' 11' 13 14 **15'** 16' **17'** 18 19 20 21 22 23 RIP Alexandre de Lur Saluces. Son Philippe now at helm. Unclassified but top quality; rich, refined, age-worthy.

Faugères St-Ém ★★→★★★ 10' 14 **15** 16' 18 19' 20 22 Sizeable GRAND CRU CLASSÉ owned by Silvio Denz. Rich, bold, modern wines. Sister CHX Péby Faugères, Rocheyron, Cap de Faugères (CAS).

Ferrand, De St-Ém ★★→★★★ 09 10' 14 15 **16** 18 19 20 (22) Big GRAND CRU CLASSÉ. Investment. More CAB FR from 21 (35%): fresh, firm, expressive.

Ferrande Grav ★★ 15 16' 18 **19 20** (22) Sizeable (100 ha) property owned by Castel. Improvement; easy-going red; creamy SÉM/SAUVS BL/GR white.

Ferrière Marg ★★★ 08 09 10' 12 14 **15** 16' **17** 18 19 20 22 23 Little-known Third Growth. Organic, bio. Dark, firm, perfumed.

Feytit-Clinet Pom ★★ →★★★ 08 09' 10' 14 **15** 16' **17** 18 19' 20 22 Tiny 6-ha property in w of plateau. 90% MERLOT on clay-gravel. Top, consistent; rich, seductive. Relatively gd value.

Fieuzal Pe-Lé ★★★ (r) 09' 10' 11 14 **15** 16' 18' 19' 20 21 22 (w) 20 21 22 Classified estate. Rich, ageable, SAUV BL-led white; rich, firm red. Second label (r/w): L'Abeille de Fieuzal.

Figeac St-Ém ★★★★ 04 05' 06 07 08 **09' 10'** 12 14 **15** 16' **17** 18' 19' 20' 21 22 23 PREMIER GRAND CRU CLASSÉ (A) on a roll. Gravelly vyd with unusual 70% CABS FR/SAUV. State-of-the-art winery. Now richer, but always elegant; needs long ageing. Visitor-friendly. Second label: Petit-Figeac.

Filhot Saut ★★ 09' 10' 11' 12 13 14 15 **16** 18 19 20 22 Second Growth; SÉM/SAUV BL/MUSCADELLE blend (60/36/4%). Richer, purer in recent yrs.

Fleur Cardinale St-Ém ★★ 10' 14 15 **16' 18 19'** 20' 21 (22) GRAND CRU CLASSÉ on flying form. Ripe, unctuous, modern. Second label: Intuition. Also a little dry white BX from 21. Organic (2024).

Fleur de Boüard, La L de P ★★ →★★★ 14 15 16' 17 18 **19 20** (22) Dark, dense, modern. Special CUVÉE Le Plus: 100% MERLOT; more extreme. Visitor-friendly (restaurant, wine bar). Second label: Le Lion.

Fleur-Pétrus, La Pom ★★★★ 09' 10' 11 14 **15 16 17'** 18 19' 20' 21 22 23 J-P MOUEIX property on plateau. Sizeable (18.7 ha) for POM. MERLOT-led with unusual 3% PETIT VERDOT. Refined, long-ageing.

Château Dauzac uses dehydrated potatoes for fining so can be labelled vegan.

Fombrauge St-Ém ★★ →★★★ 09 10 14 15 **16'** 18 19 20 22 23 Substantial GRAND CRU CLASSÉ in St-Christophe-des-Bardes. Bernard Magrez-owned. Rich, dark, creamy, opulent. Magrez Fombrauge is special CUVÉE. Visitor-friendly.

Fonbadet Pau ★★ 10' 14 15 **16' 18 19'** 20' (22) Small non-classified estate; gd value, less long-lived but reliable. Second label: Harmonie.

Fonbel, De St-Ém ★★ 15 16 18 **19 20** 22 23 Consistent, juicy, fresh, gd value. Owned by Vauthier family (AUSONE) since 1971.

Fonplégade St-Ém ★★ 12 14 15 **16'** 18' 19 20' 21 22 23 American-owned (Adams), bio GRAND CRU CLASSÉ. Previously concentrated, modern; now more fruit, balance.

Fonréaud List ★★ 09' 10' 14 15 **16'** 17 **18** 19 20 21 22 23 CRU BOURGEOIS Supérieur.

CAB SAUV-led (53%); consistent, satisfying, savoury. Dry white v.gd: Le Cygne. Second label: Légende.

Fonroque St-Ém ★★★ 09' 10' 14 15 16 18 19 20' 21 22 Côtes GRAND CRU CLASSÉ nw of St-Émilion town; bio. Medium-bodied, mineral, fresh.

Fontenil Fron ★★ 10' 14 15' 16 18' 19 20 (22) Owned by Dany and MICHEL ROLLAND. Ripe, chocolatey, opulent.

Forts de Latour, Les Pau ★★★★ 05' 08 09 10 11 12 14 15 16' 17 18 19' 20 (21) (22) Second label of CH LATOUR; authentic PAU flavour in slightly lighter format; high price. Primeur sales finished; only released when deemed ready to drink (18 in 2023), but another 10 yrs often pays.

Sauv Bl originated in the Loire; related to both Chenin Bl and the Sém of Bordeaux.

Fourcas Dupré List ★★ 10' 15' 16' 17 18 19 20 22 Well-run property, fairly consistent; medium-bodied, dry, fresh. Environmental certification.

Fourcas-Hosten List ★★→★★★ 10' 15 16 17 18 19 20 22 23 Large estate owned by Hermès connections. Organic. Finesse, precision these days. Also SAUVS BL/Gr/SÉM dry white.

France, De Pe-Lé ★★ (r) 10 14 15 16' 18 19 20 22 (w) 20 21 22 Unclassified PE-LÉ owned by Thomassin family. Ripe, modern reds. Fresh and balanced 80/20% SAUV BL/SÉM. Value.

Franc Mayne St-Ém ★★ 10' 14 15 16 17 18 19' 20 22 23 Tiny GRAND CRU CLASSÉ on côtes. 100% MERLOT. Fresh, structured. Organic.

Gaby Fron ★★ 14 15 16 18 19' 20 (22) Well-sited CANON-FRON estate. MERLOT-dominated. Can age. Organic.

Gaffelière, La St-Ém ★★★ 10' 14 15 16' 17 18 19' 20 21 22 23 Previously First Growth, declined classification in 2022. Investment, improvement; part of vyd replanted. Lots of CAB FR (40%); on fine, elegant form. Long-ageing.

Garde, La Pe-Lé ★★ (r) 14 15 16' 18 19 20 (22) (w) 20 21 (22) Unclassified, owned by DOURTHE; supple, CAB SAUV/MERLOT reds. Tiny production 90/10% SAUV BL/SÉM white. Also Mosaic from different soils.

Gay, Le Pom ★★★ 10' 11 12 14 15 16 17 18' 19' 20 22 23 Neighbour of LAFLEUR. MERLOT dominant (90%). Only 1500 cases. Rich, suave with ageing potential. Second label: Manoir de Gay. Also CH La Violette.

Gazin Pom ★★★ 09 10' 11 12 14 15' 16' 18' 19' 20 22 23 Large DOM on plateau. On v.gd form; generous (90% MERLOT), long-ageing. De Bailliencourt family owners.

Gilette Saut ★★★ 86 88 89 90 96 97 99 01 Extraordinary small Preignac CH. Stores its sumptuous wines untouched in concrete vats for 18–20 yrs; c.400–500 cases/yr. Also Ch Les Justices (SAUT).

Giscours Marg ★★★ 09 10' 11 12 14 15 16' 17 18' 19' 20' 21 22 23 Substantial Third Growth. Dutch owners Albada Jelgersma family. CAB SAUV-led (60%). Full-bodied, long-ageing MARG; recent vintages on song. Second label: La Sirène de Giscours. Little BX rosé.

Glana, Du St-Jul ★★ 15 16' 17 18 19' 20 (22) Unclassified; 65/35% CAB SAUV/MERLOT. Undemanding, robust, value. Owned by Meffre family since 1961. Second label: Pavillon du Glana.

Gloria St-Jul ★★→★★★ 09' 10' 11 14 15 16' 17 18 19' 20 21 22 23 Domaines Henri Martin owner; CAB SAUV-dominant (65%). Unclassified but sells at Fourth-Growth prices; c.18,000 cases/yr. Superb form recently.

Grand Corbin-Despagne St-Ém ★★→★★★ 08 09' 10' 14 15 16' 18' 19' 20' 21 22 23 GRAND CRU CLASSÉ discerningly run by François Despagne, gd value. Aromatic now, with riper, fuller edge. Organic. Conversion to bio. Le Chemin (POM) sister estate. Second label: Petit Corbin-Despagne.

Grand Cru Classé St-Ém 2022: 71 classified; reviewed every 10 yrs (next in 2032).

Grand Mayne St-Ém ★★★ 09' 10' 14 15 16' 17 18 19' 20 21 22 23 Impressive GRAND CRU CLASSÉ on the côtes and pied de côtes. 80/20% MERLOT/CAB FR. Consistent, full-bodied, structured.

Grand-Puy Ducasse Pau ★★★ 09' 10' 12 14 15' 16' 18 19' 20 21 22 23 Fifth Growth, steady rise in quality; 60/40% CAB SAUV/MERLOT. New winery on PAU quay inaugurated in 2023. Sister to MEYNEY.

Grand-Puy-Lacoste Pau ★★★ 06 08 09' 10' 12 13 14 15' 16' 17' 18' 19' 20 22 23 Fifth Growth famous for CAB SAUV-driven (75%+) PAU to lay down; vyd in one block around CH. Second label: Lacoste Borie.

Grave à Pomerol, La Pom ★★★ 10 12 14 15 16' 17 18 19' 20 21 22 23 Small J-P MOUEIX property on gravel soils with fine clay; value for POM. MERLOT/CAB FR (85/15%). Refined; can age.

Greysac Méd ★★ 16' 17 18 19 20 (22) CRU BOURGEOIS Supérieur. Fine, fresh, consistent. MERLOT-led. Sister to HAUT CONDISSAS.

Gruaud-Larose St-Jul ★★★★ 08 09' 10' 12 14 15' 16' 17 18' 19' 20' 22' 23 One of biggest, best-loved Second Growths. Vigorous claret to age. Organic. Recent vintages on song. Second label: *Sarget de Gruaud-Larose.*

Guadet St-Ém ★★ 10 14 15 16' 18 19 20 (22) Tiny GRAND CRU CLASSÉ. Better form recently; 7th generation at helm. Bio since 2015.

Guiraud Saut ★★★ 06 07 08 09 10' 11' 13 14 15' 16' 17 19 20 22 23 Classed-Growth SAUT; organic. More SAUV BL than usual. Two dry whites: G de Guiraud, Grand Vin Blanc Sec. Second label: Petit Guiraud. Plans for a hotel in 2025.

Gurgue, La Marg ★★ 14 15 16' 18 19 20 21 22 Plenty of PETIT VERDOT (17% in 22); organic, bio. Also FERRIÈRE.

Hanteillan, D H-Méd ★★ 15 16 18 19 20 (22) Sizeable CRU BOURGEOIS at Cissac. Approx 15,000 cases. Reliable; early drinking. Second label: CH Laborde.

Haut-Bages-Libéral Pau ★★★ 08 09' 10' 14 15' 16 18 19' 20' 21 22 23 Improving Fifth Growth. CAB SAUV-led (87% in 22); organic, bio. Reasonable value. Second label: La Chapelle de Haut-Bages-Libéral.

Haut-Bailly Pe-Lé ★★★★ 08' 09' 10' 11 12 14 15' 16' 17 18' 19' 20' 21 22 23 Top-quality Classed Growth. Refined, elegant, CAB SAUV-led; 25 yrs of Wilmers family ownership in 2023. Visitor-friendly. Second label: Haut-Bailly II (previously La Parde de H-B).

Haut-Batailley Pau ★★★ 09' 10' 11 12 14 15 16' 17 18' 19' 20' 22 23 Fifth Growth owned by Cazes family (LYNCH-BAGES). On top form; vyd expanded from 22 ha to 41 ha. Second label: Verso.

Haut-Bergeron Saut ★★ 13 14 15' 16 17' 18 19 20 (22) Family-owned, 9th generation. Consistent, unclassified. Vines in SAUT, BAR. Mainly SÉM (90%). Rich, opulent and gd value.

Haut-Bergey Pe-Lé ★★→★★★ (r) 15 16' 18' 19 20' 21 22 (w) 19 20 Non-classified. Organic, bio. Rich, bold red. Fresh, SAUV BL-led dry white, CUVÉE Paul (r).

Haut-Brion Pe-Lé ★★★★ 04 05 06 07 08 09' 10' 11' 12 13 14 15' 16' 17' 18' 19' 20' 21 22 23 Only non-MÉD First Growth in list of 1855, owned by American Dillon

---

En primeur angst

What makes an en primeur campaign a success? According to the trade, the 2022 campaign was a disaster: price rises from the CHX that misjudged the market, consumers who sat on their hands. Yet the chx will say they sold everything. They did: to the NÉGOCES, who will have to fund it until they can sell it. And the amount the top chx release en primeur every yr is maybe half their total. The 22 vintage was v.gd but by no means the best ever. Just the most expensive ever. Until the next time.

family since 1935. Prince Robert de Luxembourg titular head. Eight original archives on the history of the estate. Deeply harmonious, wonderful texture; for many, top choice of all. New cellars under construction. Wine shop. A little *sumptuous dry white* (SAUV BL/SÉM) for tycoons: 18 19 20 **21 22** 23. Also La Clarté (w) from both H-B and LA MISSION HAUT-BRION. Second label: LE CLARENCE DE HAUT-BRION (previously Bahans H-B).

Haut Condissas Méd ★★★ 15 16 17 **18 19'** 20 (22) Top wine from Jean Guyon stable (Rollan-de-By, Tour Séran). Rich, exuberant, modern. MERLOT-led (60%) plus 20% PETIT VERDOT.

Haut-Marbuzet St-Est ★★→★★★ 09 10' 15 **16 17 18** 19' 20' 21 (22) Started in 1952 with 7 ha; now 70; owned by Duboscq family. Easy to love, but unclassified; 60%+ sold directly by CH. Unctuous, matured in 100% new oak. Around 30,000 cases. CAB SAUV-led. Second label: Mac Carthy.

Haut-Sarpe St-Ém ★★ 10 14 15' **16' 18** 19 20 22 GRAND CRU CLASSÉ owned by Joseph Janoueix; MERLOT/CAB FR; ripe, modern style.

Hosanna Pom ★★★★ 09 10' 11 12 **14 15 16' 17 18** 19' 20' 21 22 23 Tiny vyd in heart of plateau. Clay/gravel soils, iron-rich subsoil. MERLOT (70%), old-vine CAB FR (30%). Created by J-P MOUEIX (1999). Power, purity, balance; needs time.

Issan, D' Marg ★★★ 08 09' 10' 11 12 14 **15' 16'** 17 18' 19' 20 21 22 23 Third Growth. Fragrant, CAB SAUV-led (60%) wines that age; incl CAB FR, MALBEC, old-vine PETIT VERDOT from 2020. Second label: Blason.

Jean Faure St-Ém ★★ 10' 14 15 **16 18'** 19' 20' 22 GRAND CRU CLASSÉ on clay, sand, gravel soils. CAB FR-led (plus MALBEC); gives fresh, elegant style; bio (2023). Second label: La Réserve.

Kirwan Marg ★★★ 08 09 10' 14 **15' 16'** 18 19' 20' 21 22 Third Growth owned by Schÿler family. More freshness, finesse, charm in past 10 yrs. Visitor-friendly. Second label: Charmes de Kirwan.

Labégorce Marg ★★→★★★ 09 10' 14 **15 16'** 17 **18'** 19 20 21 22 23 Substantial unclassified property. CAB SAUV-led (50%). Considerable investment. Ripe, modern but fresh. Second label: Zédé de Labégorce.

Lafaurie-Peyraguey Saut ★★★ 07 09' 10' 11 **13 14** 15' **16'** 17 18 19 20 21 22 23 Leading Classed Growth owned by Silvio Denz. Rich, harmonious, sweet. SÉM (93%), MUSCADELLE (1%); 250g/l residual sugar in 22. Also Grand Vin Sec (dr w).

Lafite Rothschild Pau ★★★★ **05' 06** 07 08 **09'** 10' **11'** 12 13 **14 15'** 16' 17 18' 19' 20' 21 22 23 Big (112 ha) First Growth of famously elusive perfume and style, never great weight, although more dense, sleek these days. Lots of CAB SAUV (94% in 22). Great vintages need keeping for decades. Transition to organics. More affordable, approachable (MERLOT-led) Anseillan in 18 20. Second label: CARRUADES DE LAFITE. Also CHX DUHART-MILON, L'EVANGILE, RIEUSSEC.

Lafleur Pom ★★★★ 07 08 09' **10'** 11 12 13 **14 15'** 16' 17' 18' 19' 20 21 22 23 Superb but tiny; family-owned. Elegant, intense, for maturing. Expensive. Second label: *Pensées de Lafleur.* Also gd-value CH Grand Village (BX r/w).

Lafleur-Gazin Pom ★★ 14 15 **16' 17 18'** 19 20' 21 22 23 Small, gd-value J-P MOUEIX estate. 100% MERLOT. Elegant, fresh.

> Celebratory years
>
> 2022 and 2023 were celebratory vintages for a number of CHX in BX. Olivier Bernard marked his 40th vintage at DOM DE CHEVALIER, Denis Lurton his 30th at DESMIRAIL and Gérard Perse his 25th at PAVIE, all in 2022. There will be special labels at the 1st two and specially engraved bottles at the latter. Meanwhile, in 2023, it was the 40th vintage for Suntory at LAGRANGE and the 25th for the Wilmers family at HAUT-BAILLY. How time flies when you're having fun.

Lafon-Rochet St-Est ★★★ 08 09' 10' 12 14 **15' 16' 17** 18' 19 20' 21 22 23 Fourth-Growth neighbour of cos LABORY. Christophe Congé (ex-LAFITE) in charge from 2022. On gd form; firm but zesty. Environmental approach. Second label: Les Pélerins de Lafon-Rochet.

Lagrange St-Jul ★★★ 08' 09' 10' 12 14 **15' 16' 17** 18 19' 20 21 22 23 Substantial (118 ha) Third Growth; 40 yrs of Suntory ownership in 2023. Serious investment. Consistent, fresh. Plenty of CAB SAUV these days (86% in 22). Dry white Les Arums de Lagrange. Second label: Les Fiefs de Lagrange (gd value).

Latest status symbol: a watch includes pebble from Latour vineyard. Only 18 made.

Lagrange Pom ★★ 14 15' **16'** 17 **18 19 20** 21 22 Tiny, J-P MOUEIX-owned, on n edge of plateau. 100% MERLOT. Supple, round, accessible; gd value.

Lagune, La H-Méd ★★★ 09' 10' 11 12 14 **15' 16'** 17 19 20 21 22 23 Substantial Third Growth in v. s of MÉD. On gd form; fine-edged with structure, depth. Organic, bio. Second label: Moulin de La Lagune.

Lamarque, De H-Méd ★★ 10' **14 15 16** 18 19' 20 22' Medium-sized, family-owned estate. Dates back to C11. Competent, savoury, mid-term wines; value. Lots of PETIT VERDOT (14% in 22). Second label: D de Lamarque.

Lanessan H-Méd ★★ 12 14 15' **16'** 17 **18 19'** 20 22 Classic, gd-value claret from just s of ST-JUL. Part of Aussie group TWE.

Langoa Barton St-Jul ★★★ 09' 10' 11 12 14 **15' 16' 17** 18' 19' 20 21 22 23 Small Third-Growth sister CH to LÉOVILLE BARTON; CAB SAUV-led, with MERLOT, CAB FR; charm, elegance. Owned by Barton family since 1821.

Larcis Ducasse St-Ém ★★★ 08 09' 10 14 **15' 16' 17 18** 19' 20 21 22 23 PREMIER GRAND CRU CLASSÉ on top form. Wine to mature; 80% MERLOT. On-going renovation. Second label: Murmure de Larcis Ducasse.

Larmande St-Ém ★★ 10 **14** 15 **16 18' 19'** 20 22 GRAND CRU CLASSÉ in same stable as SOUTARD. Sound but lighter weight, frame; accessible. Visitor-friendly.

Laroque St-Ém ★★→★★★ 10' 14 15 **16 17** 18' 19' 20' 21 22 Large GRAND CRU CLASSÉ. 98% MERLOT. More finesse these days.

Larose-Trintaudon H-Méd ★★ **16** 18 **19' 20** (22) CRU BOURGEOIS Supérieur. Largest vyd in MÉD (202 ha). Generally for early drinking. Environmental certification. Second label: Les Hauts de Trintaudon.

Laroze St-Ém ★★ 10' 14 15 **16' 18'** 19' 20 21 22 GRAND CRU CLASSÉ on sandy-gravel soils. MERLOT-led (70%). Lighter-framed wines but fruit, balance. Second label: La Fleur Laroze. Also Lady Laroze.

Larrivet Haut-Brion Pe-Lé ★★★ (r) 09 10' 12 14 **16' 18'** 19 20 21 22 23 Unclassified; vyd expanded from 17 ha to 75 ha. Opulent, seductive red. 50/50% MERLOT/CABS SAUV/FR. Rich, creamy, SAUV BL-led *white* 20 21 22 23. Visitor-friendly. Second label (r/w): Les Demoiselles.

Lascombes Marg ★★★ 08 09 10' 11 **14 15' 16' 17** 18 19' 20 21 22 23 Large Second Growth with chequered history. Rich, dark, opulent, modern with touch of MARG perfume. Ex-Ornellaia (*see* Italy) winemaker in charge from 2023. Second label: Chevalier de Lascombes.

Latour Pau ★★★★ 03 04 **05' 06** 07 08 **09' 10' 11 12 13 14** 15' 16' 17 18' 19' 20' 21 (22) First Growth considered grandest statement of BX. Profound, intense, almost immortal in great yrs; even weaker vintages have unique taste and run for many yrs. Sustainable and organic. Ceased en primeur sales 2012; wines now only released when considered ready to drink (15 in 2023: but still better with a few more yrs). Owned by Pinault family; technical director Hélène Génin. Second label: LES FORTS DE LATOUR. *Third label: Pauillac*; even this can age 20 yrs.

Latour à Pomerol Pom ★★★ 09' 10' 12 14 **15' 16' 17** 18 19' 20 21 22 23 J-P MOUEIX property. 100% MERLOT. Consistent, well-structured wines that age. Relative value.

Latour-Martillac Pe-Lé ★★→★★★ (r) 09' 10' 14 15' 16 17 18' 19 20 21 22 23 Cru Classé owned by Kressmann family. Fresh, fragrant red. Appetizing *white* 20 21 22 23. Usually gd value. Visitor-friendly (Best of Wine Tourism awards).

Laurets, Des St-Ém ★★ 16 18 19 20 (22) Edmond de Rothschild Heritage wine. Large estate in PUISSEGUIN ST-ÉM. Supple, round, early drinking.

Laville Saut ★★ 15 16 18 19 (22) Sizeable, non-classified Preignac estate; SÉM-dominated (85%), with SAUV BL, MUSCADELLE; lush, gd-value, botrytized.

NFTs: Malartic-Lagravière sold 150 linked to magnums of 22 within an hour.

Léoville Barton St-Jul ★★★★ 05' 08 09' 10' 11 12 13 14 15' 16' 17 18' 19' 20' 21 22 23 Second Growth owned by Anglo-Irish Bartons since 1826, Lilian Barton with daughter Mélanie and son Damien now at helm. Harmonious, classic claret; CAB SAUV-dominant (83% in 22). New gravity-flow *cuverie* with 44 vats from 2022. Second label: La Rés de Léoville Barton.

Léoville Las Cases St-Jul ★★★★ 04' 05' 08 09' 10' 11' 12 13 14 15' 16' 17' 18' 19' 20' 21 22 23 Largest Léoville and original "Super Second" owned by Jean-Hubert Delon (CLOS DU MARQUIS, NÉNIN). Elegant, complex wines built for long ageing. New gravity-fed *cuvier* from 2023. Second label: Le Petit Lion.

Léoville Poyferré St-Jul ★★★★ 08 09' 10' 11' 12 13 14 15' 16' 17 18' 19' 20' 21 22 23 In Cuvelier family hands since 1920. "Super Second" level; dark, rich, spicy, long-ageing. Second label: Pavillon de Léoville Poyferré. *Ch Moulin Riche* a separate 21-ha parcel.

Lestage List ★★ 15 16' 17 18 19' 20 (22) CRU BOURGEOIS Exceptionnel; stablemate of FONRÉAUD. Firm, ripe, toasty.

Lilian Ladouys St-Est ★★ 15 16' 17 18' 19' 20 22 23 Sizeable CRU BOURGEOIS Exceptionnel. Lorenzetti family (*see* LAFON-ROCHET, PÉDESCLAUX); investment, expansion. Organic. More finesse since 2019. Second label: La Devise de Lilian.

Liversan H-Méd ★★ 15 16' 18 19 20 (22) CRU BOURGEOIS in N H-MÉD; owned by Advini group (*see* PATACHE D'AUX). Round, savoury, early drinking.

Loudenne Méd ★★ 15 16 18 19' 20 22 Large estate owned by Christophe Gouache. Landmark C17 pink-washed *chartreuse* by river. Supple 50/50% MERLOT/CAB SAUV reds; SAUV BL-led white. DERENONCOURT consults.

Louvière, La Pe-Lé ★★★ (r) 10' 14 15 16' 17 18 19 20 21 22 (w) 20 21 22 23 Vignobles André Lurton property (run by son Jacques). Excellent white (100% SAUV BL), savoury red that can age (generally CAB SAUV-led).

Lussac, De St-Ém ★★ 16 18 19 20 (22) Top estate in LUSSAC-ST-ÉM. MERLOT-led (70%). Supple red, rosé.

Lynch-Bages Pau ★★★★ 05' 08 09' 10' 11 12 13 14 15 16' 17 18 19' 20' 21 22 23 Always popular, far higher than its Fifth-Growth rank; pricier. Rich, dense CAB SAUV-led, for ageing. Owned by Cazes family. State-of-the-art winery. Second label: Echo de Lynch-Bages. *Blanc de Lynch-Bages* (gd w). Also HAUT-BATAILLEY.

Lynch-Moussas Pau ★★ 09 10' 14 15 16 18 19' 20 21 22 23 Fifth Growth owned by Castéja family (BORIE-MANOUX). Less gravitas than top PAU, but much improved.

Lyonnat St-Ém ★★ 18 19 20 (22) Sizeable LUSSAC-ST-ÉM owned by Milhade family. MERLOT-led; consistent. Also special CUVÉE Emotion.

Malartic Lagravière Pe-Lé ★★★ (r) 10 11 14 15' 16' 17 18 19' 20' 21 22 23 (w) 19 20 21 (22) Classed Growth. Loads of investment. Environmental certification. Rich, appetizing red; fresh, creamy *white* (majority SAUV BL). Visitor-friendly. Second labels (r/w), Le Comte, La Réserve.

Malescasse H-Méd ★★ 15' 16' 17 18 19 20 (22) CRU BOURGEOIS Exceptionnel. Investment, upgrade. Ripe, fleshy, polished. B&B.

Malescot St Exupéry Marg ★★★ 09' 10' 14 15' 16' 17 18' 19 20 21 (22) Third Growth. CAB SAUV, MERLOT, CAB FR, PETIT VERDOT. Ripe, fragrant, finely structured.

Malle, De Saut ★★★ 11′ 12 13 14 15′ 16′ 17′ **18 19** (22) Second Growth. Fine, medium-bodied SAUT. Second label: Les Fleurs de Malle.

Mangot St-Ém ★★ 15 **16 18** 19 20 (22) Promoted to GRAND CRU CLASSÉ 2022; vyd e of ST-ÉM; clay-limestone. MERLOT-led (85%).

Margaux, Ch Marg ★★★★ 05′ 06′ 08 09′ 10′ 11 12 13 14 15 16′ 17 18′ 19′ 20′ 21 22 23 First Growth; most seductive, fabulously perfumed, consistent, long ageing. Owned by Mentzelopoulos family (1977). CAB SAUV-dominated (92% in 22). *Grand vin* c.36% total production. Second label: Pavillon Rouge 10′ 11 **16′ 17** 18′ 20 21 22 23. Third label: Margaux du CH Margaux. *Pavillon Blanc* (100% SAUV BL) best white of MÉD 19′ 20 **21′ 22 23**.

Marojallia Marg ★★★ 15 16 17 **18′** 19′ 20 (22) Micro-CH; big, rich, un-MARG-like wines. Acquired by MARQUIS DE TERME in 2023 (so 22 last vintage).

Marquis d'Alesme Marg ★★→★★★ 15 **16** 18 19 20 (22) 23 Third Growth revived by owning Perrodo family. Upward curve since 2010. Franco-Asian *cuvier*, vyd restructured. MARG on lush side.

Marquis de Terme Marg ★★→★★★ 09′ 10′ 14 **15 16′ 17** 18′ 19′ 20 21 22 23 Fourth Growth. Investment, progression in recent yrs, but solid side of MARG. MAROJALLIA integrated 2023. Restaurant.

Maucaillou Mou ★★ 10 14 15′ **16′ 17** 18 19′ 20 21 22 23 Dourthe family-owned. Consistent and clean, medium-term wines. Visitor-friendly. Second label: Nº 2 de Maucaillou.

Mayne Lalande List ★★ 14 15 16 **18 19** 20 (22) Full, finely textured. Also Myon de l'Enclos. B&B.

Mazeyres Pom ★★ 14 15 16′ **18 19′ 20** 21 22 Lightish but consistent. Earlier-drinking, MERLOT-led, CAB FR, PETIT VERDOT. Organic, bio.

Meyney St-Est ★★→★★★ 05′ 06 08 09′ **10′** 12 14 15′ 16′ **17** 18′ 19′ 20′ 21 (22) 23 Big river-slope vyd, superb site next to MONTROSE. Structured and age-worthy; CAB SAUV-led, but lots of PETIT VERDOT; gd value. Organic conversion from 2021. Second label: Prieur de Meyney.

Mission Haut-Brion, La Pe-Lé ★★★★ **05′** 06 07 **08** 09′ **10′** 11 12 13 14 **15′** 16′ 17′ 18′ 19′ 20′ 21 22 23 Owned by DOM Clarence Dillon since 1983. Considerable investment over past 40 yrs. Consistently grand-scale, full-blooded, long-maturing. Second label: La Chapelle de la Mission. Magnificent SÉM-led white: previously Laville Haut-Brion; renamed La Mission Haut-Brion Blanc 19′ **20′** 21′ 22 23. Second label: La Clarté.

Monbousquet St-Ém ★★★ 10′ 14 **15 16′** 18 19 20 22 23 GRAND CRU CLASSÉ on sand and gravel plain. 30 yrs devotion from owner Gérard Perse (*see* PAVIE) in 2023. Concentrated, oaky, voluptuous. Last vintage of dry white BX: 20. Second label: Angélique de Monbousquet.

Monbrison Marg ★★→★★★ 10′ 14 **15′** 16 17 18 19 20 21 22 Tiny property owned by Vonderheyden family. Delicate, fragrant. H-MÉD and rosé too.

Mondotte, La St-Ém ★★★→★★★★ 09′ 10′ 11 12 14 **15′ 16** 17 18 19′ 20′ 22 23 Tiny (4.5 ha) PREMIER GRAND CRU CLASSÉ on limestone-clay plateau; 75/25% MERLOT/ CAB FR; intense, powerful. Organic. CANON-LA-GAFFELIÈRE, D'AIGULHE same stable.

New E-2-M red AOP from 2023; wines available 2025.

Montrose St-Est ★★★★ 05′ 08 **09′ 10′** 12 13 14 **15′ 16′ 17** 18′ 19′ 20′ 21 22 23 Second Growth with riverside vyd. Famed for forceful, long-ageing claret. Vintages 1979–85 were lighter. Bouygues brothers owners. Massive environmental programme: biodiversity, geothermal station, solar panels. Second label: *La Dame de Montrose*. Third label: Tertio.

Moulin du Cadet St-Ém ★★ 14 15′ **16 18′** 19′ 20′ 22 23 Tiny GRAND CRU CLASSÉ (2.85 ha) on plateau; 100% MERLOT. Structured, lithe, fresh.

Moulinet Pom ★★ 10 15 **18** 19 20 (22) Large CH for POM: 18 ha on gravelly soils. MERLOT-led (90%). Lighter style.

Moulin Haut-Laroque Fron ★★ 14 15' 16 **18' 19'** 20' 21 22 Leading FRON. MERLOT-led. Consistent, can age.

Moulin Pey-Labrie Fron ★★ 15 16 **18 19** 20' (22) MERLOT-led CANON-FRON; organic. Hubau family owners. Sturdy, can age.

Moulin St-Georges St-Ém ★★★ 10' 14 **15' 16'** 17 18' 19' 20 22 23 Lively, fresh and harmonious; gd value at this level. Same stable as AUSONE.

Mouton Rothschild Pau ★★★★ 05' 06 07 08' **09' 10'** 11 12 13 **14** 15' 16' 17' 18' 19' 20' 21 22 23 Rothschild-owned (1853). Most exotic, voluptuous of PAU First Growths; at top of game. Modern, gravity-fed *cuvier*; museum. White Aile d'Argent (SAUV BL/SÉM) now more graceful. Second label: *Le Petit Mouton*. Also D'ARMAILHAC, CLERC MILON.

Nairac Bar ★★ 09 10 11 12 13 15 16 17 **18** 22 Second Growth owned by Tari-Heeter family. Rich but fresh, SÉM-led (90%) with SAUV BL and MUSCADELLE. Second label: Esquisse de Nairac.

Nénin Pom ★★★ 08 09' **10'** 12 14 **15' 16'** 17 18' 19' 20' 21 22 23 Owned by Domaines Delon (LÉOVILLE LAS CASES); investment. Restrained but generous, ageable; 60/40% MERLOT/CAB FR. Second label: Fugue de Nénin (gd value).

Olivier Pe-Lé ★★★ (r) 10' 14 15 **16' 18** 19' 20 21' 22 23 (w) **20 21 22 23** Vast DOM. Structured red (50%+ CAB SAUV), juicy white (75% SAUV BL). Second label (r): Le Dauphin.

Ormes de Pez St-Est ★★ 08' 09' 10' 11 **14 15' 16'** 17 18' 19 20' 22 23 Owned by Cazes family (LYNCH-BAGES). Cool, classic, age-worthy. B&B.

Ormes Sorbet, Les Méd ★★ 15 16' **18** 19 **20** (22) Reliably consistent MÉD cru owned by 9th-generation Boivert family. CAB SAUV-led (65%). Elegant, gently oaked wines.

Palmer Marg ★★★★ **05'** 08 09' **10'** 11 12 13 **14** 15' 16' **17** 18' 19' 20' 21 22' 23 Third Growth on par with "Super Seconds" (occasionally Firsts). Voluptuous wine of power, complexity and much MERLOT. Thomas Duroux general manager since 2004. Philosophy and certification bio. Sells 50% en primeur, releases rest at 10 yrs (13 in 2023). Second label: *Alter Ego de Palmer*.

Pape Clément Pe-Lé ★★★★ (r) 08 09' **10'** 12 14 **15'** 16' **17** 18' 19' 20 22 23 (w) **20 21** 22 Historic estate in Bordeaux suburbs, owned by Bernard Magrez. Dense, long-ageing reds. CAB SAUV-led (56%). Tiny production of rich, oaky white. Visitor-friendly. Second label (r/w): Clémentin.

Patache d'Aux Méd ★★ 15 16' **18 19 20** (22) Sizeable CRU BOURGEOIS owned by Advini. Classic, savoury. Usually gd value.

Pavie St-Ém ★★★★ 05' 06 08 **09' 10'** 12 13 **14** 15' 16' 17 18 19' 20' 21 22 23 PREMIER GRAND CRU CLASSÉ (A). Splendidly sited on plateau and s côtes. Intense, powerful, for long ageing; recent vintages less extreme. CHX Bellevue Mondotte and PAVIE DECESSE integrated in 2022 (specially engraved bottle). Second label: Arômes de Pavie.

Bordeaux hospitality

There are plenty of new attractions in BX these days. The Cité du Vin (opened 2016) has renewed and updated its exhibitions. There are new cellars to visit at BALESTARD LA TONNELLE, LÉOVILLE BARTON and PICHON BARON (but make an appointment). Fine dining can be had at LAFAURIE-PEYRAGUEY, MARQUIS DE TERME, PAVIE and TROPLONG MONDOT, and bistro fare at FLEUR DE BOÜARD. As to accommodation, CHX Léognan and Lafaurie-Peyraguey can oblige, and there are projects in hand for hotels at D'AGASSAC and GUIRAUD in 2025/26.

Pavie Decesse St-Ém ★★★ 08 09' 10' 12 **14 15'** 16 **17** 18 19' 20' 21 Former GRAND CRU CLASSÉ now integrated into PAVIE (2022). Tight, tannic, needs time.

Pavie Macquin St-Ém ★★★ 08 09' **10 15 16' 17** 18' 19' 20' 21 22 23 PREMIER GRAND CRU CLASSÉ (B); vyd on late-ripening limestone-clay; 80% MERLOT, rest CAB FR and 2% old CAB SAUV. Sturdy, full-bodied, needs time. Second label: Les Chênes de Macquin.

Pédesclaux Pau ★★ 09 10' **14'** 15 16' 17 18 19' 20 22 23 Underachieving Fifth Growth revolutionized by owner Jacky Lorenzetti since 2009. Organic from 2022. Lighter than top PAU, but well defined.

Mature years of top châteaux can be cheaper than 22. Drinking now, no need to wait.

Petit Village Pom ★★★ 08 09' 10' **14 15'** 16' 17 18' 19 20' 22 23 Much-improved estate on plateau. Atypical 40% CABS FR and SAUV. Lots of replanting. Suave, dense, increasingly finer tannins.

Petrus ★★★★ 04 **05'** 06 07 08 **09' 10' 11'** 12 **13 14** 15' **16' 17** 18' 19' 20' 21 22 23 (Unofficial) First Growth of POM: MERLOT solo *in excelsis*. 11.5-ha vyd on blue clay produces 2500 cases of massively rich and concentrated wine for long ageing; at a price. Winemaker Olivier Berrouet (follows in the footsteps of father Jean-Claude).

Pey La Tour Bx ★★ 18 19 **20** 22 Large DOURTHE property (176 ha). Quality-driven generic BX. Three red CUVÉES: Rés du CH (MERLOT-led) top. Also rosé, dry white.

Peyrabon H-Méd ★★ 10 15 16 17 **18 19 20** (22) Savoury CRU BOURGEOIS Supérieur in N H-MÉD; owned by Casteja family (Group BCAP).

Pez, De St-Est ★★★ 09' 10' 12 14 **15' 16' 17** 18' 19' 20 21 22 23 Dense, reliable, can age; vyd in one block. Owned by ROEDERER since 1995.

Phélan Ségur St-Est ★★★ 08 09 **10'** 12 14 **15' 16' 17** 18' 19' 20 21 22 23 Reliable, top-notch, unclassified CH with Irish origins; long, supple style. Managed by Véronique Dausse. Visitor-friendly. Second label: Frank Phélan.

Pibran Pau ★★ 10' 12 14 **15 16' 17** 18' 19' 20 21 22 23 AXA property. Earlier-drinking PAU. Almost 50/50% MERLOT/CAB SAUV.

Pichon Baron Pau ★★★★ 05' 06 07 08 **09' 10'** 11 12 **14 15'** 16' 17 18' 19' 20 21 22 23 AXA-owned. Second Growth on flying form. Powerful, long-ageing PAU at a price. Upgraded *cuvier*, new visitor facility. Second labels: Les Tourelles de Longueville (approachable: more MERLOT); Les Griffons de Pichon Baron (generally CAB SAUV-dominant).

Pichon Longueville Comtesse de Lalande (Pichon Lalande) Pau ★★★★ **05'** 06 08 09' **10'** 11 12 13 **14 15' 16' 17** 18' 19' 20' 21 22 23 ROEDERER-owned Second Growth (investment). Always among top performers; long-lived wine of famous breed. More elegance, less power than neighbour PICHON BARON. More CAB SAUV in recent yrs (78% in 22, with 5% CAB FR). Second label: *Rés de la Comtesse.*

Pin, Le Pom ★★★★ 06' 07 08' 09' **10'** 11 12 **14 15** 16' **17** 18' 19' 20' 21 22 23 Original BX cult wine, owned by the Thienpont family. Only 2.8 ha. Neighbour of TROTANOY. 100% MERLOT on deep gravel and sand; almost as rich as its drinkers; prices out of sight. Ageing potential. Also L'If (ST-ÉM), L'Hêtre (CAS). Winemaker Guillaume Thienpont of VIEUX CH CERTAN.

Plince Pom ★★ 10 14 15 **16' 18 19** 20 22 23 Lighter POM on sandy soils. MERLOT-led. Oaky when young. Moreau family-owned.

Pointe, La Pom ★★ 10 12 14 15' **16' 18** 19 20 21 22 Large, well-run estate; gd value; less intensity than top POM. Also Croque-Michotte.

Poitevin Méd ★★ 15 16 17 18 **19 20** (22) CRU BOURGEOIS Supérieur. Consistent quality, value; organic (2023).

Pontet-Canet Pau ★★★★ 05' 06' 08 09' **10'** 14 15 16' **17** 18' 19' 20 21 22 23 Large, bio, Tesseron family-owned Fifth Growth. Radical improvement has seen prices soar. CAB SAUV-led (57% in 22). Ageing in barrel and amphora. Classic PAU but generous, refined.

Potensac Méd ★★→★★★ 10' 12 14 15 16' 17 18' 19' 20' 21 22 23 Firm, long-ageing wines; gd value. Usually MERLOT-led, but lots of old-vine CAB FR too. No more Chapelle de Potensac (second label) from 22.

Pouget Marg ★★ 09' 10' 14 15' 16 18 19 20 (22) Tiny Fourth-Growth sister of BOYD-CANTENAC. CAB SAUV, MERLOT, PETIT VERDOT, CAB FR. Sturdy; needs time.

Poujeaux Mou ★★ 09 10 14 15' 16' 17 18' 19 20 21 22 23 Large MOU estate. Full, robust, ageing potential. Owned by Cuvelier family (CLOS FOURTET).

What to plant post-vineyards? Olive trees, hemp, kiwis. Sign of the (climatic) times.

Premier Grand Cru Classé St-Ém 2022: 14 classified, two ranked (A) and 12 (B). *See* box, p.103.

Pressac, De St-Ém ★★ 12 14 15' 16' 17 18' 19' 20' 21 22 GRAND CRU CLASSÉ e of St-Émilion town. Ripe, full, engaging. Second label: Tour de Pressac.

Preuillac Méd ★★ 15 16 18 19' 20 (22) Savoury, structured CRU BOURGEOIS Supérieur. MERLOT-led (54%). Also Emotion, Esprit.

Prieuré-Lichine Marg ★★★ 10' 12 14 15' 16' 17 18' 19' 20' 21 22 23 Fourth Growth owned by Ballande group. Parcels in all five MARG communes. DERENONCOURT consults. Fragrant, currently on gd form. Visitor-friendly. Second label: Confidences. Also gd Le Blanc (w).

Puygueraud Bx ★★ 15' 16' 17 18' 19 20 (22) Leading CH of tiny FRANCS-CÔTES DE BX AOP. Managed by Nicolas and Cyrille Thienpont. MERLOT-led (80%); top yrs can age a bit. Also MALBEC/CAB FR-based George. A little dry white (SAUVS BL/Gr).

Quinault L'Enclos St-Ém ★★→★★★ 15 16' 17 18' 19' 20 21 22 23 Same team/owners as CHEVAL BLANC. No longer classified. MERLOT-led, but more CABS SAUV/FR these days (37% in 22); more freshness, finesse.

Quintus St-Ém ★★★ 14 15 16' 17 18' 19' 20' 22 23 Owned by Domaine Clarence Dillon (HAUT-BRION). Composed of ex-Tertre Daugay, L'Arrosée and Grand Pontet vyds; total 42 ha. Gaining in stature but expensive. Second label: Le Dragon de Quintus. Third label: St-Émilion de Quintus.

Rabaud-Promis Saut ★★→★★★ 10 11 13 14 15' 16 17' 18 19 (22) First Growth (1855). Quality, gd value. Dejean family owners.

Rahoul Grav ★★ (r) 16' 18 19 20 21 22 23 DOURTHE property; reliable, MERLOT-led red. White: gd-value, SÉM-dominated 19' 20 22.

Ramage la Batisse H-Méd ★★ 16 18 19 20 (22) CRU BOURGEOIS Supérieur owned by La Macif insurance. CAB SAUV, MERLOT, lots of PETIT VERDOT.

Rauzan-Gassies Marg ★★★ 10 14 15 16' 18 19 20' 21 22 23 Second Growth. Effort and improvement but still lacks a little finesse. Second label: Gassies. Also L'Orme in H-MÉD.

Rauzan-Ségla Marg ★★★★ 08 09' 10' 11 12 13 14 15' 16' 17 18' 19' 20' 21 22 23 Leading Second Growth; fragrant, structured; owned by Wertheimers of Chanel. CAB SAUV-led (72% in 22). Aged in 50% new barrels. Second label: Ségla (value).

Raymond-Lafon Saut ★★★ 09' 10 11' 13 14 15' 16' 17' 18 19 20 22 Unclassified SAUT, but First-Growth quality. Neighbour of YQUEM. Rich, complex, gd-value, 80% SÉM wines that age.

Rayne Vigneau, De Saut ★★★ 11' 12 13 14 15' 16' 17 18' 19' 20 21 22 23 Substantial First Growth. Suave, age-worthy (74% SÉM). Visitor-friendly. Second label: Madame de Rayne. Also SAUV BL Le Sec (dr w).

Respide Médeville Grav ★★ (r) 16 18 19 20 (22) (w) 19 20 (22) Tiny property. Same Gonet-Médeville ownership as GILETTE. Elegant red, complex *white*.

Reynon Bx ★★ Leading CADILLAC-CÔTES DE BX estate owned by Denis Dubourdieu Domaines. MERLOT-led red 18 19' 20' 22; BX white SAUV BL (DYA).

Reysson H-Méd ★★ 16 18 **19 20** 22 CRU BOURGEOIS Supérieur owned by DOURTHE. Mainly MERLOT (90%+). Consistent; rich but fragrant.

Rieussec Saut ★★★★ 09' 10' 11' 13 14 15' **16' 17 18' 19 20** First Growth with substantial vyd in Fargues, owned by (LAFITE) Rothschild. Powerful, opulent. New bottle marked with yellow crown. No longer released en primeur. Second label: Carmes de Rieussec.

Rivière, De la Fron ★★ 16' 17 18 **19 20** 21 (22) Largest (65 ha), most impressive FRON property with C16 CH. MERLOT-led, CABS SAUV/FR, MALBEC. Formerly big, tannic; now more refined. Visitor-friendly.

Roc de Cambes Bx ★★★ 09 10' 11 14 **15' 16' 17** 18 19 20 21 22 23 Undisputed leader in CÔTES DE BOURG; 80/20% MERLOT/CAB SAUV; savoury, opulent, pricey. Same Mitjavile philosophy as TERTRE ROTEBOEUF. Also DOM de Cambes.

Rochemorin, De Pe-Lé ★★ (r) 15 16 18' **19 20** (22) (w) 19 20 (22) VIGNOBLES André Lurton property (Jacques Lurton in charge). Fleshy, earlier-drinking, dark-fruit red; aromatic white (100% SAUV BL). Fairly consistent quality.

Rol Valentin St-Ém ★★ 10' 14 15' **16' 18** 19 20' 21 22 GRAND CRU CLASSÉ; MERLOT-led, CAB FR, MALBEC. Ripe, concentrated, structured.

Rouget Pom ★★ 12 14 **15 16' 18** 19 20 22 Sizeable (for POM) estate on n edge of plateau. Owned by Burgundian Labruyère family. MERLOT-led, CAB FR. Rich, powerful, unctuous. Second label: Le Carillon de Rouget.

St-Georges St-Ém ★★ 15 16 18 **19 20** (22) This vyd represents 25% of ST-GEORGES AOP. MERLOT-led (80%), with 10% each CABS FR/SAUV; gd wine sold direct to public. Second label: Puy St-Georges (100% MERLOT).

St-Pierre St-Jul ★★★ 09' 10' 11 12 **14 15' 16' 18'** 19' 20 21 22 23 Tiny Fourth Growth owned by DOMS Henri Martin (GLORIA). CAB SAUV-led (75%). Stylish, consistent, classic. Worth following.

Sales, De Pom ★★ 10' 15 16 17 **18 19' 20'** 22' Biggest vyd of POM (47.6 ha). Investment and improvement. Honest, drinkable; can age; value. Efforts in biodiversity. Second label: CH Chantalouette.

Sansonnet St-Ém ★★→★★★ 10' 12 14 15 **16' 17 18** 19' 20 21 22 Plateau-based GRAND CRU CLASSÉ. Modern but refreshing. Visitor-friendly. Second label: Envol.

Saransot-Dupré List ★★ 10' 15 16 **18 19** 20 (22) CRU BOURGEOIS Supérieur. Four BX grapes. Firm, generous. Also gd dry white Bx.

Sénéjac H-Méd ★★ 15 **16' 18 19' 20'** (22) Cru in S H-MÉD (Pian). Consistent, well balanced. Drink young or age. Sales at property.

Serre, La St-Ém ★★ 14 15 **16' 17 18'** 19' 20' 21 22 23 Small GRAND CRU CLASSÉ on plateau. Fresh, consistent, stylish wines. J-P MOUEIX exclusivity.

Sigalas Rabaud Saut ★★★ 10' 11' 12 13 14 15' 16 **17' 18** 19' 21 22 23 Tiny First Growth. 100% SÉM; *v. fragrant and lovely*. Second label: Le Lieutenant de Sigalas. Also Le 5 Sans Soufre Ajouté (no sulphur; 60g/l sugar).

Siran Marg ★★→★★★ 08 09' 10' 14 **15' 16' 17** 18' 19' 20 21 22 23 Unclassified estate in Labarde. Substance, fragrance, can age. Miailhe family-owned. Visitor-friendly (collection of wine artefacts). Second label: S de Siran.

Sweet white is now just 0.5% of production in Bordeaux. Use it or lose it.

Smith Haut Lafitte Pe-Lé ★★★★ (r) 09' 10' 11 12 **14 15'** 16' **17** 18 19' 20 21 22 23 (w) 20 **21** 22 23 Celebrated Classed Growth with spa hotel (Caudalie). White is full, ripe and sappy; red precise and generous. Own cooperage. Royal visit from Charles III in 2023. Second labels: Les Hauts de Smith (r/w) and Le Petit Haut Lafitte (r/w).

Sociando-Mallet H-Méd ★★★ 09' 10' 11 12 14 **15' 16'** 17 18 19' 20 22 Large estate; 54/42/4% MERLOT/CABS SAUV/FR. Classed-Growth quality. Wines for ageing. Second label: La Demoiselle de Sociando-Mallet. Gîte to rent.

Sours, De Bx ★★ Large property owned by Jack Ma of Alibaba fame. New range: Quarry; Les Essences de Sours.

Soutard St-Ém ★★★ 09 10 14 **15 16'** 17 18' 19' 20' 21 22 23 *Potentially excellent* GRAND CRU CLASSÉ on limestone plateau. Owner La Mondiale insurance; massive investment, making strides in recent yrs. MERLOT-led (63%). Visitor-friendly, with B&B.

An AOP Médoc white is on cards for 2025.

Suduiraut Saut ★★★★ 09 10' 11' 13 14 15' 16' 17' **18 19'** 20' 21 22 AXA property. One of v. best SAUT; 100% SÉM, luscious quality, v. consistent. Second labels: Castelnau de Suduiraut; Lions de Suduiraut (fruitier). Dry wines: VIEILLES VIGNES, Pur SÉM and entry-level Lions de Suduiraut.

Taillefer Pom ★★ 14 15 16 **18' 19** 20' (22) Claire MOUEIX at the helm. MERLOT-led (85%+). Lighter weight but refined. Usually gd value.

Talbot St-Jul ★★★ 06 09' **10'** 11 **14 15 16 17** 18 19 20 21 22 23 Substantial Fourth Growth (110 ha) in heart of AOP. Bignon Cordier family owners. Wine rich, *consummately charming, reliable.* Approachable SAUV BL-based Caillou Blanc. Second label: Connétable de Talbot (more approachable).

Tertre, Du Marg ★★★ 09' 10' 14 **15' 16'** 17 18' 19' 20 21 22 23 Fifth Growth isolated S of MARG. Fragrant (20% CAB FR), fresh (5% PETIT VERDOT) and fruity but structured wines. Eric Boissenot consults since 2018. Second label: Les Hauts du Tertre. Also Tertre Blanc VDF dry white.

Tertre Roteboeuf St-Ém ★★★★ 05' 08 09' 10' 12 14' **15' 16' 17** 18' 19 20 21 22 23 Tiny, unclassified côtes star; concentrated, exotic; 80/20% MERLOT/CAB FR. François Mitjavile's creation; frightening prices; v.gd ROC DE CAMBES.

Thieuley Bx ★★ An E-2-M supplier of consistent-quality AOP BX (r/w); run by Sylvie and Marie Courselle; oak-aged CUVÉE Francis Courselle (r/w).

Tour Blanche, La Saut ★★★ 08 09' 10' 11' 13 14 15 16' 17 **18' 19'** 20 21 22 23 Excellent First Growth; rich, bold, powerful, on sweeter end of scale; SÉM-dominant, SAUV BL, MUSCADELLE. Second label: Les Charmilles. Also dry white Duo (Sém/Sauv Bl).

Tour Carnet, La H-Méd ★★★ 08 09' 10' 14 15 **16' 18'** 19' 20 21 22 Large Fourth Growth owned by Bernard Magrez (*see* FOMBRAUGE, PAPE CLÉMENT). Concentrated, opulent. CH CARONNE STE-GEMME acquired and integrated 2022. Second label: La Mémoire de La Tour Carnet. Also a dry white BX.

Tour de By, La Méd ★★ 14 15' 16' **18** 19' 20' 21 22 23 Substantial family-run estate in N MÉD. Popular, sturdy, reliable, CAB SAUV-led (60%) wines; can age. Environmental certification.

Tour de Mons, La Marg ★★ 15' 16' **18'** 19 20 (22) CRU BOURGEOIS Supérieur owned by Perrodo family (LABÉGORCE). Upward curve; gd value.

Tour du Haut Moulin H-Méd ★★ 10 15' 16' **18** 19 20 (22) CRU BOURGEOIS in N H-MÉD; 50% CAB SAUV. Classic wines; structured, to age.

Tour du Pas St-Georges St-Ém ★★ 15 16 **18** 19 20 (22) ST-GEORGES-ST-ÉM estate owned by Delbeck family; wines made by FLEUR DE BOÜARD team since 2021. Classic style.

Tour Figeac, La St-Ém ★★ 14 15' **16' 18'** 19' 20 21 22 23 GRAND CRU CLASSÉ neighbour of FIGEAC; 60/40% MERLOT/CAB FR; fine, floral.

Tour Haut-Caussan Méd ★★ 15 16' **18** 19 20 22 Small cru owned by Courrian family; 50/50% CAB SAUV/MERLOT on clay-limestone. Consistent, value.

Tournefeuille L de P ★★ 15' **16 18** 19 20 (22) Reliable, on clay and gravel soils. MERLOT-led (67%); round, firm, fleshy.

Tour St Bonnet Méd ★★ 15 16 **18** 19 20 22 CRU BOURGEOIS at St-Christoly; MERLOT-led; ageing in large oak *foudres.* Usually value.

Tour Saint Christophe St-Ém ★★ 16 18 19 20 21 22 Promoted to GRAND CRU CLASSÉ (2022). Same Vignobles K stable as BELLEFONT-BELCIER. Also Enclos Tourmaline (POM), Le Rey (CAS).

Trois Croix, Les Fron ★★ 15 16' 18' 19' 20 22 Fine, balanced, gd-value wines from consistent producer; 80/20% MERLOT/CAB FR.

Tronquoy St-Est ★★★ 11 12 14 15' 16' 17 18' 19' 20 21 22 23 Tronquoy-Lalande to 2019 (new label; blue wax seal). MERLOT/CAB SAUV/PETIT VERDOT; consistent, satisfying.

Troplong Mondot St-Ém ★★★ 09 10 12 13 14 15' 16 17 18' 19' 20 21 22 23 PREMIER GRAND CRU CLASSÉ (B) on limestone plateau. Lots of investment; new winery, restaurant. *Wines of power, depth*; major style change from 17; more elegance, freshness. Aymeric de Gironde in charge. Second label: Mondot.

Trotanoy Pom ★★★★ 08 09' 10' 11 12 14 15' 16' 17 18' 19' 20 21 22 23 One of jewels in J-P MOUEIX crown; 100% MERLOT since 2019; dense, powerful, long-ageing.

Trottevieille St-Ém ★★★ 09' 10' 12 14 15 16' 17 18' 19' 20 22 PREMIER GRAND CRU CLASSÉ (B) owned by BORIE-MANOUX. Greater consistency; wines long, fresh, structured; 49/46/5% MERLOT/CABS FR/SAUV. New *cuvier*, cellar, tasting room. Second label: La Vieille Dame de Trottevieille.

Valandraud St-Ém ★★★★ 09' 10 11 12 14 15' 16' 17 18 19' 20 21 22 23 PREMIER GRAND CRU CLASSÉ (B). Garage wonder turned First Growth. Formerly super-concentrated; now rich, dense and balanced. Also Virginie de V, V Bl and Clos Badon Thunevin.

Vieille Cure, La Fron ★★ 15 16' 17 18' 19' 20 22 Leading FRON estate; appetizing, fruit-evident, MERLOT-led wines. Value.

Vieux Château Certan Pom ★★★★ 06 08 09' 10' 11' 12 13 14 15' 16' 17 18' 19' 20' 21 22 23 One of the great POMS. Different in style to neighbour PETRUS; *elegance, harmony, fragrance*. Plenty of old-vine CABS FR/SAUV one of reasons. Great consistency; long-ageing. Alexandre and Guillaume Thienpont in charge.

Vieux Château St-André St-Ém ★★ 16' 17 18 19 20 22 Small MERLOT-based vyd in MONTAGNE-ST-ÉM; *gd value*. Berrouet family-owned since 1979.

Villegeorge, De H-Méd ★★ 15 16 18 19 20 22 Tiny S H-MÉD owned by Marie-Laure Lurton; CAB SAUV/MERLOT/PETIT VERDOT; light but elegant wines.

Vray Croix de Gay Pom ★★★ 10 14 15 16' 17 18' 19' 20' 22 23 Tiny vyd in best part of POM (in two blocks). More finesse of late. Organic; bio practices. Same ownership as CALON SÉGUR.

Yquem Saut ★★★★ 02 03' 04 05' 06' 07 08 09' 10' 11' 13' 14 15' 16' 17' 18' 19 20 King of sweet, *liquoreux* wines. Strong, intense, luscious; kept 2 yrs in barrel. Most vintages improve for 15 yrs+, some live 100 yrs+ in transcendent splendour; 100 ha in production (75/25% SÉM/SAUV BL). No Yquem made 51 52 64 72 74 92 2012. Makes small amount (approx 830 cases) of off-dry (5g/l sugar) 75/25% Sauv Bl/Sém "Y" (pronounced "ygrec"). Yquem promoted in top restaurants by the glass, young. Owned by LVMH; Pierre Lurton CEO.

Too much wine

At one end of the scale, BX CHX are charging record prices; at the other, oversupply, financial difficulties and the threat of abandoned vines causing the spread of diseases like flavescence dorée have persuaded the Bx authorities to grub up 9500 ha of vyd. That's about 9% of the total, accounting for a spare 500,000 hl of wine each yr. Candidates for the grubbing-up scheme will receive €6000/ha (minus tax, social charges and cost of grubbing-up) and will have to let the land lie fallow or plant trees. Those who see this as a temporary measure can also diversify into another agricultural activity. Most of the grubbing-up will take place in E-2-M.

Italy

VALLE
D'AOSTA

L Maggiore

Turin ○ LOMBAR
PIEDMONT

Genoa ○

LIGURIA

Ligurian Sea

More heavily shaded areas are
the wine-growing regions.

Abbreviations used in
the text:

Ab	Abruzzo	Mol	Molise
Bas	Basilicata	Pie	Piedmont
Cal	Calabria	Pu	Puglia
Cam	Campania	Sar	Sardinia
E-R	Emilia-Romagna	Si	Sicily
FVG	Friuli Venezia Giulia	T-AA	Trentino-Alto Adige
Lat	Latium	Tus	Tuscany
Lig	Liguria	Umb	Umbria
Lom	Lombardy	VdA	Valle d'Aosta
Mar	Marches	Ven	Veneto

If you've noticed some great releases from Italy lately, you're right.
Piedmont this year is offering the 2020 Barolos and 21 Barbarescos,
Bolgheri the 21s and 22s, Veneto the 20 and 21 Amarones: all very fine
vintages crammed with age-worthy keepers.

What else have we seen lately? 2023 saw the release of the 19 Barolos
and the 20 Barbarescos, drop-dead gorgeous wines that will age well.
In short, those are two fine vintages – and if you love the best that the
Nebbiolo grape can offer, then you need to stock up with those two
wines. Tuscany has released many excellent 20 Bolgheri and Tuscan
Coast wines that are lighter in style than usual. The mostly mono-varietal
Cabernet Francs, Cabernet Sauvignons, Merlots and blends thereof will
win over many fans because of tannic frames that are much more graceful and refined than usual. And the song remains the same in Campania,
where juicy and fruity Piedirosso, Tintore di Tramonti and Aglianico
wines from the 22 vintage and the bigger-bodied 20 Riserva wines are
plentiful and fairly unforgettable. But not just reds: look in FVG for the
21 vintage, because it delivered some of Italy's best whites
in memory. And the 21 vintage was pretty special in Sicily too, where
both white and red wines will be remembered fondly for some time.

Recent vintages

Amarone, Veneto & Friuli

2023 Ven: better than expected in difficult yr. FVG: uneven; where no hail
    or downy mildew okay; better whites.
2022 Ven: dry, gd quality. FVG: v.gd quality. Better than expected.
2021 Ven: dry, v.gd quality, less quantity. FVG: v.gd quality, uneven volume.
2020 Ven: balanced, gd quality, quantity. FVG: wet June, uneven, better whites.
2019 Low quantity. Ven: gd for Amarone, Soave. FVG: fair quality.

2018 Optimal weather conditions; gd for quantity, quality, esp fresh whites.
2017 V. difficult (non-stop rain); weedy Amarones a risk, green reds in general.
2016 V. hot; round but low-acid, big reds, chunky whites.

Campania & Basilicata

2023 V. difficult: downy mildew, hail. Small crop. What escaped is gd.
2022 Cam: classic, v.gd quality (r/w). Bas: warm and classic, v.gd.
2021 Cam: balanced, gd quality, less quantity (best for r). Bas: late harvest,
    classic, v.gd.

2020 Similar to 19. Classic, balanced but lower quantity; gd (r/w).
2019 Classic, balanced. Best for Aglianico, gd for whites.
2018 Rainy, but whites fresh, lively; sleek reds (Aglianico best).
2017 Low-volume yr of reds plagued by gritty tannins. Whites flat; Greco best.
2016 Cold spring delayed flowering, hot summer allowed catch-up. Fiano best.

Marches & Abruzzo
2023 V. difficult: downy mildew; small crop; better for whites.
2022 Mar: similar to 21, uneven. Ab: dry, better than 21. Both best for red.
2021 Hot, dry late vintage, gd quality but low yields; gd for late-ripening grapes.
2020 Uneven; quality peaks; wet June, fresh weather; late-ripening grapes gd.
2019 Difficult yr. Rainy, cold spring. Low quantity, medium quality.
2018 Patchy spring. More balanced than 17; v. high volume, gd quality (r/w).
2017 Best to forget: hot, droughty. Reds gritty, whites overripe. Low volume.
2016 Rain, cold, lack of sun = difficult yr. Lemony, figgy Pecorino probably best.

Piedmont
2023 Better than expected, though still difficult. Alto Piemonte v.gd.
2022 Better than expected, uneven quantity, gd quality.
2021 Gd, despite warm dry summer; gd quality, less quantity.
2020 Classic. Slightly less balanced than 19, but elegant; better Barbera
     than Nebbiolo.
2019 Classic vintage, more balanced than 18. Lower quantity but higher quality.
2018 Despite difficult spring, potentially classic Barolo, Barbaresco.
2017 Among earliest harvests in living memory. Can lack depth.
2016 Potentially top vintage; classic, perfumed, age-worthy Barolo/Barbaresco.
Earlier fine vintages: 13 10 08 06 04 Vintages to keep: 13 10 06 04 99 96.
Vintages to drink up: 12 11 09 08 07 03 01 98 97.

Tuscany
2023 Complicated but promising, crop reduction, but gd quality.
2022 Better than expected, high quality; gd structure, acidity for Sangiovese.
2021 V.gd (even if warm, dry) mainly for Sangiovese (better: fresher sites).
2020 V.gd, but complicated. Less power, alc than 19, elegant.
2019 Maybe one of best since 2000. Classic, balanced; gd quality, quantity.
2018 Reds gd: of steely personality, age-worthiness.
2017 Hot, v. difficult vintage. Better in Chianti Classico than coastal Maremma.
2016 Hot summer, fresh autumn; success across the region. Small crop.
Earlier fine vintages: 15 11 10 08 07 06 04 01. Vintages to keep: 10 01 99.
Vintages to drink up: 09 07 06 04 03 00 97 95 90.

Abate Nero T-AA ★★★ Roberta Lunelli runs artisanal winery, devoted to sparkling TRENTO. Top: Domini, Domini Nero, RISERVA Cuvée dell'Abate. Look for Riserva Collezione dedicated to founder Luciano L.
Abrigo, Orlando Pie ★★★ Some of most mineral, steely, refined BARBARESCOS. Top: Meruzzano (and RISERVA), Montersino, CN III (100% NEBBIOLO rosé). Trés Plus (w blend CHARD/Nascetta) v.gd.
Accornero Pie ★★★ Some of Italy's best medium-bodied reds. GRIGNOLINO sings in Bricco del Bosco (steel-aged) and Bricco del Bosco Vigne Vecchie (oak-aged). Also v.gd BARBERA Cima, Bricco Battista; new red Varigi (Ruchè).
Adanti Umb ★★★ One of three best estates in Montefalco, benchmark of DOC. Top MONTEFALCO SAGRANTINO (Il Domenico, Passito); v.gd Montefalco Rosso Riserva and GRECHETTO.

Adriano, Marco e Vittorio Pie ★★★ High quality, low prices, BARBARESCO full of early appeal. Top: Basarin (also RISERVA), Sanadaive. MOSCATO D'ASTI v.gd.

Aglianico del Taburno Cam ★→★★★ DOCG Around Benevento. Generally cooler microclimate than TAURASI. Spicier notes (leather, tobacco), herbs, higher acidity than other AGLIANICOS. Best: Fontanavecchia (RISERVAS: Grave Mora, VIGNA Cataratte), La Rivolta gd.

Aglianico del Vulture Bas ★→★★★ DOC(G) 15 17' 19 20 21' DOC after 1 yr, SUPERIORE after 3 yrs, RISERVA after 5. From slopes of extinct volcano Monte Vulture. Volcanic soils with high content of clay-rich tuff. More floral (violet), dark fruits (plum), smoke, spice than other AGLIANICOS. Top: ELENA FUCCI, GRIFALCO. Mastrodomenico (Likos), Mustocarmelitano v.gd. Also gd: Basilisco, Cantine del Notaio, Donato d'Angelo, Madonna delle Grazie, PATERNOSTER, Re Manfredi.

Alba Pie Truffles, hazelnuts and PIE's, if not Italy's, most prestigious wines: Alba, BARBARESCO, BARBERA D'ALBA, BAROLO, DOLCETTO d'Alba, NEBBIOLO D'ALBA.

Alessandria, Fratelli Pie ★★★ Since 1870 top BAROLO producer in VERDUNO. Best crus: Monvigliero, Gramolere, San Lorenzo. Barolo di Verduno, Verduno Speziale v.gd.

Almondo, Giovanni Pie ★★★→★★★★ Top ROERO estate. Best: Roero ARNEIS Bricco delle Ciliegie, Rive del Bricco. Outstanding FREISA; v.gd Roero Bric Valdiana (r).

Alta Langa Pie ★★★ DOCG The 1st METODO CLASSICO made in Italy, since mid-C19 in "underground cathedrals". Vintage only, and simply CHARD, PINOT N. Best: BANFI (Aurora 100 Mesi, Cuvée Aurora), Bera, Brandini, Cascina Cerruti, COCCHI-BAVA, Colombo (Blanc de Blancs, RISERVA 60 Mesi rosé), Contratto (For England Blanc de Noirs, Millesimato), Enrico Serafino (Riserva Zero, Riserva Zero 140), ETTORE GERMANO, GANCIA, Mirafiore (Blanc de Noirs), Monsignore, Paolo Berruti, PODERI COLLA, RIZZI, ROBERTO GARBARINO.

Alto Adige (Sudtirol) T-AA DOC Mountainous region with Bolzano its chief city (Austrian until 1919); arguably best Italian whites today but also underrated reds. Germanic vines dominate. GEWURZ, KERNER, SYLVANER, but PINOT GR too. Probably world's best PINOT BIANCO. PINOT N often overoaked; *Lagrein* in gd yrs.

Alto Piemonte Pie Cradle of PIE quality in C19 (40,000 ha). Acidic soil, exposure, climate and altitude diversity, ideal for many different NEBBIOLO expressions (here called Spanna). Main DOC(G): BOCA, BRAMATERRA, Colline Novaresi, Coste della Sesia, Fara, GATTINARA, GHEMME, LESSONA, Sizzano, Valli Ossolane. Many outstanding wines. Actually, rarely 100% Nebbiolo: small additions of Croatina, Uva Rara, Vespolina common.

Ama, Castello di Tus ★★★★ Among 1st to produce single-vyd CHIANTI CLASSICO. Gran Selezione VIGNETO Bellavista best; La Casuccia close 2nd; v.gd San Lorenzo and RISERVA Montebuoni. MERLOT L'Apparita one of Italy's three best.

Amarone della Valpolicella Ven ★★→★★★★ DOCG 11' 13 15 16 18 (19) (20) (21) CLASSICO area (from historic zone), Val d'Illasi and Valpantena (from extended zone) can make unique world-class reds from raisined grapes. Alas, many less than what they should be, despite hype. Choose carefully. (*See* VALPOLICELLA, and box p.151.)

Ambra, D' Cam ★★★ On ISCHIA; fosters rare local native grapes. Best: single-vyd Frassitelli (w, 100% Biancolella). Also v.gd (w) Ischia Bianco, Biancolella and Forastera; (r) La VIGNA dei Mille Anni (blend) and Per' 'e Palummo.

Antinori, Marchesi L&P Tus ★★→★★★★ Top CHIANTI CLASSICO (TENUTE and *Badia a Passignano*), two excellent SUPER TUSCANS (TIGNANELLO, SOLAIA) and Prunotto (PIE BAROLOS). Also gd FVG (JERMANN), La Braccesca, MONTALCINO (Pian delle Vigne).

Antoniolo Pie ★★★ Age-worthy benchmark GATTINARA. Outstanding RISERVAS Le Castelle, Osso San, San Francesco.

Argiano, Tenuta di Tus ★★★→★★★★ Since 1580. High-quality BRUNELLOS (esp RISERVA, VIGNA del Suolo); trad-style Brunello and single-vyd, modern Riserva.

Argiolas Sar ★★★ Top producer, native island grapes. Outstanding crus: Iselis (Monica, Nasco), *Turriga* ★★★★, *Vermentino* di SARDEGNA (Cerdeña) and top Antonio 100 (CANNONAU PASSITO). Bovale Korem, Cannonau RISERVA Senes, Carignano del Sulcis (Cardenera, Is Solinas) and new (sp) Argiolas METODO CLASSICO (from Nuragus grapes) v.gd.

Arnaldo Rivera Pie ★★★ Starting from vintage 13, top-quality line of Terre del BAROLO co-op. Small parcels (less than 0.5 ha) in most prestigious Barolo crus. Best: Barolo Undicicomuni (blend of grapes from best vyds in 11 villages of Barolo) Bussia, Monvigliero, Rocche dell'Annunziata, Vignarionda and new Cannubi.

Asti Pie ★→★★ NV sparkler from MOSCATO Bianco grapes, inferior to MOSCATO D'ASTI. Try Bera, Cascina Fonda, Caudrina, Vignaioli di Santo Stefano.

Attimis Maniago, Conte d' FVG ★★★ One of best trad estates; standout MALVASIA, RIBOLLA, Pignolo, SCHIOPPETTINO; Tazzelenghe knockout.

Avignonesi Tus ★★★ Large bio estate. *Italy's best Vin Santo*. Top: VINO NOBILE single-vyd Grandi Annate, Poggetto di Sopra. Also gd MERLOT Desiderio.

Azelia Pie ★★★ Distinctive, elegant BAROLOS from Luigi Scavino and son Lorenzo. Some of best crus. Top: Bricco Fiasco, Cerretta, Margheria, San Rocco, RISERVA Bricco Voghera. Also v.gd BARBERA D'ALBA, LANGHE NEBBIOLO.

Azienda agricola / agraria Estate (large or small) making wine from its own grapes.

Badia a Coltibuono Tus ★★★ One of the top producers in CHIANTI CLASSICO; every wine is worth buying – great terroirs spell non-stop success. IGT SANGIOVESE v.gd. Organic.

Banfi (Castello or Villa) Tus ★★→★★★★ Giant of MONTALCINO, but top, limited-production POGGIO all'Oro is great BRUNELLO; v.gd ALTA LANGA, Moscadello.

Barbaresco Pie ★★→★★★★ DOCG 13 14 **15** 16 18 19 20 21 Often better than BAROLO, Barbaresco's lesser reputation is undeserved. When spot-on, the gracefulness, age-worthiness and perfumed intensity are like those of no other wine in Italy – the world, really. Min 26 mths' ageing, 9 mths in wood; at 4 yrs becomes RISERVA. Two main types of soil: Serravalian (alternation of sandy

---

Top Barbaresco by MGA

BARBARESCO has four distinct communes, four distinct styles: **Barbaresco** most complete, balanced. Growers incl Asili (BRUNO GIACOSA, CA' DEL BAIO, CERETTO, PRODUTTORI DEL BARBARESCO), Martinenga (MARCHESI DI GRÉSY), Montefico (Produttori del B, ROAGNA), Montestefano (Giordano Luigi, Produttori del B, Rivella Serafino), Ovello (CANTINA del Pino, ROCCA ALBINO), Pajè (Roagna); Pora (Ca' del Baio, MUSSO, Produttori del B), Rabaja (Bruno Giacosa, BRUNO ROCCA, CASTELLO DI VERDUNO, GIUSEPPE CORTESE, Produttori del B), Rio Sordo (Cascina Bruciata, Cascina delle Rose, MUSSO, Produttori del B), Roncaglie (PODERI COLLA). **Neive** most powerful, fleshiest. Albesani (Cantina del Pino, CASTELLO DI NEIVE, MASSOLINO), Basarin (ADRIANO MARCO E VITTORIO, Giacosa Fratelli, Negro Angelo, PAITIN, SOTTIMANO), Bordini (La Spinetta), Currà (Bruno Rocca, Sottimano), Gallina (Castello di Neive, Ceretto, La Spinetta, Lequio Ugo, ODDERO), Serraboella (Cigliuti, PAITIN). **San Rocco Seno d'Elvio** readiest to drink, soft. Rocche Massalupo (Lano, TENUTA Barac), Sanadaive (Adriano Marco e Vittorio). **Treiso** freshest, most refined. Bernardot (Ceretto), Bricco di Treiso (PIO CESARE), Marcarini (Ca' del Baio), Montersino (ORLANDO ABRIGO, Rocca Albino), Nervo (RIZZI), Pajoré (Rizzi, Sottimano), Rombone (Fiorenzo Nada, Luigi Oddero).

levels and grey silty marls), on average, elegant and v. perfumed wines, not too fleshy and with perhaps a lower propensity to age (mainly in San Rocco Seno d'Elvio, Treiso); Tortonian (blue-grey marls with more or less sand), v. structured wines that age (mainly in Barbaresco, Neive). (For top crus and producers, *see* box, p.126.)

Barbera d'Alba Pie DOC Unique, luscious, sultry BARBERA, quite different from D'ASTI's more nervy, higher-acid version. AZELIA (Punta), BREZZA, BURLOTTO, CAVALLOTTO (Cuculo), CLERICO DOMENICO, CORREGGIA, CONTERNO FANTINO (Vignota), CORTESE, FRATELLI REVELLO, GERMANO ETTORE (della Madre), MASSOLINO, PODERI ALDO CONTERNO (Conca Tre Pile), PODERI COLLA (Costa Bruna), ROAGNA, SOTTIMANO, TREDIBERRI, VIETTI (Scarrone VIGNA Vecchia) make benchmarks. COGNO's Pre-Phylloxera is *hors classe*.

Barbera d'Asti Pie Huge DOCG, encompassing v. different soils (from sandy to marly) and climatic characteristics. Wines vary, but usually high acidity and fruity notes. SUPERIORE: higher quality (but often overoaked). (*See also* NIZZA.) Try BERSANO, BAVA, BRAIDA, Cascina Castlet, Colle Manora, Doglia (Bosco Donne), Marchesi Alfieri, Marchesi di Gresi (Monte Colombo), Marchesi Incisa della Rocchetta, SCARPA (La Bogliona), Spertino, TENUTA Olim Bauda (Le Rocchette), *Vietti* (La Crena).

Barbera del Monferrato Superiore Pie DOCG From soils rich in limestone, full-bodied BARBERA with sharpish tannins, gd acidity. Top: ACCORNERO, Castello di Uviglie, Iuli (Barabba, Rossore).

Barolo Pie DOCG 10' 11 12 13' 15 16' 17 19' 20 21' "King of wines and wine of kings", 100% NEBBIOLO. 2000-ha zone. Must age 38 mths before release (5 yrs for RISERVA), of which 18 mths in wood. Best are age-worthy, able to join power and elegance, with alluring floral scent and sour red-cherry flavour. Now most is single vyd, but trad a blend of vyds from different communes. The concept of "cru" is replaced (in Barolo and BARBARESCO at least) by subzones known officially as MGA (menzioni geografiche aggiuntive). Currently Barolo has 11 village mentions and 170(!) additional geographical mentions. Often underrated: Village MGA ("Barolo del Comune di…") best way to understand different Barolo terroirs. Best: "di Barolo" (ROAGNA, SCARZELLO, Virna), "di Grinzane" (Canonica), "di La Morra" (Brandini, CIABOT BERTON, GIANNI GAGLIARDO, TREDIBERRI), "di Serralunga" (ETTORE GERMANO, GIOVANNI ROSSO, PALLADINO, RIVETTO), "di VERDUNO" (FRATELLI ALESSANDRIA). Three main types of soil: Messinian (chalk-sulphur formation), less interesting wines, w slope of La Morra; Serravalian (greyish yellow/red looser calcareous marl soil and sands), Castiglione Falletto (bold), Monforte (structure), Serralunga (power); Tortonian (blue-grey compact marl soil and calcareous sands, younger), Barolo (grace), La Morra (fragrance). Newcomers to follow: La Contrada di Sorano. (For top crus and producers, *see* box, p.128.)

Barone Pizzini Lom ★★★ One of top FRANCIACORTA estates. Organic. Top: Animante (also LA, Long Ageing), Naturae (Brut), RISERVA Bagnadore (Dosage Zero).

Bartoli, Marco De Si ★★★★ One of best estates in all Italy. Marco spent life promoting "real" MARSALA, and his must be tried. Top: VECCHIO SAMPERI, 20-yr-old Ventennale. Also v.gd GRILLO (Grappoli del GRILLO and sp Terzavia), ZIBIBBO (Pietranera). Outstanding sweet Zibibbo di PANTELLERIA ***Bukkuram***.

Benanti Si ★★★★ This family turned world on to ETNA Bianco SUPERIORE ***Pietramarina*** (one of Italy's best whites) and Contrada Rinazzo. Top: (r) Etna RISERVA (Rovittello, Serra della Contessa); Selezione Contrade (Cavaliere, Dafara Galluzzo, Monte Serra, Rinazzo, Calderara Sottana). Also v.gd Lamorèmio (sp, NERELLO MASCALESE), Noblesse 48 Mesi (sp, CARRICANTE).

Berlucchi, Guido Lom ★★★ Created FRANCIACORTA wine with Franco Ziliani in 1961, hence names of wines. Top: 61 Nature, 61 Nature Blanc de Blancs, 61 NV Extra Brut, Palazzo Lana Extreme RISERVA.

Bersano Pie ★★→★★★ Large volume but gd quality. BARBERA D'ASTI, BAROLO, GRIGNOLINO, NIZZA, Ruchè, all inexpensive, delightful.

Bertinga Tus ★★★ Estate in Gaiole, CHIANTI. Best: Bertinga (SANGIOVESE/MERLOT), Punta di Adine (Sangiovese), Volta (Merlot). Original.

Biondi-Santi Tus ★★★★ Invented BRUNELLO. High quality, high in acid, tannin requiring decades to develop fully.

Bio Vio Lig ★★★ Top Ponente estate, Aimone and daughter Caterina. Outstanding Pigato Bon in da Bon; v.gd Marené, Pigato Grand Père.

Bisol Ven ★★★ Owned by FERRARI's Lunelli family; quality leader in PROSECCO. Top: CARTIZZE and Relio Rive di Guia. Also v.gd Crede, Molera and Rive di Campea.

Boca Pie DOC *See* ALTO PIEMONTE. Potentially among greatest reds. NEBBIOLO (70–90%), incl up to 30% Uva Rara and/or Vespolina. Volcanic quartz porphyry soils. Highest, freshest denomination of Alto Piemonte. Needs long ageing. *Le Piane* best. Carlone Davide, Castello Conti gd.

Bolgheri Tus DOC Mid-Maremma, on w coast, cradle of many expensive SUPER TUSCANS, mainly French variety-based. Big name and excellent quality: GAJA (Ca' Marcanda), Grattamacco. Le Macchiole, MICHELE SATTA (Marianova, Piastraia), SAN GUIDO (SASSICAIA, original Super Tuscan) and ORNELLAIA (FRESCOBALDI) are best (incl iconic 100% MERLOT Masseto).

Top Barolos by MGA

Here are a few top crus and their best producers: **Bricco Boschis** (Castiglione Falletto) CAVALLOTTO (RISERVA VIGNA San Giuseppe). **Bricco delle Viole** (BAROLO) GD VAJRA, VIBERTI. **Bricco Rocche** (Castiglione Falletto) CERETTO. **Briccolina** (Serralunga) RIVETTO. **Brunate** (La Morra, Barolo) Ceretto, FRANCESCO RINALDI, GIUSEPPE RINALDI, ODDERO, VIETTI. **Bussia** (Monforte) ALDO CONTERNO (Gran Bussia e Romirasco), ARNALDO RIVERA, Ceretto, EINAUDI, GIACOMO FENOCCHIO (also Riserva 90 Dì), Oddero (Vigna Mondoca), PODERI COLLA (Dardi Le Rose). **Cannubi** (Barolo) BREZZA, Giacomo Fenocchio, LUCIANO SANDRONE, PIRA E FIGLI – CHIARA BOSCHIS, Einaudi, Virna. **Cerequio** (La Morra, Barolo) BOROLI, GAJA. **Falletto** (Serralunga) BRUNO GIACOSA (Riserva Vigna Le Rocche). **Francia** (Serralunga) GIACOMO CONTERNO (Cascina Francia and Monfortino). **Ginestra** (Monforte) CONTERNO FANTINO (Sorì Ginestra and Vigna del Gr), DOMENICO CLERICO (Ciabot Mentin). **Lazzarito** (Serralunga) ETTORE GERMANO (Riserva), GIANNI GAGLIARDO, VIETTI. **Monprivato** (Castiglione Falletto) GIUSEPPE MASCARELLO (Mauro). **Monvigliero** (VERDUNO) Arnaldo Rivera, CASTELLO DI VERDUNO, Einaudi, FRATELLI ALESSANDRIA, GB BURLOTTO, PAOLO SCAVINO, Viberti. **Mosconi** (Monforte) Conterno Fantino, Domenico Clerico, Pira e Figli – Chiara Boschis, PIO CESARE. **Ornato** (Serralunga) Pio Cesare, PALLADINO. **Ravera** (Novello) ELVIO COGNO (Bricco Pernice), GD Vajra, Vietti. **Rocche dell'Annunziata** (La Morra) Arnaldo Rivera, Paolo Scavino (Riserva), Ratti, Rocche Costamagna, TREDIBERRI. **Rocche di Castiglione** (Castiglione Falletto) BROVIA, Oddero, ROAGNA, Vietti. **Vigna Rionda** (Serralunga) Ettore Germano, GIOVANNI ROSSO, Figli Luigi Oddero, MASSOLINO VR, Oddero. **Villero** (Castiglione Falletto) Boroli, Brovia, Giacomo Fenocchio, Giuseppe Mascarello. And the Barolo of Bartolo Mascarello blends together Cannubi San Lorenzo, Ruè and Rocche dell'Annunziata. A sommelier's delight.

Borgo del Tiglio FVG ★★★→★★★★ Nicola Manferrari (one of Italy's top white-wine makers) and his son Mattia run one of best COLLIO estates. Top is Black Label collection: Collio FRIULANO RONCO della Chiesa, MALVASIA Selezione, Rosso della Centa, Studio di Bianco esp impressive.

Borgogno, Virna Pie ★★★ Family estate run by Virna B and sister Ivana. Great-value BAROLO from famous crus: Cannubi and Sarmassa. Barolo del Comune di Barolo, Barolo Noi, RISERVA, BARBERA D'ALBA v.gd.

Boroli Pie ★★★ Achille now runs this winery, devoted to BAROLOS. Best: Brunella (monopole), Cerequio, Villero. New v.gd Langhe NEBBIOLO 1661.

Bosco, Tenute Si ★★★ Small ETNA estate owned by Sofia B, high quality. Best: Etna Rosso VIGNA Vico Prephylloxera. Piano dei Daini (r/w/rosé) v.gd.

Botte Big barrel, anything from 6–250 hl, usually 20–50, trad Slavonian but increasingly of French oak. To traditionalists, ideal vessel for ageing wines without adding too much oak smell/taste.

Braida Pie ★★★ If BARBERA D'ASTI is known today, it's thanks to the Bologna family, world ambassadors for this wine. Top: Bricco dell'Uccellone, Bricco della Bigotta and Ai Suma. Montebruna v.gd. GRIGNOLINO d'Asti Limonte one of Italy's best.

Bramaterra Pie DOC Volcanic porphyry and marine deposits. Most variegated in terms of soils. Wines tend to be lighter and less massive than the other ALTO PIEMONTE denominations. Top: Antoniotti Odilio, PROPRIETÀ SPERINO.

Brezza Pie ★★★→★★★★ Organic. Certainty for those who love trad BAROLOS. Great value, from famous crus Cannubi, Castellero and Sarmassa (esp RISERVA VIGNA Bricco); v.gd BARBERA and DOLCETTO D'ALBA, LANGHE NEBBIOLO; outstanding FREISA.

Brolio, Castello di Tus ★★→★★★ Since 1141 run by Ricasoli family. (Bettino R devised the classic CHIANTI blend.) Historic estate of CHIANTI CLASSICO. Outstanding Gran Selezione offerings.

Brovia Pie ★★★→★★★★ Since 1863, classic BAROLOS in Castiglione Falletto. Organic. Top: Ca' Mia, Garblèt Sue, Rocche, Villero. After 10 yrs again iconic DOLCETTO d'ALBA Solatio. BARBERA and Dolcetto d'Alba v.gd.

Bruna Lig ★★★ Historical Pigato producer. Best: Russeghine, U Baccan. Pigato Majè v.gd.

Brunelli, Gianni Tus ★★★ Lovely refined user-friendly BRUNELLOS (top RISERVA) and Rossos from two sites: Le Chiuse di Sotto n of MONTALCINO, Podernovone to s.

Brunello di Montalcino Tus 09 10' 12 13 15' 16' 18 19' (20') (21) DOCG World-famous, but quality all over the shop. When gd, memorable and ageless, archetypal SANGIOVESE. Problems derive mostly from greedily enlarged production area (a ridiculous 2000 ha+), much less than ideal for fickle Sangiovese and world-class wines. Recent push to turn wine into a blend has been successfully stopped (thus far, at least). Generally speaking, MONTALCINO's soils vary from the limestone-rich Galestro of the n sector (wines are sleeker, more floral and mineral, generally higher acidity), to the loamier, siltier sandy clays of the s (wines broader, more powerful). (For top producers, *see* box, p.130.)

Bucci Mar ★★★★ Villa Bucci RISERVA one of Italy's ten best whites. All wines quasi-Burgundian, v. elegant, esp complex VERDICCHIOS. All age splendidly; v.gd red Pongelli. Outstanding Vintage Collection.

Burlotto, Commendatore GB Pie ★★★★ Fabio Alessandria maintains his ancestor Commander GB Burlotto's (among 1st to make/bottle BAROLO in 1880) high quality and focus. Barolo Monvigliero and superlative FREISA best. Barolos (Acclivi, Cannubi, Castelletto), VERDUNO Pelaverga also outstanding.

Bussola, Tommaso Ven ★★★★ Self-taught maker of some of the great AMARONES, RECIOTOS, RIPASSOS of our time. The great Bepi QUINTARELLI steered him; he steers his two sons. Top TB selection.

> **Best of Brunello**
>
> Any of the below provide satisfying BRUNELLO DI MONTALCINO; the top get a ★: ★ Altesino, ★ Baricci, ★ BIONDI-SANTI, Campogiovanni, ★ Canalicchio di Sopra, Canalicchio di Sotto, Caparzo, Casanova di Neri, ★ CASE BASSE, Castelgiocondo, ★ CASTELLO DI Argiano, ★ CASTELLO ROMITORIO, Castiglion del Bosco, Ciacci Piccolomini, ★ COL D'ORCIA, ★ Collemattoni, Colombini, ★ Costanti, ★ Cupano, Donatella Cinelli, ★ Franco Pacenti, ★ FULIGNI, ★ GIANNI BRUNELLI, Giodo, Il Colle, Il Marroneto, Il Paradiso di Manfredi, La Gerla, La Magia, La Poderina, ★ Le Potazzine, ★ Le Ragnaie, Le Ripi, ★ Lisini, ★ MASTROJANNI, ★ PIAN DELL'ORINO, Pieve di Santa Restituta, POGGIO ANTICO, ★ POGGIO DI SOTTO, San Filippo, ★ Salvioni, SESTA DI SOPRA, Silvio Nardi, Siro Pacenti, ★ Stella di Campalto, Talenti, ★ TENUTA IL POGGIONE, TENUTA di Sesta, Uccelliera, Val di Suga.

Ca' del Baio Pie ★★★ Family estate; best-value producer in BARBARESCO. Outstanding Asili (RISERVA too) and Pora; v.gd Autinbej, LANGHE RIES, Vallegrande.

Ca' del Bosco Lom ★★★★ Arguably Italy's best METODO CLASSICO sparkling, famous FRANCIACORTA estate owned by Zanella family and Santa Margherita Group. Outstanding and unforgettable Dosage Zéro Annamaria Clementi RISERVA (rosé too). Great Cuvée Prestige (esp Edizione RS). Vintage Collection (Dosage Zéro, Dosage Zéro Noir) practically as gd. Excellent Bx-style Maurizio Zanella (r), PINOT N, CHARD.

Cadinu, Francesco Sar ★★★ Micro size, mega quality. Top CANNONAU di SARDEGNA (Ghirada Elisi, Ghirada Fittiloghe). Mattìo (w, rare Granatza) v.gd.

Caiarossa Tus ★★★ Dutch-owned (Ch Giscours; see Bordeaux) estate, n of BOLGHERI. Excellent Caiarossa Rosso plus reds Aria, Pergolaia.

Ca' La Bionda Ven ★★★ Some of finest VALPOLICELLA. Top: AMARONE, CORVINA.

Calcagno Si ★★★→★★★★ Lilliputian size and Brobdingnagian quality from ETNA family estate. Outstanding mineral NERELLO MASCALESE reds. Arcurìa and Feudo di Mezzo top reds; plus v.gd Ginestra (w), Nireddu (r), Romice delle Sciare (rosé).

Calì, Paolo Si ★★★ Passionate Paolo C makes numerous wines highly typical of Vittoria's sandy terroir. Top: CERASUOLO DI VITTORIA, new single-vyd Forfice, Niscia, Pruvuletta; Frappato Pruvenza. NERO D'AVOLA (r), Mood (rosé/sp) v.gd.

Caluso / Erbaluce di Caluso Pie ★★→★★★ DOCG Morainic soils giving v. interesting and mineral wines. Can be still, sparkling or sweet (Caluso PASSITO). Top: FERRANDO (Cariola), Giacometto, TAPPERO MERLO (Kin, sp). Cieck (Misobolo), Favaro (Le Chiusure), Gnavi (VIGNA Crava, sp Turbante), Orsolani, San Martin (Memento), Scelte di Vite (sp), SORPASSO v.gd.

Campania Some of Italy's greatest and most age-worthy whites, terroir-driven, full of character. Reds unfortunately less consistent due to combination of overripe grapes and too much oak, with some remarkable exceptions. Few international varieties cloud native grapes panorama. FIANO DI AVELLINO may well be Italy's best white zone, TAURASI makes better and better reds. Try BENITO FERRARA, Caggiano, CANTINE Lonardo, CANTINE MAZZELLA, *Colli di Lapio*, D'AMBRA, De Angelis, Di Prisco, Fattoria La Rivolta, FEUDI DI SAN GREGORIO, Galardi, Guastaferro, I FAVATI, La Sibilla, Luigi Maffini, *Marisa Cuomo*, MASTROBERARDINO, Molettieri, Perillo, Pierlingeri, Pietracupa, QUINTODECIMO, Reale, Rocca del Principe, Sarno 1860, SORRENTINO, Terredora, Vadiaperti. MONTEVETRANO: world-class, international, mostly CAB SAUV wine.

Canalicchio di Sopra Tus ★★★★ Top-ten BRUNELLO estate. Owner Francesco Ripaccioli is a keen observer of terroir and MONTALCINO typicity. Top: Brunello

RISERVA and single-vyd (La Casaccia, Montosoli). Brunello and ROSSO DI MONTALCINO v.gd.

Cantina A cellar, winery or even a wine bar.

Capezzana, Tenuta di Tus ★★★ Organic production from noble Bonacossi family that made Carmignano's reputation. Excellent Carmignano (Trefiano, Villa di Capezzana), UCB (SANGIOVESE), Ghiaie della Furba (Bx blend). Exceptional VIN SANTO, one of Italy's five best.

Capichera Sar ★★★★ No better VERMENTINO anywhere than that of Ragnedda family. Top Capichera, Santigaìni, VT.

Caprai Umb ★★★→★★★★ MONTEFALCO leader thanks to Marco C. Top: Montefalco (25 Anni, Spinning Beauty). Collepiano (less oak), GRECHETTO Grecante, Montefalco Rosso RISERVA (smooth, elegant) v.gd.

Carema Pie ★★★ DOC 13 15 16' 18' 20' 22' Only 22 ha, n of Turin. Steep terraces, morainic agglomerate soils for light, mineral, intense, outstanding NEBBIOLO. Top: FERRANDO, MONTE MALETTO, Murajè, SORPASSO. Chiussuma, Cella Grande, Milanesio, Produttori Nebbiolo di Carema (esp RISERVA) v.gd.

Carpineti, Marco Lat ★★★ Phenomenal bio whites from little-known Bellone and GRECO Moro, Greco Giallo varieties. Benchmark Moro, and Ludum (one of Italy's best stickies).

Cartizze Ven ★★★→★★★★ DOCG At 107 ha, this PROSECCO super-cru is the 2nd-most expensive vyd land in Italy, after BAROLO; v. steep hills in heart of Valdobbiadene showcase just how great Prosecco DOCG can be. Usually on sweet side due to fully ripe grapes. Best: BISOL, Bortolomiol, Col Vetoraz, Le Colture, Merotto, NINO FRANCO, Ruggeri.

Case Basse Tus ★★★★ Gianfranco Soldera's children keep up similar lofty level of iconic BRUNELLO. Long-oak-aged. Rare, precious.

Castel de Paolis Lat ★★→★★★ One of quality-leading estates in Lat. Best: Frascati SUPERIORE, Donna Adriana (VIOGNIER/MALVASIA del Lazio).

Castel Juval, Unterortl T-AA ★★★ Distinctive, crystalline wines. Best: WEISSBURGUNDER (Himmelsleiter). RIES (Windbichel), MÜLLER-T, PINOT N v.gd.

Castell' in Villa Tus ★★★ CHIANTI CLASSICO estate in extreme sw of zone. Wines of class, trad, excellence; v. age-worthy. Top RISERVA.

Castello Romitorio Tus ★★★→★★★★ Filippo Chia produces some of BRUNELLO's sleekest, most perfumed. Top: single-vyd Filo di Seta (also RISERVA), classic Brunello. Metafisica (w blend), Romitoro (r), ROSSO DI MONTALCINO v.gd.

Caudrina Pie ★★★→★★★★ Romano Dogliotti, one of best for MOSCATO D'ASTI. Top: ASTI La Selvatica, La Galeisa. Also gd La Caudrina, NIZZA Montevenere.

Cavallotto Pie ★★★★ Organic. Solid reference for trad BAROLO, in Castiglione Falletto. Outstanding RISERVA VIGNA San Giuseppe and Riserva Vignolo, v.gd BARBERA D'ALBA SUPERIORE Vigna Cuculo, LANGHE NEBBIOLO, FREISA.

Cave Mont Blanc VdA ★★★ Quality co-op at foot of Mont Blanc, with ungrafted indigenous 60–100-yr-old Prié Bl vines. Organic. Outstanding sparkling. Top Blanc de Morgex et de la Salle Rayon and cru La Piagne (oaked), sparkling (Blanc du Blanc, Cuvée des Guides, Cuvée du Prince, X.T.).

Bussia vyd 1st appeared on a Barolo label in 1961, thanks to Beppe Colla.

Cerasuolo d'Abruzzo Ab ★ DOC DYA ROSATO version of MONTEPULCIANO D'ABRUZZO. Can be brilliant; best (by far): Cataldi Madonna (Piè delle Vigne), EMIDIO PEPE, Praesidium, TIBERIO, VALENTINI.

Cerasuolo di Vittoria Si ★★ 14 16 17 18 19 20 (21) Blend of Frappato/NERO D'AVOLA. Only SI DOCG, in se, around city of Vittoria, best terroir for Frappato. Try COS, GULFI, OCCHIPINTI ARIANNA, PAOLO CALÌ, PLANETA, Valle dell'Acate.

Ceretto Pie ★★★★ Leading organic/bio producer of BARBARESCO (Asili, Bernadot,

Gallina), BAROLO (Bricco Rocche, Brunate, Bussia, Cannubi San Lorenzo, Prapò and new Rocche di Castiglione), plus LANGHE Bianco Blange (ARNEIS). Wines now more classic, elegant.

Cerruti, Ezio Pie ★★★ Small estate in gd area for MOSCATO: best sweet Sol, naturally dried Moscato. Also v.gd Fol (dr).

Cesanese (Comune and di Affile) Lat ★→★★★ Two grapes: Comune (more common in Olevano Romano area, s of Lat), d'Affile (in Affile and Piglio). Three wines: C del Piglio, top Casale della Ioria (Torre del Piano); C di Affile, top Colline di Affile (Le Cese); Olevano Romano C, top DAMIANO CIOLLI.

Chianti Tus ★→★★★ DOCG When gd, delightfully delicious, easy-going and food-friendly fresh red. Modern-day production zone covers most of TUS; v. big differences in topography, climate and soils among various Chianti denominations. RÙFINA is only terroir of quality comparable to historic Chianti production zone (now called CHIANTI CLASSICO).

Chianti Classico Tus ★★→★★★ DOCG 15 16' 18 19' 20' 21 No wine in Italy has improved more over past 20 yrs+, now often 100% SANGIOVESE. More than 500 producers means inconsistent quality, but best are among Italy's greatest. Made in historic (high, rocky) CHIANTI production zone between Florence and Siena in nine townships. Climate varies greatly from n to s sectors, three main soil types – Alberese (whitish marls), Galestro (clay schist) and macigno (mix of sands and compacted sands) – so potentially wines are v. different from each other. From 2019, new UGA (unità geografiche aggiuntive) only for Gran Selezione (new top level, above RISERVA). (For top producers, *see* box, below.)

Ciabot Berton Pie ★★★ Marco Oberto and his wife Federica run this family estate; best-value producer of BAROLO in La Morra. Top: Barolo 1961, crus Roggeri, Rocchettevino have distinctive single-vyd characters, LANGHE NEBBIOLO and BARBERA D'ALBA.

Ciolli, Damiano Lat ★★★ One of most interesting wineries in central Italy. Best is Cirsium, 100% Cesanese d'Affile, 80-yr-old vines; v.gd Silene. New Botte 22, Trebbiano Verde (aka VERDICCHIO)/Ottonese.

Cirò Cal ★→★★★ DOC Brisk strong red from Cal's main grape, Gaglioppo, or light, fruity white from GRECO (DYA). Best: 'A Vita, Caparra & Siciliani, Ceraudo (Dattilo), IPPOLITO 1845, *Librandi*, San Francesco (RONCO dei Quattroventi), Santa Venere, VIGNA de Franco.

Classico Term for wines from a restricted, usually historic and superior-quality area within limits of a commercially expanded DOC. *See* CHIANTI CLASSICO, SOAVE, VALPOLICELLA, VERDICCHIO DEI CASTELLI DI JESI, numerous others.

Clerico, Domenico Pie ★★★→★★★★ Influential BAROLO innovator, modernist producer of Monforte d'ALBA, esp crus Ginestra (Ciabot Mentin, Pajana), Mosconi (Percristina only in best vintages). BARBERA D'ALBA (Trevigne), Barolo Aeroplanservaj (from Baudana cru), LANGHE NEBBIOLO (Capisme-e) v.gd.

Who makes really good Chianti Classico?

CHIANTI CLASSICO is a large zone with hundreds of producers, so picking the best is tricky. Top get a ★: ★ AMA, ★ BADIA A COLTIBUONO, BROLIO, Castellare di Castellina, CASTELL' IN VILLA, ★ CASTELLO DI MONSANTO, ★ CASTELLO DI VOLPAIA, ★ FELSINA, ★ FONTODI, ★ I Fabbri, ★ ISOLE E OLENA, ★ Le Cinciole, ★ Monteraponi, NITTARDI, Nozzole, Palazzino, Poggerino, Poggiopiano, ★ QUERCIABELLA, Rampolla, RIECINE, Rocca di Castagnoli, ★ Rocca di Montegrossi, Ruffino, San Fabiano Calcinaia, SAN FELICE, ★ SAN GIUSTO A RENTENNANO, Tenuta Perano – FRESCOBALDI, ★ Vecchie Terre di Montefili, ★ Villa Calcinaia, ★ Villa La Rosa, Viticcio.

Clivi, I FVG ★★★ Wealth of old vines (in FRIULI COLLI ORIENTALI and COLLIO), even up to 90 yrs of age. Some of FVG's purest, most age-worthy and mineral wines, ranking with Italy's best whites. Top: MALVASIA and FRIULANO cru wines and also an outstanding dry VERDUZZO.

Cocchi-Bava Pie ★★★ Since 1891 producer of vermouth. Top Cocchi: ALTA LANGA (Pas Dosé, Toto Corde), Vermouth Storico di Torino and Extra Dry. Bava: BARBERA D'ASTI Stradivario, BAROLO Scarrone, NIZZA Piano Alto, Serre di San Pietro (NEBBIOLO), Ruchè.

Cogno, Elvio Pie ★★★★ Top estate; super-classy, austere, elegant BAROLOS from Ravera cru. Best: Bricco Pernice, Ravera, RISERVA VIGNA Elena (NEBBIOLO Rosé clone). Anas-Cëtta (100% Nascetta), BARBERA D'ALBA Bricco Merli, Barolo Cascina Nuova v.gd.

Col d'Orcia Tus ★★★ Top-quality MONTALCINO estate (3rd-largest) owned by Francesco Marone Cinzano. Best: BRUNELLO RISERVA POGGIO al Vento, Brunello Nastagio. BRUNELLO, GHIAIE BIANCHE (CHARD), Moscadello di Montalcino v.gd.

Colla, Poderi Pie ★★★★ Family-run winery based on experience of Beppe Colla. Classic, trad, age-worthy. Top: BARBARESCO Roncaglie, BAROLO Bussia, LANGHE Bricco del Drago, new RISERVA Beppe Colla and Bonmè (vermouth). ALTA LANGA Pietro Colla, NEBBIOLO D'ALBA, PINOT NERO, RIES v.gd.

Colli = hills; singular: colle. **Colline** (singular collina) = smaller hills. *See also* COLLIO, POGGIO.

Colli di Lapio Cam ★★★ Clelia Romano's estate is Italy's **best Fiano** producer. Outstanding FIANO Clelia. GRECO DI TUFO, TAURASI Andrea v.gd.

Colli di Luni Lig, Tus ★★→★★★★ DOC nr Spezia. VERMENTINO, Albarola whites; SANGIOVESE-based reds easy to drink, charming. Top: Giacomelli, Il Monticello, La Baia del Sole, Linero, LUNAE, Ottaviano Lambruschi.

Collio FVG ★★→★★★★ DOC Famous white denomination, unfortunately moved steadily to nonsensical Collio Bianco blend rather than highlight terroir differences of its communes, incl coolish San Floriano and Dolegna, warmer Capriva. Happily, Collio boasts glut of talented producers: BORGO DEL TIGLIO, Castello di Spessa, Gradis'Ciutta, Gravner, La Castellada, Livon, Marco Felluga, Podversic, Primosic, Princic, **Radikon**, Renato Keber, RONCO dei Tassi, RUSSIZ SUPERIORE, **Schiopetto**, Venica & Venica, VILLA RUSSIZ.

Colterenzio CS / Schreckbichl T-AA ★★★ Cornaiano-based main player among ALTO ADIGE co-ops. Top whites (Lafoa SAUV BL and CHARD, PINOT BIANCOS Berg and LR) and Lafoa reds (CAB SAUV, PINOT N). Cru range v.gd.

Conegliano Valdobbiadene Ven ★→★★ DOCG DYA Name for top PROSECCO: may be used separately or together. Extremely steep hills; quality should be better.

Conterno, Aldo Pie ★★★★ Top estate of Monforte d'ALBA, 25 ha for only 80,000 bottles of highest quality. Top BAROLOS Cicala, Colonello, Granbussia and esp Romirasco; Bussiador CHARD. BARBERA D'ALBA, LANGHE NEBBIOLO, Quartetto (r blend) v.gd.

Conterno, Giacomo Pie ★★★★ Monfortino – one of best wines of Italy. Outstanding BARBERAS, BAROLOS. Owns Nervi in GATTINARA.

Conterno Fantino Pie ★★★→★★★★ Organic. One of top producers of excellent modern-style BAROLO crus at Monforte: Castelletto (VIGNA Pressenda), Ginestra (Sorì Ginestra, Vigna del Gris), Mosconi (Vigna Ped). Ginestrino, iconic Monprà (NEBBIOLO/BARBERA blend) gd; Bastia CHARD (one of PIE's best).

Contini Sar ★★★ Benchmark VERNACCIA DI ORISTANO, oxidative-styled whites (like dry Sherry). Antico Gregori one of Italy's best whites. Amazing Flor 22 and RISERVA; gd I Giganti (r).

Contrada di Sorano, La Pie ★★→★★★ Micro-size and mega-quality estate. Top: BAROLO, FAVORITA, LANGHE NEBBIOLO.

ITALY

Cornelissen, Frank Si ★★★★ One of ETNA's top producers, esp for red. Practically all crus outstanding. Don't miss Magma (from vyd at 910m/2986ft, planted in 1910), usually SI's most expensive wine, and Munjebel crus CS, SC, Cuvée VA (r/w) and Perpetuum (using perpetual solera).

Corincino, Fattoria Mar ★★★ Organic, trad estate now run by Valerio Canestrari (Lucio's son), specialist in VERDICCHIO DEI CASTELLI DI JESI. Top: Cenobita, Gaiospino (also Fumè), Stracacio, Stragaio (also Fumè). Coroncino, Il Bacco v.gd.

Correggia, Matteo Pie ★★★ Organic. Leading producer of ROERO (RISERVA Rochè d'Ampsej, Val dei Preti), Roero ARNEIS, plus BARBERA D'ALBA (Marun) and Roero Arneis Val dei Preti (aged 6 yrs).

Cretes, Les VdA ★★★ Costantino Charrère is father of modern VALLE D'AOSTA viticulture, he saved many forgotten varieties. Outstanding *Petite Arvine*, incl Rebàn Pas Dosé; Cuvée Bois CHARD (one of Italy's best), Fumin, Neige d'Or (w blend), Torrette.

Cristo di Campobello, Baglio del Si ★★→★★★ Bonetta family estate just e of Agrigento. Top: Grillo La Luci, NERO D'AVOLA Lu Patri. Solid wines.

Crotta di Vegneron, La VdA ★★→★★★ Quality co-op in Chambave. Top La Griffe des Lions line (Fumin, Nus MALVOISIE); v.gd Chambave MUSCAT Attente, Chambave Superieur and sparkling range Quatremillemètres Vins d'Altitude.

CS (cantina sociale) Cooperative winery.

Cuomo, Marisa Cam ★★★ Fiorduva is *one of Italy's greatest whites*; v.gd red RISERVAS (Furore, Ravello), Furore (r/w), Ravello (r/w).

Custodi delle Vigne dell'Etna, I Si ★★★→★★★★ Estate run by Mario Paoluzi. Member of consortium I VIGNERI. Outstanding ETNA (r) Aetneus, RISERVA Saeculare; (w) Contrada Caselle. Etna whites (Ante, Contrada Muganazzi) and rosé v.gd.

Dal Forno Romano Ven ★★★★ VALPOLICELLA, AMARONE, RECIOTO (latter not identified as such any more) v. high quality; vyds outside CLASSICO zone but wines great.

Derthona Pie ★→★★★ Wine from Timorasso grapes grown only in COLLI Tortonesi. One of Italy's most *interesting whites*, like v. dry RIES from Rheinhessen (*see* Germany). Best: Boveri Giacomo (Piazzera, Lacrime del Bricco), La Colombera (Il Montino), Mariotto (Pitasso), Ricci, ROAGNA (Montemarzino), VIGNETI MASSA, VIETTI.

Di Barrò VdA ★★★ Small family estate, top quality from typical VDA grapes. Best: (r) Mayolet, Torrette Sup (Ostro), (w) Petite ARVINE.

DOC / DOCG Quality wine designation: *see* box, p.153.

Dogliani Pie ★→★★★ DOCG Varietal DOLCETTO. Some to drink young, some for moderate ageing. Chionetti, Clavesana, EINAUDI, Pecchenino, TREDIBERRI, Versio all gd.

Summit of Etna

Some of Italy's most exciting wines come from this famous volcano. Vines grow up to 1000m (3281ft) on SI's e coast. *Contrada* is Si's way to express cru: differences in soil, altitude and age of lava flows. Of Etna's 133 *contrade*, the greatest number are in Castiglione di Sicilia (46), Randazzo (25) and Linguaglossa (10). Following producers make gd to great wine (top get a ★): Alberelli di Giodo, ★ BENANTI, Calabretta, ★ CALCAGNO, Cottanera, Cusumano Alta Mora, DONNAFUGATA, ★ FRANK CORNELISSEN, ★ GIROLAMO RUSSO, Graci (Arcuria, Feudo di Mezzo), ★ GULFI, ★ I CUSTODI DELL'ETNA, ★ I VIGNERI, PALMENTO COSTANZO, ★ PIETRADOLCE, TASCA D'ALMERITA, TENUTE BOSCO (VIGNA Vico), ★ TENUTA DI FESSINA, ★ TENUTA DELLE TERRE NERE, Statella (Pignatùni Vecchie Vigne), Tornatore (Pietrarizzo, Trimarchisa), ★ VINI FRANCHETTI.

Donnafugata Si ★★→★★★ Classy range incl: (r) ETNA Rosso (Contrada Fragore, Marchesa, Sul Vulcano), Mille e Una Notte, Tancredi; (w) Chiaranda, Lighea. MOSCATO PASSITO di PANTELLERIA Ben Ryé v. fine.

Due Terre, Le FVG ★★★ Small family-run FRIULI COLLI ORIENTALI estate. Top: Sacrisassi Rosso (SCHIOPPETTINO/REFOSCO). MERLOT, Sacrisassi Bianco (w) v.gd.

Einaudi, Luigi Pie ★★★ Founded late C19 by ex-president of Italy, 52-ha estate in DOGLIANI. Solid BAROLOS from Bussia, Cannubi, Monvigliero, Terlo and new Villero. Barolo Ludo, Dogliani from VIGNA Tecc v.gd.

Etna has some of oldest ungrafted vines in Italy: c.140 years old.

Enoteca Wine library; also shop or restaurant with ambitious wine list. There is a national enoteca at the *fortezza* in Siena.

Etna Si ★★→★★★ DOC (r) 14' 15 16' 17 19' 20 21 (22) Remarkable development; 900 ha on n slopes, high-altitude, volcanic soils. Etna Rosso typically 90/10% blend of NERELLOS MASCALESE/Cappuccio, while Etna Bianco can be pure CARRICANTE or incl CATARATTOS Comune or Lucido. (*See also* box, p.134.)

Favati, I Cam ★★★ Rosanna Petrozziello runs this high-quality family winery. Top: Etichetta Bianca (white label) range (FIANO, GRECO, TAURASI).

Fay Lom ★★★ Run by Fay family in VALTELLINA since 1971. Alpine wines. Top: SFORZATO (RONCO del Picchio), Valgella (Carteria RISERVA, Il Glicine).

Felline Pug ★★★→★★★★ Gregory Perucci was pioneer in rediscovery of PRIMITIVO and Susumaniello vines. Top: PRIMITIVO DI MANDURIA (Cuvée Anniversario, Dunico, Giravolta, ZIN). Edmond Dantès 24 Mesi (sp VERMENTINO), Sum (Susumaniello), Pietraluna (NEGROAMARO), Verdeca (w) v.gd.

Felluga, Livio FVG ★★★→★★★★ Consistently fine, age-worthy FRIULI COLLI ORIENTALI, esp blends Abbazia di Rosazzo and Terre Alte; Bianco Illivio, FRIULANO (esp cru Sigar), *Pinot Gr* (esp cru Curubella), SAUV BL Potentilla; MERLOT/REFOSCO blend Sossó; PICOLIT (Italy's best?).

Felsina Tus ★★★ CHIANTI CLASSICO estate of distinction in se of zone. Best (100% SANGIOVESE): Gran Selezione Colonia, classic RISERVA Rancia and IGT Fontalloro.

Fenocchio, Giacomo Pie ★★★→★★★★ Small but outstanding Monforte d'ALBA-based BAROLO cellar; trad style. Crus: Bussia (also RISERVA 90 Dì), Cannubi, Catsellero, Villero. Outstanding FREISA, one of Italy's 2–3 best.

Ferrando Pie ★★★→★★★★ Historic, iconic producer of outstanding Caluso Cariola (one of best), CAREMA Black Label. Also v.gd C White Label.

Ferrara, Benito Cam ★★★ Maybe Italy's best GRECO DI TUFO producer (Terra d'Uva, VIGNA Cicogna). Talent shows in excellent TAURASI (Vigna Quattro Confini).

Ferrari – Tenute Lunelli T-AA ★★★★ TRENTO maker of one of two best Italian METODO CLASSICOS. Outstanding Giulio Ferrari (RISERVA del Fondatore, Rosé and new Selezione 2004) and Riserva Bruno Lunelli 2006 (2nd vintage since 1995); v.gd CHARD-based Brut Riserva Lunelli, Perlè Bianco (gd value), Perlè Zero, PINOT N-based Perlè Nero. TENUTE Lunelli: Castelbuono (MONTEFALCO) Umb, Margon T-AA (Chard, Pinot N), Podernuovo Tus.

Fessina, Tenuta di Si ★★★→★★★★ Jacopo Maniaci continues Silvia Maestrelli's path, in one of youngest and best ETNA estates. Elegant wines. Best: EB A' Puddara (w), Il Musmeci (r/w) and new red Il Musmeci RISERVA Speciale RS (dedicated to Roberto and Silvia). Erse Moscamento 1911 (r) v.gd.

Feudi di San Gregorio Cam ★★★ Much-hyped CAM producer, with DOCGS FIANO DI AVELLINO (Pietracalda, RISERVA *Campanaro*), GRECO DI TUFO Cutizzi, TAURASI Riserva Piano di Montevergine. Look for *FeudiStudi* range (most expressive vyds, selected every yr among 700 sites) and Storie Feudi line.

Feudo di San Maurizio VdA ★★★★ Outstanding wines from rare native grapes CORNALIN, Mayolet and Vuillermin; last two rank among Italy's greatest reds.

Try (r) Torrette (and SUPERIORE) and Ch de Sarre (NEBBIOLO); (w) GEWURZ and Petite ARVINE.

Feudo Montoni Si ★★★★ Exceptional estate in upland E SI. Best: NERO D'AVOLA Lagnusa, Vrucara; v.gd CATARRATTO del Masso (w), GRILLO della Timpa (w), Perricone del Core (r), PASSITO Bianco (sw). Authentic wines.

Fiano di Avellino Cam ★★→★★★★ DOCG 16 18 19' 20 21 Can be either steely (most typical) or lush. Best: Cantina del Barone, Ciro Picariello, COLLI DI LAPIO, Di Prisco, FEUDI SAN GREGORIO, I FAVATI, MASTROBERARDINO, Pietracupa, Rocca del Principe, QUINTODECIMO, TENUTA Sarno, TRAERTE (Vadiaperti).

Fino, Gianfranco Pug ★★★★ Greatest PRIMITIVO, from old, low-yielding bush vines. Outstanding Es among Italy's top 20 reds and Es Selezione Red Label. Jo (NEGROAMARO), Se (Primitivo) v.gd.

Florio Si ★★→★★★★ Historic quality maker of MARSALA. Specialist in Marsala Vergine Secco. Best: RISERVA Donna Franca, Targa; v.gd Baglio Florio.

Fongaro Ven ★★★★ Classic-method Lessini Durello (100% Durella). High quality, even higher acidity, age-worthy. Top: RISERVAS (Brut, Pas Dosé). Pas Dosé v.gd.

Fonterutoli Tus ★★★ Historic CHIANTI CLASSICO estate of Mazzei family at Castellina. Characterful wines. Notable Chianti Classico Gran Selezione: Badiola, Castello Fonterutoli, Vicoregio 36 and outstanding Ipsus (Caggio vyd). IGT Siepi (SANGIOVESE/MERLOT). Also owns Tenuta di Belguardo (Maremma), Zisola (SI).

Fontodi Tus ★★★★ One of v. best CHIANTI CLASSICOS. Top: Flaccianello (100% SANGIOVESE); Gran Selezione VIGNA del Sorbo and San Leolino; Filetta di Lamole. IGT SYRAH Case Via among best of that variety in TUS.

Foradori T-AA ★★★ Much-loved Elisabetta F is "lady of Trentino wine" making outstanding *Teroldego* but lovely macerated, amphora-aged Incrocio Manzoni and Nosiola. Look for TEROLDEGO Morei and Sgarzon (also amphora-aged Cilindrica), Nosiola Fontanasanta (w). Top remains TEROLDEGO-based Granato.

With frico (cheese pie from Friuli) drink Friulano.

Franchetti, Vini Si ★★★→★★★★ ETNA estate (former Passopisciaro) run by Franchetti (*see* TENUTA DI TRINORO), contributor to fame of Etna. Outstanding Rosso Franchetti (PETIT VERDOT/Cesanese d'Affile) and NERELLO MASCALESE single *contrada*. Best: Contrada C, Contrada G, Contrada S; v.gd Contrada R. New Contrada PC (CHARD).

Franciacorta Lom ★★→★★★★ DOCG Italy's zone for top-quality METODO CLASSICO fizz. Soils extremely complex (50+ different types). Two large sectors: e generally most elegant, freshest wines; w generally broadest, richest. Top: BARONE PIZZINI, CA' DEL BOSCO, Cavalleri, MOSNEL, TERRA MORETTI (Bellavista, Contadi Castaldi), UBERTI, VILLA, VILLA CRESPIA. Also v.gd: Ca' del Vent, Cola-Battista (Extra Brut, Millesimato Dosaggio Zero), Majolini, Monte Rossa, Ricci Curbastro.

Frascole Tus ★★→★★★★ Most n winery of most n CHIANTI RÙFINA zone, small estate run organically by Enrico Lippi. Top: Chianti Rùfina, VIN SANTO

Frescobaldi Tus ★★ ·★★★★ Ancient noble family, leading CHIANTI RÙFINA pioneer at NIPOZZANO estate (look for ★★★ **Montesodi**), also BRUNELLO from Castelgiocondo estate, MONTALCINO. Sole owner of LUCE estate (Montalcino), ORNELLAIA (BOLGHERI), TENUTA Perano (top: CHIANTI CLASSICO Gran Selezione Rialzi). Also vyds in COLLIO (Attems), Maremma (Ammiraglia), Montespertoli (Castiglioni), Gorgona Island (state prison).

Friuli Colli Orientali FVG ★★→★★★★ DOC 15 16 20 21 (was COLLI Orientali del Friuli) Hilly area of FVG next to COLLIO. Unlike latter, not just whites, but outstanding reds and v.gd stickies from likes of red Pignolo, SCHIOPPETTINO, Tazzelenghe and white PICOLIT, VERDUZZO FRIULANO. Top: Aquila del Torre, d'Attimis, Ermacora, Gigante, La Sclusa, LA VIARTE, LE DUE TERRE, LIVIO FELLUGA,

MIANI, Meroi, RONCHI DI CIALLA, VIGNA PETRUSSA. Volpe Pasini (Zuc di Volpe range) Ramandolo DOCG is best sweet Verduzzo (look for Anna Berra). Picolit can be Italy's best sweet: Aquila del Torre, Livio Felluga, Marco Sara, Ronchi di Cialla, VIGNA Petrussa often amazing.

Friuli Isonzo FVG ★★★ DOC (previously just Isonzo). One of the world's best flatland wine denominations. High-alc, powerful, rich, unfailingly complex whites, from gravel-rich and clay-loam soils and a downright hot mesoclimate. Best: LIS NERIS, RONCO DEL GELSO, VIE DI ROMANS. Also gd: Borgo Conventi, Pierpaolo Pecorari.

Friuli Venezia Giulia A ne region hugging Slovenian border, home to Italy's best whites (along with ALTO ADIGE). Hills to ne give best, but alluvial seaside regions (DOC from Annia, Aquileia, Latisana) improving markedly. DOCs Carso, COLLIO, F COLLI ORIENTALI, F ISONZO best.

Frizzante Semi-sparkling, up to 2.5 atmospheres, eg. MOSCATO D'ASTI, much PROSECCO, LAMBRUSCO and the like.

Fucci, Elena Bas ★★★★ AGLIANICO DEL VULTURE Titolo from 55–70-yr-old vines in Mt Vulture's Grand Cru; one of Italy's 20 best, now also RISERVA and SUPERIORE. Organic. By Amphora and Pink Edition also v.gd.

Fuligni Tus ★★★★ Outstanding, trad: BRUNELLO (top RISERVA), ROSSO DI MONTALCINO.

Gagliardo, Gianni ★★★ High-quality BAROLOS from six different crus. Best: Castelletto, Lazzarito VIGNA Preve, Castelletto, Monvigliero, Mosconi. Iconic Fallegro (Favorita) v.gd.

Gaja Pie ★★★★ Old family firm at BARBARESCO led by eloquent Angelo G; daughter Gaia G following. One of Italy's top wineries. Best: Barbaresco (Costa Russi, Sorì San Lorenzo, Sorì Tildìn and classic Barbaresco), BAROLO (Conteisa, Sperss). Splendid CHARD (Gaia e Rey). Also owns Ca' Marcanda in BOLGHERI (Ca' Marcanda top, v.gd Magari, Promis), Pieve di Santa Restituta in MONTALCINO.

Gancia Pie Famous old brand of ASTI. Best ALTA LANGA ★★★ Cuvée (120, 60).

Garbarino, Roberto Pie ★★★ One of most talented young producers of ALTA LANGA DOCG. Top: Le Rapide (PINOT N/CHARD). Il Viaggio (Chard) and La Sorgente (Pinot N) v.gd.

Gattinara Pie **13** 15 16' 17 18 19' 21 Best known of a cluster of ALTO PIE DOC(G)s based on NEBBIOLO. Steep hills; wines suitable for long ageing. Best: Antoniolo, CANTINA del Signore, Iarretti Paride, Nervi, Torraccia del Piantavigna, TRAVAGLINI. *See also* ALTO PIEMONTE.

Gavi / Cortese di Gavi Pie ★→★★★ DOCG At best, subtle dry white of CORTESE grapes. Best: *Bruno Broglia*/La Meirana, Castellari Bergaglio (Rovereto, Rolona), Castello di Tassarolo, Chiarlo, La Giustiniana, La Mesma (Indi, RISERVA), LA SCOLCA, Nicola Bergaglio (Minaia), Villa Sparina.

Germano, Ettore Pie ★★★→★★★★ Family Serralunga estate run by Sergio G and wife Elena. Top BAROLOS: Cerretta, RISERVA Lazzarito, outstanding VIGNA Rionda. ALTA LANGA (also RISERVAS Blanc de Noirs and Blanc de Blancs, both 65 mths), BARBERA D'ALBA SUPERIORE della Madre, Barolo Prapò, Del Comune di Serralunga, LANGHE RIES Hérzu all v.gd.

Ghemme Pie ★★→★★★ DOCG NEBBIOLO (at least 85%), incl up to 15% Uva Rara and/or Vespolina. Mainly morainic agglomerate soils of friable pebbles and rich in minerals, poor and not v. fertile (actually, youngest among those of Alto Piemonte). Top: *Antichi Vigneti di Cantalupo* (Collis Braclemae, Collis Carellae), Ioppa (Balsina), Rovellotti (RISERVA); v.gd Torraccia del Piantavigna (VIGNA Pelizzane). *See also* ALTO PIEMONTE.

Ghizzano, Tenuta di Tus ★★★ Historic bio estate on Pisa's hills; non-interventionist. Best: (r) Nambrot (Bx blend), Il Ghizzano; new Mimesi Project (r/w).

Giacosa, Bruno Pie ★★★★ Now run by daughter Bruna; wines still top. Splendid iconic trad-style BARBARESCOS (Asili, Rabajà), BAROLOS (Falletto, Falletto VIGNA Rocche). Top wines (ie. RISERVAS) get famous red label. Amazing METODO CLASSICO Brut (one of best in PIE), ROERO ARNEIS (w), Valmaggiore (r).

Gini Ven ★★★ Gini family since 1500s; bio estate. Best: SOAVE CLASSICO Contrada Salvarenza Vecchie Vigne, La Froscà. AMARONE RISERVA Scajari and RECIOTO DI SOAVE v.gd.

Girlan, Cantina T-AA ★★→★★★ Quality co-op. Top Solisti (PINOT NS VIGNA Ganger, Trattmann; VERNATSCH) and Flora (PINOT BL) ranges.

Giuseppe Cortese Pie ★★★ A trad producer of outstanding BARBARESCO Rabajà (also RISERVA). Also gd Barbaresco, LANGHE NEBBIOLO, Scapulin (CHARD).

Grappa Pungent spirit made from grape pomace (skins, etc., after pressing), can be anything from disgusting to inspirational. What the French call "marc".

Greco di Tufo Cam ★★→★★★ DOCG Better versions among Italy's best whites (tannic, oily) made with local GRECO (different from Cal's also outstanding Greco Bianco). Best: BENITO FERRARA (VIGNA Cicogna), COLLI di Lapio, FEUDI DI SAN GREGORIO (Cutizzi, Goleto), I FAVATI, *Mastroberadino*, Pietracupa (G), QUINTODECIMO, TRAERTE (Tornante). Bambinuto, Terredora (Terre degli Angeli) v.gd.

Grifalco Bas ★★★→★★★★ Small estate in high-quality Ginestra and Maschito subzone. Purity, trad. Best: AGLIANICO DEL VULTURE SUPERIORE Daginestra, Damaschito. Gricos, Grifalco v.gd.

Grignolino Pie DYA Two DOCS: Grignolino d'ASTI, Grignolino del Monferrato Casalese. At best, light, perfumed, crisp, high in acidity, tannin. D'Asti: Bersano, BRAIDA, Cascina Tavijin, Crivelli, Incisa della Rocchetta, Spertino, TENUTA Garetto. Monferrato Casalese: Accornero (Bricco del Bosco and Bricco del Bosco Vigne Vecchie – oaked), Bricco Mondalino, Castello di Uviglie, PIO CESARE.

Grosjean VdA ★★★ Top quality, native grapes; best CORNALIN, Premetta. Vigne Rovettaz one of VDA's oldest, largest.

Guerrieri Rizzardi Ven ★★→★★★ Noble family making top AMARONE, Bardolino: Amarones Calcarole, Villa Rizzardi (cru). SOAVE CLASSICO Costeggiola v.gd.

Gulfi Si ★★★★ Best producer of NERO D'AVOLA in SI; 1st to bottle single-*contrada* (cru) wines. Organic. Outstanding: Nerobufaleffj, Nerosanlorè; iconic Nerojbleo; new RISERVAS. Also v.gd (r) CERASUOLO DI VITTORIA CLASSICO, Nerobaronj, NeroMàccarj; (w) Carjcanti. Interesting Pinò (PINOT N), ETNA red Reseca.

IGT (indicazione geografica tipica) Increasingly known as IGP (indicazione geografica protetta). (*See* box, p.153.)

Inama Ven ★★★ One of SOAVE's and COLLI Berici's most important producers, making some of denomination's best. Top: Soave CLASSICO (Carbonare, Du Lot, Foscarino and new I Palchi Grande Cuvée); CARMENÈRE RISERVA Oratorio di San Lorenzo (r) and Bradisismo (r blend).

Ippolito 1845 Cal ★★→★★★ Since 1845 in heart of CIRÒ. Best: Cirò Bianco Mare Chiaro (GRECO BIANCO); Cirò Rosato Mabilia, red Cirò (Liber Pater, RISERVA COLLI del Mancuso).

Ischia Cam ★★→★★★ DOC DYA Island off Naples, green volcanic tuff soils, own grape varieties (w: Biancolella, Forastera; r: Piedirosso, also found in CAM). Frassitelli and VIGNA del Lume vyds best for Biancolella. Best: CANTINE MAZZELLA, Cenatiempo (Kalimera), D'AMBRA.

Isole e Olena Tus ★★★★ Top CHIANTI CLASSICO estate now owned by EPI group. Superb red IGT Cepparello. Outstanding CHIANTI CLASSICO, CHARD, VIN SANTO. Also v.gd CAB SAUV, SYRAH.

Kaltern, Cantina T-AA ★★★ Quality co-op close to Caldaro lake. Top Quintessenz range. Look for limited-edition Kunst Stück (to celebrate grape that best interprets the vintage) and new sparkling Brut Nature.

Köfererhof T-AA ★★★→★★★★ Great whites: KERNER, SYLVANER; MÜLLER-T excellent.

Lageder, Alois T-AA ★★★ Famous ALTO ADIGE producer. Most exciting are single-vyd varietals: CAB SAUV Cor Römigberg; CHARDS Gaun, Löwengang; GEWURZ Am Sand; PINOT N Krafuss; MCM (MERLOT Vecchie Viti).

Lagrein Alto Adige T-AA ★★→★★★ DOC 16' 18' 20 21' Alpine red with deep colour, rich palate (plus a bitter hit at back); refreshing pink *Kretzer rosé* made with LAGREIN. Top ALTO ADIGE: CANTINA Bolzano (Taber), CS Terlano, IGNAZ NIEDRIST, LAGEDER, MURI GRIES, TIEFENBRUNNER.

Lambrusco E-R ★→★★★ DYA The 17 different Lambrusco grapes (five mostly planted) make for highly distinct wines. When gd, delightful fizzy fresh, lively red that pairs divinely with rich, fatty fare. DOCS: Best: **Grasparossa** Cleto Chiarli (Enrico Cialdini), Moretto (Monovitigno and VIGNA Canova), Pederzana (Canto Libero Semi Secco), *Vittorio Graziano* (Fontana dei Boschi); **Maestri** Ceci, Dall'Asta; **Marani** Medici Ermete; **Salamino** Cavicchioli, Luciano Saetti, Medici Ermete; **Sorbara** Cavicchioli (Cristo Secco, Cristo Rose), Cleto Chiarli (Antica Modena Premium), Medici Ermete, PALTRINIERI.

Langhe Pie The hills of central PIE, home of BAROLO, BARBARESCO, etc. DOC name for several Pie varietals plus Bianco and Rosso blends. Those wishing to blend other grapes with NEBBIOLO can at up to 15% as LANGHE NEBBIOLO – a label to follow.

Langhe Nebbiolo Pie ★★→★★★ Like NEBBIOLO D'ALBA (Nebbiolo 85%+) but from a wider area: LANGHE hills. Unlike N d'Alba, may be used as a downgrade from BAROLO or BARBARESCO. Try ALDO CONTERNO, AZELIA, BOROLI, BREZZA, BURLOTTO, CIABOT BERTON, CLERICO, ETTORE GERMANO, FRANCESCO RINALDI, GIACOMO FENOCCHIO, GIOVANNI ROSSO (Ester Canale), GIUSEPPE RINALDI, LA CONTRADA DI SORANO, MASSOLINO, PALLADINO, PIO CESARE, SCARZELLO, TREDIBERRI, VAJRA, VERSIO.

With pasta and beans in Ischia, enriched with mussels, drink (w) Ischia Biancolella.

Lessona Pie DOCG *See also* ALTO PIEMONTE. NEBBIOLO (at least 85%). Mostly clay-free marine sandy soils, rich in minerals. Elegant, age-worthy, fine bouquet, long savoury taste. Best: PROPRIETÀ SPERINO. Colombera & Garella, La Prevostura, Massimo Clerico, Noah, TENUTE Sella v.gd.

Librandi Cal ★★★ Top producer pioneering research into native Cal varieties; Best: CIRÒ (*Riserva Duca San Felice* ★★★), IGT Asylia (w GRECO Bianco), Efeso (w Mantonico), Gravello (CAB SAUV/Gaglioppo blend), Megonio (r Magliocco).

Liguria ★→★★★ Narrow ribbon of extreme mtn viticulture produces memorable (w) PIGATO, VERMENTINO, (r) ROSSESE DI DOLCEACQUA varieties. Riviera di Levante (in e): De Battè, Giacomelli, La Baia del Sole, Lunae, Ottaviano Lambruschi (Vermentino). Cinque Terre is beautiful and Sciacchetrà (sw) one of Italy's best stickies. Riviera di Ponente (in w): Alessandri, BIO VIO, BRUNA, Ka' Manciné, Maccario, Rocche del Gatto, TENUTA di Selvadolce (Pigato), Terre Bianche, Terre Rosse. For Ormeasco di Pornassio (r) made with Ligurian biotype of DOLCETTO: Cascina Nirasca, Fontanacota, Maffone. *See also* ROSSESE DI DOLCEACQUA.

Lis Neris FVG ★★★ Top ISONZO estate for whites. Best: FRIULANO (Fiore di Campo), PINOT GR (Gris), SAUV BL (Picol), Confini (w blend).

Lo Triolet VdA ★★★ Top PINOT GR producer. v.gd Fumin, Torrette, GEWURZ, MUSCAT.

Luce Tus ★★★ FRESCOBALDI's estate. Luce SANGIOVESE/MERLOT blend for oligarchs. Lovely Luce BRUNELLO DI MONTALCINO.

Lugana ★★→★★★ DOC DYA Much-improved white of S Lake Garda, rivals gd SOAVE next door. Main grape Turbiana (was TREBBIANO di Lugana). Best: Ca' dei Frati (esp *Brolettino*), Cavalchina, Corte Sermana, Le Morette, MONTE DEL FRÀ, Ottella, Roveglia, TOMMASI.

Lunae, Cantine Lig ★★★ Owned by Bosoni family in COLLI DI LUNI. Terroir-expressive. Best: VERMENTINO (Cavagino, Etichetta Nera, Numero Chiuso). Rare Vermentino Nero v.gd.

Lungarotti Umb ★★→★★★ Leading producer of TORGIANO. Star wines DOC Rubesco, DOCG RISERVA *Monticchio*. Also Giubilante, MONTEFALCO SAGRANTINO, Sangiorgio (SANGIOVESE/CAB SAUV), VIGNA Il Pino (VERMENTINO/GRECHETTO/TREBBIANO).

Macchiole, Le Tus ★★★★ Organic. One of few native-owned wineries of BOLGHERI; one of 1st to emerge after SASSICAIA, makes *Italy's best Cab Fr* (Paleo Rosso), one of best MERLOT (Messorio), SYRAH (Scrio).

Maculan Ven ★★★ Quality pioneer of Ven. Excellent CAB SAUV (Fratta, Palazzotto). Best known for sweet Torcolato (esp RISERVA Acininobili).

Malvasia delle Lipari Si ★★★ DOC Luscious sweet, from one of many MALVASIA varieties. Best: Caravaglio, Fenech, Marchetta, TENUTA Capofaro (Dydime, VIGNA di Paola), Tenuta di Castellaro. Hauner gd.

Malvirà Pie ★★★→★★★★ Top ROERO producer. Organic. Best Roero single vyd: (r/w) Renesio, Trinità; (w) Saglietto. New ARNEIS RISERVA Saglietto.

Manduria (Primitivo di) Pug ★★→★★★ DOC Cradle of PRIMITIVO, alias ZIN, so expect gutsy, alc, sometimes Porty wines. Best: FELLINE, GIANFRANCO FINO, MORELLA. Try producers, located in Manduria or not: Cantele, Commenda Magistrale (Supremo), PIETRAVENTOSA, Polvanera, TENUTE Chiaromonte, Vetrere.

Marchesi di Grésy Pie ★★★ Historic BARBARESCO producer since 1797, from Martinenga cru (monopole). Best: Gajun, Martinenga, RISERVA Camp Gros. BARBERA D'ASTI Monte Colombo v.gd.

Marrone, Agricola Pie ★★★ Small estate, gd-value BAROLOS. Top: Bussia, Pichemej. ARNEIS, BARBERA D'ALBA SUPERIORE, Favorita, San Carlo (r) all gd.

Marsala Si ★→★★★★ DOC Once-famous fortified of SI. Can be dry to v. sweet; best is bone-dry Marsala Vergine. *See also* MARCO DE BARTOLI.

Veneto has largest area under vines in Italy: 100,000 ha.

Mascarello Pie ★★★★ Two top producers of BAROLO: Bartolo M, of Barolo, whose daughter Maria Teresa continues her father's highly trad path (outstanding FREISA, BARBERA D'ALBA, LANGHE NEBBIOLO); Giuseppe M, of Monchiero, whose son Mauro makes v. fine, trad-style Barolo from the great *Monprivato* vyd in Castiglione Falletto. Both deservedly iconic.

Masi Ven ★★→★★★ Archetypal yet innovative producer of Verona, led by inspirational Sandro Boscaini; v.gd Rosso Veronese *Campo Fiorin* and Osar (Oseleta). Top AMARONES: Campolongo di Torbe, Costasera. Masi Wine Estates: Canevel (CARTIZZE, Valdobbiadene Campofalco), Conti Bossi Fedrigotti (Fojaneghe Bx blend, Trento Conte Federico), Serego Alighieri (Amarone Vaio Armaron).

Maso Martis T-AA ★★★ Owned by Stelzer family. Reference for TRENTO organic. Top: Madame Martis Dosaggio Zero Limited Edition, Monsieur Martis Rosé (PINOT M), DosaggioZero RISERVA. AL-MA 800 MÜLLER-T v.gd.

Massa, Vigneti Pie ★★★ Walter M brought Timorasso (w) grape back from nr extinction. Top: Coste del Vento, Montecitorio, Sterpi. Anarchia Costituzionale (MOSCATO Bianco), BARBERAS Monleale and Bigolla all v.gd.

Massolino Vigna Rionda Pie ★★★ One of finest BAROLO estates, in Serralunga. Top: long-ageing VIGNA Rionda RISERVA (Black Label). Excellent Margheria, Parafada, Parussi, new BARBARESCO Albaneri. LANGHE NEBBIOLO v.gd.

Mastroberardino Cam ★★★ Historic top-quality producer of mtn Avellino province. Top: Stilema range, *Taurasi* (Radici RISERVA) and More Maiorum (blend of GRECO and FIANO).

Mastrojanni Tus ★★★ Classic BRUNELLOS from Castelnuovo dell'Abate. Top: VIGNA Schiena d'Asino, Vigna Loreto. ROSSO DI MONTALCINO v.gd.

Mazzella, Cantine Cam ★★★ Siblings Nicola and Vera M's high-quality winery on ISCHIA island. Top: single-vyd Biancolella VIGNA del Lume. Ischia Biancolella and Forastera, Villa Campagnano (w blend) v.gd.

Meroi FVG ★★★ Dynamic estate. Top: CHARD Dominin, FRIULANO, MALVASIA Zittelle Durì, RIBOLLA GIALLA, SAUV BL Zitelle Barchetta; (r) REFOSCO Dominin.

Metodo classico (MC) or tradizionale Italian for "Champagne method".

Miani FVG ★★★★ Enzo Pontoni is Italy's best white-wine maker. Top: FRIULANO (Buri, Filip), RIBOLLA GIALLA Pettarin, SAUV BL Zitelle. CHARD Zitelle, Sauv Bl Saurint, MERLOT, REFOSCO Buri v.gd.

Mirizzi and Montecappone Mar ★★★ Two estates owned by Gianluca Mirizzi focus on VERDICCHIO DEI CASTELLI DI JESI. Mirizzi on marly sandstone, deep slopes; organic, trad winemaking. Top: Ergo, Ergo Sum RISERVA, sparkling Millesimè Pas Dosè. Montecappone on calcareous clay, reductive winemaking. Top: Federico II, Riserva Utopia.

Molettieri, Salvatore Cam ★★★ Outstanding RISERVA VIGNA Cinque Querce, TAURASI. FIANO DI AVELLINO Apianum, GRECO DI TUFO gd.

Molino, Mauro Pie ★★★ High-quality BAROLO producer in La Morra. Top: Conca. Excellent: Bricco Luciani, Gallinotto, La Serra.

Monacesca, Fattoria La Mar ★★★ Family-run estate, Aldo Cifola in charge. Top VERDICCHIO DI MATELICA. Best: RISERVA Mirum, Terra di Mezzo (longer ageing). Outstanding Mirum 30 Year (multi-vintage blend). Criptico (VERDICCHIO/ CHARD) v.gd.

Monsanto, Castello di Tus ★★★ Historic, top-quality CHIANTI CLASSICO estate. Top: Il Poggio Gran Selezione (1st single-vyd Chianti Classico), iconic RISERVA and IGT Fabrizio Bianchi (r SANGIOVETO Grosso, w CHARD).

Montalcino Tus Hilltop town in province of Siena, fashionable and famous for concentrated, expensive BRUNELLO and more approachable, better-value ROSSO DI MONTALCINO, both still 100% SANGIOVESE.

Monte del Frà Ven ★★→★★★ Owned by Bonomo family; v.gd value. Top: AMARONE (Lena di Mezzo, RISERVA), Custoza (Bonomo Sexaginta, Ca' del Magro). Bardolino (Bonomo), LUGANA v.gd.

Montefalco Sagrantino Umb ★★★→★★★★ DOCG Once sweet PASSITO only (still best wine of area), drier version is Italy's most powerfully tannic red that requires optimal growing seasons to show best. Top: ADANTI, Antano Milziade, Bocale, CAPRAI (25 Anni, Collepiano, Spinning Beauty), Pardi. Bocale, Castelbuono (Carapace), Lorenzo Mattoni, LUNGAROTTI, Terre della Custodia v.gd.

Monte Maletto Pie ★★★ Gian Marco Viano is one of most talented young producers in Italy. Best: CAREMA Sole e Roccia, single-vyd La Costa.

Montepulciano d'Abruzzo Ab ★★→★★★ DOC (r) **16** 18 19 20' 22 Thanks to new generation of winemakers, Ab's wines (MONTEPULCIANO, TREBBIANO D'ABRUZZO too) never been better. Reds can be either light, easy-going or structured, rich. Best: Cataldi Madonna (Piè delle Vigne, Tonì), EMIDIO PEPE, Filomusi Guelfi, Praesidium, TIBERIO (Archivio, Colle Vota), Torre dei Beati (Cocciapazza, Mazzamurello), Valle Reale and of course *Valentini* (best, age-worthy).

Montevertine Tus ★★★★ Organic estate in Radda. Outstanding IGT Le Pergole Torte, world-class, pure, long-ageing SANGIOVESE; v.gd Montevertine.

Montevetrano Cam ★★★ Iconic CAM AZIENDA. Superb IGT Montevetrano (AGLIANICO/ CAB SAUV/MERLOT); v.gd Core Rosso (Aglianico) and Core Bianco (FIANO/GRECO).

Morella Pug ★★★→★★★★ Gaetano M and wife Lisa Gilbee make outstanding PRIMITIVO (La Signora, Mondo Nuovo, Old Vines) from c.90-yr-old vines. Also v.gd Mezzarosa rosé (Primitivo/NEGROAMARO), Mezzogiorno (FIANO).

Morellino di Scansano Tus ★→★★★ DOCG 16' 17 18 19' 20 21' Maremma's famous SANGIOVESE-based red is better when cheerful, light than overoaked, gritty. Best: Fattoria dei Barbi, *Le Pupille* (plus RISERVA), Moris Farms, PODERE 414, POGGIO ARGENTIERA, Roccapesta, TENUTA Belguardo.

Moris Farms Tus ★★★ One of 1st new-age producers of TUS Maremma. Top: iconic

IGT Avvoltore (rich SANGIOVESE/CAB/SYRAH), MORELLINO DI SCANSANO (regular, RISERVA). But try Rosato Rosamundi, VERMENTINO.

Moscato d'Asti Pie ★★→★★★ DYA Similar to DOCG ASTI, but usually better grapes; lower alc, lower pressure, sweeter, fruitier, often from small producers. Best DOCG MOSCATO: Ca' d'Gal, *Caudrina* (La Galeisa), Forteto della Luja, Mongioia, *Saracco*, Vignaioli di Santo Stefano. BRAIDA, GD VAJRA RIZZI v.gd.

Mosnel Lom ★★★→★★★★ Barzanò family-run organic winery in FRANCIACORTA, since 1836. Elegance, complexity, long ageing. Top: EBB, Nature, Pas Dosé RISERVA, Riedizioni Late Release Vintage.

Muri Gries T-AA ★★→★★★ Monastery in Bolzano suburb of Gries; trad and still top producer of LAGREIN ALTO ADIGE DOC. Best: Abtei Muri, Klosteranger.

Musso Pie ★★★ Musso family-run BARBARESCO estate, since 1929. Underrated. Top: Barbarescos Pora (also RISERVA), Rio Sordo.

Nals Margreid T-AA ★★★ Small quality co-op making mtn-fresh whites (esp PINOT BIANCO Sirmian), CHARD RISERVA, new cuvée (w) Nama.

Nebbiolo d'Alba Pie ★★→★★★ DOC 15 16' 18 19' 21 (100% NEBBIOLO) Sometimes a worthy replacement for BAROLO/BARBARESCO, though it comes from a distinct area between the two. Best: BREZZA, BRUNO GIACOSA, CERETTO, Hilberg-Pasquero, LUCIANO SANDRONE, ORLANDO ABRIGO, PAITIN, PODERI COLLA.

Neive, Castello di Pie ★★★ Historic estate, owns single greatest cru of all BARBARESCO, famous Santo Stefano (Albesani MGA). Top Barbarescos: Gallina, Santo Stefano (also RISERVA). Also v.gd (r) Albarossa, Barbarossa.

Niedrist, Ignaz T-AA ★★★ LAGREIN Berger Gei RISERVA is reference. So are RIES, WEISSBURGUNDER (Limes, Berg), BLAUBURGUNDER Riserva. CHARD (vom Kalk), SAUV BL (Limes, Porphyr & Kalk), Trias (w blend) v.gd.

In past 15 yrs Glera vine (Prosecco) has tripled area under vine: 38,900 ha now.

Nino Franco Ven ★★★→★★★★ Owner Primo F makes large volumes of top-notch PROSECCO that age surprisingly well. Among finest: Grave di Stecca Brut, Primo Franco Dry, Rustica di San Floriano Brut, Rustico. Excellent CARTIZZE.

Nipozzano, Castello di Tus ★★★→★★★★ FRESCOBALDI estate in RÙFINA, e of Florence, making excellent CHIANTI Rùfina. Top: IGT *Montesodi*, Nipozzano RISERVA (esp Vecchie Viti). Mormoreto (Bx blend) v.gd.

Nittardi Tus ★★→★★★ Reliable source of quality modern CHIANTI CLASSICO (Casanuova di Nittardi, RISERVA). German-owned; oenologist Carlo Ferrini.

Nizza Pie ★★→★★★ DOCG (100% BARBERA) Only from best exposed sites of 19 villages around town of Nizza Monferrato; also RISERVA. Needs time. Best: Bava, BERSANO, Cacina Garitina (900, Riserva), Chiarlo (La Court), Doglia Gianni, ODDERO, Olim Bauda (also Riserva), TENUTA Garetto, Villa Giada, Vinchio Vaglio.

Nössing, Manni T-AA ★★★★ Outstanding KERNER, GRÜNER V, MÜLLER-T Sass Rigais, SYLVANER. Benchmark wines.

Occhio di pernice Tus "Partridge's eye". Type of VIN SANTO made predominantly from black grapes, mainly SANGIOVESE. *Avignonesi's is definitive*.

Occhipinti, Arianna Si ★★★ Cult producer, deservedly so. Organic. Top: CERASUOLO DI VITTORIA CLASSICO Grotte Alte, Il Frappato.

Oddero Pie ★★★→★★★★ Traditionalist La Morra estate for excellent BAROLO (Brunate, Bussia RISERVA, Villero, outstanding VIGNA Rionda Riserva), BARBARESCO (Gallina) crus, plus other serious PIE wines. Also v.gd-value Barolo, RIES.

Oltrepò Pavese Lom ★→★★★ Multi-DOC, lots of varietals, blends from Pavia province: MC best. Barbacarlo, Bruno Verdi, Conte Vistarino (METODO CLASSICO 1865, PINOT N Bertone), Isimbarda, Mazzolino, Travaglino.

Ornellaia Tus ★★★★ 15 16' 18 19' 20 21 Fashionable, indeed cult, estate nr BOLGHERI now owned by FRESCOBALDI. Top wines of Bx grapes/method: Bolgheri DOC

Ornellaia, IGT Masseto (MERLOT), Ornellaia Bianco (SAUV BL/VIOGNIER); gd Bolgheri DOC Le Serre Nuove and POGGIO alle Gazze (w).

Orvieto Umb ★→★★★ DOC DYA One of few areas of Italy where noble rot occurs spontaneously and often. Sweet late-harvest can be memorable. Off-dry Amabile less in favour today but delicious. Top: Barberani (Luigi e Giovanna), but sweet Calcaia just as gd. Bigi, Cardeto, *Castello della Sala*, Decugnano dei Barbi, Palazzone. Sergio Mottura (Lat) gd.

Ottin VdA ★★★ Elio O is one of top interpreters of VDA terroir. Best: PINOT N (also L'Emerico), Petite ARVINE Nuances (one of best), Torrette Superieur.

Paitin Pie ★★★ Pasquero-Elia family has been bottling BARBARESCO since C19. Today back on track making "real" Barbaresco from cru Serraboella in large barrels. Sorì Paitin Vecchie Vigne is star; v.gd new Barbaresco (Basarin, Faset), BARBERA D'ALBA (Campoline), NEBBIOLO D'ALBA.

Palladino Pie ★★★ Family estate, talented interpreter of Serralunga BAROLO. Top: Ornato, RISERVA San Bernardo. BARBERA D'ALBA, Parafada v.gd.

Palmento Costanzo Si ★★→★★★ 18 ha in several ETNA *contradas*. Top: (r) Contrada Santo Spirito, Etna Prefillossera, Nero di Sei; (w) Bianco di Sei, Etna Contrada Santo Spirito.

Paltrinieri E-R ★★→★★★ One of top three LAMBRUSCO producers. Among 1st to produce 100% L di Sorbara. Best: Leclisse, Secco Radice, La RISERVA.

Pantelleria Si ★★★ Windswept, black volcanic) earth SI island off Tunisian coast, famous for superb MOSCATO d'Alessandria stickies. PASSITO versions dense/intense. Try MARCO DE BARTOLI (Bukkuram), DONNAFUGATA (Ben Ryé), Ferrandes, Vinisola (A'mmare, Arbaria, Zefiro).

Parusso, Armando Pie ★★★ Excellent BAROLO. Best: Bussia (and RISERVAS Munie, Rocche), Mariondino. Mosconi, Perarmando v.gd.

Passito Si, Tus, Ven One of Italy's most ancient and characteristic styles, from grapes dried briefly under harvest sun (in s) or over a period of weeks or mths in airy attics – a process called *appassimento*. Best-known versions: AMARONE/RECIOTO, VALPOLICELLA/SOAVE (VEN); VIN SANTO (TUS); Pantelleria (SI). Try Loazzolo, MONTEFALCO, ORVIETO, Torcolato. Never cheap.

Pavese Ermes VdA ★★★ One estate, one grape: Prié Bl, with ungrafted vines up to 1219m (4000ft). Top: Blanc de Morgex et de la Salle (Classic, Le 7 Scalinate, Nathan), Ninive (sw), sparkling MC Pavese (XLVIII and LX, mths of ageing).

Pepe, Emidio Ab ★★★ Artisanal winery, 15 ha, bio/organic. Top: MONTEPULCIANO D'ABRUZZO. PECORINO, TREBBIANO D'ABRUZZO (Old Vines) gd.

Petrussa, Vigna FVG ★★★ Small family estate, high-quality wines. Best: PICOLIT, Richenza (indigenous w grapes cuvée, old vines), SCHIOPPETTINO di Prepotto (and RISERVA).

Pian dell'Orino Tus ★★★★ Small MONTALCINO estate, committed to bio. BRUNELLO seductive, technically perfect, Rosso nearly as gd. Many epic wines.

Piane, Le Pie ★★★★ BOCA DOC resurfaced thanks to Christoph Kunzli: v.gd (r) Maggiorina, Mimmo (NEBBIOLO/Croatina), Nebbiolo, Piane (Croatina); (w) Bianco (Erbaluce).

Picolit FVG ★★→★★★ DOCG 13 15 16' 17 18 (20') Potentially Italy's best sweet (most from air-dried grapes; rare late-harvests even better), but plagued by poor versions that don't speak of the grape. Texture ranges from light/sweet (rare) to super-thick (PASSITO). Best: Aquila del Torre, d'Attimis, I Comelli, LIVIO FELLUGA, Marco Sara, Perusini, RONCHI DI CIALLA, Valentino Butussi, VIGNA PETRUSSA. Also v.gd: Ermacora, Girolamo Dorigo, Paolo Rodaro.

Piedmont / Piemonte In ne, bordering France to the w. Turin is capital. Main areas: ALTO PIEMONTE, Monferrato, LANGHE, ROERO. With TUS, Italy's most important region for quality (10% of all DOC[G] wines). No IGTS allowed. Grapes incl BARBERA, Brachetto, CORTESE, DOLCETTO, FREISA, GRIGNOLINO, MALVASIA di Casorzo, Malvasia di Schierano, MOSCATO, NEBBIOLO, Ruchè, Timorasso. *See also* BARBARESCO, BAROLO.

Pieropan Ven ★★★★ Andrea and Dario, Leonildo's sons, now run winery. Organic. Cru *La Rocca* still ultimate oaked SOAVE; Calvarino best of all. Outstanding new Calvarino 5 (blend of Calvarino 08–12). Plus v.gd AMARONE, RECIOTO DI SOAVE (Le Colombare).

Pietradolce Si ★★★→★★★★ Faro bros own vyds in key ETNA crus, often pre-phylloxera vines. Top: (r) Barbagalli, Feudo di Mezzo, Rampante, Santo Spirito; (w) Sant'Andrea (100% CARRICANTE); (r/w) Archineri. Precise wines.

Pietraventosa Pug ★★★ Small family estate, one of top producers of PRIMITIVO di Gioia del Colle. Top: Allegoria, RISERVA. Rosé Est-Rosa.

Pievalta Mar ★★★ Founded by BARONE PIZZINI; bio. Top: VERDICCHIO DEI CASTELLI DI JESI (RISERVA San Paolo, Tre Ripe and sp Perlugo).

Pio Cesare Pie ★★★ Veteran ALBA producer; BAROLO, BARBARESCO in modern (barrique) and trad (large cask-aged) versions. Particularly gd NEBBIOLO D'ALBA, *a little Barolo at half the price*. Best: Single-vyd (Bricco, Mosconi, Ornato) and Classic (Pio, dedicated to Pio Boffa) collections. Also gd Barolo Chinato and vermouth.

Pira e Figli – Chiara Boschis Pie ★★★★ Organic. Must-visit estate. Top: Cannubi, Mosconi, Via Nuova. BARBERA D'ALBA SUPERIORE and LANGHE NEBBIOLO v.gd.

Planeta Si ★★★ Leading SI estate with vyds all over island, incl Menfi (GRILLO Terebinto), Noto (NERO D'AVOLA Santa Cecilia, PASSITO di Noto), Vittoria (CERASUOLO Dorilli, Frappato), most recently on ETNA (NERELLO MASCALESE Eruzione 1614). Also gd Cometa (FIANO). Reliable.

Podere Tus Small TUS farm, once part of a big estate.

Poggio Tus Means "hill" in TUS dialect. **Poggione** means "big hill".

Poggio Antico Tus ★★★ Paola Gloder looks after 32-ha estate, one of highest in MONTALCINO at c.500m (1640ft). Restrained, consistent, at times too herbal.

Poggio Argentiera Tus ★★★ Maremma estate owned by TUA RITA: freshness, drinkability. Best: Capatosta (95% SANGIOVESE), MORELLINO DI SCANSANO.

Poggio di Sotto Tus ★★★★ Small MONTALCINO estate with a big reputation recently. Top: BRUNELLO, RISERVA, ROSSO, trad character with idiosyncratic twist.

Poggione, Tenuta Il Tus ★★★ MONTALCINO estate, in s; consistently excellent BRUNELLO, Rosso. Top: Brunello RISERVA VIGNA Paganelli. VIN SANTO v.gd.

The best Pinot Noirs in Italy

Everybody loves PINOT N, and Italy is no different. Like everywhere else, Italians have been making it for decades; and just like everywhere else, the growing pains have been real. Only in the past 15 yrs has Italian Pinot Nero become interesting: best (by far) from ALTO ADIGE and, recently, PIE; other places, eg. TUS, are too hot/low-lying for there to be much hope for success. But there are always exceptions. FVG LE DUE TERRE. **Lom** Conte Vistarino (Pernice). **Pie** Colombo (Maxima), PODERI COLLA (Campo Romano), SARACCO. **Sic** GULFI (Pinò). **T-AA** (Italy's best PINOT N wines, esp those from the AA vyds of Egna, Mazzon, Pinzon; note that in AA, Pinot N is often called by the German name BLAUBURGUNDER): ALOIS LAGEDER (Krafuss), Brunnenhof (Mazzon), Castel Juval, Ferruccio Carlotto (Filari di Mazzon), GIRLAN (VIGNA Ganger), Gottardi (also Riserva), Hofstatter (Barthenau), NIEDRIST, TERLANO (Monticol). **Tus** FONTODI (Case Via), FRANCHETTI (Sancaba). **VdA** Les Cretes (Revei), GROSJEAN (Les Frères), Lo Triolet, OTTIN (L'Emerico).

Pomino Tus ★★★ DOC (r) 15 16 18 19' 20 21 Appendage of RÙFINA, with fine red and white blends (Il Benefizio). Virtually a FRESCOBALDI exclusivity.

Potazzine, Le Tus ★★★★ Organic estate of Gorelli family just s of MONTALCINO; vyd is quite high. Outstanding BRUNELLO (and RISERVA), ROSSO: serious and v. drinkable. Try them at family's restaurant in town.

Prà Ven ★★★★ Leading SOAVE CLASSICO producer: Colle Sant'Antonio, Monte Grande, Staforte. Excellent AMARONE (15 top), VALPOLICELLA La Morandina.

Produttori del Barbaresco Pie ★★★ One of Italy's earliest and best co-ops. Excellent trad, classic BARBARESCO plus crus Asili, Montefico, Montestefano, Ovello, Pora, Rio Sordo. Super value.

Proprietà Sperino Pie ★★★★ Top estate of LESSONA. One of best of ALTO PIEMONTE run by Luca De Marchi. Outstanding BRAMATERRA, Lessona (and RISERVA Covà). 'L Franc (one of best Italian CAB FR), Rosa del Rosa (NEBBIOLO/Vespolina rosé), Uvaggio (r blend) all v.gd.

Prosecco Ven ★–★★ DOC(G) DYA Prosecco is the wine, GLERA the grape variety. Quality is higher in the Valdobbiadene. Look for: Adami, Biancavigna, BISOL, Bortolin, Canevel, Carpenè-Malvolti, Case Bianche, Col Salice, Col Vetoraz, Gregoletto, La Riva dei Frati, Le Colture, Mionetto, Najma, NINO FRANCO, Ruggeri, Silvano Follador, Zardetto.

Puglia The "heel" of Italy. Many gd-value reds from likes of Bombino Nero, NEGROAMARO, PRIMITIVO, Susumaniello and Uva di Troia grapes. Bombino Bianco, aromatic Minutolo and Verdeca most interesting whites. Castel del Monte, Gioia del Colle Primitivo, PRIMITIVO DI MANDURIA, SALICE SALENTINO best denominations.

Querciabella Tus ★★★ Top CHIANTI CLASSICO estate, bio since 2000. Top: IGT Camartina (CAB/SANGIOVESE), Batàr (CHARD/PINOT BL), Chianti Classico (RISERVA, Gran Selezione). Mongrana (VIOGNIER/VERMENTINO), Palafreno (MERLOT) v.gd.

Quintarelli, Giuseppe Ven ★★★★ Arch-traditionalist artisan producer of sublime VALPOLICELLA, RECIOTO, AMARONE. Daughter Fiorenza and sons now in charge, altering nothing, incl the ban on spitting when tasting.

Quintodecimo Cam ★★★→★★★★ Oenology professor/winemaker Luigi Moio's beautiful estate. Outstanding TAURASI (VIGNA Grande Cerzito, Vigna Quintodecimo), Grande Cuvée Luigi Moio (w blend of native grapes). Great AGLIANICO, FIANO D'AVELLINO, GRECO DI TUFO.

Ragnaie, Le Tus ★★★ Makes trad BRUNELLOS revealing essence of SANGIOVESE. Top: Casanovina Montosoli, Passo del Lume Spento, V.V.

Recioto della Valpolicella Ven ★★★→★★★★ DOCG Sweet-wine marketing problems mean this trad Italian beauty is being made less and less. Shame, esp as always much better than many disappointing overly sweet/tannic AMARONE. Top: Brigaldara, Roccolo Grassi, Secondo Marco, TEDESCHI, TOMMASO BUSSOLA.

Recioto di Soave Ven ★★★→★★★★★ DOCG SOAVE from half-dried grapes: sweet, fruity, slightly almondy; sweetness is cut by high acidity. *Drink with cheese*. Best: Anselmi, Coffele, GINI, PIEROPAN, SUAVIA, Tamellini. Often v.gd from Ca' Rugate, Pasqua, PRÀ, Trabuchi.

Refosco (dal Peduncolo Rosso) FVG ★★ 15 16 19' 20 21 Most planted native red grape of region. Best from FRIULI COLLI ORIENTALI DOC. Top: MIANI, Ronchi di Cialla, VIGNA PETRUSSA, Volpe Pasini. Jacuss, La Viarte, LIVIO FELLUGA, MEROI gd.

Revello, Fratelli Pie ★★★ Small family estate makes delicious BAROLO from some of La Morra's best crus (Rocche dell'Annunziata, Conca, Gattera) and new Cerretta. L'Insieme (NEBBIOLO/BARBERA/CAB SAUV) v.gd.

Riecine Tus ★★★→★★★★ SANGIOVESE specialist at Gaiole since 70s. Riecine di Riecine, La Gioia (100% Sangiovese) potentially outstanding; Tresette (MERLOT).

Rinaldi, Francesco Pie ★★★ Paola and Piera R make classic, elegant BAROLOS.

Top: Brunate, Cannubi (also RISERVA), Rocche dell'Annunziata. Classic Barolo, LANGHE NEBBIOLO, Langhe FREISA v.gd.

Rinaldi, Giuseppe Pie ★★★ Marta and Carlotta R produce some of most iconic LANGHE wines. Top BAROLO, LANGHE NEBBIOLO, FREISA and new Barolo Bussia.

Riserva Wine aged for a statutory period, usually in casks or barrels.

Rivetto Pie ★★★ Enrico R is one of most talented young winemakers; bio. Top: BAROLOS Briccolina, Leon. BARBERA D'ALBA, Barolo Serralunga, LANGHE NEBBIOLO, Langhe Nascetta (w) v.gd.

Rizzi Pie ★★★→★★★★ Sub-area of Treiso, commune of BARBARESCO, where Dellapiana family looks after 35 ha. Organic. Top: Barbaresco Pajorè, Rizzi RISERVA Boito. ALTA LANGA, Barbaresco (Nervo, Rizzi), MOSCATO D'ASTI, vermouth v.gd. Mineral, steely wines.

Roagna Pie ★★★★ Old vines, massal selection, organic, wild yeast, long maceration and long ageing in large oak casks. Outstanding BARBARESCO Crichet Pajet (also RISERVA), BAROLO and Barbaresco Vecchie Viti ("old vines") range and Riservas "Black Label". Barbaresco Pajè, Barolo Pira, Timorasso Montemarzino and new Barbarescos (Albesani, Gallina) and Barolos (Del Comune di Barolo, Rocche di Castiglione) v.gd.

Rocca, Albino Pie ★★★→★★★★ Foremost producer of elegant, sophisticated BARBARESCO: Cottà, Ovello VIGNA Loreto, RISERVA, Ronchi.

Rocca, Bruno Pie ★★★→★★★★ Family estate run by Francesco and Luisa, Bruno's children. BARBARESCO with more trad style. More elegance than power. Top: Currà, Maria Adelaide, Rabajà, RISERVAS. BARBERA D'ASTI, LANGHE NEBBIOLO v.gd.

Roero Pie ★★→★★★ DOCG 14 16' 18 19' 20 21 Wilder, cooler compared to LANGHE. Wines have typically moderate alc and tannin, gd elegance, freshness, aromatic profile. NEBBIOLO (r) and ARNEIS (w). Best: ★ BRUNO GIACOSA, Ca' Rossa, Cascina Chicco, Cornarea, ★ GIOVANNI ALMONDO, ★ MALVIRÀ, ★ MATTEO CORREGGIA, Morra, Negro, Rosso, Taliano, Val del Prete, Valfaccenda.

Romagna Sangiovese Mar ★★→★★★ DOC At times too herbal and oaky, but often well-made, even classy SANGIOVESE red. Try Condè, Condello, Drei Donà, Fattoria Zerbina, Nicolucci, Papiano, Ronchi di Castelluccio, Tre Monti. Tenuta Mara (Guiry, Maramia) v.gd.

Ronchi di Cialla FVG ★★★→★★★★ Leading FVG estate, in Cialla subzone of FRIULI COLLI ORIENTALI, run by Rapuzzi family, devoted to local old native grapes. Best: Ciallabianco (blend of RIBOLLA GIALLA/VERDUZZO/PICOLIT), Picolit di Cialla, SCHIOPPETTINO. REFOSCO dal Peduncolo Rosso di Cialla, Sol (dr Picolit) v.gd.

Ronco Term for a hillside vyd in NE Italy, esp FVG.

Ronco del Gelso FVG ★★★→★★★★ Tight, pure ISONZO. Regional benchmarks: FRIULANO Toc Bas, MALVASIA VIGNA della Permuta, PINOT GR Sot lis Rivis. Latimis (w blend), RIES Schulz, MERLOT v.gd.

Rosato General Italian name for rosé. Other rosé names incl Chiaretto from Lake Garda; CERASUOLO from Ab; Kretzer from ALTO ADIGE.

Rossese di Dolceacqua, or Dolceacqua Lig ★★→★★★ DOC Interesting reds. Intense, salty, spicy; greater depth of fruit than most. Best: Ka' Manciné, Maccario-Dringenberg (Curli, Luvaira, Posaù, Sette Cammini), Terre Bianche (Bricco Arcagna), TENUTA Anfosso. Poggi dell'Elmo v.gd.

Rosset VdA ★★→★★★ Innovative young winery. Best: CHARD 770, SYRAH 870.

Rosso, Giovanni Pie ★★★ Davide R is a talented interpreter of Serralunga BAROLO. Best: Cerretta, LANGHE NEBBIOLO Ester Canale Rosso, Serra, Vignarionda Ester Canale. Langhe Nebbiolo, ROERO ARNEIS v.gd. Also in ETNA.

Rosso di Montalcino Tus ★★→★★★ 13 15 16 18 19' 20 21 DOC for earlier-maturing wines from BRUNELLO grapes, usually from younger or lesser vyd sites; bargains exist.

Rosso Piceno / Piceno Mar ★→★★ DOC 18 19 (20) Blend of MONTEPULCIANO (35%+) and SANGIOVESE (15%+). SUPERIORE means it comes only from far s of region. Try BUCCI, Garofoli, MONTECAPPONE (Utopia). Boccadigabbia, Moncaro, Monte Schiavo, Saladini Pilastri, Santa Barbara, TENUTA DI TAVIGNANO, Velenosi v.gd.

Rùfina Tus ★★→★★★ Most n subzone of CHIANTI, e of Florence, is by far best and most interesting non-CHIANTI CLASSICO denomination. Highest of all Chiantis, so refined, age-worthy. Soils are varied and incl limestone, sand, Galestro, Alberese, marly clays and others. Top: Colognole, Fattoria SELVAPIANA Bucerchiale, Frascole, Il Pozzo, Lavacchio, NIPOZZANO (RISERVA, Vecchie Viti see FRESCOBALDI).

Russiz Superiore FVG ★★→★★★ LIVIO FELLUGA's brother Marco est vyds in various parts of FVG. Now run by Marco's granddaughter Ilaria. Wide range. Best: Col Disôre (COLLIO Bianco blend), PINOT GRIGIO. PINOT BIANCO RISERVA v.gd.

Russo, Girolamo Si ★★★→★★★★ Giuseppe R is one of three or four best ETNA producers. Among 1st on Etna to bottle crus separately. Top: (r) Caldera Sottana, Feudo, Feudo di Mezzo, San Lorenzo; (w) Nerina, San Lorenzo.

Salento Pug ★→★★★ Home to Italy's best rosé from NEGROAMARO (alongside Ab's CERASUOLO from MONTEPULCIANO). Plus v.gd red Negroamaro, with a bit of help from MALVASIA Nera, and now red from local Susumaniello. Best: Conti Zecca (Nero, Rodinò), Cupertinum (quality CS: Copertino Rosso RISERVAS, Negroamaro, Settantacinque; Spinello dei Falconi rosé); Leone de Castris (Five Roses); Rosa del Golfo (VIGNA Mazzi classic, rosé). See also SALICE SALENTINO.

Salice Salentino Pug ★★→★★★ DOC 16 17 20' 22 Best known of Salento's too many NEGROAMARO-based DOCS. RISERVA after 2 yrs. Try Apollonio (Mani del Sud), Cantele, Claudio Carta (Riserva Moros), Conti Zecca (Cantalupi), Due Palme (Riserva Selvarossa), Feudo di Guagnano (Riserva Cupone), Leone de Castris (Riserva), Le Vigne di San Marco (Salicale), Masseria Li Veli.

The smallest MGA of Barbaresco? Rabajà-Bas (4.4 ha).

Salvioni Tus ★★★★ (aka La Cerbaiola) Iconic small, highest-quality MONTALCINO estate. BRUNELLO, ROSSO DI MONTALCINO among v. best available.

Sandrone, Luciano Pie ★★★→★★★★ Modern-style ALBA. Deep BAROLOS: Aleste (was Cannubi Boschis), Le Vigne, Vite Talin. Also gd NEBBIOLO D'ALBA Valmaggiore.

San Felice Tus ★★★ Historic winery, owned by Gruppo Allianz, run by Leonardo Bellaccini. Fine CHIANTI CLASSICO and RISERVA POGGIO Rosso from Castelnuovo Berardenga. Also gd BRUNELLO DI MONTALCINO Campogiovanni, IGT *Vigorello* (1st SUPER TUSCAN, from 1968).

San Giusto a Rentennano Tus ★★★★ Top CHIANTI CLASSICO estate. Organic. Outstanding: IGT Percarlo (SANGIOVESE) and La Ricolma (MERLOT); Chianti Classico (and RISERVA Le Baroncole); Vin San Giusto (PASSITO).

San Guido, Tenuta Tus See SASSICAIA.

San Leonardo T-AA ★★★★ Top Trentino estate of Marchesi Guerrieri Gonzaga. Main wine is Bx blend, *San Leonardo* (now released 1 yr later). CARMENÈRE, Villa Gresti (MERLOT/Carmenère), RIES, TRENTO (sp, esp new RISERVA 16) v.gd.

San Lorenzo, Fattoria Mar ★★★ Age-worthy VERDICCHIOs from Montecarotto, bio/organic. Top: Campo delle Oche (also Integrale), Il San Lorenzo Bianco. Il San Lorenzo Rosso (SYRAH), Le Oche v.gd. VIGNA La Gattara (r).

San Michele Appiano T-AA ★★★ Historic co-op; *mtn-fresh whites* a speciality brimming with varietal typicity, drinkability. Best: Appius (selected by Hans Terzer), Sanct Valentin, The Wine Collection; v.gd PINOT BL Schulthauser.

Santadi Sar ★★★ Best SAR co-op (and one of Italy's), esp for Carignano del Sulcis (Rocca Rubia RISERVA, *Terre Brune*). Villa di Chiesa (w blend), Latinia (PASSITO), VERMENTINO DI SARDEGNA (Cala Silente) v.gd.

Saracco, Paolo Pie ★★★★ Top MOSCATO D'ASTI; v.gd CHARD, LANGHE RIES, PINOT N.

Sardinia / Sardegna Italy's 2nd-largest island is home to world-class whites and reds. Try VERMENTINO DI GALLURA, VERMENTINO DI SARDEGNA (fruitier, less mineral), Sherry-like VERNACCIA DI ORISTANO, NURAGUS, Nasco, Semidano. CANNONAU (GARNACHA), Carignano, most famous reds. Bovale, Monica, Pascale just as gd.

Sartarelli Mar ★★★ High-quality VERDICCHIO DEI CASTELLI DI JESI CLASSICO. Top: Balciana, Milletta RISERVA, Tralivio.

Sassicaia Tus ★★★★ 10 13 15' 16' 18 19' 20 21' Italy's sole single-vyd DOC (BOLGHERI), a CAB (SAUV/FR) made on First-Growth lines by Marchese Incisa della Rocchetta at TENUTA SAN GUIDO. More elegant than lush, made for age – and often bought for investment, but hugely influential in giving Italy a top-quality image; 16 extremely elegant, one of best recent yrs.

Satta, Michele Tus ★★★ Virtually only BOLGHERI grower to succeed with 100% SANGIOVESE (Cavaliere). Best: BOLGHERI Marianova, Piastraia.

Scarpa Pie ★★★ Historic trad winery in NIZZA Monferrato. Top BARBERA D'ASTI La Bogliona, Rouchet (Ruchè); v.gd BARBARESCO Tettineive, Freisa.

Scarzello Pie ★★★ Classic, refined BAROLO. Top: Boschetti, Sarmassa. BARBERA D'ALBA, LANGHE NEBBIOLO v.gd.

Scavino, Paolo Pie ★★★ Modernist BAROLO producer of Castiglione Falletto: Bric del Fiasc, Monvigliero, Prapò, Ravera, Rocche dell'Annunziata.

Schiava Alto Adige T-AA ★ DOC DYA Schiava (VERNATSCH in German): blend of the three main Schiava varieties (Gentile, Grigia, Grossa). Used to make DOC wines called Lago di Caldaro, St-Magdalener (Santa Maddalena). Light- to medium-bodied, v. fresh, pleasant red. Best: cs Bolzano, Caldaro, GIRLAN, Merano.

Schiopetto, Mario FVG ★★★ Legendary late COLLIO pioneering estate now owned by Rotolo family; v.gd DOC FRIULANO, SAUV BL, *Pinot Bl*, RIBOLLA GIALLA and IGT blend Blanc des Rosis, etc.

Scolca, La Pie ★★★ Among 1st to make GAVI known in world, with legendary Black Label. Best: Gavi dei Gavi (Black Label, Limited Edition), Soldati D'Antan (and SPUMANTE Millesimato).

Sella & Mosca Sar ★★→★★★ Major SAR grower-merchant. *See* TERRA MORETTI.

Selvapiana Tus ★★★★ RÙFINA organic estate among Italian greats. Best: RISERVA Bucerchiale, IGT Fornace; but even *basic Chianti Rùfina is a treat*. Also fine red Petrognano, POMINO, Riserva VIGNETO Erchi.

Sesta di Sopra Tus ★★★ High-quality BRUNELLO (top RISERVA), ROSSO DI MONTALCINO.

Sesti – Castello di Argiano Tus ★★★ Distinctive, refined yet flavourful BRUNELLOS from Sesti family estate; trad-style. CLASSICO Brunello and RISERVA Phenomena equally gd, if different.

Sforzato / Sfursat Lom ★★★ DOCG Sforzato di VALTELLINA is made AMARONE-like, from air-dried NEBBIOLO grapes. Ages beautifully. Best: FAY (RONCO del Picchio). Dirupi (Vino Sbagliato), Mamete Prevostini (Albareda, Corte di Cama), Nino Negri (Cinque Stelle), Triacca all v.gd. *See* VALTELLINA.

Sicily The Med's largest island, modern source of exciting original wines and value. Native grapes (r Frappato, NERELLO MASCALESE, NERO D'AVOLA; w CARRICANTE, CATARRATTO, Grecanico, GRILLO, INZOLIA), plus internationals. The vyds are on flatlands in w, hills in centre, volcanic altitudes on Mt Etna.

Soave Ven ★★→★★★ DOC Famous, hitherto underrated Veronese white. Soils: mix of mainly volcanic or calcareous elements. Wines from volcanic soils of CLASSICO zone can be intense, saline, v. fine, quite long-lived. Best: Ca' Rugate, Casato 1922 (Vite Torta), GINI, INAMA, PIEROPAN, PRÀ, SUAVIA. Agostino Vicentini (Il Casale), Coffele (Alzari), Nardello (Monte Zoppega), Roccolo Grassi (Broia) v.gd. *See also* RECIOTO.

Solaia Tus ★★★★ 15 16' 18 19' 21 CAB/SANGIOVESE by ANTINORI; needs age.

Sorpasso Pie ★★★ Vittorio Garda is one of most talented young winemakers in PIE. Top: CALUSO, CAREMA. Elegant, refined.

Sorrentino Cam ★★→★★★ Benni S makes top (r/w) Lacryma Christi (5 Viti, VIGNA Lappillo). Best: AGLIANICO Don Paolo (r), Caprettone (Benita 31), Catalò (w) gd.

Sottimano Pie ★★★→★★★★ Family estate. One of most inspired in BARBARESCO (crus: Basarin, Cottá, Currá, Fausoni, Pajoré). BARBERA D'ALBA, DOLCETTO D'ALBA, LANGHE NEBBIOLO v.gd.

Speri Ven ★★★ VALPOLICELLA family estate. Organic; trad style. Top: AMARONE Sant'Urbano, RECIOTO DELLA VALPOLICELLA (La Roggia).

Spumante Sparkling.

Strette, Le Pie ★★★ Makes gd-value BAROLO Best: Bergera Pezzole, Corini Pallaretta, LANGHE Nas-cëtta del Comune di Novello (also single-vyd Pasinot).

Suavia Ven ★★★ Tessari sisters produce v. refined SOAVE CLASSICO. Top: Le Rive (GARGANEGA), Massifitti (TREBBIANO di Soave), Soave Classico (and Monte Carbonare); I Luoghi (The Places) project (Garganega).

Südtirol T-AA German name for ALTO ADIGE.

Superiore Wine with more ageing than normal DOC and 0.5–1% more alc. May indicate a restricted production zone, eg. ROSSO PICENO Superiore.

Super Tuscan Tus Wines of high quality and price developed in 70s/80s to get around silly laws then prevailing. Now, esp with Gran Selezione on up, scarcely relevant. Wines still generally considered in Super Tuscan category, strictly unofficially: BERTINGA, Ca' Marcanda, Flaccianello, Guado al Tasso, Messorio, ORNELLAIA, Redigaffi, SASSICAIA, SOLAIA, TIGNANELLO.

Alto Adige has largest grapevine in the world: 300m²+, 350 years+, Versoaln grape.

Tappero Merlo Domenico Pie ★★★ Roots in the past, eyes to the future and Erbaluce grape as life partner. Top: Acini Perduti (80/20% rare MALVASIA Moscata/Erbaluce), ERBALUCE DI CALUSO (Cuvée des Paladins, Kin). Bohemien (PASSITO) v.gd.

Tasca d'Almerita Si ★★★ New generation runs historic TENUTE. Top: (r) Regaleali (NERO D'AVOLA-based *Riserva del Conte*); (w) CHARD VIGNA San Francesco, Nozze d'Oro. Also v.gd: Capofaro (MALVASIA delle Lipari – Didyme, Vigna di Paola), Sallier de la Tour (SYRAH La Monaca), Tascante (ETNA r – Contrada Rampante, Contrada Sciaranuova Vigna Vecchia), Whitaker (GRILLO Mozia).

Taurasi Cam ★★★ DOCG 12 13 15 16 19 20 21' The 1st DOCG in S Italy. Best is AGLIANICO of CAM. None so potentially *complex, demanding, ultimately rewarding*. With 17 communes, four subzones: nw, w, Taurasi, s. Top: BENITO FERRARA, COLLI DI LAPIO, Contrade di Taurasi (Vigne d'Alto, Coste), Di Prisco, Donnachiara (and RISERVA Per Umberto), FEUDI DI SAN GREGORIO, I FAVATI, Guastaferro (and Riserva V.V. Primum), MASTROBERARDINO, Perillo, QUINTODECIMO, SALVATORE MOLETTIERI.

Tavignano, Tenuta di Mar ★★★ Organic. One of best VERDICCHIO DEI CASTELLI DI JESI producers. Top: Misco (and RISERVA). Villa Torre v.gd.

Tedeschi Ven ★★★ Bevy of v. fine VALPOLICELLA, AMARONE. Best new Amarone La Fabriseria, Capitel Monte Olmi, Maternigo, RECIOTO Capitel Monte Fontana. Amarone Marne 180 and Valpolicella La Fabriseria v.gd.

Tenuta An agricultural holding (*see* under name – eg. SAN GUIDO, TENUTA).

Terlano, Cantina di T-AA ★★★★ High-quality co-op, benchmark PINOT BL. Outstanding LAGREIN RISERVA Porphyr, Pinot Bl Riserva Vorberg, Primo *Terlaner I* Grande Cuvée (Pinot Bl/SAUV BL/CHARD), *Rarity* (w special editions, aged min 10 yrs on lees), Sauv Bl Quarz, Terlaner Cuvée Riserva Nova Domus. GEWURZ Lunare and iconic Terlaner (Pinot Bl/Sauv Bl/Chard) v.gd.

Teroldego Rotaliano T-AA ★★→★★★ DOC Trentino's best local grape makes seriously tasty wine on flat Campo Rotaliano. Top: *Foradori*. Cipriano Fedrizzi (Due Vigneti), Dorigati (Diedri), Mezzacorona (Musivum, Nos) gd.

Terra Moretti Lom, Sar, Tus ★★★→★★★★ Three regions, six estates owned by Moretti family. In FRANCIACORTA: Bellavista with new chef de caves Richard Geoffroy, ex-Dom Pérignon (top Pas Operé, Vittorio Moretti; v.gd Alma Non Dosato, Teatro alla Scala Brut), Contadi Castaldi (Pinot Nero, Zéro). In SAR: Sella & Mosca (top I CAB SAUV Marchese di Villamarina, Tanca Farrà, Cannonau Mustazzo; top w Torbato Terre Bianche Cuvée 161, VERMENTINO DI GALLURA Monte Oro.) In TUS: Acquagiusta La Baiola, Petra (Petra, Quercegobbe), Teruzzi (VERNACCIA DI SAN GIMIGNANOS Isola Bianca, RISERVA Sant'Elena).

Terre Nere, Tenuta delle Si ★★★★ Marc de Grazia shows great wine can be made from NERELLO and CARRICANTE, on coveted n side of Mt Etna. Top: Cuvée delle Vigne Niche, Guardiola and pre-phylloxera La VIGNA di Don Peppino. Le Vigne di Eli v.gd. Look for new ER Bocca d'Orzo (monopole) and EB Montalto.

Teularju Sar ★★★ Family estate, dedicated to CANNONAU and its ancient biotypes. Top: crus ("Ghiradas") Cara'Gonare, Ocruarana.

Tiberio Ab ★★★★ Outstanding TREBBIANO D'ABRUZZO Fonte Canale (60-yr-old vines), one of Italy's best whites; MONTEPULCIANO D'ABRUZZO Archivio, Colle Vota (both single vyd; CERASUOLO D'ABRUZZO (one of best ROSATOS in Italy). PECORINO also exceptional.

Tiefenbrunner T-AA ★★★→★★★★ Christof runs one of most historical estates in Turmhof Castle in S ALTO ADIGE. Wide range of mtn-fresh white and well-defined red varietals, esp 1000m (3281ft)-high MÜLLER-T *Feldmarschall*, one of Italy's best whites, now also late-harvest. Top: VIGNA range: CHARD Au, CAB SAUV Toren, SAUV BL Rachtl. Linticlarus range: Chard, LAGREIN, PINOT N v.gd.

Tignanello Tus ★★★ 16' **17 19** 20 21 Dense SANGIOVESE/CAB SAUV, from ANTINORI.

Tommasi Ven ★★★ Now 4th generation in charge, elegant wines. Top: AMARONE (RISERVA Ca' Florian, iconic De Buris), LUGANA Riserva Le Fornaci, VALPOLICELLA Rafael. Classic. Other estates in Bas (Paternoster), OLTREPÒ PAVESE (TENUTA Caseo), PUG (Masseria Surani), Ven (Filodora).

Torgiano Umb ★★ DOC ★★→★★★ Riserva DOCG **13** 15 16 19' 20 21 Range gd to excellent red. Top: LUNGAROTTI *Vigna Monticchio* Rubesco RISERVA. Keeps many yrs.

Torrette VdA ★→★★★ DOC Blend based on Petit Rouge and other local varieties. Best: Torrette Superieur. Anselmet, D&D, DI BARRÒ, Didier Gerbelle, OTTIN, FEUDO DI SAN MAURIZIO, GROSJEAN, LES CRETES, LO TRIOLET gd.

Traerte Cam ★★★ Raffaele Troise, v. talented maker of Torama, one of Italy's best whites (100% Coda di Volpe Bianca). Top: GRECO DI TUFO Tornante, GRECO Fuori Limite Le Vecchie Vigne, FIANO DI AVELLINO Aipierti.

Tramin, Cantina T-AA ★★★ Quality co-op with benchmark GEWURZ. Outstanding Epokale, Nussbaumer, Terminum, (CHARD) Troy, (PINOT GR) Unterebner. Best: Selezioni range the highest expression.

Travaglini Pie ★★★ Solid producer of GATTINARA. Best: RISERVA, Tre Vigne. Coste della Sesia, Gattinara, METODO CLASSICO Nebolé (NEBBIOLO) v.gd.

Trebbiano d'Abruzzo Ab ★→★★★★ DOC DYA Generally crisp, simple, but TIBERIO'S (Fonte Canale) and VALENTINI'S are *two of Italy's greatest* whites. Cirelli, EMIDIO PEPE, La Valentina, Terraviva, Valle Reale v.gd.

Trediberri Pie ★★★ Dynamic estate. Top: BAROLO Rocche dell'Annunziata (best value). New BARBERA D'ALBA, Barolo Berri, LANGHE NEBBIOLO gd.

Trento T-AA ★★→★★★★ DOC High-quality METODO CLASSICO fizz. Top: ABATE NERO, FERRARI, MASO MARTIS (esp Blanc de Blancs Brut, Madame Martis RISERVA), SAN LEONARDO. Cembra (Oro Rosso), Cesarini SFORZA, Letrari v.gd.

Trinoro, Tenuta di Tus ★★★★ Individualist TUS red estate, pioneer in DOC Val d'Orcia.

Heavy accent on Bx grapes in flagship TENUTA di Trinoro, also in Camagi, Palazzi, Magnacosta, Tenagli. *See also* VINI FRANCHETTI (ETNA).

Tua Rita Tus ★★★★ As new BOLGHERI in 90s, 1st producer of possibly Italy's greatest MERLOT in Redigaffi (25th anniversary: 19); outstanding *Giusto di Notri* Bx-blend, SYRAH Per Sempre, Keir (amphora). Also owns POGGIO ARGENTIERA in Maremma (best: Capatosta, MORELLINO DI SCANSANO).

Tuscany / Toscana Home of world's top SANGIOVESE. CHIANTI CLASSICO, BRUNELLO DI MONTALCINO, RÙFINA best, but BOLGHERI just as gd and world-class for international grapes (CAB FR, MERLOT), but SASSICAIA (CAB SAUV) most famous.

Uberti Lom ★★★→★★★★ Historic estate, excellent interpreter of FRANCIACORTA's terroir. Outstanding Comarì del Salem, Dequinque (blend of 15 yrs), Quinque (blend of 5 yrs). Dosaggio Zero Sublimis RISERVA, Francesco I v.gd.

Vajra, GD Pie ★★★→★★★★ Leading BAROLO producer in Vergne. Outstanding Bricco delle Viole, LANGHE FREISA Kyè. Barolos (Coste di Rose, Ravera), DOLCETTO Coste & Fossati, Langhe RIES, Serralunga's Baudana Barolos (Cerretta) gd.

Valentini, Edoardo Ab ★★★★ Collectors seek CERASUOLO D'ABRUZZO, MONTEPULCIANO D'ABRUZZO, TREBBIANO D'ABRUZZO; among Italy's v. best. Age-worthy, trad.

Valle d'Aosta ★★→★★★ DOC Italy's smallest region makes some of its best reds/whites, but hard to find. Soil of morainic origin (heterogeneous glacial deposits of gravel sands). Famous names incl Arnad-Montjovet, Blanc de Morgex (w/sp from Prié Bl), Chambave (local biotype of w MUSCAT), Donnas (NEBBIOLO-based), Nus MALVOISIE (with PINOT GR), Torrette (r mostly Petit Rouge). Lovely wines from (r) Cornalin, Mayolet and Premetta; (w) Petite ARVINE and CHARD.

Valle Isarco T-AA ★★ DYA ALTO ADIGE DOC for seven Germanic varietal whites made along Isarco (Eisack) River, ne of Bolzano. Top: Abbazia di Novacella, Eisacktaler, KÖFERERHOF, Kuenhof, MANNI NÖSSING. Also gd GEWURZ, MÜLLER-T, RIES, SILVANER.

Valpolicella Ven ★→★★★★ DOC(G) Light, easy-going red (Valpol), medium-bodied to powerfully alc, rich, tannic (AMARONE) and super-sweet (RECIOTO). Popular RIPASSO, between Valpol and Amarone, but few noteworthy. (*See* box, below.)

Valpolicella Ripasso Ven ★★→★★★ DOC 13 15 16 18 19 20 21' In huge demand, so changes from 2016. Used to be only from VALPOLICELLA SUPERIORE re-fermented (once only) on RECIOTO or AMARONE grapeskins to make a more age-worthy wine. Now can blend 10% Amarone with standard Valpol and call it Ripasso. Best: Brigaldara, BUSSOLA, CA' LA BIONDA, PRÀ, SPERI, Tamburino Sardo, TEDESCHI, TOMMASI, ZENATO.

Valtellina Lom ★→★★★ DOC/DOCG Rare e-w valley, just s of Swiss border. Soils are sandy-loamy. Home of CHIAVENNASCA. Best labelled Valtellina SUPERIORE (five subzones: Grumello, Inferno, Maroggia, Sassella, Valgella), *see* SFORZATO. Top: ArPePe (Grumello RISERVA Sant'Antonio, Inferno Fiamme

---

Valpolicella: the best

Time to take gd VALPOLICELLA more seriously. AMARONE DELLA VALPOLICELLA and RECIOTO DELLA VALPOLICELLA are now DOCG, while RIPASSO has new rules. Following producers make gd to great (★) wine: Allegrini, Begali, Bertani, BOLLA, Boscaini, ★ Brigaldara, BRUNELLI, ★ BUSSOLA, Ca' la Bianca, ★ CA' LA BIONDA, Ca' Rugate, Campagnola, CANTINA Valpolicella, Castellani, Corteforte, Corte Sant'Alda, CS Valpantena, ★ DAL FORNO, ★ GUERRIERI RIZZARDI, Le Ragose, Le Salette, ★ MASI, ★ Mazzi, MONTE DEL FRÀ, Nicolis, ★ PRÀ, ★ QUINTARELLI, ★ Roccolo Grassi, Secondo Marco, ★ Serego Alighieri, ★ SPERI, ★ Stefano Accordini, ★ TEDESCHI, ★ TOMMASI, Valentina Cubi, Venturini, ★ Viviani, ZENATO, Zeni.

Antiche, Nuova Regina, Sassella Rocce Rosse), Dirupi, FAY, Mamete Prevostini (Sassella Sommarovina).

Vecchio Samperi Si *See* MARCO DE BARTOLI.

Venissa Ven ★★★ Owned by BISOL family. Beautiful vyd on island of Mazzorbo in Venice lagoon. Top: Venissa (100% rare w Dorona). Rosso Venissa (Bx blend) v.gd. Unique wines.

How many castles are there in Verdicchio dei Castelli di Jesi? 25. Plenty of sightseeing.

Verdicchio dei Castelli di Jesi Mar ★★→★★★ Versatile white from nr Ancona on Adriatic; light and quaffable or sparkling or structured, complex, long-lived (esp RISERVA DOCG, min 2 yrs old), usually lighter and more floral than those of Matelica. Montecarotto more structured. Cupramontana more vibrant. Also CLASSICO. Best: *Bucci*, CORONCINO, Edoardo Dottori (Kochlos, Nardì), FATTORIA SAN LORENZO, Garofoli (Podium, Serra Fiorese), Marotti Campi (Salmariano), MONTECAPPONE, PIEVALTA, SARTARELLI, TENUTA DI TAVIGNANO.

Verdicchio di Matelica Mar ★★→★★★ Higher acidity level, but also more body, alc and intense minerality, than wines of Jesi; so longer-lasting though less easy-drinking young. Lower-lying vyds grow on alluvial soils, while higher hillsides have complex soils of calcarenites, marl, limestone, gravel and conglomerates. RISERVA is likewise DOCG. Top: Belisario (Cambrugiano), Bisci, Borgo Paglianetto (Jera Riserva, Petrara, Vertis), Collestefano, LA MONACESCA.

Verduno Pie ★★★ DOC DYA Berry and herbal flavours. Top: Arnaldo Rivera, Cadia, CASTELLO DI VERDUNO, Diego Morra, FRATELLI ALESSANDRIA (Speziale), GB BURLOTTO, Gianluca Colombo, Reverdito.

Verduno, Castello di Pie ★★★ Husband/wife team, v.gd terroir-driven BARBARESCO Rabajà and Rabajà-Bas, BAROLO Massara and Monvigliero (also RISERVA), VERDUNO Basadone.

Verduzzo FVG ★★→★★★ DOC (FRIULI COLLI ORIENTALI) Full-bodied white from local variety. Ramandolo (DOCG) is well-regarded subzone for sweet. Top: I CLIVI, Marco Sara, Scubla.

Vermentino di Gallura Sar ★★★ DOCG More flinty and saline than VERMENTINO DI SARDEGNA. Different soils characterized by pink granite (rarity in Italy) with high acidity and minerality. Maybe best in Italy. Top: CANTINA di Gallura (Canayli), Capichera, CS del Vermentino (Funtanaliras), Masone Mannu (top Costarenas), Petrizza, Roccaìa), Mura (Sienda), Pala (Stellato), Paolo Depperu (Ruinas), SELLA & MOSCA (Monteoro), Surrau.

Vermentino di Sardegna Sar ★★ DOC DYA From anywhere on SAR; generally fruitier (less structured) and offer earlier, uncomplicated appeal compared to VERMENTINO DI GALLURA. Best: ARGIOLAS, Deiana, Mora e Memo, Quartomoro, *Santadi, Sella & Mosca*.

Vernaccia di Oristano Sar ★→★★★★ DOC Flor-affected wine, similar to light Sherry, a touch bitter and full-bodied. Delicious with bottarga. Must try. Top: CONTINI (★ Antico Gregori, Flor 22, RISERVA). Orro, Serra, Silvio Carta gd.

Vernaccia di San Gimignano Tus ★★→★★★ Better at entry level than RISERVA. Top: Fontaleoni (VIGNA Casanuova), Giovanni Panizzi, Guicciardini Strozzi/Fattoria di Cusona (1933), La Lastra, Sono Montenidoli (Fiore), Turizzi (Sant'Elena).

Versio, Francesco Pie ★★★ Young talented winemaker in BARBARESCO. Top: refined Barbaresco, DOGLIANI, LANGHE NEBBIOLO.

Viarte, La FVG ★★→★★★ Organic estate of FRIULI COLLI ORIENTALI; v.gd terroir-driven FRIULANO, SCHIOPPETTINO di Prepotto, Tazzelenghe.

Viberti Pie ★★★ High-quality, classic BAROLO (Bricco delle Viole, La Volta, Monvigliero, San Pietro), RISERVAS. BARBERA D'ALBA, LANGHE NEBBIOLO v.gd.

Vie di Romans FVG ★★★★ Gianfranco Gallo has built up his father's ISONZO estate to top status. Outstanding Climat line (six different CHARDS, from six different sites, for authentic terroir expression), Flors di Uis blend, Isonzo PINOT GR Dessimis, MALVASIA, SAUV BL Piere and Vieris. Pinot Gr Dessimis v.gd.

Vietti Pie ★★★★ Organic estate at Castiglione Falletto owned by Krause Group but still run by Luca Currado and Mario Cordero. Characterful. Textbook BAROLOS: Brunate, Cerequio, Lazzarito, Monvigliero, Ravera, Rocche di Castiglione, Villero RISERVA. Plus v.gd BARBERA D'ALBA, BARBERA D'ASTI, BARBARESCO, DERTHONA.

Vigna (or vigneto) A single vyd, generally indicating superior quality.

Vigneri, I Si ★★★★ Consortium of growers, also ETNA estate within that consortium, run by Salvo Foti, greatest expert on NERELLO MASCALESE and all Etna varieties. Consortium focus on bush-trained vines, native grape varieties and respect for the land. Outstanding: ETNA Bianco SUPERIORE (VIGNA di Milo, Palmento Caselle), ETNA Rosso (Vinupetra and Viti Centenarie). Also v.gd Aurora (w), I Vigneri (r), Vinudilice (rosé).

Villa Lom ★★★ Owned by Bianchi family, in small medieval hamlet (C15) in FRANCIACORTA. Consistent. Best sparkling: Diamant Pas Dosè, Emozione Brut Millesimato and RISERVA, Selezione Riserva.

Villa Crespia Lom ★★★ Family estate in FRANCIACORTA, organic. Top: Brut Millè RISERVA, Dosaggio Zero Numero Zero and Riserva del Gelso. Brut Millè v.gd.

Villa Russiz FVG ★★★ Historic estate for DOC COLLIO, v.gd SAUV BL and MERLOT (esp de la Tour selections), CHARD, FRIULANO, PINOTS BL/GR.

Vino Nobile di Montepulciano Tus ★★→★★★ 15 16 17 18 19 20 21 The 1st Italian DOCG (1980). Prugnolo Gentile (SANGIOVESE)-based, from TUS town MONTEPULCIANO (distinct from grape). Recent focus on single vyds. Complex, long-lasting Sangiovese expression, often tough, drying tannins. Top: AVIGNONESI, Boscarelli (Costa Grande, Nocio, RISERVA Sotto Casa), Dei (Bossona, cru Madonna della Querce), La Braccesca, Poliziano, Salcheto. Bindella, Fattoria del Cerro, Fattoria della Talosa, Montemercurio, Valdipiatta gd. Riserva after 3 yrs.

Vin Santo / Vinsanto / Vino Santo T-AA, Tus ★★→★★★★ DOC Sweet PASSITO, usually TREBBIANO, MALVASIA and/or SANGIOVESE in TUS (Vin Santo), Nosiola in Trentino (Vino Santo). Versions from TUS extremely variable, anything from off-dry and Sherry-like to sweet and v. rich. May spend 3–10 unracked yrs in small barrels called *caratelli*. *Avignonesi's is legendary*; plus CAPEZZANA, FELSINA, FRASCOLE, ISOLE E OLENA, Rocca di Montegrossi, SAN GIUSTO A RENTENNANO, SELVAPIANA, Villa Sant'Anna, Villa di Vetrice. *See also* OCCHIO DI PERNICE.

Volpaia, Castello di Tus ★★→★★★★ CHIANTI CLASSICO estate at Radda; v.gd; organic. Top Balifico (SANGIOVESE/CAB SAUV), Chianti Classico RISERVA, Gran Selezione Coltassala (Sangiovese/Mammolo).

Zenato Ven ★★★ Garda wines: v. reliable, sometimes inspired. Also AMARONE, LUGANA, SOAVE, VALPOLICELLA. Look for labels RISERVA Sergio Zenato.

What do the initials mean?

DOC (denominazione di origine controllata) controlled denomination of origin, cf. AOP in France.

DOCG (denominazione di origine controllata e garantita) "G" = "guaranteed". Italy's highest quality designation. Guarantee? It's still caveat emptor.

IGT (indicazione geografica tipica) geographic indication of type. Broader and more vague than DOC, cf. IGP in France.

DOP / IGP (denominazione di origine protetta / indicazione geografica protetta) "P" = "protected". The EU's DOP/IGP trump Italy's DOC/IGT.

MGA (menzione geografica aggiuntiva) or UGA (additional geographical units), eg. subzones, cf. crus in France.

Germany

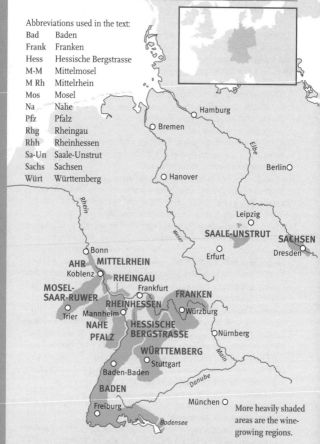

Abbreviations used in the text:

Bad	Baden
Frank	Franken
Hess	Hessische Bergstrasse
M-M	Mittelmosel
M Rh	Mittelrhein
Mos	Mosel
Na	Nahe
Pfz	Pfalz
Rhg	Rheingau
Rhh	Rheinhessen
Sa-Un	Saale-Unstrut
Sachs	Sachsen
Würt	Württemberg

More heavily shaded areas are the wine-growing regions.

German wine is Riesling: discuss. This identity has deep historical roots and has been revitalized by growers over the past 30 years. But of course German wine is not exclusively Riesling; as recently as the 60s, the most widely planted vine was Silvaner. And at the heart of German wine, there is another grape: Pinot Noir. There are many indications that it came to Lake Constance from Burgundy during the medieval warm period in the ninth or tenth century. Now the climate is getting warmer again, so not surprisingly Pinot Noir, and Chardonnay in its wake, are becoming more important. Before climate change began to be felt, Pinot Noir was a bit of an also-ran in Germany. Now there are wines to compete with any. When you talk to young growers, you often realize that they respect the Riesling tradition and continue it, but what they really love are the Burgundy varieties. That Pinot love: it never lets go.

Recent vintages

Mosel

Don't drink them too young. Certainly, Mosels are delicious v. soon after bottling, but to enjoy their max complexity, allow Grosses Gewächs (GG) a min of 3 yrs, Kabinett 3–5 yrs, Spätlese 5–7 yrs, Auslese 7–10 yrs.

2023 Conditions improved just in time and lasted: mid-weight wines of fine balance.
2022 Another dry, hot summer. Sept rain complicated harvest.
2021 Mildew, rain, harvest into Nov, lighter wines, outstanding freshness and balance.
2020 3rd yr running of drought, gd quality, quantity.
2019 Low quantity (-25%, Ruwer -40%: frost), but textbook raciness.
2018 Powerful, low acidity (but better than 2003). Crystal-clear TBA.
2017 Low yield (frost) = high extract.
2016 Balanced wines.
2015 Warm yr, rich Trocken, Spätlesen, Auslesen to keep.
Earlier fine vintages: 12 11 09 08 07 05 04 03 01 99 97 95 94 93 90 89 88 76 71 69 64 59 53 49 45 37 34 21.

Rheinhessen, Nahe, Pfalz, Rheingau, Ahr

Rhg tends to be longest-lived of all German regions, improving for 15 yrs or more, but best wines from Rhh, Na and Pfz can last as long – and this applies not only to Spätlese and Auslese; GGs undoubtedly have potential to age for 10 yrs+ too. The same holds for Ahr V reds and their peers from Bad and other regions of the s.

2023 Spring wet, summer dry, hail too (Rhh, Bad). Sept wet, warm; Oct fine. Ries better than Pinot N, but tight selection crucial.
2022 Hot, dry yr, mixed results: cool nights, but also rain. Pinots often better than Ries.
2021 Classical yr like those of 80s, gd acidity, moderate alc, intense flavours.
2020 Early and fast harvest, mid-weight wines.
2019 Drought, heatwaves, rain. Excellent Ries with gd acidity.
2018 Record summer, powerful wines. Growers allowed to acidify.
2017 Roter Hang and Mittelhaardt outstanding: freshness combined with extract.
2016 Quality and quantity mixed.
2015 Hot, dry summer. Rhg excellent, both dry and nobly sweet.
Earlier fine vintages: 12 11 09 08 05 03 02 01 99 98 97 96 93 90 83 76 71 69 67 64 59 53 49 45 37 34 21.

Acham-Magin Pfz ★★★ Family estate at FORST; vines in Kirchenstück, Jesuitengarten, Pechstein. Organic; crisp, age-worthy wines. Restaurant too, continuously open since 1712.

Adams, Simone Rhh ★★★ PhD oenologist putting emphasis on vibrant freshness of INGELHEIM's calcareous soils. Best: single-vyds Auf dem Haun and Pares.

Adelmann, Graf Würt ★★→★★★ Estate est 1297, kept young by count Felix A, wide range: lush Süssmund RIES, tight Oberer Berg LEMBERGER, finely tuned red cuvées, skin-fermented Ries Neben Frank, or even GRÜNER V.

Adeneuer, J.J. Ahr ★★★ Prime producer, best usually Gärkammer, from enclave in famous Kräuterberg, planted with ancient Kastenholz clone of PINOT N.

Ahr Small river valley s of Bonn; PINOT N of outstanding complexity from slate. Terrible flood in July 21 destroyed buildings and equipment, but vintage saved by helicopter sprays. Best: ADENEUER, BERTRAM-BALTES, Brogsitter, BURGGARTEN, DEUTZERHOF, KREUZBERG, Kriechel, MEYER-NÄKEL, Nelles, Riske, SCHUMACHER, SERMANN, STODDEN. Also gd co-ops: Dagernova, Mayschoss-Altenahr.

Aldinger, Gerhard Würt ★★★→★★★★ Outstanding family estate at Fellbach nr Stuttgart. Reliable (RIES, LEMBERGER, PINOT N), and inventive: Brut Nature SEKT, TROLLINGER ALTE REBEN Blanc de Noirs, magnificent Mönchberg Ries EISWEIN 21.

Assmannshausen has mineral springs – until 1945 it was a spa and bathing resort.

Alte Reben Old vines. But no min age.

Amtliche Prüfungsnummer (APNr) Official test number for quality wine. Useful for discerning different lots of AUSLESE a producer has made from the same vyd.

Assmannshausen Rhg ★★→★★★★ Steep Höllenberg (45 ha) produces delicate *Spätburgunder* with 50 yrs+ ageing potential. Growers: Allendorf, Berg, BISCHÖFLICHES WEINGUT RÜDESHEIM, CHAT SAUVAGE, HESSISCHE STAATSWEINGÜTER, KESSELER, König, KRONE, KÜNSTLER, SAALWÄCHTER, SOLVEIGS.

Aust, Karl Friedrich Sachs ★★★ Fine family estate (brilliant TRAMINER, PINOT N) nr Dresden, brand-new winery at foot of steep, terraced Goldener Wagen vyd.

Ayl Mos ★→★★★ All vyds known since 1971 by name of historically best site: Kupp. Growers: BISCHÖFLICHE WEINGÜTER TRIER, *Lauer*, Vols, ZILLIKEN.

Bacharach M Rh ★→★★★ Small, idyllic Rhine-side town; centre of M RH RIES. Growers: JOST, KAUER, RATZENBERGER.

Baden Huge sw region and former Grand Duchy, 15,000 ha stretch 300 km+. There are nine districts with v. different conditions, eg. BODENSEE, KAISERSTUHL, MARKGRÄFLERLAND, ORTENAU.

Barth, Wein- und Sektgut Rhg ★★→★★★ Family estate at HATTENHEIM, 22 ha; specialize in finely chiselled RIES SEKT from single vyds (Hassel, Schützenhaus).

Bassermann-Jordan Pfz ★★★ Famous historic estate producing powerful RIES from DEIDESHEIM and FORST: trad GGS; experimental vinifications (Ries Ancestrale, amphora CAB SAUV).

Battenfeld-Spanier Rhh ★★★→★★★★ Passionate HO Spanier (*see also* KÜHLING-GILLOT) is leading grower in calcareous sites at Hohen-Sülzen, Mölsheim and ZELLERTAL (auction RIES about to get cultish), bio. Brilliant Brut Nature SEKT.

Becker, Friedrich Pfz ★★★★ Age-worthy, terroir-driven PINOT N (Heydenreich, Kammerberg, Sankt Paul) from SÜDPFALZ. Some vyds actually lie across border in Alsace.

Becker, J.B. Rhg ★★→★★★ Delightfully old-fashioned, cask-aged (and long-lived) dry RIES, SPÄTBURGUNDER at Walluf and Martinsthal. Mature vintages (back to 90s) great value.

Bercher Bad ★★★ KAISERSTUHL family estate, v. reliable from ORTSWEIN up to GG, long experience in barrique ageing of PINOT BL/GR/N.

Bergdolt Pfz ★★★ Organic estate at Duttweiler, known for food-friendly WEISSBURGUNDER GG Mandelberg, mineral RIES, taut SPÄTBURGUNDER. Stunning SEKT (Brut Nature Fluxus).

Bernkastel M-M ★→★★★★ Centre of M-M, misrepresented by Kurfürstlay GROSSLAGE (avoid!). Rightly famous sites: Alte Badstube am Docterberg, Badstube, DOCTOR, Graben, Johannisbrünnchen, Lay.

Bernkasteler Ring Mos One of two MOS growers' associations organizing an auction every Sept, eg. MOLITOR, THANISCH Erben Müller-Burggraef.

Bertram-Baltes Ahr ★★★ Shooting stars in AHR. Early picking, moderate use of new oak, and ageing on lees bring fresh, dense, racy SPÄTBURGUNDER from prime vyds.

Bischel Rhh ★★★ VDP family estate in Appenheim, outstanding RIES GGS Heerkretz, Hundertgulden 19' 21', Scharlachberg.

Bischöfliches Weingut Rüdesheim Rhg ★★★ Not to be confused with BISCHÖFLICHE WEINGÜTER TRIER: 9 ha of best sites in ASSMANNSHAUSEN, RÜDESHEIM. Age-worthy, dense *Pinot N.* (Cellarmaster Peter Perabo vinified legendary vintages at KRONE before.) Brilliant 20s.

Bischöfliche Weingüter Trier Mos ★★ 130 ha of potentially 1st-class historic donations. Not v. reliable; do not buy without prior tasting.

Bocksbeutel Frank Belly-shaped bottle dating back to C18, today only permitted in FRANK and village of Neuweier, BAD.

Bodensee Bad Idyllic district of S BAD and on (particularly dynamic) Bavarian shore of Lake Constance, at altitude: 400–580m (1312–1903ft). Dry, elegant MÜLLER-T, light, firm SPÄTBURGUNDER.

Boppard M Rh ★→★★★ Wine town of M RH with GROSSE LAGE Hamm, an amphitheatre of vines. Growers: Heilig Grab, Lorenz, M Müller, Perll, WEINGART. Unbeatable *value*.

Brauneberg M-M ★★★ →★★★★ Excellent full-flavoured RIES from Juffer and Juffer-Sonnenuhr vyds. Growers: *F Haag*, KESSELSTATT, M Conrad, MF RICHTER, Paulinshof, Sankt Nikolaus Hospital, SCHLOSS LIESER, THANISCH, *W Haag*.

Bremer Ratskeller Town-hall cellar in N Germany's commercial town of Bremen, founded in 1405, UNESCO World Heritage Site. Oldest wine is a barrel of 1653 RÜDESHEIMER Apostelwein.

Breuer Rhg ★★★→★★★★ Exquisite RIES from RAUENTHAL, RÜDESHEIM and LORCH. Nonnenberg transforms austerity into age-worthiness, Berg Schlossberg 90' 93' 96' 97' 02' 08' **12' 13' 14** 15' 16 17' 18 19 20 21' has depth at 12% alc, Pfaffenwies full of floral elegance.

Buhl, Reichsrat von Pfz ★★★ Historic PFZ estate at DEIDESHEIM. Several changes in cellar, unstable quality but still 1st-class sites.

Bürgerspital zum Heiligen Geist Frank ★★★ Ancient charitable estate with great continuity: only six directors in 180 yrs. Whites trad-made from best sites in/

Geology of German Pinot

German PINOT N is now so gd that we can take a look at what influences style – and of course, it's terroir. Let's focus here on soil. Prepare for a spot of geology. **Slate** gives Pinot almost RIES-like elegance, fruit-driven, quite powerful in warm yrs, but always kept in balance by fine acidity. Locations: AHR, ASSMANNSHAUSEN, LORCH, MOS. **Buntsandstein** (or **sandstone**) gives Pinot an iron-mineral kick and extremely fine yet firm tannins. Locations: Bürgstadt, Klingenberg (textbook: FÜRST). **Limestone** gives Pinot power and spiciness, and it allows an inherent "coolness" to shine through in the wine, however dense it may be. Locations: Breisgau (Malterdingen), MARKGRÄFLERLAND, INGELHEIM, N PFZ (Kallstadt, Laumersheim, ZELLERTAL), SÜDPFALZ. Layers of the fossiliferous **Keuper formation** produce Pinot that tends to be similar to those from limestone, with a slightly more herbaceous flavour and a little less tannic power. Location: WÜRT. **Volcanic** weathering gives Pinot firmness, tension and capacity to age, sometimes with tufa-like flavours. Locations: KAISERSTUHL, NA, SACHS. **Granite** and **gneiss** create Pinots of vertical structure, which develop a luscious fruit with bottle-age. Locations: parts of Breisgau, ORTENAU (both BAD).

around WÜRZBURG, eg. SILVANER GG from monopole Stein-Harfe 15' 16' 17' 18' 19' 20' 21' 22, RIES Randersacker Pfülben 20' 21' 22'.

Burggarten Ahr ★★★ PINOT N from best sites in lower AHR, tight, aromatic, outstanding Alte Lay 20', but not much left after flood.

Bürklin-Wolf, Dr. Pfz ★★★→★★★★ Estate with 30 ha of best MITTELHAARDT vyds, incl FORST (Jesuitengarten, Kirchenstück, Pechstein); bio. Forerunner of VDP classifcation (1994).

Busch, Clemens Mos ★★★★ Steep Pündericher Marienburg farmed by hand, bio. Seven GGs from different parcels, eg. Felserrasse (mineral, deep), Raffes (power, balance), Rothenpfad (silky, balsamic). Also Res range (2 yrs barrel ageing).

Castell'sches Fürstliches Domänenamt Frank ★★★ Ferdinand Fürst zu Castell vigorously increases quality: SILVANER GG Schlossberg 11 12 14 15' 16 17' 18, now sold only 5 yrs after harvest, ERSTE LAGE Silvaners (Hohnart 22', Kugelspiel 22) outstanding value.

Chat Sauvage Rhg ★★★→★★★★ Burgundy in RHG: dense PINOT N from ASSMANNSHAUSEN, JOHANNISBERG, LORCH, RÜDESHEIM; crisp CHARD.

Christmann Pfz ★★★→★★★★ VDP President Steffen C, bio pioneer, now joined by daughter Sophie, PINOT N expert. Estate owns only classified vyds. Also CHRISTMANN & KAUFFMANN.

Christmann & Kauffmann Pfz ★★★ SEKT estate, est 2019 by Sophie and Steffen C and ex-Bollinger cellarmaster (*see* France) Mathieu K. Triple-digit codes on labels: 101 = RIES-based, 1st disgorgement; 203 = PINOTS N/BL/CHARD-based, 3rd disgorgement.

Clüsserath, Ansgar Mos ★★★ Tense TRITTENHEIM Apotheke RIES by Eva Clüsserath-WITTMANN (married to Philipp W). KABINETTS delicious.

Corvers-Kauter Rhg ★★★ Organic estate at Mittelheim, 37 ha, textbook dry RIES from RAUENTHAL (Baiken), RÜDESHEIM, Marcobrunn, occasionally also TBA; PINOT N from ASSMANNSHAUSEN.

Crusius, Dr. Na ★★→★★★ Family estate at TRAISEN. Young Rebecca C brings fresh air, combining finesse, expression.

Dautel Würt ★★→★★★★ Christian D produces CHARD, PINOT N, also PINOT BL, LEMBERGER, in a Burgundian spirit. Breathtaking S Chard 20: flinty, rich, with distinctive minerality.

Deidesheim Pfz ★★→★★★★ Centre of MITTELHAARDT (also economically). Many vyds compete for 1st place, eg. Grainhübel, Kalkofen, Langenmorgen. Top growers: BASSERMANN-JORDAN, Biffar, BUHL, BÜRKLIN-WOLF, CHRISTMANN, Fusser, MOSBACHER, SECKINGER, Siben, Stern, VON WINNING; gd co-op.

Deutzerhof Ahr ★★★ Quality pioneer in AHR in 90s, now top again; GGS (Mönchberg, Eck) and Res range (Grand Duc).

Diel, Schlossgut Na ★★★→★★★★ Caroline D follows father: exquisite *GG Ries*, best usually Burgberg. Magnificent SPÄTLESEN, serious *Sekt* Cuvée Mo and Goldloch RIES.

Doctor M-M Emblematic steep vyd at BERNKASTEL, place where TBA was invented 1921 by THANISCH. RIES of unique balsamic flavours from 3.2 ha, five owners: both Thanisch estates, WEGELER (1.1 ha), Lauerburg and local Heiligen Geist charity (0.26 ha, leased until 2024 to MOLITOR, SCHLOSS LIESER).

Dolde, Helmut Würt ★★→★★★ Some of Germany's highest vyds (up to 530m/1739ft), meticulously managed by retired grammar-school teacher. Stunning SILVANERS, delicate SPÄTBURGUNDER, serious pét-nat.

Dönnhoff Na ★★★★ Outstanding in every respect: solid basic wines, excellent GGS (balance, ageing potential), and fruity and nobly sweet wines of great distinction. Usually best: Hermannshöhle; other vyds not far behind.

Egon Müller zu Scharzhof Mos ★★★★ 59 71 83 90 01 03 15 18 19 20 21 22 23 Legendary

SAAR family estate at WILTINGEN, treasury of old vines. Racy SCHARZHOFBERGER RIES among world's greatest: sublime, vibrant, immortal. *Kabinetts* feather-light, long-lived (but meanwhile costly).

Einzellage Individual vyd site. Never to be confused with GROSSLAGE.

Emrich-Schönleber Na ★★★ Werner S and son Frank make precise RIES from Monzingen's classified Frühlingsplätzchen and Halenberg vyds.

Erden M-M ★★★ →★★★★ Village on red slate soils; RIES (dr/sw) with rare spiciness, delicacy. GROSSE LAGE: Prälat, Treppchen. Growers: BREMER RATSKELLER, Erbes, JJ Christoffel, LOOSEN, MAX F RICHTER, MERKELBACH, MOLITOR, Mönchhof, Rebenhof, Schmitges.

Erste Lage Classified vyd, 2nd-from-top level in VDP classification, similar to Burgundy's Premier Cru.

Erzeugerabfüllung Analogous to GUTSABFÜLLUNG, but also allowed on the labels of co-ops.

Escherndorf Frank ★★★ Village with steep GROSSE LAGE Lump ("scrap" – as in tiny inherited parcels). Marvellous *Silvaner*, RIES (dr/sw). Growers: Fröhlich, H SAUER, R SAUER, Schäffer, zur Schwane.

Eser, August Rhg ★★→★★★ Fine Oestrich family estate known for elegant RHG RIES (dr/sw); gd PINOT N too.

Feinherb Imprecisely defined trad term for wines with around 10–30g/l sugar.

Forst Pfz ★★→★★★★ Famous MITTELHAARDT village; Kirchenstück was PFZ's highest taxed vyd in 1828 tax map. Pechstein, Jesuitengarten, Ungeheuer vyds almost equally outstanding. Top growers: ACHAM-MAGIN, BASSERMANN-JORDAN, BÜRKLIN-WOLF, H Spindler, Margarethenhof, MOSBACHER, VON BUHL, VON WINNING, WOLF.

Franken / Franconia Region of distinctive dry wines, esp SILVANER, often bottled in round-bellied flasks (BOCKSBEUTEL).

Fricke, Eva Rhg ★★★ Dense, full-bodied, even silky RIES from 17 ha at KIEDRICH and LORCH.

Fürst, Weingut Frank ★★★ →★★★★ *Spätburgunders* 97' 03' 05' 09 10' 15' 16' 17 18' 19 20 21 of great finesse from red sandstone (most dense, Hundsrück; most powerful, Schlossberg; most typical, Centgrafenberg). Also tight CHARD in burgundian style, and underrated RIES.

Gallais, Le Mos EGON MÜLLER ZU SCHARZHOF 2nd estate, with 4-ha monopoly Braune Kupp at WILTINGEN. AUSLESEN can be exceptional.

Geisenheim Rhg Town primarily known for Germany's university of oenology/ viticulture. GROSSE LAGE Rothenberg (WEGELER) less famous but one of RHG's best.

Grosse Lage / Grosslage: spot the difference
Up to now, German wine labels can say GROSSLAGE or GROSSE LAGE. They are not the same: the former is a mix of usually hundreds of ha of secondary vyds, the latter refers to the exact opposite – to a top single vyd, an EINZELLAGE, a German "Grand Cru" according to the classification set up by growers' association VDP. Until now, a *Grosslage* could disguise itself as a single vyd: who would know if Forster Mariengarten is an *Einzellage* or a *Grosslage*? (It's Gross.) But luckily, this is not the end of the story: after 2026, a *Grosslage* name will not be allowed to be mentioned together with a village name. Instead of Forster Mariengarten, it must be written: region Mariengarten. The term *Bereich* will also be replaced by region. *Bereich* means district within an *Anbaugebiet* (region). *Bereich* on a label should equally be treated as a flashing red light; the wine is a blend from arbitrary sites within that district. Do not buy.

160 |

GG (Grosses Gewächs) "Great/top growth". The top dry wine from a VDP-classified GROSSE LAGE.

Goldkapsel / Gold Capsule Mos, Na, Rhg, Rhh Designation (and bottle seal) mainly for AUSLESE and higher; v. strict selection of grapes, which should add finesse and complexity, not primarily weight and sweetness. Lange Goldkapsel (Long Gold Capsule) even better. Not a legal term.

Graach M-M ★★★→★★★★ Small village between BERNKASTEL and WEHLEN. GROSSE LAGE vyds: Domprobst, Himmelreich, Josephshöfer. Growers: *J.J. Prüm*, Kees-Kieren, KESSELSTATT, LOOSEN, MOLITOR, MAX F RICHTER, S.A. PRÜM, SCHAEFER, *Selbach-Oster*, Studert-Prüm, WEGELER.

Grans-Fassian M-M ★★★ Catharina Grans (13th generation) has treasure of prime sites at TRITTENHEIM, PIESPORT, Leiwen. Kitsch-free RIES (dr/sw), drive, balance.

Griesel & Compagnie Hess ★★★ SEKT startup (2013) at Bensheim, known for crisp dry style, eg. RIES Rés Perpétuelle, Granit F PINOT N (both Brut Nature).

Gröhl Rhh ★★→★★★ Young Johannes G advocates v. early picking for bitingly acidic RIES, eg. ROTER HANG KABINETT.

Grosse Lage Top level of VDP classification, but only for VDP members. Dry wine from a Grosse Lage site is called GG. Note, not on any account to be confused with GROSSLAGE. Stay awake, there.

Grosser Ring Mos Group of top (VDP) MOS estates, whose annual Sept auction at TRIER sets world record prices.

Grosslage Term destined, maybe even intended, to confuse: a collection of secondary vyds without identity. Not on any account to be confused with GROSSE LAGE. Newest legislation stipulates term "region" must precede *Grosslagen* name; mention of village together with *Grosslage* (eg. Piesporter Michelsberg) no longer permitted, but transition period lasts until 2026.

Gunderloch Rhh ★★★→★★★★ Historical NACKENHEIM estate portrayed in Carl Zuckmayer's play *Der fröhliche Weinberg* (1925). Deeply mineral Rothenberg RIES both TROCKEN (GG 15 16 17' 18' 19' 20 21' 22) and sweet. New VERSTEIGERUNGSWEIN/GG from Rothenberg parcel Fenchelberg. *Kabinett Jean-Baptiste* is perfect match for spicy dishes.

Gut Hermannsberg Na ★★★ Historic Prussian state dom at NIEDERHAUSEN, now in private hands. RIES GGS (eg. Kupfergrube) need time to develop. Also stylish guesthouse.

Gutsabfüllung Estate-bottled, and made from own grapes.

Gutswein Entry-level wine, no vyd or village designation, but only producer's name. Ideally, produced from own grapes, but is not always the case.

Haag, Fritz Mos ★★★★ BRAUNEBERG's top estate; Oliver H is more modern in style than late father Wilhelm. *See* SCHLOSS LIESER.

Nine floating barrels

The AHR V flood of July 2021 destroyed – as with so many estates – all the buildings at the MEYER-NÄKEL winery, and the entire 2020 harvest, all 350 barrels, simply floated away. One barrique almost made it into the Atlantic: a wine-lover from Nijmegen in the Netherlands sent an email and a photo of a Meyer-Näkel branded barrel that he had found in the reeds while he was walking on the beach. Alas, the wine had leaked. Dörte and Meike Näkel were only able to recover nine intact barrels, either in the immediate vicinity of the winery or in neighbouring villages. These nine barrels were bottled individually in 2023. Thanks to the cellar book, the contents of each barrel could be traced. Barrels 1, 2 and 5 contained Pfarrwingert, 7 Kräuterberg, 3 and 9 Hardtberg. If these bottles don't become collector's items, what will?

Haag, Willi Mos ★★→★★★ BRAUNEBERG family estate, led by Marcus H. Old-style RIES, mainly sweet, rich but balanced, inexpensive.

Haart, Reinhold M-M ★★★→★★★★ Best estate in PIESPORT, with important holding in famous Goldtröpfchen ("gold droplet") vyd. RIES SPÄTLESEN and higher PRÄDIKAT wines are *racy, copybook Mosels.*

Haidle Würt ★★★→★★★★ Moritz H uses cool climate of Remstal area for wines of distinctive freshness. Outstanding LEMBERGER GGS Berge, Gehrnhalde, and RIES Pulvermächer.

Halbtrocken Medium-dry with 9–18g/l unfermented sugar, inconsistently distinguished from FEINHERB.

Hallgarten Rhg ★★→★★★★ Village situated away from River Rhine in heights; vyds (eg. Jungfer, Hendelberg) more and more sought after with climate change. Growers: FÜRST LÖWENSTEIN, KÜHN, H Nicolai, PRINZ, Querbach, SPREITZER.

Hattenheim Rhg ★★→★★★★ Town famous for its *Brunnen* ("well") vyds (Nussbrunnen, Wisselbrunnen), which have water-bearing layers underneath, and for legendary STEINBERG high above the village. Estates: BARTH, HESSISCHE STAATSWEINGÜTER, Kaufmann, Knyphausen, Ress, Schloss Reinhartshausen and SPREITZER.

Heger, Dr. Bad ★★★ KAISERSTUHL estate known for parcel selections from volcanic soils in Achkarren and IHRINGEN, young Katharina and Rebecca H now work alongside father Jochim H. Best: Winklerberg Vorderer Berg (PINOTS N/GR/BL) from steep terraces, and Häusleboden Pinot N from old Clos de Vougeot (*see* France) cuttings, planted 1956.

Heitlinger / Burg Ravensburg Bad ★★→★★★ Two leading estates of Kraichgau, N BAD, under same ownership: Heitlinger more elegant, Burg Ravensburg more full-bodied.

Hessische Bergstrasse Germany's smallest wine region (460 ha), n of Heidelberg.

Hessische Staatsweingüter Hess, Rhg ★★→★★★★ State dom with vinotheque in KLOSTER EBERBACH; 238 ha in top sites all along RHG and HESSISCHE BERGSTRASSE, rich stock of mature wines back to 1706.

Hey, Weingut ★★★ Leading estate in e, at Naumburg, SA-UN. Impressive RIES GG from Steinmeister vyd.

Heymann-Löwenstein Mos ★★★ Sarah L has taken over from father Reinhard, continues to produce terroir-minded, non-conformist RIES from steep terraces at WINNINGEN, nr Koblenz.

Hochheim Rhg ★★→★★★★ Town e of main RHG, on River Main, rich RIES from loess and limestone soils (best usually Domdechaney, Hölle, Kirchenstück). Growers: Domdechant Werner, Flick, HESSISCHE STAATSWEINGÜTER, Himmel, Im Weinegg, KÜNSTLER.

Hock A trad English term for Rhine wine, derived from HOCHHEIM.

Hornstein, Simon Würt ★★→★★★ Gifted young grower making name for CHARD from Bayerischer BODENSEE: balanced Seehalde and bitingly mineral Sonnenbichl. Trained at Paul and Sebastian FÜRST.

Hövel, Weingut von Mos ★★★ Passionate Max von Kunow, now joined by ex-KESSELSTATT cellarmaster Wolfgang Mertes, takes light, crystalline SAAR style to highest level. Superb SCHARZHOFBERG VERSTEIGERUNGSWEIN KABINETT 22. Brilliant 22 GGS too.

Huber, Bernhard Bad ★★★→★★★★ PINOT N Wildenstein, Sommerhalde and ALTE REBEN have generous fruit, and world fame. Same holds for Julian H's tight, demanding CHARD.

Ihringen Bad ★→★★★ Village in KAISERSTUHL known for fine PINOTS N/GR/BL on steep volcanic Winklerberg. Top growers incl DR. HEGER, Konstanzer, Michel and Stigler.

Ingelheim Rhh ★★→★★★★ Town with limestone banks under vyds, and historic fame for PINOT N. Dynamic estates ADAMS, Bettenheimer, Dautermann, NEUS, SAALWÄCHTER, Schloss Westerhaus, Wasem and Werner put wines back on map.

Iphofen Frank ★★→★★★ Town in E FRANK (Steigerwald area = altitude) famous for rich, aromatic, well-ageing SILVANER from gypsum soils in Julius-Echter-Berg and neighbouring vyds. Growers: Arnold, Emmerich, JULIUSSPITAL, Popp, RUCK, Seufert, Vetter, Von der Tann, Weigand, WELTNER, *Wirsching*, Zehntkeller.

Johannisberg Rhg ★★→★★★★ Legendary SCHLOSS JOHANNISBERG has made town's name synonymous with RIES; other wineries incl CHAT SAUVAGE, JOHANNISHOF (Eser), Prinz v. Hessen, Schamari-Mühle. GROSSLAGE (avoid!): Erntebringer.

Johannishof (Eser) Rhg ★★→★★★ Family estate with vyds at JOHANNISBERG, RÜDESHEIM: RIES with perfect balance of ripeness and steely acidity.

Jost, Toni M Rh ★★★ Leading estate in BACHARACH with monopoly Hahn, now led by Cecilia J.

Jülg Pfz ★★→★★★★ Dense PINOT N, sharply mineral CHARD, SAUV BL from limestone soils at SCHWEIGEN. Top: Opus Oskar (named after Johannes J's grandfather).

Juliusspital Frank ★★★ Ancient WÜRZBURG charity with top vyds all over FRANK, known for firmly structured *dry Silvaners* that age well. New director 2023.

Kaiserstuhl Bad Extinct volcano nr Rhine in S BAD, notably warm climate, black soil. Altitudes up to 400m (1312ft). PINOTS N/GR of class, renown.

Kanzem Mos ★★★ SAAR village with steep GROSSE LAGE vyd Altenberg (green and grey slate, weathered red rock). Growers: BISCHÖFLICHE WEINGÜTER TRIER, Cantzheim (plus guesthouse), VAN VOLXEM, VON OTHEGRAVEN.

Karthäuserhof Mos ★★★ Historic RUWER estate with emblematic neck-only label. After mixed results over past decade, a new team: Mathieu Kauffmann (ex-Bollinger, *see* France), Dominik Völk (ex-VAN VOLXEM).

Kauer M Rh ★★→★★★★ Randolf K is professor of organic viticulture at GEISENHEIM; daughter Anne now about to take over family estate at BACHARACH, aiming at fresher, crisper style.

Keller, Franz Bad *See* SCHWARZER ADLER.

Keller, Klaus Peter Rhh ★★★★ Star of RHH, cultish for ALTE REBEN RIES G-Max from undisclosed (calcareous) parcel, and GGS Hubacker, Morstein. Also Ries from NIERSTEIN (Hipping, Pettenthal), M-M (PIESPORT Schubertslay). Record prices at auction.

Kesseler, August Rhg ★★★★ August K's 85 ASSMANNSHAUSEN Höllenberg PINOT N was start of new German Pinot N miracle. Meanwhile, long-time employees taken over.

Kesselstatt, Reichsgraf von Mos ★★ Top vyds on Mosel and tributaries, 46 ha. After death of visionary Annegret Reh-Gartner, not yet back in smooth waters.

Kiedrich Rhg ★★→★★★★ Top village, almost monopoly of WEIL estate; other growers (eg. FRICKE, Knyphausen, PRINZ VON HESSEN) own only small plots. Famous church and choir.

Kloster Eberbach Rhg Atmospheric C12 Cistercian abbey in HATTENHEIM, where *The Name of the Rose* was filmed. Domicile of HESSISCHE STAATSWEINGÜTER.

Klumpp Bad ★★★ Top famliy estate in Kraichgau, N BAD, led by brothers Markus and Andreas K, esp fruit-driven PINOT N, refined PINOT GR from Rothenberg vyd at Bruchsal.

> Don't forget the sun lotion
> Grapes can get sunburned; and when they do, they get bitter. To the taste, that is. Solution: spray them with kaolin – keeps grapes cool, doesn't affect photosynthesis. And it looks just like sun cream.

Knebel Mos ★★★ Family estate in top form at WINNINGEN. Refined TBA, and elegant, aromatic dry wines.

Knewitz Rhh ★★★ Practically unknown 10 yrs ago; today VDP member, and one of RHH's leaders. Best: CHARD Res, RIES Hundertgulden 15' 16' **17' 18** 19' 20' 21' 22'. Organic.

Knipser Pfz ★★★→★★★★ Top estate in N PFZ, best for age-worthy PINOT N (15' RdP a monument), CHARD and specialities like Gelber Orleans, SYRAH, Cuvée X (Bx blend).

The first Syrah planted in Germany: 1994. Who'd have thought?

Königin Viktoriaberg Rhg ★★→★★★ Historic RIES vyd at HOCHHEIM, today run by Flick estate, Wicker. After 1845 visit, Queen Victoria granted owner right to rename vyd as "Queen-Victoria-mountain".

Kranz, Weingut Pfz ★★★→★★★★ Top estate at Ilbesheim, S PFZ. Intense RIES, SPÄTBURGUNDER, WEISSBURGUNDER from classified Kalmit vyd. Organic.

Kreuzberg, H.J. Ahr ★★★ Prime producer. Best: Devonschiefer R PINOT N, Hardtberg FRÜHBURGUNDER.

Krone, Weingut Rhg ★★★ Famous SPÄTBURGUNDER estate with a treasure of old vyds in ASSMANNSHAUSEN, run by WEGELER.

Kühling-Gillot Rhh ★★★★ Top bio estate, run by Caroline Gillot and husband HO Spanier. Best in outstanding range of ROTER HANG RIES: GG Rothenberg Wurzelecht from ungrafted vines.

Kühn, Peter Jakob Rhg ★★★→★★★★ Obsessive bio vyd management and long macerations shape **nonconformist but exciting** RIES; Res RPJK Unikat aged 4 yrs in cask. St Nikolaus and Doosberg GGS reliable at highest level.

Kuhn, Philipp Pfz ★★★→★★★★ Outstanding estate at Laumersheim, N PFZ: RIES (eg. Saumagen, Schwarzer Herrgott, VERSTEIGERUNGSWEIN Philippsbrunnen from ZELLERTAL), age-worthy SPÄTBURGUNDER, and terrific specialities CHARD, SAUV BL, VIOGNIER.

Künstler Rhg ★★★ Gunter K's family estate at HOCHHEIM has vyds and GGS in every part of RHG, incl ex-Schönborn vyd in MARCOBRUNN; trad; reliable style.

Kuntz, Sybille Mos ★★★ Progressive organic 12-ha estate at Lieser, esp Niederberg-Helden vyd. Pioneer of MOS TROCKEN; intense wines, one of each ripeness category, intended for gastronomy, listed in many top restaurants.

Kurek, Jonas Würt ★★→★★★ Young grower at Nonnenhorn, on Bavarian shores of BODENSEE. Trained with Julian HUBER, makes outstanding Seehalde PINOT N.

Laible, Andreas Bad ★★★ Crystalline dry RIES from Durbach's Plauelrain vyd (granite). Younger brother Alexander has own estate.

Landwein Technically "ggA" (*see* box, p.172), meant to label wines with only broadly defined origin. But now popular among ambitious growers to avoid official quality testing (eg. because of spontaneous fermentations, or low sulphur levels). Best known: Brenneisen, Enderle & Moll, Forgeurac, Greiner, Höfflin, Nieger, Vorgrimmler, WASENHAUS, ISEREISEN (all BAD); Drei Zeilen, Vetter, Weigand (FRANK); Schmitt (RHH); Konni & Evi (SA-UN).

Lauer Mos ★★★ Fine, precise SAAR RIES: tense, poised. Parcel selections from huge Ayler Kupp vyd. Best: Kern, Schonfels, Stirn.

Leitz, Josef Rhg ★★★ Important RÜDESHEIM estate, 160 ha, producing anything from respectable discount RIES to outstanding GGS (Berg Schlossberg 21'). Inexpensive, reliable Eins-Zwei-Dry label.

Loersch, Weingut M-M ★★→★★★ Fine family estate (since 1640) with energetic KABINETT and aromatically complex dry wines from 1st-class vyds (TRITTENHEIM Apotheke, PIESPORT Goldtröpfchen).

Loewen, Carl Mos ★★★ Produces RIES of complexity, with best vyd Longuicher

Maximin Herrenberg (planted 1896, ungrafted). Try entry-level Ries Varidor too excellent *value*.

Loosen, Weingut Dr. M-M ★★→★★★★ Ernie L is Germany's most important RIES ambassador; his wines convince from entry-level Blauschiefer, Rotschiefer and even Dr. L from bought-in grapes, over nine different GGs and four Res wines (2 yrs cask-ageing) up to cultish Prälat AUSLESE. New projects incl Tradition range for KABINETT, SPÄTLESE with less sweetness, and extended barrel-ageing (3, 5, 8 yrs) for dry wines. *See also* WOLF; Appassionata, J Christopher (Oregon, US); Ch Ste Michelle (Washington State, US).

Lorch Rhg ★→★★★ Village in extreme w of RHG, conditions more M RH-like than Rhg-like. Sharply crystalline wines, both RIES, PINOT N. Best: BREUER, CHAT SAUVAGE, FRICKE, KESSELER, SOLVEIGS, von Kanitz.

Löwenstein, Fürst Frank, Rhg ★★★ Princely estate, classic RIES from HALLGARTEN (RHG), unique SILVANER, Ries from ultra-steep Homburger Kallmuth (FRANK).

Marcobrunn Rhg Historic 7-ha vyd in Erbach, VDP-classified GROSSE LAGE. Potential for rich, long-lasting RIES. Growers: CORVERS-KAUTER, HESSISCHE STAATSWEINGÜTER, Höhn, Knyphausen, KÜNSTLER, PRINZ, Schloss Reinhartshausen, von Oetinger.

Markgräflerland Bad District s of Freiburg, cool climate nr Black Forest, limestone soils. Typical GUTEDEL a pleasant companion for local cuisine. Pinot varieties increasingly successful.

Markgraf von Baden Bad ★★→★★★ Important noble estate (112 ha) at Salem Castle (BODENSEE) and Staufenberg Castle (ORTENAU).

Mathis, Gebrüder Bad ★★★ Young couple (3rd generation) taken over family estate (formerly known as Kalkbödele) on Tuniberg. Stylish PINOT N (Rosenloch 20'), CHARD, PINOT BL from vyds next to a lime plant.

Maximin Grünhaus Mos ★★★★ Maximin von Schubert taken helm at supreme RUWER estate; v. trad winemaking shapes herb-scented, *delicate, long-lived Ries*. To be taken more seriously each yr: creamy WEISSBURGUNDER, elegant PINOT N.

Merkelbach M-M ★★→★★★ Tiny estate at ÜRZIG, 1.4 ha. Brothers Alfred and Rolf (RIP 2023) M handed over day-to-day business to SELBACH-OSTER, but wine still made in bros' cellar.

Meyer-Näkel Ahr ★★★→★★★★ Refined PINOT N from steep terraces at Walporzheim Kräuterberg 13' 15' 16' 17' **18** 19' 21 and Dernau Pfarrwingert 15' 16' 17 18' 19 21. Vintage 20 almost completely lost in flood (*see box, p.160*). In Portugal (Quinta da Carvalhosa), S Africa (Zwalu, with Neil Ellis).

Mittelhaardt Pfz North-central and best part of PFZ, incl DEIDESHEIM, FORST, RUPPERTSBERG, WACHENHEIM; largely planted with RIES.

Mittelmosel Central and best part of MOS, a RIES Eldorado, incl BERNKASTEL, BRAUNEBERG, GRAACH, PIESPORT, WEHLEN, etc.

Mittelrhein ★★→★★★ Dramatically scenic Rhine area, nr tourist magnet Loreley. *Steely, underrated Ries.* Today's vyds a quarter of size (466 ha) they were in 1980.

Molitor, Markus M-M, Mos ★★★→★★★★ Perfectionist, trad winemaking from 120 ha in 24 EINZELLAGEN – almost 100 different bottlings/yr. Capsules indicate degree of sweetness (white = dry, green = off-dry, golden = sweet). *See* DOM SERRIG.

Mosbacher Pfz ★★★ Some of best GG RIES of FORST, refined rather than massive; trad ageing in big oak casks.

Mosel Growing area for the lightest of German RIES, 8575 ha, 62% RIES. Conditions on the RUWER and SAAR tributaries (also subsumed under "Mosel" in wine law) significantly different.

Nackenheim Rhh ★→★★★★ ROTER HANG village famous for *Rhh's richest Ries*, superb TBA from Rothenberg on red shale. Top: *Gunderloch*, KÜHLING-GILLOT, Marbé-Sans, SCHÄTZEL.

Germany's quality levels

The official range of qualities and styles in ascending order is (take a deep breath):

1 **Wein** Formerly known as Tafelwein. Light wine of no specified character, mostly sweetish.

2 **ggA (geschützte geographische Angabe)** or protected geographical indication, formerly known as LANDWEIN. Dryish Wein with some regional style. Mostly a label to avoid, but some thoughtful estates use the Landwein designation to bypass official constraints.

3 **gU (geschützte Ursprungsbezeichnung)** or protected designation of origin. Replacing QUALITÄTSWEIN. Up to now, only six small-scale appellations in the narrower sense of the word approved by the EU.

4 **Qualitätswein** Dry or sweetish wine with sugar added before fermentation to increase its strength, but tested for quality and with distinct local and grape character. Don't despair.

5 **Kabinett** Lightest of German wines, dry/dryish, unsugared, subtle yet long-lived, production complicated by climate change: altitude vyds needed, and early, speedy picking.

6 **Spätlese** Late-harvest. One level riper and sweeter than KABINETT. Needs to be aged for 5 yrs at least. Dry SPÄTLESE (or what could be considered as such) is today mostly sold under Qualitätswein designation (even if not sugared).

7 **Auslese** Wines from selective picking of super-ripe bunches affected by noble rot (*Edelfäule*). Unctuous, but – trad – elegant rather than super-concentrated; 99% are sweet, but specialists (J.B. BECKER, Koehler-Ruprecht) show Auslese TROCKEN can be elegant too.

8 **Beerenauslese (BA)** Luscious sweet wine from exceptionally ripe, individually selected berries concentrated by noble rot.

9 **Eiswein** Made from frozen grapes with the ice (ie. water content) discarded, thus v. concentrated: of BA ripeness or more. Outstanding Eiswein vintages: 98 02 04 08. Less and less produced in past decade: climate change is Eiswein's enemy.

10 **Trockenbeerenauslese (TBA)** Sweetest, most expensive category of German wine, extremely rare, viscous and concentrated, with dried-fruit flavours. Made from selected dried-out berries affected by noble rot (botrytis). Half-bottles a gd idea.

Nahe Tributary of the Rhine and dynamic region (4230 ha), with couple of famous (eg. DIEL, DÖNNHOFF, SCHÄFER-FRÖHLICH) and dozens of lesser-known producers, excellent *value*. Great soil variety.

Neipperg, Graf von Würt ★★★→★★★★ One of most reliable estates in all Germany, stronghold of elegance (LEMBERGER, SPÄTBURGUNDER), but also PINOT BL, RIES. Outstanding MUSKATELLER TBA 18. Count Philipp N's uncle Stephan makes wine at Canon-la-Gaffelière in St-Émilion (*see* Bordeaux) and elsewhere.

Neus Rhh ★★★ Revived historic estate at INGELHEIM, excellent PINOT N (best: Pares).

Niederhausen Na ★★→★★★★ Village known for RIES from Hermannshöhle vyd and neighbouring steep slopes. Growers: CRUSIUS, *Dönnhoff*, GUT HERMANNSBERG, Jakob Schneider, Mathern.

Nierstein Rhh ★→★★★★ Avoid by any means GROSSLAGE Gutes Domtal designation. Genuine Nierstein RIES is rich, complex: Hipping, Oelberg, Pettenthal. Growers: Bunn, Gehring, GRÖHL, GUNDERLOCH, Guntrum, Hofmann, Huff (both), KELLER, KÜHLING-GILLOT, Manz, SCHÄTZEL, ST-ANTONY, Strub.

Ockfen Mos ★★→★★★ SAAR village known for GROSSE LAGE Bockstein. Growers:

KESSELSTATT, M MOLITOR, OTHEGRAVEN, SANKT URBANS-HOF, VAN VOLXEM, WAGNER, ZILLIKEN. Historical Geisberg now re-cultivated (Van Volxem).

Odinstal, Weingut Pfz ★★→★★★ Highest PFZ vyd, 150m (492ft) above WACHENHEIM; bio farming, low-tech vinification bring pure GEWÜRZ, RIES, SILVANER.

Oechsle Scale for sugar content of grape juice. Until 90s, more Oechsle meant better wine. But climate change has altered game.

Baden is co-op land: 72% of vineyard, 14,000 co-op members. Safe, but no thrills.

Oppenheim Rhh ★→★★★ Village s of ROTER HANG with different soil (limestone) and no direct Rhine influence. Growers: GRÖHL, Guntrum, Kissinger, KÜHLING-GILLOT, Manz. Spectacular C13 church.

Ortenau Bad ★★→★★★ District around and s of city of Baden-Baden. Mainly RIES (locally called Klingelberger) and SPÄTBURGUNDER from granite soils.

Ortswein The 2nd rank up in VDP's pyramid of qualities: a village wine, many bargains. *See* next entry.

Ortswein aus Ersten Lagen Rhh New designation of VDP RHH indicating village wine grown in classified vyds. Typically, blend of different ERSTE LAGE sites. Funnily enough, no Erste Lage single-vyd wines in Rhh.

Östreicher, Richard Frank ★★★ Organic viticulture, low-interventionist winemaking give concentrated CHARD Rossbach, flinty SILVANER Maria im Weingarten, smoky PINOT BL Hölzlein.

Othegraven, von Mos ★★★ Family estate owned by German TV star Günther Jauch, with important holdings in superb Altenberg at KANZEM. KABINETT and SPÄTLESE VERSTEIGERUNGSWEIN among SAAR's finest.

Palatinate Pfz English for PFALZ.

Pfalz The 2nd-largest German region, 23,698 ha, balmy climate, Lucullian lifestyle. MITTELHAARDT RIES legendary; SÜDPFALZ produces outstanding PINOTS N/BL, plus CHARD. ZELLERTAL now fashionable: cool climate.

Piesport M-M ★→★★★★ Village in M-M for rich, aromatic RIES from famous Goldtröpfchen vyd. Growers: GRANS-FASSIAN, Hain, Joh Haart, Julian Haart, KESSELSTATT, LOERSCH, *Reinhold Haart*, SANKT URBANS-HOF, SCHLOSS LIESER. Avoid GROSSLAGE Michelsberg.

Prädikat Legally defined category of ripeness at harvest. *See* QMP and box, p.172.

Prinz, Weingut ★★★ Distinctly fresh, elegant RIES from HALLGARTEN's altitude vyds; organic. KABINETT GOLDKAPSEL can be magnificent. Now also MARCOBRUNN.

Prüm, J.J. Mos ★★★★ 59 71 76 83 90 03 11 15 18 19 20 21 22 Legendary WEHLEN estate; also BERNKASTEL, GRAACH. Delicate but extraordinarily long-lived wines with finesse, recognizable character.

Prüm, S.A. Mos ★★→★★★ Old estate at WEHLEN. Saskia Antonia P took over 2017, noticeable improvements.

QbA (Qualitätswein bestimmter Anbaugebiete) "Quality Wine", controlled as to area, grape(s), vintage. May add sugar before fermentation (chaptalization). Intended as middle category, but VDP obliges its members to label their best dry wines (GGS) as QbA. New EU name gU is scarcely found on labels (*see* box, p.165).

QmP (Qualitätswein mit Prädikat) Top category, six levels according to ripeness of grapes: KABINETT to TBA. (*See* box, p.165.) No sugaring of must or other forms of enrichment allowed.

Ratzenberger M Rh ★★★ Jochen R, 3rd generation, had 10 ha of vines and took over another 10 ha on steep slopes at BACHARACH (2017). Full range: sound, typical M RH RIES, occasionally with magnificent BA, TBA.

Rauenthal Rhg ★★→★★★★ *Spicy, austere but complex* RIES from inland slopes. Baiken, Gehrn, Rothenberg vyds contain GROSSE LAGE, ERSTE LAGE parcels, while neighbouring Nonnenberg (monopole of BREUER) is unclassified, despite its equal quality.

Raumland Rhh ★★★ SEKT house with deep cellar and full range of fine cuvées; 1st Sekt-only estate to become VDP member. Best: CHARD Brut Nature (disgorged after 10 yrs), sensational (and rare) MonRose 07' 09'.

Rebholz, Ökonomierat Pfz ★★★ Top SÜDPFALZ estate: bone-dry, best usually RIES GG Kastanienbusch from red schist, also outstanding CHARD, SPÄTBURGUNDER.

Restsüsse Unfermented grape sugar remaining in (or added in the form of süssreserve to) wine to give it sweetness. Can range from 1g/l in TROCKEN to 300g in TBA.

Rheingau Birthplace of RIES, famous for substantial, age-worthy wines with steely backbone (dr/sw). Soils are either pyhillite, schist, quarzite (in mtn villages) or limestone, loess, river sediments nr Rhine. Only 3200 ha (8th-biggest region). Small but increasing amounts of SPÄTBURGUNDER.

Rheinhessen Germany's largest region by far (27,312 ha and rising), between Mainz and Worms. Much *Fasswein* (bulk wine), but also treasure trove of well-priced wines from gifted young growers.

Richter, Max F M-M ★★→★★★ Fine, reliable M-M estate wealthy in prime vyds at BRAUNEBERG, ERDEN, GRAACH, WEHLEN: full, aromatic RIES (dr/sw).

Riffel Rhh ★★★ Family estate, bio, known for purist style, to put Bingen's once-famous Scharlachberg (red soils) back on map.

Rings Pfz ★★★→★★★★ Dense, emphatically fresh RIES and SPÄTBURGUNDER from prime sites in N PFZ.

Roter Hang Rhh ★★→★★★★ Leading RIES area of RHH (NACKENHEIM, NIERSTEIN). Name ("red slope") refers to red shale soil.

Ruck, Johann Frank ★★★ Spicy, age-worthy RIES, SCHEUREBE, SILVANER, TRAMINER from IPHOFEN.

Rüdesheim Rhg ★★→★★★★ Tourist magnet in RHG. Unique RIES from Berg (mtn) vyds on slate (Kaisersteinfels, Roseneck, Rottland, Schlossberg). Full-bodied but never clumsy, esp gd in off-yrs. Best: Allendorf, BISCHÖFLICHES WEINGUT RÜDESHEIM, *Breuer*, CHAT SAUVAGE, CORVERS-KAUTER, HESSISCHE STAATSWEINGÜTER, JOHANNISHOF, Jörn Wein, *Kesseler*, KÜNSTLER, *Leitz*, Prinz von Hessen, Ress.

Ruwer Mos ★★→★★★★ Tributary of MOS nr TRIER, cool and late-ripening, esp renowned for dry RIES. Best: Beulwitz, Karlsmühle, KARTHÄUSERHOF, KESSELSTATT, MAXIMIN GRÜNHAUS.

Saale-Unstrut Small but fine ne region (847 ha) around confluence of these two rivers 50 km w of Leipzig. Terraced vyds have Cistercian origins. Best: Böhme, Böhme und Töchter, Born, Gussek, HEY, Kloster Pforta, Konni & Evi (LANDWEIN), Pawis, Proppe.

Saalwächter, Carsten Rhh ★★★ Shooting star at INGELHEIM, known for outstanding Silv Grauer Stein, elegant CHARD, delicate PINOT N (Ingelheim and ASSMANNSHAUSEN).

Saar Mos Tributary of Mosel, bordered by steep slopes. Most austere, steely, *brilliant Ries* of all, consistency favoured by climate change.

Viticulture is spreading to the islands: Föhr, Rügen, Sylt already have vineyards.

Sachsen Region in Elbe V around Meissen and Dresden. Characterful dry whites, TRAMINER a speciality. Best: AUST, Drei Herren, F Fourré, Gut Hoflössnitz, Rothes Gut, SCHLOSS PROSCHWITZ, SCHLOSS WACKERBARTH, Schuh, SCHWARZ and ZIMMERLING.

St-Antony Rhh ★★→★★★★ NIERSTEIN organic estate. Exceptional vyds, known for sturdy, ageable ROTER HANG RIES. Steep slopes all worked by hand.

GERMANY

Salm, Prinz zu Na, Rhh ★★→★★★ Owner of Schloss Wallhausen, vyds there and at BINGEN (RHH); ex-president of VDP.

Salwey Bad ★★★→★★★★ Leading KAISERSTUHL estate, forerunner of fresher PINOTS N/GR style as early as 2008. Best: GGS Henkenberg Pinot Gr, Steingrubenberg and Kirchberg PINOT BL, Henkenberg and Kirchberg Pinot N. Stunning Pinot Gr/CHARD Sieben Winter 16, aged 7 yrs in cask.

Sankt Urbans-Hof Mos ★★★ Large family estate (45 ha) led by Nik Weis, vyds along M-M and SAAR; vine nursery too. Limpid RIES, impeccably pure, racy, age well.

Sauer, Horst Frank ★★★ Man who put FRANK on sweet-wine map. Sensational BA, TBA from ESCHERNDORF's steep Lump vyd. Daughter Sandra now in charge.

Sauer, Rainer Frank ★★★ Top family estate producing seven different dry SILVANERS from ESCHERNDORF's steep slope Lump. Best: GG am Lumpen, and L.

Schaefer, Willi Mos ★★★ Willi S and son Christoph finest in GRAACH, 4.2 ha in over 100 parcels; MOS RIES at its best, pure, crystalline, feather-light.

Schäfer-Fröhlich Na ★★★→★★★★ Family estate in NA, spontaneously fermented RIES of great intensity, GGS incl Bockenau Felseneck, Kupfergrube, Schlossböckelheim Felsenberg.

Scharzhofberg Mos ★★→★★★★ Superlative SAAR vyd, 28 ha: a rare coincidence of microclimate, soil and human intelligence to bring about the perfection of RIES. Top: EGON MÜLLER, KESSELSTATT, VAN VOLXEM, VON HÖVEL.

Schätzel Rhh ★★→★★★★ Low-alc, high-tannin RIES from prime ROTER HANG sites, sometimes irritating, but almost always fascinating, eg. Fuchs (declassified NIERSTEIN Hipping, aged many yrs in cask without sulphur), NV Steiner from SOLERA (*see* Spain). Brilliant Pettenthal KABINETT.

Schloss Johannisberg Rhg ★★★→★★★★ Historic RHG estate and Metternich mansion, place where SPÄTLESE was invented (1775); 100% RIES, owned by Henkell (Oetker group). Seal colour indicates wine type. Currently on top form and in conversion to organic. Goldlack and Ex Bibliotheca Subterranea TROCKEN are pricey, but entry-level Gelblack shows nobility of site too.

Schloss Lieser M-M ★★★★ Thomas Haag, elder brother of Oliver (FRITZ HAAG), produces painstakingly elaborate RIES (dr/sw) from BRAUNEBERG, Lieser (Niederberg Helden) PIESPORT, WEHLEN. Hotel Lieser Castle has no ties to the wine estate.

Schloss Ortenberg Bad ★★→★★★ Was underperforming; taken over 2021 by hotelier Thomas Althoff (Schloss Bensberg, St. James's Hotel & Club), remarkable progress since.

Schloss Proschwitz Sachs ★★→★★★ New team brings notable improvements in Prince zur Lippe's 70-ha estate. Top: WEISSBURGUNDER, SPÄTBURGUNDER, delicious TRAMINER Brut SEKT.

Schloss Rattey ★→★★★ Hotel and winery in ne state of Mecklenburg-Vorpommern, 30 ha, remarkable dry Solaris (PIWI grape, *see* p.12).

Schloss Vaux Rhg ★★→★★★★ Co-owned by PRINZ ZU SALM. SEKT house, best known for single-vyd RIES Sekt.

Spätburgunder or Pinot Noir?

German PINOT N is historically known as SPÄTBURGUNDER. But today, many growers prefer to call it Pinot N. Some growers make a distinction: they call the wines from Burgundy clones Pinot N, and those from German Pinot genetics Spätburgunder. But not everyone does it that way. Many vyds are a mix of clones anyway, so it doesn't really make a difference. In one respect, however, the word Spät(=late)-Burgunder is outdated: In the last decade, Pinot N has consistently been one of the earliest-picked varieties.

Schloss Wackerbarth ★★→★★★ Saxon state dom on outskirts of Dresden, conceived as experience winery, with restaurant, park, events, 190,000 visitors/yr. Also wine-wise on top form. Best: ALTE REBEN, Protze RIES TROCKEN, TRAMINER SPÄTLESE, all from Radebeul's Goldener Wagen vyd.

Schnaitmann Würt ★★★→★★★★ Excellent barrel-aged reds from Fellbach nr Stuttgart. Whites (eg. RIES, SAUV BL), SEKT (Evoé!), and wines from lesser grapes (SCHWARZRIESLING, TROLLINGER) tasty too.

Market share of Grosslage wines is falling: below 15% now. Still 15% too much.

Schneider, Markus Pfz ★★ Shooting star in Ellerstadt. Full range of soundly produced, trendily labelled wines.

Schoppenwein Café (or bar) wine, ie. wine by the glass.

Schumacher, Paul Ahr ★★★ Perfectionist grower at Marienthal, only 4 ha. Age-worthy PINOT N: Kräuterberg 12 13 **15' 16** 17' 18 19' 20' 21. Outstanding Trotzenberg 21', from yr of catastrophic flood.

Schwarz, Martin Sachs ★★★ Perfectionist grower (6 ha) at Meissen, SACHS: CHARD, RIES, PINOT N – and, believe it or not, NEBBIOLO.

Schwarzer Adler Bad ★★★→★★★★ Michelin-starred restaurant and top estate at Oberbergen, KAISERSTUHL: PINOTS N/BL/GR and CHARD to show France is nr.

Schwegler Würt ★★★→★★★★ Family estate, 11 ha, red blends full of charcter: Beryll, Granat, Saphir. Powerful CHARD.

Seckinger Pfz ★★→★★★ Three brothers from Niederkirchen/MITTELHAART making name for RIES from DEIDESHEIM in style of Vin Nature but without becoming too extreme. Organic.

Sekt ★→★★★★ German sparkling. Avoid cheap offers: bottle fermentation is not mandatory. Serious Sekt producers incl ALDINGER, Bardong, BARTH, BATTENFELD-SPANIER, BERGDOLT, BREUER, BUHL, DIEL, F John, GRIESEL, GUT HERMANNSBERG, H Bamberger, HEYMANN-LÖWENSTEIN, LAUER, Leiner, MAX F RICHTER, Melsheimer, MOLITOR, RAUMLAND, Reinecker, Schembs, SCHLOSS VAUX, SCHWARZER ADLER, Solter, S Steinmetz, Strauch, WAGECK, WEGELER, Wilhelmshof, ZILLIKEN.

Selbach-Oster M-M ★★★ Scrupulous family estate with excellent vyd portfolio, known for classical style and focus on sweet PRÄDIKAT wines.

Sermann, Lukas Ahr ★★→★★★ Young grower in Altenahr, village worst affected by 2021 floods. Resilient: made BA 21, opened small restaurant 22. Superb: Im Eck ALTE REBEN (30–80 yrs) PINOT N, RIES TROCKEN from ungrafted vines.

Serrig, Dom Mos ★★★ A 25 ha-estate in one piece, bought 2016 by MARKUS MOLITOR, mostly newly planted and now sold via Place de Bordeaux (*see* Bordeaux).

Solveigs Rhg ★★→★★★★ PINOT N from red slate at ASSMANNSHAUSEN and LORCH, only 2 ha, organic. Best: plots Micke 13' 15' **16'** 18' 19' 20', Present 09' 12 13' 15' 16' 18' 19' 20'.

Sonnenuhr M-M Sundial. Name of vyds at BRAUNEBERG, Pommern, WEHLEN and Zeltingen.

Spreitzer Rhg ★★★ Deliciously *racy, harmonious* RIES from vyds in HATTENHEIM, Mittelheim, Oestrich. Mid-price range ALTE REBEN a bargain. Breathtaking TBA, EISWEIN (esp Würtzgarten GOLDKAPSEL 22').

Staatsweingut / Staatliche Weinbaudomäne State wine estates or doms exist in BAD (IHRINGEN, Meersburg), NA (Bad Kreuznach), PFZ (Neustadt), RHG (HESSISCHE STAATSWEINGÜTER), RHH (OPPENHEIM), SACHS (Wackerbarth), SA-UN (Kloster Pforta), WÜRT (Weinsberg).

Steinberg Rhg ★★★ Walled-in vyd above HATTENHEIM, est by Cistercian monks 700 yrs ago: a German Clos de Vougeot (*see* France). Monopoly of HESSISCHE STAATSWEINGÜTER. Best parcels have unique soil: clay with fragments of decomposed schist in various colours.

Stein-Berg Frank Best parcels of famous Stein vyd at WÜRZBURG (39 ha out of 71 ha), since 2020 acknowledged by EU as GU (in sense of AOP, *see* France).

Steinwein Frank Wine from WÜRZBURG's best vyd, Stein. Goethe's favourite. Only six producers: BURGERSPITAL, JULIUSSPITAL, L Knoll, Meinzinger, Reiss, Staatlicher Hofkeller. Hugh J once tasted the 1540 vintage.

Stodden Ahr ★★★→★★★★ AHR SPÄTBURGUNDER with Burgundian touch, best usually ALTE REBEN and Herrenberg GOLDKAPSEL.

Sturm, Martin M Rh ★★→★★★★ Journalist turned grower, winemaker; perfectionistic CHARD, RIES, PINOT N from most n part of M RH. Organic.

Südpfalz Pfz S PFZ on Alsace border known for Pinots (r/w). Best: BECKER, DR. WEHRHEIM, JÜLG, KRANZ, Leiner, Minges, Münzberg, REBHOLZ, Siegrist.

Taubertal Bad, Frank, Würt ★→★★★ Cool-climate river valley, divided by Napoleon into BAD, FRANK, WÜRT sections. SILVANER (limestone soils), local red Tauberschwarz. Hofmann, Schlör, gd co-op at Beckstein.

Thanisch, Weingut Dr. M-M ★★★ BERNKASTEL estate, founded 1636, famous for its share of the DOCTOR vyd. After family split in 1988, two homonymous estates with similar qualities: Erben (heirs) Müller-Burggraef (more modern), Erben Thanisch (VDP, classical style).

Trier Mos The n capital of ancient Rome, on the MOSEL, between RUWER and SAAR. Big charitable estates have cellars here among awesome Roman remains.

Trittenheim M-M ★★ →★★★ Racy, textbook M-M RIES if from gd plots within extended Apotheke vyd. Growers: A CLÜSSERATH, Clüsserath-Weiler, E Clüsserath, F-J Eifel, GRANS-FASSIAN, LOERSCH, Milz.

Trocken Dry. Defined as max 9g/l unfermented sugar. Generally: the closer to France, the more Trocken wines.

Ürzig M-M ★★★ →★★★★ MOS village on red sandstone and red slate, famous for ungrafted old vines and *unique spicy Ries* from Würzgarten vyd. Growers: Berres, Christoffel, Erbes, *Loosen*, MERKELBACH, *Molitor*, Mönchhof, Rebenhof.

Van Volxem Mos ★★★ Historical SAAR estate revived by obsessive Roman Niewodniczanski. Low yields from top sites bring about monumental, mostly dry RIES. Spectacular castle-like new cellar building in a Saar lunar nr WILTINGEN.

VDP (Verband Deutscher Prädikatsweingüter) Influential association of 200 premium growers setting highest standards. Look for its eagle insignia on wine labels and for GG logo on bottles. VDP wine is usually a gd bet. President is Steffen CHRISTMANN.

Versteigerungswein ★★★★ Wines of extraordinary quality, auctioned off by one of the historic growers' associations (ie. BERNKASTELER RING or VDP), easily recognized by a sticker on the bottle stating the auction from which the bottle was purchased.

German vintage notation

The vintage notes after entries in the German section are mostly given in a different form from those elsewhere in the book. If the vintages of a single wine are rated, or are for red wine regions, the vintage notation is identical to the one used elsewhere (*see* p.6). But for regions, villages or producers, two styles of vintage are indicated:

Bold type (eg. **22**) indicates classic, ripe vintages with a high proportion of SPÄTLESEN and AUSLESEN; or in the case of red wines, gd phenolic ripeness and must weights.

Normal type (eg. 23) indicates a successful but not outstanding vintage.

Generally, German white wines, esp RIES, can be drunk young for their intense fruitiness or kept for a decade or even two to develop their potential aromatic subtlety and finesse.

Villa Wolf Pfz ★★→★★★ WACHENHEIM estate, leased by Ernst LOOSEN of BERNKASTEL. Quality sound, consistent rather than dazzling.

Wassmer Bad ★★★ These two brothers – Fritz and Martin – started 25 yrs ago by (separately) growing strawberries and asparagus; today both of them make wine too. Fritz is one of the finest producers of Pinot varieties in Breisgau, esp full-bodied, rich Herbolzheim Kaiserberg CHARD and PINOT N. Martin is a top producer of Pinot varieties in MARKGRÄFLERLAND, esp tight, vertical Dottingen Castellberg CHARD and Pinot N.

Wachenheim Pfz ★★★ Celebrated village with, according to VDP, NO GROSSE LAGE vyds. See what you think. Top growers: Biffar, BÜRKLIN-WOLF, Karl Schäfer, ODINSTAL, WOLF, Zimmermann (bargain).

Wageck Pfz ★★★ Family estate at Bissersheim known for CHARD, PINOT N (best: Geisberg), SEKT and Portugieser ALTE REBEN (planted 1931).

Wagner, Dr. Mos ★★→★★★ Christiane W follows four generations in producing crisp dry and off-dry SAAR RIES from prime vyds in OCKFEN and Saarstein.

Wagner-Stempel Rhh ★★★ Seriously crafted RHH wines from Siefersheim nr NA border. Best usually powerful RIES GGS Heerkretz 05 08 11' **15** 18 21.

Wasenhaus Mos ★★★ Burgundy-inspired PINOT N Bellen, Kanzel and PINOT BL Möhlin from limestone sites in MARKGRÄFLERLAND, all vines farmed by hand, all wines labelled as LANDWEIN.

Weedenborn Rhh ★★★ Gesine Roll is SAUV BL expert, her wines (Res, Terra Rossa) have great density and freshness without superficiality. Grande Res unites best barrels of CHARD, Sauv Bl.

Wegeler M-M, Rhg ★★→★★★★ Important estate in Oestrich and BERNKASTEL (both in top form) plus a stake in the famous KRONE estate of ASSMANNSHAUSEN. Geheimrat J brand (TROCKEN RHG RIES) is on a par with the GGS. Old vintages available: Vintage Collection.

Wehlen M-M ★★★→★★★★ Wine village with legendary steep SONNENUHR vyd expressing RIES from slate at v. best: rich, fine, everlasting. Top: J.J. PRÜM, Kerpen, KESSELSTATT, LOOSEN, MAX F RICHTER, MOLITOR, Pauly-Bergweiler, S.A. PRÜM, Sankt Nikolaus Hospital, SCHLOSS LIESER, SELBACH-OSTER, Studert-Prüm, THANISCH, W SCHÄFER, WEGELER.

Wehrheim, Dr. Pfz ★★★ SÜDPFALZ family estate known for outstanding Kastanienbusch Köppel RIES, PINOT N, Mandelberg WEISSBURGUNDER.

Weil, Robert Rhg ★★★★ Outstanding estate in KIEDRICH of great qualitative consistency, GROSSE LAGE vyd Gräfenberg gives superb sweet KABINETT to TBA, and GG. Parcel-selection Monte Vacano available only by subscription.

Weingart M Rh ★★★ Passionate grower at Spay, vyds in BACHARACH, BOPPARD (esp Hamm Feuerlay). Refined, taut RIES, low-tech in style, superb value. Also v.gd PINOT N.

Weingut Wine estate.

Weissherbst Pale-pink wine, made from a single variety, often SPÄTBURGUNDER; v. variable quality.

Weltner, Paul Frank ★★★ Family estate at Rödelsee in cool, high-altitude Steigerwald. Densely structured, age-worthy SILVANER from underrated Küchenmeister vyd.

Wiltingen Mos ★★→★★★★★ Heartland of the SAAR. SCHARZHOFBERG crowns a series of GROSSE LAGE vyds (Braune Kupp, Braunfels, Gottesfuss, Kupp). ORTSWEIN usually a bargain.

Wind, Katrin Pfz ★★→★★★ Shooting star at Arzheim. Straightforward but nuanced wines, eg. Kalmit FRÜHBURGUNDER and SPÄTBURGUNDER, RIES.

Winning, von Pfz ★★★→★★★★ DEIDESHEIM estate with prime vyds there and at FORST. *Ries of great purity*, terroir expression, fermented in partly new *fuder* casks.

GERMANY

Winningen Mos ★★ →★★★ Lower MOS town nr Koblenz; powerful dry RIES. GROSSE LAGES: Röttgen, Uhlen. Top: HEYMANN-LÖWENSTEIN, KNEBEL, Kröber, R Richter.

Wirsching, Hans Frank ★★★ Renowned estate in IPHOFEN known for classically structured dry RIES, *Silvaner*. Occasionally crystal-clear BA, TBA: breathtaking Julius-Echter-Berg Ries TBA 22'.

Wittmann Rhh ★★★ Leading bio estate; pure, zesty dry RIES GGS Brunnenhäuschen 13', Kirchspiel, Morstein 08 11 12' 15 16 **17** 18 19' 20 21'. Top Morstein ALTE REBEN selection La Borne.

Wöhrwag Würt ★★★ Family estate at Untertürkheim (district of Stuttgart), long known for some of best RIES in WÜRT. Now also successful with LEMBERGER, PINOT N and Bx-blend *Cuvée X*, always in a finely chiselled and fresh style that nevertheless matures v. well.

Wöhrle Bad ★★★ Organic pioneer (30 yrs+) in Breisgau. Top GGS (eg. Kirchgasse GRAUBURGUNDER, SPÄTBURGUNDER, Teufelslochgasse CHARD).

Württemberg Dynamic s region nr Stuttgart, many young growers eager to experiment. Best usually LEMBERGER, SPÄTBURGUNDER, red blends. Light and bright trad TROLLINGER has renaissance. Only 30% white varieties. RIES needs altitude vyds.

Würzburg Frank ★★→★★★★ Great Baroque city on the Main, famous for its best vyd Stein (STEINWEIN, STEIN-BERG).

Zellertal Pfz ★★→★★★★ Area in N PFZ, high, cool, recent gold-rush: BATTENFELD-SPANIER, KP KELLER, PHILIPP KUHN have bought in Zellertal's best vyd Schwarzer Herrgott or neighbouring RHH plot Zellerweg am Schwarzen Herrgott. Local estates incl Bremer, Full, Janson Bernhard.

Ziereisen Bad ★★ →★★★★ Outstanding estate in MARKGRÄFLERLAND, advocating LANDWEIN. Best: SPÄTBURGUNDERS from small plots – Rhini, Schulen, Talrain. Jaspis = old-vine selections. Top: GUTEDEL 10⁴ (provocatively priced at €125) has great terroir expression.

Zilliken, Forstmeister Geltz Mos ★★★→★★★★ SAAR family estate, unique track record of mature fruity and nobley sweet *Ries from Saarburg Rausch* and OCKFEN Bockstein. Dorothee Z follows father's path of elegance, delicacy (eg. AUSLESE GOLDKAPSEL 21', TBA 18'); v.gd SEKT and Ferdinand's gin.

Zimmerling, Klaus Sachs ★★★ Small, perfectionist estate, VDP, one of 1st est after Berlin Wall came down. Best vyd: Königlicher Weinberg (King's vyd) nr Dresden.

EU terminology

Germany's part in new EU classification involves, firstly, abolishing the term Tafelwein in favour of plain **Wein** – this is, up to now, the only visible change on labels. LANDWEIN is still called Landwein, even if its bureaucratic name would be **geschützte geographische Angabe (ggA)**, or protected geographical indication. Brussels generally allows continued use of est designations. **Geschützte Ursprungsbezeichnung (gU)**, or protected designation of origin, should technically be replacing QUALITÄTSWEIN and QUALITÄTSWEIN MIT PRÄDIKAT but is, up to now, mainly in place for large geographical units such as AHR, BAD, FRANKEN, etc. Since it's hard and time-consuming (4–6 yrs) to get recognition for a village- or vyd-specific gU, only six such gUs were in place by end of 2023: Bürgstadter Berg (see WEINGUT FÜRST), WINNINGEN Uhlen (parcel-specific Blaufuesser Lay, Laubach, Roth Lay, see HEYMANN-LÖWENSTEIN), WÜRZBURGER STEIN-BERG, and Monzinger Niederberg (NA). Another gU, IPHOFEN Echter-Berg (see WIRSCHING), is in the application process. The existing predicates – SPÄTLESE, AUSLESE and so on (see box, p.165) – stay in place; the rule for these styles hasn't changed and isn't going to.

Luxembourg

Vineyards (1200 ha) lie upstream of the more famous parts of the Moselle, on limestone, with more in common with Chablis than Piesport. Only 13% is Riesling. Müller-Thurgau (aka Rivaner) prevails. Auxerrois and Crémant fizz are specialities. Most whites have some sweetness – often too much, now that high acidity levels are a thing of the past. Labels don't specify dry or off-dry. Drought is becoming more of a problem. In summer 2022, it only rained a third of the usual amount. And the number of hours of sunshine was the highest since 1947.

Alice Hartmann ★★★→★★★★ Rich, slightly off-dry RIES from prime sites (Wormeldange Koeppchen). In Burgundy (St-Aubin), Mittelmosel (Trittenheim).

Aly Duhr ★★★ Carefully crafted wines, spontaneously fermented Koeppchen RIES (organic) shows terroir, oaked Monsalvat (80/20% CHARD/AUXERROIS) with food.

Bernard-Massard ★→★★★ Big producer, esp Crémant. Top: Ch de Schengen/Thill and Clos des Rochers. Sekt in Germany too.

Gales ★★→★★★ Reliable, stylish. Best in a series of balanced Crémant: Heritage 16 Brut Nature, gd Domaine et Tradition whites. Cellar labyrinth worth seeing.

Kox, R&L ★★★ Avant-garde with a sense of craftsmanship: planting trees in the vyd (Orchard series, eg. Mosella Ries 22'), Cremant without added sulphur, Kvevri RIES. Also foot-trodden old-vine ELBLING (Rhäifrensch).

Pauqué, Ch ★★★→★★★★ Passionate Abi Duhr bridges gap between Burgundy and Germany: extract-laden, dense dry RIES (eg. Paradäis, Sous la Roche-Rue, "15hl"), balanced sweet Ries, barrel-fermented CHARD Clos de la Falaise.

Ruppert, Henri ★★★ RIES TBA-style (*see* Germany), PINOT N Ma Tâche (yes, really).

Schram ★★→★★★ SYLVANER (Kurschels), on Franken-like (*see* Germany) Keuper soils.

Sunnen-Hoffmann ★★★ Round and aromatic concrete-egg RIES Wintrange Felsbierg, and old-school full-bodied Domaine et Tradition PINOT GR.

Other good estates: Bentz, Cep d'Or, Desom, Häremillen, Kohll-Leuk, Krier Frères, Mathes, Mathis Bastian, Schmit-Fohl, Schumacher-Lethal. Doms Vinsmoselle is a union of co-ops.

Belgium

Belgium's growing wine industry now counts c.300 producers and c.1000 hectares of vineyards across all provinces, with Hainaut and Limburg as frontrunners. They make fresh, food-friendly, cool-climate wines, mainly sparkling or white and in premium price brackets. Most sell locally: at cellar doors, specialist retailers, wine bars, restaurants and increasingly at fairs, markets and oenotourism events. Exports are rising, albeit from a low base. Main grape varieties are Auxerrois, Chardonnay, Pinots Blanc/Gris/Noir and Riesling, alongside Johanniter, Regent and Solaris. Promising results also with Acolon, Gamay, Muscaris and Souvignier Gris. Best recent vintages: 22 18.

Try Agaises, Aldeneyck, Beekborne, Bioul, Bon Baron, Bousval, Chant d'Eole, Chapitre, Chenoy, Clos d'Opleeuw, Crutzberg, Cruysem, d'Hellekapelle, Entre-Deux-Monts, Genoels-Elderen, Gloire de Duras, Haksberg, Hoenshof, Kitsberg, Oud Conynsbergh, Petrushoeve, Pietershof, Pres De Gand, Ravenstein, Ry d'Argent, Schorpion, Septem Triones, Steinberg, Stuyvenberg, Ten Gaerde, Ter Weyden Bosch, Vandersteene, Vandeurzen, Vin de Liège, Waes, Wijnfaktorij.

Spain

Abbreviations used in the text:

SPAIN

Alel	Alella	P Vas	País Vasco
Alic	Alicante	R Bai	Rías Baixas
Ara	Aragón	Rib Sac	Ribeira Sacra
Bier	Bierzo	Rib del D	Ribera del Duero
Bul	Bullas	Rio	Rioja
Cád	Cádiz	R Ala	Rioja Alavesa
Can	Canary Islands	R Alt	Rioja Alta
C-La M	Castilla-La Mancha	R Or	Rioja Oriental
		Rue	Rueda
C y L	Castilla y León	Som	Somontano
Cat	Catalonia	U-R	Utiel-Requena
C de Bar	Conca de Barberá	Vcia	Valencia
Cos del S	Costers del Segre		
Emp	Empordà		
Ext	Extremadura		
Gal	Galicia		
Jum	Jumilla	PORTUGAL	
La M	La Mancha	Alen	Alentejo
Mál	Málaga	Alg	Algarve
Mall	Mallorca	Bair	Bairrada
Man	Manchuela	Bei Int	Beira Interior
Mén	Méntrida	Dou	Douro
Mont-M	Montilla-Moriles	Lis	Lisboa
Mont	Montsant	Mad	Madeira
Mur	Murcia	Min	Minho
Nav	Navarra	Set	Setúbal
Pen	Penedès	Tej	Tejo
Pri	Priorat	Vin	Vinho Verde

How rapidly Spain has changed! Fifty years ago, the dictator Franco was still alive; Spain was not to enter what is now the EU for another decade or so. The majority of today's denominations did not exist. The DOs of Cava, Ribera del Duero, Priorat were all still to come. Twenty-five years on, with the turn of the millennium, Spain was on the verge of international recognition: new projects were starting up, with the influence of the next generation, who had been able to travel, to study and make wine worldwide. Now, in 2025, Spain has come of age. The classics – Rioja and Jerez – have become more polished. Producers have returned to the vineyards to replace the high-yielding vines favoured in the 1970s and 80s with more appropriate plant material. The fashion for international varieties – Cabernet, Syrah, Merlot – has thankfully faded, to be replaced by the search for long-ignored local varieties, often overlooked with the replanting after phylloxera. Styles of winemaking have changed in such a short time, as winemakers look back to traditional containers, such as clay amphorae and concrete tanks, and to traditional methods. Welcome back to *clarete*, the light red with its crunchy freshness. Welcome

back to the unfortified wines of the Sherry zone and Montilla-Moriles. The DOP regulations remain a straitjacket, but more and more producers are flexing their muscles and choosing to fight their way out. Yet the coming years bring new demands to manage climate change: the search for different pruning methods; different varieties; higher-altitude sites. Despite that, the first quarter-century, 2025, is a moment for celebration. Spain can look forward to 2050 with great confidence.

Recent Rioja vintages

2023 Difficult: drought in many areas. Lower yields. Depends on producer.

2022 A few v. hot summer days. Lower yields. Generally lighter wines.

2021 V. promising; deep-coloured structured reds, fine ageing potential.

2020 Difficult yr. Fresh wines, moderate alc.

2019 Low yield, overall fine quality, officially *excelente*. Some wines outstanding.

2018 Gd yr with generous yields, lower alc, fresh wines.

2017 Dramatic frost. What was left is v.gd. Enjoy now or soon.

2016 Largest harvest since 05, well-balanced wines, plenty to like.

2015 Top wines gd as 10, rich, full of character. Savour now, best are keepers.

2014 After two small vintages, return to quality, quantity. Drink soon.

Aalto Rib del D ★★★→★★★★ Stylish, polished wines. Two labels: Aalto and flagship PS (from 200 plots). Best with 10 yrs+ ageing. Winemaker MARIANO GARCÍA. Owner Masaveu also has Enate (SOM), Fillaboa (R BAI), Murua (RIO) and v.gd Asturias cider (Valverán).

Abadía Retuerta C y L ★★→★★★ Luxury, thy name is Abadía Retuerta, hotel and winery. No expense spared at Spain's newest VINO DE PAGO. Just outside RIB DEL D. Serious single-vyd reds, eg. Pago Garduña SYRAH, Pago Valdeballón CAB SAUV, PV PETIT VERDOT. Michelin-starred restaurant. Novartis-owned.

Águila, Dominio del Rib del D ★★→★★★★ Jorge Monzón proves there is another face to RIB DEL D: crisp, delicate, occasionally playful. His pale *clarete* is refreshing; field-blend Peñas Aladas, exceptional.

Álava / País Vasco / Basque Country ★→★★★★ Stretching s from the TXAKOLIS of the Atlantic to RIO, Álava is home to a people with a proud history and their own language. Young, trad R Ala wines use carbonic maceration. R Ala known for old vines, different village characters. Campaigns for regional identity encouraging some producers to break from Rio to unite under an Ala umbrella.

Algueira Rib Sac ★★→★★★ Exceptional producer in RIB SAC, expert in its extreme viticulture on vertiginous river banks. Fine selection of elegant wines from local varieties. Outstanding is Merenzao (aka Jura's TROUSSEAU), almost burgundian in style.

Alicante ★→★★★ Take a closer look. Spiritual home of MONASTRELL: spicy reds and rare, trad, unfortified *Fondillón*. But also dry white from formerly unloved MOSCATEL de Alejandría coming to fore; and local (r) Giró. Top: ARTADI, GUTIÉRREZ DE LA VEGA, PEPE MENDOZA CASA AGRÍCOLA. Also Finca Collado, Les Freses, Murviedro.

Allende, Finca R Alt ★★→★★★★ Top (in all senses) BODEGA at BRIONES in merchant's house with tower looking over town to vyds, run by irrepressible Miguel Ángel de Gregorio. Outstanding white.

Almacenista Man, Sherry Sherry stockholder; cellars wines for BODEGAS to increase or refresh stocks. Important in MANZANILLA production. Can be terrific. Few left; many have changed direction and now sell direct to consumers, eg. EL MAESTRO SIERRA, GUTIÉRREZ COLOSÍA.

Alonso del Yerro Rib del D, Toro ★★→★★★ Stéphane Derenoncourt (*see* France) entices elegance from RIB DEL D's extreme continental climate. Vintages from 16 on showing great delicacy. Family business, estate wines. Top: María. Paydos is TORO. Owner María del Yerro chairs Grandes Pagos (*see* PAGO).

Alta Alella Cat ★★→★★★ Family business with toes in Med, closest to Barcelona. Excellent CAVAS, fine, full-bodied Pansa Blanca (XAREL·LO), sweet red Dolç Mataró from MONASTRELL. Organic. Separate Celler de les Aus is brand for min-intervention, no-added-sulphur wines.

Alvear Ext, Mont-M ★★ →★★★★ Historic. Superb array of PX in MONT-M; gd FINO CB and Capataz, lovely sweet SOLERA 1927, unctuous DULCE Viejo; v. fine vintage. RAMIRO IBÁÑEZ of SANLÚCAR advises on Miradas still wines aged under FLOR.

Añada Vintage.

Anza R Ala ★★ Elegance from Diego Magaña, part of impressive, well-travelled new generation in RIO.

Aragón Former mighty medieval kingdom, stretching s from Pyrénées, home to Calatayud, CAMPO DE BORJA, CARIÑENA, Som DOPS. Once a land of bulk wine, co-ops, now gaining attention for new generation recuperating old vines, incl GARNACHA, MACABEO, Moristel (r). Producers: ESCOCÉS VOLANTE, Familia NAVASCUÉS, FRONTONIO, SAN ALEJANDRO CO-OP.

Arizcuren Rio ★★ Javier A trained as architect, designs wineries in RIO, incl his own urban BODEGA in downtown Logroño (worth a visit, as is trad cave in cliffs in

Quel town). Specializes in GARNACHAS at altitude from R OR, Mazuelo (CARIÑEÑA; relatively rare as single variety in Rio) and amphora wine. One to watch.

Artadi Ala, Alic, Nav, P Vas ★★→★★★★ Juan Carlos López de Lacalle makes wine within RIO DOP but prefers to label with ÁLAVA origin. Single-vyd focus: luxuriant La Poza de Ballesteros; dark, stony El Carretil; outstanding El Pisón. Also in ALIC (r El Sequé), NAV (r Artazuri, ROSADO DYA). Izar-Leku TXAKOLÍ (w) from Getaria.

Artuke Rio ★★→★★★ Brothers Arturo and Kike de Miguel have transformed family's wines. One of new generation of "Rioja 'n' Rollers" now seriously gd. Exponent of villages in R Ala. Gloriously elegant, subtle use of large oak. Two top single vyds: El Escolladero, on limestone; La Condenada, on iron-rich sandstone.

Astobiza Ala ★★ In smallest of TXAKOLÍ DOPS, v. fine, advised by Ana Martín (*see* CASTILLO DE CUZCURRITA). Mineral Malkoa; also gin.

Atlantic wines Gal, P Vas, Rio Unofficial term for bright, often unoaked whites with firm acidity. Increasingly used to describe crisp, delicate reds, esp in R BAI, or TXAKOLÍS. Claimed by JEREZ. Describes cool-climate influences on specific vintages, eg. in inland GAL DOPS, and RIO. Not forgetting CAN in mid-Atlantic.

Axarquía Beautiful mtn region inland from MÁL, worth a visit, renowned for sweet wines. *See also* BENTOMIZ, Mál.

Barbadillo Cád, Man ★→★★★★ From supermarket to superb. Astonishing portfolio of v. fine Sherries. Sherry guru Armando Guerra works with Montse Molina seeking out specialities from cellars, incl unfortified PALOMINO. Pioneered MANZANILLA EN RAMA. Top-of-range Reliquía, esp AMONTILLADO, PALO CORTADO. Plenty to enjoy. Blanco de Albariza finally updates simple Castillo de San Diego from Palomino FINO, the long-time bestseller. Also Vega Real (RIB DEL D), BODEGA Pirineos (SOM).

Barrio de la Estación Rio The "station quarter" of Haro, from where trains shipped wine to Bx when latter's vines were destroyed by phylloxera. Now home to seven top wineries: BODEGAS Bilbaínas (CODORNÍU), CVNE, Gómez Cruzado, LA RIOJA ALTA, LÓPEZ DE HEREDIA, MUGA, RODA. Annual open-house tastings; *see* barrioestacion.com.

Belondrade C y L, Rue ★★→★★★ Consistent leader in VERDEJO as it should be but so rarely is. Didier B was early (1994) exponent of finesse in RUE, and lees ageing.

Bentomiz, Bodegas Mál ★★→★★★ Dutch by birth, Spanish by adoption: Clara (winemaker) and André (chef) are welcoming hosts in AXARQUÍA, inland from MÁL. Learn how they make sweet MOSCATEL, MERLOT. Rare dry Romé (rosé). New: CAVA with PENEDÈS grapes and Bentomiz *licor de expedición*.

Bhilar, Bodegas R Ala ★→★★ David Sampedro Gil single-minded pioneer in El Villar. Focus on vyds, old vines, horses in vyd; bio. Whites are textured, reds show elegance. Phinca Revilla Sexto Año spends 6 yrs in oak, homage to trad whites of RIO. Phinca Lali is dense, spicy red from a centenarian vyd.

Bideona R Ala ★→★★★ Young producer, v. promising (incl two MWs). Aims to reflect specific terroirs. Founded when RIO regulated use of village name on wines not made in that village, Bideona used abbreviations, eg. V1BN4 for Villabuena. Wines are more than just a play on words. Part of Península Viticultores (C y L, CEBREROS, GREDOS, TXAKOLÍ de Bizkaia).

Bierzo ★→★★★★ Looking for a different flavour in Spain? Find it in aromatic, mid-weight, often crunchily fresh reds from MENCÍA in nw. On slate soils they become perfumed, *Pinot-like*. The DOP shot to international fame with RAÚL PÉREZ and Ricardo Pérez Palacios (no relation). Take care: quality is uneven. Look for CÉSAR MÁRQUEZ, DESCENDIENTES DE J PALACIOS, Raúl Pérez, plus Dominio de Tares, Losada, Luna Berberide, Mengoba, MICHELINI, Peique, Veronica Ortega. Also fine GODELLO (w).

Bilbao, Ramón Rib del D, Rio, Rue, R Bai ★→★★★ Part of huge Zamora company

SPAIN

(producer of Licor 43). Research-driven BODEGAS incl RIB DEL D for Cruz de Alba bio. In R OR delivering fresh GARNACHA at altitude. Newest winery in Rio is Lalomba, paradise of tailor-made concrete tanks, with two single-vyd reds and Provençal-style ROSADO.

Bodega A cellar; a wine shop; a business making, blending and/or shipping wine.

Butt Sherry 600-litre barrel of long-matured American oak used for Sherry. Filled 5/6 full, allows space for FLOR to grow, protecting wine from oxygen and consuming nutrients. Trend for wineries – and whisky distillers – to use former butts for maturation for Sherry influence – eg. CVNE Monopole Clásico, BARBADILLO Mirabras.

Callejuela Man, Sherry ★★→★★★ Blanco brothers have vyds in some of Sherry's most famous PAGOS. Sherries and VINOS DE PASTO incl Las Mercedes from Añina Pago. Part of TERRITORIO ALBARIZA.

Campo de Borja Ara ★→★★ Self-proclaimed "Empire of GARNACHA". Heritage of old vines, plus young vyds = 1st choice for gd-value Garnacha, now starting to show serious quality: Alto Moncayo, Aragonesas, Borsao.

Campo Viejo Rio ★→★★ Biggest RIO brand. In addition to value RES, GRAN RES, covers all main categories. Part of Pernod Ricard (*see also* YSIOS).

Canary Islands ★→★★★ Seven main islands, nine DOPS. Tenerife has five of them. Favourite of vine-hunters: unusual varieties, old vines, distinct microclimates, volcanic soils, unique pruning. Dry white LISTÁN (aka PALOMINO) and Listán Negro, Marmajuelo, Negramoll (TINTA NEGRA), Vijariego. MOSCATELS, MALVASÍAS, incl fortified El Grifo from Lanzarote. Top: Borja Pérez, ENVINATE, SUERTES DEL MARQUÉS; try also Viñátigo. In volcano-hit La Palma: Victoria Pecis Torres (esp Malvasía Volcánica). Lanzarote: El Grifo, Puro Rofe. Gran Canaria: TAMERÁN. Overall, plenty of dull wine for tourists.

Cangas ★→★★ Isolated DOP in wild Asturias just beginning to be known. Unique varieties USP: fresh Albarín Blanco, crunchy reds from Albarín Negro, Verdejo Negro and, most promising, Carrasquín. Producers: Dominio de Urogallo, Monasterio de Corias, VidAs.

Can Sala Cava ★★★★ Exceptional CAVA winery still belonging to Ferrer family, former owners of FREIXENET. Cava de Paraje, from PARELLADA.

Cariñena Ara ★→★★ The one DOP that is also the name of a grape variety. Co-op country transformed by talented winemakers. ESCOCÉS VOLANTE; Jorge NAVASCUÉS. Bold, characterful, value.

Casa Castillo Jum ★★→★★★★ One of Spain's greats, José María Vicente, proves JUM can be tiptop. Family business high up in *altiplano*. Outstanding MONASTRELLS, esp PIE FRANCO.

Castaño Mur Yecla is trad bulk-wine country, but Castaño stands apart. Castaño Dulce a modern classic sweet MONASTRELL.

Castell d'Encús Cos del S ★★→★★★★ Shades of a philosopher-king, Raül Bobet (also of PRI Ferrer-Bobet) constantly planning. At over 1000m (3281ft) he can make *superbly fresh, original wines*. Grapes fermented in C12 granite *lagares*. Natural micro-reserve. Acusp PINOT, Ekam RIES, Thalarn SYRAH all classics.

Castilla y León ★→★★★ Spain's largest wine region. Diversity means exciting discoveries. DOPS: Arlanza, Arribes, BIER, Cigales, RUE, Sierra de Salamanca (one to watch, with red Rufete grape), Tierra de León, Tierra del Vino de Zamora, TORO, Valles de Benavente, Valtiendas. Catch-all DOP Vino de la Tierra de Castilla y León can be source of v. fine wines, eg. Barco del Corneta, Máquina y Tabla. Top: ABADÍA RETUERTA, MARQUÉS DE RISCAL (VERDEJO), Mauro, Ossian, Prieto Pariente. Recuperating unique grapes, eg. Cenicienta, Juan García, Puesta en Cruz.

Castillo de Cuzcurrita R Alt ★★ Lovely walled vyd and castle, v. fine RIO. Inky, pure, single-vyd Tilo.

Castillo Perelada Emp, Nav, Pri, Rio ★→★★ Glossy tourist destination: hotel, casino, Michelin restaurant, striking winery. Vivacious value CAVAS. Also modern red blends. Rare 12-yr-old, SOLERA-aged Garnatxa de l'EMPORDÀ. Casa Gran del Siurana (PRI) v. fine. Owns Chivite (NAV), Salceda (RIO).

Catalonia Vast umbrella DOP, covers whole of Cat: seashore, mtn, in-between. Top chefs and top BODEGAS. Actual DOP too large to have identity.

Cava ★→★★★ Spain's trad-method sparkling; 90%+ made in PEN. Cava de Guarda, youngest, min 9 mths' age. Cava de Guarda Superior, incl all older wines, all certified organic by 2025. Res (min 18 mths), Gran Res (min 30 mths). Single-vyd Cava de Paraje (min 36 mths), low or no dosage. Brut Nature v. common in top categories; XAREL·LO becoming more highly rated for ageability; MACABEO less able to tolerate climate change. New: Elaboradores Integrales: producers who grow/make/bottle their own wines. Regulatory changes partly driven by breakaway producer groups, eg. CLÀSSIC PENEDÈS, Conca del Ríu Anoia and CORPINNAT, plus RIO now has own category of trad-method sparkling not called Cava. Latest initiatives give potential for recognition of Cava's top-quality wines. *See* ALTA ALELLA, CAN SALA, CODORNÍU, MESTRES, JUVÉ Y CAMPS.

Cebreros C y L ★→★★ Young (2017) DOP illustrating dynamic development of GREDOS, with distinct zones identifying themselves. As elsewhere, GARNACHA (r) dominates; also Albillo Mayor (w). Look for Daniel Ramos, Rico Nuevo, Ruben Díaz, Soto Manrique, TELMO RODRÍGUEZ.

Count them: number of bubbles in 100ml Cava at 6°C (43°F) after 4 hours = 1m.

Celler del Roure Vcia ★→★★ Interested in TINAJAS? Then visit this BODEGA in S VCIA. Impressive underground cellar of vast *tinajas* buried up to necks; gd, fresh, elegant. Cullerot, Parotet, Safrà from local varieties. Many old houses in Alforins district have trad *tinajas*, none quite so remarkable as this.

César Florido Sherry ★→★★★ Master of MOSCATEL, since 1887, working with the underrated sweet-style Sherry. Explore gloriously scented, succulent: Dorado, Especial, Pasas. Based in CHIPIONA.

Chipiona Sherry Sandy coastal zone, source of MOSCATEL. Best: floral delicacies, far less dense than PX.

Clàssic Penedès Pen Category of DOP PEN for trad-method fizz, stricter rules than CAVA; min 15 mths' ageing, organically grown grapes. Members incl Albet i Noya, Colet, Loxarel, Mas Bertran.

Clos Mogador Pri ★★→★★★ René Jnr's father, René Barbier, was one of PRI's founding quintet and mentor to many. One of 1st wineries to gain a Vi de Finca designation. Lovely Manyetes CARIÑENA.

Codorníu Raventós Cos del S, Pen, Pri, Rio ★→★★★★ Historic art nouveau CAVA winery worth a visit. Single-vyd, single-variety Cavas de Paraje Calificado trio v. fine. Mass-market Cavas continue to improve. Elsewhere, Legaris in RIB DEL D has v.gd village wines; Raimat in COS DEL S is Europe's largest organic estate; BODEGAS Bilbaínas in RIO has bestseller VIÑA Pomal – back on form. Jewel is outstanding PRI SCALA DEI, which it part owns.

Colección de Toneles Centenarios Alic ★★★★ Superb aged FONDILLÓN: forgotten casks being revived, commercialized under brand Luis XIV. Limited release.

Conca de Barberà Cat Small DOP once a feeder of fruit to large enterprises, now some excellent wineries, incl Abadía de Poblet, TORRES.

Consejo Regulador Organization that controls a DOP; each DOP has its own. Quality as inconsistent as wines they represent: some bureaucratic, others enterprising.

Contino R Ala ★★→★★★★ Estate incl one of RIO's great single vyds, making Viña del Olivo. Winemaker Jorge NAVASCUÉS. CVNE-owned. Known for use of GRACIANO.

Corpinnat Cat ★★→★★★★ Independent group of producers of trad-method fizz, more stringent quality than CAVA: Can Descregut, Can Feixes, GRAMONA, Júlia Bernet, Llopart, Mas Candí, Nadal, Pardas, RECAREDO, Sabaté i Coca, Torelló.

Corrales, Viña Sherry ★★★ PETER SISSECK's BODEGA in JEREZ, FINO from PAGO Balbaína, 8–9-yr-old EN RAMA. Aim is single-vyd Sherries, in time, from organic vyds. Viña La Cruz is AMONTILLADO from Pago Macharnudo.

Costers del Segre ★→★★★ Geographically divided DOP combines mountainous CASTELL D'ENCÚS and lower-lying Castell del Remei, Raimat.

Cota 45 Sherry ★★ From thoughtful, ever-interesting SANLÚCAR winemaker RAMIRO IBÁÑEZ. Ube is PALOMINO from different famous PAGOS, eg. Carrascal, Miraflores. Saline, appley, unfortified, briefly matured in Sherry BUTTS. Reveals strong terroir differences. *See also* DE LA RIVA, WILLY PÉREZ.

Crianza Declaration of wine age – not quality – in RIO. Indicates use of oak. Must be min 2 yr old; reds min 1 yr in oak barrels, whites and ROSADOS min 6 mths.

Cuentaviñas Rio ★★ Personal project of Eduardo Eguren, son of Marcos (SIERRA CANTABRIA), in Peciña (San Vicente de la Sonsierra). Old vine (1923) El Tiznado. One of new generation in RIO.

Cusiné, Tomás C de Bar, Cos del S ★★→★★★ Winemaker leading innovative group: wines incl Finca collection, Tomás Cusiné blends. In MONT, C DE BAR, COS DEL S.

CVNE R Ala, R Alt ★★→★★★★ One of RIO's great names, based in Haro's BARRIO DE LA ESTACIÓN, owns 545 ha vyds. Pronounced *"coo-nee"*, Compañia Vinícola del Norte de España, founded 1879. Four Rio wineries: CONTINO, CVNE (incl Real de Asúa), Imperial, VIÑA Real. Most impressive at top end. Also wineries in R BAI (La Val); CAVA (Roger Goulart), RIB DEL D (Bela), VALDEORRAS (Virgen del Galir).

How long does Sherry keep opened? Fino/Manzanilla 1 wk in fridge. Others: 1 yr+.

Daniel Gomez Jiménez-Landi Mén ★★→★★★ Pioneer in new generation of GARNACHA producers, making wines at higher altitude across GREDOS (CEBREROS, Mén, etc). Uvas de la Ira, modern classic.

De Alberto Rue ★★★ Exceptional demijohn- and SOLERA-aged oxidative VERDEJO: caramel and walnut, vanilla and raisin.

Dinastía Vivanco R Alt ★→★★ Family business in Briones known for varietal wines and *outstanding wine museum* in Briones. Impressive trad-method sparkling RIO.

DO / DOP (denominación de origen / protegida) DOP replaced former DO category.

Dominio de Atauta Rib del D ★★→★★★★ Star among elegant wines of RIB DEL D's Soria province. Pre-phylloxera vyds; v. different from typically bold wines of DO.

Dulce Sweet. Can be late-harvest, botrytis, or fortfied. Seek out treasures: ALTA ALELLA, BENTOMIZ, GUTIÉRREZ DE LA VEGA, OCHOA, TELMO RODRÍGUEZ, TORRES. Also EMPORDÀ, MÁL, TXAKOLÍ, Yecla.

El Escocés Volante Ara, Cal ★→★★★ Scot Norrel Robertson MW was flying winemaker in Spain, hence the brand. Focus on old bush-vine GARNACHA grown at altitude, often field blends. Individual, characterful wines, part of movement transforming ARA; v. fine, single parcels.

El Maestro Sierra Sherry ★★★ Discover how a JEREZ cellar used to be. Run by Mari-Carmen Borrego Plá, following on from her mother, the redoubtable Pilar. Fine AMONTILLADO 1830 VORS, FINO, OLOROSO 1/14 VORS.

El Puerto de Santa María Sherry Just five BODEGAS remain, incl GUTIÉRREZ COLOSÍA, OSBORNE (gd wine bar). Puerto FINOS are less weighty than JEREZ, not as "salty" as SANLÚCAR. Lustau's EN RAMA trio shows differences of Sherries aged in the three different towns.

Empordà Cat ★→★★ One of number of centres of creativity in CAT, incl CASTILLO PERELADA, Celler Martí Fabra, Pere Guardiola, Vinyes dels Aspres. Sumptuous natural sweet wine from Celler Espolla: SOLERA GRAN RES.

Envínate Alm, Can, Rib Sac ★→★★★ Sparkling quartet of winemakers unlocking lesser-known regions: Almansa (Albahra), RIBEIRA SACRA (Lousas) and Tenerife (Táganan).

Equipo Navazos Man, Mont-M, Sherry ★★★→★★★★ Academic Jesús Barquín and Sherry winemaker Eduardo Ojeda pioneered négociant approach to Sherry, bottling individual BUTTS. Not just JEREZ: v. fine MONT-M selections.

Espumoso Means "sparkling", but confusing: incl cheap, injected-bubble wine as well as quality trad-method – like CAVA.

Fernando de Castilla Sherry ★★→★★★★ Gloriously consistent quality. Antique range all qualify as VOS or VORS, but label doesn't say so. Complex Antique FINO is fortified to historically correct 17% abv. OLOROSO and PX Singular v.gd. Plus v. fine brandy, vermouth, vinegar. Favoured supplier to EQUIPO NAVAZOS.

Finca Sandoval Man ★→★★ Consultant winemaker JAVIER REVERT making impressive changes. Top: La Rosa.

Flor Sherry Spanish for "flower": refers to the layer of *Saccharomyces* yeasts that typically grow and live on top of FINO/MANZANILLA Sherry in a BUTT 5/6 full. Flor consumes oxygen and other compounds ("biological ageing") and protects wine from oxidation. It grows a thicker layer nearer the sea at EL PUERTO and SANLÚCAR, hence finer character of Sherry there. VINO DE PASTO often aged for a short time with flor. Growing interest in flor winemaking elsewhere in Spain.

Fondillón Alic ★→★★★ Fabled unfortified *rancio* semi-sweet wine from overripe MONASTRELL. Matured in oak for min 10 yrs; some SOLERAS of great age. Unfairly fallen out of fashion, production shrinking too fast: Brotons (v. fine 64′ 70′), MG Wines, COLECCIÓN DE TONELES CENTENARIOS.

Freixenet Cava, Pen ★→★★★ Biggest CAVA producer. Best known for black-bottled Cordón Negro. CAN SALA is Cava de Paraje. Plus: Morlanda (PRI), Solar Viejo (RIO), Valdubón (RIB DEL D), Vionta (R BAI). Also Finca Ferrer (Argentina), Gloria Ferrer (US), Katnook (Australia). Owned by sparkling giant Henkell.

Frontonio Ara ★→★★★ Fernando Mora MW and Mario López continue to make waves, seeking out old-vine GARNACHA, GARNACHA BLANCA. Also v.gd MACABEO, from old-vine El Jardin de la Iguales vyd.

Galicia Spain's nw corner. Isolation has ensured rare varieties. Outstanding whites, esp RAFAEL PALACIOS; delicate, fresh reds, esp ALGUEIRA, DESCENDIENTES DE J PALACIOS, ZARATE (*see* MONTERREI, R BAI, RIB SAC, RIBEIRO, VALDEORRAS).

García, Mariano & Sons C y L, Rib del D, Rio Mariano G is a fixture in N and NW Spain. For many yrs winemaker at VEGA SICILIA. Co-founded AALTO and launched Mauro (C Y L). He and sons Eduardo and Alberto also run Garmón Continental (RIB DEL D), San Román (TORO). Arrived in RIO 2020 in Baños de Ebro.

Genérico Rio If there's no age category shown on the RIO bottle – such as RES – then it's a *genérico*. *Genéricos* need not follow all DOP rules on ageing (such as barrel size, min ageing). Unattractive and unhelpful name, but can be v.gd or outstanding. Case of needing to know producer.

González Byass Cava, Cád, Rib del D, Rio, Sherry ★→★★★★ Family business (1845). Cellarmaster Antonio Flores is debonair presence. From the *Tío Pepe* SOLERA, Flores extracts fine EN RAMA and **glorious Palmas series** (latter celebrated 1st decade 2020). Consistently gd. Exceptional 1975 AMONTILLADO. Boutique hotel (1st hotel in a working BODEGA in JEREZ). Other wineries: Beronia (RIO), Pazos de Lusco (R BAI), improving Vilarnau (CAVA), VIÑAS del Vero (Som); Dominio Fournier (RIB DEL D); plus (not so gd, but popular) Croft Original Pale Cream Sherry. Finca Moncloa, close to Jerez, produces still reds.

Gramona Cat, Pen ★★→★★★★★ Specialist in long-aged trad-method sparkling, esp Enoteca, *III Lustros*, *Celler Batlle*. Drove founding of CORPINNAT. Next-generation cousins Leo and Roc G run business, also v. fine L'Enclòs de Peralba; bio.

Gran Reserva In RIO, red Gran Res ages min 60 mths, of which min 2 yrs in

225-litre barrel, min 2 yrs in bottle. Whites and ROSADOS age min 4 yrs, of which 6 mths in barrel. Seek out superb old Rio vintages, often great value.

Gredos, Sierra de C y L ★→★★ A mtn region nw of Madrid. Renowned for new-wave GARNACHA. Best: pale, ethereal. DOPS gradually appearing: CEBREROS, Madrid, MÉN. Producers: 4 Monos, Bernabeleva, Canopy, Comando G, DANIEL GOMEZ JIMÉNEZ-LANDI, Marañones, TELMO RODRÍGUEZ.

Guita, La Man ★→★★★ Classic *Manzanilla* distinctive for sourcing fruit from vyds close to maritime SANLÚCAR. Grupo Estévez-owned (also VALDESPINO).

Gutiérrez Colosía Sherry ★→★★★ Rare remaining riverside BODEGA in EL PUERTO. Family business. Former ALMACENISTA. Excellent old PALO CORTADO.

Gutiérrez de la Vega Alic ★→★★★ Remarkable BODEGA specializing in sweet wine. In ALIC, but no longer in DOP, after disagreement over regulations. Expert in MOSCATEL, FONDILLÓN. Daughter Violeta now leading business alongside own project Curii (with partner Alberto Redrado, focus on Giró r).

Hidalgo, Emilio Sherry ★★★→★★★★ Outstanding family BODEGA. All wines (except PX) start by spending time under FLOR. Excellent unfiltered 15-yr-old La Panesa FINO, thrilling 50-yr-old AMONTILLADO Tresillo 1874, rare Santa Ana PX 1861.

Hidalgo-La Gitana Man ★★→★★★★ Historic (1792) SANLÚCAR firm. MANZANILLA La Gitana a classic. Finest Manzanilla is single-vyd Pastrana Pasada, verging on AMONTILLADO. Outstanding VORS, incl Napoleon Amontillado, Triana PX, Wellington PALO CORTADO.

Ibáñez, Ramiro Mont-M, Sherry Leading thinker in returning Sherry country to v. best of its old ways. Co-author with WILLY PÉREZ of book on their research. SANLÚCAR native, winemaker (eg. COTA 45), influential consultant to others, eg. ALVEAR (MONT-M), VIÑA CORRALES (PETER SISSECK). Member TERRITORIO ALBARIZA.

Grapes returning to Sherry: Beba, Cañocazo, Mantúos Castellano / Pila, Perruño.

Jerez de la Frontera Capital of Sherry region. "Sherry" is corruption of C8 "Sherish", Moorish name of city. Pronounced "hereth". In French, Xérès. Hence DOP is Jerez-Xérès-Sherry. MANZANILLA has own DOP: M-SANLÚCAR DE BARRAMEDA.

Joven Young, unoaked wine.

Jumilla Mur ★→★★★ Arid vyds in mtns n of Mur with heritage of old MONASTRELL vines. Top: CASA CASTILLO. Promising new-generation bio project BODEGAS Cerrón.

Juvé y Camps Cava, Pen ★★→★★★ Consistently gd CAVA. Stalwart is Res de la Familia (though qualifies as Gran Res), La Capella is Cava de Paraje.

Lalomba Rio ★→★★★ Ambitious winery of RAMÓN BILBAO. Paradise of concrete tanks, with two single-vyd reds and Provençal-style ROSADO.

La Mancha C-La M ★→★★ Don Quixote country; Spain's least impressive (except for its size) wine region, s of Madrid. Key source of grapes for distillation to brandy, particularly neutral AIRÉN. Too much bulk wine, yet excellence still possible: MARTÍNEZ BUJANDA's Finca Antigua and newbie VERUM.

López de Haro Nav, Rio, Toro ★→★★★ Entrepreneurial pair from Badarán in RIO making reliable value BODEGA Classica; v.gd GRAN RES. Also El Pacto (Rio); Aroa (NAV), Bardos (RIB DEL D), Matsu (TORO).

López de Heredia R Alt ★★→★★★★ Haro's oldest (1877), a family business in the BARRIO DE LA ESTACIÓN with wines that have become a cult. Take a look at "Txori-toki" tower and Zaha Hadid-designed shop. See how RIO was made (as it still is, here). Cubillo is younger range with GARNACHA; darker Bosconia; delicate, ripe *Tondonia*. Whites have seriously long barrel- and bottle-age; GRAN RES ROSADO is like no other. No shortcuts here.

Lupier, Dom Nav ★→★★★ Put NAV and its GARNACHA back on map, rescuing old vines to create two exceptional wines: bold El Terroir, ethereal La Dama; bio. One to watch: RAÚL PÉREZ now in charge.

Lustau Sherry ★★★→★★★★ Benchmark Sherries from JEREZ, SANLÚCAR, EL PUERTO. Originators of ALMACENISTA collection; each one is worth trying. Only BODEGA to produce EN RAMA from three Sherry towns. Consistently excellent.

Málaga ★→★★★ MOSCATEL-lovers should explore hills of Mál. TELMO RODRÍGUEZ revived ancient glories with subtle, sweet **Molino Real**. Barrel-aged No. 3 Old Vines Moscatel from Jorge Ordóñez is gloriously succulent. BENTOMIZ has impressive portfolio. Also Sierras de Mál DOP.

Mallorca ★→★★★ Uneven quality, some v.gd, some simply prestige projects. Can be high-priced and hard to find off island: 4 Kilos, Ánima Negra, Bàrbara Mesquida, Biniagual, Binigrau, Can Ribas, Miquel Gelabert (with wide array), Son Bordils, Toni Gelabert, Tramuntana. Reds blend trad varieties (Callet, Fogoneu, Mantonegro) plus CAB, SYRAH, MERLOT. Whites improving fast. DOPS: Binissalem, Pla i Llevant.

Manchuela ★→★★★ Take another look: making waves are JAVIER REVERT at FINCA SANDOVAL and PONCE, quietly superb, working with BOBAL and field blends.

Marqués de Cáceres R Alt, Rue, R Bai ★→★★★ Famous for introducing French techniques in 70s. Fresh (w/rosé). Modern Gaudium; trad classic GRAN RES. In RUE and R BAI.

Marqués de Murrieta R Alt, R Bai ★★★→★★★★ Between them, the marquesses of RISCAL and Murrieta launched RIO. At Murrieta, the step change in quality continues with new BODEGA on estate. Two styles, classic and modern: Castillo Ygay GRAN RES is one of Rio's trad greats. Latest release of Gran Res Blanco is **86**. Dalmau is impressive contrast, glossy modern Rio, v. well made. **Capellania** is fresh, taut, complex white, one of Rio's v. best; v. pale, crisp Primer Rosé from MAZUELO. In R BAI, relaunched Pazo de Barrantes shines gloriously; La Comtesse, brilliantly intense (ALBARIÑO).

Marqués de Riscal C y L, R Ala, Rue ★★→★★★ Riscal is living history of RIO, able to put on a tasting of every vintage going back to 1st, 1862. Take your pick of styles: reliable RES, modern Finca Torrea, balanced GRAN RES. Powerful **Barón de Chirel Res**. The Marqués launched RUE (1972) and today makes vibrant DYA SAUV BL, VERDEJO and v.gd Barón de Chirel Verdejo, though prefers to put wines in C y L not Rue. Eye-popping Frank Gehry hotel attached to Rio BODEGA.

Márquez, César Bier ★★→★★★ Relatively new entrant in Valtuille. Nephew of RAÚL PÉREZ. MENCÍA and GODELLO. Outstanding El Val Godello.

Mas Doix Pri ★★→★★★★ Star of PRI. Doix's treasure are old vines, esp superb CARIÑENA (grape). Top – all blueberry and velvet, astonishingly pure, named after yr vyd was planted – is *1902*, **Tossal d'en Bou**, one of few Gran Vinya Clasificada. Also v. fine old-vine GARNACHA *1903*, **Coma de Casas**. Murmuri and Salix (w).

Mas Martinet Pri ★★→★★★ Sara Pérez is daughter of one of original PRI quintet. Stays independent of that history. Vociferous, adventurous, ready to try new approaches: TINAJAS, demijohns, blends.

Mendoza, Abel R Ala ★★→★★★ For knowledge of RIO villages and varieties, Abel and Maite M have few equals. Discover no fewer than five varietal whites. Grano a Grano are only-the-best-berry-selected TEMPRANILLO and GRACIANO.

Merino, Miguel R Alt ★★ Son of famous father with same name, Miguel Jnr growing the winery: classics, yes, but also varietal Mazuelo, single-vyd wines.

Mestres, Cava Pen ★★→★★★ Specialist in aged CAVAS; 1st producer of Brut Nature (no dosage) Cava, in 1945. Fascinating Cavateca series with different disgorgement dates, and time in bottle.

Michelini Nav, Rio ★★ The Michelinis (parents) from Argentina have an old-vine project in BIER. Son Matias has est himself in RIO.

Monasterio, Hacienda Rib del D ★★★ PETER SISSECK co-owns/consults, where he 1st started in RIB DEL D. More accessible in price, palate than his DOMINIO DE PINGUS.

Monterrei Gal ★→★★★ Small DOP on Portuguese border, with traces of Roman winemaking. GODELLO, MENCÍA, the grapes. Best by far: Quinta da Muradella (José Luis Mateo) and gd-value Candea (Mateo with RAÚL PÉREZ).

Montilla-Moriles ★→★★★ Andalusian DOP nr Córdoba. Unfairly still in JEREZ's shadow; PX makes unfortified dry FINOS but also sweetest wines from sun-dried grapes. *Albariza* soils. Top wines superbly rich, some long ageing in SOLERA. Trend for dry whites aged in large amphorae. Top: ALVEAR, PÉREZ BARQUERO, TORO ALBALÁ. Important source of PX for use in Jerez DOP.

Montsant Cat ★→★★★ Tucked in around PRI, the gd-value neighbour. Fine GARNACHA BLANCA (Acústic). Reds worth exploring: Can Blau, Capçanes, Domènech, Espectacle, Joan d'Anguera, Mas Perinet, Masroig, Venus la Universal.

Muga R Alt ★★→★★★★ Does not put a foot wrong. Two styles: classical GRAN RES *Prado Enea*; modern, powerful *Torre Muga*. Family business with siblings, cousins. Also pale ROSADO; elegant white; lively trad-method sparkling.

Mustiguillo Rib del D ★★→★★★ Toni Sarrión led renaissance of unloved BOBAL grape, also Merseguera (w); created VINO DE PAGO Finca El Terrerazo with top Quincha Corral. Also at Hacienda Solana (RIB DEL D).

Navarra ★→★★★ Revival led by GARNACHA. Always in shadow of neighbour RIO. Early focus on international varieties confused its identity. Producers: DOM LUPIER, Chivite, Nekeas, OCHOA, Tandem, VIÑA ZORZAL. Also sweet MOSCATELS.

Navascués Ara ★★ Jorge N, one of new generation transforming ARA. In addition to family winery, where he makes eg. Cutio, he's winemaker at CONTINO, and CVNE properties in GAL.

Michelin's 1st Spanish sommelier of yr: Josep "Pitu" Roca of El Celler de Can Roca.

Numanthia Toro ★★→★★★★ One of TORO's heavyweights. Founded by Egurens of SIERRA CANTABRIA, who sold to LVMH. Exceptional, powerful wines gradually becoming more elegant. Top Termanthia comes round with 10 yrs of age.

Ochoa Nav ★→★★ Ochoa *padre* led modern growth of NAV, with focus on CAB, MERLOT. Winemaker daughter Adriana calls her range 8a, a play on her surname, developing different styles, incl Mil Gracias GRACIANO; fun, sweet, Asti-like sparkling MdO; classic MOSCATEL.

Osborne Sherry ★★→★★★★ Historic BODEGA in EL PUERTO, treasure trove, incl AOS AMONTILLADO, PDP PALO CORTADO. Owns former Domecq VORS incl 51–1a Amontillado. FINO Quinta and mature Coquinero Fino typical of town. Wineries in RIO (Montecillo), RUE, RIB DEL D.

Pago de Carraovejas Rib del D ★★★ Refined, elegant, from a winery strikingly situated on slopes below Peñafiel's romantic castle; on-site Ambivium, Michelin-starred restaurant. The business – Alma Carraovejas – growing at pace buying/founding BODEGAS. Owns VIÑA MEÍN - EMILIO ROJO (RIBEIRO), Marañones (GREDOS), Milsetentayseis (RIB DEL D), Ossian (top-quality VERDEJO producer in C Y L). Newest Aiurri (RIO), Tricó (R BAI).

Pago / Vino de Pago / Grandes Pagos *Pago* is a vyd, usually with est name, ie. Sherry's *pago* Miraflores and *pago* Balbaína. **Vino de Pago** is officially the top category of DOP; actually, not always. Typically Vinos de Pago are found in less famous zones. Not to be confused with **Grandes Pagos**, the network of mainly family-owned estates. Some are Vinos de Pago, but not all.

Palacio de Fefiñanes Gal ★★→★★★★ Reliable DYA R BAI ALBARIÑO. Two superior styles: barrel-fermented 1583 (yr winery was founded, oldest of DOP); super-fragrant, lees-aged III. Visit palace/winery at Cambados.

Palacios, Álvaro Bier, Pri, Rio ★★★→★★★★ Almost single-handedly built modern reputation of Spanish wine by his obsession with quality. One of quintet that revived PRI. Has driven recent designations from village to Grand Cru: Gran

Vi de Vinya. In RIO, at PALACIOS REMONDO, restoring reputation of R OR and its GARNACHAS. In BIER with nephew Ricardo at DESCENDIENTES DE J PALACIOS.

Palacios, Descendientes de J Bier ★★★→★★★★ MENCÍA at its best. Ricardo Pérez P, Álvaro's nephew, grows old vines on steep slate; bio. Floral Pétalos and Villa de Corullón gd value; Las Lamas and Moncerbal are different soil expressions, one clay, one rocky. Exceptional *La Faraona* (only one barrel), grows on tectonic fault.

Palacios, Rafael Vald ★★★→★★★★ Impossible to find fault with Rafael's wines. In VALDEORRAS, focus on GODELLO across many rocky parcels (*sortes*). Lovely Louro do Bolo; As Sortes, a step up; *Sorte O Soro*, surely Spain's best white. Sorte Antiga (old vines), v. delicate orange wine, Sorte Souto (tiny production, late harvest).

Palacios Remondo ★★→★★★ ÁLVARO P has put deserved spotlight on R OR and its GARNACHAS. Complex Plácet (w) originally created by brother RAFAEL P. Top: Quiñón de Valmira from slopes of Monte Yerga.

Pasto, Vino de Sherry ★→★★★ White from the Sherry zone, from Sherry grapes, but unfortified, revival of a former style. Grapes are sun-dried for a day, then wine aged in Sherry casks. Can have distinct *albariza* (chalky) soil character and some FLOR aromas. Growing in popularity. A delicate introduction to Sherry. BODEGAS DE LA RIVA, COTA 45 Reventón, LUIS PÉREZ La Escribana. Needs to form own DOP.

Pazo de Señorans Gal ★★★ Consistently excellent ALBARIÑOS from glorious R BAI estate. Outstanding Selección de Añada, min 30 mths on lees, proof v. best Albariños age beautifully.

Penedès Cat ★→★★★★ Region w of Barcelona, most diverse of CAT. Mix of soils, mix of varieties, a little mixed in message. XAREL·LO could be star; 1st DOP to be 100% organic. Best: Agustí Torelló Mata, Alemany i Corrio, Can Rafols dels Caus, GRAMONA, Jean León, Parés Baltà, TORRES.

Pepe Mendoza Casa Agrícola Alic ★→★★ After a long career in family wine business (Enrique Mendoza), Pepe launched his personal project in 2016, with great success focusing on elegant Giró (r), MONASTRELL, MOSCATEL. Blends, varietals, experimental wines.

Pérez, Raúl Bier ★★→★★★★★ A star, but avoids celebrity. Renowned for finesse, non-intervention. Provides generous house-room for new winemakers in cellar in BIER. Magnet for visiting (eg. Spanish, Argentine) winemakers. Outstanding Vizcaina Mencías; *El Rapolao* exceptionally pure. Other projects incl DOM LUPIER.

Pérez, Willy Sherry With RAMIRO IBÁÑEZ leading return to old ways in JEREZ, researching and reviving practices, trads, rare varieties, terroirs – and jointly writing the history. Interest in unfortified PALOMINO. Projects incl VINO DE PASTO DE LA RIVA. Founder member TERRITORIO ALBARIZA.

Pérez Barquero Mont-M ★→★★★ Leading producer of MONT-M: Gran Barquero FINO, AMONTILLADO, OLOROSO; La Cañada PX. Supplier to EQUIPO NAVAZOS.

Pie franco Ungrafted vine, on own roots. Typically on sandy soils where phylloxera could not penetrate. Some 110 yrs+ – many in TORO, some in C Y L, RUE.

Pingus, Dominio de Rib del D ★★★→★★★★ One of RIB DEL D's greats. Tiny bio winery of Pingus (PETER SISSECK's childhood name), made with old-vine TINTO FINO, shows refinement of variety in extreme climate. Flor de Pingus from younger vines; Amelia is single barrel named after wife. PSI uses grapes from growers, long-term social project to encourage them to stay on land. *See also* VIÑA CORRALES, HACIENDA MONASTERIO.

Pomares, Eulogio R Bai ★★→★★★★ No better way to understand R BAI and ALBARIÑO than with his wines. Winemaker for ZARATE; launched eponymous project.

Ponce Man ★★→★★★ Juan Antonio P has single-mindedly transformed family business into pre-eminent producer in DOP. One of leaders building reputation of BOBAL; bio. PIE FRANCO bottling: PF.

Priorat ★★ ·★★★★ Some of Spain's finest. Named after former monastery tucked under craggy cliffs. Key is *llicorella* (slate) soil. Best show remarkable purity, finesse, sense of place; Pri has pioneered classification pyramid from village wines through Vi de Vila to Gran Vi de Vinya. After a period when CAB, SYRAH were thought best, producers have returned to trad CARIÑENA, GARNACHA and have toned down new oak. Source of superb elegance.

Raventós i Blanc Cat ★·★★★ Pepe R led historic family business out of CAVA in 2012. Created Conca del Riu Anoia for high-quality sparklings with strict controls; bio. Wines: De Nit ROSADO, Mas del Serral, ringingly pure Textures de Pedra. Can Sumoi estate natural-wine project (2017), incl XAREL·LO, pét-nats.

In Priorat, vines must be 70 to be "old". In Rioja, mere 35-year-olds qualify.

Recaredo Pen ★★ ·★★★★ Outstanding producer of trad-method sparkling, small family concern, celebrated centenary 2024. Wines aged under cork, not crown cap; still hand-disgorges. Top: precise, mineral *Turó d'en Mota*, from vines planted 1940, ages brilliantly; classic Res Particular; Enoteca library releases. Member CORPINNAT. Celler Credo: still wines, low in alc, strikingly pure. All bio.

Remelluri, La Granja Nuestra Señora R Ala ★★·★★★ TELMO RODRÍGUEZ's family property; v. fine white blend; old-vine TEMPRANILLOS; focus on exceptional old GARNACHA single vyds, ethereal wines. Organic.

Remírez de Ganuza R Ala ★★·★★★ Fernando R de G hit 100-point jackpot with 2004 GRAN RES from his well-selected vyds around Samaniego. Diversifying with new owner: excellent Olagar Gran Res Blanco, also Iraila GARNACHA.

Reserva (Res) Has actual meaning in RIO. Reds: aged min 3 yrs, of which min 1 yr in oak of 225 litres and min 6 mths in bottle. Whites and ROSADOS: min 2 yrs age, of which min 6 mths barrel. Note: age does not mean quality.

Revert, Javier Vcia ★·★★★ Remarkably pure Med wines from family vyds, local grapes, eg. Tortosí, Trepadell and others. Three wines: Micalet, Sensal, Simeta, a benchmark. Also updating wines at FINCA SANDOVAL.

Rías Baixas Gal ★·★★★★ Atlantic DOP in GAL split in five subzones, mostly DYA. Best: Forjas del Salnés, Fulcro, Gerardo Méndez, Martín Códax, PALACIO DE FEFIÑANES, Pazo de Barrantes (MARQUÉS DE MURRIETA), *Pazo de Señorans*, Terras Gauda, ZÁRATE. Land of *minifundia*, tiny landholdings. Until recently Spain's premier DOP for whites, now like RUE at risk of overproduction. ALBARIÑO is variety here; v. best can age, reaching burgundian elegance. A few reds, strikingly fresh, crisp.

Ribeira Sacra Gal ★★·★★★ Magical DOP with vyds running dizzyingly down to River Sil. Some impressive, original, fresh, light MENCÍA reds: Adegas Moure, ALGUEIRA, Castro Candaz, Dominio do Bibei, Guímaro, Rectoral de Amandi.

Ribeiro Gal ★·★★★ Historic region, famed in Middle Ages for Tostado (sw). Promising textured whites made from GODELLO, LOUREIRO, Treixadura. Some reds, fresh, crunchy. Top: Casal de Armán, Coto de Gomariz, Finca Viñoa, VIÑA MEÍN - EMILIO ROJO.

Ribera del Duero Gal ★·★★★★ Ambitious DOP with great appeal in Spain, created 1982. Anything that incl AALTO, HACIENDA MONASTERIO, PINGUS, VEGA SICILIA has to be serious. Domestic demand for oaky concentration. At last, elegance breaking through. Wineries in Soria (to e) provide most delicate wines (DOMINIO DE ATAUTA, Dominio de Es, DOMINIO DEL AGUILA). Try ALONSO DEL YERRO, PAGO DE CARRAOVEJAS. Also: Arzuaga, Bohórquez, Cillar de Silos, Garmón, Hacienda Solano, Tomás Postigo, Valduero. *See* C Y L neighbours ABADÍA RETUERTA, Mauro.

Rioja ★·★★★★ Spain's most famous wine region. Three subregions: R Ala, R Alt and R OR. Two key provinces: La Rioja and ÁLAVA, with NAV to e. Growing political differences between provinces and between producers and the CONSEJO

REGULADOR reflected in proposal for some Ala producers to separate from DOP. Introduction of Viñedo Singular category was criticized, but gradually est itself; trad-method sparkling permitted since 2017, v. promising, esp Bilbaínas, Conde Valdemar, URBINA, VIVANCO. New generation of producers also taking different approaches, diversifying trad image of Rio.

Rioja Alta, La R Ala, R Alt, R Bai ★★ →★★★★ For lovers of classic RIO, a favourite choice. Standard keeps going up. *Gran Res 904* and GRAN RES 890 are stars. But rest of range from *Ardanza* down to Arana, Alberdi each carry classic house style; all qualify as Gran Res. Also owns R ALA modern-style Torre de Oña, R BAI Lagar de Cervera, RIB DEL D Áster. Hard to fault.

Rioja Oriental Rio Name of what was Rioja Baja. Renamed to remove pejorative sense of "baja" as "low", and to identify fact it is most e or oriental (and largest) subregion of RIO. Was poor relation, rapidly gaining attention for its GARNACHA, led by PALACIOS REMONDO. Also RAMÓN BILBAO's Lalomba; ARIZCUREN in town of Quel (worth a visit).

Riva, De La Sherry ★★ →★★★ Project from WILLY PÉREZ and RAMIRO IBÁÑEZ based on abandoned De La Riva BODEGA. Exceptionally fine.

Roda R Alt, Rib Del D ★★→★★★ At far tip of BARRIO DE LA ESTACIÓN. TEMPRANILLO specialist: polished Roda, Roda I, Cirsion, approachable Sela, recent release of first white. Also RIB DEL D BODEGAS La Horra, Corimbo (w), Corimbo I.

Rosado Rosé. The trad dark rosados of NAV were defeated by Provence pinks. Spain has fought back with pale hues, esp SCALA DEI's Pla dels Àngels (PRI), MARQUÉS DE MURRIETA's Primer Rosé (RIO), DOMINIO DEL ÁGUILA Pícaro Clarete (RIB DEL D).

Rueda C y L ★→★★★ Spain's response to SAUV BL: zesty VERDEJO. Mostly DYA. Too much poor quality. Exceptional SOLERA-aged BODEGAS DE ALBERTO. New Gran Vino quality category for older vines, lower yields. Chapirete Prefiloxérico v.gd.

Saca Sherry A withdrawal of Sherry from the SOLERA (oldest stage of ageing) for bottling. For EN RAMA wines, most common *sacas* are in *primavera* (spring) and *otoño* (autumn), when FLOR is richest, most protective.

Sánchez Romate Sherry ★★ →★★★ Historic (1781) BODEGA with wide range, also sourcing and bottling rare BUTTS for négociants and retailers; 8-yr-old *Fino Perdido*, nutty AMONTILLADO NPU, PALO CORTADO Regente, excellent VORS Amontillado and OLOROSO La Sacristía de Romate, unctuous Sacristía PX.

Sanlúcar de Barrameda Man, Sherry Sherry on River Guadalquivir. Port where Magellan, Columbus, admiral of Armada set sail. Humidity in low-lying cellars encourages FLOR. Sea air said to encourage "saltiness". Wines aged here qualify for DOP MANZANILLA-Sanlúcar de Barrameda.

Scala Dei Pri ★★→★★★ Tiny vyds of "stairway to heaven" cling to craggy slopes. Part-owner CODORNÍU. Winemaker Ricard Rofes, leader in GARNACHA revival, expresses exceptional terroir, esp in single-vyd *Mas Deu*, Sant'Antoni. Also unusual GARNACHA BLANCA/CHENIN BL blend.

Spain makes its mark on La Place de Bordeaux with eight fine wines.

Sierra Cantabria R Ala, Toro ★★★ Exceptional family business run by brothers Marcos (winemaker) and Miguel Ángel Eguren. Elegant, single-vyd, low-intervention. Reds, all TEMPRANILLO. Also Viñedos de Paganos, Señorío de San Vicente, both RIO, Teso la Monja in TORO. Next-generation cousins have own R ALA wineries: Eduardo at CUENTAVIÑAS, Koldo at Ukan.

Sierra de Toloño R Ala ★★ Sandra Bravo's wines are all about elevation, cool climate, purity; assisted by old vines, field blends, neutral oak and time in amphora. Bravo indeed!

Sisseck, Peter Rib del D, Sherry Dane who attracted world interest to RIB DEL D with DOMINIO DE PINGUS starting to work magic on JEREZ. His purchase with a partner of FINO VIÑA CORRALES plus vyd in PAGO Balbaína, has re-energized sector. His statement "Sherry is the best white wine in Spain" has worked wonders. Also at Ch Rocheyron (in Bx).

Solera Sherry System for blending Sherry, less commonly Madeira (*see* Portugal), plus specialities such as DE ALBERTO Dorado and res wine of GRAMONA. Consists of topping up progressively more mature BUTTS with younger wines of same sort from previous stage, or *criadera*. With FINOS, MANZANILLAS it maintains vigour of FLOR. For all wines gives consistency; refreshes mature wines.

Suertes del Marqués Can ★★ Start here in discovering new-wave wineries in Tenerife. Unique local *trenzado* (plaited) vines. Edición 1 (r/w) v.gd. Worth a visit. Owner Jonatán García advises at TAMERÁN.

Tamerán Can ★★ Impressive Gran Canaria project from local boy and former UK (Man City) football star David Silva, working with Jonatán García of SUERTES DEL MARQUÉS (Tenerife). Subtle, delicate wines.

On Place de Bordeaux: Adega Algueira, CVNE, De la Riva, Marqués de Riscal, Telmo Rodriguez.

Telmo Rodríguez, Compañía de Vinos Mál, Rib del D, Rio, Toro ★★→★★★★ Groundbreaking winemaker Rodríguez returned to family base REMELLURI in RIO but continues with Pablo Eguzkiza: in ALIC (Al-Murvedre), Cigales (Pegaso), MÁL (*Molino Real* MOSCATEL), RIB DEL D (Matallana), RUE (Basa), TORO (Dehesa Gago), Valdeorras (DYA Gaba do Xil GODELLO, plus three exceptional r single vyds). Return to Rio and BODEGA Lanzaga has led to work on recuperating old vyds, esp exceptionally pure La Estrada, Las Beatas, Tabuérniga. Latest release Yjar, from Rio's SIERRA DE TOLOÑO, sell-out on Place de Bordeaux.

Terra Alta Cat Top GARNACHA country, with 90% of CAT'S GARNACHA BLANCA vyds, and 75% of Spain's. Deliciously complex, textured wines. Producers: Bárbara Forés, Celler Piñol, Edetària, Herencia Altés, Lafou.

Territorio Albariza Sherry Network of new-wave producers in JEREZ dedicated to *albariza* soils, and leading producers of VINO DE PASTO. Members incl Alejandro Muchada (Muchada-Leclapart), Joaquín Gómez (Meridiano Perdido), PETER SISSECK, Primitivo Collantes (Chiclana), RAMIRO IBÁÑEZ (COTA 45), WILLY PÉREZ (Luis Pérez), the brothers Blanco (CALLEJUELA). Not part of Sherry DOP, may form their own.

Tinaja Aka amphora. *See* A Little Learning. In Spain, widely used, and also eg. by ALVEAR, CELLER DEL ROURE, MAS MARTINET, SIERRA DE TOLOÑO. Prestige wineries such as NUMANTHIA also investing.

Toro ★→★★★★ Small DOP on the Duero. Famed for bold reds from Tinta del Toro (phenotype of TEMPRANILLO, similar but not identical). Today best more restrained, but still firm tannic grip. Glamour from VEGA SICILIA-owned Pintia, LVMH-owned NUMANTHIA, and early investor the Egurens of SIERRA CANTABRIA, now owners of Teso la Monja. San Román, owned by MARIANO GARCÍA and family, also working with GARNACHA and v.gd zesty MALVASÍA Castellana (w). Growing trend for Garnacha, a lighter alternative to trad reds. Also: Dominio del Bendito, Fariña, Las Tierras de Javier Rodríguez, Matsu.

Toro Albalá Mont-M ★★→★★★★ Why is MONT-M not better known? Toro Albalá has a historic treasure trove of wines from PX, incl AMONTILLADO Viejísimo, sumptuous Don PX Convento Selección 31, v.gd Gran Res 90.

Torres Cat, Pri, Rib del D, Rio, R Bai ★★→★★★★ Torres family never stops. After 150 yrs they might ease off, but Miguel Jnr runs business, sister Mireia is technical director and runs Jean León, Miguel Snr busy on many eco fronts. Clear pyramid of quality. Top is Torres Antología, outstanding Catalan terroir collection: Bx blend *Res Real*, top PEN CAB *Mas la Plana*; C DE BAR duo (burgundy-like *Milmanda*, one of Spain's finest CHARDS, tiptop *Grans Muralles* blend of local varieties); single-vyd *Mas de la Rosa* will become a Gran Vi de Vinya (top category of PRI) in due course. Also Camino de Magarín (RUE), La Carbonera (RIO), PAGO del Cielo (RIB DEL D), Pazo Torre Pezelas (R BAI). Also famous, consistent, gd-value portfolio, eg. Viña Sol. Pioneer in Chile. Marimar T est in Sonoma (US).

Tradición Sherry ★★→★★★★ Fabulous collection of VOS/VORS Sherries. Must-visit for its outstanding collection of Spanish art. Based on oldest-known Sherry house (1650), fascinating archives.

Txakoli P Vas ★→★★ Wines from the Basque Country DOPS: ÁLAVA, Bizkaya, Getaria. Once were DYA acidic wines poured into tumblers from a height to add to spritz. Bizkaya wines, with less exposed vyds, have depth, ageability. Top: Ameztoi, ASTOBIZA, Doniene Gorrondona, Izar-Leku (from ARTADI), Txomín Etxaníz. Also Gorka Izagirre, with Michelin three-star restaurant Azurmendi.

Urbina Rio ★★→★★★ For lovers of gloriously mature RIO. Seemingly bottomless store of fine aged wines.

Valdeorras Gal ★→★★★★ Warmest, most inland of GAL's DOPS, named after the gold (*oro*) the Romans mined. GODELLOS more interesting than many ALBARIÑOS. RAFAEL PALACIOS's Godello miraculously gd. TELMO RODRÍGUEZ's MENCÍA v. fine. Also Godeval, Valdesil.

Valdepeñas C-La M ★→★★ Big DOP s of LA MANCHA, and historic favourite for cheap reds.

Valdespino Sherry ★★→★★★★ Winemaker Eduardo Ojeda oversees Inocente FINO from top Macharnudo single vyd, rare oak-fermented Sherry (EN RAMA bottled by EQUIPO NAVAZOS). Plus terrific dry AMONTILLADO Tío Diego; outstanding 80-yr-old *Toneles* MOSCATEL, JEREZ's v. best. Owned by Grupo Estévez (OWNS LA GUITA).

Valencia ★→★★ Was known for bulk wine, and still supplies supermarket sweet, fortified MOSCATEL. News is it's on the move, with higher-altitude old vines and min-intervention winemaking: eg. Aranleon, Baldovar 923, CELLER DEL ROURE, El Angosto, JAVIER REVERT, Los Frailes, Rafael Cambra.

VDT (Vino de la Tierra) Table wine usually of superior quality made in a demarcated region without DOP. Covers immense geographical possibilities; category incl many prestigious producers, non-DOP by choice to be freer of inflexible regulation and use varieties they want. (*See* Super Tuscan, Italy.)

Vega Sicilia Rib del D, Rio, Toro ★★★★ Carries a heavy burden of history, its reputation placing it above fashion. In Alvarez family ownership for four decades. Wines built to last. Valbuena has 5 yrs in oak and bottle, Único has almost 10 yrs in oak of different sizes and in bottle. Res Especial, NV blend of three vintages. Neighbouring Alión (modern take on RIB DEL D). Pintia (TORO) now much fresher. Macán (RIO), joint venture with Benjamin de Rothschild, going in right direction. Oremus in Tokaj (*see* Hungary), in addition to sweet wine, has electrically fresh dry FURMINT Petracs. Latest project: R BAI.

Verum C-La M ★ Elias López in Tomelloso, heart of Spain's AIRÉN-growing, brandy-distilling industry. Yet his wines from old vines, TINAJAS make him one to watch.

Viña Literally, a vyd.

Viña Meín - Emilio Rojo Gal ★★★ Rojo's eponymous wine is Treixadura blend with thrilling freshness. Star of RIBEIRO, v. fine (r/w). Now owned by RIB DEL D PAGO DE CARROVEJAS group. Rojo remains to advise, with winemaker Laura Montero.

Vinegar Mont-M, Sherry ★→★★★ A trad unwanted by-product of winemaking that Sherry producers did not wish to publicize. All change now with a controlled process. Favourites incl FERNANDO DE CASTILLA, TORO ALBALÁ GRAN RES.

Williams & Humbert Sherry ★→★★★★ Historic BODEGA famed for classic brands: Dry Sack, Winter's Tale AMONTILLADO, As You Like It OLOROSO (sw). Winemaker Paola Medina pioneering specialities: organic Sherry, Vintage Sherries.

Ysios Rio ★→★★ Winery in every picture book for its undulating roof by Calatrava. Pernod Ricard-owned.

Zárate Gal ★★→★★★ El Palomar is from centenarian vyd, one of DOP's oldest, on own rootstock, aged in *foudre*. Fontecon is unusual rosé. Fascinating set of local single-variety reds.

Zorzal, Viña Nav ★→★★★ Family business transformed by entrepreneurial new generation. Young, gd-value wines (GRACIANO). Old-vine GARNACHA (Malayeto); works with MATIAS MICHELINI; Jorge NAVASCUÉS consults.

Sherry styles

Palomino Fino Dominant grape of Sherry zone. Strong trend to unfortified PALOMINO aka VINO DE PASTO, eg. COTA 45, Muchada-Leclapart, Primitivo Collantes.

Manzanilla From SANLÚCAR, v. dry, biologically aged. Serve cool with seafood, eg. I Think (EQUIPO NAVAZOS), LA GUITA.

Manzanilla Pasada With 7 yrs+, where flor is dying, starting to turn into AMONTILLADO; v. dry, complex, eg. LUSTAU'S ALMACENISTA Cuevas Jurado.

Fino Dry, biologically aged in any of the 8 Sherry towns (except Sanlúcar); weightier than MANZANILLA; min age 2 yrs (as Manzanilla) but don't drink so young. Trend for mature FINOS aged 7 yrs+, eg. EMILIO HIDALGO. Trend to cellar and age Finos and Manzanillas in bottle.

Fino Viejo New category for DOP JEREZ, parallel to Manzanilla Pasada. Min 7 yrs+.

En Rama Sherry as if bottled directly from BUTT; not clarified or cold stabilized, low filtration = max flavour. Understood to refer to Manzanilla and Fino, but any Sherry bottled this way is En Rama. SACA typically when flor is most abundant, in spring.

Amontillado Started as Fino, then protective FLOR died. Oxidative ageing gives complexity. Naturally dry, eg. Lustau Amontillado del Castillo. If sweetened, indicated by "medium" label.

Palo Cortado Between Amontillado and v. delicate OLOROSO. Difficult to identify with certainty, eg. BARBADILLO Reliquía, Fernando de Castilla Antique.

Oloroso Typically not originally aged under flor. Naturally ultra-dry, superbly savoury, even fierce. May be sweetened and sold as CREAM, eg. Emilio Hidalgo Gobernador (dr), Old East India (sw).

Cream Blend sweetened with grape must, PX and/or MOSCATEL for a commercial medium-sweet style.

Pedro Ximénez (PX) Raisined sweet, from partly sun-dried PX grapes. Unctuous, decadent, bargain. Sip with ice cream, eg. Emilio Hidalgo Santa Ana 1861, Lustau VORS.

Moscatel Aromatic appeal, around half sugar of PX, eg. Lustau Emilín, VALDESPINO Toneles.

VOS / VORS Age-dated Sherries, some of treasures of Jerez BODEGAS. Wines assessed by carbon dating to be 20 yrs old+ are VOS (Very Old Sherry/Vinum Optimum Signatum); 30 yrs old+ are VORS (Very Old Rare Sherry/Vinum Optimum Rare Signatum). Also 12-yr-old, 15-yr-old examples. Applies only to Amontillado, Oloroso, PALO CORTADO, PX, eg. VOS Hidalgo Jerez Cortado Wellington. Some VORS wines softened with PX; sadly producers may overdo the PX.

Vintage / Añada Sherry with declared vintage. Runs counter to trad of SOLERA. Formerly private bottlings now winning public accolades, eg. WILLIAMS & HUMBERT series, Lustau Sweet Oloroso Añada 1997.

Portugal

The best defence against climate change seems to be native grape varieties: they often have the inate ability to deal with extremes. Portugal has hundreds of native varieties, and they – plus field blends, amphorae in the cellar and high-altitude vines – are all contributing to better, fresher, unique wines, Port and Madeira included. The natural and low-intervention movement is finally taking off, with many new projects now widely available in Lisbon and Porto restaurants.

Recent Port vintages

Vintage, the king of Port, is silently changing. Robotic-foot treading, improvement of spirits quality and precision viticulture are making VPs more approachable than ever. Everyone wins: more value-for-money LBVs and single-quinta Ports, but also more high-end, limited-edition, single-vyd special cuvées (eg. Stone Terraces, Vinha da Pisca, Vargellas Vinhas Velhas). Previously, a Vintage was "declared" only when a wine is outstanding by shippers' own standards. Now, some producers "declare" a Vintage every yr, while also making single-quinta wines, arguably with less structure and longevity. To taste heaven: 63 66 70 77 94 00 07 09 11 17 18 (yes, v. young VP is a treat).

2023 Increased production, gd quality if harvested before rain.
2022 Smaller quantities but overall gd quality, some excellent.
2021 Gd quality; gd weather conditions: mild July after fairly wet winter. Best: Graham's Stone Terraces, Noval, Nacional, Ramos Pinto.
2020 Challenging yr; tiny vols of v. concentrated Graham's, Warre's Vinhas Velhas, Vargellas, Noval, Nacional, Ventozelo, Gaivosa Amphitheatrum.
2019 Balance, freshness but less structure. Best: Niepoort, Noval (incl Nacional), Pintas, Vesúvio.
2018 Gd quality, declaration for some, esp Dou Superior. Best: Ferreira, Noval, Sandeman, Taylor's, Vesúvio.
2017 Superlative yr, widely declared; v. hot, dry, compared to historic 1945.
2016 Classic yr, widely declared. Great structure, finesse.
2015 Controversial yr; v. dry, hot. Declared by many (drink: Niepoort, Noval) but not Fladgate, Sogrape or Symington.
2014 Excellent from vyds that ducked September's rain; production low.
2013 Single-quinta yr; mid-harvest rain. Stars: Fonseca Guimaraens, Vesuvio.
2012 Single-quinta yr. Stars: Malvedos, Noval. Elegant, drink now.
Earlier fine vintages: 09 07 03 00 97 94 92 91 87 83 80 77 70 66 63 45 35 31 27.

Recent table-wine vintages

2023 Portugal avoided weather crisis; v.gd whites; elegant reds.
2022 V. v. dry; light, fruity whites; elegant low-alc reds.
2021 Quality, quantity; v.gd whites and fresh, elegant reds.
2020 Gd quantity overall; v.gd whites; pick your red producer.
2019 No rain, cool summer; v.gd quality all around. Keep.
2018 Heavy rains; v. low yields. Aromatic whites, concentrated reds.
2017 3rd consecutive fine vintage; v.gd quality all around. Keep for yrs.
2016 Quality v.gd for those who had patience. Keep for yrs.

See Portugal map p.174

Açor, Domínio do Dão ★★★ Ambitious boutique project making stunning old-vine, single-variety range from ENCRUZADO, Bical, Jaen, Tinta Pinheira.

Açores / Azores ★→★★★★ Portugal's volcanic-wine darling. Unique mid-Atlantic archipelago with three DOCs: Pico, Biscoitos, Graciosa. Dominated by sea-threatened vines often protected by difficult-to-cultivate *currais* (pebble walls). Successful and up-and-coming winemakers make stony, saline whites from indigenous varieties Arinto dos Açores, *Terrantez do Pico*, VERDELHO. Try ★★ Adega do Vulcão, ★★★ Azores Wine Company, ★★★ Cerca dos Frades, ★★ Magma, ★★★ Pico Wines. Late-harvest/fortified *licoroso* is sweet treat.

AdegaMãe Lis ★→★★★ Ambitious estate just n of Lisbon owned by codfish group Riberalves. Fresh, bright, age-worthy Atlantic-influenced whites v.gd. Dory range (esp ARINTO, *Viosinho*) gd value. Top-notch Terroir range is mineral, saline, oak-aged white blend. *Estate restaurant* serves great bacalau/wine pairings.

Aldeia de Cima Alen ★★★★ Luisa Amorim's (QUINTA NOVA) personal project blends heritage and modernity. Fresher terroir, old vines, alternative ageing (amphora, concrete, oak vats) makes superb, age-worthy range, esp top GARRAFEIRA (r/w) trad aged in 3000-litre oak vats.

Alentejo ★→★★★ Large, popular, reliable, hot, dry region known for fruit-forward reds. Pioneer in hot-climate sustainability leading to fresher wines. Subregional diversity allows for other styles: mineral, seaside Costa Vicentina (VICENTINO); fresh, high-altitude PORTALEGRE (CABEÇAS DO REGUENGO, RUI REGUINGA, Teixinha's ★★ Fonte de Souto); fresh Vidigueira (Cortes de Cima, ROCIM); earthy, ancient clay amphora VINHO DE TALHA DOC (★★ XXVI Talhas, Rocim). Classics often made with ALICANTE BOUSCHET, TOURIGA N, TRINCADEIRA, SYRAH: CARTUXA, ESPORÃO, Herdade dos Grous, JOÃO PORTUGAL RAMOS, JOSÉ DE SOUSA, MALHADINHA NOVA, MOUCHÃO. Watch: ALDEIA DE CIMA, ★★ Fita Preta.

Ameal, Quinta do Vin ★★★ Benchmark boutique estate run by ESPORÃO. Organic, age-worthy LOUREIRO pioneer. Varietal gd value; racy single-vyd Solo Único, v.gd oaked *Res*. Bico Amarelo gd value.

Andresen Port ★★→★★★★ Historic, Portuguese-owned house with superb TAWNIES: v.gd 20-yr-old; ethereal *Colheitas* 1900' 1910' (bottled on demand) 68' 80' 91' 92' 97' 00' 03' 05'. Pioneered age-dated WHITE PORTS: 10-, 20-, v.gd 40-yr-old.

Aveleda Vin ★→★★ Most popular, largest VIN available worldwide. Makes gd-value, reliable white range, esp ALVARINHO, LOUREIRO, Parcela, Solos. Expanding: now owns top estate VALE D. MARIA (DOU), ★★ D'Aguieira (BAI), ★ Villa Alvor (Alg). Also gd visitor centre close to Porto.

Bacalhôa Vinhos Alen, Lis, Set ★★→★★★★ Group with eponymous brand. Top: age-worthy, v.gd QUINTA da Bacalhôa Bx blend incl CAB SAUV 1st planted 1974, also used in iconic red *Palácio da Bacalhôa*. MOSCATEL DE SETÚBAL barrels, incl rare

---

Keep it light

Thirsty for light, aromatic, juicy red fruit (strawberry, cherries)? Most often found in: BASTARDO, CASTELÃO, PINOT N, Rufete grapes and palhete or clarete styles. Favourites have a ★. **Alg** Casteleja. **Alen** ★ Cabeças do Reguengo, XXVI Talhas. **Azores** Wine Company Rosé Vulcânico. **Bair** ★ Gilda. **Bei Int** Rui Roboredo MADEIRA Natural, QUINTA da Biaia 750. **Dão** ★ Casa de Mouraz (Nina, Palhete), Saes Altitude. **Dou** ★ Conceito BASTARDO, Frey Palhete, ★ NIEPOORT (Bastardo, Nat'Cool, Voyeur), ★ MUXAGAT Tinta Franscica, Proibido à Capela, ★ Quinta Maria Izabel Bastardo, Uivo Semi. **Lis** COZs, Espera Nat'Cool, Marinho, ★ MONTE BLUNA Tinta Miúda, Viúva Gomes. **Mad** Atlantis. **Sét** Primeur de Trois. **Tej** Casal das Freiras, Menina d'Uva. **Trás-os-Montes** ★ Arribas, Menina d'Uva. **Vin** Soalheiro Oppaco.

Roxo; gd fruit-forward ALEN Quinta do Carmo reds. Popular: Catarina, Serras de Azeitão (SET). Owns several art museums.

Bairrada ★★→★★★★ Atlantic-influenced DOC famous for world-class, age-worthy, structured BAGA (often v. old vines), citrus whites Bical, Cercial. Try ★★★ BÁGEIRAS, ★★ Casa de Saima, CAVES SÃO JOÃO, *Filipa Pato*, *Foz de Arouce*, *Giz by Luis Gomes*, *Kompassus*, LUÍS PATO, ★★ São Domingos, ★★★ *Sidónio de Sousa*, *Vadio*. Watch: ★★★ *Mira do Ó*, ★★ NIEPOORT. Look for Baga Bair for v.gd sparkling to pair with local *roast suckling pig*.

Sparkling Baga Bairrada: all white and pink. No red; red fizz is so often a bad idea.

Barbeito Mad ★★→★★★★ Highly regarded boutique producer. Elegance: unique, single-vyd, single-cask FRASQUEIRAS; outstanding 20-, 30-, 40-yr-old MALVASIAS, 50-yr-old BASTARDO; historic series honours Mad's US popularity in C18, C19. Growing range of v.gd, mineral, salty white *table wines*.

Barca Velha Dou ★★★★ Portugal's most expensive, sought-after red; 1st made in 1952. Cellar-release only in exceptional yrs: 91' 95' 99 00 **04** 08' 11'. Can't afford it? Try v.gd *Res Especial*, released in non-BV yrs, from CASA FERREIRINHA's best barrels: 89' 94' 97' 01' **07** 09 14. Both last decades. Tip: luckily (and arguably) 89' 94' 97' 01' 09 14 could have been BV.

Blandy's Mad ★★→★★★★ Reputed family-run firm. Top-notch, unique, library of old stocks: FRASQUEIRA (BUAL 1920' 57' 66' 72' 76', MALMSEY 88' 77' 81' 91', SERCIAL 68' 75' 80' 88' 90', Terrantez 75' 77' 80', VERDELHO 76 79' 82'); v.gd 20-yr-old Malmsey, *Terrantez* and COLHEITAS (Bual **96 08 09 10**, Malmsey **99 04 07 10**, Sercial **02 08 09 10**, Verdelho **00 08 09 10**). Superb *50-yr-old Malmsey*. Expensive, rare MCDXIX blends 11 yrs between 1863 and 2004. Unique 77 Listrão from Porto Santo Island. Affordable RAINWATER, and Atlantis table-wine range. Unmissable, historic *Funchal lodges*.

Boavista, Quinta da Dou ★★★★ Fine, Cima-Corgo estate, run by SOGEVINUS. Superb, age-worthy old field blends: 80-yr-old vines, single-vyd spicy Oratório and piney Ujo; seductive *Res* blends old and new vines; new-oak-aged Vinha do Levante.

Bual (or Boal) Mad Classic grape for medium-sweet MAD: tangy, smoky; balances acidity/sweetness. Perfect match for hard cheeses or alone. Look for thrilling old vintages.

Cabeças do Reguengo Alen ★★→★★★ Boutique estate, trad winemaking. Fresh, low-intervention range from high-altitude, v. old field blends in PORTALEGRE. Try cement-fermented Vira Cabeças (incl r/w grapes). Cosy wine tourism.

Canteiro Mad Natural, slow-warming ageing in humid lodges (now also TINTA NEGRA). Used for more expensive MAD. Superior to ESTUFAGEM.

Carcavelos Lis ★★★ Tiny production, hidden gem. Unique, mouthwatering, gripping, off-dry fortified from seaside DOC. Try Villa Oeiras.

Cardo, Quinta do Bei Int ★★ Historic 90-yr-old estate, revamped by new owners. Star winemakers (also LÉS-A-LÉS) make elegant, fresh, high-altitude (750m/2461ft), bio range: top-notch Grande Res (w), single-vyd **Lomedo** (w), Pombal (r); gd-value Cardo, Res (r/w) labels.

Cartuxa, Adega da Alen ★★→★★★★ Historic ALEN firm. Flagship, full-bodied Pêra Manca (r) draws connoisseurs; v.gd, age-worthy, best-buy *Cartuxa Res*; v.gd single-variety Scala Coeli changes every yr. Popular EA range.

Carvalhais, Quinta dos Dão ★→★★ SOGRAPE-owned classic DÃO estate. Consistent, age-worthy: gd oak-aged, flinty ENCRUZADO; sumptuous RES (*esp w*); earthy *Alfrocheiro*; floral TOURIGA N; dense, top red Único; unusual, rich Branco Especial. Popular: Duque de Viseu, Grão Vasco.

Cazas Novas Vin ★★→★★★ Young firm, owns largest Avesso vyd, benchmark VIN: crisp COLHEITA, lees-aged Pure and v.gd Origens.

Chocapalha, Quinta de Lis ★★★ Coastal family-run estate. Age-worthy. Winemaker Sandra Tavares da Silva (WINE & SOUL) makes vibrant, *mineral, saline whites* (v.gd CHARD, RES, old-vine ARINTO CH, new Arinto Antigo from old vyds); v.gd Vinha Mãe; gd-value red, esp CASTELÃO.

Chryseia Dou ★★★★ Prestigious, consistent, fine, progressively more elegant TOURIGA-driven red. Born from SYMINGTON FAMILY ESTATES, Bruno Prats (Bx) partnership. *Post Scriptum* v.gd value.

Don't mention screwcaps in Portugal. Not popular – yet.

Churchill Dou, Port ★★★ Family-run Port house, v.gd reds: gd-value Churchill's Estates Grafite range, esp Grande RES. Top Port: Dry WHITE PORT, 20-, 30-yr-old, unfiltered LBV, VINTAGE PORT. Charming C19 guesthouse.

Cockburn's Port ★★→★★★ Refreshed, younger image, SYMINGTON-owned house, consistently gd: Special RES aged longer in wood than others; vibrant LBV aged 1 yr less; v.gd single-QUINTA dos Canais; drier, fresher style of VINTAGE PORT. Cocktail-ready Tails of the Unexpected.

Colares Lis ★★★ Historic treasure-trove DOC with windswept, ungrafted vines on sand. Europe's w-most vyds. Age-worthy: tannic Ramisco reds and crisp, saline MALVASIA whites. Best: ★★★ Adega Regional de Colares, ★★★ Viúva Gomes, ★★ Casal Santa Maria.

Colheita Mad, Port Single-yr TAWNY Port. Drink on release; nutty, oxidative, delicious. Cask-aged: min 7 yrs, often 50 yrs+, rare superb 100 yrs+ bottled on demand. Bottling date printed on label (look for recent dates). Best (serve chilled): ANDRESEN, DALVA, GRAHAM'S, KOPKE, NIEPOORT, NOVAL, POÇAS, TAYLOR'S. Also MAD, cask-aged min 5 yrs.

Cossart Gordon Mad ★★★ Oldest MAD shipper (1745) known for fine, drier style; v.gd single-yr bottlings. New releases: Colheitas (VERDELHO 09', Bual 06', Malmsey 08' 95'), FRASQUEIRA (Verdelho 75'). MADEIRA WINE COMPANY-owned.

Crasto, Quinta do Dou, Port ★★★ →★★★★ Prestigious family-run estate with striking hilltop pool/lodge. Top field-blend, single-vyd, lush, complex, expensive reds Vinha da Ponte and Vinha Maria Teresa. Popular, seductive old-vyd *Res* gd value. Superb varietals, esp age-worthy TINTA RORIZ. Dou Superior range gd value.

Croft Port ★★→★★★ Historic house; sweet, fleshy VINTAGE PORT; v.gd-value, single-quinta *Quinta da Roêda*. Superlative old-vine *Sērikos 17'*. Popular: Indulgence, Pink Rosé Port, Triple Crown. FLADGATE-owned. Visitor centre in Pinhão.

Crusted (Port) Port's wallet-friendly secret. Seductive, luscious, rare, age-worthy NV style. Blend of two or more vintage-quality yrs, aged up to 4 yrs in casks, 3 yrs in bottle. Forms deposit ("crust"), so decant. CHURCHILL, DOW'S, FONSECA, *Niepoort*.

Dalva Port ★★★ →★★★★ Quality-focused house, 1st-class TAWNY stocks: superb COLHEITAS, 10-, 20-, 30-, 40-, 50-yr-old dry white range, stunning *golden white* 52' 63' 71' 89'. Excellent new 50-yr-old. Organic Port range Pure v.gd. Table wines gd-value. Owned by GRANVINHOS.

Dão ★★ →★★★★ Historic DOC undergoing silent quality revolution. Elegant, food-friendly, age-worthy reds and flinty ENCRUZADO-based whites. Often called Portugal's Burgundy but not v. similar. Modern projects CASA DA PASSARELLA, TABOADELLA add prestige. Classics incl ★★ Boas Quintas, ★ Cabriz, ★★ CARVALHAIS, ★★ Casa de Santar, ★ Lusovini, ★★ Ribeiro Santo. Try low-intervention ★★ António Madeira, organic CASA DE MOURAZ, 1st-class ★★★★ Druida, characterful João Tavares de Pina. Top designation: Dão Nobre ("noble"): ★★★ Vinha do Contador. Best buy: rare, age-worthy, GARRAFEIRAS. Watch: ★★ DOMÍNIO DO AÇOR, ★★ Terra Chama, ★★★ Textura.

DOC (denominação de origem controlada) Quality wine designation. Increasingly ignored by wine-lovers. Newer denomination DOP rarely used.

Dona Maria Alen ★★★★ Once a cheeky gift by the king to his mistress, now a reputed estate. Charismatic owner Júlio Bastos and winemaker Sandra Gonçalves make superb, classic, age-worthy range with native and French varieties: foot-trodden, old-vine ALICANTE BOUSCHET reds esp Grande RES, Júlio B. Bastos; v.gd single-variety (esp PETIT VERDOT), elegant Amantis; v.gd-value *estate label*.

Douro ★→★★★★ Historic, dreamy UNESCO World Heritage Site made of hard-to-work steep hills. Famous for Port, increasingly for quality table wine (Dou DOC) and tourism. Powerful, structured reds; fine, high-altitude whites. Three subregions (cooler Baixo Corgo, milder Cima Corgo and warmer, fast-expanding Dou Superior). Vinhas Velhas (old vines) now regulated: min 40 yrs+ old, low yields, min four varieties. Some are 100 yrs+ field blends (30+ varieties) planted in terraces of unforgiving schist. Best: ALVES DE SOUSA, *Boavista*, *Casa Ferreirinha* incl top *Barca Velha*, *Chryseia*, CHURCHILL, CRASTO, *Maria Izabel*, *Niepoort*, NOVAL, QUINTA NOVA, Quanta Terra, RAMOS PINTO, *Vale D. Maria*, ★★★ Vale Meão, *Vesuvio*, *Wine & Soul*. Watch ★★ Carolina, ★★ Costa do Pinhão, KRANEMANN, *Luis Seabra*, ★★ Manoella, ★★ MENIN.

Dow's Port ★★★★ Historic, reputed SYMINGTON-owned house making age-defying, drier-style VINTAGE PORT. Legendary yrs: 27 45 55 63 66 70 80 94; recent: 07' 11' 16' 17'. In non-declared yrs, v.gd single-QUINTAS do Bomfim (19 20 21), *Senhora da Ribeira* (15 18). Pinhão highlight: *Bomfim visitor centre*, v.gd restaurant.

Duorum Dou, Port ★★→★★★ DOU Superior venture between iconic winemakers: JOÃO PORTUGAL RAMOS (ALEN) and José Maria Soares Franco (ex-CASA FERRERINHA/BARCA VELHA). Top, aged several yrs pre-release O. Leucura; v.gd-value range with fine RES, new fruity Altitude (r/w). Popular: Tons, COLHEITA. Dense VINTAGE PORT from 100-yr-old vines v.gd; LBV gd value.

Esporão Alen ★★→★★★ Dynamic, leading 50-yr-old ALEN wine and olive-oil pioneer, now eco-focused: top-notch rare Torre do Esporão; fine GARRAFEIRA-like wood-aged Private Selection (creamy SÉM w and rich, dense r). High-quality, fruit-focused, modern RES. Popular: Monte Velho, new Res. Interests in DOU (Murças), VIN (AMEAL).

Espumante Sparkling. Wallet-friendly gem, best are age-worthy, made in BAIR since 1890 (try Abibes, Aliança, Marquês de Marialva, Poço do Lobo, São Domingos, São João). BAGA Bair is quality designation. Távora-Varosa gd value. Undisputed best: DOU's ★★★ VÉRTICE.

Estufagem Mad State-of-the-art MAD heating process (up to 50°C/122°F) for faster ageing, characteristic scorched-earth tang in entry-level wines.

Falua Tej ★→★★ French-owned estate undergoing multi-region expansion led by Antonina Barbosa: Barão do Hospital auspicious VIN project (esp LOUREIRO); QUINTA de São José (v.gd DOU range); Quinta do Mourão (v.gd PORT stocks). Falua range incl gd-value Conde de Vimioso (RES a step up), gd Res (r/w, esp Sommelier Edition). Best: stony-soil Vinha do Convento (r/w).

Ferreira Port ★★★→★★★★ Historic, prestigious SOGRAPE-owned house. Stand-out 11' 16' 18', top Vinhas Velhas 16', v.gd-value single-QUINTA do Porto 17' 19' 20'. Elegant TAWNY v.gd value: Dona Antonia RES, 10/20/30-yr-old. GAIA visitor centre.

Plan your weekend: Port cellars in Gaia, but Dou wineries 1-hour drive from Porto.

Ferreirinha, Casa Dou ★★→★★★★ Large, highly reputed SOGRAPE-owned brand. Home to iconic Barca Velha, rare Res Especial, age-worthy, 1st-class *Quinta da Leda*, v.gd-value Vinha Grande. Consistent fine-wine range, esp elegant *Castas Escondidas*, single-variety Tinta Francisca. Popular: Esteva, Papa Figos.

Fladgate Port Large, independent family-owned firm, now expanding to table wine. Owns leading Port brands (CROFT, FONSECA, Krohn, TAYLOR's); growing travel empire incl hotels, in Lisbon, Pinhão, Porto, GAIA, Michelin-starred The

Yeatman, WOW (World of Wine) Gaia visitor centre. Newly acquired from Ideal Drinks: Pedra (VIN), Bella (DÃO), Colinas de São Lourenço (BAIR).

Fonseca Port ★★★→★★★★ FLADGATE-owned house from 1815. Reputed, age-defying VINTAGE PORT 63' 70' 94' 97' 11' 16' 17'. Superb *Fonseca Guimaraens* 13' 15' 18' 19'. Single-QUINTA Panascal; v.gd 20-, 40-yr-old TAWNY; Bin 27 popular, gd value.

Comporta: long beaches, seaside restaurants, great wine shop. Book now.

Fonseca, José Maria da Alen, Set ★→★★★★ Family-run firm, 7th generation. Jewel in crown is fortified *Moscatel de Setúbal*, esp stocks of old MOSCATEL. Stunning *20-yr-old Alambre* and *Moscatel Roxo*, lavish *Superior* 55' 66 71. Table-wine range: top-notch, dense Hexagon (r/w); gd-value single-variety DSF range and popular BSE, João Pires, Lancers, Periquita. Owns v.gd-value, ALEN classic *José de Sousa*.

Foz de Arouce Bei At ★★★★ Hidden gem, esp older vintages. JOÃO PORTUGAL RAMOS's family-run BAIR outpost making age-worthy, classics: characterful Cercial, TOURIGA N/BAGA blend, top-notch old-Baga-vines *Vinhas Velhas*.

Frasqueira Mad Highly sought-after, top MAD category. Aged min 20 yrs in CANTEIRO, usually much longer. Single yr (aka Vintage), single (noble) variety. Bottling date on label. Best: BARBEITO, MADEIRA WINE COMPANY.

Gaia, Vila Nova de Dou, Port Historic home of major Port shippers. Working cellars now also tourist attractions, incl cable car, boat tours, hotels (The Yeatman, Michelin-starred), museums (WOW), restaurants/bars (Enoteca 17·56, Vinum). Best cellars: Cálem, COCKBURN'S, FERREIRA, GRAHAM'S, SANDEMAN, TAYLOR'S. Double-deck bridge: best place to admire sunset and city of Porto.

Garrafeira Term for aged wine, esp ALEN, BAIR, DÃO. Underrated, great value. Reds aged for min 30 mths (often much longer), min 1 yr in bottle. Whites need 12 mths, min 6 in bottle.

Global Wines Bair, Dão ★★→★★★ Large DÃO-based firm. Fine, age-worthy Vinha do Contador range (dense red; rare, creamy, organic Grand Jury white); popular, gd-value Cabriz (esp RES) and Casa de Santar (esp Res, superb Nobre). Interests in nearby regions: Encostas do Douro (DOU), Grilos, Monte da Cal (ALEN), Lourosa (VIN) and QUINTA do Encontro (BAIR), incl striking visitor centre.

Graham's Port ★★★→★★★★ Highly reputed SYMINGTON-owned 200-yr-old house with striking lodge, restaurant in GAIA. Top-notch VINTAGE PORT 27' 63' 66' 85' 91' 94' 97 00' 03' 07' 11' 16' 17' 20' (delightful at release); lavish Stone Terraces 11' 15' 16' 17' 21'; v.gd-value single-QUINTA dos Malvedos 12 15 18' 19'. CRUSTED, RES RUBY Six Grapes, LBV all gd value. Superb TAWNY range: attractive 20-, 30-, 40-yr-old; luscious Single Harvest (COLHEITAS) collection 40' 50' 52' 61' 63' 69' 72' 82 94' 97 03. Ne Oublie VERY VERY OLD TAWNY is 1882 bottled history.

Granvinhos Port ★→★★ Ex-Gran Cruz. Owns: boutique DALVA, Port's largest exporting brand Porto Cruz (volume, cocktails), Porto Presidential. Portfolio: GAIA museum, bar; Porto hotel; DOU Ventozelo. Owned by La Martiniquaise.

Grous, Herdade de Alen, Dou ★★→★★★ Prestigious eco-focused estate: RES (rich, oak-aged w; ripe, fine r); fruity Moon Harvested, best-barrels 23 Barricas labels; thrilling cement-aged *Concrete*. Underrated DOU outpost: QUINTA de Valbom.

Henriques & Henriques Mad ★★→★★★★ Superior MAD shipper. Thrilling *20-yr-olds (Malvasia, Terrantez)*, 50-yr-old TINTA NEGRA; top-notch FRASQUEIRAS (some aged in bourbon barrels): BASTARDO 27, BUAL 00' 09, VERDELHO 32 57, SERCIAL 28 71' 01', Terrantez 54'. Entry-level range gd value. Owned by La Martiniquaise.

Justino's Mad ★→★★★★ Largest MAD shipper, some gems. Best: Terrantez *50-yr-old* and 78' (oldest in cask), MALVASIA 64' 68' 88' 97'. Try also: SERCIAL 97', TINTA NEGRA 99'. Makes popular Broadbent label. Owned by La Martiniquaise.

Kopke Port ★→★★★★ Oldest Port house, now making table wines. Known for thrilling TAWNY (COLHEITAS 35' 40' onwards) and remarkable WHITE PORT (esp now-rare 35' 40' and 20-, 30-, 40-, *50-yr-old*). São Luiz DOU range, incl v.gd Winemaker's Collection (esp Rufete). SOGEVINUS-owned.

Kranemann Wine Estates Dou ★★–★★★ Renovated historic estate with quality range, esp v.gd high-altitude whites. RES; gd-value, fresh Hasso (r/w), new single-variety Tinta Barroca, Rabigato; v.gd 10-, *20-*, 30-yr-old TAWNY.

LBV (Late Bottled Vintage) Port Wallet-friendly, widely available alternative to VINTAGE PORT. Now as gd as last decade's Vintage Port. Cask-aged 4–6 yrs (twice as long as VP) for early drinking. Try v.gd, age-worthy, unfiltered versions FERREIRA, NIEPOORT, NOVAL, RAMOS PINTO, SANDEMAN, TAYLOR'S, WARRE'S. Serve lightly chilled: chocolate's best friend or a luscious dessert on its own.

Lés-a-Lés ★★ Tiny coast-to-coast project recovering trad varieties, methods; v.gd unique range, esp Távora-Varosa, Trás-os-Montes.

Lisboa ★→★★★ Underrated coastal region balancing large firms with wave of quality-focused, dynamic, often organic producers. Great-value, age-worthy reds: CHOCAPALHA, ★★★ *Monte Bluna*, top SYRAH pioneer MONTE D'OIRO. Historic, singular COLARES microclimate and dry, racy Bucelas (ARINTO-based w, great-value ROMEIRA). Try ADEGAMÃE, QUINTA DE SANT'ANA, ★★ Pancas (age-worthy range), ★★ Pinto (value blends). Young, often natural, producers refocus region on Arinto, CASTELÃO: ★★ Casal Figueira, ★★ COZs, ★★ Espera, ★★ Hugo Mendes, ★★ Humus, ★★ Marinho, ★★ Serradinha, ★★★ *Vale da Capucha*, ★★ Viuva Gomes.

Lopes, Márcio Dou, Vin ★★→★★★ Dynamic star winemaker. *Pequenos Rebentos* range (gd-value ALVARINHO/LOUREIRO), top Caminho; DOU (Permitido/Proibido).

Maçanita, António Alen, Dou ★★→★★★ Star winemaker/consultant, many regions, plus wine tourism. Home ALEN (popular Sexy, seductive Fita Preta, v.gd Palpite, trad Chão dos Eremitas), AZORES (superb *Terrantez do Pico*, old-vine Vinha dos Utras), sister-led DOU (Letra A, F range), MAD (rare, thrilling Porto Santo island).

Madeira ★→★★★★ Island and DOC, cliff-hanging vines, mouthwatering wines. Only eight firms making world-famous fortified. Treasured decades-old stocks. Best: BARBEITO, MADEIRA WINE COMPANY. Value: BORGES, HENRIQUES & HENRIQUES, JUSTINO'S, ★★ Pereira d'Oliveira, ★ Faria & Filhos, ★ Madeira Vintners. Watch: table wines rise, ★★ Atlantis, ★★★ BARBEITO; unique wines from Porto Santo.

Madeira, Rui Roboredo Bei Int, Dou ★★→★★★ High-altitude pioneer; v.gd mineral *Pedra Escrita (r/w)*, top, eponymous old-vines label (DOU); great-value *Beyra* range, esp *Jaen*, Grande RES, GARRAFEIRA (BEI INT). Popular: Castello d'Alba.

Madeira Wine Company Mad Reputed, largest MAD firm, led by 7th-generation Chris Blandy. Owns BLANDY'S, COSSART GORDON, Leacock, Miles.

Malhadinha Nova, Herdade da Alen ★★★ Reputed Soares-family S ALEN bio estate, high-end *country house*. Age-worthy range, incl *estate label*; rich, late-released Marias da Malhadinha; piney, dense ALICANTE BOUSCHET *Menino António* and CAB SAUV Pequeno João. Old-vine (1949) Vale Travessos (r/w) v.gd; single-variety, often single-vyd range gd. High-altitude PORTALGRE outpost v.gd: Teixinha.

Malvasia (Malmsey) Mad Sweetest, richest of MAD's noble varieties. Sharp tang makes for thrilling, luscious end to a meal. Look for older yrs.

For bargains, look for underrated high-altitude Beira Interior, Dão, Trás-os-Montes.

Maria Izabel, Quinta Dou ★★★ Brazilian-owned estate revival; v.gd, consistent range made with Dirk NIEPOORT, esp QUINTA, top-notch old-vine Vinhas da Princesa (r/w), unique Sublime range (light, complex Sublime r, oak-aged w). Rare, pricey BASTARDO.

Mateus Rosé ★ Bestseller. Light, fresh, off-dry bubbly rosé with dry edition.

Mendes, Anselmo Vin ★★★→★★★★ "Mr. Alvarinho": benchmark minerality. Try lees-aged *Contacto* (now owned by SYMINGTON); classic, crisp Muros de Melgaço; superb, flinty Parcela Única. Muros Antigos great value.

Menin Dou ★★ Ambitious new firm to watch. Brazilian entrepreneurs hired star winemaker Tiago ALVES DE SOUSA to make classy range, incl RES (r/w), single-variety labels, top-notch Grande Res, New Legacy and D. Beatriz.

Monte Bluna Lis ★★★ Classy Atlantic-influenced boutique project, high-altitude vyds n of Lisbon: top-notch ARAGONÊZ-based Blunissima; fine, elegant, rare native-variety *Tinta Miúda*; seductive *Res* and TicTac range.

Monte d'Oiro, Quinta do Lis ★★→★★★ Atlantic-influenced, Hermitage-inspired bio family estate started with Chapoutier's vines. Fine range: SYRAH/VIOGNIER *Res*; v.gd Viognier *Res*; 1st-class Ex Aequo Syrah/TOURIGA N label; thrilling new 100% ARINTO. Entry-level range gd value.

Monte da Ravasqueira Alen ★★→★★★ Family-run estate, now part of new WINESTONE group. Consultant winemaker David Baverstock (ex-ESPORÃO) makes consistent range, esp Premium, ALICANTE BOUSCHET. Single-vyd Vinhas das Romãs (r/w) gd value.

Morgado do Quintão Alg ★★ Restored 1800 family estate. Winemaker Joana Maçanita (sister of ANTÓNIO M) makes sandy-soil, old-vine, native-variety range: Negra Mole (elegant: rosé, *clairet*; CASTELÃO (estate r); amphora (blends both).

Moscatel de Setúbal Set ★★→★★★★ Luscious MOSCATEL-made fortified treasure. Thrilling, exotic, sweet, esp richer *Roxo* and superlative *Superior*. Best: JOSÉ MARIA DA FONSECA (100-yr-old+ stocks). V.gd: BACALHÔA VINHOS, ★★ Horácio Simões. Value: ★★ Palmela Wine Company, ★★ Piloto. Pair with crème brûlée, hard, salty cheeses, or the right company.

Mouchão, Herdade de Alen ★★★ Classic family-run estate, fine foot-trodden range: large-barrel-aged *estate red* (1st bottled 1949); unique ALEN fortified Tonel 3-4; v.gd-value perfumed *Ponte* (r) and old-vine *Dom Rafael* (r/w).

Mouraz, Casa de Dão ★★★ A bio pioneer. Vibrant, authentic range: eponymous label, natural Bolinha, *clairet* Nina; gd-value Air. Best: v.gd 80-yr-old vine *Elfa*; top-notch 100-yr-old-vines Boot.

Muxagat Dou ★★★ Boutique estate, distinct, elegant. Best: rare high-altitude Rabigato-based *Xistos Altos*; v.gd varietal reds, unique *Cisne* (blends r/w grapes), 100% Tinta Francisca.

Nicolau de Almeida Dou ★★★ Boutique project; grandfather created BARCA VELHA. Fine, seductive, tense Monte Xisto; v.gd elegant Órbita, Oriente.

Niepoort Bair, Dou, Dão ★★→★★★★ Multi-region family-run firm led by larger-than-life DOU pioneer Dirk, now son Daniel. Fine, bold, age-worthy range: v.gd Redoma esp *Res* (w); 1st-class Batuta; *Charme; Coche* (w); single-vyd, structured Robustus; elegant, fresh amphora-aged *Voyeur* and 130-yr-old-vines *Turris*. Diálogo/Fabelhaft is gd-value globetrotter. Popular Nat'cool easy-drinking, low-intervention range. Other regions: BAIR (esp GARRAFEIRA, Poeirinho, VV), DÃO (esp Conciso), VIN. Port range v.gd, often superb: VINTAGE PORT 45' 87' 00' 15'

Pink renaissance

You thought you knew Portuguese rosé? These are the new wave. Favourites have a ★. **Alg** Arvad. **Alen** ★ Fonte Souto, João Dona Maria Amantis, MONTE DE RAVASQUEIRA Heritage, Portugal Ramos Vinha da Rosa. Azores Wine Company Rosé Vulcânico. **Bair** ★ Giz, ★ Kompassus, Principal Tête de Cuvée, Prior Lucas Fénix P. **Bei Int** QUINTA da Biaia 750. **Dão** ★ PASSARELLA O Fugitivo, TABOADELLA Caementa. **Dou** ★ ALVES DE SOUSA Rosa Celeste, Bons Ares, KOPKE, Manoella, Paulo Coutinho Fusion, ★ Poço do Lobo, Quanta Terra Phenomena, VALLADO, Ventozelo. **Lis** ★ Casal Sta Maria Mar de Rosas, CHOCAPALHA, ★ Dona Aninhas, ★ MONTE BLUNA (Res, TicTac), MONTE D'OIRO, ★ Quinta Nova, Redoma, Síbio. **Mad** MAÇANITA Vilões. **Sét** DSF.

17' 19', trad *Pisca*, organic Bioma; great-value **Crusted**; unique demijohn-aged *Garrafeira*; ethereal 1983 VV; TAWNY v.gd, esp bottle-aged COLHEITAS. Private GAIA cellar requires booking.

Noval, Quinta do Dou, Port ★★★→★★★★ Historic AXA-owned (1993) estate reputed for Port, now table wines. Port: v.gd **Vintage** released every yr; jewel-in-crown *Nacional* 00' 01' 03' 04' 11' 16' 17' 19' 21' from 2.5 ha ungrafted vines; v.gd unfiltered LBV; superior **Colheitas**, 20-, 40-yr-olds. DOU range: top-notch, single-plot, v. old field-blend Vinhas da Marka, do Passadouro; v.gd, age-worthy RES (oak-aged *Viosinho-based* w, classic r); gd-value Cedro (r/w); elegant, single-variety PETIT VERDOT, SYRAH, TOURIGA N. Owns ★★ Passadouro.

Touriga Nacional: chameleon of Portugal. Different profile in every region.

Offley Port ★★ Historic 1737 house. Fruit-driven, gd-value VINTAGE PORT, unfiltered LBV. Cocktail-ready Clink. Owned by SOGRAPE.

Pacheca, Quinta da Dou, Port Historic estate famous for sleep-in-barrel hotel; gd-value table wines. Owner group Terras & Terroir expanding: ★★ Caminhos Cruzados, esp Teixuga (DÃO), Ortigão (BAIR), Rocha (ALEN).

Passarella, Casa da Dão ★★→★★★★ Historic estate revival by DÃO star Paulo Nunes. Benchmark: fine, late-release **Vindima** 09' 11 (80-yr-old field blend); classy Villa Oliveira range, esp oaked ENCRUZADO, dense, 80-yr-old-vine Pedras Altas; v.gd-value single-variety *Fugitivo* range.

Pato, Filipa Bair ★★★ Star bio BAGA couple, "wines with no makeup". Fine, silky, v.-old-vine reds, esp *Nossa Missão*, *Nossa Calcario* (also v.gd w). Seductive, amphora-aged Post-Quercus, new chestnut-aged Castanea.

Pato, Luis Bair ★★→★★★★ Opinionated, non-conformist, modern BAIR pioneer. Father of FILIPA P. Expert in *age-worthy, single-vyd Baga* (Barrio, Barrosa, Pan) and Pé Franco (ungrafted) wines (bright, sandy-soil *Ribeirinho*); age-worthy whites (rich, single-vyd Vinha Formal, sharp Parcela Cândido, fine *Ribeirinho*). Try now: v.gd-value VINHAS VELHAS (r/w), BAGA Rebel.

Pereira d'Oliveira Mad ★★→★★★★ Founded 1880, now 5th generation. Vast stocks of bottled-on-demand FRASQUEIRA, many available at travel-back-in-time touristy cellar door. Ask nicely for C19 vintages: MOSCATEL 1875, SERCIAL 1875, Terrantez 1880, rare *Bastardo 1927*.

Pico Wines ★★ Largest, oldest AZORES CO-OP, undergoing revolution. Star winemaker Bernardo Cabral makes quality volcanic range: gd-value Frei Gigante, Terras de Lava; v.gd salty, single-variety range ARINTO/Terrantez do Pico/VERDELHO. Top: Rola Pipa, 100-yr-old-vine *Gruta das Torres*. Delicious 10-yr-old Licoroso.

Poças Dou, Port ★★→★★★ Family-owned, 100-yr-old+ firm with reputed Dou, growing table-wine range. Old Tawny stocks: fine 20-, *30-*, 40-yr-old, COLHEITAS fabulous 90-yr-old+ 1918. LBV, VINTAGE PORT v.gd. Top-notch: sumptuous, oaked Branco da Ribeira (w); *Fora da Série* range (esp *Vinho da Roga*); Símbolo (with Hubert de Boüard of Bx). Plus gd-value RES.

Pormenor Dou ★★★ Boutique min-intervention project. Elegant, mineral, high-altitude field-blend *Trilho*; firm, austere A de ARINTO; creamy yet vibrant, high-altitude *Pormenor Res*; v.gd-value entry-level (r/w).

Portalegre Alen ★→★★★★ Old, now trendy n subregion, winemaker's dream (high altitude, cooler climate, old field-blend vyds). Trendsetters: ★★ CABEÇAS DO REGUENGO, RUI REGUINGA, *Susana Esteban*, ★★ Tapada do Chaves. Early trend-followers: ESPORÃO, MALHADINHA (Teixinha), SOGRAPE (Série Ímpar), SYMINGTON (Fonte Souto).

Quinta Estate. "Herdade" in ALEN.

Quinta Nova Dou ★★★→★★★★ Historic estate with *charming hotel*, river views. Owned by Amorim (cork) family, led by Luisa A and star winemaking team.

Remarkable cork-taint-free range: fine, rich oaked Mirabilis (r/w); outstanding rich and layered Vinha Centenária range (100-yr-old vines: *Tinta Roriz* or TOURIGA N); superior 100-yr-old-vines Aeternus; v.gd-value (r/w) *Grainha*, Pomares. DÃO outpost: TABOADELLA.

Rainwater Mad Once-popular, still seductive chilled apéritif. Lighter, drier style of MAD aged min 5 yrs, usually TINTA NEGRA.

Ramos, João Portugal Alen ★→★★★ An ALEN pioneer, now led by new generation. Popular gd-value brands incl: Marquês de Borba, Vila Santa, VINHAS VELHAS. Best: Marquês de Borba RES, Estremus, single-vyd range. Outposts: VIN, DOU (DUORUM), Beira Atlântico (FOZ DE AROUCE).

Ramos Pinto Dou, Port ★★★→★★★★ Historic estate, Port and growing DOU range: popular Bons Ares, great-value Duas Quintas (r/w), classy *Res* (r), top-notch Ervamoira. Best Ports: TAWNY 10-yr-old, 1st-class, vibrant 20-yr-old; v.gd VINTAGE PORT, incl single-quintas Bom Retiro, Ervamoira. Owned by Champagne Roederer (*see* France).

Real Companhia Velha Dou, Port ★→★★★ Oldest (1756) wine firm in Portugal, now run by young generation. DOU: fine Carvalhas, esp v.gd old-vines (r/w); international-variety Cidrô, incl popular oaked CHARD and seductive, fine *Marquis* (TOURIGA N/CAB SAUV); bio, native-variety Síbio, esp whites; gd-value Aciprestes, Evel; best-in-class Grandjó late-harvest. Port brands gd value: RCV, Carvalhas, Delaforce, Royal Oporto, Silva Reis. Superb GAIA wine bar.

Reguinga, Rui Alen, Tej ★★★ Consultant's own brand. ALEN, PORTALEGRE: v.gd, high-altitude, old-vines *Terrenus* range, incl 100-yr-old-vine *Vinha da Serra* (w). Tej: Rhône-inspired *Tributo*, MARSANNE/ROUSSANNE/VIOGNIER Vinha da Talisca.

Reserve / Reserva (Res) Port Bottle- or oak-aged. Each region has its rules. Usually higher quality, not always. Grande Reserva is respected. In Port, bottled without age indication: often gd-value RUBY, TAWNY.

Rocim Alen ★★→★★★ Dynamic firm, VINHO DE TALHA-revival pioneer. Best: fine Grande Rocim (dense, piney ALICANTE BOUSCHET r; firm, oaky ARINTO w), late-release Crónica #328 and 1st-class *Vinha da Micaela*. Clay-pot range v.gd: foot-trodden, polished *Clay Aged* (r); elegant Amphora (r/w). Also gd old-vine, single-vyd Olho de Mocho (r/w), bio Alicante Bouschet Indígena. Other regions: seductive old-field-blend DOU Bela Luz; fine DÃO *O Estrangeiro* (r/w). Try collaborations with BARBEITO, NIEPOORT, Lenz Moser (Austria).

Romeira, Quinta da Lis ★★ Historic Bucelas estate. Atlantic-influenced, ARINTO-based range v.gd value: Prova Regia, Morgado Sta Catherina. Owned by SOGRAPE.

Rosa, Quinta de la Dou, Port ★★★ Classic, family-run estate, charming riverside guesthouse. Jorge Moreira (Poeira) makes gd-value range: La Rosa, RES (r/w); Passagem label. Best PORT: v.gd LBV, 30-yr-old TAWNY, VINTAGE PORT.

Rozès Dou, Port ★★ Vranken-Pommery (*see* France) PORT house: gd LBV from warmer DOU Superior; gd Terras do Grifo table wines (fine RES, Grande Res).

Ruby Port Major PORT style/category. Bottle-aged, fruitier (vs TAWNY); yrs in wood before bottling: VINTAGE PORT (2), LBV (4–6), RES (6). Also name for most simple, young, cheap, often delicious sweet Port.

Sandeman Port Port ★★→★★★ Historic SOGRAPE-owned house famous for caped-man image, now modern labels; v.gd-value range: *20*-, 30-, 40-, 50-yr-old TAWNY, unfiltered LBV. VINTAGE PORT back on form.

Where to eat/drink: casual

Best wine spots: **Eat** (Dou) Casa dos Ecos, Seixo. (Lis) Corrupio, Lota d'Ávila, Ofício, Prado, Taberna da Rua das Flores, Velho Eurico. (Porto) Almeja, Casario, Cozinha das Flores, Rogégio do Redondo, Vinum. **Drink** (Lis) Black Sheep, Insaciável, Pinot Bar. (Porto) Prova.

Sant'Ana, Quinta de Lis ★★★ Historic, idyllic, family-run estate known for crisp, saline whites: v.gd ALVARINHO, ARINTO, esp pricey Marreco. Age-worthy reds. Exquisite, rare *Ramisco*.

São João, Caves Bair ★★ →★★★ Historic firm with vast 100-yr-old stock, new owners. Famous for cellar releases. Two regions: BAIR (Frei João, Poço do Lobo); DÃO (Porta dos Cavaleiros).

Tapas in Spain. Petiscos in Portugal. Same principle, just as good.

Seabra, Luis Dou, Vin ★★★ A min-intervention, star winemaker (ex-NIEPOORT) makes elegant single-vyd range. DOU: v.gd Indie, *Xisto Cru* (r/w), Ilimitado. VIN: fine lees-aged ALVARINHO *Granito Cru*.

Sercial Mad Aka Esgana-Cão. Racy, tart, driest style of MAD. *Supreme apéritif;* perfect with smoked fish or caviar.

Setúbal, Península de Set ★ →★★★ Seaside region s of Lisbon, home of world-class fortified MOSCATEL DE SETÚBAL. Table wines: look for crisp whites, gd CASTELÃO-focused reds. Popular: Adega de Pegões, BACALHOA, Casa Ermelinda Freitas, JOSÉ MARIA DA FONSECA. Try small producers: ★★ Brejinho da Costa, ★★ Horácio Simões, ★★ *Pegos Claros*, ★★ Piloto, ★★ Portocarro, ★★★ Trois.

Soalheiro, Quinta de Vin ★★ →★★★ Leading, dynamic ALVARINHO firm in Monção e Melgaço; gd-value Classico; mineral *Granit;* fine, subtly barrel-fermented *Primeiras Vinhas;* oaked RES.

Sogevinus Dou, Port Large group, Port plus growing gd table-wine range (★★ São Luiz, top-notch QUINTA DA BOAVISTA). Owns centenary houses: ★★ →★★★ Barros (v.gd-value COLHEITAS from every decade since 30s; v.gd 20-, 30-, 40-yr-old Tawny); ★ →★★★ Burmester (elegant, gd-value TAWNY: 20-, 40-yr-old, Colheitas; delectable 30-, 40-yr-old WHITE PORTS;); ★ →★★★ Cálem (bestseller, entry-level Velhotes; 10-, 40-yr-old TAWNY); KOPKE. Three popular visitor centres in GAIA.

Sogrape Alen, Dou, Vin ★ →★★★★ Largest wine firm in Portugal known globally for MATEUS ROSÉ. ALEN: gd-value Herdade do Peso. DÃO: CARVALHAIS. DOU: v.gd CASA FERREIRINHA, iconic BARCA VELHA. LIS: v.gd-value QUINTA DA ROMEIRA. VIN: Azevedo. Port: FERREIRA, OFFLEY, SANDEMAN. Growing fine-wine range: *Antónia Adelaide Ferreira*, 100-yr-old+ vine Legado, *Série Ímpar*. Global interests incl Argentina (Finca Flichman); Chile (Los Boldos); NZ (Framingham); Spain (LAN, Santiago Ruiz).

Sousa, Alves de Dou, Port ★★ →★★★ Family-run table-wine pioneer making classic, v.gd, structured *Quinta da Gaivosa*, unique late-released RES Pessoal; fine, sought-after old-vine field-blends Abandonado, Vinha de Lordelo; refined Port, esp Gaivosa, single-vyd Amphitheatrum.

Sousa, José de Alen ★★ →★★★ Historic estate keeping ALEN trad alive. Portugal's largest (100+) TALHA collection. Best: *talha*-based *Mayor* and *J.* Spicy, ripe *José de Sousa* and RES gd value. Owned by JM DA FONSECA.

Symington Family Estates Dou, Port ★★ →★★★★ Historic, family-run, B Corp-certified PORT firm undergoing quiet table-wine revolution, while running top Port houses COCKBURN'S, DOW'S, GRAHAM'S, VESUVIO, WARRE'S. Table wine: CHRYSEIA, fruit-driven Vesuvio, thrilling high-altitude DOU whites (esp *Pequeno Dilema*, Ilustres Desconhecidos). Altano RES, *Contacto* (still made by ANSELMO MENDES), Pombal, Post Scriptum all gd value. Fabulous historic 1890 Lodge visitor centre/restaurant in GAIA. Outposts: high-altitude ALEN/PORTALEGRE Fonte Souto (try top-notch Taifa); new VIN property. Now co-owner of VÉRTICE, and Hambledon (*see* England).

Taboadella Dão ★★★ Amorim-family DÃO project with QUINTA NOVA's star team. Top, elegant, oaked Grande Villae (r/w); seductive varietal range, esp *Alfrocheiro*, ENCRUZADO; delicious *Caemenda* (r). v.gd-value, unoaked entry-level Villae.

Talha, Vinho de Alen ALEN DOC. Popular in other regions. Ancient clay-amphora Roman trad getting new attention. Vinification: some whole-bunch, 5–6-wk maceration in decades-old amphorae, now hunted treasures. Best: CARTUXA, ★★ Gerações da Talha, ★★ José Piteira, ROCIM, ★★ XXVI Talhas, esp *Mestre Daniel.*

Wine fairs to visit: Essência do Vinho Porto, Simplesmente Vinho (small producers).

Tawny Port ★ ⋆★★★★ Oxidative, nutty, sweet, wood-aged crowd-pleaser Port style. Ready to drink on release, lasts 2 mths after opening. Serve chilled. Perfect dessert on its own, with crème brûlée or dry, salty, hard cheese. Try age-dated wines for added complexity: 10-, 20-, 30-, 40, new 50-yr-old; single-yr, cask-aged COLHEITAS up to 100 yrs, incl luscious, expensive *Very Very Old Tawny* (80-yr-old+). Best in class: ANDRESEN, DALVA, GRAHAM'S, KOPKE, NIEPOORT, NOVAL, Otima (WARRE'S), POÇAS, RAMOS PINTO, TAYLOR'S, VASQUES DE CARVALHO. Cheap RES (6 yrs in wood) a wallet-friendly treat.

Taylor's Port ★★ ⋆★★★★ Historic shipper, FLADGATE's jewel in the crown. Impressive range of top Port wines. VINTAGE PORTS 63' 66' 70' 77' 94' 97' 00', single-QUINTAS (Terra Feita, Vargellas) and rare, splendid Vargellas VINHA VELHA from 70-yr-old+ vines. Outstanding TAWNY range (some from v.gd old stocks of reputable Krohn brand), esp v.gd 20-, 30-, 40-yr-old, 50-yr-old Golden Age, 1863' single-harvest, Scion, Kingsman Edition (average 90 yrs old); new VERY VERY OLD PORT, a luscious, decadent liquid treasure.

Vadio Bair ★★★ Luis Patrão's underrated BAGA-focused boutique project: v.gd, age-worthy, classic. *Estate label* and Grande Vadio.

Vale D. Maria, Quinta do Dou, Port ★★ ⋆★★★ Reputable, now AVELEDA-owned. Rich DOU range: v.gd *estate label*, single-vyd Vinha do Rio, *Vinha da Francisca* and new top-notch, rare cellar-release Vinha do Moinho. Oak-aged whites gd: VVV, Vinha do Martim; Dou Superior range gd value. LBV, RES, VERY OLD TAWNY, VINTAGE PORT all gd.

Vale Meão, Quinta do Dou ★★★ Aristocratic family-run estate, birthplace of BARCA VELHA (now made elsewhere). Fine, dense-yet-fresh, age-worthy range incl iconic top red; v.gd single-vyd varietal range Monte Meão; gd-value Meandro (r); gd VINTAGE PORT.

Vallado, Quinta do Dou ★★ ⋆★★★ Famous Régua-based firm, modern hotel/winery; v.gd-value organic DOU Superior; v.gd RES field-blend Sousão range; gd 10-, 20-, 30-, 40-, 50-yr-old TAWNY; top-notch, single-vyd, old-vine Coroa, Granja, 100-yr-old-vine Adelaide red; thrilling, rare, pre-phylloxera 1888 VERY OLD TAWNY.

Van Zellers & Co Dou, Port ★★★ A DOU table-wine pioneer Cristiano Van Zeller and daugther Francisca, back after selling QUINTA DO VALE D. MARIA. High-quality range, as expected: benchmark CV – Curriculum Vitae (r/w); v.gd VZ (r/w). Port v.gd, esp stylish 20-yr-old COLHEITA range 34 35 40 50 76. Also three superb one-off C19 Colheitas, at a price.

Vasques de Carvalho Dou, Port ★★★ Boutique firm, est 2012 from inherited family cellars, stock, vyds. Liquid jewellery: fine, pricey, stylish *10-, 20-, 30- and 40-yr-old Tawny*; v.gd 10-, 20-yr-old WHITE PORTS; gd VINTAGE and DOU range. Charming lounge/shop in GAIA.

Verdelho Mad Classic MAD grape. Sweeter than SERCIAL, but drier than BUAL. Try with Japanese food for a surprise; gd apéritif with hard cheese. Popular in Mad table wine.

Vértice Dou ★★★ ⋆★★★★ Portugal's best fizz, half-owned by SYMINGTON; v.gd-value Gouveio, Millésime. Remarkable, high-altitude, 84-mth-aged PINOT N.

Very Very Old Tawny Port ★★★★ Bottled history. Wines aged for decades (min

80 yrs) in wood. Still available: 1900, 1910 (ANDRESEN), 1918 (POÇAS), 5G (WINE & SOUL), Honore (CRASTO), Kingsman, Ne Oublie (GRAHAM'S), Scion, VV (NIEPOORT), VVOT (TAYLOR'S).

Vesuvio, Quinta do Dou, Port ★★★ ⋯★★★★ Magnificent, historic SYMINGTON-owned riverside QUINTA where Port still foot-trodden, on par with best. Fruit-driven DOU range: consistently v.gd old-vine estate red; gd-value second label **Pombal do Vesuvio** and Comboio.

Vicentino Alen ★★ Vicentine-coast pioneer, making fresh, saline Atlantic-influenced range: ALVARINHO, ARINTO, SAUV BL, PINOT N, SYRAH; gd-value entry-level label.

Vinhas Velhas Old vines. Widespread national treasure. Age/meaning varies by region, now regulated in DOU (min 40-yr-old vyds, min four-variety field blend, low yield).

Vinho Verde ★ ⋯★★★ Portugal's most exported wine region. Borders rainy Galicia/Spain. Famous for spritzy whites, increasingly high quality, influx of new players: FALUA, FLADGATE, GRANVINHOS, SYMINGTON, WINESTONE. Best by subregion: top ALVARINHO from Monção e Melgaço (**Anselmo Mendes**, ★★ Barão do Hospital, **Luis Seabra**, MÁRCIO LOPES, ★★★ Regueiro, ★★ **Santiago**, SOALHEIRO); elegant LOUREIRO from Lima (AMEAL, bio ★★ Aphros); characterful Avesso from Baião (★★ bio A&D, ★★ Covela); Cávado (★★ Azevedo); Amarante (Casa de Cello, ★★ Casa de Vilacetinho). Large brands with cheap, off-dry and slightly fizzy wines: Adega de Monção, Adega Ponte da Barca, Casal Garcia, Gazela, Muralhas.

Vintage Port Port One of world's greatest classics. Aged patiently in bottle after 2 yrs in wood. Made only in v. finest yrs (aka "classic" or "declared" yrs), increasingly made back-to-back due to precision viticulture/winemaking. Single-QUINTA VPs made in non-declared yrs. Rare, superlative **special editions**: Capela (VESUVIO), Sērikos (CROFT), Stone Terraces (GRAHAM'S), Vinha da Pisca (NIEPOORT). Unfiltered, throws deposit, always decant. Look for an old vintage to touch heaven, or young for a sweet treat.

Warre's Port ★★★→★★★★ Underrated SYMINGTON-owned historic Port house. Rich, long-ageing VINTAGE and unfiltered LBV, elegant QUINTA da Cavadinha, racy **20-yr-old Tawny Otima**.

White Port Port Category undergoing revival with high-quality labels: age-dated 10-, 20-, 30-, or 40-yr-old v.gd (ANDRESEN, KOPKE, Quevedo, Vieira de Sousa); superb, rare COLHEITAS (**Dalva, Kopke**). Lágrima is cheap, v. sweet. Base of popular, refreshing Port & Tonic cocktail.

Wine & Soul Dou, Port ★★★ ⋯★★★★ Reputable estate, often old vines: v.gd oak-aged **Guru**; complex, powerful Pintas; delicious, elegant, field-blend **Pintas Character**. QUINTA da Manoella range gd value, top-notch VINHAS VELHAS and Vinha Alecrim; crisp, high-atititude **Vinha do Altar** (w). Elegant Ports incl 10-yr-old, VINTAGE. Superlative 100-yrs+ VERY VERY OLD TAWNY 5G.

Winestone Alen, Dou, Lis, Port, Vin New group by José de Mello family, ambitious multi-region portfolio: MONTE DA RAVASQUEIRA (ALEN); Wiese & Krohn (Port); Quinta de Pancas (LIS); long-term loan of QUINTA do Cotto (DOU) and Paço do Teixeiró (VIN).

PORTUGAL

Switzerland

Abbreviations used in the text:

Aar	Aargau
Ber	Bern
Gris	Grisons
Luc	Lucerne
Neu	Neuchâtel
Schaff	Schaffhausen
Thur	Thurgau
Tic	Ticino
Val	Valais
Vd	Vaud
Zür	Zürich

S wiss wine is at a crossroads. Should it look for international fame? Or should it remain a self-sufficient business aimed at loyal local customers? The older generation of growers devoured the books of the great Bordelais oenologist Émile Peynaud, while the young are busy on Instagram. The older generation transformed Swiss wine: light-coloured, easy-to-drink Blauburgunder turned into seriously burgundian red. Ticino Merlot is no longer a light trattoria wine. Valais rediscovered its own varieties. Switzerland exports hardly anything, and imports lots. Prices are high – so Swiss wine will never be a star of the supermarket. But it is already a hidden champion in the top league: compare the price of a superb bottle of Pinot Noir with its cousins on the other side of the Jura in Beaune or Nuits. And where else can you get breathtakingly independent local varieties such as Cornalin, which can also mature for 20 years, for the price of a mid-range Bordeaux? At the moment, though, non-Swiss might have to factor in the cost of the fare. That changes things a bit.

Recent vintages

2023 Another rollercoaster season: rain at harvest, hail in Tic.
2022 Warm and dry yr, generally gd quantity, quality.
2021 Frost, hail, mildew: tiny crop. Lighter wines, sound quality, v.gd whites.
2020 Early, small, 20–40% less: uneven flowering, drought, v.gd quality.
2019 Rain at harvest time, esp in e; Vd and Val better.
2018 Powerful, round wines all over the country.
Earlier fine vintages: 17 15 09 05 90, (Pinot N) 13 10, (Dézaley) 99 97.

Aigle Vd ★→★★★ Popular CHASSELAS AOC, best from Plantour hill on moraine soil.

AOC Equivalent of France's appellation contrôlée; 62 AOCs countrywide.

Auvernier, Ch d' Neu ★★→★★★ Important estate (60 ha), typical NEU CHARD, CHASSELAS, OEIL-DE-PERDRIX, PINOT N (best: single-vyd Les Argiles 15' 18'). Henry Grosjean is 15th generation of his family.

Bachtobel, Schlossgut Thur ★★★ Family estate (since 1784): refined PINOT N labelled 1–4 (higher number = better quality), gd SAUV BL.

Bad Osterfingen Schaff ★★★ Historic spa (est 1472), now restaurant and wine estate. Michael Meyer's PINOTS BL/N v. fine food matches.

Badoux, Henri Vd ★★ AIGLE Les Murailles (classic lizard label) is most popular Swiss brand. Ambitious Lettres de Noblesse series has gd barrel-aged YVORNE.

Baumann, Ruedi Schaff ★★★ Family estate at Oberhallau. Beatrice, Ruedi, son Peter best known for PINOT N (eg. Ann Mee, R, ZWAA).

Bern Capital and canton, wine villages on Lake Biel and Lake Thun. Top growers: Andrey, Johanniterkeller, Keller am See, Krebs & Steiner, Schlössli, Schott (bio).

Besse, Gérald Val ★★★ Sarah B converted excellent family estate to organic. One of many SPÉCIALITÉS in steep terraces up to 600m (1969ft) is *Ermitage Les Serpentines* 15 16 17 18 19 (MARSANNE on granite soils, planted 1945).

Bonvin Val ★★→★★★ Old name of VAL, intriguing local grapes: *Nobles Cépages* series (eg. HEIDA, PETITE ARVINE, SYRAH).

Swiss Army drinks up to 70,000 litres local wine/year: less than 50cl/head.

Bovard, Louis Vd ★★→★★★ Keeper of the grail in DÉZALEY (La Médinette 99' 00' 05' 07' 11' 12' 15' **16 17' 18'** 19 20 21 22); other AOCs equally reliable. Doyen Louis-Philippe B, now 90, joined by Fabio Bongulielmi.

Calamin Vd ★★★ GRAND CRU of LAVAUX, 16 ha of deep calcareous soils on a landslide, CHASSELAS tarter than nearby DÉZALEY.

Chablais Vd ★★→★★★ Wine region at upper end of Lake Geneva around AIGLE and YVORNE. Name is from Latin *caput lacis*, head of the lake.

Chappaz, Marie-Thérèse Val ★★★→★★★★ Small bio estate, famous for tiny quantities of nobly sweet Ermitage (MARSANNE) and Petite ARVINE 06' 07' 15' 18. In 2020, 54 litres of "grain par grain" in essencia style (*see* Hungary).

Colombe, Dom La Vd ★★→★★★ Bio estate at FÉCHY, led by Raymond Paccot and daughter Laura. Age-worthy CHASSELAS Brez, terracotta-aged field-blend white (Curzilles), SAVAGNIN Amédée.

Constantin, Thierry Val ★★★ Passionate grower at Pont de la Morge, 7 ha of steep slopes, outstanding SYRAH Anastasi (ex-L'Odalisque).

Cortaillod Neu PINOT N stronghold on shores of Lake Neuchâtel, eponymous low-yielding local clone. Best: PORRET.

Côte, La Vd ★→★★★ A breadbasket of CHASSELAS: 2000 ha w of Lausanne on Lake Geneva, v. variable quality. Villages incl FÉCHY, Mont-sur-Rolle, Morges.

Cruchon Vd ★★★ A bio producer of LA CÔTE, now led by young Catherine C, lots of SPÉCIALITÉS. Top: PINOT N from local clone Servagnin dating back to C15 (Raissennaz 10' 13' 15' 17', Servagnin 18' 19' 20').

Dézaley Vd ★★★ LAVAUX GRAND CRU on steep slopes of Lake Geneva, 54 ha; planted in C12 by Cistercian monks. Potent CHASSELAS develops with age (7 yrs+). Best: DUBOUX, *Fonjallaz*, LEYVRAZ, *Louis Bovard*, MONACHON, Ville de Lausanne.

Dôle Val ★→★★ VAL's answer to Burgundy's Passetoutgrains: PINOT N plus GAMAY for light, quaffable red.

Donatsch Gris ★★★ Martin D has made a name for spectacular auction results, esp PINOT N Res Privée. Local grape Completer a SPÉCIALITÉ.

Duboux, Blaise Vd ★★★ Family estate in LAVAUX. Rich, mineral CALAMIN, DÉZALEY.

Féchy Vd ★→★★★ Famous though unreliable AOC of LA CÔTE, mainly CHASSELAS.

> **Wine regions**
> Switzerland has six major wine regions: VAL, VD, GENEVA, TIC, Trois Lacs
> (NEU, Bienne/BER, VULLY/Fribourg) and German Switzerland (Aar, GRIS,
> SCHAFF, St Gallen, Thur, ZÜR and some smaller wine cantons).

Fendant Val ★→★★★ Full-bodied VAL CHASSELAS, recognizable by its balsamic scent, ideal for fondue or raclette.

Fläsch Gris ★★★→★★★★ Village of Bündner Herrschaft known for PINOT N from schist and limestone. Lots of gd estates, esp members of Adank, Hermann, Marugg families. *Gantenbein* is outstanding.

Flétri / Mi-flétri Late-harvested grapes for sweet/slightly sweet wine.

Fromm, Georg Gris ★★★ Top grower in MALANS, bio, known for light-coloured, subtle, age-worthy single-vyd PINOT N.

Gantenbein Gris ★★★★ Star growers Daniel and Martha G in FLÄSCH. PINOT N is famous, but CHARD (tiny quantity) even more intriguing.

Geneva 1400 ha of vines remote from the lake (vyds there belong mainly to the VD canton). Growers: Balisiers, Clos des Pins, GRAND'COUR, Les Hutins, Novelle.

Germanier, Jean-René Val ★★→★★★ Reliable FENDANT Les Terrasses, SYRAH Cayas, local AMIGNE from schist at Vétroz (dr/sw).

Gialdi Tic ★★→★★★★ Prime producer in TIC. Bought-in grapes from small producers in mtn-altitude vyds produce outstanding MERLOT Sassi Grossi 06 07 **09** 11 12 13' 15 16' 18' 19 20' (no 21 produced).

Glacier, Vin du (Gletscherwein) Val ★★★ A sort of Alpine "Sherry" from rare Rèze grape of Val d'Anniviers, aged in larch casks. Taste at Grimentz town hall.

Grain Noble ConfidenCiel Val Quality label for authentic sweet wines. Berries must be concentrated on the vine.

Grand'Cour, Dom Gen ★★★ Leading estate of GENEVA, 25 varieties on 15 ha, outstanding CABS FR/SAUV blend Grand'Cour 03' **05 07 09** 13' 15' 16' 17 18' 19'.

Grand Cru Val, Vd Inconsistent term, used in VAL and VD, sometimes linked to specific varieties or restricted yields, or to designations like clos, ch, abbaye. Only few are classifications of a vyd site (eg. CALAMIN, DÉZALEY).

Grisons (Graubünden) A mtn canton, German- and Rhaeto-Romanic-speaking. PINOT N king. Most famous part is called Bündner Herrschaft, comprises four villages (FLÄSCH, Jenins, Maienfeld, MALANS): 6000 inhabitants, 329 growers.

Hammel, Maison Val, Vd ★→★★★★ Merchant with 15 doms. Dom de Crochet Cuvée Charles Auguste SYRAH/CABS SAUV/FR **06'** 09 10 11' 12 13' 15 16' 17 18' 19.

Hubervini ★★→★★★ Family estate (7 ha) led by Jonas H, best known for MERLOT/CAB FR blend Montagna Magica 01' 03' 09' 15' 19.

Johannisberg Val Name for SILVANER in VAL, often off-dry or sweet; great with fondue. Excellent: *Dom du Mont d'Or.*

Kartause Ittingen Thur ★→★★★ Former Carthusian monastery, now a hotel, restaurant, museum, farm, owned (and beautifully restored) by the Canton of Thurgau. Fine PINOTS N/GR Kirchwingert.

Lavaux Vd ★★→★★★★ 30 km of steep s-facing terraces e of Lausanne; UNESCO World Heritage Site. Uniquely rich, mineral CHASSELAS. GRANDS CRUS CALAMIN, DÉZALEY, several village AOCs.

Leyvraz, Pierre-Luc Vd ★★★→★★★★ Perfectionist grower at LAVAUX, now joined by young André Bélard; terroir-led ST-SAPHORIN Les Blassinges, age-worthy DÉZALEY.

Litwan, Tom Aar ★★★ Bio grower at Schinznach; 5 ha. Substantial CHARDS Büel, Wanne, and single-vyd PINOT N (Auf der Mauer, Chalofe, Rüeget).

Maison Carrée, La Neu ★★★ Family estate, est 1827, 10 ha; v. trad winemaking incl use of old wooden press, esp delicately scented PINOT N (Auvernier, Hauterive, single-vyd, old-vines Le Lerin).

Malans Gris ★★→★★★★ Village in Bündner Herrschaft. Top PINOT N producers: DONATSCH, FROMM, Liesch, Studach, Wegelin. Late-ripening local grape Completer (Giani Boner has ungrafted vines) gives a long-lasting phenolic white.

Maye, Simon & Fils Val ★★★ Raphaël Maye is best known for SYRAH Vieilles Vignes 05 09 10′ 11 12 13 15′ 16′ 17 18′. But other SPÉCIALITÉS (eg Païen) are excellent too.

Mémoire des Vins Suisses Union of 58 leading growers in effort to create stock of Swiss icon wines, prove ageability. Oldest from 99.

Mercier, Denis Val ★★★→★★★★ Meticulous vyd management produces aromatic wines from outstanding FENDANT and DÔLE to SYRAH and rare CORNALIN 05 06′ 08′ 09′ 10′ 11′ 12 13′ 15′ 16 17 18′ 19 20′.

Monachon, Pierre Vd ★★★ Crisp, mineral and extremely reliable DÉZALEY Les Côtes Dessus and ST-SAPHORIN Les Manchettes 15′ 18′ 21′.

Mont d'Or, Dom du Val ★★→★★★★ Emblematic VAL estate on schist soils, owned by SCHENK, famous for nobly sweet JOHANNISBERG Saint-Martin 06′ 09′ 11′ 15′ 16 20. Also v.gd dry wines (RIES Amphytrion).

Morcote, Castello di Tic ★★★ Castle ruin and eponymous 14-ha winery, converted to bio by 3rd-generation owner Gaby Gianini. Excellent Riserva 17 18′ 19′ 20′.

Neuchâtel ★→★★★ 606 ha around city and lake on calcareous soil. Slightly sparkling CHASSELAS; exquisite, local PINOT N clone (CORTAILLOD). Best: CH D'AUVERNIER, Dom de Chambleau, Kuntzer, LA MAISON CARRÉE, PORRET, TATASCIORE.

Oeil de perdrix "Partridge's eye": PINOT N rosé, originally from NEU, now elsewhere.

Ottiger, Weinbau Luc ★★→★★★ Subtle PINOT N *Rosenau* proves that Lake Lucerne has a suitable wine-growing climate.

Pircher Zür ★★★→★★★★ Gianmarco Ofner continues work of retired Urs P, esp complex PINOT N Stadtberger Barrique 05′ 06′ 08 10 15′ 16′ 17 18′ 19′ 20′. Having worked in the MOSEL (*see* Germany), Ofner has now planted RIES too.

Porret Neu ★★→★★★★ Leading family estate at CORTAILLOD with Burgundian approach to CHARD, PINOT N (best: Cuvée Elisa).

Provins Val ★→★★★ Co-op with 4000+ members, Switzerland's biggest producer, 1500 ha, 34 varieties. Sound entry-level, gd oak-aged Maître de Chais range, ambitious (even overambitious) red cuvées (Clos Corbassières, Défi Noir).

Riehen, Weingut Bas ★★→★★★★ Boutique winery in eponymous town; Hanspeter Ziereisen (*see* Germany) and merchants Jacqueline and Urs Ullrich collaboration; CHARD, PINOT N of distinction, potential.

Rouvinez Vins Val ★→★★★ A VAL giant at Sierre; after success of cuvées La Trémaille (w) and Le Tourmentin (r), huge takeovers: BONVIN (2009), Imesch (2003), Caves Orsat (1998).

Ruch, Markus Schaff ★★★ Excellent, ultra-rare PINOT N from Hallau (Chölle old vines, Haalde, Buck), Gächlingen (Schlemmweg); 3.5 ha. Also amphora MÜLLER-T and Cidre.

St Jodern Kellerei Val ★★→★★★ VISPERTERMINEN co-op famous for *Heida Veritas* from ungrafted old vines 09′ 10 15 16 17 18′ 21′.

Visperterminen (1000m/3281ft altitude), has desert-like soils: 65% sand. Bad for phylloxera, good for Heida.

St-Saphorin Vd ★→★★★ Neighbour AOC of DÉZALEY, lighter but equally delicate. Best: LEYVRAZ, MONACHON.

San Giorgio, Tenuta Tic ★★★ Fine family estate led by Mike Rudolph, 7 ha. Best: Bx-blend Arco Tondo, MERLOT Crescendo.

Schaffhausen Schaff ★→★★★ A flood of cheap supermarket wines, but also top growers: BAD OSTERFINGEN, BAUMANN, RUCH, Stamm.

Schenk SA Vd ★→★★★ Wine giant with worldwide activities, based in Rolle, founded 1893. Sound wines (esp VD, VAL); substantial exports.

208 |

Schwarzenbach, Hermann Zür ★★★ Family estate on Lake Zürich with historical merit: during building boom of 50s, family held on to vyds instead of selling as building land. A 3rd of vyd devoted to local grape Räuschling. Best: single-vyd Seehalden 07' 09' 10' 15' 17' 18' 19' 20 21'. Many other SPÉCIALITÉS too.

Spécialités / Spezialitäten Quantitatively minor grapes producing some of best Swiss wines, eg. GEWURZ, PINOT GR, Räuschling, or Completer in German Switzerland; Bondola in TIC; Cornalin, Humagne (Bl/N) or JOHANNISBERG, MARSANNE, SYRAH in VAL.

Stucky-Hügin Tic ★★★→★★★★ MERLOT pioneer. Best: Conte di Luna (Merlot/ CAB SAUV), Soma (Merlot/CAB FR), Temenos (Completer/SAUV BL).

Tatasciore, Jacques Neu ★★★ Powerful (and rare) NEU PINOT N.

Ticino ★→★★★★ Italian-speaking. MERLOT (leading grape since 1948) in a taut style. Best: Agriloro, CASTELLO DI MORCOTE, Chiericati, Delea, GIALDI, HUBER, Kopp von der Crone Visini, Pelossi, STUCKY, Tamborini, Valsangiacomo, Vinattieri, ZÜNDEL.

Trécord, Dom de Vd Small family estate at Ollon, glorious Rés de la Famille: lemon cream spiked with herbs.

Tscharner, von ★★★ Family estate at Reichenau Castle; tannin-laden PINOT N named after father Gian-Battista 05 06' 09' 13' 15' 16' 17 18' 19'. New wines less trad in style.

Valais (Wallis) Largest wine canton, in dry, sunny upper Rhône V. Best MARSANNE, SYRAH rival French legends. Many exquisite local varieties.

Vaud (Waadt) On shores of Lake Geneva, place where CHASSELAS gives most complex terroir expression. Many fine family estates, big houses incl Bolle, HAMMEL, Obrist, SCHENK.

Visperterminen Val ★→★★★ Upper VAL vyds, esp for HEIDA. One of highest vyds in Europe (at 1000m/3281ft+; called Riben). Try Chanton, ST JODERN KELLEREI.

Vully, Mont Fri, Vd ★→★★★ AOC on shores of Lake Murten, split between cantons Fribourg (116 ha) and VD (46 ha). Best: Ch de Praz, Chervet, Cru de l'Hôpital, Javet & Javet, Petit Ch.

Yvorne Vd ★★→★★★ CHABLAIS village with vyds on detritus of 1584 avalanche, eg. BADOUX, Ch Maison Blanche, Commune d'Yvorne, Dom de l'Ovaille.

Zündel, Christian Tic ★★★→★★★★ Small bio estate, famous for elegance: MERLOT/ CAB SAUV Orizzonte 16' 17 18' 19'; CHARD Velabona.

Zürich Biggest city and largest wine-growing canton in German Switzerland, 610 ha. Mainly BLAUBURGUNDER. Best: Besson-Strasser, E Meier, Gehring, Lüthi, PIRCHER, SCHWARZENBACH, Staatskellerei, Zahner.

Zürichsee Schwyz, Zür Dynamic AOC uniting vyds of cantons ZÜR and Schwyz on shores of Lake Zürich.

Zur Linde, Weingut Aar ★★★ Photographer Michel Jaussi renovated listed building in Linn; makes dense, round PINOT N.

Zwaa Schaff ★★★ Collaboration: BAUMANN (calcareous, deep soil) and BAD OSTERFINGEN (light, gravelly). PINOT N 09' 13' 15' 16 17 18 19; PINOT BL/CHARD equally long-lasting.

The original appellation?
Trust the Swiss to think of it 1st. "This" being appellation contrôlée – perhaps. Thierry Grosjean, owner of CH D'AUVERNIER in NEU, in compiling a list of all the crises his family has survived since they took over ch and vyd in 1603, discovered that when Switzerland fell under French rule after the French Revolution, and lost many trad markets as a result, the region's wine-growers tried to boost sales by issuing certificates of origin for their wines. Rather a gd idea, as it turned out.

Austria

Abbreviations used in the text:

Burgen	Burgenland
Carn	Carnuntum
Kamp	Kamptal
Krems	Kremstal
Nied	Niederösterreich
Stei	Steiermark
S Stei	Südsteiermark
Therm	Thermenregion
Trais	Traisental
V Stei	Vulkanland Steiermark
Wach	Wachau
Wag	Wagram
Wein	Weinviertel
W Stei	Weststeiermark

This tiny patch of vineyards close to the Alps – less than 1% of the world's total – is producing outstanding quality. Grüner Veltliner is the local star grape, peppery and good at all quality levels; Riesling, more pernickity and rarer, can be brilliantly taut and pure. Pinot Blanc and Chardonnay are catching up fast, as are the reds. Blaufränkisch has grown out of its overoaked phase. The Sekt Österreich regulation (founded 2015) has encouraged more and more good sparklers. Organic wine-growing flourishes: 22%, of which 15% biodynamic. Natural wines are a big thing and are done well: they suit the climate, or vice versa.

Recent vintages

2023 Variable: Stei wet, Burgen dry, Nied ideal, all perfect autumn, v.gd quality.

2022 Hot, dry summer, changeable spring/autumn: v. ripe wines, less acidity.

2021 Changeable summer, ideal autumn: balanced, ripe wines, gd acidity.

2020 Some disease pressure, some hail. Balanced and classic.

2019 Dream vintage boasting both ripeness and freshness.

2018 Heatwave yr: ripe wines; gd and plentiful.

Alzinger Wach ★★★★ 18 19' **20 21'** 22 WACH elegance to the max. Clear-cut, long-lived RIES and GRÜNER V. Iconic 21' Ries Steinertal.

Ambrositsch, Jutta Vienna ★★★ 20 21' 22 23 Delicious field blends. R in cooperation with WACHTER-WIESLER, pét-nat with STRAKA. Great HEURIGE in VIENNA: Buschenschank in Residence open c.8 wkds/yr.

Angerhof-Tschida Burgen ★★★★ 19 21' 22 Hans Tschida in ILLMITZ. Try crystalline TBA, BA (*see* Germany) aromatic grapes like SCHEUREBE. Rare Eiswein 20.

Braunstein, Birgit Burgen ★★★★ 17 18 19' 20' 21' 22 23 Individualistic bio star of Leithaberg: BLAUFRÄNKISCH, CHARD. Try skin-fermented PINOT BL Brigid.

Bründlmayer, Willi Kamp ★★★★ 18 19 20 21' 22 Iconic producer, now organic: GRÜNER V Lamm, RIES, esp Alte Reben, Heiligenstein. Six styles of Sekt. More elegant than ever. Francophile reds.

Burgenland Region bordering Hungary. Warmer than NIED; red BLAUFRÄNKISCH, ZWEIGELT prevalent. Shallow Neusiedlersee, eg. at Rust and in SEEWINKEL, created ideal botrytis conditions, but now endangered by drought.

Carnuntum Nied Region e of VIENNA, accomplished fresh reds, esp ZWEIGELT and cuvées. Look for BLAUFRÄNKISCH from Spitzerberg. Try Artner, Auer, Glatzer, G Markowitsch, Kellerkünstler, Netzl, Taferner.

DAC (Districtus Austriae Controllatus) Mission complete: 18 DAC. Provenance- and quality-based appellation system for regional typicity; 13 have hierarchy inspired by Burgundy – Regional, Ort (village), RIED (cru) – CARN, KAMP, KREMS, Leithaberg, Rosalia, S STEI, Therm, Trais, V STEI, WACH, WAG, WIENER GEMISCHTER SATZ, W STEI. Eisenberg has no village category. RUSTER AUSBRUCH is exclusively sweet. Mittelburgenland, Neusiedlersee, WEIN all divide between Res and Regional.

Diwald, Martin Krems ★★★ 18 19 20 21' 22 Organic from 1976, upward-moving since Martin took over; refined GRÜNER V, rare Frühroter Veltliner.

Domäne Wachau Wach ★★★★ 19' 20 21' 22 World-class co-op. GRÜNER V, RIES Achleiten, Kellerberg a must. Brand-new SMARAGD Ries Brandstatt, Grüner V Kirnberg. Experimental Backstage wines.

Ebner-Ebenauer Wein ★★★★ 18' 19' 20 21' 22 Driving force. Single-vyd GRÜNER V and old-vine PINOT N, ST-LAURENT. Four fine fizzes, some rare.

Edlmoser Vienna ★★★★ 18 19' 20 21 22 Leading winery in S VIENNA. Refined, mineral white, powerful red. Try PINOT BL Ried Himmel at superb HEURIGE.

Erste Lage Single-vyd quality designation of ötw wineries: 109 so far.

Federspiel Wach VINEA WACHAU middle category of ripeness, min 11.5%, max 12.5% abv. Understated, gastronomic wines as age-worthy as SMARAGD.

Feiler-Artinger Burgen ★★★★ 19 20' 21 22 Intuitive bio maker of complex whites, fine-boned reds, stellar RUSTER AUSBRUCH in historic Baroque house in RUST.

Frischengruber, Weingärtnerei Wach ★★★ 18 19 20 21 22' Hero of s bank of Danube with RIES and GRÜNER V Kreuzberg in refined, cool style.

Fritsch, Weinlaubenhof Wag ★★★ 18 19' 20 21' 22 23 Fine-tuned wines in all colours; bio. Try sublime RIES Mordthal; juicy ROTER VELTLINER and elegant GRÜNER V, both Steinberg; PINOT N.

Fritz, Josef Wag ★★★ 19 20 21 22 23 Leading producer of delicate ROTER VELTLINER, sophisticated spiciness, longevity. Try all.

Geyerhof Krems ★★★★ 18 19 20 21' 22 Historic estate. Super-bio credentials since 1988. Wonderful GRÜNER V, RIES, notable entry-level Stockwerk.

Quartet in four parts
All, perhaps, about to come back into fashion: GRÜNER V – now world-famous – was never endangered, but ROTER VELTLINER definitely was. It's super-difficult in the vyd, but its wines, high in extract with refined spiciness, are excellent with food. Then there are THERM's ZIERFANDLER/ROTGIPFLER; 100 yrs ago these were off-dry superstars, but lost their reputation when fashions changed in the 80s and 90s. Today, Therm DAC might help them back to old glory. (Roter V, Rotgipfler, Roter Traminer take their names from their reddish skins when ripe.) NEUBURGER is the fourth: for a long time it was considered a wannabe-Pinot – it's soft, powerful with a subtle hint of almonds.

Grabenwerkstatt Wach ★★★★ 20' 21 22 In cool SPITZER GRABEN; bio. Elegant, exquisite RIES from old vines on steep terraces: Brandstatt, Kalkofen, Trenning.

Grassl, Philipp Carn ★★★★ 18 19 20 21' Regional leader. Impressive ZWEIGELT Schüttenberg, gorgeous PINOT N, ST-LAURENT.

Groiss, Ingrid Wein ★★★ 18 19' 20 21' 22 23 Revives old vyds, specializes in GEMISCHTER SATZ, peppery GRÜNER V. Lovely RIES Auf der Henne.

Huge replanting in years after 1985. Now vines are 30 years+: one reason for quality.

Gut Oggau Burgen ★★★ 17 18 19 20' 21 Mouthwatering wines, eye-catching labels at this bio estate. Most are blends with Pannonian sense of place.

Harkamp S Stei ★★★★ 18' 19 20 21 22 Fascinated by any kind of sparkling; pét-nats too. Among top three in Austria, best in STEI; try all.

Heinrich, Gernot & Heike Burgen ★★★ 17 18 19' 20 21' 22 Made name with BLAUFRÄNKISCH and cuvées; now focus on natural wines of any colour. Try all Freyheit wines and BLAUFRÄNKISCH newbie Out of the Dark.

Herrenhof Lamprecht V Stei ★★★ 19 20 21' 22 Renegade grower in V STEI. Focus on field blends. Adorable FURMINT. Try any from Buchertberg.

Heuriger New wine. **Heurige:** inn; growers serve own wines, local food – integral to Austrian culture. Called Buschenschank outside VIENNA.

Hirsch Kamp ★★★★ 18 19' 20 21' 22' Better every yr; RIES, GRÜNER V from Heiligenstein, Lamm. Pristine new Ries Heiligenstein-Rotfels.

Hirtzberger, Franz Wach ★★★★ 18 19' 20 21' 22 Iconic winery now run by Franz Jnr. Elegance replaces opulence. Single-vyd RIES, GRÜNER V (Honivogl, Singerriedel).

Huber, Markus Trais ★★★ 19 20' 21 22 23 Emblematic of fine-boned TRAIS style from limestone with GRÜNER V, RIES. Citrus brilliance, radiance, slenderness.

Jurtschitsch Kamp ★★★★ 18 19 20 21' 22 German-Austrian couple reinvented successful winery by going bio. Better than ever. Stellar interpretations of RIES Loiserberg, Heiligenstein-Steinwand, GRÜNER V Käferberg. Also fizz, pét-nats.

Kamptal Nied DAC; region with rounder style, lower hills, impressive minerality, precision (gd sp). Top vyds: Heiligenstein, Käferberg, Lamm, Loiserberg, Seeberg. Try Allram, Aichinger, Arndorfer, Hiedler, Rabl, Steininger (for sp).

KMW Klosterneuburger (viticultural research station) Mostwaage (must weight) – Austrian unit of sugar content of juice in grams sugar/1000g must. 1° KMW = 4.86° Oechsle (*see* Germany). 20° Brix = 83° Oe.

Knoll, Emmerich Wach ★★★★ 13 19' 20 21 22 Famous for long-lived wines, esp Vinothekfüllung bottlings. Crystalline pure RIES, GRÜNER V RIED Schütt.

Kopfensteiner Burgen ★★★ 17' 18 19 20 21 In front row of Eisenberg producers; go for graceful BLAUFRÄNKISCH from meagre soils of RIED Saybritz.

Kracher Burgen ★★★★ 10' 13 15' 16 17 18 19 20 21 Brilliant, complex, botrytized: Kollektion, top TBA (*see* Germany). Library releases of sweet 10/15/20/25 yrs later; NV Noble RES, blend of different yrs. Note GRÜNER V under Sohm & Kracher.

Kremstal DAC; top for authentic GRÜNER V, RIES. Try Buchegger, Nigl, Philipp Bründlmayer, Thiery-Weber, Vorspannhof Mayer, Zöller.

Lackner Tinnacher S Stei ★★★★ 18 19' 20 21' 22 23 Precise, mineral SAUV BL, PINOT (w). Try PINOT BL, RIED Eckberg; Sauv Bl, Ried Welles; any from Ried Steinbach, the heart-and-soul vyd here.

Lesehof Stagård Krems ★★★★ 18 19 20 21' 22' 23 Bold, electric RIES from single vyd to experimental Steinzeug; bio. Try RIES Steiner Hund, also GRÜNER V Stein (village wine), ravishing entry-level Urban.R and RIES Handwerk.

Lichtenberger González Burgen ★★★ 18 19 20 21' 22 Spanish-Austrian couple showing best side of Leithaberg (r/w). NEUBURGER Leithaberg DAC, or BLAUFRÄNKISCH Vorderberg.

Loimer, Fred Kamp ★★★★ 17 18 19' 20 21' 22 23 Individualistic bio producer of long standing. Famed for GRÜNER V, RIES, esp single-vyds Seeberg, Steinmassl. Increasingly elegant PINOT N and *lovely sparkling* (NV/Vintage). Try sparkling GROSSE RES Langenlois or Grosse Res Gumpoldskirchen.

Malat Krems ★★★★ 18 19 20 21' 22 Clean-cut, concentrated RIES, GRÜNER V (single-vyds Gottschelle, Silberbichl). Pioneering PINOT N producer. Three top sparklers.

Mantlerhof Krems ★★★ 18 19' 20 21 22 Long-time expertise with ROTER VELTLINER, long-lasting wines from loess soils; bio pioneer. Always worth a visit.

Moric Burgen ★★★★ 15 16 **17** 18 19' 20 21 22 Cult producer, rebellious mastermind of focused, deservedly famed BLAUFRÄNKISCH – worth trying any vintage, any style. Three top cru RIEDS: Kircherg, Maissner, Schwemmer. Working with young Hungarian winemakers: Hidden Treasures.

Muhr, Dorli Carn ★★★★ 17 18 19' 20' 21 Silky, fine-boned BLAUFRÄNKISCH. PR-cum-winemaker revived limestone slopes of SPITZERBERG; 20 unparalleled elegance.

Müller Klöch V Stei ★★★ 19 20' 21' 22 23 Proof that trad GEWÜRZ from Klöch doesn't need residual sugar. Try Gelber Traminer RIED Seindl, Gewürz Ried Hochwarth.

Neumayer ★★★★ 18 19' 20 21' 22 23 Doyen in limestone-dominated Trais. Started from scratch with PINOT BL in 86. Still top with precise, crystalline GRÜNER V (Zwirch), RIES (Rothenbart).

Neumeister V Stei ★★★★ 18 19' 20 21' 22' World-class address for outstanding SAUV BL and Pinots. Try Sauv Bl ALTE REBEN, MORILLON Moarfeitl, PINOT BL Klausen. Notable PINOT GR, PINOT N.

Niederösterreich (Lower Austria) Region incl 60.5% of country's vyds. Danube area in w (KAMP, KREM, TRAIS, WACH, WAG), WEIN (ne) and CARN, THERM (e, s).

Nikolaihof Wach ★★★★ 13 15 **17** 19' 20 21' 22 One of world's 1st bio wine estates. Exemplary, pure, textured GRÜNER V, Ries; look for late-release Vinothek series.

Nittnaus, Anita & Hans Burgen ★★★★ 18 19 20' **21'** 22 Mastermind behind Pannobile and Leithaberg; bio pioneers. Famous Commondor (r blend). Try precise single-vyd CHARD Bergschmallister, Freudshofer; BLAUFRÄNKISCH Jungenberg, Lange Ohn. Next generation doing own alternative thing in family winery: Manila.

Ott, Bernhard Wag ★★★★ 18 19' 20 21' 22 23 Iconic bio producer: salty, savoury GRÜNER V of increasingly fine-boned elegance, esp RIED Rosenberg, Spiegel, Stein vyds. Fass 4 is cult.

ÖTW (Österreichische Traditionsweingüter) Carn, Kamp, Krems, Therm, Trais, Vienna, Wag Association of 77 top growers in seven areas. Prominent emblem on bottles. *See* ERSTE LAGE.

Pichler, FX Wach ★★★★ 15 18 19' 20 21' 22 Legendary estate, long-lived GRÜNER V, RIES; top WACH sites. Most recent top vintage 21. Has left VINEA WACHAU.

Pichler, Rudi Wach ★★★★ 17 19' 20 21' 22 Next generation in charge. Magnificent RIES from crus Hochrain, Kirchweg; GRÜNER V from Achleiten, Hochrain.

Pichler-Krutzler Wach ★★★★ 18 **19** 20 21 22' Energetic, thrilling single-vyd RIES Kellerberg and Loibenberg. GRÜNER V outstanding: esp In der Wand, Pfaffenberg Alte Reben. Organic (2022).

Pittnauer, Gerhard & Brigitte Burgen ★★★★ **19** 20' 21' 22' Renowned for gracefully ageing BLAUFRÄNKISCH, PINOT N, ST-LAURENT. Serious skin-fermented wines, fresh pét-nats. Perfect Day, Red Pitt, Rosé Dogma... try all, expect the unexpected.

Wein aus Österreich

As everywhere, rules don't suit everybody. Austrian wine rules were introduced after 1985, current law dates from 2009, and for the refuseniks there is Wein aus Österreich: lowest category in hierarchy, intended for v. simplest, cheapest wines, and (as everywhere) being co-opted for natural wines or anything that doesn't fit the rules. Try GUT OGGAU, Hartmut Aubell, PREISINGER, SCHNABEL, TSCHIDA, ZILLINGER.

Prager Wach ★★★★ 18 19′ 20 21′ 22 Toni Bodenstein, philosopher/winemaker, involving son Martin step by step. Family passion RIES: 60% of all vyds. Also spellbinding GRÜNER V Stockkultur.

Preisinger, Claus Burgen ★★★★ 19′ 20′ 21′ 22′ Highly experimental bio winemaker, offering classic reds BLAUFRÄNKISCH, PINOT N, ZWEIGELT and whites PINOT BL, GRÜNER V, also crown-capped fizzy Puszta Libre (r). Try Sweden + BURGEN in a glass – rhubarb juice and red wine Fruktinger.

Prieler Burgen ★★★★ 18 19′ 20′ 21′ 22′ Tightly textured BLAUFRÄNKISCH, needs bottle-age, esp Goldberg and Marienthal; master of compelling age-worthy, profound PINOT BL from Leithaberg, eg. Alte Reben, Steinweingarten.

Proidl Krems ★★★ 18 19 20 21′ 22 Reliably brilliant GRÜNER V, RIES, both from Ehrenfels vyd. Even better since son Patrick joined. Try library Ries releases.

Reserve (Res) Must have min 13% abv plus longer ageing period in winery.

Ried Cru. Compulsory term for single-vyd bottlings since 2016. *See* riedenkarten.at.

Ruster Ausbruch DAC; botrytized sweet wines (TBA class, *see* Germany); 1st mentioned 1634. Produced exclusively in Baroque town Rust, BURGEN. Best: FEILER-ARTINGER, SCHRÖCK, TRIEBAUMER, WENZEL.

Sabathi, Erwin S Stei ★★★★ 17′ 18′ 19 20 21′ 22 Best known for elegant, profound, age-worthy MORILLON, SAUV BL.

Sabathi, Hannes S Stei ★★★★ 18 19 20 21′ 22′ 23 Leading estate, esp single-vyd SAUV BL Kranachberg. Revived vyds in Graz under Falter Ego label.

Salomon-Undhof Krems ★★★★ 18 19 20 21′ 22 23 Consistently showing best of Krems; elegant, lean GRÜNER V, RIES, single-vyds Kögl, Pfaffenberg, Wachtberg.

Sattlerhof S Stei ★★★★ 18 19′ 20′ 21′ 22 Wonderful under father Willi, effortlessly brilliant since bio under sons Alex, Andy. Top crus Kranachberg, Sernauberg, monopole Pfarrweingarten. Try all, also standout village DAC SAUV BL Gamlitz.

Sausal S Stei Subregion of schist and limestone; vyds up to 600m (1969ft). Small enclave, extraordinarily elegant RIES, SAUV BL, also BLAUFRÄNKISCH, PINOT N.

Schauer S Stei ★★★ 18 19 20 21′ 22 Light-bodied but consistently profound whites from schisty SAUSAL: RIES, SAUV BL, esp notable PINOT BL Höchtemmel.

Schloss Gobelsburg Kamp ★★★★ 18 19′ 20 21′ 22 Cistercian-founded estate, run by Michael Moosbrugger, ÖTW boss and classification mastermind; exquisite GRÜNER V, RIES worth ageing. Tradition series and single-vyds Gaisberg, Grub, Heiligenstein, Lamm, Renner. Fine sparkling. Also elegant PINOT N, ZWEIGELT.

Schnabel - Ermihof S Stei ★★★ 18′ 19 20 21′ 22 Beautifully stubborn producer in SAUSAL; natural wines (r/w) that age gracefully. Try fine-boned BLAUFRÄNKISCH, elegant PINOT N, crus Hochegg, Koregg, Kreuzegg.

Schröck, Heidi Burgen ★★★★ 18 19 20 21 22 Doyenne of RUSTER AUSBRUCH on dry-wine mission. Note dry FURMINT. Working with twin sons Georg and Johannes.

Schuster, Rosi Burgen ★★★★ 18 19′ 20 21 22′ Formerly famous for bold reds, now all about purity. Son Hannes introduced more elegance, focus on FURMINT, BLAUFRÄNKISCH, ST-LAURENT. Try ravishing Aus den Dörfern (r/w) and Dorfkultur (r/w); any Blaufränkisch or St-Laurent.

Seewinkel Burgen Region e of Neusiedlersee; was ideal for botrytis, but now drier every yr. Small salt lakes almost dry, can be refilled by winter rain (eg. 2023/24).

Sekt Austria PDO for best sparkling. Entry level, 9 mths on lees; RES, 18 mths on lees; Grosse Res, 36 mths on lees (trad mandatory for both Res).

Sepp Moser *See* VITIKULTUR MOSER.

Smaragd Wach Ripest category of VINEA WACHAU, min 12.5% abv but can exceed 14%; dry, potent, age-worthy. In past, often botrytis-influenced but dry.

Spitzerberg Carn Sub-appellation; limestone and schist, renowned for fine-grained, profound BLAUFRÄNKISCH.

Spitzer Graben Wach Cool side valley nr Spitz. Steepest terraces, v. dry, meagre soils give excellent NEUBURGER, RIES. Interesting, off-beaten-track wineries: GRABENWERKSTATT, Martin Muthenthaler, VEYDER-MALBERG.

Stadlmann Therm ★★★★ 18 19' 20 21' 22 Exemplary, clear-cut ZIERFANDLER/ROTGIPFLER, esp single-vyds Mandelhöh, Tagelsteiner. Subtle, poetic PINOTS BL/N.

Steiermark (Styria) Most s region; aromatic, expressive dry whites, esp SAUV BL and Pinots. *See* S STEI, V STEI, W STEI.

Steinfeder Wach Lightest VINEA WACHAU category for dry wines, max 11.5% abv. Difficult to produce in warming conditions, barely exported.

Stift Göttweig ★★★ 18 19' 20 21' 22 Prominent hilltop Benedictine abbey surrounded by vyds; crystalline GRÜNER V Gottschelle, RIES Pfaffenberg.

Straka, Thomas Burgen ★★★ 18 19' 20' 21' 22' Reinvented whites in S BURGEN by experiments with WELSCHRIESLING. Try all (w).

Südsteiermark DAC; region close to Slovenian border, famed for elegant, v. aromatic MORILLON, MUSKATELLER, SAUV BL from breathtakingly steep slopes. Try Ewald Zweytick, Jaunegg, Landesweingut Silberberg (wine-grower's school), Primus am Grassnitzberg, Tamara Kögl, Warga-Hack.

Tement S Stei ★★★★ 12 13 18' 19 20' 21' 22 Incredible subtlety, age-worthiness, esp MORILLON, SAUV BL. Top sites: Grassnitzberg, Zieregg. Try Zieregg RES Sauv Bl, top yrs only. Now run by brothers Armin and Stefan T.

Thermenregion Nied DAC (with vintage 2023). Spa region s of VIENNA. Home to rare ROTGIPFLER, ZIERFANDLER; historic PINOT N and ST LAURENT hotspot. Many styles; try Alphart, Alphart am Mühlbach, Gebeshuber.

Tinhof, Erwin Burgen ★★★ 12 18 19' 20 21 22' 23 Below-the-radar but exquisite bio Leithaberg estate. Specialist for PINOT BL, NEUBURGER, esp RIED Golden Erd – vintages back to 12. Try ST-LAURENT Feiersteig and village Eisenstadt.

Trapl, Johannes Carn ★★★ 18 19' 20' 21' 22 Renegade wunderkind with expressive, site-specific reds. Floral BLAUFRÄNKISCH (SPITZERBERG), PINOT-esque ZWEIGELT.

Triebaumer, Ernst Burgen ★★★★ 13 18 19' 20 21 22 Iconic RUST producer, now next generation; bio. Try BLAUFRÄNKISCH legend Mariental, also as late release (from 13), and then all the rest.

Tschida, Christian Burgen ★★★★ 18 19' 20' 21' 22' No interest in compromise, min intervention. Cult in natural-wine circles. Notable range Himmel auf Erden, elegant, subtle, but don't expect continuity in names or styles. Try any.

Umathum, Josef Burgen ★★★★ 13 18 19' 20' 21' 22 Originally famous for reds, ZWEIGELT and ST-LAURENT, today bio legend, all colours. Exceptionally elegant reds, revived rare Lindblättrige grape. Try Austria's best Zweigelt: single-vyd Hallebühl, also BLAUFRÄNKISCH Kirschgarten, Cuvée Rosa rosé.

Velich ★★★★ Legend CHARDS Darscho, Tiglat. Less oaked than past. Try any vintage.

Veyder-Malberg Wach ★★★ 18 19' 20 21' 22' Terroir fanatic, old vines up to 70 yrs, steep terraces in SPITZER GRABEN; vyds elsewhere in WACH. Try GRÜNER V, RIES.

Vienna (Wien) 133 wineries, 582 ha vyds within city borders – not bad at all. Wine ancient trad, badly reputed at times, but recently reignited focus on quality. Local field blend enshrined as WIENER GEMISCHTER SATZ DAC (2013). *Heurigen among vines; visit a must.* Recommended: Christ, Fuchs-Steinklammer, Rotes Haus. Best crus: Bisamberg, Maurerberg, Nußberg.

Take public transport to Vienna's vineyards: bus 38A, or tram D or tram 43.

Vinea Wachau Wach Pioneering quality growers' association. Ripeness scale for dry wine: FEDERSPIEL, SMARAGD and STEINFEDER. Exists parallel to official WACH DAC. Some growers leaving: climate change makes VW styles difficult.

Vitikultur Moser Krems ★★★★ 18 19' 20' 21' 22 New name of Sepp Moser. Growers since 1848, family ties with Lenz Moser. Run by Nikolaus M, early bio adopter, plus next generation. Exemplary GRÜNER V, also RIES, long-lived CHARD.

Vulkanland Steiermark DAC; was famous for GEWÜRZ from Klöch. Now renowned for MORILLON, Pinots, SAUV BL. Best: Frauwallner, Krispel, Ploder-Rosenberg, Scharl, Winkler-Hermaden.

Wachau Nied DAC. Danube region of world repute for age-worthy GRÜNER V, RIES. Parallel to VINEA WACHAU (STEINFEDER/FEDERSPIEL/SMARAGD). Try Högl, Johann Donabaum, Macherndl, Muthenthaler, Tegernseerhof. Note newcomers: PAX, Wabi-Sabi, WEINGÄRTNEREI FRISCHENGRUBER.

Fancy staying with a top grower? Many offer rooms, cottages, apartments.

Wachter-Wiesler, Weingut Burgen ★★★ 18 19 20' 21' 22 Fine-boned, elegant, silky BLAUFRÄNKISCH with a twist, from iron clay and green schist of Eisenberg DAC. Great ageing potential. Also entry-level Handgemenge (r/w/rosé).

Wagram Nied DAC (based on GRÜNER V, RIES, ROTER VELTLINER). Region w of VIENNA. Deep loess ideal for spicy Grüner V. Best: FRITSCH, JOSEF FRITZ, Leth, Nimmervoll, OTT.

Weingut Stadt Krems Krems ★★★ 17 18 19' 20 21' 22 Brilliant municipal estate, 31 ha within city limits. GRÜNER V, RIES slightly riper, rounder than WACH, crystalline, expressive at top level; gd single vyds, value entry-level.

Weinviertel DAC ("Wine Quarter") Largest region, GRÜNER V in classic, RES, Grosse RES versions. Region once slaked VIENNA's thirst, now quality counts. Base wine for Viennese Sekt houses like Schlumberger, home of excellent fizz by EBNER-EBENAUER and ZUSCHMANN-SCHÖFMANN. For still, try Christoph Bauer, Dürnberg, Faber-Köchl, Fidesser, Gruber-Röschitz, Gut Hardegg, Neustifter, Obenaus, Rücker, Schödl Family, Uibl.

Wellanschitz Burgen ★★★ 18 19' 20 21 22 23 Family winery with excellent, profound, complex BLAUFRÄNKISCH from mica schist. Try Blaufränkisch Sonnensteig. Also unconventional, complex wines by son Stefan: Kolfok.

Weninger, Franz Burgen ★★★★ 18 19' 20 21' 22 Brooding hand-harvester; expressive and seductive terroir wines. Outstanding BLAUFRÄNKISCH, single-vyds Hochäcker, Kirchholz. Brilliant FURMINT.

Wenzel, Michael ★★★★ 18 19 20 21' 22' Quiet man, speaks loudly through excellent natural wines in white, red and sometimes also sweet. A lot of shades of FURMINT. Try all.

Weststeiermark DAC; super-crisp rosé Schilcher from Blauer Wildbacher grape (r), grown on 527 ha of total 658 ha. Different styles: trad rosé, rare sweet, modernist sparkling, natural and orange. Try natural-wines expert Franz Strohmeier, Langmann vulgo Lex.

Wiener Gemischter Satz Vienna DAC. Revived historic co-planted/fermented field blends of white grapes in VIENNA. Complex. Try Christ, Fuhrgassl-Huber, Hajszan-Neumann, Mayer am Pfarrplatz. Called Gemischter Satz or Mischsatz outside Vienna: try GROISS.

Wieninger, Fritz Vienna ★★★★ 18 19' 20 21' 22 23 Mastermind behind VIENNA's quality renaissance; bio from the bottom of his heart. Exemplary WIENER GEMISCHTER SATZ Nussberg, Rosengartl. Great PINOT N. Also experimental winery Hajszan-Neumann in Grinzing.

Wohlmuth S Stei ★★★★ 18 19 20 21 22' Towering winery, 200-yr trad. Subtle, dazzling CHARD, RIES, SAUV BL, esp from single-vyds Edelschuh, Gola, Hochsteinriegl; gd reds. Recultivating RIES in steepest terraces.

Zillinger, Herbert Wein ★★★★ 18 19 20 21' 22' 23 Splendid, complex GRÜNER V; bio. Try Kalkvogel, Hirschenreyn.

Zuschmann-Schöfmann ★★★ 18 19' 20 21' 22 23 Couple with focus on excellent trad-method sparkling. Entry-level GRÜNER V SEKT AUSTRIA of exceptional quality. Also RIES Grosse Res Ralessen, Rosé Brut Res.

England

English wine is changing again – just when you hadn't quite caught up with the last changes. Fizz still rules, but the lure of Essex's warm Crouch Valley is strong for still wines. There are some noteworthy Pinots from Essex and good rosés from everywhere; Chardonnays too. For fizz, be discriminating. The biggest producers, and the cheapest, aren't necessarily the best; and the super-expensive ones are not twice as good as the next tier down. Abbreviations: Buckinghamshire (Bucks), Cornwall (Corn), East/West Sussex (E/W Sx), Essex (Esx), Hampshire (Hants), Herefordshire (Her), Oxfordshire (Oxon), Wiltshire (Wt).

All Angels Berks Classic shortbread notes with plenty of acidity, gd. Subtle rosé too.

Ambriel W Sx Small, ambitious, delicacy and depth. Cloud Ten is tops.

Balfour Kent ★★ Rosé is gd flagship; much focus on still, done well.

Blackbook Urban winery, bought-in grapes, vinified in S London; min intervention, small lots.

Black Chalk Hants ★★ Taut, pure, but released a bit too young now.

Breaky Bottom E Sx ★★★★ Fabulous wines, tiny vyd, eccentric owner. Richness and tension, layered flavours.

Bride Valley Dorset ★★ New local owners. Wine focused on fruit, not lees character.

Camel Valley Corn ★★ ⋯★★★ Flavoursome wines; vivid, vibrant.

Candover Brook Hants Fresh, citrus, rather gd. Delicate rosé. Made at Hambledon.

Chapel Down Kent Much improved; younger wines cleaner, fresher. ★★ Kit's Coty (still/sp).

Coates & Seely Hants ★★★★ As gd as ever. Lovely Blanc de Blancs. All detailed, precise.

Cottonworth Hants Length and depth gd here. Best: Classic Cuvée.

Court Garden E Sx Family-owned, on the Downs. Rich, elegant style.

Danbury Ridge Esx ★★★ Exemplary still CHARD, PINOT N of depth, elegance, from warm Crouch V. Octagon is bigger, richer.

Denbies Surrey Large, commercial. Marked toastiness in fizz. Still wines light.

Digby Hants, Kent, W Sx ★★★ New Blanc de Blancs a joy: yellow fruits, saline. Everything v.gd, actually. Visit tasting room in Arundel.

Everflyht E Sx Vines v. young, so wines lack depth, but promising.

Exton Park Hants ★★★ RB (Res Blend) wines put this in top tier. Grace, depth, tension; high acidity, so needs age of res wines.

Folc ★★ Floral, smoky, well-made pink: probably UK's best.

Grange, The Hants ★★★ Still quite new, but doing everything well. Classic lemon shortbread flavours.

Branching out

Roots in Champagne, head in the air: that's English wine now. Those classic sparklings are now establishment, and all sorts of other things are going on in small vyds and urban wineries – and in the corners of those establishment establishments. Try pét-nats whenever you see them, and if you spot Bonkers Zombie Robot Alien Monsters from the Future Ate My Brain Sur Lie, try it: it's from Dermot Sugrue and is possibly the longest English wine name to date. Others to watch: Blackdown Ridge (W Sx), Busi Jacobsohn (Sx fizz, a bit Marmite), Cary Wine Estate (Kent), Castle Brook (gd fizz made at RIDGEVIEW), Coolhurst (fizz, W Sx), Higham (Suffolk), Itasca (contract winemaker), London Cru (urban winery), The Secret Vyd.

Gusbourne Kent, W Sx ★★★★ 51°N is tops and super-pricey, but single-vyd fizz nearly as gd and half the price. Beautiful.

Hambledon Vineyard Hants ★★★ New owners Berry Bros and Symington Group (*see* Portugal) should give firm footing. Superb rich, saline Première Cuvée.

Harrow & Hope Bucks ★★ Well made, classic, v. pleasing. Rich, deep Blanc de Noirs.

Good vermouth now, often from, ahem, not the top wine producers. Properly bitter.

Hart of Gold Her ★★ Made at RIDGEVIEW; lemony, biscuity; attractive. Also vyds in Maury (*see* France): The Dom of the Bee.

Hattingley Valley Hants ★★★ Baked apple and brioche, crisp and taut, always impeccably made.

Henners E Sx ★★ Nice biscuity, reliable Brut and cherry-spice Rosé. Always elegant, delicate, structured.

Herbert Hall Kent ★★→★★★ Precision, tension, ripeness; v.gd limited-edition Kirsty's Blanc de Blancs.

Highweald W Sx Lovely poise and layered complexity; toasty Rosé; gd weight. From Sx High Weald clay and greensand.

Hoffmann & Rathbone E Sx ★★ Firm, well-made wines from bought-in fruit.

Hugo, Dom Wt Natural, bio, stylish, characterful, tense, fiercely saline fizz.

Hundred Hills Oxon ★★★ Young, ambitious. Tense, saline wines from chalky slopes, umpteen different cuvées.

Langham Wine Estate Dorset ★★ Corallian has lovely lemon-blossom flavours; Culver is rich, poised. Pretty Rosé.

Leckford Estate Hants Waitrose's own estate, vinified by RIDGEVIEW. Nicely mature, gd fruit, straightforward.

Litmus Based at DENBIES but separate. Tiny parcels, experimental, v. often excellent.

Nyetimber W Sx ★★★★ Standard v. high across board, with 1086 for luxury market. Tillington fine, detailed. Wines of substance, finesse.

Plumpton College E Sx ★★ UK's only wine college; attractive wines, well made (as they should be).

Pommery England Hants Own grapes now being used; nicely elegant wine, a step up from Pommery Champagne (*see* France).

Raimes Hants Tense, fresh style; gd fruit. Made at HATTINGLEY V.

Rathfinny E Sx ★★★ Chalk in excelsis: tight, taut, precise, needs age. Big operation, gd tourism.

Ridgeview E Sx ★★ Weighty wines, chunkier than most English fizz now. Big range.

Riverview Esx Crouch V ripeness in still CHARD, PINOT N, plus elegance.

Roebuck W Sx ★★ Weight and richness gd – opulent Blanc de Noirs – complex and focused.

Simpsons Kent ★★ Fond of oak flavours; try with food. Also gd still wines.

Squerryes Kent Rich, autolytic character, ripe and focused. Vintage Brut weighty.

Sugrue South Downs E Sx ★★★★ Dermot S has more vyds now and endless energy. Enormous depth, complexity, tension. Plus gin made from PINOT M.

Trotton W Sx Spectacular Sparkling (that's the brand, not a description) elegant, fine, well made; gd still BACCHUS/PINOT GR.

Vagabond ★★ Urban winery in S London using bought-in grapes. Min intervention, skilful, v.gd.

Westwell Kent ★★★ Pure, taut and fine Pelegrim fizz; still wines adventurous, fairly light.

Wiston W Sx ★★★★ Perfect elegance. Steely, tense style that repays bottle-age. Look out for tiny amounts of still.

Wyfold Oxon ★★ Nicely elegant wines from Laithwaite-owned vyd. Same family has Windsor Great Park Vyd, from – well, yes.

Central & Southeast Europe

More heavily shaded areas are the wine-growing regions.

Abbreviations used in the text:

Bal	Balaton	N/S Pann	North/South Pannonia
Cri & Mar	Crişana & Maramureş	Pod	Podravje
Cro Up	Croatian Uplands	Pos	Posavje
Dalm	Dalmatia	Prim	Primorje
Dan P	Danubian Plain	Sl & CD	Slavonia & Croatian Danube
Dob	Dobrogea	Thr L	Thracian Lowlands
Is & Kv	Istria & Kvarner	Tok	Tokaj
Mold	Moldovan Hills	Trnsyl	Transylvania
Mun	Muntenia & Oltenia Hills	U Hun	Upper Hungary

HUNGARY

Central Europe's most important wine country, all about fresher elegant reds based on local Kékfrankos, Kadarka, rescued rare red Csókaszőlő and more. Local white favourite Olaszrizling, whose homeland is the inland sea of Lake Balaton, is finding new favour, offering much more than spritzers. Hungary has two-thirds volcanic bedrock: look for freshness and vibrancy.

Ancient Mangalica pigs, curly coats, nearly went extinct – the original sheep-pig.

Aszú Tok Noble rot, extreme shrivelling define Aszú berries – always picked one by one. Resulting sweet wine maybe world's best thanks to balance of sweetness and vibrant acidity, incredibly long-lived too. Most label as 5-PUTTONYOS (min 120g/l sugar) or sweeter, richer 6-Puttonyos (min 150g/l sugar, often higher).

Balassa Tok ★★★ Small personal winery for fine dry FURMINT, esp Szent Tamás, plus gorgeous Villő Aszú, lovely SZAMORODNI; v.gd Ikrek (sp) jointly with GIZELLA.

Balaton Dynamic region around Hungary's inland sea; n shore is volcanic, suiting Hungarian favourite OLASZRIZLING, plus new plantings of old varieties KÉKNYELŰ, FURMINT. RIES and elegant CAB FR, KÉKFRANKOS, MERLOT. Around Badacsony and Szent György-hegy: 2HA, Borbély, Földi Bálint, Folly Arboretum, Gilvesy, Laposa, Sabar, Szászi, Szeremley, ValiBor, Villa Sandahl, Ujvári. Balatonfüred-Csopak n of lake: Dobosi, Figula, Homola, Jasdi, Liszkay, St Donát, organic Zelna. Bal Uplands: somló and Zala, try Bussay, Pálffy. Balatonboglár on s shore (riper): Budjosó, GARAMVÁRI, Ikon, Kislaki, KONYÁRI, bio Kristinus, Légli, TÖRLEY.

Barta Tok ★★★→★★★★ Highest vyd in region, plus beautifully renovated Rákóczi mansion. Vivien Ujvári crafts super-elegant wines, esp Öreg Király FURMINT, HÁRSLEVELŰ and fun entry-point Egy-Kis. Glorious SZAMORODNI, superb ASZÚ.

Béres Tok ★★→★★★ Beautiful estate; family created popular remedy, Béres drops. Rich ASZÚ, gd dry, esp Diókút HÁRSLEVELŰ, Lőcse FURMINT. Pleasant new fizz.

Bikavér ★→★★★ "Bull's Blood". PDO in EGER and SZEKSZÁRD, unique bottles – best are some of Hungary's top reds. Oak-aged, based on KÉKFRANKOS, min four varieties. Szekszárd requires min 5% KADARKA: Eszterbauer, HEIMANN, Markvart, Meszáros, Schieber, Sebestyén, Szeleshát, TAKLER, Tüske, Vesztergombi, VIDA. Eger: Superior, Grand Superior for restricted yield, longer ageing. Best Egri Bikavér: BOLYKI, Bukolyi Marcell, Csutorás, GÁL TIBOR, Grof Buttler, KOVÁCS NIMRÓD, ST ANDREA, Tóth Ferenc, Thummerer.

Bock, József S Pann ★★→★★★★ Bold VILLÁNY reds: Bock Libra, Capella, selection wines.

Bolyki N Hun ★★ Dramatic winery in a quarry in EGER, great labels, appealing juiciness: v.gd Egri Csillag, Meta Tema, rosé and BIKAVÉR.

Csányi S Pann ★→★★ Largest winery in VILLÁNY. Much-improved entry-level varietals, plus premium Ch Teleki, serious, structured Kővilla.

Danube (Duna) Duna Largest region on Great Plain, lighter wines. Three districts: Csongrád, Hajós-Baja (Koch), Kunság (Frittmann, Font, Gedeon, Szentpéteri). New PDOs Monor, Soltvadkert.

Degenfeld, Gróf Tok ★★→★★★ Stunning castle hotel, organic vyds. Try Terézia HÁRSLEVELŰ, Zomborka FURMINT, excellent barrel-select ASZÚ.

Demeter, Zoltán Tok ★★★★ Legendary winemaker with passion for old vines, excellent vyd selections. Pioneer of PEZSGŐ (sp) in TOK and one of best. Fine Anett and Eszter SZAMORODNIS, superb ASZÚ.

Dereszla, Ch Tok ★★→★★★ Consistent gd-value producer for dry FURMINT, ASZÚ, reliable PEZSGŐ. Excellent bistro. Also try flor-aged dry SZAMORODNI Experience.

Disznókő Tok ★★★★ Dramatic estate with gd restaurant. Superb, silken sweets that keep beautifully – one of v. few to make ASZÚ every yr. Wonderful *Kapi* cru in top yrs; v.gd 1413 SZAMORODNI. Consistent dry wines: new Szamorodni Száraz 2018.

Dobogó Tok ★★★ Superb family winery. Benchmark ASZÚ 6-PUTTONYOS and late-harvest *Mylitta*, excellent long-lived; dry FURMINT, esp Úrágya vyd selection.

Dűlő Named single vyd or cru. Increasing emphasis on vyd selections of FURMINT for dry and sweet. Top *dűlő* in TOKAJ incl Betsek, Bomboly, Király, Mézes-Mály, Nyúlászó, Szent Tamás, Úrágya, Urbán.

Eger N Hun The s-facing slopes of Bükk Mtns, for cooler-climate reds, esp BIKAVÉR, KÉKFRANKOS, PINOT N, SYRAH and fragrant fresh whites. Egri Csillag, "Star of Eger" (dr w Carpathian-grape blend). Try Bukolyi, Csutorás, Gróf Buttler, Kaló Imre (natural), Petrény, Thummerer, Tóth Ferenc.

Essencia / Eszencia Tok Rare, pricey, free-run trickle of syrup from ASZÚ grapes, min 450g/l residual sugar, barely ferments. Reputed to raise the dead.

Etyek-Buda N Pann Rolling limestone hills, increasing emphasis on gd fizz, plus expressive, crisp white (esp SAUV BL), decent PINOT N. Top: ETYEKI KÚRIA, HARASZTHY, Hernyák, Kertész, Nyakas, Rókusfalvy, TÖRLEY Sparkling Cellar.

Etyeki Kúria N Pann ★★ Top ETYEK-BUDA winery, noted for SAUV BL, elegant reds (esp Red, PINOT N). Winemaker Meresz Sandor also has natural project; try *Zenit*.

Figula Bal ★★→★★★ Family winery in BAL, v.gd selections of OLASZRIZLING, esp Sáfránkert, Száka. Excellent blends: Köves, Szilénusz.

Gál Tibor N Hun ★★ Appealing Egri Csillag, fine KADARKA, gd vyd BIKAVÉR.

Garamvári Bal ★★ Leading PEZSGŐ specialist, esp FURMINT Brut, Evolution Rosé; gd Garamvári varietals; top is Sinai-hegy CAB FR. Lellei label for great-value varietals.

Gere, Attila S Pann ★★★→★★★★ Standard-setting family winery in VILLÁNY: Attila Cuvée, Kopar Cuvée, *Solus Merlot*, Villányi Fr (CAB FR). Also gd varietals plus rare historic Fekete-Járdovány.

Gizella Tok ★★★→★★★★ Small, impeccable range; tiny family estate worked by horse. Delicious dry cuvée, superb SZAMORODNI, glorious ASZÚ.

Grand Tokaj Tok ★→★★ Largest winery in TOK. Best wines under Grand Tokaj label guided by highly regarded Karoly Áts. Late-harvest Arany Késői is appealing, stylish dry FURMINT Kővágó, v.gd ASZÚ.

Haraszthy N Hun ★★ Beautiful ETYEK-BUDA estate for expressive SAUV BL, aromatic Sir Irsai (w/rosé), complex The Champ (sp).

Heimann S Pann ★★→★★★ Family winery in SZEKSZÁRD, intense Alte Reben (old-vine) KÉKFRANKOS, Barbár, Franciscus. Next-generation Heimann & Fiai offshoot, local grapes, natural fermentation (vyd selections Kekfrankos, KADARKA).

Hétszőlő Tok ★★★ Historic cellar and organic vyd on TOKAJ Hill itself. Try elegant Kis-Garai FURMINT, fine ASZÚ.

Heumann S Pann ★★★ German/Swiss-owned estate in Siklós part of VILLÁNY making great *Kékfrankos Res*, CAB FR La Trinitá, delicious rosé, classy SYRAH.

Hilltop Winery N Pann ★★ In Neszmély. Reliable well-made, gd-value varietals; gd Kamocsay Premium range (CHARD, Ihlet Cuvée).

Holdvölgy Tok ★★→★★★ Super-modern winery in MÁD, TOK's youngest winemaker. Complex, dry Vision, Expression, plus v.gd Eloquence SZAMORODNI.

Juliet Victor Tok ★★★ Ambitious investment by founder of Wizz Air. Excellent vyd FURMINTS (notable *Bomboly, Király*), superb rich SZAMORODNI, ASZÚ.

Kikelet ★★★ Lovely, ageable HÁRSLEVELŰ and elegant FURMINT vyd selections from a tiny family cellar owned by French winemaker and her Hungarian husband.

Királyudvar Tok ★★★ Pioneering private winery in old royal cellars at Tarcal, bio. Top: FURMINT Sec, Henye PEZSGŐ, Cuvée Ilona (late-harvest), flagship Lapis ASZÚ.

Konyári Bal ★★→★★★ Pioneering estate s of lake, son of founder in charge. Try Loliense (r/w), Jánoshegy KÉKFRANKOS, MERLOT Sessio, age-worthy Páva.

Kovács Nimród Winery N Hun ★★→★★★ In heart of EGER. Try Battonage CHARD, Sky FURMINT, Rhapsody BIKAVÉR, Blues KÉKFRANKOS, 777 PINOT N, NJK.

Kreinbacher Bal ★★→★★★ Leading producer of PEZSGŐ, based in SOMLÓ, always FURMINT in blend; v.gd Classic Brut, superb *Prestige Brut*. Also gd still: Öreg Tokék, Selection Furmint, HÁRSLEVELŰ.

Mád Tok Historic village surrounded by top vyds, with protected origin/quality scheme. Leading: Árvay, Áts (family project of Karoly Áts, also of GRAND TOKAJ), BARTA, Budaházy, Demetervin (Mád FURMINT, Úrágya DŰLŐ), HOLDVÖLGY, JULIET VICTOR, Lenkey (unique, long-aged, complex), Mád Hill, Orosz Gabor, Pelle (Szent Tamas Furmint, PEZSGŐ), ROYAL TOKAJI, SZEPSY, TOKAJI Classic.

Mad Wine Tok ★★ Sizeable winery in MÁD (with bistro) selling under Mád label. New Mád Moser FURMINT MM5 and MM55, jointly with Lenz Moser (Austria).

Malatinszky S Pann ★★★ Organic VILLÁNY cellar. Barrel-fermented Maghari impresses, plus long-lived Kúria CAB FR, v.gd Rozé.

Mátra N Hun ★→★★ Overlooked volcanic region for lively whites, gd rosé, elegant reds. Try Balint, Benedek (gd PINOT N, KÉKFRANKOS), Centurio (esp Diós, Liberty), Gábor Karner, NAG (try Föld és Ég range), Nagygombos (rosé), Sol Montis.

Mór N Pann Small region, fiery local Ezerjó; CHARD, OLASZRIZLING; ★★ *Csetvei Winery*.

Oremus Tok ★★★→★★★★ Part of Vega Sicilia (*see* Spain) stable: dry FURMINT Mandolás better than ever. Also fine, elegant SZAMORODNI, ASZÚ.

Pajzos-Tokaj Tok ★★→★★★ Notable estate, vyds in warmer Pajzos and cooler

Megyer. T range is consistent fruity varietals, Selection for vyd wines aged in oak. Also fantastic flor-aged dry SZAMORODNI, excellent ASZÚ.

Pannonhalma N Pann ★★→★★★ 800-yr-old abbey. Look for top Hemina blends plus v.gd SAUV BL. Tricollis blends gd entry point.

Patricius Tok ★★→★★★ Steely, vibrant dry FURMINTS, incl organic range. PEZSGŐ, new focus. Amazing long-lived ASZÚ.

Pezsgő Hungarian for sparkling; growing trend. PDO TOK must be bottle-fermented.

Puttonyos (Putts) Sweetness indication for TOK ASZÚ, min 120g/l sugar for 5 Puttonyos, 150g/l for 6 Puttonyos. Was the number of 25-kg *puttonyos* or hods of Aszú grapes added to each 136-litre barrel (*gönci*) of base wine. Now more about stylistic balance of sweetness, acidity.

Royal Tokaji Wine Co Tok ★★★→★★★★ MÁD winery leading rebirth of TOK. (Hugh Johnson was co-founder 1990.) New focus on FURMINT only for v.gd ASZÚ, esp excellent 6-PUTTONYOS single-vyd. Blue label is benchmark 5-Puttonyos. Also look for small parcels of By Appointment, plus consistent Late Harvest and dry.

St Andrea N Hun ★★★→★★★★ Modern BIKAVÉR (fruity Áldás, single-vyd Hangács, barrel-selection **Merengő**, flagship *Nagy-Eged-Hegy, Agapé selection*). Also gd Egri Csillag (w): Napbor, Örökké. FURMINT-based Mária is white flagship.

Sauska S Pann, Tok ★★★→★★★★ Returning expat, superb wineries in VILLÁNY, TOK and new space-age PEZSGŐ cellar. Champenois consultant Regis Camus. Reds always impress, esp CAB FR, Cuvée 7, Cuvée 5. Consistent dry FURMINT, plus complex vyd selections Medve and Birsalmás; v.gd refined sparkling.

Hungary has its own cowboys – horsemen of the great plains called Csikósok.

Somló Bal Dramatic extinct volcano; firm, mineral white, esp Juhfark (sheep's tail). Small wineries dominate. Try Fehervari, *Kolonics*, KREINBACHER, Moric, Royal Somló, Somlói Apátsági, Somlói Vándor, Spiegelberg, Tornai.

Sopron N Pann Across the lake from Burgenland (*see* Austria). Fine reds, esp signature KÉKFRANKOS on old schist rocks. Standard-setter: bio WENINGER. Also look for Luka, organic Steigler, Taschner, Vincellér.

Szamorodni Tok Name of Polish origin for TOK made from whole bunches, partial botrytis or less shrivelled berries. Gaining popularity: more authentically Tok than late-harvest. *Édes* (sweet) is min 45g/l sugar (usually sweeter), 6 mths' oak ageing. Try BALASSA, BARTA, Bott, DEMETER ZOLTÁN, Demetervin, GIZELLA, HOLDVÖLGY, JULIET VICTOR, KIKELET, Kvaszinger, MAD WINE, Maison aux Pois, OREMUS, Pelle, SZEPSY, TOKAJ-NOBILIS. Best dry (*szaraz*) versions flor-aged like Sherry, try Breitenbach, CH DERESZLA, Harsanyi, *Pajzos*, ROYAL TOKAJI, *Tinon*.

Szekszárd S Pann Famous for rich reds, increasing focus on elegant BIKAVÉR, KÉKFRANKOS, reviving lighter KADARKA. Try Dúzsi (rosé), Eszterbauer, Fritz, HEIMANN, Lajver, Markvárt, Sebestyén, Szent Gaál, TAKLER, Tüske, VESZTERGOMBI, VIDA.

Szepsy Tok ★★★★ Quality in a different league. Now guided by István Jnr, with focus on complex, terroir-selected dry FURMINT (esp Bányász, Percze, Szent Tamás, Urbán), though don't ignore v.gd estate Furmint. Gorgeous sweet SZAMORODNI and superb ASZÚ, incl recent single-vyd releases.

Takler S Pann ★★ Family estate; ripe, supple SZEKSZÁRD reds. Best: Res selections of BIKAVÉR, CAB FR, KÉKFRANKOS.

Tinon, Samuel Tok ★★★ Frenchman in TOK since 1991. Long-ageing, complex ASZÚ in more trad style, with long maceration, oak-ageing; gd vyd-selected FURMINT. Wonderful, flor-aged dry *Szamorodni*.

Tokaj-Nobilis Tok ★★★ Fine, small organic estate run by Sarolta Bárdos. Excellent dry Rány & Barakonyi FURMINT, v.gd ASZÚ, Benchmark for Furmint PEZSGŐ.

Tokaj / Tokaji Tokaj is the town and region; Tokaji the wine. Producers to try (without own entry): Árvay, Áts, Bardon, Basilicus, Bodrog Borműhely, Bott Pince, Breitenbach, Budaházy, Carpinus, Demetervin, Erzsébet, Espák, Füleky, Harsányi, Hommona Atilla, Karádi-Berger, Kvaszinger, Lenkey, Maison aux Pois, Orosz Gábor, Pelle, Pendits, Peter, Présello, Sanzon, Szarka, Szóló, TR, Zsirai.

Törley ★ →★★ Reliable, gd-value DYA international and local varieties (labels incl Chapel Hill, St Stephen's Crown, Talisman); György-Villa for better selections. Major fizz producer (esp Gala, Hungaria, Törley labels), v.gd classic-method François, based on history of sparkling back to 1886.

Goulash/guylás, originally a soup, not a stew, made from dried meat by cowboys.

Tornai Bal ★★ Signficant SOMLÓ estate; gd-value entry-level varietals. Excellent, weighty, mineral Top Selection FURMINT, HÁRSLEVELŰ, Juhfark.
Tűzkő S Pann ★★ Antinori-owned estate; gd CAB FR, KÉKFRANKOS, MERLOT, TRAMINI.
Vesztergombi ★★→★★★ Family SZEKSZÁRD estate impressing with next generation at helm. Look for Alpha, BIKAVÉR, Kétvölgy KÉKFRANKOS.
Vida S Pann ★★→★★★ Multi-generation family winery in SZEKSZÁRD. Appealing entry-point Tündértánc and wonderful BIKAVÉR, *Bonsai (old-vine) Kadarka*, Hidaspetre KÉKFRANKOS, La Vida.
Villány S Pann Most s region. Serious ripe Bx varieties, esp top-performing CAB FR – labelled Villányi Franc with rules for premium and super-premium. Juicy KÉKFRANKOS, PORTUGIESER. High quality (without own entries): Bakonyi, Gere Tamás & Zsolt, Günzer Tamás, Hummel, Jackfall, Jammertal, Kiss Gabor, Koch Csaba, Lelovits, Maul Zsolt, Polgar, Riczu, Ruppert, Stier, Tiffán, Wassmann (bio).
Vylyan S Pann ★★→★★★ Red specialist in VILLÁNY for fruity Classicus range, new-wave amphora Variáció, more serious premium KÉKFRANKOS, Montenuovo, rare Csóka, top vyd selections (Mandulás CAB FR), plus flagship Duennium Cuvée.
Weninger N Hun ★★★ Standard-setting bio winery in SOPRON run by Austrian Franz W Jnr. Superb single-vyd *Steiner Kékfrankos*; try Frettner CAB FR, Rózsa too.

BULGARIA

This is an ancient wine country with roots in Thrace, dotted with amazing historical and cultural sites. The wine industry continues to shrink – today smaller but better, with a scene of private estates and projects rebuilding the local-grape story and increasing focus on single vineyards. Finally, there are some great wine bars and restaurants for a memorable wine experience and top local food.

Varna gold treasure, found 1972: 3000 items, 6.5 kg, oldest golden treasure known.

Alexandra Estate Thr L ★★ VERMENTINO, rosé v.gd; reliable Res. New orange, RUBIN.
Angel's Estate Thr L ★★ Part of Purcari Wineries Group (*see* Moldova). Stallion range for rich supple red blends, Deneb for v.gd varietals, Angels for value.
Bessa Valley Thr L ★★★ One of 1st true estates, French consultancy. Try Enira, v.gd SYRAH and Enira Res, excellent *Grande Cuvée*.
Better Half Thr L ★★★ Intriguing, small-batch wines from a garage winery using amphorae and concrete eggs. Try reds and Dalakov Kvevri range.
Bononia Dan P ★★ Historic brewery building-turned-winery, close to Danube; v.gd Istar CHARD, GAMZA in several styles, Istar CAB FR.
Borovitsa Dan P ★★★ Low-intervention, small-parcel wines from nw. Special Selection is top range, incl age-worthy Dux and Ogy's Legacy. Great Terroirs for old-vine versions of GAMZA, Cuvée Bella Rada (RKATSITELI), Sensum.
Boyar, Dom Thr L ★ →★★★ Large modern winery, dramatic painted tanks. Reliable entry-point ranges Bolgaré, Deer Point; mid-range Elements, Quantum. Top: single-vyd Solitaire (MERLOT). Boutique Korten cellar: Grand Vintage, Natura.

Bratanov Thr L ★★ Low-intervention family estate in Sakar: Try 3 Blend (r/w), sur-lie CHARD, Tamianka (MUSCAT), excellent *Syrah Sans Barrique*, CAB FR.

Burgozone Dan P ★★ Sizeable vyd overlooking Danube; fresh, fruity varietally pure wines. Collection wines a step up: Eva, Iris Creation.

Copsa, Ch Thr L ★★ In heart of Rose V, producing one of best MISKET Cherven called AXL. Also gd SAUV BL and improving reds.

Dragomir Thr L ★★→★★★ Big, bold reds with RUBIN as star grape, esp in long-lived Pitos, Res. Fruity unoaked Sarva range (Dimyat, MAVRUD, Rubin) gd.

Georgiev / Milkov ★★→★★★ Exciting personal project of two top winemakers, based on old vines, local grapes. Recommended: MAVRUD, RUBIN, pét-nat, Why Not MISKET, new appealing light red Mixtape, based on PAMID.

Haralambievi Dan P ★★ Young family winery in n, already impressing with Royal Rouge CAB FR, fresh vibrant RUBIN, crisp lively whites.

Katarzyna Thr L ★★ Supple, ripe, well-made wines. Flagship Res impresses, also Encore SYRAH, 16 Harvests MAVRUD, MERLOT.

Logodaj Thr L ★★ STRUMA winery for super-ripe reds; esp Nobile Early MELNIK, v.gd rosé, fine bottle-fermented *Satin*.

Maryan Dan P ★★ Family winery. Res (r), Ivan Alexander (r), Sense of Tears DIMIAT.

Medi Valley Thr L ★★→★★★ Own vyds at 550m (1804ft) nr Rila Monastery; v.gd reds, esp Great Bulgarian, Incanto Black, MELNIK 55; fine VIOGNIER.

Menada, Dom Thr L ★ Large producer. Tcherga blends, Vulk RUBIN/CAB SAUV.

Midalidare Estate Thr L ★★→★★★ Immaculate boutique winery. Some of country's best *trad-method sparkling*, plus v.gd reds, esp Grand Vintage.

Minkov Brothers Thr L ★→★★★ Large but consistent winery, esp premium Oak Tree and v.gd Enoteca. Cycle is solid entry-point range.

Miroglio, Edoardo Thr L ★★★ Significant Italian/Bulgarian estate. Now focus on local grapes: excellent Elenovo MAVRUD, RUBIN; fruit-forward Prometheus Mavrud. PINOT N (Blanc de Noir, Res), classic fizz (Brut Rosé, Blanc de Blanc) v.gd.

Orbelia Thr L ★★ Family winery in STRUMA V; v.gd Via Aristotelis range, also Estate Res, esp MELNIK. Fun pét-nat from Sandanski MISKET.

Orbelus Thr L ★★ Organic STRUMA winery. Vibrant Orelek whites, gd MELNIK 55.

Rossidi Thr L ★★→★★★ Pioneering winery nr Sliven. Top concrete-egg-fermented CHARD; v.gd MAVRUD, RUBIN, excellent SYRAH.

Rumelia Thr L ★★ MAVRUD specialist, v.gd: Rumelia Res, Erelia, unoaked Merul.

Salla Estate Dan P ★★ Precise SAUV BL, RIES, Vrachanski MISKET and TRAMINER. Elegant CAB FR.

Santa Sarah Thr L ★★→★★★ Quality pioneer's estate. Bin reds v.gd. Privat flagship.

Stephan Pirev Wines ★★→★★★ Personal project of respected winemaker. Eager v.gd, esp CHARD, SYRAH, Red Blend.

> **New faces**
> It's an ever-changing scene in Bulgaria, with new projects like Wine Hippies, Bottled Opinions, Bulgarian Reloaded and more. Newer wineries worth watching (without own entries): Aya Estate, Bendida (v.gd MAVRUD, RUBIN), Ch Avli (PINOT N), Damyanov, DeVina (DIMIAT, Vrachanski MISKET), Downtown Urban, Four Friends, Gorun (superb CAB FR), Kapatovo, Lakeside, Libera Estate, Odessos (v.gd vyd CAB FR, RIES, Pinot N, Dimiat), Pink Pelican (Tamianka), Red Church, Rosalea (Rubin Writer's Wine), ROXS, Rupel, Staro Oryahovo (Varnenski Misket), Stratsin, Tipchenitza (gd orange MISKET), Uva Nestum, Varbovka (GAMZA), Via Verde, Via Vinera (Heritage Mavrud, orange Dimiat), Villa Yustina (Monogram, Four Seasons Rubin rosé), Yalovo (Old School Dimiat, Gamza), Zaara Estate, Zornitza.

Struma Valley Thr L Dramatic wine region surrounded by mtns: don't miss the sand pyramids and quaint historic town of Melnik. Focus on local grapes: MELNIK 55, Sandanski MISKET, Shiroka Melnik (aka Broadleafed Melnik). Look for: Augeo, Aya Estate (esp Ayano Shiroka Melnik), Damianitza (Redark, Uniqato), Damyanov (try Broadleafed Melnik, Keratsuda Orange), Kapatovo (PETIT VERDOT, GRENACHE/MOURVÈDRE/SHIRAZ), Libera (Hotovo, Melnik 55, Orange Keratsuda), Mihovi (Keratsuda), Rupel, Uva Nestum, Via Verde (esp Expressions Sandanski Misket), Zlaten Rozhen, Zornitza.

Terra Tangra Thr L ★★ Large estate in Sakar, organic red vyds; gd MALBEC, MAVRUD (r/rosé), serious Roto.

Tohun Dan P ★★ Precise, refreshing whites and rosé, esp Barrique CHARD, Tohun rosé, promising Tohun CAB/MERLOT.

Tsarev Brod Dan P ★★ Innovative estate in n. Try Amber CHARD, Evmolpia (r/rosé), rare local Gergana (new sp), pét-nat RIES, SAUV BL Res, v.gd Ries Icewine.

Villa Melnik Thr L ★★ Family estate, focus on local grapes, esp MAVRUD, MELNIK. Rare Varieties label, esp Melnik Jubilee, Ruen. Impressive Aplauz Res.

Villa Yambol Thr L ★ Fruity varietals and blends in Kabile range, gd value.

Vinex Slavyantsi Thr L ★→★★ "Fair for Life"-certified for supporting local ethnic community. Reliable well-priced varietals and blends, esp Leva brand.

Yamantiev's Thr L ★→★★★ Sound, commercial Kaba Gayda, SHIRAZ. Excellent *Marble Land (r)* and Yamantiev's Grand Res CAB SAUV.

Zagreus Thr L ★★ Organic vyd, MAVRUD in all styles: white, rosé and complex Vinica from semi-dried grapes. Three Generations blend gd.

Zelanos Thr L ★★ Pristine winery/wines. Try fresh (Red) MISKET, PINOT GR, elegant Z series CAB FR, PINOT N.

SLOVENIA

The next generation is taking the reins in Slovenia, with more women involved too, rebelling against the tradition of handing vineyards to the oldest male heir. This all makes for dynamism, fresh ideas and new approaches – in both elegant, classic wine styles and the small but burgeoning area of skin-contact and low-intervention wines. And it's beautiful, green, forested country, with amazing restaurants and great hiking. It should be on your radar.

Top dining destination: Hiša Franko. Ana Roš is chef. Book well ahead.

Albiana Pos ★★ Lovely family vyds in DOLENJSKA: try sparkling, esp rosé. Also gd SILVANER, MODRA FRANKINJA Alto.

Batič Prim ★★ Low-intervention VIPAVA estate. Angel range noted, also Zaria (w).

Bjana Prim ★★★ Superb PENINA specialist in BRDA. All trad method. Cuvée Prestige, Blanc de Noirs/Blancs, Rosé Brut particularly gd.

Brda Prim Top-quality region of hilly terraced vyds. Wineries without own entry worth trying: Benedetič, Blažič, Bužinel, Dobuje, Domačija Bizjak, Dom Vicomte De Noüe-Marinič, Emeran Reya, Klinec, Kristančič, Medot, Moro, Mulit, Nebó, Ronk, Schumacher Wines, Zalatel, Zanut.

Burja Prim ★★★★ Low-intervention, organic VIPAVA estate, focus on local grapes. Try Burja Bela, Burja N (PINOT N), Burja Reddo; v.gd vyd selections in top yrs.

Dolenjska Pos Improving region, moving on from trad sharp red Cviček. Look for: ALBIANA, Dular, FRELIH, Klet Krško (Turn Classic, Premium ranges), Kobal, Kozinc, Štemberger. Local Žametovka/Žametna Crnina proving great for sparkling, esp Dom Slapšak, FRELIH.

Dolfo Prim ★★→★★★ Family winery in BRDA: gd Spirito PENINA, consistent fresh, mineral REBULA. Serious Gredič, Res labels.

Dveri-Pax Pod ★★→★★★ Historic Benedictine-owned estate nr Maribor. Bright precise whites; v.gd old-vine selections, esp FURMINT Ilovci, plus age-worthy BLAUFRÄNKISCH, excellent *Furmint Penina*.

Erzetič Prim ★★ Family winery since 1725, bio, next-generation winemaker. New Orbis range aged in five woods is superb.

Check out rare "cave dragons" – blind salamanders, only found in karst caves.

Ferdinand Prim ★★★ Hilltop estate and dramatic winery. Delicious cross-border Sinefinis (sp, with Gradis'ciutta, Italy), excellent Epoca (r/w).

Frelih Pos ★★ Mother/daughter team making v.gd PENINA, MODRA FRANKINJA, SILVANER, plus modern interpretation of trad Cviček.

Frešer Pod ★★ Organic estate, 7th generation, fine PINOT N, gd Markus RIES.

Gašper Prim ★★★ Impressive brand of Gašper Čarman with KLET BRDA: v.gd MALVAZIJA, REBULA Selekcija, Markisa rosé, fruity Palamida, excellent CAB FR.

Gross, *Vino* Pod ★★ Low-intervention terroir wines from steep terraces. Try Gorca and Iglič FURMINTS, Colles SAUV BL, RIES and impressive Furmint Brut Natur.

Guerila Prim ★★ Estate in VIPAVA; bio, v.gd MALVAZIJA, PINELA, BARBERA, CAB FR.

Herga Pod ★★ Highly regarded winemaker Mitja H took over former Kupljen estate. Promising start with own style, esp CHARD, PINOT GR, SAUV BL, PINOT N.

Hiša Joannes Protner Pod ★★ Passionate about RIES, plus gd PENINA, CHARD, PINOT N from bio estate.

Istenič Pos ★★ Pioneering fizz specialist. Try Prestige Extra Brut, Gourmet Rosé, No. 1 Brut and new Rare Brut Natur.

Istria (Slovenska Istra) The Slovenian part of the peninsula; main grapes: MALVAZIJA, REFOŠK. Best: Bordon, Brič, Korenika & Moškon (bio), MonteMoro, Pucer z Vrha, Rodica (organic), SANTOMAS, Steras (superb Epulon, Saurin Malvazija), VINAKOPER, Zaro.

Jakončič Prim ★★★ BRDA producer: v.gd Carolina range, skin-contact Uvaia PINOT GR.

Kabaj Prim ★★★ French-led BRDA estate making complex skin-contact whites and bold reds. Also restaurant/rooms.

Klet Brda Prim ★★→★★★ Slovenia's largest co-op continues to set quality and environmental standards. Fresh Quercus range v.gd, unoaked Krasno. Bagueri vyd selections excellent, esp REBULA. Impressive De Baguer range incl superb flagship A+ (r/w), single-vyd MERLOT, Rebula. Produces v.gd Schumacher wines.

Kobal Pod ★★ Boutique winery in Halože: v.gd fruit-focused white-label range, more structured black label and Bajta for long skin contact and pét-nat.

Kogl Pod ★★ Historic estate nr Ormož (1542). Appealing fresh Mea Culpa whites, more complex Magna Domenica.

Krapež, *Vina* Prim ★★ VIPAVA family producer. Now organic, tending towards longer macerations. Top: Lapor Belo, Rdeče.

Kras Prim Most noted for TERAN PDO made from REFOŠK, also gd MALVASIA, Vitovska. Try Čotar, Marko Fon, Štoka, Vinakras.

Kristančič Prim ★★ Family estate in BRDA: new Artwork range is v.gd, plus Cristatus PENINA, top cuvée Pavó.

Marijan Simčič, *Dom* Prim ★★★★ Benchmark classic varietal range, v.gd cru selection from older vines, selected plots. Superb single-vyd old-vine Opoka range, esp wonderful CHARD, SAUV VERT, MERLOT, PINOT N Breg. Also gd Teodor blends. Leonardo (sw) consistently glorious.

Marof Pod ★★→★★★ No-compromise estate. Grand Vin for vyd selections: Bodonci SAUV BL, Kramarovci CHARD, Mačkovci Frankinja. Also v.gd Goričko varietals.

Movia Prim ★★★→★★★★ Charismatic Aleš Kristančič with son Lan, bio. Excellent Veliko range, esp Belo (w), showstopping *Puro Rosé (sp)*, *Rdeče (r)*. New Kapovolto (sp). Also admired for long-macerated orange Lunar.

Pasji Rep Prim ★★ Next-generation organic, bio VIPAVA estate; v. well-made wines, esp lovely MERLOT Breg, plus Jebatschin blends, PINOT N, Zelen.

Penina Name for quality sparkling, Charmat or trad method.

Podravje Largest region, covering ŠTAJERSKA SLOVENJIA and Prekmurje. Vibrant, dry whites, esp FURMINT, SAUV BL, lighter reds. Hotbed for new wineries/next-generation winemakers.

Posavje Region in se covering DOLENJSKA, Bizeljsko-Sremič, Bela Krajina (Metlika, Prus, Šturm, ŠUKLJE). Focus building on v.gd fresh fizz, elegant MODRA FRANKINJA. Izbor (sw) can be excellent: great acidity.

Primorje / Primorska Region in w covering Slovenian BRDA, ISTRIA, KRAS, VIPAVA.

Puklavec Family Wines Pod ★★→★★★ Large family winery, consistent expressive whites in Puklavec & Friends and Jeruzalem Ormož ranges; v.gd Seven Numbers label, amazing archive wines from 70s.

Pullus (Ptujska Klet) Pod ★→★★ Reliable fresh bright Pullus label; G range and sweet wines impress.

Radgonske Gorice Pod ★→★★ Historic sparkling cellar, top-selling Srebrna (silver) PENINA. Also gd classic-method Selection Brut, long-aged Millesimé CHARD.

Santomas Prim ★★→★★★ Benchmark producer of REFOŠK, from organic grapes. Also v.gd Mezzo Forte (r), SYRAH.

Ščurek Prim ★★★ Family estate in BRDA, five sons; gd varietal entry-point wines. Superb *Rebula Up*, attractive Stara Brajda (r/w), new Zero Brut PENINA.

Simčič, Edi Prim ★★★★ Beautiful family winery and standard-setter in BRDA. Excellent Fojana, Kozana vyd selections and some of country's top reds, esp barrel-selection Kolos, Kozana MERLOT. Classic range, Lex blends v.gd.

Štajerska Slovenija Pod Major region in e, incl important districts of Haloze, Ljutomer-Ormož, Maribor. New winery association. Crisp, vibrant whites, elegant lighter reds and top sweet. Try Dom Ciringa, Doppler, Familija, FREŠER, Gaube, Heaps Good Wine, Horvat, Jaunik, Meum, M-simply good wines, Roka, Sanctum, SiSi Druzovič, Statera, Valdhuber, Zlati Grič.

Steyer Pod ★★ TRAMINER specialist in ŠTAJERSKA, esp Vaneja.

Šuklje ★★→★★★ Standard-setting small family estate, with terroir focus in Bela Krajina: Lozice SAUV BL, Lodoma and excellent Vrbanjka MODRA FRANKINJA.

Sutor Prim ★★★→★★★★ Excellent small producer from VIPAVA. Lovely Sutor White, fine CHARD, elegant MERLOT-based red.

Tilia Prim ★★→★★★ Tagline is "House of Pinot", reflecting passion for PINOT N in all styles, from refined sparkling via juicy estate to top age-worthy selections. Also expressive Sunshine whites, appealing Rubido red blend.

Verus Pod ★★★ Fine, beautifully made, vibrant whites: v.gd FURMINT, PINOT GR, refined RIES, aromatic SAUV BL. Great value too.

Vinakoper Prim ★★ Large ISTRIAN winery, local-grape focus esp MALVAZIJA, REFOŠK. Look for Capo d'Istria, Capris, Rex Fuscus labels.

Vipava Prim Dramatic valley noted for *Burja* wind in PRIM. Try Benčina, Bizjak, Fedora, Ferjančič, JNK, Koglot, Lepa Vida, Lisjak, Marc, Miška, Mlečnik, Poljšak, Saksida, Štokelj, Vina Ušaj Ussai, Wipach. Also keep an eye on promising newcomer Grof.

Vipava 1894 Prim ★→★★ Large winery in VIPAVA. Lanthieri range, Terase MALVAZIJA.

Rebula: the future?
BRDA and VIPAVA's most important native grape, capable of excellent quality. At its best on steep terraces on well-drained flysch bedrock, called *opoka* locally. The wine regions' secret weapon in coping with climate change, thanks to its deep roots seeking water through fractured bedrock. It's drought-tolerant too.

CROATIA

Sun, sea, island escapes and amazing historic sites still work magic in bringing thirsty tourists to Croatia (many cities, like Dubrovnik, are now restricting cruise ships), so most Croatian wine is enjoyed in situ – alongside amazing fish, cheeses, olive oil and truffles. The revival of local grapes with unpronounceable names (Kujundžuša or Svrdlovina, anyone?) continues, while indigenous Malvazija Istarska has become an established medal-winner on the world stage. So much to explore.

Ante Sladić Dalm ★★ Next-generation family winery focusing on v.gd versions of local grapes, esp Lasina, Oya Noya Debit, Plavina.

Antunović Sl & CD ★★ Boutique winery next to Danube, making elegant Tradition GRAŠEVINA, gd CHARD sur lie. Pioneering female winemaker-owner, with son.

Arman, Marijan Is & Kv ★★ Family estate for consistent fresh MALVAZIJA and always impressive G Cru from selected plot. Also gd TERAN.

Badel 1862 ★→★★ Largest and oldest wines and spirit producer in Croatia. Best: polished, ripe Korlat (r). Also owns Duravar, Ivan Dolac.

Benvenuti Is & Kv ★★★ Family winery run by two brothers. Notable Santa Elisabetta TERAN, excellent Anno Domini and new Livio range in honour of late father. Amazing San Salvatore MUŠKAT.

BIBICh Dalm ★★→★★★ Family estate from C15. Bas de Bas is flagship; also look for excellent R6 blend and local Debit.

Bire Dalm ★★→★★★ Rare Grk, esp single-vyd Defora from Lumbarda on Korcula.

Boškinac Dalm ★★→★★★ Highly regarded boutique hotel and winery on Pag Island: impressive Cuvée (r). Superb Ocu (w) from rare Gegić.

Bura-Mrgudić Dalm ★★ Weighty, trad, but gd Bura PLAVAC MALI. Also modern Benmosche DINGAČ, ZIN.

Cattunar Is & Kv ★★ Hilltop winery for MALVAZIJA from ISTRIA's four different soils.

Clai Is & Kv ★★ Organic, natural wine pioneer. Try: Baracija MALVAZIJA, Sv Jakov Malvazija, Ottocento blends.

Coronica Is & Kv ★★→★★★ Pioneer of quality wines from TERAN; Gran Teran is age-worthy benchmark. Also v.gd Gran MALVAZIJA and fresh DYA version.

Croatian Uplands Međimurje is coolest, focus on vibrant Pušipel (aka FURMINT), expressive SAUV BL: try Cmrečnjak, DK Vina, Horvat, Jakopić, Kocijan, Kopjar, Lovrec, Štampar, Steiner. Moslavina is notable for mineral-fresh Skrlet (look for Florijanović, Košutić, Romić). Plešivica for great sparkling, precise Sauv Bl, RIES and is orange/amphora hotspot, esp Griffin Ivančić, Korak, *Šember*, TOMAC.

Dalmatia Sunny rocky coastline and islands from Zadar to Dubrovnik. Divided into N Dalm, The Hinterland, S-central Dalm. Unique varieties, exciting producers.

Damjanić Is & Kv ★★→★★★ Just-opened new winery, taking family wines to next level; v.gd Borgonja (aka BLAUFRÄNKISCH), Clemente (r/w), Justina MALVAZIJA.

Dingač Dalm Croatia's 1st PDO since 1962 for weighty reds from PLAVAC MALI, on steep sea-facing slopes of Pelješac peninsula. Try Benmosche, BURA-MRGUDIĆ, Crna Ovca, KIRIDŽIJA, Korta Katarina, Madirazza, SAINTS HILLS, SKARAMUČA, Vinarija Dingač.

Enjingi, Ivan Sl & CD ★★ Legendary natural-wine maker in SLAVONIA. Noted for GRAŠEVINA, long-lived Venje.

Enosophia Sl & CD ★→★★★ Previously Feravino. Best: Miraz (v.gd CAB FR, Frankovka), also Trs No. 5 GRAŠEVINA.

Fakin Is & Kv ★★★ "Fakin good wines" is winery motto, and this young winemaker delivers. Exciting top labels La Prima MALVAZIJA, Il Primo TERAN. Also try fresh Malvazija and latest release Teran.

Galić Sl & CD ★★★ Space-age winery: refined CHARD, Crno 9, GRAŠEVINA, PINOT N.

Grabovac Dalm ★★→★★★ Family winery in inland DALM impressing with Kujundzuša, Modro Jezero Ris, Trnjak.

Gracin Dalm ★★ →★★★ Professor Leo G pioneered revival of BABIĆ: complex, herby, elegant. Also as sweet Prošek and in v.gd Kontra blend made with KIRIDŽIJA.

Grgić Dalm ★★ Founded by California legend Mike Grgich (RIP 2023) of Judgement of Paris fame: bold, trad PLAVAC MALI, typical POŠIP on Pelješac peninsula.

Hvar Dalm Island with UNESCO listing for Stari Grad Plain and its vyd *chora*, dating to C4 BCE. Noted for PLAVAC MALI. Carić, PZ Svirče, TOMIĆ, ZLATAN OTOK.

Iločki Podrumi Sl & CD ★→★★ Historic cellar from 1450, continuous production since. GRAŠEVINA specialist, also gd TRAMINAC. Try Premium, Principovac labels.

Istria Adriatic peninsula, more a country within a country. Versatile local MALVAZIJA Istarska is main grape and red TERAN (must be labelled Hrvatska Istra – Teran). Best (without own entry): Banko Mario, Bastian, Cossetto, Degrassi, Deklić, Dobrovac, Dom Koquelicot, Franković, Ferenac, Ipša, Kadum, Medea, Meneghetti, Milan Budinski (Omo), Misal Peršurić (sp), Novacco, Piquentum, Radovan, Rossi, Roxanich, San Tommaso, Sosich, Trapan, Veralda, Vivoda, Zigante.

Kabola Is & Kv ★★→★★★ Immaculate organic estate, wines to match. MALVAZIJA as fizz, young wine, cask-aged Unica and superb Amfora. Also Amfora TERAN.

Kiridžija Dalm ★★ Modern DINGAČ, PLAVAC MALI v.gd. Also Kontra JV with GRACIN.

Komarna Dalm Newest wine region since 2013: all organic, on precipitous slopes by sea. Try Rizman, SAINTS HILLS Sv Roko, Volarević. Watch Deak, Terra Madre.

Korta Katarina Dalm ★★ Croatian winery with US roots and luxury hotel on Pelješac overlooking Korcula: gd POŠIP, weighty PLAVAC MALI, esp Reuben's Res.

Never put your handbag on floor in Balkans: it's said you will never have any money.

Kozlović Is & Kv ★★★→★★★★ Stunning family winery and pioneer of modern winemaking in region continues to raise standards. Benchmark entry-point MALVAZIJA, TERAN and superb Santa Lucia selections.

Krajančić Dalm ★★→★★★ Owner Luka is guru for all styles of POŠIP (try 1214 Statut, Intrada, Opera, Sur Lie), now joined by excellent PLAVAC MALI (esp Zaglav).

Krauthaker Sl & CD ★★★ Pioneer and GRAŠEVINA specialist from Kutjevo: as dry, sweet, vyd-selection Mitrovac. Also try Zelenac (aka ROTGIPFLER).

Kutjevo Cellars Sl & CD ★★ Large producer with cellar from 1232; gd-value, consistent GRAŠEVINA main focus. Also premium De Gotho, lovely Icewine.

Kvarner Is & Kv Bay and islands off ISTRIAN coast. White Žlahtina is main focus from fizz to PROŠEK (Ivan Katunar, Katunar Winery, Pavlomir, Šipun) and revived Sansigot red (Grand Village, Ivan Katunar, Katunar).

Laguna, Vina Is & Kv ★★→★★★ Signficant winery at Poreč on *terra rossa*, new winemaker. Vina Laguna for gd-value varietals, premium Festigia range for better vyd selections, esp MALVAZIJA; gd Blanc de Moi (sp).

Markus Fine Wines ★★→★★★ Ambitious new project, Canadian investor, top winemakers. Superb POŠIP, and BABIĆ (complex, from 70–80-yr-old vines).

Matošević Is & Kv ★★★ Benchmark, age-worthy MALVAZIJA: Alba, Alba Antiqua, Alba Robinia (in acacia). Grimalda vyd selections v.gd.

Pilato Is & Kv ★★ Consistently gd family winery; v.gd MALVAZIJA, esp ★★★ sur lie.

Prošek Dalm Trad sweet wine, from sun-dried local grapes. Also made in KVARNER; 1st mention 1556. Legal battles with Italy, which claims similarity to Prosecco.

Saints Hills Dalm, Is & Kv ★★→★★★★ Two estates in DALM, ISTRIA. Consultant Michel Rolland (*see* France): v.gd Frenchie (w), Nevina (w), Posh POŠIP, Sv Roko PLAVAC MALI, one of best DINGAČ .

Skaramuča Dalm ★★ Reliable, decent value, family-run winery. Elegance range best for PLAVAC MALI, POŠIP.

Slavonia / Croatian Danube This e wine region is heartland of GRAŠEVINA. Mostly whites planted, improving reds. Try Adzić, **Antunović**, Belje, ENJINGI, ENOSOPHIA, Erdutski Vinogradi, GALIĆ, KRAUTHAKER, KUTJEVO, Mihalj, Royal Hill, Sontacchi, Terra Slavonia, Zlatno Brdo. Slavonia also famous for its oak.

Stina Dalm ★★ Dramatic steep vyds on Brač Island. PLAVAC MALI (Majstor label, top Remek Djelo). Also v.gd POŠIP, Tribidrag, Vugava.

Testament Dalm ★★→★★★ Organic estate in historic area at Šibenik: v.gd POŠIP, BABIĆ, Tribidrag. Fun Dalmatian Dog (r/w). Sister winery Black Island on Korcula makes gd Merga Victa POŠIP.

Tomac Cro Up ★★★ Family winery and amphora pioneer nr Zagreb; bio. Excellent *qvevri* wines, plus Rockstar RIES, trad-method sparkling.

Tomaz Is & Kv ★★ Family winery pushing boundaries in ISTRIA. Seriously impressive Barbarossa TERAN, complex MALVAZIJA Sesto Senso.

Tomić Dalm ★★ Bold wines from leading personality on HVAR; organic PLAVAC MALI; gd reds (esp Plavac Barrique); PROŠEK Hectorovich (sw).

Zlatan Otok Dalm ★★ Famous family winery from HVAR with vyds also at Makarska, Šibenik. Noted for ripe reds, gd DYA POŠIP.

Zure Dalm ★★→★★★ Specialist in Grk vine from Lumbarda on Korcula. Look for Grk Bartul, Reventon sur lie. Also gd PLAVAC MALI, POŠIP.

BOSNIA & HERZEGOVINA, KOSOVO, MONTENEGRO, NORTH MACEDONIA, SERBIA

New wineries continue to pop up, most with quality ambitions. International grapes are often preferred domestically, but local varieties are also becoming increasingly good – turning from ugly workhorse grapes to wines of real beauty in the best cases. Sadly, many of the best wines aren't exported, and locals and tourists will pay well for the most exciting.

Bosnia & Herzegovina White Žilavka is star, esp from sun-drenched karst vyds around Mostar. Juicy, supple red Blatina, darker, more structured Trnjak gaining attention. Try Andrija, Begić, bio Brkić (Mjesečar, Žilavka), Carska Vina Grgo Vasilj (Premium Blatina, David, Gregorius Žilavka), Hercegovina Produkt, Jungić (Premium CAB FR, Šikar), Matić (Con Brio), Nuić (Blatina, MERLOT), Puntar (Saint, Žilavka), Rubis (CAB SAUV, Signorina rosé), Škegro (Krš range, Carsus Blatina), Tvrdos Monastery (VRANAC), Vera (Harmonia, Prima Vera), Vilinka (Selekcija, Žilavka, X-Line), Vinarija Čitluk (Teuta range), Vino Milas (Blatina Res, Žilavka), Vukoje (Carsko-Vino, Žilavka, Vranac).

Kosovo Recognized as independent by c.100 countries after declaring independence in 2008, but still has two wine laws – its own and Serbia's. Total is 2823 ha under wine grapes, two-thirds red, and 37 wineries. Largest region is Dukagjini (Metohija in Serbian rules), with Rahovec the largest zone. Stonecastle and Old Cellar (Bodrum i Vjeter) biggest. Smaller names like Labi, Lakićević, Sefa, Suhareka improving, esp most planted grape: Vranç (aka VRANAC). Other important grapes: GAMAY, Prokupac, Smederevka (aka DIMIAT), WELSCHRIESLING.

8000-year-old remnants of world's oldest village (on stilts) found near Lake Ohrid.

Montenegro Inky-dark VRANAC dominates 2992 ha under vine; 13-jul-Plantaže has 2310-ha single vyd (world's largest), 95% of wine production and is leader in viticultural research, discovering likely local origins of Vranac and Kratošija (aka ZIN). Generally gd, esp Vranac: Pro Corde, v.gd Stari Podrum. Small wineries getting better: Keković, Lipovac, Priča, Rajković, Rupice, Savina, Sjekloča.

North Macedonia Emphasis now on quality bottled wine, esp flagship VRANEC (local spelling), with ageing potential, capable of terroir expression. Giant Tikveš has French-trained winemaker, intensive research programme; Babuna, Barovo, Bela Voda single vyds impress. Consistent Luda Mara, Alexandra Cuvée, oaked Dom Lepovo. Other gd mid/larger wineries: Bovin (Alexandar, Era), Ch Kamnik (Cuvée Prestige, Spark, Ten Barrels, Terroir), Dalvina (Dioniz, Hermes), Ezimit, Imako (Constellation, Black Diamond), Lazar (Erigon r, Kratošija), Popov (Kratošija, CARMENÈRE), Popova Kula (Stanušina w/rosé), Stobi (esp Vranec Veritas), Venec (Orle, 56 Res). New small family wineries association (under 30,000 litres): Eros, Kartal, Maksimilian, Paradžik, Peshkov, Popovi, Sarika.

A Serbian wine called Bermet was served on the *Titanic*. Ice, madam?

Serbia Quality commitment. Hosts Wine Vision by Open Balkan. 500 wineries+. International and revived local grapes, Prokupac, Grašac (aka WELSCHRIESLING), Bagrina, Morava, Neoplanta, Probus. Try Aleksandrović (Regent Res, Rodoslov, Trijumf range), Aleksić (Amanet, Biser, Žuti Cvet), Arsenijević, Bikicki (Uncensored TRAMINER), Budimir, Chichateau, Čokot (Experiment, Radovan Prokupac), Despotika, Deurić (Aksiom r/w, Morava, Probus 276), Djoković, Doja (Breg Prokupac, Prokupac), Erdevik, Jovac, Grabak, Ivanović (No. 1/2, Prokupac), Janko, Kovačević, Lastar, Matalj (Bagrina, Kremen, Kremen Kamen, Zemna), Matijašević (Belina, Bukovski, Sovinoa, Tri Doline), Milanović (Probus), Maurer (KADARKA 1880), Radovanović, Sagmeister (FURMINT Kanias, Šapat, Rajković, Tarpoš, Temet, Todorović (organic), Tonković, Virtus, Zvonko Bogdan (Cuvée No. 1, Icon Campana Rubimus), Verkat, Veritas, Vinčić, Vinum.

CZECHIA

A new generation of vintners, 35 years on from the change of regime, is taking the helm in the nation's many small and medium-sized family wineries, bringing fresh ideas: natural wines, of course, and an emphasis on the genius loci of the site. Environmental concerns are important to them too. Two regions: Bohemia (Boh) and Moravia (Mor).

Bisenc – Petr Kunc Mor ★★→★★★ Organic producer: RIES of many styles, from light linden flower to heady botrytized. Remarkable SYLVANER, PINOT N.

Cibulka, Víno Mor ★★★ Family enterprise working organically. Impressive PÁLAVA, WELSCHRIESLING, but accent on red blends CAB SAUV/MERLOT in Mor oak, and six different Sekts, incl intriguing Blauer Silvaner, Cikáda, Clos Portz Insel.

Hartman, Jiří Mor ★★ Small producer of burgundian-style (r/w) in picturesque cellar-settlement typical of Slovácko area. Also v.gd RIES, WELSCHRIESLING.

Lobkowicz, Bettina Boh ★★→★★★ Swiss-born ex-princess produces admirable PINOT N Barrique Selection, trad-method Blanc de Noirs Brut. Also RIES, v.gd-value entry-level Lady Lobkowicz (r/w/rosé).

VOC: local quality-based appellation modelled on Austrian DAC.

Naturvini Mor ★★★ Patrik Staško makes aromatic PÁLAVA (TRAMINER X MÜLLER-T), expressive PINOT GR, WELSCHRIESLING from foot of Pálava Hills, 90% bio.

Nepraš & Co Mor ★★★ Architect Radek N produces vibrant Maidenstein PINOT BL, RIES, SAUV BL. Also opulent Gravettien Grande Cuvée CAB SAUV/MERLOT.

Porta Bohemica Boh ★★ Outstanding Frühroter Veltliner, RIES. Try also interesting blends Charpin (CHARD/PINOT N), natural MüVé.

Skalák Wine Cellars Mor ★★ Family enterprise, emphasis on rich, aromatic whites (Pálava, PINOT GR, SAUV BL) and terroir.

Springer, Jaroslav Mor ★★★ Jaroslav S and son Tomáš make remarkable single-vyd Záhřebenské CHARD, PINOT N. Flagship burgundy-style Roučí Pinot N v.gd.

Stávek, Richard Mor ★★→★★★ Dedicated terroirist. Best sites: Kolberg, Odměry, Špigle-Bočky, Veselý. Orange and pét-nat hits in Japan, US (NY).

Vican Mor ★★★ Film producer Tomáš V est 2015. WELSCHRIESLING, Pálava, PINOT GR from Kienberg vyd. Top: Karel Roden Edition. Try SYLVANER, Yellow MUSCADELLE.

Wilomenna Boh ★★→★★★ Boutique family winery on volcanic Central-Boh Uplands nw of Prague. Clear-cut CHARD, RIES, SAUV BL. Unusual varieties (Rubinet), blends (Provocateur, Rozmarné Cuvée JM), trad-method Sekt Wilomenna Brut.

SLOVAKIA

Although area under vine still decreases, emphasis is now on own vineyards, traditional varieties and fewer chemicals. Rosé is the new "in". Six wine regions: Central/Eastern/Southern Slovakia (C/E/S Slo), Lesser Carpathians (L Car), Nitra (Nit), Tokaj (Tok).

Belá, Ch S Slo ★★★ Fine Mosel-style RIES by joint Egon Müller (*see* Germany) and Miroslav Petrech venture; Alibernet (ALICANTE BOUSCHET X CAB SAUV), PINOT N.

Dubovský & Grančič L Car ★★ Small dynamic winery. Admirable St George edition (classic RIES, WELSCHRIESLING) plus two fine sparklers.

Dudo, Miroslav L Car ★★★ CAB SAUV, also unusual Devín (TRAMINER x Veltliner Rotweiss), Dunaj (Muscat Bouschet x Oporto x ST-LAURENT), MUSCAT Ottonel.

Elesko L Car ★★ Unique concept in Modra, wine capital of Lesser Carpathians, combining ultra-modern facilities with gastronomy, featuring art gallery with Warhol originals. Elegant modern wines exclusively from own grapes.

Fedor Malík & Sons L Car ★★★ Family winery, mainly whites. Notable red crosses Hron (Abouriou x Castets, SW France), Rudava (Castets x Tenturier/Aleatico/Puchljakovskij); blends Sahral, Professeur, Hrom (Thunder). Modragne fizz.

J&J Ostrožovič Tok ★★★ Pure dry FURMINT, Lipovina (HÁRSLEVELŰ) and Yellow Muscadelle plus admirable Tok styles ranging from Samorodné (Szamorodni) to Tokajský výber (Aszú) 3–6 Putňový (Puttonyos). Esencia (Eszencia) yr 2000.

Karpatská Perla L Car ★★→★★★ Important producer specializing in zesty RIES (Kramáre, Suchý Vrch single vyds) and quaffable GRÜNER V (Ingle, Noviny).

Magula L Car ★★★ Family facility with bio principles: GRÜNER V, WELSCHRIESLING. Exquisite Frankovka (BLAUFRÄNKISCH) grown on loess in single-vyd Rosenberg.

Pivnica Brhlovce Nit ★★→★★★ Photographer Ján Záborský est 2011. Artisanal volcanic wines in troglodyte dwellings. Try youthful Pesecká Leánka (FETEASCĂ REGALĂ) Happiness: happy combination of fruit and hardy earthiness.

Vinovin – Peter Ščepán L Car ★★ Wide range of distinctive varietals. Note CAB FR, Devín, Dunaj (*see* DUDO).

ROMANIA

Local red Feteascǎ Neagrǎ continues to lead the native-grape charge, with great quality in areas that were previously too cool, like Transylvania, Cotnari and Satu Mare. But you will have to visit to taste Romania's best, which is rarely exported.

Avereşti, Domeniile Mold ★★ Significant private estate, only producer of local Zghihară, v.gd Busuioacă. Look for Diamond, Nativus labels.

Avincis Mun ★★ In DRĂGĂŞANI, possibly Romania's most beautiful estate: gd Cuvées Grandiflora, Petit & Alexis. Excellent Negru de Drăgăşani. Also try Crâmpoşie Selecţionată (still and sp). Only producer of rare Alutus, just released.

Balla Géza Cri & Mar ★★→★★★ Consistently gd family estate; vyds up to 400m (1312ft) on Miniş Hills. Excellent Stone Wine (CAB FR, Cadarca, FETEASCĂ NEAGRĂ, FURMINT). Also try Clarus (sp) from Cadarca, Mustoasa grapes.

Banat Dynamic region in w. Try Agape Artă & Natură, Crama Aramic, CRAMELE RECAŞ, Petro Vaselo, Thesaurus.

Bauer Winery Mun ★★→★★★ Excellent low-intervention winery of Oliver and Raluca B (also at PRINCE ŞTIRBEY). Intriguing, limited-edition batches from old vines: CAB SAUV, PETIT VERDOT, Novac (rosé), CRÂMPOŞIE (s/sw), SVS (SAUVIGNONASSE).

Bogdan, Domeniul Dob ★★ Ambitious bio vyd (Romania's 1st) in DOBROGEA. Try Patrar and rich but beautifully made Primordial FETEASCĂ NEAGRĂ.

Romania has salt mines – you can even row on a lake deep in Turda Salt Mine.

Budureasca Mun ★→★★ Modern DEALU MARE estate, British winemaker. Best labels: Noble 5, Origini, Vine-in-Flames export range. Look for PINOT N, SHIRAZ, TĂMÂIOASĂ ROMÂNEASCĂ.

Corcova Roy & Dâmboviceanu Mun ★★ Renovated historic royal cellar, superb vyds. Bright fresh whites, rosé. More serious reds repay some age.

Cotnari, Casa de Vinuri Mold ★★ Only Romanian producer using only local varieties. Try dry Busuioacă de Bohotin, Colocviu (GRASĂ de Cotnari). Also Millesime (sp), Vladoianu FETEASCĂ NEAGRĂ.

Cotnari Winery Mold ★ Dominant large producer in DOC of same name. Mostly dry and semi-dry whites from local grapes. Aged sweet Collection can impress.

Crişana & Maramureş Cooler region in nw. Look for BALLA GEZA, Carastelec (v.gd Carassia bottle-fermented sp), Darabont Family (esp Urme), Dradara (FETEASCĂ REGALĂ), organic Nachbil (BLAUFRÄNKISCH, FETEASCĂ NEAGRĂ, orange Grünspitz), low-sulphite wines from Weingut Edgar Brutler.

Dagon Mun ★★→★★★ Small, impressive quality-focused vyd. Best: Clearstone FETEASCĂ ALBĂ, Sandridge old-vine FETEASCĂ NEAGRĂ.

Davino Winery Mun ★★★★ Excellent producer in DEALU MARE. Focus on blends for v.gd, age-worthy Dom Ceptura, Flamboyant, Rezerva, Revelatio (w); v.gd FETEASCĂ NEAGRĂ under Purpura Valahica label.

Dealu Mare / Dealul Mare Mun Means "Big Hill"; regarded as Romania's Tuscany. Top: AURELIA VISINESCU, BUDUREASCA, Crama Mierla Alba, DAGON, DAVINO, Domeniile Franco-Române, Domeniile Tohani – Apogeum, Gramofon, ICONIC ESTATE, LACERTA, LICORNA, SERVE, Prince Matei, VIILE METAMORFOSIS.

Dobrogea Sunny region by Black Sea. Improving: Alcovin-Macin (Curtea Regala), Alira (rosé, SAUV BL, MERLOT), BOGDAN (bio), Dropia (BABEASCA NEAGRĂ), Histria (v.gd Ammos, Nikolaos CAB SAUV, rosé), La Sapata (bio, focus on Băbească Neagră), Rasova (Sur Mer, Imperfect), VITICOLA SARICA NICULIŢEL (ALIGOTÉ, Caii de Letea, FETEASCĂ NEAGRĂ), Vladoi (Alb Cuvée, Anca Maria TĂMÂIOASĂ).

DOC Romanian term for PDO: 40 registered. Sub-categories incl DOC-CMD: harvest at full maturity. DOC-CT: late harvest. DOC-CIB: noble harvest. PGI is vin cu indicatie geografică, or simply IG.

Drăgăşani Mun Plateau and hills in OLTENIA; unique grapes incl Crâmpoşie Selecţionată, Negru de Drăgăşani, Novac. Dynamic wineries, esp AVINCIS, BAUER, Mennini, PRINCE ŞTIRBEY.

Iconic Estate Mun ★→★★ Try gd-value commercial La Umbra range, Colina Pietra blends; historic Rhein & Cie (gd sp); Hyperion top label.

Jidvei Trnsyl ★→★★ Romania's largest single vyd, 2500 ha+. Best: Owner's Choice (with Marc Dworkin of Bulgaria's Bessa V); Eiswein and Extra Brut (sp).

LacertA Mun ★★ A gd estate in DEALU MARE: Cuvée IX (r), Cuvée X (w), SHIRAZ.

Licorna Wine House Mun ★★ Small DEALU MARE estate. Try Serafim for local grapes, Bon Viveur for international blends. Anno top selection.

Liliac Trnsyl ★★★ Impeccable Austrian-owned estate, Alsace consultant. Crisp fine whites, elegant reds, delicious sweet Nectar, Icewine with Kracher (*see* Austria).

Metamorfosis, Viile Mun ★★→★★★ Part Antinori-owned (*see* Italy) estate in DEALU

MARE. Top: Cantvs Primvs, esp FETEASCĂ NEAGRĂ; v.gd Coltul Pietrei SAUV BL, Via Marchizului Negru de DRĂGĂȘANI, PINOT N; reliable Metamorfosis range.

Moldovan Hills Largest region in ne. Fresh whites, rosé; refined reds incl AVEREȘTI, Gramma (quirky labels, bright, fresh), Hermeziu (esp Busuioacă de Bohotin), Strunga (v.gd FETEASCĂS ALBĂ/NEAGRĂ). Try also Gîrboiu (Bacanta, Epicentrum, Tectonic labels, special focus on local Șarba).

Muntenia & Oltenia Hills Major region in s. DOC areas: DEALU MARE, Dealurile Olteniei, DRĂGĂȘANI, Pietroasa, Sâmburești, Stefanești, Vanju Mare.

Oltenia Up-and-coming region in overlooked sw: Catleya, CORCOVA, CRAMA OPRIȘOR, Domeniul Coroanei Segarcea, Mosia Galicia Mare.

Oprișor, Crama Mun ★★ → ★★★ Consistent German-owned winery; reliable La Cetate range, v.gd Crama Oprișor CAB SAUV, Jiana Rosé, Rusalca Alba; top *Smerenie* (r).

Petro Vaselo Ban ★★ Organic vyd in BANAT; focus on sparkling from charmat Bendis to serious Kotys; fruity basic range, more serious Melgris, Otarnita, Ovas; PV is top experimental range.

Prince Știrbey Mun ★★★ Pioneering estate in DRĂGĂȘANI. Fine, vibrant dry whites from local varieties, esp Crâmpoșie Selecționată, FETEASCĂ REGALĂ, TĂMÂIOASĂ, impressive local reds (Negru de Drăgășani, Novac) and fine complex sparkling.

Recaș, Cramele Ban ★★ → ★★★ Success story for exports and now domestic market. Modern; long-standing Australian, Spanish winemakers. Multiple labels, incl entry-point Calusari, Paparuda, Schwaben Wein, Wildflower. Mid-range: Regno Recaș, Sole, Solo Quinta. Excellent premium Cuvée Uberland, La Stejari, Selene.

SERVE Mun ★★ → ★★★ The 1st private winery continues vision of founder Count Guy de Poix: v.gd Terra Romana (Cuvée Amaury w, Cuvée Sissi rosé, FETEASCĂ NEAGRĂ). Top: *Guy de Poix Feteasca Neagra*. Iconic Cuvée Charlotte.

Tohani Mun ★★ → ★★★ Large winery with S African winemaker; same ownership as flagship Apogeum FETEASCĂ NEAGRĂ.

Transylvania Cool mtn plateau encircled by Carpathians, great wildlife. Crisp whites; increasingly lighter, elegant reds. Producers without own entry: Jelna (esp Navicella r), La Salina (Issa label for gd NEUBERGER, RIES, PINOT N), Lechburg.

Villa Vinèa Trnsyl ★★ Stylish wines from a cool hilly vyd nr Târnave. Top: Diamant, GEWURZ, FETEASCĂ REGALĂ, RUBIN.

Vișinescu, Aurelia Mun ★★ Female-led DEALU MARE estate, gd Artisan label for local grapes. Top brand: Anima, v.gd *Fete Negre* from selected FETEASCĂ NEAGRĂ.

Viticola Sarica Niculițel Dob ★ → ★★ Large winery, vyds. Caii de la Letea for gd ALIGOTÉ, FETEASCĂ NEAGRĂ, rosé; gd multi-vintage Quintessence Res. Owns Domeniile Prince Matei (DEALU MARE).

MALTA

Malta and Gozo's unique native grapes (and 20 internationals), varied geology, hot/dry climate (irrigation is fundamental), phylloxera resistance, bush-farmed old vines and passionate winemakers are reviving 2000 years of winemaking tradition. Natives Girgentina (nuanced, high-acid whites) and Gellewza (rosés and light-bodied reds) are often blended for greater structure (the usual suspects: Chardonnay/Syrah). Also good idiosyncratic Syrah and savoury Merlot wines (oak alert!); Sangiovese and Vermentino have fans too. The 800 hectares are (maybe?) best for reds, but locals prefer whites, given the heat. Three appellations: DOK Malta, DOK Gozo and IGT Maltese Islands (wines of both). In Malta, try Delicata (Gellewza Medina, Gellewza Frizzante), Marsovin (Cassar of Malta traditional fizz), Mar Casar (natural wines), Antinori-owned Meridiana (good Vermentino Astarte), Zafrana. In Gozo, try Bacchus, Ta'Mena, Tal-Massar. Best are boutique wines: hard to find outside of the archipelago.

Greece

Native Greek grapes are like no others: aromatic and fresh, with good acidity even in scorching heat – all you need from wines that are made to complement food. You'll find most of that scorching heat in Crete; Santorini or Attica are freshened by sea breezes, and this is where you'll find the greatest elegance. The islands are some of the most challenging places on earth to grow vines, but they've been doing it a long time; they've got the hang of it. Assyrtiko and Agiorgitiko are well known abroad now; look for others, like Liatiko or Robola. Abbreviations: Aegean Islands (Aeg), Attica (Att), Central Greece (C Gr), Ionian Islands (Ion), Macedonia (Mac), Peloponnese (Pelop), Thessaloniki (Thess).

Aivalis Pelop ★★★ Producer in NEMEA, cult following, esp for "4" and Armakas reds. Full, new-oak style, demands ageing.

Alpha Estate Mac ★★★→★★★★ Largest vyd owner in Greece, a leading KTIMA defining AMYNTEO. Ktima A (r/w): modern and fruit-focused. Barba Yiannis XINOMAVRO from century-old vines: opulent but detailed.

Amynteo Mac (POP) Captivating, elegant XINOMAVRO (r/rosé/sp) from coolest Greek POP, at 600m (1968ft)+ altitude. More continental French than Med.

Argyros Aeg ★★★★ Top SANTORINI producer; largest vyd owner on island, prices beyond reasonable. Sumptuous VINSANTOS out of this world, Evdemon and Gerontampelo exemplary, reserved yet concentrated.

Avantis Aeg, C Gr ★★★ Boutique wineries in Evia and SANTORINI (called Anhydrous). Top: Agios Chronos (SYRAH/VIOGNIER); Icon in Santorini. On the rich side.

Biblia Chora Mac ★★★ Polished, superb KTIMA. Ovilos (r/w) rivals Bx in style at triple the price. Ever-expanding empire, with sister wineries in Pelop (Dyo Ipsi), SANTORINI (Mikra Thira), GOUMENISSA (Mikro Ktima) and NAOUSSA.

Boutari, J & Son ★→★★★ Historic brand in transition mode under new ownership; trad style overall, excellent value, esp *Grande Res Naoussa* to age 40 yrs+.

Carras, Dom Mac ★★ Historic estate at Halkidiki, recently changed hands, again. Work in progress.

Cephalonia Ion Island famous for mineral, floral ROBOLA (w) and getting famous for dry, herbaceous, tannic MAVRODAPHNE (r). Many excellent growers; for many the next SANTORINI.

Dalamaras Mac ★★★→★★★★ Prodigious producer in NAOUSSA, at top of XINOMAVRO game. Top bottlings are ethereal, dazzlingly complex.

Dougos C Gr ★★★ Ambassador for RAPSANI. Reds are broad and top-class, like Old Vines or MAVROTRAGANO, yet Tourtoura is v. elegant.

Douloufakis Crete ★★★ VIDIANO pioneer. Several versions, all round and expressive, from sparkling to amphora. Try spicy Liatiko Grande Res.

Economou, Ktima Crete ★★★★ One of great artisans of Greece; unicorn status. Latest (and late) releases more natural in style, not for faint-hearted.

Gaia Aeg, Pelop ★★★ Exquisite range from NEMEA, SANTORINI. *Gaia Estate* is top Nemea, ditto for flinty Ammonite Santorini. Stylish, refined.

Gentilini Ion ★★★ Historic CEPHALONIA winery, incl *steely Robola*, esp R24. Benchmark dry MAVRODAPHNE Eclipse (r) is v. precise, tannic, imposing.

Gerovassiliou, Ktima Mac ★★★ Trendsetter on repeat. Practically created MALAGOUSIA genre, smooth and peachy. Don't overlook delicious reds. Link with BIBLIA CHORA.

Goumenissa Mac ★★→★★★ (POP) Excellent XINOMAVRO/Negoska (r), rounder than NAOUSSA. Try Chatzyvaritis (lean), Ligas (wild), Mikro KTIMA (modern), TATSIS (full-on natural).

Hatzidakis Aeg ★★★ Legent of SANTORINI; children of Haridimos H now in charge. Louros, Nyhteri, Skytali, Rambelia all impeccably balanced heavyweights.

Karamolegos Aeg ★★★ Small SANTORINI winery, excellent restaurant on top. Rare bottlings (esp Pyritis, Louroi, Pappas) complex, broad-shouldered.

Karanika Mac ★★★ Arguably best sparkling in Greece; razor-sharp ASSYRTIKO/ XINOMAVRO Brut showing the way.

Karydas, Ktima Mac ★★★ Tiny, amazing vyd in NAOUSSA, crafting complex, herbaceous, age-worthy XINOMAVRO. Hidden jewel, crazy value.

Katogi Averoff Epir, Mac ★★→★★★ Historic Katogi a popular range. Rossiu di Munte (firm, reserved) from 1000m (3281ft)+, one of highest vyds in Europe, while Inima, from across Mac, more forward.

Katsaros Thess ★★★ Tiny KTIMA on Mt Olympus. Ktima red nods at Bx and ages for two decades. Buttery Stella CHARD an ambitious addition.

Kechris ★★→★★★ ASSYRTIKO-based The Tear of the Pine, possibly *world's best Retsina*: full of zing, just a note of pine perfume. Fantastic wine, no kidding.

Kir-Yianni Mac ★★→★★★ NAOUSSA and AMYNTEO originally, now owns SIGALAS in SANTORINI. Stylistically, most modern of the trad.

Ktima "Estate" in Greek. Increasingly seen on labels.

Lazaridi, Costa Att, Mac ★★★ KTIMA in Drama and Att (Oenotria Land). Top: Cava Amethystos CAB FR. Michel Rolland (*see* France) consults, and you can taste it. Plantings in high Drama promising: try lifted MALAGOUSIA.

Lazaridi, Nico Mac ★→★★★ Originally from Drama. Huge range. Top: Perpetuus (r/w). Old-school approach.

Loïc Pasquet (Liber Pater, Bx) behind €700-a-pop rosé from Naxos. Value? Up to you.

Lyrarakis Crete ★★★ *Single-vyd versions* extraordinary. Winery that introduced Dafni, Melissaki, Plyto grapes. Serious, low-key, detailed wines.

Malvasia Group of four POPs recreating famous medieval "Malmsey". Not MALVASIA, but local varieties. POPs are Monemvassia-M in Laconia, M of Paros and M Chandakas-Candia, M of Sitia (from Crete). Lush but never cloying.

Manoussakis Crete ★★★ Initially Rhône-inspired, with help from Dom Pegau, now focusing on Greek varieties: ASSYRTIKO, full MUSCAT of Spinas, VIDIANO and Romeiko (r). Opulent, ripe.

Mantinia Pelop (POP) High-altitude, cool mtn plateau. Crisp, lifted, almost Germanic whites from *Moschofilero*. Excellent fizz next big thing.

Mercouri Pelop ★★ Greece's most beautiful KTIMA on w coast; v.gd dry MAVRODAPHNE/REFOSCO, Italian rather than Greek in style. Must-visit.

Monemvassia Winery - Tsimbidi Pelop ★★→★★★ Only producer of POP MALVASIA-Monemvassia (sw) and godfather of Kydonitsa: try textured, waxy Mature.

Mylonas Att ★★→★★★ Young Stamatis M crafts fine Savatiano in many guises. Mouthwatering, but with true sense of sunny Attican sky.

Naoussa Mac ★★★→★★★★ (POP) Breathtaking XINOMAVRO. Best on par in quality, style (but at fraction of price) with Barolo: firm, linear, otherworldly. Top: DALAMARAS, KARYDAS, KIR-YIANNI, THIMIOPOULOS, many others. Can age for 10 yrs++, premium versions far more.

Nemea Pelop ★★→★★★ (POP) AGIORGITIKO reds: fresh to classic to exotic. Try Driopi from TSELEPOS (French-inspired), AIVALIS (New World-style), GAIA (pristine), Ieropoulos (oak), Mitravelas (modern), PALYVOS (fruit-focused), PAPAÏOANNOU (classic), SKOURAS (polished).

Oeno P ★★★★ New venture of Paris Sigalas, founder of KTIMA SIGALAS. Premier Cru prices, but Grand Cru quality. ASSYRTIKO at its elegant grandest.

Palyvos Pelop ★★→★★★ KTIMA in NEMEA making big-framed, age-worthy reds with AGIORGITIKO and French varieties, from SYRAH to VIOGNIER.

GREECE

Papagiannakos Att ★★→★★★ Original mouthpiece of Savatiano, Vassilis P shows dry-farmed old vines of Att can produce wines of grace, vivacity. Try Vientzi.

Papaioannou Pelop ★★★ Put NEMEA on map. Top: Microclima, Palea Klimata (old vines), Terroir. Four-square reds that keep for ages. AGIORGITIKO at its trad finest.

Pavlidis Mac ★★★ KTIMA in Drama. NZ-like Thema (w) ASSYRTIKO/SAUV BL, Alma is a layered premium rosé. Emphasis range, incl AGIORGITIKO, Assyrtiko, moves away from oak and high alc.

POP Greek equivalent of AOP (appellation d'origine protégée).

Rapsani C Gr XINOMAVRO-based POP on Mt Olympus – the (dry) Nectar the gods feasted on. Made famous by Tsantalis; now DOUGOS, THIMIOPOULOS and others. Softer than NAOUSSA.

Retsina New-wave Retsinas (GAIA, KECHRIS, natural-style Kamara) have freshness, character – impeccable food wine, great alternative to Fino Sherry. Used to be longest nail in coffin of Greek wine, now its rising star.

Samos Aeg ★★→★★★ (POP) Island famed for sweet MUSCAT BL – typical but at its finest. Main producer is co-op; try fortified Anthemis and sun-dried Nectar. Old bottlings are steals. New producers emerging, eg. Nopera, plus dry wines.

Santorini Aeg ★★★→★★★★ Dramatic, windy volcanic island with white (dr/sw) wines to match, from century-old gnarled vines. Luscious VINSANTO, salty, *bone-dry Assyrtiko*. Even with prices rising given huge tourism/land grab pressure, cheapest ★★★★ whites around, age for 20 yrs.

Santo Wines Aeg ★★→★★★ Successful SANTORINI CO-OP. Rich Grande Res, complex VINSANTOS. Lovely veranda next to winery is place to be.

Semeli C Gr, Pelop ★★ Vast range, gd value. Main focus on NEMEA (try Grand Res) and MANTINIA (esp Thea). Soft, approachable style.

Sigalas Aeg ★★★★ Original winery of Paris S, now in v. able hands of KIR-YIANNI. Kavalieros, Nychteri out of this world, marble statue-like beauty, proportions.

Skouras Pelop ★★★ Ever-evolving, quality-oriented KTIMA. Lean, wild-yeast Salto MOSCHOFILERO. Megas Oenos a fine-boned classic. Try solera-aged Labyrinth, complex Peplo rosé. *Recioto*-like (*see* Italy) Titanas is rare Mavrostyfo.

Tatsis Mac ★★★ Natural producer in GOUMENISSA. Not obtrusive; intense, defined.

Thimiopoulos Mac ★★★★ Superstar producer in NAOUSSA and RAPSANI (Terra Petra). Approachable but thought-provoking XINOMAVROS. Single-vyd range is breathtaking, larger-volume cuvées made from same cloth.

T-Oinos Aeg ★★★★ Putting Tinos on the global wine map, with ASSYRTIKO and MAVROTRAGANO of epic proportions. Expensive, esp Rare range, but worth it. Stéphane Derenoncourt (*see* France) consults.

Tour Melas, La C Gr ★★★★ Top-drawer KTIMA in Achinos. Idylle rosé rules the market. Convincingly Médoc-like La Tour Melas and Palies Rizes both top, with eye-popping prices. Amazing B&B.

Tselepos Pelop ★★★ Leader in MANTINIA, NEMEA (Driopi) and SANTORINI (Canava Chrysou). Top cuvées, by father Yiannis and son Aris, velvety, rare masterpieces.

Vassaltis Aeg ★★★ Small establishment in SANTORINI. Gramina and Plethora quirky but convincing.

Vinsanto Aeg ★★★★ Sun-dried, cask-aged luscious but highly acidic ASSYRTIKO and Aidani from SANTORINI that can age forever. Insanely low yields.

Tinos

Mykonos and SANTORINI are crowded; Santorini is getting expensive. Where next? Tinos, another beautiful Cyclades island. T-OINOS is leader, but try Kalathas (Vorias), Vaptistis (Antara), Volacus (MALAGOUSIA), X-Bourgo (r). ASSYRTIKO and MAVROTRAGANO are main varieties, but check out Rozaki, Potamisi or Mavrithiriko.

Eastern Mediterranean & North Africa

EASTERN MEDITERRANEAN

This region is defined by religion and strife. Wine is mainly made by Christians in Cyprus and Lebanon, by Jews in Israel and by Muslims in Turkey. Let's hope that wine rises above politics and is a unifying factor. If more wine was drunk and less coffee, maybe things would be calmer.

CYPRUS

Altitude (up to 1500m/4921ft) and no phylloxera (so plenty of ancient vines) are keys to success on this sunny dry island. Explore the wineries in the hills, native grapes and single-vyd wines; also modern versions of possibly world's most ancient wine, Commandaria.

Cypriot Halloumi cheese dates back to the medieval Byzantine period.

Aes Ambelis ★→★★ Family winery for sound varietals. Try floral/spicy Morokanella, more trad fortified COMMANDARIA.

Argyrides Vineyards **★★→★★★** Beautiful 4th-generation winery run by one of Cyprus's few women winemakers/owners. Standard-setting *Maratheftiko*, plus v.gd VIOGNIER, MERLOT/CAB SAUV, MOURVÈDRE.

Commandaria Rich, sweet PDO; sun-dried XYNISTERI and/or MAVRO; mentioned by Hesiod in 800 BCE, may be oldest wine in continuous production. New unfortified versions from small producers: KYPEROUNDA, TSIAKKAS, ZAMBARTAS. For more trad fortifieds: AES AMBELIS, St Barnabas (KAMANTERENA), St John (KEO).

Constantinou ★→★★ Family winery; dry reds, esp Shiraz, best.

Ezousa ★→★★ Small winery focusing on terroir wines, impressing with XYNISTERI.

Kamanterena (SODAP) ★ Large co-op in Paphos hills, been facing challenges, now under new management. Kamanterena label for sound local varietals. Project X for superior single-vyd versions, plus gd trad St Barnabas COMMANDARIA.

KEO ★ Large drinks group and brewer with winery at Mallia. Notable trad-style St John COMMANDARIA.

Kyperounda **★★→★★★** *Petritis* showcases ageability of XYNISTERI, plus terroir releases from East and West vyds. Juicy, entry-point Andessitis (r), new easy-drinking MARATHEFTIKO. Excellent own-vyd flagships: *Epos* white (CHARD), red (CAB SAUV, SYRAH). Lovely modern COMMANDARIA.

Makarounas ★★ Promising young organic winery with experimental approach. Try zesty Vasilissa, Promara from amphora, juicy Yiannoudi.

Tsiakkas **★★→★★★** Standard-setting, high vyds, organic, focus on local grapes. Highlights: (w) *Promara*, XYNISTERI, elegant Exelixis; (r) v.gd Vamvakada (aka MARATHEFTIKO); fine Mouklas MAVRO; excellent *Yiannoudi*; new red flagship Anagennisis blend of local varieties. Fantastic, fruity, modern COMMANDARIA.

Vasilikon, K&K Winery **★★** Family winery, known for consistent XYNISTERI, juicy Ayios Onoufrios red blend, long-lived Methy. Also new single-vyd Xynisteri, jasmine-scented Vasilissa, complex robust LEFKADA.

Vlassides ★★→★★★ Family winery, quality pioneer, famous for SHIRAZ. New emphasis on local varieties, esp excellent Alátes XYNISTERI, *Óroman* based on Yiannoudi. Winery flagship is Artion, entry point is fruit-driven Grifos range.

Vouni Panayia ★★ Family winery all about local grapes, limited batches: Alina XYNISTERI, MARATHEFTIKO, Morokanella, Promara, Spourtiko.

Zambartas ★★→★★★ Australia-trained winemaker making v.gd single-vyd range: Margelina from centenarian vines, XYNISTERI, Not Orange rosé. Zambartas range v.gd, top SHIRAZ/LEFKADA. Superb, just-released Melusine COMMANDARIA.

ISRAEL

Not an easy year; disrupted by war. Wineries on an emergency footing. However, despite the constraints, vineyard work and winemaking continues, at least providing a feeling of continuity and normality. Life goes on.

1848 ★★ Best of Shor family, winemakers since 1848; v.gd CAB FR, Argaman.

Abaya ★★ Rehabilitates abandoned vyds. Gluggable, natural CARIGNANS.

Agur ★★→★★★ Rejuvenated. Well-crafted Blanc, Rosé and Kessem (r).

Ahat ★★ Quality *garagiste*. Superb CHENIN BL, complex ROUSSANNE/VIOGNIER, rosé.

Amphorae ★→★★ Beautiful winery; gd white and rosé. Wine-tourism pioneer.

Barkan-Segal ★→★★ Large winery owned by Israel's largest brewery. Barkan: Cherry-berry Argaman. Gold popular brand. Segal: whole-cluster SYRAH.

Carmel ★→★★ Historic, est by Rothschild 1882. Largest winery. Big-selling brands: Selected, Private Collection. Quality label: Carmel Signature.

Castel, Dom du ★★★★ Pioneer Judean Hills. Grand Vin is complex, layered Bx blend. Consistent excellence. Plush Petit Castel, great-value second label. Fresh rosé. Burgundian "C" Blanc du Castel (CHARD). Fragrant La Vie, mainly SAUV BL.

Clos de Gat ★★★ Genuine estate. Powerful SYRAH; gd CHARD. Chanson (w) gd value.

Cremisan ★→★★ Palestinian winery. Monastery est 1885, pioneer of local varieties. Other Palestinian wines: Kassis promising vigneron. Philokalia natural, artisan.

Dalton ★★→★★★ Galilee pioneer. English-Israeli family. Vibrant Majestic CARIGNAN, mouthfilling PETITE SIRAH. Citrus PINOT GR. New Family Collection label.

Feldstein ★★→★★★ Argaman pioneer, Dabouki specialist. Complex Gilgamesh.

Flam ★★★→★★★★ Flam bros. Med-style winery. New Judean Hills vyd on ancient terraces. Elegant Bx-blend Noble, classy CAB SAUV. Fruity-forward SYRAH. Classico always great value. Fragrant white (SAUV BL/CHARD). Crisp rosé.

Galil Mountain ★→★★ Fruit only from Upper Galilee. Leader in sustainability. Vibrant GRENACHE. Yiron gd value. Bold single-vyd PETIT VERDOT.

Golan, Ch ★★→★★★ Geshem, v.gd Med blends. Prestige Eliad. Naveh kosher label.

Gva'ot ★★ Researching local varieties. PINOT N best in Israel. Prestige Masada.

Jezreel Valley ★→★★★ Mainly known for characterful, oaky Argaman and CARIGNAN.

Lahat ★★★ Rhône specialist. Enchanting GSM, peppery SYRAH. ROUSSANNE/VIOGNIER can age. Innovative use of amphorae.

Lewinsohn ★★★ Graceful SYRAH; v.gd CHARD. Rare whole-cluster red. Crisp rosé.

Margalit ★★→★★★ Father and son specialize in Bx varieties. Complex CAB FR.

Mia Luce ★★→★★★ *Garagiste*. Rhôney SYRAH, superb MARSELAN, fine COLOMBARD.

Mika ★★ Steely SAUV BL/ROUSSANNE blend; v.gd whites; elegant PETIT VERDOT.

Nana ★★ High-elevation desert vyd. Excellent CHARD, CHENIN BL.

Oryah, Ya'acov ★★ Creative artisan. Pioneer of orange wines. Always experimenting.

Pelter ★★ Popular brand. Light, fragrant SAUV BL. Matar ★→★★ kosher.

Pinto ★→★★ Desert start-up. Bright entry-level wines. Spicy SHIRAZ.

Psagot ★→★★ Fast-growing. Peak is succulent Med blend. New fizz.

Razi'el ★★★ Ben Zaken family (CASTEL). Barrel-aged gastro rosé; fine-textured, focused Med blend. Handcrafted trad-method fizz: NV, Rosé.

Recanati ★★→★★★ Specialist in Med varieties like CARIGNAN, MARSELAN, PETITE SIRAH. Opulent, bold Special Res. New winery in operation.

Sea Horse ★★ Idiosyncratic. Quirky Counoise. Intriguing Oz (CINSAULT/GRENACHE).

Shiloh ★★→★★★ Built new winery. CAB SAUV: robust, rich, oaky. Regular award-winner. Honi v. drinkable. Prestige Mosaic.

Shvo ★★★ Non-interventionist winemaker, a true vigneron. Super-rustic chewy red, rare Gershon SAUV BL, fresh BARBERA, characterful rosé.

Sphera ★★★→★★★★ Whites only. Cool-climate White Concept varietals; gd mouthfeel, texture, precision, intensity. Well-defined First Page blend. Complex, rare White Signature (SEM), gd for ageing. Delicate trad fizz.

Desert grape pips, dated 900 CE, genetically v. close to known varieties Be'er, Syriki.

Tabor ★→★★ Ecological vyds. Whites best, esp ROUSSANNE, SAUV BL; gd CHENIN BL.
Tel ★★ N Golan exquisite RIES, fresh GRENACHE, herbaceous CAB FR.
Teperberg ★ →★★ Since 1870. Largest family winery. Legacy CAB FR, PETITE SIRAH excellent; gd value at every price point.
Tulip ★★ Works with adults with special needs; gd SYRAH, SAUV BL. Maia, Med style.
Tura ★→★★ Central Mtns. Full-flavoured Mountain Peak, fleshy MERLOT.
Tzora ★★★★ Leader in white awakening and terroir-led, precision winemaking. Beautiful high-altitude Shoresh vyd. Talented winemaker (MW). Wines show intensity, balance, elegance. Crisp, complex, mineral Shoresh Bl; Judean Hills (r/w) outstanding value. Graceful Misty Hills (CAB SAUV/SYRAH) with finesse.
Vitkin ★★→★★★ ABC icebreaker. Quality CARIGNAN pioneer. Quality PETITE SIRAH. Floral PINOT N. Complex GRENACHE BL. Great-value entry-level (r/w/rosé).
Vortman ★→★★ Passionate vigneron; N Coastal; v.gd COLOMBARD, chewy Levant (r).
Yarden ★★→★★★★ Cutting-edge viticulture. Sustainability pioneer. King of CAB SAUV, with ageing ability. PINOT GR gd. Superb Blanc de Blancs (sp). Second label: Gamla. SANGIOVESE of interest. Mt Hermon (r) big-selling blend.
Yatir ★★→★★★ Desert winery, forest vyds. Velvet Yatir Forest (r). Value Mt Amasa. Complex PETIT VERDOT. Less expensive: Darom by Yatir.

LEBANON

Muscular, international blends still dominate, but there are more terroir-driven wines made with an increasing range of native varieties like Asmi N, Aswad Karesh, Jouzani, Marini, Meksassi, Merwah. More extended skin-contact whites, often in amphorae. Unoaked, moderately extracted "heritage" Rhône varieties CARIGNAN, CINSAULT and GRENACHE are consolidating their reputation as Lebanon's best-performing reds, while high-altitude (1000m/3281ft+) CHARD, SAUV BL, VIOGNIER, as well as ASSYRTIKO, SAPARAVI, continue to impress.

One of alleged tombs of Noah – the first vigneron – is near Chateau Ksara, Bekaa V.

Coteaux du Liban ★★ CINSAULT blend and varietal crunchy rosé, plus old-vine Cinsault, Obeideh, VIOGNIER varietals. Young winemaking couple. Watch.
Couvent Rouge ★★★ Remote, E Bekaa winery dedicated to swapping cannabis fields for vyds. Range of easy-drinkers (r/w/rosé), posher oaked SYRAH and VIOGNIER, plus fun white and rosé pét-nat, both with with local Obeideh.
Heritage, Ch A branch of arak-making Touma family. Charismatic winemaker Dargham Touma (aka Dr D) makes hefty Family Res CAB SAUV/SYRAH; Plaisir du Vin and nine-variety, Cinsault-led blend called, you guessed it, Nine. Plus SAUV BL, VIOGNIER, MUSCAT Blanc de Blancs.
Ixsir ★★→★★★ High vyds across Lebanon; stony SYRAH-based blends, floral whites and prestige El red. Altitudes range and Grande Res Rosé excellent.
Karam ★★★ S Lebanon's 1st winery. Owner retired airline pilot. Extensive range incl local Meksassi (w), ALBARIÑO; SEM/SAUV BL/VIOGNIER Cloud 9 a bestseller. Also value Maison (r), TOURIGA N varietal. CAB/SYRAH/MERLOT St John more polished.
Kefraya, Ch ★★→★★★★ Innovative; French winemaker. Les Exceptions varietals; local Aswad Karesh (r), SAPERAVI in amphorae; complex *Comte de M*, oaky Comtesse de M, famous Blanc de Blanc, fruity Les Breteches, plus white, rosé.

Ksara, Ch ★★★ Est 1857; Ch red is the icon. More innovative now: old-vine CARIGNAN and local Merwah. Consistent, v.gd value. Blanc de Blancs, CHARD outstanding. Gris de Gris "adult" rosé. Cuveé du Printemps superb summer red.

Marsyas, Ch ★★ Powerful flagship CAB/SYRAH, thrilling CHARD/SAUV BL. Diffusion range B-Qa de Marsyas. Also Satyr range (unoaked Cab, Sauv Bl). Owner of complex ★★★ Bargylus (Syria), miracle wines made in impossible conditions.

Massaya ★★ Terraces de Baalbeck: refined GSM. Entry-level Les Colombiers v.gd value. Also Cap Est (r) from E Bekaa vyds on Anti-Lebanon Mtns. Punchy rosé and elegant, floral white fermented at high altitude in 2nd winery in Mt Lebanon. High-profile, Châteauneuf and St-Émilion partners.

Mersel Natural wines, pét-nat; reviving ancient Jouzani, Marini, plus Merwah, Obeideh, often in amphorae. Varietal CINSAULT. Destined for cult status.

Musar, Ch ★★★→★★★★ 02 03 05' 09 10 11 12 13 14 15 16 *Unique recognizable style.* Best after 15–20 yrs in bottle. Flagship red still most famous, but Obeideh/ Merwah (w) arguably more interesting; ages indefinitely. Second label: Hochar (r) now higher profile. Musar Jeune is softer, easy-drinking.

Oumsiyat, Ch Mt Lebanon winery; no-nonsense, easy-drinking Bx/Rhône blends and varietals that, as well as usual suspects, incl ASSYRTIKO, Obeidy [sic].

St Thomas, Ch ★→★★★ Old Bekaa arak producers and grape farmers. French-trained great-grandson Joe Touma nailing it with Les Gourmets "cadet" range of red (aromatic CINSAULT), white, rosé. Textured Obaidy [sic] and muscular, high-altitude PINOT N. Vintage "Chateau" wines ageing well.

Sept ★★★ Pioneer *garagiste*. Skin-contact Merwah, Obeideh; other min-contact varietals VIOGNIER, GRENACHE, haunting SYRAH.

Tourelles, Dom des ★★→★★★★ Winery (C19), run by dynamic Fouzi Issa. Blockbuster SYRAH, gd Marquis des Beys (r/w). Top old-vine CARIGNAN, CINSAULT, Obeideh/ Merwah blend and skin-contact Merwah; equally gd classic red. Classy rosé.

Wardy, Dom ★★ Varietal pioneer: CINSAULT, Obeideh, SAUV BL, VIOGNIER. Also trad French blends, incl outstanding, easy-drinking red.

TURKEY

Possibly the best wines are from international varieties, but those from local varieties are far more interesting. Many wineries don't understand that yet.

What did the Hittites ever do for us? "Wiyana" is the Hittite word for wine.

Buzbag ★ Main brand since 40s. Rustic ÖKÜZGÖZÜ/BOĞAZKERE (Kayra). Better now.
Chamlija ★★→★★★ Terroir wines; v.gd CABS SAUV/FR. Aromatic Papaskarasi.
Corvus ★→★★ Bozcaada island. Intense, oaky New World style.
Doluca ★→★★ Three generations. Villa Doluca gd value. Sarafin noble varieties.
Kalpak ★★→★★★ Deep, rich, full-bodied Bx blends; min intervention.
Kavaklidere ★→★★★ Largest winery. Cote d'Avanos NARINCE. Pendore ÖKÜZGÖZÜ.
Kayra ★→★★ Plush ÖKÜZGÖZÜ, tannic BOĞAZKERE, fresh NARINCE. Owned by Diageo.
Likya ★→★★ Revives lost varieties. Arkeo label incl vibrant Fersun.
Pasaeli ★→★★★ Innovative champion of local varieties. Kalkarasi Blush v. drinkable.
Sevilen ★→★★ Large winery offering value; SAUV BL, SYRAH best.
Suvla ★→★★ Full-bodied Bx-blend Sur; fruity SYRAH backed by oak.
Urla ★★ Big-spend winery. NERO D'AVOLA/Karasi is concentrated, spicy.

Notable names in North Africa & Eastern Levant
Jordan Zumot (Saint George). **Morocco** Amal, ★★ Baccari (Première de Baccari), Castel Group, ★ Celliers de Meknès (Ch Roslane), La Ferme Rouge, ★→★★ Ouled Thaleb (*Tandem/Syrocco*), ★→★★ Val d'Argan (Orian r), Zouina. **Syria** ★★★ *Bargylus*. **Tunisia** Neferis.

Asia & Black Sea & Caucasus

ASIA

China What to drink here? PETIT MANSENG is not a variety that jumps to mind when we think of Chinese wine. Although little grown, Petit Manseng is possibly China's best-performing white in ratio to its modest production. Shandong's Taila Winery is a serial award-winner with its cracking Vendange Tardive. Longting, another Shandong stalwart, has just launched a v. convincing dry Petit Manseng with a screwcap. RIES also performs well, incl Hebei's Canaan Wine Estate, Ningxia's Dom du 1er Juin and Xinjiang's Silk Road. China's best unoaked CHARD – reminiscent of Chablis (see France) – is Jiabeilan Baby Feet Chard by multi-award-winning winemaker Zhang Jing. Pernod Ricard's Helan Mtn Res Chard, while oaked, is equally fine and elegant. China's fixation on CAB SAUV continues. Lafite's Dom de Long Dai from Shandong commands eye-watering prices, as does Moët-Hennessy's Ao Yun in Yunnan. China's own and best Bx blend is Jiabeilan Res. Lower priced, it equals in quality. Other producers to look out for incl Grace Vyd, Kanaan Winery, Li Family, Silver Heights, Tiansai and Xige Estate. CoPower Jade Fei Tswei and Dom Chanson produce excellent pure CAB FR. As for MARSELAN – (Cab Sauv x Grenache) – the best are unoaked or see v. little wood. Although a latecomer to the variety, Jiabeilan Baby Feet has shot straight to the top rank. Joining this elite group are Ch Kings and Jade Vyd. Ch Rongzi's unoaked PINOT N bristles with varietal expression. Overachiever Jiabeilan and Dom du 1er Juin join the leaders.

Will China ever turn to making reds that taste of fruit, not furniture?

India Expect upfront, juicy wines that match the local food. There's plenty of oak, and reds are lush. There are c.70 producers; some is exported, but not much. The climate isn't suited to wine-growing, but try Fratelli, Grover Zampa (Bx styles; Michel Rolland consults, see France), KRSMA, M/S Akluj, Sula (The Source GRENACHE Rosé, oaked SAUV BL), Vallonné, plus Chandon and York fizz. Main regions: Andhra Pradesh, Karnataka, Maharashtra states (CHARD, CHENIN BL, Sauv Bl, RIES, VIOGNIER, Grenache, TEMPRANILLO and CAB SAUV).

Koshu is versatile: goes with sushi, sashimi, tempura.

Japan News here is the Burgundian-Japanese collaboration between De Montille (see France) and Hokkaido: PINOT N making waves, also CHARD, KERNER, ZWEIGELT. Chitose Kimura Vyd Pinot N is impressive, also KERNER. Staying in the northerly island, Camel Farm continues to dazzle with BLAUFRÄNKISCH. Innovative growers are looking for alternatives to Bx varieties, which have difficulty ripening fully. Ch Mercian Mariko Vyd SYRAH in Nagano adds to the discussion. Japan's finest bottle-fermented fizz is even more reminiscent of Champagne now that climate change has been producing increasingly ripe fruit in France. Grace Blanc de Blancs, Chard with min 5 yrs on lees, is gd. Based in Yamanashi, birthplace of Japanese wine, Grace is benchmark for KOSHU, from screwcap entry-level, eg., to single-vyd Cuvée Misawa, 1st subregional Koshu, planted in Akeno. Best Koshu are without oak, and Sanwa Shurui produces a worthy version. Other names to look for: Aruga Branca, Ch Mars, Dom Hide, Haramo, Huggy Wine, Kurambon, L'Orient, Lumiere, Manns Wines, Marquis, Mercian, Morita Koshu Winery, Soryu and Suntory's single-vyd Tomi No Oka.

BLACK SEA & CAUCASUS

The war in Ukraine continues at the time of writing. Despite the losses and damages, wineries are upbeat. Production hasn't halted. The Caucasus countries cling to their millennia-old wine heritage, which is now modern again. "Ancient world" wines of Georgia and Armenia, produced with long skin macerations and vinified in amphorae, are in demand among wine geeks, millennials, adepts of natural winemaking. Azerbaijan, known for brandy, is now emerging as a quality wine producer. Moldova, with its value-driven wines, aims for a higher level. Curiosities can be found in Uzbekistan and Kazakhstan.

Armenia Tiny country with fascinating wines and gd brandy. Local wine trad is as old as Georgia's, with a shared use of amphorae, known here as *karas*. Distinctively Armenian are (w) Voskeat and (r) Areni (can be superb), Akhtanak, Karmrahyut. Phylloxera-free vyds at high altitude are common. Try Armenia Wines and Hin Areni or boutique ArmAs, Old Bridge, Tushpa, Van Ardi, Voskeni, Voskevaz, v.gd Zorah.

Georgia *Qvevris* are synonymous with Georgian winemaking. Clay vessels, mostly enormous, are used for skin-macerated fermentation and ageing of Georgian whites and reds. The practice goes back unbroken for 8000 yrs: new experiments involve temp control, different sizes and rosé wines. Ancient methods coexist with modern production. A host of indigenous varieties is unique, with around 40 in commercial use. Red-star SAPERAVI is great in full-bodied, tannic and age-worthy wines. Acidic white RKATSITELI, mainly from Kakheti, has prompted the phenomenon of orange/amber wines. White Chinuri, Kisi, Mtsvane of note. There is a winery roughly for every 30 people in Georgia. Better-known names: Badagoni, Ch Mukhrani, Jakeli, Khareba, Marani, Papari V, Shumi Winery, Tbilvino, Teliani V, Tsinandali Estate, Vazisubani Estate.

Moldova Neighbouring Ukraine and Romania, Moldova has more vyds than S Africa and boasts the largest cellars in the world. Production offers value at all price levels. Backed by long history and fame in tsarist Russia, it has yet to realize its modern potential. International grapes dominate, but worth seeking local: (w) FETEASCĂS ALBĂ/REGALĂ, Viorica, (r) FETEASCĂ NEAGRĂ, Rară Neagră. Try unusual red blend Negru de Purcari (CAB SAUV/SAPERAVI/Rară Neagră) and Icewine. Leading producers: Cricova (sp), Milestii Mici, Purcari Winery. Plus gd to excellent quality: Asconi, Castel Mimi, Ch Vartely, Et Cetera, Fautor, Gitana, Lion Gri, Vinăria Bostavan, Vinăria din Vale.

Russia Sentiment here, backed by politicians, is to drink local wine, but choices are limited and often unexciting; vyds are in s. Natural conditions best by Black Sea and River Kuban. Harsh climate in Don V requires vines to be buried in winter. Reds are better than whites. Indigenous tannic Krasnostop has est itself as the signature red grape; also Sibirkovy (w) and Tsimliansky (r) can be gd. Most winemaking is about international grapes, esp red Bx varieties, ALIGOTÉ, CHARD, RIES. At the time of writing, Russia is of course under international sanctions.

Ukraine There's never been such awareness of Ukrainian wine as now. The war has damaged vyds, destroyed wineries, limited human resources, hiked costs, but work doesn't stop. Stretching from the Black Sea to Carpathian Mtns and Kyiv, vyds cover 36,000 ha. Russian-invaded Crimea accounts for sought-out premium wines, esp Oleg Repin, Uppa Winery. Odessa is largest Ukrainian wine area: Beykush Winery, Bolgrad, Esse, Guliev Wines, Kolonist, Stoic (former Prince Trubetskoy Winery), Satera, Shabo, Veles, Villa Tinta. Fizz has important heritage: ArtWinery, Novy Svet, Odessavinprom, Zolotaya Balka. Historic fortified styles have niche too: Ch Chizay, Koktebel, Massandra, Solnechnaya Dolina.

United States

NORTH COAST
Mendocino
Sierra Foothills
Anderson Valley
Redwood Valley
Clear Lake
Clear Lake
Sacramento
Lake Tahoe
NEVADA
Sonoma Coast
Northern Sonoma
Sacramento
El Dorado
Shenandoah Valley
Amador
Napa Valley
Carneros
Coombsville/Oak Knoll
Sonoma Valley
Lodi
Clarksburg
Calaveras
San Francisco
Livermore Valley
Santa Cruz Mountains
Santa Clara Valley
CENTRAL VALLEY
San Joaquin
Monterey
Salinas
Carmel Valley/
Santa Lucia Highlands
Arroyo Seco
San Lucas
CENTRAL COAST
Fresno
Pacific Ocean
Paso Robles
CALIFORNIA
San Luis Obispo
Edna Valley/Arroyo Grande Valley
Santa Maria Valley
Santa Barbara
Sta Rita Hills
Santa Ynez Valley
Santa Barbara
Los Angeles

UNITED STATES

Abbreviations used in the text
(*see also* principal viticultural
areas pp.245, 262, 268):

Arroyo GV	Arroyo Grande Valley, CA
Clark	Clarksburg, CA
Coomb	Coombsville, CA
Mad	Madera, CA
Oak K	Oak Knoll, CA
PNW	Pacific Northwest
San LO	San Luis Obispo, CA
Santa Cz Mts	Santa Cruz Mountains, CA
Son	Sonoma, CA

Anyone who thinks they know US wine now probably doesn't. Yes, those luxury-market Napa Cabs are still there. But the rest of the country – including much of California – is moving further and further away from that model. Local conditions determine what can be grown, and yes, there are plenty of candidates for the luxury market in other states – but also plenty of experimental plantings and experimental cellar techniques, all aimed at producing wines that reflect their origin, that taste authentic, as if somebody got down into the vineyard, ran the soil through their fingers and thought. And for anybody interested in Pinot Noir, there are some sensational examples.

American Viticultural Areas
With no production rules or trad to protect, AVAs are only loosely comparable to appellations contrôlées. Administered by the US government's TTB, they are instead guides to location – and climate, soil, market – and are a wine-minded alternative to state or county labels. Whether a region within a state or a traits-based overlap such as high-toned Columbia Gorge shared by WA and OR, or NY, PA, OH's cool, water-tempered Lake Erie, there are 269 est AVAs – and a steady queue of applied and pending. Most (149) are in CA, which boasts a wealth of nested AVA subregions, some hyperfocused, like Napa V's Stags Leap District. While an AVA label indicates a min higher standard at the federal level (state and county labels mean 75% provenance, AVA promises 85%), some states have stricter rules: OR famously demands 100% for the former, 95% for the latter. AVA approval standards are rigorous: petitions must show distinguishing features verifiable on US Geological Survey maps, and how they affect viticulture inside vs outside the petitioned zone – whose proposed name must be one historically applied to the area. The TTB says AVAs allow "producers to better describe the origin of their wines and... consumers to better identify wines". Some even translate to higher prices.

Arizona (AZ)

Well-est regions, wineries; high quality, dynamic industry. High desert climate allows gd ripening: Sonoita and Verde V limestone-based; Willcox volcanic-based. Best varieties: Iberian, Med, Bx, with MALVASIA leading white. Wineries incl: **Arizona Stronghold** ★★★ two ranges – everyday Provisioner, top Arizona Stronghold. Tuscan blend Mangus (r) v.gd. **Bodega Pierce** grown in Willcox AVA; Malvasia (w), PINOT N rosé. **Caduceus Cellars** ★★★ consistent quality leader with Nagual del Sensei SAGRANTINO top; also v.gd Dos Ladrones (w), Primer Paso (r). Owned, along with sibling winery Merkin Vyds, by musician Maynard James Keenan. **Callaghan Vyds** ★★★ excellent Iberian and Bx styles; flagship Caitlin's PETIT VERDOT/CAB SAUV (r), TEMPRANILLO-led Padres (r); Malvasia (w) Love Muffin. **Ch Tumbleweed** ★★ old vyds; compare single-vyd/single-variety Cimarron Vyd wines. **Dos Cabezas WineWorks** emphasis on blends; Aguileron (r), Meskeoli (w). **Javelina Leap Vyd & Winery** SYRAH, Tempranillo, ZIN signatures. **Page Springs Cellars** Rhône specialist, esp Syrah Clone series and single-vyd ROUSSANNE. **Pillsbury Wine Company** ★★ owned by film-maker Sam Pillsbury; estate-grown, wild-yeast Rhône varieties; SHIRAZ-based Guns and Kisses (r). **Rune Wines** low-intervention winemaking, mainly Rhône varieties; graphic, illustrated labels. **Sand-Reckoner** ★★ dry aromatic Malvasia, rich Tempranillo.

California (CA)

After decades of increasing wine consumption, younger buyers are exiting wine, and this is a legitimate concern for the industry worldwide. Next gens are increasingly opting for pre-mixed cocktails, alcoholic seltzers and mocktails over wine. Maybe the expensive, klutzy, "natural" wines made from mediocre grape varieties foisted on young consumers were uninspiring. PINOT N, ZIN, SAUV BL are delivering great CA wines. All are exciting for the same reason: winemakers are leaning into fresh, focused, zippy, less-complicated wines from outstanding fruit, and that fruit is all being grown in the proper place. CA's heritage grape, Zin, has zagged abruptly from bombastic to balanced and elegant in recent yrs, all for the better. Sauv Bl makers cribbing notes from NZ are producing more direct, coherent, refreshing whites with a sense of place and distinctly CA character. Pinot N has been an emergent marvel in CA since the 90s, but in the past 10 yrs, it's hit an entirely different gear in NorCal. It might not be burgundy, but it's damn fine. After yrs of drought and fires, CA wine is looking strong again. Analysis suggests CA has suffered less dramatic climate change than many places to date. The pressing question: who will buy this great wine?

Recent vintages

CA is too diverse for simple summaries. There can certainly be differences between the N, Central and S thirds of the state, but no "bad" vintages in over a decade. Recent relief from drought and autumn fires appreciated!

2023 Lower crop, but v. high quality after long, cool season. Late, great harvest.
2022 Spring frosts = smaller crop; state-wide Sept heatwave not ideal, but expect concentration, high quality.
2021 Small crop but high quality. Fires hurt El Dor Co, parts of Lake County.
2020 Small crop: great whites. Fire issues, but some early picked wines v.gd.
2019 Solid harvest. Minor late losses in Alex V to fires, smoke taint.
2018 Bumper crop of great quality, but smoke issues in Lake County.
2017 Wildfires in Napa, Son after most grapes picked; quality mostly v.gd.
2016 Gd quality: reds/whites show great freshness, charm.
2015 Dry yr, low yields, but quality surprisingly gd, concentrated.

Principal viticultural areas

There are well over 100 AVAs in CA. Below are the key players.

Alexander Valley (Alex V) Son. Warm region in upper Son. Best known for gd Zin, Cab Sauv on hillsides.
Amador County (Am Co) Warm Sierra County with wealth of old-vine Zin; Rhône grapes also flourish.
Anderson Valley (And V) Mend. Pacific fog and winds follow Navarro River inland. Superb Pinot N, Chard, sparkling, v.gd Ries, Gewurz, some stellar Syrah.
Atlas Peak E Napa. Exceptional Cab Sauv, Merlot.
Calistoga (Cal) Warmer n end of Napa V. Red-wine territory esp Cab Sauv.
Carneros (Car) Napa, Son. Cool AVA at n tip of SF Bay; gd Pinot N, Chard; Merlot, Syrah, Cab Sauv on warmer sites, v.gd sparkling.
Coombsville (Coomb) Napa. Cool region nr SF Bay; top Cab Sauv in Bx style.
Diamond Mountain Napa. High-elevation vines, outstanding Cab Sauv.
Dry Creek Valley (Dry CV) Son. Top Zin, gd Sauv Bl; gd hillside Cab Sauv, Zin.
Edna Valley (Edna V) San LO. Cool Pacific winds; v.gd Chard.
El Dorado County (El Dor Co) High-altitude inland area surrounding Placerville. Some real talent emerging with Rhône grapes, Zin, Cab and more.
Howell Mountain Napa. Briary Napa Cab Sauv from steep, volcanic hillsides.
Livermore Valley (Liv V) Suburban, gravelly, warm region e of SF, gd potential.

Mendocino County (Mend) Large county n of Son County, incl warm Red V and cool And V.

Mendocino Ridge (Mend Rdg) Mend. Emerging region, dictated by elevation over 365m (1198ft). Cool, above fog, lean soils.

Monterey County (Mont) Big ranches in Salinas V: affordable Chard, Pinot N in cool, windy conditions. Carmel V bit warmer, Arroyo Seco moderate.

Mount Veeder Napa. High mtn vyds for gd Chard, Cab Sauv.

Napa Valley Cab Sauv, Merlot, Cab Fr. Look to sub-AVAs for meaningful terroir-based wines, and mtn areas for most complex, age-worthy.

Oakville (Oak) Napa. Prime Cab Sauv territory on gravelly bench.

Paso Robles (P Rob) San LO. Popular with visitors. Reds: Rhône, Bx varieties.

Pritchard Hill (P Hill) E Napa. Elevated, woodsy, prime terrritory for Cab Sauv.

Red Hills of Lake County (R Hills) N extension of Mayacama range; great Cab Sauv country.

Redwood Valley (Red V) Mend. Warmer inland region; gd Zin, Cab Sauv, Sauv Bl.

Russian River Valley (RRV) Son. Pacific fog lingers; Pinot N, Chard, gd Zin on benchland.

Rutherford (Ruth) Napa. Outstanding Cab Sauv, esp hillside vyds.

Saint Helena (St H) Napa. Lovely balanced Cab Sauv.

Santa Barbara County (Santa B) County n of LA; transverse valleys, several notable subzones, cool and warm.

Santa Lucia Highlands (Santa LH) Mont. Higher elevation, s-facing hillsides, great Pinot N, Syrah, Rhônes.

Santa Maria Valley (Santa MV) Santa B. Coastal cool; gd Pinot N, Chard, Viognier.

Sta Rita Hills (Sta RH) Santa B. Excellent Pinot N.

Santa Ynez (Santa Ynz) Santa B. Rhônes (r/w), Chard, Sauv Bl best bet.

Sierra Foothills (Sierra Fhills) El Dor Co, Am Co, Calaveras County. All improving.

Sonoma Coast (Son Coast) A v. cool climate; edgy Pinot N, Chard, Syrah.

Sonoma Valley (Son V) Note Son V is area within Son County; gd Chard, v.gd Zin, excellent Cab Sauv from Son Mtn sub-AVA.

Spring Mountain Napa. Elevated Cab Sauv, complex soil mixes and exposures.

Stags Leap (Stags L) Napa. Classic red, black-fruited Cab Sauv; v.gd Merlot.

West Sonoma Coast (W Son Coast) Exceptionally cool, marine-influenced parts of Son Coast: Chard, Pinot N, Syrah.

Acorn RRV ★★→★★★ Preserving CA heritage making lively co-fermented field blends from historic Alegria vyd, featuring ZIN plus 17 other mixed black grapes.

Acumen Napa ★★★→★★★★ Pedigreed, hillside Atlas Peak Cabs (mostly) from volcanic terroir; winemaker Phillip Titus (CHAPPELLET). Not cheap, but legit, and age-worthy. I do love *Mountainside* SAUV BL, CAB SAUV.

Alma de Cattleya RRV ★★★ Colombian-born Bibiana González Ravé, with mad CV making wine in Europe and US at 1st-tier wineries, stakes her own claim in CA. Resonant, unpretentious, affordable PINOT N; sublime CHARD. Not to be missed.

Andrew Murray Vineyards Santa Y ★★★ SYRAH leads Rhône pack, but white VIOGNIER, ROUSSANNE, fresh GRENACHE BL hits too.

Anthill Farms Son Coast ★★★ Three hard-working WILLIAMS-SELYEM alumni: lively, ethereal cool-climate PINOT N, SYRAH, old-vine, head-trained CHARD from coastal SON COAST, AND v. Great-value AND v Pinot N. Serious up-and-comer.

Aperture Son ★★★→★★★★ Winemaker Jesse Katz been on steep trajectory for two decades, now controls more land and facilities, finally his own brand. One to watch. Excellent Bx-inspired reds.

A. Rafanelli Winery Dry CV ★★★→★★★★ Generations of family wisdom contributing expertise to superb ZIN-based reds in sweet terroir for Zin.

Balletto RRV ★★→★★★ Refreshingly from-the-heart, pure CA across board at loveable prices, most notably classically proportioned RRV CHARD.

Barnett Spring Mtn ★★★ Under-the-radar mtn-top gem managed by David Tate, who also makes CHARD, PINOT N from SON V. Screaming gd wines across board, towering views, plus 1st-rate NAPA V CAB SAUV – all well worth drive up mtn.

Beaulieu Vineyard (BV) Napa V, Ruth ★★★→★★★★ Iconic Georges de Latour Private Res CAB SAUV is back in fine form; spin-off branded wines are serviceable down the line. Bouncing back!

Beckmen Vineyards Santa B ★★★ Exceptional, Rhône-inspired; innovative family winery firmly committed to bio agriculture. Affordable, excellent Cuvée le Bec red blend popular nationwide.

Bedrock Wine Co Son V ★★★ Morgan Peterson's label is a paean to historic ZIN vyds, techniques. Wisdom of ages seen through clear young eyes.

Beringer Napa ★★→★★★★ Private Res CAB SAUV, single-vyd Cabs serious, age-worthy. Historic ST H location well worth a visit. CHARD now quite gd.

Bevan Cellars N Coast ★★★★ Boutique brand (mostly subscription) from Russel B, collector-turned-winemaker. Exceptional wines from select sites in NAPA, SON. Age-worthy Tin Box CAB SAUV (Napa V), Dry Stack SAUV BL (Bennet V, Son) v.gd.

B. Kosuge Wines Son ★★★ Ex-SAINTSBURY winemaker Byron K devotes himself to subtle, refined PINOT N from N Coast. SON COAST Pinot N, sublime, well priced.

Blue Farm Son Formidable Donum Estate alum Anne Moller-Racke finally pilots her own PINOT N-driven project in SON from CAR to Fort Ross-Seaview – 1st-rate farming, 1st-rate wines, with a few tasty whites on side.

Bogle Central V, Lodi ★★ Solid, under-$15, grocery-store, family-owned brand delivers ever-reliable varietal wines from Lodi, Clark and now more coastal zones, all aged in barriques without oak flavour additives. Respect!

Boisset Collection Napa V, Son ★★★ Ambitious portfolio of sustainably farmed estates and brands assembled by Burgundy-born *boulevardier* Jean-Charles Boisset (*see* France): historic BUENA VISTA, DELOACH, Lyeth, Wattle Creek (SON COUNTY); JCB and Raymond (NAPA V), excellent quality across board.

Bokisch Vineyards Lodi ★★→★★★ Legit Lodi favourite with enthusiastic followers champions Iberian varieties; great TEMPRANILLO plus superb ALBARIÑO, GRACIANO, flirty Rosado.

Bonny Doon Mont ★★★ You can't not love Randall Grahm, Willy Wonka envisioner of everything plausible in CA wine. *Vin gris* is superb, juicy Clos de Gilroy GRENACHE, Le Cigare Volant blend a legit CA Rhône classic. Latest Popelouchum project just getting rolling.

Bonterra Mend ★★→★★★ Long-time leader in organic, bio growing, Fetzer spin-off has stayed true to mission against all odds, despite changes in control, still makes grounded, eco-friendly wines. Salute.

Brewer-Clifton Santa B ★★★★ Steve B makes appreciably nerdy, cool-climate wines balancing locale's rich latitude with whole-cluster fermentation and no new oak. 3D CHARD is immersive.

Buena Vista Son V ★★→★★★ Historic winery, est 1857, bedazzled by owner Jean-Charles BOISSET (DELOACH, Raymond Vyds) with period-costume tours, lights and animatronics straight outta Disneyland. Try The Count's Selection SYRAH.

Cade Howell Mtn ★★★ Superb mtn wines: CAB SAUV, SAUV BL produced in stunning, ultra-modern winery. Partnership of wealthy Getty family, CA Governor Newsom, GM J Conover.

Calera ★★★→★★★★ Josh Jensen (RIP 2022) sought limestone and altitude for PINOT N, CHARD on Mt Harlan. Sold to The Duckhorn Portfolio in 2017, wines still outstanding. Everyone should try epic Jensen Pinot N once in their life – CA wine history in a bottle.

Carlisle Son V ★★★ Best way to save historic vyds is to make extraordinary wines from them. Mike Officer crafts brilliant ZIN-based field blends from N CA, preserving history with updated growing tech. Rhône reds also notable.

Carneros, Dom Car ★★★→★★★★ Taittinger (*see* France) outpost, led by women (currently Remi Cohen), for decades executes one of best Blanc de Blancs sparkling in CA, Le Rêve. Other bubblies and PINOT N also superb.

Caymus Napa V ★★★ Popular status brand. Special Selection CAB SAUV, esp iconic, but on rich, sappy end of current style spectrum.

Turns out Syrah is a hella finicky grape. Struggle for excellence in CA continues.

Chanin Wines Santa B, Sta RH ★★★ Low-input SANTA B winery making accurate, mineral CHARD, focused PINOT N and peppery, varietal SYRAH from Schlock Family vyd. Becoming influential.

Chappellet Napa V ★★★★ Rugged P HILL property has delivered savoury, age-worthy, madrone scrub-laced CAB SAUV for decades. Signature-series Cab Sauv is flat-out killer and beats any NAPA rival for value. Dry CHENIN BL, tangy treat if a bit spendy. Also owns formidable PINOT N, CHARD-themed Sonoma-Loeb brand.

Chimney Rock Stags L ★★★→★★★★ Latina winemaker Elizabeth Vianna elevated Terlato STAGS L property to next level. Relatively affordable Elevage Bx blend glowing introduction to brand.

Cline Car ★★★ Stalwart family operation delivers on affordable varietal offerings, with some exotic, old-vine, single-vyd ZIN and Rhône bottles. Eucalypt-inflected Small Berry MOURVÈDRE from Big Break vyd hyper-cool.

Constellation Brands ★→★★★ Publicly traded major wine/beer/spirits company owns famed ROBERT MONDAVI brand, Meiomi, The Prisoner, Woodbridge and many more inernational brands. Lately re-focusing on beer and cannabis products, but still a big dipper in the wine biz.

Continuum Napa V, St H ★★★★ Tim Mondavi est his bona fides with 2nd-generation, top-tier P HILL estate making impeccable CAB SAUV. Second label: Novicium, from younger vines.

Corison Napa V ★★★ Cathy C stays on course, producing elegant NAPA V CAB SAUV; was often an outlier but has proven her strength with ever-focused age-worthy Kronos vyd Cab Sauv.

Covenant Napa V ★★★ Professional wine-writer, saxophonist-turned-winemaker Jeff Morgan makes CA's best kosher wines (Hagafen also deserves shout-out), sourced from terrific sites in NAPA V, SON V and beyond.

Cuvaison Car ★★★ Quiet historic property, making great wine yr after yr. Top marks to CHARD, PINOT N from CAR estate; gd CAB SAUV, SYRAH, from MT VEEDER. Single Block bottlings: lovely rosé, slinky, sexy Méthode Béton SAUV BL.

Dalla Valle Oak ★★★★ A 1st-rate hillside estate transitioning to 2nd generation. Maya CAB SAUV is legendary, eponymous Cab Sauv a cult wine, Dalle Valle Collina edition *the best* younger-vine, relatively affordable entry to luxury NAPA Cab. Get some.

Daou P Rob ★★★ Ambitious estate just sold to Australia's Treasury Estates for whopping $900m price tag. Makes fine CAB SAUV from elevated w-side P ROB.

Dashe Cellars Dry CV, N Coast ★★★ RIDGE veteran Mike D makes tasteful, affordable and balanced DRY CV and ALEX V ZIN from urban winery in Alameda, CA. Terrific old-vine CARIGNANE, zesty GRENACHE rosé leaning natural, but sound.

Davis Bynum RRV ★★★ Acquisition by Rodney Strong proved fruitful for this RRV stalwart. Superb SAUV BL might even outshine fine CHARD, PINOT N.

DeLoach Winery Son ★★★ Flamboyant maestro Jean-Charles BOISSET saw gd value in progressive organic, bio-oriented winery making great CHARD, PINOT N. Solid down-to-earth investment, if not his sexiest.

Denner P Rob ★★★ Well-farmed Templeton Gap estate making fine Rhône-inspired reds and more, acquired in 2022 by E&J GALLO. Ditch Digger red blend a personal fave and a loose translation of my last name (*see* Contributors list).

Diamond Creek Napa V ★★★★ Extraordinary longevity of CAB SAUV from iconic sites like Volcanic Hill and Gravelly Meadow makes some of most coveted, collectable wines of NAPA V.

Dominus Estate Napa V ★★★★ Moueix-owned (*see* France). Herzog de Meuron-designed winery is epic, but not open to hoi polloi. Gravelly terroir in cool S NAPA is indisputably great. Second label: Napanook also great. You can buy the wine, but you can't pet the vines.

Drew Family And V, Mend ★★★→★★★★ A MEND RDG visionary making minimalist, savage PINOT N from AND V and higher up hills. Look for estate Field Selections Pinot N from Mend Rdg, SYRAH from coastal Valenti vyd. Hunt these down.

Dry Creek Vineyard Dry CV ★★★ Standard-bearer on its A-game. Trustworthy, Loire-inspired, grassy FUMÉ BL and other SAUV BL always delicious, CHENIN BL and all reds better than ever; great stop nr Healdsburg. What's not to love? ZIN/Bx-blend Mariner also better than ever.

Duckhorn Vineyards Napa V ★★★→★★★★ Crowd-pleasing and ultra-consistent CAB SAUV and MERLOT, incl legendary Three Palms vyd, gd SAUV BL. Second label Decoy is hugely successful and excellent value. Publicly traded parent company The Duckhorn Portfolio also owns the Migration brand (N Coast CHARD and PINOT N), GOLDENEYE (AND V), CALERA, KOSTA BROWNE, SONOMA-CUTRER and Canvasback (in WA).

Dutton-Goldfield RRV ★★★ Classical cool-climate CA CHARD, PINOT N from RRV-based powerhouse grower; not super-edgy or risky, maybe a gd thing.

Eberle P Rob ★★→★★★ Former Penn State footballer is literally a giant of Central Coast wine history and one of 1st to explore potential of SYRAH in P ROB. Dependable, classically proportioned wines.

Edmunds St. John Sierra Fhills ★★★ Energy over power is the motto of Berkeley *garagiste* and academic Steve Edmunds. Bone-Jolly GAMAY from EL DOR CO, a perfect introduction.

Emeritus RRV ★★★→★★★★ Emergent estate, three home dry-farmed (!) vyds making focused, structured PINOT N under supervision of gifted winemaker Dave Lattin. Hallberg Ranch bottlings exquisite, singular in style.

Etude Car ★★★ Ever-trustworthy brand that always succeeded at making great CAB SAUV, PINOT N under same roof, using same attentive techniques. Now owned by TWE (*see* Australia), but legacy stays true. Pinot N Rosé to die for.

Far Niente Napa V ★★★→★★★★ Pioneer of generous CAB SAUV, CHARD. Hedonism with soul. Dolce: celebrated dessert wine. Also Nickel & Nickel single-vyd Cabs.

Farrell, Gary RRV ★★★ Namesake founder long gone, but wines still terrific despite a few ownership changes, much thanks to winemaker Theresa Heredia, Farrell's hand-picked successor. Basic RRV CHARD beams brightly, Hallberg and Fort Ross single-vyd PINOT N among top offerings.

Flowers Son Coast ★★★→★★★★ Pioneer next to Pacific now owned by Huneeus Vintners; CHARD, PINOT N remain great illustrations of that climate, elevation.

California's spectrum of Pinot Noir
California PINOT N has remarkable terroir and climate diversity along the cool Pacific coast. SANDHI leans elegant in otherwise fruit-saturated SANTA B neighbourhood, FOURSIGHT delivers *en pointe* AND V juice, GARY FARRELL serves textbook velvety RRV, LUCIA offers refined Central Coast style, ETUDE CAR holds down a smooth, sandy loam Car style. They're all making outstanding wines that can compete with the world's best.

Foppiano Son ★★→★★★ Honest RRV wines loaded with sunny fruit and little pretence. Note PETITE SIRAH, SAUV BL.

Fort Ross Vineyard Son Coast ★★★ Dazzling high-elevation estate, a stone's throw from Pacific; zesty CHARD, terrific, savoury PINOT N, surprisingly gd PINOTAGE (!).

Foursight And V ★★★ Family operation making consistent PINOT N, a few whites and bubbly nr Boonville. Tireless promoters of region, and wines deliver. Zero New Oak Pinot N sees only used barrels.

Keeping up with the Jacksons? Gallos are snatching up boutique brands/vyds in CA.

Foxen Santa MV ★★★ Homey Foxen Canyon winery, founded 1985, with steady hand for PINOT N; try Block 8 from Bien Nacido Vyd. Intriguing, cool-climate Heritage SYRAH from home estate.

Freemark Abbey Napa V ★★★ Classic name claimed by JACKSON FAMILY WINES in 2006, improved. Great-value single-vyd Bosché, Sycamore CAB SAUV bottlings.

Frog's Leap Ruth ★★★ John Williams is a pioneer of bio viticulture in CA. He coaxes best out of NAPA V floor with elegant CHARD, refreshing SAUV BL, supple, juicy CAB SAUV, MERLOT and brambly ZIN.

Gallo, E&J ★→★★★ Biggest wine company in world, titan in under-$20 sector with dozens of major CA brands, incl Apothic, Barefoot, Louis Martini. Recent buys: Black Box, Clos du Bois, ROMBAUER, Jayson, RAVENSWOOD. Gallo of Sonoma makes excellent wines from owned vyds; lately been buying boutique brands like DENNER, MASSICAN.

Gloria Ferrer Car ★★★ Exceptional CA bubbly. Toast to decades-long team of owners, growers, winemakers that made this Freixenet-owned venture extraordinary. All wines v.gd, Vintage Royal Cuvée best.

Goldeneye And V ★★★→★★★★ Well-conceived and managed estate winery with three principal vyds. PINOT N on ripe side, but undeniably delicious, esp The Narrows vyd. Bubbly also special, and visitors welcome.

Green & Red Napa V ★★★ Back-to-the-land hippie winery, founded in early 70s by Jay Heminway, still cranks out mouthwatering SAUV BL and some killer ZIN, one specifically blended for Chez Panisse in Berkeley.

Greenwood Ridge And V ★★★ Recharge your Tesla at cosy octagonal redwood tasting room in Philo; array of well-made wines, esp PINOT N, ZIN. Vintage CA spirit at its best.

Gundlach Bundschu Son V ★★★ Terrific wines, welcoming vibe, popular tasting destination, with adventurous cool Huichica Fest music concerts for hipster set. Best: GEWURZ, CAB SAUV, MERLOT.

Hall Napa V ★★★→★★★★ Glitzy ST H winery makes great NAPA CAB SAUV, but bewildering variety of selections. Signature offering best, velvety SAUV BL, MERLOT among best in CA. Also owns coastal CHARD, PINOT N brand Walt.

Halter Ranch P Rob ★★→★★★ Boasting 200 acres+ of sustainably farmed vyds on P ROB's w-side, Halter reckons large as premium grower and winery in AVA. Solid CAB SAUV, SYRAH. PICPOUL a sprightly surprise.

Hanzell Son V ★★★ Pinot pioneer of 50s still making CHARD, PINOT N from estate vines. Both reward cellar time. Mineral Chard still thrilling. Sebella Chard (young vines) all bright, crisp fruit.

Harlan Estate Napa V ★★★★ Concentrated, robust CAB SAUV from W Oakville bench, cult Cab with long waiting list from Meadowood Resort owner Bill H. Resort rebuilding after 2020 fires, but vyds intact. Wines made by Cory Empting.

Harney Lane Lodi ★★ Family-owned with a century+ of grape-growing under belt. Old-vine ZIN from Home Ranch and Lizzy James vyds the stars, but ALBARIÑO, TEMPRANILLO also impress as Iberian grapes gain momentum in Lodi.

Hartford Family Son Coast ★★★ Winemaker Jeff Stewart is quietly killing it at this

JACKSON FAMILY winery, with small batches of CHARD, PINOT N, ZIN from sites up and down N Coast. Taut Seascape Chard, subtle Fog Dance Pinot N (Green V).

HdV Wines Car ★★★ A gem: fine complex CHARD with honed edge; PINOT N from Larry Hyde with Aubert de Villaine of DRC (*see* France); v.gd CAB SAUV, SYRAH.

Hendry Oak K ★★★ Classic, soulful, minimalist wines, est 1939. Note brambly, distinctive CAB SAUV, ZIN (try Block 28) from cool pocket. Never disappointing.

Hirsch Son Coast ★★★→★★★★ Edgy, influential; nervy, high-acid, moderately oaked CHARD, PINOT N nr Fort Ross. In ideal yrs excellent produce.

Hope Family P Rob ★★★ Paso visionary Austin H bangs out some fine Rhône reds from Templeton Gap and CAB SAUV under his eponymous label, plus affordable Liberty School varietals, complex Treana brand blends. Experienced, dependable.

Inglenook Oak ★★★ Director FF Coppola's legendary estate. Rubicon CAB SAUV is flagship proprietary red; v.gd CHARD, MERLOT. Showpiece mansion is spectacular, popular with international visitors.

Jackson Family Wines ★★→★★★★ Visionary, continually expanding privately held company, massive vyd owner in CA and beyond, with remarkable empire of stellar properties. Holdings focus on elevated sites, high-quality terroir. Owns popular Kendall-Jackson brand plus ritzier BREWER-CLIFTON, Cardinale, Copain, Edmeades, FREEMARK ABBEY, HARTFORD FAMILY, La Crema, La Jota, Lokoya, MAGGY HAWK, Matanzas Creek, Murphy Goode, Siduri, Verité. Jackson Estate series great for N Coast mtn CAB SAUV. Uniformly high-quality wines.

Jessie's Grove Lodi ★★→★★★★ Deep roots in Lodi, est 1868, home to some seriously old ZIN vines. Boss Greg Burns knows Zin inside out: it shows in fine, generous wines. The Westwind Zin is potent, also ALBARIÑO, VERMENTINO.

Jordan Alex V ★★★ Showcase estate generates elegant, balanced, Bx-faithful CAB SAUV for devoted following; CHARD, now sourced from RRV, delivers lemony, mouthwatering panache.

Joseph Phelps Vineyards ★★★★ Insignia Bx blend a CA benchmark luxury wine. NAPA V CAB SAUV and Hyde Vyd SYRAH also dazzle. Freestone coastal wines also worth a gander.

Josh N Coast ★★ Shooting-star brand from Joseph Carr. Solid varietal bulk brand successfully competing with affordable E&J GALLO offerings.

Keenan Spring Mtn ★★★ Just one of many reliably rocksteady mtn wineries in NAPA V. CAB SAUV is age-worthy, but don't sleep on structured MERLOT.

Keller Estate Son Coast ★★★ One more eg. of balanced, elegant CA wine from cool coastal regions. CHARD, La Cruz vyd PINOT N from Petaluma Gap delightful.

Kistler Vineyards RRV ★★★→★★★★ Style of CHARD, PINOT N adapted over time, wines only improved. Decadent, but balanced, nutty Les Noisetiers CHARD from SON V, exceptional.

Kornell, Paula Napa V ★★★→★★★★ This 2nd-generation bubbly specialist brings the party with outstanding CA fizz: 1st-rate Brut and Brut Blanc de Noirs. Seek.

Younger generation deserting wine. Is problem weird/natty wines marketed to them?

Kosta Browne Son Coast ★★★★ Top-notch, moon-shot PINOT N, CHARD, under The Duckhorn Portfolio umbrella, making world-class wines at world-class prices. Keefer Ranch Pinot insanely gd, and don't sleep on flinty Chards (One Sixteen). They ain't cheap.

Kutch N Coast ★★★→★★★★ Jamie K produces some prime coastal PINOT N consistently. Currently developing a home ranch, he sources from other top sites outside textbook sources. Delivers consistently, like McDougall Ranch Pinot N (vyd at c.305m/1000ft), precise, expressive, special wines.

Ladera Napa V ★★★ Brand has been through some changes, but hillside Napa CAB SAUVS, SAUV BL from NZ winemaker still damn gd.

Lang & Reed Mend, Napa ★★★ If you're interested in CA CAB FR, start here. John Skupny's wines capture perfume, litheness of variety, with NAPA generosity. Also delicious MEND CHENIN BL.

Lindquist Family – Verdad Arroyo G, Arroyo Seco ★★★ Rhône Ranger Bob L's pivot toward Spain, incl authentic-ish ALBARIÑO, TEMPRANILLO from bio Sawyer Lindquist vyd in nearby EDNA V. *Muy bueno.*

New-wave Sauvignon Blanc: it's finally refreshing. Took a while.

Littorai And V, Son Coast ★★★★ Burgundy-trained maestro Ted Lemon's N Coast CHARD, PINOT N are nervy, coastal and seeking global audience. Small lots, but all sleek, exciting. Thrilling Cerise, Savoy, Wendling Vyd offerings.

Lohr, J P Rob ★★→★★★ Arguably among best value in CA, from CAB SAUV to MERLOT to SYRAH. Everything under $20 is well worth it. Cuvée Pau and Cuvée St. E pay homage to Bx. Don't miss seductive, floral Beaujolais-like Wildflower Valdiguié.

Long Meadow Ranch Napa V ★★★→★★★★ Smart, holistic vision, incl destination winery with restaurant, cattle on organic farm. Supple, age-worthy, fresh CAB SAUV has reached ★★★★ status; lively Graves-style SAUV BL.

Lucia Santa LH ★★★ Access to great vyds and 2nd-generation knowledge has positioned Jeff Pisoni well. Impressive CHARD, PINOT N. Central Coast, SANTA LH brand to watch, Juicy Lucy GAMAY, delicious.

Macchia Lodi ★★★ One of Lodi's most accomplished winemakers, Tim Holdener vacuums up medals in blind tastings yr after yr. Speciality is balanced old-vine ZIN, but also interesting SANGIOVESE, TEROLDEGO; PETITE SIRAH v.gd.

MacRostie RRV, Son Coast ★★★ Tasting room a post-modern beauty; minimalist screwcapped wines 1st rate. Lovely PINOT N, SYRAH; SON COAST CHARD a delight. Get on the bus.

Maggy Hawk And V ★★★ Copain alumna Sarah Wuethrich heads JACKSON FAMILY team crafting great CHARD, PINOT N in deep end (cold part) of AND V. Don't just drink it, visit new tasting room.

Massican ★★★ Only whites from ex-Larkmead whizz Dan Petroski. Just sold to E&J GALLO; Dan stays on for now. Direct wines with some fermentation complexity, SAUV BL, CHARD, PINOT GRIGIO all impressive.

Masút Mend ★★★ Newish elevated Eagle Peak property, run by Ben and Jake Fetzer, shines. Estate PINOT N ethereal. Will inspire others to explore area.

Matthiasson Napa V ★★★ Mostly certified organic vyd sources in NAPA, making trendy, relatively low-alc CAB SAUV, REFOSCO, VERMENTINO; v. hip.

Mauritson Dry CV ★★★ Clay M, 6th-generation grower, captains extraordinary holdings in elevated Rockpile district; wines only got better under his two decades. ZIN is flagship, of course; CAB SAUV, SAUV BL also excellent.

Medlock Ames Son ★★★ Winery on Bell Mtn with reliably delicious, bio, round, mostly Bx reds made under respected consultant Jean Hoefliger. Sharp wines, labels, Healdsburg tasting room. Classy.

Melka Napa V, Son V ★★★★ Jewel-box holding of great Napa consultant Philippe M and wife Cherie, comprises hillside properties in CAL (NAPA v) and Knights V (SON). Limited, pricey, coveted. Mostly CAB SAUV, Bx blends, stellar MERLOT.

Michael Mondavi Family Napa V ★★★→★★★★ This Mondavi scion might be best known for his Folio import biz, but he makes great wines too. The M CAB SAUV from ATLAS PEAK is killer. Animo Cab Sauv, SAUV BL also formidable.

Miraflores Sierra Fhills ★★★ Marco Cappelli left NAPA V to set up in Sierra Mtns; vinifies sublime, broad array from estate and region he rightly believes in.

Mi Sueno Napa V ★★★ Rolando started dishwashing at a NAPA resort, worked his way up at wineries. Lorena's family worked vyds, bought property. Together they make excellent wine, every bit as gd as their story.

Montelena, Ch Napa V ★★★ Epic, elevated, historic Mayacamas castle property with sublime grounds so worth a visit. CAB SAUV can be a bit wild, CHARD shocked world at 1978 Judgement of Paris tasting.

Morgan Santa LH ★★★→★★★★ Dan Morgan Lee's organically farmed ranch overdelivers with killer CHARD, PINOT N across board. Double L vyd offerings top the charts.

Mount Eden Vineyards Santa Cz Mts ★★★→★★★★ Gorgeous vistas from high vyd, one of CA's 1st boutique wineries, with Burgundian clones dating back to Martin Ray days. Taut, mineral CAB SAUV, PINOT N, stunning CHARD since 1945. Inspired by Burgundy, but pure rugged CA character.

Nalle Dry CV ★★★ Refined craftsmanship-level ZIN, impeccable, elegant claret-style reds. Great family-owned stop nr Healdsburg.

Navarro And V ★★★ Long-time cool-climate N CA outpost reliably delivers fresh, affordable, minimalist, delicious GEWURZ, PINOT N and everything in between. Wine-club subscription you won't regret.

New Clairvaux Central V ★★★ NAPA scion Aimée Sunseri makes impressive hot-climate whites and reds at remote Franciscan monastery nr Chico. The ASSYRTIKO is fruity, electric, PETITE SIRAH polished, smooth.

Obsidian Ridge Lake ★★★ Star of Lake County extension of Mayacamas mtn range. Super CAB SAUV, SYRAH from hillside vyds, volcanic soils scattered with glassy obsidian. Half Mile Cab 1st-rate. Also owns Poseidon brand from CAR.

Opus One Oak ★★★★ Mouton Rothschild family-controlled (*see* Bordeaux) CAB SAUV estate always intended to glamour international markets, and it still does.

O'Shaughnessy Howell Mtn ★★★★ Outstanding elevated outpost atop HOWELL MTN putting out stellar CAB SAUV that's built to last. Worth seeking out.

Patz & Hall N Coast ★★★★ James H one of CA's most thoughtful winemakers; culls fruit from top vyds from Central Coast to MEND. Style is generous, tasteful, super-reliable. Zio Tony *Chard* v. special, lemony, electric, opulent.

Paul Hobbs Wines N Coast ★★★→★★★★ Hugely influential winemaker since 90s, working in CA and a lot in S America. Terroir-expressive single-vyd CHARD, CAB SAUV, PINOT N, SYRAH always impressive. Don't sleep on these wines.

Pax Mend, Son ★★★ Cult-level New World SYRAH from coastal and hillside sites since 2000 for less than cult-follower prices. Fresh TROUSSEAU Gr and GAMAY also available at The Barlow tasting room in Sebastopol.

Peay Vineyards Son Coast ★★★→★★★★ Standout brand from coldest elevated zones. Finesse-driven CHARD, PINOT N, SYRAH superb. Second label: Cep, v.gd, esp rosé. Weightless, ethereal wines that reckon international appreciation.

Philip Togni Vineyard Spring Mtn ★★★ No bling, just beauty, and long life.

Pine Ridge Napa V ★★★ Outstanding CAB SAUV from several vyds. Estate STAGS L bottling, silky, graceful. Lively CHENIN BL/VIOGNIER innovative classic.

Pisoni Family Vineyards Santa LH ★★★ A 2nd-generation Central Coast PINOT N legend, with refined Pinot N, CHARD. Cheeky second label Lucy incl exceptional CA GAMAY, refreshing Pico Blanco, white blend of PINOTS GR/BL.

Presqu'ile Santa MV ★★★ Cool-climate estate with ocean views and lovely SANTA MV PINOT N aged in neutral barrels; spicy, slightly gamey SYRAH.

Pride Mountain Napa V, Spring Mtn ★★★→★★★★ Epic Mayacamas mtn-top estate

---

White Pinot Noir

If you love Blanc de Noirs bubbly, try it without the bubbles. Higher-acid, brisk, white PINOT N is trending hard recently, perhaps as a way of salvaging smoke-tainted grapes. (Pay no attention to that man behind the curtain!) MAGGY HAWK, DOM CARNEROS Pinot Clair, The Prisoner Blindfold and Waits-Mast versions all commendable.

straddles NAPA V/SON border. Superb, bold CAB SAUV; amazing MERLOT. Tasting appointments required and worth the drive up. Call ahead.

Quintessa Ruth ★★★★ Well-conceived, gorgeous, single-wine estate owned by Chilean international wine-wizard Augustin Huneeus. That one red Bx blend is special and justifies three-figure price.

Quivira Dry CV ★★★→★★★★ Bio property of Pete and Terri Kight, helmed by accomplished winemaker Hugh Chappelle, sells estimable SAUV BL, ZIN with integrity and balance.

Qupé Santa B ★★★ One of original Central Coast SYRAH champions, Bien Nacido offerings still outstanding and CC Syrah still impressive despite departure of founder Bob LINDQUIST. The trad continues so far.

Radio-Coteau Son Coast ★★★ Notable new-wave PINOT N, serious coastal SYRAH and old-vine, dry-farmed ZIN. Bulletproof CHARD, Zin, but Pinot N steals show. Veg gardens, cider orchard, goats, chickens, honeybees and cats gild the lily.

Ramey Son ★★★→★★★★ Influential David R delivers flinty, reductive burgundian-style whites in his Hyde, Ritchie and RRV CHARD. Reds gd, but his Chards should be *de rigueur* tasting at UC Davis winemaking school.

Rancho Sisquoc Santa MV ★★→★★★★ Rustic tasting room and historic chapel deliver satisfying spectrum of Bx styles and great visitor experience, with outstanding CHARD, CAB FR, PINOT N.

Ravenswood ★★★ CONSTELLATION-owned, but single-vyd ZIN still from remarkable sites like Bedrock, Old Hill, Teldeschi. "No wimpy wines" motto still applies.

Red Car Son Coast ★★★ Hip brand with colourful label making precise CHARD, lacy, fruit-forward PINOT N and killer rosé.

Ridge N Coast, Santa Cz Mts ★★★★ Hi, natty wine kids! Ridge represents decades of natural winemaking with min additives, local oak and 1st-class terroir in Monte Bello CAB SAUV, one of greatest, most age-worthy Cabs in CA. Also a champ of ingredient labelling and transparency. Watch and learn.

Rivers-Marie Napa V ★★★→★★★ Private label of acclaimed vintner and consultant Thomas Rivers Brown (Schrader) and partner Genevieve Marie Welsh features superb varietals. Reservations required at Hwy 128 tasting room in CAL. Wicked Herb Lamb CAB SAUV.

Robert Mondavi Winery ★★→★★★ Once iconic, now a corporate concern. Top wines still pretty gd; everything in between mostly okay.

Rodney Strong Vineyards Son ★★★ Strong indeed, across board; 14 vyds producing sinewy coastal CHARD, PINOT N, citrus SAUV BL, super ALEX V CAB SAUV from Alexander's Crown, Rockaway vyds.

Roederer Estate And V ★★★★ Adventurous Champagne Roederer (*see* France) venture brought glamour to AND V sparkling. Finesse off charts, esp luxury cuvée L'Ermitage. Also makes Scharffenberger now. Dom Anderson PINOT N among best of AVA too.

Rombauer Napa V ★★★ Buttery CHARD is calling card, but sunny MERLOT, CAB SAUV also deliver juicy CA fruit.

St Jean, Ch Son V ★★★ Solid on all fronts, but consensus flagship for decades has been Cinq Cépages: five Bx varieties. Nectarine-rich Robert Young CHARD also a classic.

"Natural" is complicated

Some "natural" wine producers are quietly backing away from the N word as it becomes harder and more expensive to buy organic grapes. Most "sustainable" growing programmes in CA allow the use of artificial fertilizers and herbicides, making it inconvenient to adhere to already vague purity standards.

Saintsbury Car ★★★ Regional pioneer and benchmark still making exciting, highly relevant PINOT N, CHARD, yummy Vincent Vin Gr of Pinot N rosé. Lee vyd Swan clone Pinot is vibrant, velvet.

St-Supéry Napa ★★★ Should be on any wine-lover's radar, if only for the eternally killer SAUV BL programme. Dollarhide Ranch bottling is legendary; reds solid too.

Sandhi Sta RH ★★★ Former sommelier Raj Parr's visionary SANTA B winery producing Burgundy-inspired low-alc wines with balance, restraint. Not an easy feat at this latitude.

If CA keeps making these balanced Zins, my honey might stop adding ice cubes.

Sandlands Napa V ★★★→★★★★ Tegan Passalacqua rescues ancient, sandy, pre-phylloxera vyds from CA; boutique small batches of ultra-premium wine.

Saracina Mend ★★→★★★ Beautiful, sustainably farmed estate owned by Taub family. Wide range of solid, wholesome wines. Try the Soul of Mendocino co-ferment red. Best yet to come, methinks.

Saxum P Rob ★★★ Famed for opulent, heady Rhône-inspired reds – perhaps a bit too heady for some. James Berry Vyd blend is flagship.

Schramsberg Napa V ★★★★ A 2nd-gen CA bubbly specialist not afraid to compete with Champagne, and keeps up well. Memorable tours of historic caves by reservation. Classic Blanc de Blancs.

Scribe Son ★★★ Hipster gentleman-farmer aesthetic seduces younger set. Tasting room (SON CO) pours well-made esoterica like SYLVANER, ST-LAURENT and exceptional Van der Kamp PINOT N, aged in neutral oak.

Sea Smoke Sta RH ★★★ Cultish, high-end, opulent PINOT N and excellent bubbly made in strictly estate-driven model, with incredible continuity of leadership, talent. Luscious wines, but drink them while they're fresh.

Shafer Vineyards Napa V, Stags L ★★★→★★★★ Solid brand, widely respected. Hillside Select CAB SAUV a lavish CA classic; Relentless SYRAH/PETITE SIRAH blend an artful in-house invention. One Point Five, beautiful Cab Sauv for money.

Shannon Ridge Lake ★★→★★★ Grand, undulating, high-elevation estate overlooking Clear Lake. Terrific reds and whites from PETITE SIRAH to SAUV BL, esp Res series. Great value. Second label: Vigilance, a big seller.

Smith-Madrone Napa V ★★★→★★★★ Indie old-school outpost founded by Smith bros in 1971 atop SPRING MTN, featuring Euro-inspired, balanced CAB SAUV and exotic, trend-eschewing old-vine RIES. Worth a visit.

Smith-Story And V, Son V Always hustling, shared-dream couple makes plucky, v.gd wines and sometimes German RIES from where Eric cut his winemaking teeth. Sometimes the story is everything.

Sojourn Son ★★★ Angelina Mondavi-owned, single-vyd, N-Coast project; top NAPA V CAB SAUV (Oakville Ranch) and PINOT N (Gap's Crown) SON COAST shine bright.

Sonoma-Cutrer Vineyards Son ★★★ Big, successful RRV brand just sold to The Duckhorn Portfolio; SON COAST CHARD still impresses major audience.

Spottswoode St H ★★★★ Sublime estate always chasing perfection with every sustainable/organic/bio bona fide ever invented. Estate Cabs thrilling with modest alc. Second wine: Lyndenhurst, superb, value CAB SAUV. Spottswoode SAUV BL always zesty, immaculate. Stand and clap.

Staglin Family Vineyard Ruth ★★★★ Refined CAB SAUV from 2nd-generation, family-owned estate on RUTH Benchlands. Always impressive, and a leader, never just another cow in the herd.

Stag's Leap Wine Cellars Stags L ★★★ Founder sold to Ste Michelle Wine Estates (WA), gd to see quality held. Flagship CAB SAUV (top Cask 23, Fay, SLV).

Steven Kent Winery ★★★ SK Mirassou is hands-down the best winemaker in LIV V, lately zeroing-in on area's great potential for CAB FR. L'Autre Côte best.

Storybook Mountain Napa V ★★★ Dr. Jerry Seps's fairytale CAL estate makes some of most stylish, classically proportioned ZIN in CA. Classic Eastern Exposures.

Tablas Creek P Rob ★★★→★★★★ When it comes to Rhône and Med varieties, nobody does it better; makes me feel sad for rest. Enlightened regenerative farming begets glorious, well-edited red/white (latter rare in P ROB); CA elite. A wine club worth joining.

Terre Rouge / Easton Sierra Fhills ★★★ Exceptional red producer in AM CO sporting Rhône and ZIN offerings with equal aplomb. Affordable Tête-à-Tête red blend a steal, Ascent SYRAH reliably special.

Toulouse ★★★ Dark horse (goose?) from Philo, CA, making excellent PINOT N, terrific GEWURZ, Valdiguè. Founded in 2002 by Oakland Fire Dept captain and flight-attendant wife. Sustainably farmed too.

Trefethen Family Vineyards Oak K ★★★ Underappreciated winery in cool Oak K deserves more credit; CHARD, delicious dry RIES, elegant CAB SAUV, MERLOT.

Trinchero Family Estates Napa V ★→★★★ Bewildering slew of labels, incl mass-market Sutter Home; esp pleasing CAB SAUV under Napa Wine Co label.

Turkovich Central V ★★ Impressive Yolo County operation over Vaca range from NAPA, min coastal influence; tight, fresh wines from warm-climate grapes that fit the bill. Try The Boss, racy, clean, powerful blend of PETITE SIRAH, PETIT VERDOT and more. Great prices.

Turley Wine Cellars P Rob ★★★★ Sells mostly to mailing list. Brilliant brambly old-vine ZINS from vyds scattered across state. True CA treasures.

Turnbull Oak ★★★ Outstanding entry-level estate CAB SAUV. Black-label estate Cab also thrilling with gravelly kick, and don't sleep on luscious, tropical SAUV BL.

Vineyard 29 Napa V ★★★→★★★★ Top winemaker Philippe MELKA's fingerprints all over gorgeous CAB SAUV at maturing estate venture; gd but oaky SAUV BL.

Volker Eisele Family Estate Napa V ★★★ Special site tucked way back in Chiles V continues to overdeliver with CAB SAUV and more. Looking for an adventure?

Williams-Selyem RRV ★★★ Legendary SON PINOT N since 70s; handcrafted, low-intervention, with loyal following. Rochioli vyd (RRV) put N CA PINOT N on map.

Zaca Mesa Santa B ★★★ OG Rhône variety leader planted SYRAH in 1978, delivering boss wines for five decades. Z red blend graceful, affordable.

Colorado (CO)

Cool-climate varieties best, experimentation with hybrids owing to climate; low-humidity high-desert terroir moderates climate extremes. Two AVAs: Grand V more Bx, Rhône varieties; West Elks cooler, more Alsace, Burgundy. **Alfred Eames** ★ historic producer; Carmine (r) lauded. **Bookcliff** new ownership; awarded SYRAH. **Carboy** ★★ four wineries, tasting rooms; splashy new Grand Cuvée (sp CHENIN BL). **Carlson** history of fruit and sweet wines; gd dry GEWURZ, LEMBERGER and St. Vincent (r) hybrid. **Colterris** ★ top bottlings of each Bx red; Coral White CAB SAUV is signature. **Jack Rabbit Hill Farm** ★ only certified bio winery in state; elegant PINOTS N/M, Alsace whites. **Plum Creek Winery** Bx reds plus gd CHARD, pét-nat. **Sauvage Spectrum** ★★ quality Italian, Bx reds; MALBEC, TEROLDEGO lead. **Snowy Peaks** ★★ v.-high-altitude, Rhône, Bx and hybrids; look for Rhône blend Élevé (r), MUSCAT (sw). **Stone Cottage Cellars** high-elevation, Alsace white specialist, racy GEWURZ, PINOT GR. **Sutcliff Vyds** outlier in frontier area Four Corners, Bx varieties. **The Storm Cellar** focus on high-elevation white, rosé; aromatic ALBARIÑO, Gewurz best.

Georgia (GA)

Shares Blue Ridge Mtns with VA, NC; two AVAs, in hills n of Atlanta: Bx styles, CHARD, PETIT MANSENG, PINOT N, unusual hybrids. **Cloudland** Lomanto, Lenoir,

PETIT VERDOT. **Crane Creek** hybrid focus, try Enotah (Chardonel fermented in Hungarian oak), Noiret. **Engelheim** awarded Traminette. **Habersham** three ranges (Southern Harvest for se native Muscadine). **Sharp Mtn** GEWURZ, SANGIOVESE. **Stonewall Creek** structured Norton. **Three Sisters** AVA-range Vidal Bl, CAB FR. **Tiger Mtn** Petit Manseng, TOURIGA N. **Wolf Mtn** awarded Blanc de Blancs range. **Yonah Mtn Vyds** Marian's Meritage is co-ferment MERLOT-led Bx. Savannah-centred s: Muscadine (**Tilford** bio), fruit wine (trad blackberry), some v.gd.

Idaho (ID)

Nascent region on rise with mere 75 wineries, 526 ha. Warm days, cool nights give ripe, fresh fruit. What works best where is being explored, but SYRAH, VIOGNIER already clear standouts.

Cinder Wines Snake RV ★★ Melanie Krause (ex-Ch Ste Michelle, *see* WA) makes velvety SYRAH, stainless VIOGNIER. Valentina standout Bx blend.

Colter's Creek ★★ Benchmark producer in Lewis-Clark V; pure, elegant SYRAH, Rhône-style blends.

Huston Vineyards Snake RV ★ Chicken Dinner RIES blend a surprising delight. MALBEC pure, varietally correct.

Rivaura ★★ Lewis-Clark V estate, with highly regarded consulting winemaker. One to watch, esp SYRAH.

Ste Chapelle Snake RV ★ ID's founding winery (1975), also largest. Focus on sweet whites, soft reds. Well-priced quaffers.

Sawtooth Winery Snake RV ★ One of ID's oldest, est 1987. Now owned by WA's Precept. Makes tasty estate RIES, SYRAH, TEMPRANILLO.

Maryland (MD)

Emerging e-coast state; E Shore sandy soils, hills of Garrett and Allegheny mtns, blue-crab-rich Chesapeake Bay checks freezing winters, stifling summers. Reliable ripeners SAUV BL, MERLOT, PETIT VERDOT; also ALBARIÑO, chosen hybrids.

Black Ankle ★★★ Setting MD viticulture, vinification standards since 2008: spontaneous ferment, dry-farmed. Barrel-ferm CHARD, plus SAUV BL, MOURVÈDRE, SYRAH. Library wines incl unforgettable Bx Crumbling Rock, Estate, Slate; ALBARIÑO, Chard.

Old Westminster ★★★ Family farm, spontaneous-ferment cult wines, plus native varieties. Taut, beguiling ALBARIÑO among best in e. Serious pricey pét-nats, CHARD to GAMAY. Electric Chard concrete-aged. Red blends (Bx/Chambourcin/BLAUFRÄNKISCH) elevated by climate, incl top Rev. Cool Ridge vyd PETIT VERDOT, wild, meditative, lasting. Burnt Hill CABS, Petit Verdot, PINOT N, Marquette.

Philosophy ★★★ Top local fruit, plus own vyd. High-alt ALBARIÑO, CHARD, Chambourcin, CAB FR, PETIT VERDOT. Premium wines raised in Baltimore's The Wine Collective: Floral Cab Fr; pithy VIOGNIER; meaty, cherry Femme Noire aged red blend, complex elegance. New MUSCAT pét-nat, Chambourcin rosé.

Other good estates: Big Cork (1st post-Prohibition winery), Boordy, Bordeleau (Bx), Catoctin Breeze, Crow, Dodon, Elk Run, Linganore, Sugarloaf Mtn.

Massachusetts (MA)

Two AVAs: Martha's Vyd and SE New England shared with CT, RI. Cool Atlantic climate moderated by Gulf Stream. Many fruit wines, some v.gd. CHARD, GEWURZ, PINOTS N/BL/GR, RIES, some Cayuga; Concord developed here 1849; 25+ small producers. **Alfalfa Farm** CAB SAUV, awarded blueberry wine. **Black Birch** CAB FR, Traminette. **Glendale Ridge** Cab Fr, Corot N, VIDAL BL. **Truro Vyds** Cab Fr, MERLOT in ocean-breezed vyd. **Westport Rivers** farm, forest, Chard, GRÜNER V, Pinot N (also Blanc de Blancs, 36 mths). **Willow Spring** Léon Millot Res.

Michigan (MI)

The "Third Coast" on huge Lake Michigan (LM Shores AVA), glacial hills, nearby **Good Harbor** v.gd Blanc de Blancs/Noirs. Leelanau and Old Mission Peninsula AVAs since 80s, still best bets. Pinots, CHARD, GEWURZ, RIES; CAB FR, MERLOT, TEROLDEGO; hybrids (top Petite Pearl, Vignoles; Itasca coming) and cherries (**Ch Chantal**'s gd Cerise Noir, 80% PINOT N, the rest Montmorency cherry). Versatility: **Karma Vista**'s peppery SYRAH; **Lemon Creek**'s dark-fruit SHIRAZ. State classics: **Brys Estate** Ries to gd Merlot, Cab Fr braving cold Traverse City; **Ciccone** (founded 1998 by Madonna's dad) PINOTS BL/GR, DOLCETTO; **Left Foot Charly** BLAUFRÄNKISCH; **Mawby** Blanc de Blancs, de Noirs, rosé (sp); **Modales** Pinot N, long-ferment Ries, Blaufränkisch, oak or concrete, native yeasts; **St. Julian** Braganini, esp Cab Fr; **Verterra** Pinot Bl.

Missouri (MO)

Official state grape Norton (r) one of best US hybrids along with Vignoles (w) and Chambourcin (r). Wineries incl: **Adam Puchta** fortifieds, heady dry Res Vignoles (w). **Augusta Winery** Chambourcin, Chardonel. **Hermannhof** rich, structured Norton can age; try Chardonel, Vignoles (w). **Les Bourgeois** Chardonel, Norton. **Noboleis Vyds** juicy Chambourcin, oak-aged VIDAL. **Röbller Vyd** ★★ structured Le Trompier N (r) ages well, rich Vignoles Res. **Stone Hill** complex lauded Norton, v.gd Chardonel, SEYVAL BL, Vidal. **TerraVox** ★★ champion of hybrid and native varieties; Norton dry/fortified leads efforts.

Nevada (NV)

Few wineries use NV grapes. Most import grapes from CA or make flavoured/fruit wines. Hybrid Frontenac (r) is star. **Ardure Wines** Sonoma winery, vyd nr Lake Tahoe, low-intervention; v.gd Frontenac. **Artesian Cellars** ★ Pahrump V, Battle Born range from NV grapes: v.gd, dry crisp RIES; oak-aged, textured SEM.

New Jersey (NJ)

50+ wineries, some among best in E US; four AVAs. Bx, Italian varieties in gravelly maritime Outer Coast Plain (incl Cape May); limestone, granite Warren Hills in n for elegant BLAUFRÄNKISCH, GEWURZ, GRÜNER V, RIES, PINOT N, SYRAH. Try also Almathea, Bellview, Sharrott, White Horse, Working Dog.

Tackling climate change: compost, new varieties, sell local; no capsules, tilling.

Alba ★★★ Limestone, granite in Warren Hills AVA. One of largest PINOT N plantings on E Coast. Burgundy aspiration, incl earthy Grand Res; excellent CHARD, gd GEWURZ, RIES, CAB FR, PINOT GR.

Auburn Road ★★ Barrel-ferment CHARD Res; Bx style with Chambourcin backbone (Eidolón), and without (Gaia); PETIT VERDOT.

Beneduce Vineyards ★★★ Family estate, farm. BLAUFRÄNKISCH, CAB FR, PINOT N (spicy, cool fruit). Intermezzo GEWURZ (dr). Super Tuscan-inspired Mangione; Chambrusco Chambourcin, Modena style. Pét-nats incl Blaufränkisch, GEWURZ. New: BARBERA, DOLCETTO; acqua-pazza (piquette but Italian, honey-ferment).

Hawk Haven ★★★ Cape May Peninsula; glacial, river quartz; ocean air. Complex, structured CAB SAUV, v.gd CAB FR, MERLOT; dry RIES is Meyer lemon-plush. Steely ALBARIÑO. Flagship Q, lasting Bx. Fizz technology, quality focus, incl precise Blanc de Noirs; could incl US-rare serious Charmat soon.

Mount Salem ★★★ Austrian varieties, Burgundy methods to match terroir: masterful Matthias; Pattenburg BLAUFRÄNKISCH, ST-LAURENT, ZWEIGELT; barrel-fermented CHARD, GRÜNER V. Three CAB FR. Wild ferments. Trying out San Marco hybrid.

Unionville ★★★ Single-vyd Burgundy takes: CHARDS, serious pét-nat too; PINOT N.

Savoury CAB FR (with Chambourcin, no malo). Sourland Ridge Red (Bx style). Rhone-ish Mistral Rouge SYRAH, fanciful Hunterdon Mistral Blanc (MARSANNE/ROUSSANE/VIOGNIER) v.gd, also as 10 yrs+ library wines.

William Heritage ★★★ Outer Coastal Plain. Chewy complex Blanc de Noirs; top Blanc de Blancs. Co-ferment Grenache/Syrah rosé, Provence-style. Top CHARD, vibrant French, Austrian oak (ferment/age). Citrus SAUV BL Res, short maceration. Three-site co-ferment CAB FR. Cool maritime Bx-inspired Norman's Vyd CABS FR/SAUV, 10 yrs+. Deep, red-berried Cab Sauv-led BDX.

New Mexico (NM)

Oldest wine-growing region in US. High-altitude vyds moderate warm climate. Early emphasis on sparkling. **Black Mesa** ★★ MONTEPULCIANO, PETITE SIRAH; off-dry Abiquiu (w), Traminette/SEYVAL BL. **DH Lescombes Family Vyds** Bx focus; also Italian, Rhône. **Gruet** ★★ trad-method fizz from local grapes, now W Coast grapes. **La Chiripada** ★ oldest NM winery, signature CAB SAUV, bright, crisp Kabinett-style RIES (*see* Germany). **Luna Rossa Winery** largest grower in NM, estate vyds; v.gd range of Italian varieties. **Noisy Water** ★★ farms historic cool-climate Engle Vyd; large range, incl orange, Wild Ferment, top Demigod Cab Sauv and El Cabron Viejo Sang. **Vivác** ★★ excellent Abbot SYRAH; v.gd Italian-style Divino.

New York (NY)

Wide-ranging cool-climate vinifera experience, 150 yrs of French-American hybrids and a culture of experimentation keep US's 3rd-largest producer innovative, as does a statewide sustainability programme. Winters are freezing, but lakes, rivers and the ocean are moderating influences. Look for BLAUFRÄNKISCH, CAB FR, PINOT N, SYRAH, RIES, GEWURZ, RKATSITELI, notable dry hybrids, top trad sparkling, single-site bottles; 11 AVAs incl Finger Lakes (sunlight hours equal Napa's in fewer days), Hudson River Region (complex soils, microclimates), Lake Erie (cooler spring, warm ripening autumns), Long Island (maritime, bio pioneer). Abbreviations: Finger L, Hudson RR, Long I, Niag (Niagra Escarpment), N Fork (North Fork).

Is Aravelle the future? New vine, rot-proof, said to be like Riesling: first bottles 2024.

21 Brix ★★ Estate on Lake Erie with 1st-rate CHARD, GEWURZ, GRÜNER V, RIES; aromatic BLAUFRÄNKISCH, CAB SAUV; v.gd PINOT N. Serious Noiret. VIDAL Icewine.

Arrowhead Spring Vineyards ★★★ Estate (est 2006) on Niag, starring PINOT N; Bx blends. CAB FR, SYRAH: 13% abv and cool-climate acidity. Focused CHARD.

Bedell Long I ★★★ Pre-eminent estate. Native yeasts, maritime climate, powerful, saline wines: Musée (MERLOT/PETIT VERDOT/MALBEC) top label; next, Taste Red (base SYRAH/Merlot), Gallery 19 (CHARD/VIOGNIER, barrel, best yrs). Look for small batches. Winemaker's *Sun, Sea, Soil, Wine* book is N Fork masterclass.

Bloomer Creek Finger L ★★★ Wild-ferment, organic. Three bio-minded sites: Auten GEWURZ, RIES; Cayuga PINOT N; Morehouse Rd CHARD. Co-ferments gd, also skin-fermented whites.

Boundary Breaks Finger L ★★★ Germanic RIES, ageable, several styles. Ovid Line pleases all; refreshing Icewine. Earthy early-pick GEWURZ. The Harmonic: gd cool Bx blend, MERLOT-led.

Channing Daughters Long I ★★★ Estate famed for beachy terroir via experiments: natural ferment, Italian varieties. Textured, ageable FRIULANO; cool-maritime LAGREIN; Ramato PINOT GR (*see* p.21); REFOSCO. Playful CHARDS: complex single-vyd Hamptons; salty no-oak sites blend; L'Enfant Sauvage in *botti*, on lees. Single-site floral PETIT VERDOT. Research is CAB SAUV-led, earthy, tart fruit. Local-

> **Getting crosser**
> The climate is getting hotter, drier, more humid, more everything: the
> E US needs new grapes. In VA, project ViRV (cofounded with Ithaca,
> NY, scientist) is hunting for them. They have to be VA-disease resistant,
> commercially viable, act like vinifera in cellar. Winners are likely to be
> crosses of vinifera (from CAB FR to ALBARIÑO, maybe CHARD) and others
> (from *V. amurensis* to *Muscadinia rotundifolia*). But it will take a decade.

aromatics vermouth, seasonal. Watch new MERLOT (Sculpture Garden adds
TEROLDEGO/BLAUFRÄNKISCH). Library blends (r/w).

Element Winery Finger L ★★★ Smart use of difficult climate: magical, necessary
blends like co-ferment PINOT N/SYRAH/GRENACHE; releases only when ready
(now: CHARD, CAB FR, SYRAH 17; Blanc de Blancs 21, out 2031). Library incl 10-yr+
Cab Fr. Two more ranges: young fresh In Our Element; Can't Stop/Won't Stop
blend. Colloquial: estate, tiny quantities by plot.

Fjord Hudson RR ★★★ Sustainable; benchmark ALBARIÑO in e. Top spontaneous-
ferment CAB FR, GAMAY; v.gd CHARD Icewine; ageable MERLOT, also in serious
blend with BLAUFRÄNKISH/Cab Fr. Field blend: SAPERAVI/Blaufränkish/Cab Fr.

Floral Terranes Long I ★★★ Fruit from N Fork, wild ferment in garage for
concentrated, wild, moody wines. Coiled, textured RIES; maritime (stems-incl)
PETIT VERDOT; ferocious, delicious MERLOT, CAB FR and earthy Amarena cherry
CAB SAUV. Ciders, most yrs, incl apples foraged in untended orchards.

Forge Cellars Finger L ★★★ Seneca Lake, e-side, precise single-site RIES. Single-vyd
PINOT N: Tango Oaks, cool-climate classic; Leidenfrost, lifted flower.

Fox Run Finger L ★★★ Range of RIES v.gd; rare Res CAB FR, LEMBERGER; CAB SAUV,
MERLOT. Winemaker Peter Bell mentored many of Finger L's greatest.

Frank, Dr. Konstantin Finger L ★★★ Founder of vinifera in Finger L, winery on
Keuka Lake. Flagship: Lena Res: five Bx grapes, magnifique. US-rare Siberian/
N China Amur, rustic elegance. Amber RKATSITELI, precise. Old Vines PINOT N,
1958 vyd; CAB FR, 50 yr+ vines. SAPERAVI, robust, dark. Masterful trad-method
a focus: RIES Brut Nature 30 mths+, Keuka Lake Blanc de Blanc [sic] (CHARD);
Blanc de Noirs; Brut Natures 19, old-vine PINOTS M/GR.

Hermann J Wiemer Finger L ★★★ Top US RIES name, many bottlings, some single-
vyd. Top e nursery. Experimental Julia vyd incl rare Gouais Bl. Fine GEWURZ
(vines among NY's oldest), CAB FR (stems incl), PINOT N and superlative fizz,
some 10 yrs+. Owns historic Standing Stone (SAPERAVI aged in acid-taming
sandstone; Blanc de Blancs from 1974 vyd; old-vine Ries). Testing NEBBIOLO.

Hickory Hollow Finger L ★★★ Seneca Lake. Lauded low-intervention: CHARD, RIES
(incl 10-yr+ solera), GEWURZ, PINOT BL (Extra Brut too), MERLOT. Winemaker's
Nathan K range: library Ries, neutral-oak CAB FR, PINOT N. Chëpika bottles:
Catawba, Delaware fine pét-nat.

Hosmer Finger L ★★★ On Cayuga Lake, vyd est 1972; RIES, incl limited bottlings.
Also CHARD, CAB FR; 80s PINOT N vines, some for Blanc de Noirs.

Keuka Lake Vineyards Finger L ★★★ Vivacious RIES, incl Falling Man from steep
slopes; v.gd CAB FR. Hybrids incl Vignoles and cult Alsatian Leon Millot.

Lakewood Vineyards Finger L ★★★ A 3rd-generation estate; gd Res CAB FR; everyday
bottle too. Impressive GEWURZ, PINOTS GR/N, multiple RIES.

Liten Buffel ★★★ Estate in Niag, two PINOT N, PINOT GR Ramato (*see* p.21), RIES
(whole-cluster; also skin-contact). Co-ferment BLAUFRÄNKSICH/SAUV BL. Wild
yeasts in neutral oak, no filtering, no sulphur. Noble rot some yrs.

Macari Long I, North F ★★★ Clifftop estate focused on plot, massal selection,
bio. Horses cult PETIT VERDOT pét-nat. SAUV BL: clean, grassy Katherine's Field;
concrete Lifeforce (perfumed CAB FR too). Breakwater CHARD: Burgundy method

shows off Long I quality. Top yrs Alexandra, Bergen Road; 21 latest. Ethereal, structured PINOT N, savoury Cab Fr, herbal MERLOT (incl library, 20 yrs+).

McCall Long I, North F ★★★ Top PINOT N, incl single-vyd, Res, rosé; gd CAB FR, SAUV BL; red Bx blends. Also French-origin Charolais cattle.

Milea Hudson RR, rolling, foggy hills; CAB FR passion. Solid BLAUFRÄNKISCH. Heritage Project is tasty, rare, restoration-minded French-US varieties: Valvin MUSCAT; smart Burdin/Chambourcin and Le Colonel/Chelois blends.

Millbrook Hudson RR ★★★ Estate 1st to grow vinifera in Hudson V: CHARD, RIES, PINOT N. Single-vyd Tocai (FRIULANO), CAB FR. Acidity lets reds age a few yrs.

Paumanok Long I ★★★ Complex cool-climate CHARD, SAUV BL, CAB FR, MERLOT; spontaneous ferments, low sulphur. Assemblage: Bx-style, only best yrs. Grand Vintage Merlot. Racy CHENIN BL, ageable. Blanc de Blancs, 36 mths lees. Old Roots Merlot; Bx-style 15 still fresh; Cab Fr, now or 5 yrs; exciting ALBARIÑO.

Ravines Finger L ★★★ Seneca Lake. Inspired RIES: single-vyd Argetsinger, Falls 16, White Springs. SAUV BL, concentrated top GEWURZ. Flagship focused Argetsinger PINOT N; Limestone Springs vyd CAB FR; MERLOT, Bx. New: GAMAY on Keuka Lake.

Red Newt Finger L ★★★ Renowned RIES, top US quality. Focused on terroirs, incl Seneca Lake crus. Viridescens, Bx-style from best sites. Elegant GEWURZ, GRÜNER V, PINOT GR. Single-vyd CAB FR, PINOT N, SYRAH. Bistro, local produce.

Red Tail Ridge Finger L ★★★ Seneca Lake. Wild ferment; super CHARD, RIES; elegant BLAUFRÄNKISCH, LAGREIN, PINOT N, ZWEIGELT. TEROLDEGO sells out. Sparkling: Blanc de Noirs, pét-nats; Sekt; NV (solera, 08 start) Perpetual Change.

Shaw Vineyard Finger L ★★★ On Seneca Lake, quieter w side. Focus on Res: full-bodied CAB SAUV, MERLOT, PINOT N; clear-cut GEWURZ, RIES on fine lees; barrel-aged Ries too. Orange, blends incl Gewurz, PINOT GR, SAUV BL.

Sheldrake Point Finger L ★★ Cayuga Lake. Exuberant cool-climate GAMAY; fresh, earthy Bx blends; multiple RIES; single-plot PINOT GR, MUSCAT Ottonel; MERLOT, also v.gd rosé, CAB FR, also trad-method sparkling. Unwooded CHARD.

Silver Thread Finger L ★★★ Small-batch cellar blends; CHARD 40-yr+ vines, RIES; CAB FR, PINOT N, MERLOT all v.gd, bio. Terroir-convinced: vyd soils match surrounding forest's, solar-powered, vegan.

Sparkling Pointe Long I ★★★ Convincing *fizz*; French winemaker, Champagne grapes, loam soil. Cuvée Carnaval range (r/w/rosé) lets MERLOT into mix, MUSCAT (in w). Topaz Impérial Rosé: CHARD/PINOTS N/M.

Suhru Long I ★★★ NY maritime, glacial-soil SHIRAZ, 10 yrs+. New: PETIT VERDOT. Ember is Bx (21: TEROLDEGO not MALBEC), age-worthy; CAB FR, MERLOT, Teroldego. Rich SAUV BL, MACARI-grown; lees-deepened PINOT GR; takes hybrid La Crescent seriously, rich acidity; Blanc de Noirs 18–24 mths. Owns innovative Lieb Cellars.

Weis Vineyards Finger L ★★ Keuka Lake. Winemaker trained in Mosel (*see* Germany). RIES from dry to botrytized. Red mainstays PINOT N to SAPERAVI. Now estate vines: CHARD, Ries; CAB FR, Saperavi.

You want noble rot ? Wölffer, Nathan K, Silver Thread. Humidity, lots of waterways.

Whitecliff Hudson RR ★★ Vegan, site-, soils-driven, incl quartz-rich historic Olana slope for v.gd barrel-aged CAB FR, GAMAY. PINOT N from limestone ridge. Res wines: robust RIES, stony CHARD (also trad-method fizz). Serious hybrids: Noiret-led reds, Traminette, VIDAL Bl whites.

Wölffer Estate Long I ★★★ Premier S Fork estate. Classical: Blanc de Blancs, 42 mths, 20 yrs+; Noblesse Oblige luminous vintage rosé fizz, 36 mths; Christian's Cuvée PINOT N or MALBEC; perfumed single-vyd Pinot N Landius; rich maritime SAUV BL Antonov, 5 mths+ lees. New: red blend 0-alc by osmosis, gd fruit, no warmth; massal TREBBIANO Toscano; range of rosés (original set off Hamptons craze) incl own-rooted CAB SAUV, MERLOT; focused, creamy Grandioso.

North Carolina (NC)

Six AVAs. New steep, tiny Crest of the Blue Ridge (try **Marked Tree**; herbal CAB FR). Coastal Atlantic (**Sanctuary Vyds** TEMPRANILLO, SYRAH/TANNAT co-ferment). Piedmont in Blue Ridge Mtns (Italy-tuned **Raffaldini** top *appassimento* skills, v.gd MONTEPULCIANO – Grande Riserva blend, premium Patrimonio; hilly **Dynamis**, luxury focused on CAB SAUV.) Yadkin V (was tobacco plots, now **Jones Von Drehle**, **Junius Lindsay**, **RayLen**, **Shelton**, **Stony Knoll**, **Surrey**). Fine Wines of NC lifts wine (and food) grown/made in state.

Ohio (OH)

Lake Erie moderates continental winters; five AVAs; C19 fame as Wine Belt (esp Catawba), still learning new ways. **Debonné** since 70s. Family-run **Ferrante** Grand River Valley AVA: DOLCETTO, PINOT N, gd CHARD, RIES. **Laurentia** concrete-tank whites. **Markko** Lake Erie Chard, CAB SAUV, Pinot N; in 1968 learned from NY's Dr. Frank to plant Ohioan vinifera. **M Cellars** RKATSITELI, Bx-style. Site-focus **Vermillion V**: granite, clay CABS; sandstone, loam ARNEIS, MALBEC; limestone LEMBERGER, MOSCATO GIALLO, PINOT N (compost soil).

Oklahoma (OK)

Ozark Mtn only AVA, shared with MO and Arkansas. Hybrids most important; some gd Bx. Chambourcin (r) top variety. **Clauren Ridge** gd Meritage. **Pecan Creek Winery** excellent Barrel Res Chambourcin, estate CAB SAUV. **Sabatia** hybrid specialist, v.gd Chambourcin, Chardonel (w). **Sparks Vyd & Winery** sweet specialist. **Waddell Vyds** awarded Vignoles.

Oregon (OR)

Oregon is often assumed to be wet yr round. In reality, the state is warm and dry all summer long, with only the winters seeing heavy rains. This, and the abundance of small premium-quality producers, has resulted in OR having the highest percentage of organic/bio vyds of any state in the US. The focus on quality not quantity has resulted in it being the only growth market left on the US West Coast. Its PINOT N and CHARD regularly outclass burgundy in blind tastings. Prices are climbing as recognition grows.

Recent vintages

2023 Warm. Heatwave at véraison reduced yield. Projected gd quality.
2022 Cool growing season, small, reduced yield. Excellent wines.
2021 Hot, dry; concentrated, balanced acidities. Approachable young.
2020 Wildfires: widespread smoke taint in Will V. S OR less so; Rog V esp gd.
2019 What used to be classic: cool, wet = elegant, restrained. Age-worthy.
2018 Hot, dry; deeply coloured, concentrated, age-worthy; S OR smoke issues.
2017 Bumper crop of excellent quality; Col G smoke issues.
2016 Warm; balanced wines, moderate alc.
2015 Hot; abundant quantity; plush, ripe.

Principal viticultural areas

Columbia Gorge (Col G) is split between WA and OR. Experimentation, variety, sustainable viticulture.
Rocks District of Milton-Freewater (Walla Walla V [Walla]) entirely in OR, producing dense, age-worthy Syrahs. Grenache is up and coming.
Southern Oregon (S OR) warmest growing region, encompasses much of W OR, s of Will V: s sub-AVA Rogue V (Rog V) incl Applegate (App V); n sub-AVA Umpqua V (Um V) incl Elkton OR and Red Hill Douglas County. Rhône

and Spanish varieties best. Quality is spottier than Will V but future promising.
Willamette Valley (Will V) sub-AVAs Chehalem Mts (Ch Mts), Dundee Hills
(Dun H), Eola-Amity Hills (E-A Hills), Laurelwood District (LD), Lower Long
Tom, McMinnville (McM), Mt Pisgah, Polk County, Ribbon Ridge (Rib R),
Tualatin Hills, Van Duzer Corridor (Van DC), Yamhill-Carlton (Y-Car).
Pinots Bl/Gr, Ries and Gamay excel; beautiful Chard; Pinot N remains star.

Go to Carlton Winemakers Studio, Will V: taste with 12 producers under one roof.

Abacela Um V ★★★ The US's 1st TEMPRANILLO: Fiesta, Barrel Select, South East
Block Res, Paramour increasing quality. Classic Private Selection ALBARIÑO.

Abbott Claim Y-Car ★★★★ Antony Beck owner (*see* Graham Beck, S Africa). Organic,
dry-farmed. Flinty CHARD, impeccably balanced PINOT N. Age.

Adelsheim Chehalem Mtns ★★★ Classic, fruity, lightly oaked Breaking Ground
PINOT N and Staking Claim CHARD reliably v.gd value and well distributed.

Antica Terra Will V ★★★★ Spicy, microbial PINOT N. Opulent, golden, tannic CHARD.
Tasting experiences here lauded.

Antiquum Farm Will V ★★★★ Grazing-based regenerative viticulture. Complex,
concentrated, expressive PINOTS GR/N with beautiful fine tannins.

Archery Summit Dun H, E-A Hills ★★★ Rich and structured Summit and Arcus
PINOT N age-worthy. Gorgeous new tasting room.

Arterberry Maresh Dun H ★★★ One of oldest estates in WILL V, much dry-farmed,
own-rooted. Delicate, red-fruit, earthy PINOT N: Maresh Vyd, Old Vines, Weber.

A to Z Wineworks S OR ★ Value-priced, soundly made, fruit-forward wines.

Audeant Will V ★★★★ Concentrated, age-worthy, single-vyd PINOT N.

Beaux Frères Rib R ★★★ Majority-owned by Champagne Henriot (*see* France).
Mikey Etzel still in charge of winemaking. Stars remain estate bottlings, esp
elegant, earthy Belles Soeurs PINOT N.

Bergström Will V ★★★★ Estate fruit (100%) since 2020. Organic; elegant, powerful
wines. Sigrid CHARD v. age-worthy, La Spirale and Le Pre du Col PINOT N.

Bethel Heights E-A Hills ★★★ Now run by 2nd generation (est 70s). Precise, focused
PINOT N with layered fruit.

Big Table Farm Will V ★★★★ Holistic farm with animals, vegetables, wine.
Complex, concentrated, esp Elusive Queen CHARD, SYRAH, all single-vyd PINOT N.

Brick House Rib R ★★★★ All bio farming; all native ferments. Hands-on, family
winemaking team. Excellent Cascadia CHARD, Les Dijonnais PINOT N and older
vintages of Cuvée du Tonnelier (replanted 2018).

Brooks E-A Hills ★★★ Family estate, bio wines. Exceptional perfumed RIES (dr to
sw; up to 20 cuvées; try Ara, Bois Joli, Estate). Also v.gd fruity Rastaban PINOT N.

Cameron Dun H, Rib R ★★★★ One of OR's best-kept secrets. Opulent yet age-
worthy CHARD, esp Clos Electrique. Structured, age-worthy PINOT N, esp Arley's
Leap. Entry DUN H cuvées incredible value. Fun NEBBIOLO from RIB R.

Carriere, J.K. Will V ★★★★ Exquisitely balanced, nuanced, earthy PINOT N, v. age-
worthy. Vespidae excellent, Lola even more elevated; worth price tag.

Corollary Wines Will V ★★★ Elevated trad-method sparkling.

Crowley Wines Will V ★★★ Tyson C makes classic, graceful PINOT N. Two new
CHARDS (Helen, Phoebe) standout, laser-focused Helen 22 esp gd.

David Hill Vineyards & Winery Tua ★★★ Planted 1966. Organic; Alsace varieties;
classic Blackjack (original-vine PINOT N). Discovery Series experimental, natural.

Drouhin Oregon, Dom Dun H, E-A Hills ★★★ Owned by Drouhin family (*see*
France), made by Véronique Boss-D. Restrained Arthur CHARD, Laurène PINOT N
v.gd, firm, best aged. Sister label Roserock in E-A HILLS.

Élevée Winegrowers Will V ★★★ Exploration of sub-AVAs of WILL V with single-vyd
sources. Classic, structured, showcase terroir.

> Pinot Noir: pick your style
> THE EYRIE, DOMAINE DROUHIN deliver OR classic elegance and restraint;
> Shea Wine Cellars, Dom Serene lean into structure, oak in a fruit-
> forward style; SOTER carries torch for premium trad-method PINOT N
> sparkling; The Marigny caters to natural crowd. Up to you.

Elk Cove Will V ★★→★★★ Family-owned, 400 acres, dry-farmed, some own-rooted, 1st vintage 1977. Single-vyd PINOT N more complex, dark-fruited than entry levels, Clay Court, outstanding Five Mtn and Mt Richmond; v.gd PINOTS BL/GR.

Et Fille Will V ★★★ Family-owned/operated; small estate plot and six sustainably farmed vyds in WILL V. Outstanding Gabriella PINOT N, toasty Père Honneur (sp).

Evening Land E-A Hills ★★★ Label that revolutionized OR CHARD. Precise, mineral La Source and Summum CHARD, earthy PINOT N with nuanced oak.

Evesham Wood Will V ★★★ Incredible-value, age-worthy and complex PINOT N.

Eyrie Vineyards, The Dun H ★★★★ Dry-farmed, organic, no-till, min-intervention winemaking. Oldest producer in WILL V, original vines planted 1965. Elegant, age-worthy, low-alc. Incredible library releases; CHARD, Daphne, PINOT GR, Sisters, original South Block PINOT N bottlings textural wonders.

Flâneur Wines Will V ★★★ Excellent-value entry-level CHARD, PINOT N. More structured Cuvée Constantin, La Belle Promenade.

Goodfellow Will V ★★★ Sources fruit from dry-farmed vyds. Complex, elegant; Durant CHARD, Lewman PINOT GR, Heritage Nº 15 Whistling Ridge PINOT N.

Gran Moraine Will V ★★★ Part of Jackson Family Wines OR (*see* CA), specializing in trad-method sparkling, restrained CHARD, bright structured PINOT N.

Hamilton Russell Oregon Will V ★★★ Anthony and Olive HR invested in OR to complement S African wines. Restrained, structured PINOT N. Elegant CHARD.

Hope Well Wine E-A Hills ★★★ Made by regenerative agriculture warrior Mimi Casteel. Beautiful CHENIN BL.

Hundred Suns Will V ★★★ Firm, vibrant PINOT N, age-worthy structure.

Johan Van D ★★★ Dry-farmed, bio, no-till estate vyd. Owned by Mini Banks, also of Cowhorn. Unique CHARD, PINOTS GR/N; v.gd earthy Nils Pinot N.

King Estate Will V ★★ Estate now largest bio producer in US. Appley PINOT GR core of portfolio, a dozen PINOT N, fruit-forward CHARD, GEWURZ, SAUV BL, fizz.

Lavinea Will V ★★★ Owned by EVENING LAND alums Isabelle Meunier and Greg Ralston. Entire portfolio of lithe, fine-boned PINOT N.

Lingua Franca E-A Hills ★★★ Stylish CHARD (Bunker Hill, Estate, Sisters), balanced PINOT N (Mimi's Mind, The Plow). Now owned by Constellation Brands (*see* CA).

Loop de Loop Col G ★★★ Organic, dry-farmed, no-till. Ethereal, red-fruited, spicy PINOT N, Four Winds esp excellent.

Love & Squalor ★★★ Decidedly superior RIES, GAMAY. Great value.

Martin Woods Winery Will V ★★★ Talented winemaker Evan Martin sources from myriad AVAs. Excellent earthy GAMAY, PINOT N. Unusual white varieties.

Morgen Long Will V ★★★★ CHARD specialist. Laser-focused acid, mineral, citrus, well-integrated oak. Incredibly ageable. Seven Springs, X Omni standouts.

Nicolas-Jay Will V ★★★ More Burgundians in OR: Jean-Nicolas Méo of Dom Méo-Camuzet (*see* France) and music entrepreneur Jay Boberg. Bold, structured Momtazi, concentrated Own-Rooted PINOT N.

Patricia Green Cellars Will V ★★★ Excellent, red-fruited, moderate-weight, single-vyd PINOT N. Estate Bonshaw Block, Estate Etzel Block, Mysterious, Notorious superb. Rare OR SAUV BL.

Ponzi Lau ★★→★★★ Owned by Champagne Bollinger (*see* France). Avellana CHARD, Aurora PINOT N v.gd; fruit-forward Classico, Tavola Pinot N gd value.

Résonance Will V ★★★ Jadot's (*see* France) OR project, winemaker Guillaume

Large. Découverte CHARD, Estate PINOT N best, most age-worthy. Need vigorous decant when young.

Ribbon Ridge Winery Rib R ★★★ Ridgecrest label gd-value, textured: GRÜNER V, RIES, GAMAY, PINOTS GR/N. Aged Pinot N from RIB R label outstanding, elegant.

Rose & Arrow Will V ★★★★ Micro-production; age-worthy PINOT N from winemaker Felipe Ramirez and terroir consultant Pedro Parra. All outstanding. Second label: Alit, v.gd value if you subscribe.

Sequitur Rib R ★★★ Another project from BEAUX FRÈRES' Etzel family (vyds border). CHARD, PINOT N focused, fine. Labels, names change annually.

Sokol Blosser Will V ★★→★★★ Estate and Orchard Block PINOT N, structure, length.

Soter Will V ★★★★ Tony S, CA legend, shines with balanced, age-worthy CHARD, PINOT N, bubbly. Estate-grown Mineral Springs Ranch, all bio, has best portfolio. Planet Oregon for value.

Oregon Chardonnay with oysters is a winning combo. Try Brickhouse Cascadia.

Tan Fruit Will V ★★★★ Jim Maresh (ARTERBERRY MARESH) CHARD project, sourcing vyd designates around WILL V. Eyrie, Oak Grove, Fairview incredibly different but all v.gd.

Troon App V ★★→★★★ The 2nd regenerative organic vyd in US. Excellent textural Estate VERMENTINO, SYRAH (Siskiyou best). Rest of portfolio tends towards funky light reds, orange (Glou Glou GRENACHE, Kubli Bench Amber).

Walter Scott E-A Hills ★★★★ Family-owned, focused on vyd sources. Precise, linear, buzz-worthy CHARD. Earthy, balanced PINOT N, well-integrated oak. GAMAY also excellent. Freedom Hill, Sojourner, X-Novo vyds top list. Age-worthy.

Willamette Valley Vineyards Rocks, Will V ★★ Many shareholder/owners; extensive vyds, mostly value CHARD, PINOT N, premium Elton. Rocks District now home to Maison Bleue, Pambrun.

Winderlea Will V ★★★ Vibrant single-vyd PINOT N. Legacy, Weber, fizz v.gd; all bio.

Pennsylvania (PA)

Continental climate, humidity. ALBARIÑO v.gd, esp **Galen Glen**, **Maple Springs**. GRÜNER V, PINOT N, Bx varieties. Many Italians: BARBERA to FIANO. Lake Erie-softened nw. Milder in se: **Va La** cult Avondale field blends, incl CORVINA, 11 NEBBIOLO clones, funky rosato; **Vox Vineti** Nebbiolo, Bx-style. Central Lehigh V: **Galen Glen**, windy, 305m (1000ft) up; **Stone Cellar** range from oldest vines: Grüner V, gd sparkling; **Stony Run** v.gd Brut 18, plush Albariño. Try also **Allegro**, reliable since 70s; **Fero Vyds** bright LEMBERGER, celebrated SAPERAVI; **Karamoor**; **Mazza** Lake Erie TEROLDEGO; **Mural City Cellars** Philly urban winery, serious natural style; **Penns Woods** SAUV BL, PINOT N; **Presque Isle** DORNFELDER; **Vynecrest**; **Waltz** CAB FR; **Wayvine** gd barrique-aged native Carmine (also MERLOT blend). Local sommeliers' favourite: **Armstrong V** Chambourcin (Cab Fr, Merlot gd too).

Pennsylvania wine stalwart Galer closed. To become botanical garden again, maybe.

Rhode Island (RI)

Smallest state, just ne of NY's North Fork across cold-tempering Sound; Bx-style reds, PINOT N, CHARD. **Carolyn's Sakonnet** GEWURZ, blends CAB FR/Chancellor. **Diamond Hill** synthetics-free farming, barrel-aged Pinot N. **Greenvale** min-touch family estate, Sakonnet River, v.gd Chard, natural-ferment PINOT GR *ramato* (*see* p.21), smart-oak MALBEC, MERLOT. **Mulberry Vyds** Pinot Gr, SYRAH. **Newport** Gewurz, Bx-style. **Verde** biology prof-turned-farmer on lake: Cab Fr-led blend Surveyor, awarded St Croix.

Texas (TX)

Texas Hill Country (THC) and Texas High Plains (THP) major AVAs; THC has subregions, THP does not. Other regions outside AVAs incl N TX, nr Dallas, and E TX towards Louisiana. Portuguese and Med varieties best in High Plains. Rhône and Bx varieties best in THC. Hybrids excel in E TX.

Ab Astris ★★ Textured, refined; Bx-style, Rhône varieties plus others. TANNAT esp elegant for variety. Avignon blend (r), worthy homage to Châteauneuf.

Adega Vinho Specialist in Iberian and Rhône varieties based on Estate Bilger Family Vyds. TOURIGA, TEMPRANILLO and Pordosol Tempranillo blend excellent. Refreshing style for big reds.

Becker Vineyards ★★ Bold, ripe, oaky Bx-style, Rhône styles; compare CAB SAUV in various bottlings. Noteworthy GSM.

Bending Branch Winery ★★★ Big reds. Known for outstanding TANNAT; also v.gd Iberian and Med: PETITE SIRAH, SAGRANTINO, Souzão. Experiments with lesser-known grapes.

Brennan Vineyards ★★ Intense with elegance; outside AVAs. Top dry VIOGNIER; v.gd white Rhône blend Lily and structured NERO D'AVOLA Super Nero.

Duchman Family Winery ★★★★ Italian stars here: excellent MONTEPULCIANO, v.gd AGLIANICO, SANGIOVESE; crisp, light TREBBIANO, VERMENTINO; all benchmarks for TX. Sources grapes from older High Plains vyds.

Enoch's Stomp ★ Superb fortifieds from Blanc du Bois and Lenoir in NE TX, outside AVAs. Also v.gd orange Villard Blanc, red Norton.

Fall Creek Vineyards ★★★ Several ranges: Super-premium ExTerra from Salt Lick vyds; Classics: CHENIN BL, SAUV BL.

Texas High Plains similar to east Washington: continental climate, hot summers.

Haak Winery ★★★ Age-worthy vintage Madeira-style Blanc du Bois and Jacquez are classic, world-class. Dry herb-and-citrus Blanc du Bois also v.gd.

Hilmy Cellars ★★ One of largest vyds in Hill Country. Rhône, Bx varieties, plus TEMPRANILLO. Excellent Tejas Bl Rhône blend (w), v.gd inky PETIT VERDOT, structured Tempranillo.

Kerrville Hills ★★★ John Rivenburgh produces leathery TANNAT, supple PICPOUL Bl, and textbook SEM, among other quality offerings.

Kuhlman Cellars Rhône, Bx red blends, plus ROUSSANNE. Try ripe, rich Estate wines: Kuhlmanation (r/w), Roussanne. Calcaria ALBARIÑO blend also gd.

Lewis Wines ★★★★ Focus on single-vyd Iberian varieties, esp ALICANTE BOUSCHET, TINTA CÃO, TOURIGA N. Leading TEMPRANILLO, v.gd crisp CHENIN BL and red-fruited estate rosé.

Llano Estacado ★★→★★★ Consistently excellent full-bodied 1836 (r/w); Super Tuscan-styled Viviana (r/w) also gd. Excellent small-lot experimental bottlings through wine club.

Lost Draw Cellars ★★★ Same group as William Chris Vyds. Award-winning pét-nat PINOT M. Compare single-vyd or THC/THP bottlings of MOURVÈDRE, SANGIOVESE, TEMPRANILLO.

McPherson Cellars ★★★ Pioneering TX wine family. Restrained, balanced Iberian, Rhônes, plus heritage-vyd SANGIOVESE. Age-worthy ROUSSANNE Res. Excellent varietal ALICANTE BOUSCHET, CARIGNAN, CINSAULT.

Messina Hof Winery ★★ Bold, oaky. SAGRANTINO pioneer; CAB FR consistent award-winner. Range of sweet.

Pedernales Cellars ★★★ Rhône, Spanish grapes, structured style. Benchmark VIOGNIER, TEMPRANILLO. GSM excellent. Co-founder Julie Kuhlken's PhD in philosophy shows in thoughtful, meditative wines that can age.

Perissos Vineyard and Winery Italian focus, plus Spanish. Big reds, incl excellent AGLIANICO, TEMPRANILLO, and ever-evolving Racker's Blend.

Southold Farm and Cellar All the trends, incl carbonic, skin contact, field blends, here. Names, labels change annually. Try skin-contact whites and carbonic reds.

Spicewood Vineyards ★★★★ Sibling winery to RON YATES. Estate-grown wines of finesse, elegance, vibrancy. Outstanding signature Good Guy field blend (r); taut and textured The Independence Bx blend (r); refined Battle of Toro TOURIGA N/TEMPRANILLO.

Wedding Oak ★ Leading AGLIANICO producer. Outstanding Castanet CINSAULT rosé. Excellent flagship Tioja TEMPRANILLO blend. Big, textured ROUSSANNE. Heady and fruity ZIN.

William Chris Vineyards ★★★★ Terroir-expressive. Best-in-class single-vyd bottlings of MOURVÈDRE. Flagship Enchante (r) and Hunter (r) also v.gd. LOST DRAW CELLARS same group.

Yates, Ron ★★★ Single-vyd Friesen CAB SAUV and TEMPRANILLO/CAB SAUV/MERLOT best. GRENACHE rosé also v.gd. Focus on Rhône, Spanish, Italian varieties.

Vermont (VT)

With mtns, harsh winters, brief sunny summers, frost, hail and humidity, those who dare plant vyds share fruit: hybrids like Frontenac N, La Crescent plus BLAUFRÄNKISCH, RIES in extreme n terroirs. Masterful apple-grape blends. Many bio-farmed, natural-thinking, like pioneers **La Garagista** (rosé from Brianna steeped with other hybrid skins, r, w). Several VT mentees: **Iapetus** (experimental side, weighty L'ACADIE BL, Marquette pét-nats); **Shelburne Vyds** (Marquette Res); fizz-focused **Zafa Wines**. **Ellison Estate** beguiling hybrids. **Lincoln Peak** incl nouveau Marquette. **Stella 14** by MS, spontaneous-ferment Frontenacs N/Bl, Marquette.

Virginia (VA)

Continental climate; challenge is to beat humidity, winter freeze, harvest-time hurricanes; wide grower knowledge-sharing helps. More planting on heights, esp Shenandoah V. Elegant outcomes statewide in classical (CAB FR, MERLOT, PETIT VERDOT; stars of central and s) and experimental (hardy, rich, high-acid PETIT MANSENG; NEBBIOLO, TANNAT, select hybrids). CAB SAUV; VIOGNIER too.

Ankida Ridge ★★★ Top, ageable, precise PINOT N: possibly best in VA. Steep, ancient-granite slopes up to 590m (1800ft) in Blue Ridge Mtns; farm incl chickens, Katahdin sheep. CHARD; Blancs de Noirs; thoughtful GAMAY. Co-owns Stinson: v.gd wait-for-it Meritage, acidity-driven ripe fruit.

Barboursville ★★★ In Monticello: rolling hills, cattle, inn. Mainstays PETIT VERDOT for best-vintage blend Octagon. Nascent VIOGNER; VERMENTINO (esp Riserve); FALANGHINA's oiliness. NEBBIOLO Res age 10 yrs+; Italian focus incl FIANO Res. Monticello ideal CAB FR Res, 99 still energetic. Paxxito is luscious VIDAL/MUSCAT Ottonel. Blanc de Noirs from PINOT M.

Blenheim ★★ In hilly Charlottesville, earthy estate ALBARIÑO, GRÜNER V; round ROUSSANNE; pithy RKATSITELI (80s vines); local-sourced Monticello CAB FR; Painted Red Bx blend, labels by founder/musician Dave Matthews. Base of Oenoverse Club, an access and opportunity initiative.

Cana Vineyards ★★ Rosé-serious. N VA farmland CABS SAUV/FR, MERLOT. Unité Res (Bx r). Also MALBEC, TEMPRANILLO.

Capstone Vineyards ★★ High-altitude, LINDEN neighbour; CHARD, CHENIN BL, Bx blend estate-bottled since 2023.

Early Mountain ★★★ Rich, earthy Eluvium. Rise in best yrs: 19 21 latest, incl TANNAT.

Five single-site CAB FR: Quaker Run is lush. Elegant, age-worthy PETIT MANSENG. White-blend Intention in Petit Manseng's best yrs: 19 20 out now.

Glen Manor Vineyards ★★ Historic farm, 5th generation. Vines on steep rocky slopes in Blue Ridge Mtns 305m (1000ft)+ up. Began with SAUV BL, now joined by rich CAB FR from 20–30-yr-old vines, off-dry PETITS MANSENG/VERDOT.

King Family Vineyards ★★★ French winemaker, MERLOT-based Meritage worth waiting for; peppery red-fruit CAB FR; classic VIOGNER; top tiny-production *vin de paille*-style PETIT MANSENG. Experimental Small-Batch Series, incl skin-contact Viogner. SAVAGNIN planted 2020. Winemaker's own Dom Finot incl fresh, serious, single-vyd PETIT VERDOT rosé (no sulphites), CAB FR, TANNAT.

Linden ★★★ Estate founded in 80s by early believer in site over fruit. Notable high-altitude sites: rich, mineral CHARD; vivacious SAUV BL; savoury PETIT VERDOT; elegant, complex Bx-style reds often require ageing. Some library wines; vertical pours in tasting room.

Midland ★★★ Old family farm, limestone soils 400m (1312ft) up. Clever CHARD; peppery BLAUFRÄNKISCH; structured CAB FR; top PETIT MANSENG; RIES. No-dosage Blanc de Blancs 18, ageing well. New high plantings incl resistant MERLOT Kanthus. Family's custom-crush Common Wealth is also VA-wine co-op, think tank, tasting room. Winemaker makes *Lightwell Survey* too, bold co-ferments: earthy Cab Fr/Petit Manseng; astounding Ries-assisted Petit Manseng; three whites/Chambourcin.

Pollak ★★ Estate since 2003, international style: Creamy PINOT GR; lush, spicy VIOGNIER; heftier CABS FR/SAUV, MERLOT, Meritage.

Ramiiisol ★★★ Monticello AVA in Blue Ridge Mtns foothills. No-expense-spared CAB FR, holistic-terroir focus incl iron-rich granite gneiss parcels, forest, top Italian cooperages. Complex lasting vintages, 16–20 ethereal, wild site blends; since 21 single-vyd trials, bottles may follow. MONTEPULCIANO as v.gd rosato inspired by Cerasuolo (*see* Italy).

Rausse, Gabriele / Vino dal Bosco ★★★ Small, quality estate in forest nr Monticello, NE Italian sensibility, French technology. Single-vyd CAB FR, MERLOT, MALBEC; MALVASIA Bianca. New Blanc de Noirs. Vino dal Bosco: *méthode ancestrale*, amber wines.

RdV Vineyards ★★★★ Red blends from granite hillside. Elegance, complexity, power: MERLOT-led Rendezvous; CAB SAUV-led Lost Mountain VA's 1st $100 wine.

Veritas ★★★ Solid estate, steep forest vyds. Concentrated, floral CAB FR can age 10 yrs+. PETIT VERDOT too. Long-macerated Bx-style Monticello Res: dark fruit, leather, acidity. Restrained SAUV BL, richer VIOGNIER; CHARD in no oak; Res and trad-method Scintilla, up to 5 yrs on lees.

Washington (WA)

Hot days give ripe fruit flavours, while cool nights lock in acidity. Result: wines that sit between New and Old Worlds, approachable on release, while offering terrific ageability. Being in CA's massive shadow makes them underpriced relative to their quality. It's all a wine-lover's dream. However, limited production means the reality is you'll have to work to find them.

Principal viticultural areas

Columbia Valley (Col V) Huge AVA in central and E WA, with a touch in OR. High-quality Cab Sauv, Merlot, Ries, Chard, Syrah. Key sub-divisions incl Yakima Valley (Yak V), Red Mtn, Walla Walla.

Red Mountain (Red Mtn) Sub-AVA of Col V and Yak V. Hot region known for Cabs and Bx blends.

Walla Walla Valley (Walla) Sub-AVA of Col V with own identity and vines in WA and OR. Home of important boutique brands and prestige labels. Syrah, Cab Sauv and Merlot.

Yakima Valley (Yak V) Sub-AVA of Col V. Focus on Merlot, Syrah, Ries.

Abeja Col V, Walla ★★★ WALLA winery; high-quality COL V CHARD, CAB SAUV.

Amavi Walla ★★ A v.gd estate: Walla CAB SAUV, SYRAH, SEM.

Andrew Will Col V, HH Hills, Yak V ★★★★ 10' 12' 14' 16 Winemaker (2nd-generation) Will Carmada focuses on reserved, age-worthy style. Sorella flagship.

Avennia Col V, Yak V ★★★ 10 12' 14' 16' 18' 21 Benchmark Woodinville producer focuses on old vines, earlier picking. Sestina Bx blend tops. Gravura Bx blend v.gd value. Lydian value label.

Baer Winery Col V ★★★ Woodinville stalwart dedicated to luscious Stillwater Creek Vyd red blends. MERLOT-based Ursa consistent standout.

Betz Family Col V ★★★→★★★★ 10 12' 14' 16' 18' 19 One of Woodinville's founding wineries makes top-quality Bx-style, Rhône styles for 25 yrs+. All noteworthy. Père de Famille CAB SAUV flagship. Untold Story gd value. SUNU label (OR).

Browne Family Col V ★ Brand from wine giant Precept. CAB SAUV the highlight.

Cadence Red Mtn ★★★ 10' 12' 14 16' 17' 19' Ben Smith focuses on Bx blends from estate vyd. Immortal wines with emphasis on structure, class. All standouts that punch well above their weight. Coda from declassified barrels exceptional value.

Cairdeas Col V ★★★ Rhône specialist making everything from blends to rarely seen grape varieties.

Canvasback Red Mtn ★★ A WA brand for Napa's The Duckhorn Portfolio, with v.gd CAB SAUV.

Cayuse Walla ★★★★ 10 11 12' 14 16' 19 Vigneron Christophe Baron planting in cobblestone soils helped put WALLA on map. Cult, mailing list-only, with yrs-long wait. Stratospheric scores, steep prices on secondary market, but worth it. Sister wineries Hors Categorie, Horsepower, No Girls also top quality. Double Lucky v.gd value.

Pinot Noir is queen in Oregon; but in Washington, Cabernet Sauvignon is king.

Charles Smith Wines Col V ★★ Eponymous winemaker spun off brand to wine-giant Constellation before The Wine Group (both CA) took over in 2022. Focus on value RIES, CAB SAUV, MERLOT.

Col Solare Red Mtn ★★★→★★★★ 10 12' 14 18 RED MTN partnership between CH STE MICHELLE and Antinori (*see* Italy); CAB SAUV with complexity, longevity.

Columbia Crest Col V ★★ →★★★ Sister winery to CH STE MICHELLE, all about quality, value. Well-priced, v.gd Grand Estates label; Res wines cut above, esp CAB SAUV.

Columbia Winery Col V ★ One of WA's founding wineries, now owned by E&J Gallo (*see* CA).

Corliss Col V ★★★→★★★★ 08' 10 12' 14 16 Cult producer, extended ageing in barrel/bottle. Sister winery Tranche focuses on Blue Mtn fruit. Secret Squirrel value brand.

Côte Bonneville Yak V ★★★ A 2nd-generation winery, estate wines from DuBrul, highly regarded vyd. Extended bottle-age before release. *Train Station* v.gd value.

DeLille Col V, Red Mtn ★★★ 10' 12' 14' 16 18 19 Among Woodinville's founding wineries, 30 yrs in 2022. High-end Bx, Rhône styles; D2, Four Flags v.gd value. Chaleur Bl often state's best white. Métier new entry-level project.

Devison Walla ★★★ Attention-getting wines with voice, incl state's best SAUV BL, MALBEC, rosé. Above the Flood outrageously gd Rhône-style blend.

Dossier Col V ★★★ New winery from Seattle businessman and a former NFL player. Focus on sophisticated hedonism.

Doubleback Walla ★★★ 10' 12 16 18 Ex-footballer Drew Bledsoe's winery isn't a vanity project; classy, elegant estate WALLA CAB SAUV. Bledsoe Family sister winery. Bledsoe-McDaniels new OR PINOT and WA SYRAH project.

Dunham Walla ★★ Long-time WALLA producer of v.gd CAB SAUV, SYRAH. Trutina & Three-Legged Red gd value.

Dusted Valley Walla ★★ Focus on COL V, WALLA, from value Boomtown to high-end single-vyd offerings. Stained Tooth SYRAH consistent standout.

Echolands Walla ★★★ MS/MW makes food-friendly Bx styles, SYRAH, GRENACHE.

Figgins Walla ★★★★ 08 10 12 14 16 18 Winemaker, 2nd-generation Chris F (LEONETTI), focuses on single vyd in Upper Mill Creek. Structured Bx blends. Patience/decanting required.

Force Majeure Red Mtn ★★★→★★★★ Todd Alexander left Napa's Bryant Family Vyd to take reins at all-estate winery using RED MTN and WALLA fruit. Big, bold style. Among best in state.

Gorman Col V, Red Mtn ★★★ Hedonism: rich, ripe wines. Evil Twin CAB SAUV/SYRAH calling card. Devil You Know/Don't v.gd value. Ashan CHARD project.

Gramercy Walla ★★★ 10 12' 13 16 18 19 Founded by a MS, emphasis on lower-alc/oak, higher-acid, food-friendly wines. Speciality earthy SYRAH, herby CAB SAUV. Lower East value label.

Grosgrain Walla ★★ Champion of underdog varieties, eg. sparkling LEMBERGER.

H3 Col V ★ Spin-off from COLUMBIA CREST. Value CAB, MERLOT, Red Blend.

Januik Col V ★★★ 10 12' 18 19 Consistent quality, value Bx varieties and blends. Some of state's best CHARD. Novelty Hill sister winery. Son Andrew has eponymous label.

J Bookwalter Winery Col V ★★★ Long-time producer of hedonistic, old-vine red blends. Readers v.gd value.

Seattle might be Rain City but E WA wine country gets same rainfall as Gobi Desert.

Kevin White Winery Yak V ★★★ Micro-producer of high quality, outrageous value. The trick? Getting them before they're gone.

K Vintners Col V, Walla ★★★ Founder Charles Smith made his name with cattle-brand-style black-and-white labels, cultish, single-vyd SYRAH, Syrah/CAB SAUV blends. Sixto CHARD-focused sister winery. Also CasaSmith, Substance, ViNo.

Latta Col V ★★★ Ex-K VINTNERS winemaker Andrew L; stunning single-vyd GRENACHE, MALBEC, MOURVÈDRE, SYRAH. Latta Latta v.gd value. Disruption, Kind Stranger side projects, value.

L'Ecole Nº 41 Walla ★★★ 10 12' 14 16 18 One of WALLA's founding wineries. Superb-value COL V wines, higher-tier Walla offerings. Ferguson flagship Bx blend. CHENIN BL, SEM v.gd value.

Leonetti Walla ★★★★ 08 10' 12' 14 18 19 WALLA's founding winery with well-deserved cult status. Steep prices for all-estate, cellar-worthy CAB SAUV, MERLOT, SANGIOVESE; Res Bx-blend flagship.

Liminal Red Mtn ★★★→★★★★ New cult producer of high-elevation RED MTN reds and whites that demand attention.

Long Shadows Walla ★★★→★★★★ Brings globally famous winemakers to WA to make one wine each. Feather Cab by Randy Dunn (Napa). Poet's Leap RIES one of best in state. All worth seeking.

Luke Col V ★★ Producer of well-priced Wahluke reds that way overdeliver.

Mark Ryan Winery Red Mtn, Yak V ★★★ Original Woodinville "grape killer" known for big, bold style. But there's refinement too. Dissident v.gd value. MERLOT-based Long Haul and Dead Horse CAB SAUV stand out. Second label: Board Track Racer, gd value.

Northstar Walla ★★★ When MERLOT was WA's guiding star, this producer helped lead way. Decades later, it still does. CH STE MICHELLE sister winery.

Owen Roe Yak V ★★★ Producer of YAK V CAB SAUV, SYRAH and Bx blends that all emphasize restraint.

Pacific Rim Col V ★★ Oceans of tasty, inexpensive, eloquent Dry to Sweet and Organic. For more depth, single-vyd releases.

Passing Time Col V ★★★→★★★★ Former pro-quarterbacks Dan Marino, Damon Huard focus on appellation-specific CAB SAUV. Winemaker Chris Peterson (AVENNIA). Horse Heaven Hills tops. Quickly earning cult status.

Pepper Bridge Walla ★★★ Estate wines, Bx style, from top WALLA sites. Structured, classy. Time in cellar required.

Quilceda Creek Col V ★★★★ 04' 07 10 12' 14' 16' 18' Flagship producer of WA, cult CAB SAUV known for richness, layering, ageing potential. One of most lauded in world. Sold by allocation. Buy if it you can find it – and if you can afford to.

Reininger Walla ★★ Long-time producer of tasty reds. Helix second label.

Reynvaan Family Walla ★★★ 10' 11 12' **14** 16 18 Wait-list winery focusing on estate vyds in Rocks District, Blue Mtn foothills. Reds get raves – deservedly so – but don't miss whites.

Ste Michelle, Ch Col V ★★→★★★ State's founding winery offers gd value (r/w), plus estate offerings and higher-end Res. World's largest RIES producer, dry and off-dry COL V exceptional value.

Savage Grace Yak V ★★ Producer of low-oak, low-alc, low-intervention, single-vyd wines with something to say.

Saviah Walla ★★★ Long-time producer of high-quality/value-ratio estate wines. The Jack label gd value.

Seven Hills Winery Walla ★★★ 10 12' **14** 16 18 One of WALLA's founding wineries, now owned by CA's Crimson Wine Group. MERLOT v.gd value.

Sleight of Hand Walla ★★★ Audiophile Trey Busch focuses on Bx blends and Rhône styles. Seek Funkadelic SYRAH from Rocks District. Renegade value label.

Sparkman Red Mtn, Yak V ★★★ Woodinville "grape killer" producer focuses on power, diversity, making two-dozen-plus wines. Ruby Leigh, Stella Mae Bx blends consistent standouts. Kingpin top CAB SAUV.

Spring Valley Walla ★★★ CH STE MICHELLE property focusing on estate reds. Uriah MERLOT Bx blend the headliner.

Syncline Col V ★★★ Columbia Gorge: focus on fresh Rhône styles. Subduction Red v.gd value. Sparkling GRÜNER V insider wine. PICPOUL consistent standout.

The Walls Walla ★★★ Former Pride (Napa, *see CA*) winemaker Sally Johnson Blum now in charge. Opulent RED MTN and WALLA reds.

Trothe HH Hills ★★★→★★★★ 19 20' New producer reaching for brass ring of cult status. Quality is stratospheric. So are prices.

Two Vintners Col V ★★★ Woodinville producer; some of WA's best Rhône-styles.

Valdemar ★★★ WALLA outpost for Spain's Bodegas Valdemar. Huge investments in vy'd, winery.

Walla Walla Vintners Walla ★★ Long-time producer: luscious CABS FR/SAUV, MERLOT.

Waterbrook Walla ★ One of state's oldest wineries, now owned by wine-giant Precept; focus on value.

Woodward Canyon Walla ★★★★ 07 10 12' 14 16 18 Founding WALLA producer (now 2nd generation); Bx focus; CHARD among state's best; Old Vines CAB SAUV.

WT Vintners Yak V ★★★ Sommelier-winemaker Jeff Lindsay-Thorsen picks earlier, pulls back oak on single-vyd GRÜNER V, GRENACHE, SYRAH.

Wisconsin (WI)

American Wine Project (est 2018) leads vibrant industry focused on cold-hardy hybrids (Brianna, SEYVAL BL; Frontenac, Marquette), incl pét-nat, piquette.

Wollersheim Winery (est 1840s) v.gd estate wines, eight varieties.

Mexico

If you expect big, bold reds from Mexico, you won't be disappointed. Not much gets exported. Baja California, with its maritime-influenced Mediterranean climate, produces more than 75%, and subregion Valle de Guadalupe has the most wineries. Other states – including historic Coahuila and high-altitude areas of Zacatecas, Aguascalientes, Guanajuato and Querétaro – are making great strides in quality. Vineyards tend to be at high altitude and have cool nights.

Adobe Guadalupe ★★★★ Destination winery and inn. Serafiel blend (CAB/SYRAH) top: wines named after archangels or gardens. Jardín Secreto blend (TEMPRANILLO-based) expresses region. Jardín Mágico SAUV BL, lively, fresh.

Bichi ★★ Name means "naked" in local language: natural winemaking, min intervention, old organic dry-farmed vyds. Try Pet Mex pét-nat from unknown grape or Bichi Blanco skin-ferment CHENIN BL.

Bruma Valle de Guadalupe Winery and luxury destination resort in Valle de Guadalupe. Try Ocho Tinto (r) from CAB SAUV/PETITE SIRAH.

Carrodilla, Finca La Organic/bio. Rich, ripe, pricey. Varietal CAB SAUV, SHIRAZ, TEMPRANILLO, CHENIN BL all gd. Best: red Canto de Luna blend.

Casa de Piedra ★★★ Modern winery/winemaking; 1st project of prolific Hugo d'Acosta. Vino de Piedra CAB SAUV/TEMPRANILLO oaky, structured, age-worthy.

Casa Vieja, La Hand-destemming, natural yeasts, no sulphur, no oak flavours; 120-yrs-old+ ungrafted Mission (PAÍS); skin-contact PALOMINO most interesting.

Corona del Valle Winery/restaurant destination. TEMPRANILLO/NEBBIOLO is star; also try GRENACHE rosé, SAUV BL, varietal reds.

Cuna de Tierra In Dolores Hidalgo, Guanajuato. Architecturally significant, award-winning winery and wines. NEBBIOLO, SYRAH, MALBEC stand out.

Henri Lurton, Bodegas ★★ Lurton family (Bx). Refined CAB SAUV, CARMENÈRE, SAUV BL. CHENIN BL a highlight. Try inky PETITE SIRAH and elegant NEBBIOLO. Winemaker is ex-Ch Brane-Cantenac (*see* Bordeaux).

LA Cetto Italian heritage. Exported, well known abroad. High-altitude, juicy, value: Res Privada range (NEBBIOLO, PETITE SIRAH). CHENIN BL largest production.

Lomita, Hacienda La Renowned for winery, restaurant and murals. Organic; CHENIN BL/SAUV BL shines, award-winning Tinto de la Hacienda (r).

Mina Penelope Winemaker Verónica Santiago at helm, one of growing number of women making wine here. Julio 14 (SYRAH-driven GMS blend) is signature. Others have NEBBIOLO focus, but also on-trend amber, rosé.

Monte Xanic ★★★ The 1st modern premium winery, excellent CAB SAUV, v.gd MERLOT. Try SAUV BL, unoaked CHARD, fresh CHENIN BL. Top: Calixa blend (r), NEBBIOLO Limitada. High-elevation PINOT N breaks new ground.

Paralelo ★★ Created by Hugo d'Acosta to explore same variety made identically from different terroirs. Ensamble Colina (hillside vines); Arenal (old river bed).

San Miguel, Viñedo Largest winery in Guanajuato nr San Miguel de Allende. Best for reds. Try Latiendo (MALBEC/SYRAH/MERLOT); also Malbec Res and CAB SAUV.

Tres Valles ★★ Grapes sourced from three subregions: Valle de San Vicente Ferrer, Valle de San Antonio de las Minas and Valle de Guadalupe. TEMPRANILLO, SANGIOVESE, MERLOT all gd. Better blends incl top Kuwal.

Vena Cava ★★★ Winery features reclaimed fishing boats. Wine/dining/architecture destination. Well priced, organic. Top: CAB SAUV, SAUV BL, TEMPRANILLO.

Vinaltura ★ In Querétaro: high-altitude vyds, high desert climate. Terruño blends excel: Bajio (MERLOT/MALBEC/TEMPRANILLO), Blanco (French/German varieties).

Canada

No longer known only for ultra-sweet Icewine, Canada produces
styles that range from racy traditional-method sparkling and pure
Rieslings to elegant Pinot Noirs and robust reds. Most vineyards benefit
from nearby oceans, lakes and rivers that lengthen growing seasons and
moderate otherwise deadly winter cold. Matching varieties to the many
different sites is on-going, and the successes are evident in the bottle.

Ontario

Cool-climate influenced by lakes Ontario and Erie. Key varieties: CHARD, RIES,
CAB FR, GAMAY, PINOT N. Three Geographical Indications: Niagara Peninsula
(Niag), most important, has two regional and ten sub-appellations; Prince
Edward County (PEC); Lake Erie North Shore (LENS).

Industrial archeology: Pelee Island has ruins of 1st commercial winery, 1866.

Bachelder Niag ★★★★ Thomas B worked in Burgundy and OR, has encyclopedic
knowledge of Niag. Top-notch, elegant plot-specfic CHARD, GAMAY, PINOT N.

Cave Spring Niag ★★★ Pioneer specialist in taut dry Niag RIES (some old vines),
impressive range (fresh r/w/sp and Icewine).

Clos Jordanne Niag ★★★★ Owned by Arterra. Modelled on Burgundy, several tiers of
elegant CHARD, PINOT N. Highlight: Le Grand Clos.

Closson Chase Niag ★★ Early (1998) PEC winery specializing in elegant CHARD,
PINOT N. Notable Grande Cuvée.

Flat Rock Cellars Niag ★★ Specialist in stylish CHARD, RIES, PINOT N. Highlights:
Gravity Pinot N, Nadja's Vyd Ries.

Henry of Pelham Niag ★★ Reds esp solid, notably Speck Family Res Baco N; v.gd
fizz, esp racy Cuvée Catharine Carte Blanche Blanc de Blancs.

Hidden Bench Niag ★★★★ Superb winery, strengths in elegant CHARD, CAB FR,
PINOT N. Highlights: Terroir Caché (r blend), Tête de Cuvée Chard.

Leaning Post Niag ★★ Wide portfolio, incl clone-specific CHARD, single-vyd PINOT N.
Notable: rich Senchuk Vyd Pinot N.

Pearl Morissette Niag ★★★ Exciting, pure wines, esp CHARD, RIES, CAB FR, PINOT N.
Highlights: Irrévérence (w blend), Chamboué Pinot N. Superb restaurant.

Southbrook Vineyards Niag ★★ Organic, biodiverse, with chickens, sheep. Juicy
(r/w/sp). Notable: Triomphe CAB FR, Triomphe Orange.

Stanners Vineyard PEC ★★★ Garagiste with juicy CHARD, PINOT GR, PINOT N. Notable:
Cuivré Pinot Gr, Narrow Rows Pinot N.

Stratus Niag ★★★ Elegant blends (Stratus White, Red), growing emphasis on
CAB FR, GAMAY. Charles Baker, same property, makes bright-acid RIES.

Tawse Niag ★★★ Impressive vyd-specific pure PINOT N, CHARD. Note Robyn's Block
Chard, Spark! (sp). Also spirits.

Two Sisters Niag ★★★ Destination winery strong on flavourful CAB FR and other
Bx reds. Highlights: Blanc de Franc (sp).

Vineland Estates Niag ★★ Founded 1979 by Mosel's Weis family to grow RIES. Many
clone-specific, pure (r/w). Legacy Infinity Vintage CAB FR (stylish multi-vintage).

British Columbia

Cool- and warm-climate regions. Key varieties: PINOT N, CHARD, PINOT GR,
MERLOT, CAB SAUV, CAB FR, SYRAH. Nine Geographical Indications incl:
Okanagan Valley (Ok V), most important by far, sub-appellations
proliferating; Similkameen Valley (Sim V); Vancouver Island (Van I).

CANADA

> **The island wines of Canada**
> Three dozen Canadian wineries are on islands, where vines benefit
> from the moderating influence of water: Van I and several of the Gulf
> Islands (Pacific coast); Prince Edward Island and Cape Breton Island
> (Atlantic coast); Pelee Island (Lake Erie); Île d'Orléans (St Lawrence
> River). Top Pacific-coast island producers incl Alderlea (Van I), Sage
> Hayward (Saturna Island).

1 **Mill Road** Ok V ★★ New winery to watch, esp refined PINOT N (Black Pine), CHARD (East Kelowna Slopes).

Blue Grouse Van I ★★ Small, owned by California's Jackson Family; v.gd crisp CHARD, PINOT GR, PINOT N.

Blue Mountain Winery Ok V ★★★★ Stellar reputation for bright sparkling, elegant CHARD, PINOT N. Highlight: River Flow Block 23 Pinot N.

Clos du Soleil ★ Winery in Sim V, emphasizing flavourful Bx varieties/blends. Flagships: Signature (r), Capella (w).

Haywire Ok V ★★ Lovely lively wines, esp PINOT GR, GAMAY, PINOT N. Standout: Secrest Mtn Vyd Gamay, Pinot N.

Little Engine Ok V ★★ Focus on rich, elegant CHARD, PINOT N. Notable Platinum Tier, esp Chard, CAB FR, Pinot N.

Martin's Lane Winery Ok V ★★★★ Top-notch elegant single-vyd PINOT N, RIES from sites throughout Ok V. Stellar: Fritzi's Vyd Pinot N.

Mission Hill Family Estate Ok V ★★★ Destination winery, spectacular architecture. Large portfolio classic styles; fine top tiers, incl flagship Oculus (elegant r blend).

Osoyoos Larose Ok V ★★★★ French-owned; Bx-style reds, planted 1998, produce elegant, cellar-worthy Grand Vin, second wine Pétales d'Osoyoos.

Phantom Creek Ok V ★★★ Opulent facilities, fine estate, single-vyd textbook CABS SAUV/FR, SYRAH; whites from Sim V. Top: Kobau Vyd Cuvée (r blend).

Poplar Grove Ok V ★★ Early (1993) winery, stylish portfolio (r/w/rosé), many reserved for club members. Notable: Legacy (r blend), North Block SYRAH.

Quails' Gate Ok V ★★ Pioneer (1989) with strengths in balanced, layered CHARD, PINOT N. Top tier: Stewart Family Res.

Roche Wines Ok V ★★★ Founded by couple with Bx roots (Ch Les Carmes Haut-Brion); stunning Bx blends (Château tier) and succulent PINOT N.

Tantalus Ok V ★★ Old (70s/80s) CHARD, PINOT N, RIES vines produce gorgeous still and sparkling. Note Old Vines Ries, Ries Brut, Res Pinot N.

Tightrope Winery Ok V ★ NZ-trained owners produce attractive range of flavourful, balanced wines; note BARBERA, SYRAH.

Unsworth Vineyards Van I ★ Bright wines (r/w/sp); highlights incl Cuvée de l'Île (PINOT N sp), Saison Vyd Pinot N.

Canada has a desert, of all things; s of Ok V, grows vines, short, hot summer.

Nova Scotia & Québec

Nova Scotia Small cool-climate region of about 20 wineries on Atlantic coast. Hybrids and vinifera, notable for crisp white (Tidal Bay line) and sparkling. Benjamin Bridge ★★ top-notch vibrant fizz (trad method/pét-nat): Brut Rés (CHARD, PINOT N), Nova 7 (off-dry from hybrids). Blomidon ★ racy fizz from hybrids/vinifera: Cuvée L'ACADIE, Brut Rés; high-acid still (r/w).

Québec Cold climate, becoming cool in the s thanks to warming temps. Varieties mainly hybrid, with slowly increasing vinifera, esp CHARD, PINOT N. Many small wineries, some v. promising. Les Pervenches ★ small emerging organic producer with crisp Chard, juicy Pinot N.

South America

CHILE

Aco	Aconcagua
Bío	Bío-Bío
Cach	Cachapoal
Casa	Casablanca
Cho	Choapa
Col	Colchagua
Coq	Coquimbo
Cur	Curicó
Elq	Elqui
Ita	Itata
Ley	Leyda
Lim	Limarí
Mai	Maipo
Mal	Malleco
Mau	Maule
Rap	Rapel
San A	San Antonio

Abbreviations used in the text:

ARGENTINA

Cata	Catamarca
La R	La Rioja
Luján	Luján de Cuyo
Men	Mendoza
Neu	Neuquén
Pat	Patagonia
Río N	Río Negro
Sal	Salta
San J	San Juan
Uco	Uco Valley

South Atlantic Ocean

CHILE

Carmenère or Cabernet? That used to be the question. But today Chile is so much more than just a country of rich, plummy reds. The diversity of varieties and regions continues to grow day by day, with ever-more-intrepid winemakers pushing the boundaries to north and south. Vineyards keep creeping higher into the Andes, and now stretch to the coast and even beyond: vines have reached the Easter Islands. There is racy Riesling and spicy Sauvignon Gris; there is ethereal Cinsault and pretty Pinot Noir. Chile has evolved.

Recent vintages
Generalization in Chile is tough, but overall 22 18 most exciting of decade; 21 gd and cool, while 23 20 19 17 hotter.

Chile's newest, most extreme vyd? Chile Chico, 46.54°S.

Aconcagua Broad, historic region ranging from cool coast (top for SAUV BL, PINOT N) to balmy inland and mtn regions where rich reds (esp CAB SAUV, SYRAH) reign.

Almaviva Mai ★★★★ The 1st New World wine to reach Bordeaux's La Place, this outpost of Mouton Rothschild (*see* Bordeaux) is still one of Chile's top red blends. Opulent and indulgent, from Puente Alto of MAI.

A Los Viñateros Bravos Ita ★★→★★★ Natural wines under visionary winemaker Leo Erazo. Top for cru CINSAULT.

Altaïr Wines Rap ★★★→★★★★ Top CACH red blend by SAN PEDRO increasingly vibrant under hand of Gabriel Mustakis. Second label, Sideral, also worth the hunt.

Antiyal Mai ★★★ Brilliant mind in bio production, Alvaro Espinoza makes some true gems. Top value for age-worthy reds.

Apaltagua Col ★★ Diverse range covering all bases. CARMENÈRE Grial is top pour, from 70-yr-old ungrafted vines.

Aquitania, Viña Mai, Mal ★★★ Ranges from perfumed CAB SAUV (try Lazuli) to full-bodied PINOT N, CHARD.

Arboleda, Viña Aco ★★ Refreshing coastal vibe from ERRÁZURIZ stable; v.gd value.

Baettig, Vinos Mal, Mau ★★★ Top indie label by renowned winemaker. Excellent CHARD, PINOT N (MAL), now joined by old-vine CAB SAUV (MAU).

Bío-Bío Southerly region with plethora of old vines (top PAÍS, field blends) and new. Keep your eye on future potential for PINOT N, RIES, SAUV BL.

Bouchon Mau ★★→★★★ Ever innovative, estate continues to push historic MAU region into future. Excellent Granito SEM, crunchy PAÍS, stylish Bx blends.

Caliboro Mau ★★★ Sustainable, old-vine estate; Chile's 1st regenerative viticulture under Count Cinzano (Italy). Handsome Med reds, unctuous sweet MUSCAT.

Calyptra Cach ★★→★★★ Family winery high in Andes, and now over mtns in Argentina too. Expect old vintages and niche styles of fortified, sweet, sparkling.

Carmen, Viña Casa, Col, Mai ★★→★★★★ Modern wines from Chile's oldest winery. Best: off-beat DO range, vibrant Delanz, age-worthy Gold, but all offer top value.

Casablanca Largest coastal region, with over 5700 ha. Top for SAUV BL, SYRAH, PINOT N but now GRENACHE, MALBEC too. Generally cool, fresh style.

Casa Marín San A ★★★→★★★★ Extremely coastal (just 4 km from Pacific) estate with mother-and-son winemakers. Top SAUV BL, racy RIES.

Casas del Bosque Casa, Mai ★★→★★★ Stunning estate on rolling hills. Punchy SAUV BL, meaty SYRAH best, esp Pequeñas Producciones line.

Casa Silva Col, S Regions ★★→★★★ Historic family producer with warming CARMENÈRE (try Microterroir), gd-value reds. Most thrilling wines come from deep s, Lago Ranco in Osorno: top RIES, PINOT N.

Clos des Fous Cach, Casa, S Regions ★★→★★★ Niche range of terroir-driven wines from around Chile. Textural PINOT N, zippy CHARD, flamboyant red blends.

Concha y Toro Central V ★→★★★★ Biggest of Chile, no. 6 in world. Covers most bases, but top Don Melchor Bx blend (MAI), Amelia PINOT N (LIM), consistent Gravas and Terruño line. Marques de Casa Concha v.gd mid-range, Casillero del Diablo reliable entry-level. *See also* ALMAVIVA, TRIVENTO (Argentina).

Cono Sur Bío, Casa, Col ★★→★★★ Hard to beat for value; COL-based but making

---

Pinot charms Chile

Evasive PINOT N has beguiled winemakers for decades but is finally hitting its stride, with some top terroirs coming to the fore. The white soils of LIM produce some of country's best: Amelia, RETA, TABALÍ. In the central coast, ERRÁZURIZ Las Pizarras, LEYDA, MATETIC, MORANDÉ standout; MAU hits high notes with LABERTINO, MIGUEL TORRES Escaleras de Empedrado. Any hope for the deep s? Definitely: AQUITANIA Sol de Sol, CLOS DE FOUS, P.S. GARCIA, UNDURRAGA TH, VINOS BAETTIG.

well-defined varietal wines all over (try SAUV BL, SYRAH, CAB SAUV). World's largest *Pinot N* producer too.

Cousiño Macul Mai ★★→★★★ Making wine here since 1856. Family winery with top CAB SAUV (try Lota), engaging Finis Terrae blends.

Elqui Valley is one of top spots for Chilean SYRAH, also herbaceous SAUV BL. Runs from coast to tippy-top of Andes.

Emiliana Bío, Casa, Rap ★★→★★★ Impressive bio credentials working to scale. Winemaker Noelia Orts offers reliability in Adobe, but more exciting are Coyam, Salvaje blends.

Errázuriz Aco, Casa ★★→★★★★ One of Chile's best, and putting ACO on map. Las Pizarras CHARD is world-class, Don Maximiliano is a Chilean classic, and Aco Costa range offers vibrancy. *See also* SEÑA, VIÑA ARBOLEDA, VIÑEDO CHADWICK.

Falernia, Viña Elq ★★ The 1st to push for fine wine in ELQ. *Appassimento*-style CARMENÈRE is revelation, PEDRO XIMÉNEZ is ideal apéritif wine.

Garcés Silva, Viña San A ★★→★★★ Major grower and premium producer. Amayna is full-bodied range, Boya is fresher. Solera SAUV BL is a novelty.

Haras de Pirque Mai ★★→★★★ Antinori's (*see* Italy) mtn MAI outpost making serious, age-worthy Bx reds: v.gd CAB SAUV, CAB FR.

Itata Region in s, still struggling to make its comeback, with old vines aplenty but disappearing fast. Shame as home to some of most exciting CINSAULT, MUSCAT, PAÍS in world.

Koyle Col, Ita ★★→★★★ Leading bio estate making fresh, vibrant wines. Cerro Basalto offer excellent, juicy reds; Koyle Costa zippy SAUV BL.

Laberinto Mau ★★★→★★★★ Rafael Tirado is MAU's only mtn producer. Lone hero making top volcanic wines: RIES, SAUV BL, PINOT N all fab.

Lapostolle Cach, Casa, Col ★★→★★★★ Impressive bio estate in Apalta with classic Bx reds, building up to top Clos Apalta blend. Stunning winery.

Leyda, Viña Col, Mai, San A ★★→★★★ Viviana Navarrete is one of leading coastal winemakers, making top-value SAUV BL, PINOT N, SYRAH from LEY, but also age-worthy Lot range.

Limarí Chile's n star with sought-after CHARD, PINOT N. Cool coastal region with limestone soils and promising future.

Longaví Ita, Mau ★★★ Utterly gluggable Glup! wines from PAÍS, CARIGNAN, CINSAULT and more. More serious Cru range offers Chile's best CHENIN BL.

Luis Felipe Edwards Central V ★★ Large stable, over 45 different brands, covering over 2000 ha and dozens of varietals. Macerao is playful entry-level orange.

Maipo Surrounding Santaigo – at centre of Chilean wine. Best: CAB SAUV, Bx blends due to sunny, mtn climate and gravel soils, but almost every variety grown here.

Malleco Growing region in deep s, known for volcanic soils, cool climate, plenty of rainfall. Top: CHARD, RIES, PINOT N. Mainly small producers.

Martino, De Cach, Casa, Elq, Ita, Mai, Mau ★★→★★★★ Family winery driven by brothers Marco and Sebastian. Based in central MAI but making wines in ITA too, with innovative *tinaja* range and classy Single Vyd range.

Matetic Casa, San A ★★★ →★★★★ One of Chile's most underrated producers: stellar lineup, all bio. Corralillo, top value, EQ, cut above. Best: CHARD, PINOT N, SYRAH.

Maule Gnarly old vines, driving renaissance of dry-farmed CARIGNAN (*see* VIGNO), SEM, PAÍS here; while Bx varieties offer more structured styles.

Montes Casa, Col, Cur, Ley ★★→★★★★ Father and son continue to move the dial in Chile, with vyds from Zapallar to Chiloe. While coast offers coolest expressions, it is juicy, warming Apalta reds that made Montes famous. *Folly Syrah* is rightfully an icon of Chile.

MontGras Col, Ley, Mai ★★ Everyday wines mainly from COL. Highlights: Intriga CAB SAUV (MAI), zippy Amaral whites (Ley).

CHILE

Montsecano Casa ★★★ Cult bio wines. Best known PINOT N, but try CHARD, MALBEC.

Morandé Casa, Mai, Mau ★★→★★★ Almost 30 yrs old and still growing, now under Ricardo Baettig. Classic lineup in Morandé, but more playful in Adventure range.

Neyen Col ★★★ Old vines in Apalta (planted 1890), silky CAB SAUV/CARMENÈRE.

Odfjell Cur, Mai, Mau ★→★★★ Coastal MAI estate with vines in MAU too. Top: CARIGNAN (*see* VIGNO), red Bx blends, MALBEC.

Pedro Parra y Familia Ita ★★ Chile's top terroir expert turns his hand to cellar, focused on jazz-themed labels and precise, mineral wines from old vines.

Pérez Cruz, Viña Mai ★★→★★★ A trad producer in heart of MAI with penchant for structured, firm Bx varieties.

Pisco Served sour or solo, pride of Chile. Mainly grown and distilled in n, esp ELQ.

Polkura Col ★★→★★★ Long-standing apostle of Col SYRAH, Sven Bruchfeld is indie producer making hearty, characterful reds.

P.S. Garcia Ita, Mal, Mau ★★→★★★ Felipe G's v.gd indie brand with diverse varietals from Durif to MOURVÈDRE.

Quebrada de Macul, Viña Mai ★★→★★★ Age-worthy CAB SAUV and Bx blends under Viña Peñalolén and Domus Aurea labels.

Rapel Umbrella term covering Col and Cach.

RE, Bodegas Casa ★★★ Pablo Morande, father and son, make eccentric range in CASA and MAU, from skin-contact to unconventional red CHARD/PINOT N blend.

Reta Lim, Mau ★★★ Exciting wines from seasoned winemaker Marcelo Retamal: LIM CHARD and MAU MALBEC among Chile's best.

San Antonio San A Baby brother to neighbouring CASA, but with cooler edge – LEY is best-known subregion.

San Pedro Cur ★→★★★ Large producer spanning all levels. At bottom is forgettable Gato Negro, at top is age-worthy Cabo de Hornos CAB SAUV. Inbetween, hunt down gd-value 1865 range: v.gd SYRAH (ELQ), Tayu PINOT N (MAL). (*See* LA CELIA; ALTAÏR, TARAPACÁ in Chile.)

Santa Carolina, Viña Mai ★★→★★★ Historic winery, with broad base. Luis Pereira CAB SAUV is top; El Pacto is exciting new range, incl Romano grape.

Santa Rita Mai ★★→★★★★ One of biggest and oldest, but plenty of modern innovation, esp in Floresta range – try CHARD (LIM), CAB FR (Col). *Casa Real Cab Sauv* is legendary.

Seña Aco ★★★★ Rich, silky, age-worthy Bx blend by folks from ERRÁZURIZ.

Tabalí Lim ★★→★★★★ Region's most prolific and high-profile producer. Talinay offers outstanding CHARD, SAUV BL, PINOT N (try Pai), SYRAH.

Tarapacá, Viña Casa, Ley, Mai ★★ Large producer, not to be confused with n wine region of same name; vyd surrounded by mtns, river – effectively a clos, albeit a big one, where almost any variety is possible. Best: Grand Res Blend series.

Torres, Miguel Cur ★★→★★★★ Spain's Torres family continues to innovate with increasingly vibrant wines under Eduardo Jordan. Los Inqueitos MALBEC is remarkable, Escaleras de Empedrado is complex PINOT N planted on schist terraces in MAU, Manso de Velasco is seriously old-vine CAB SAUV (115 yrs).

Undurraga Casa, Ley, Lim, Mai ★→★★★ Capable Rafael Urrejola leads pack in large winery. Terroir Hunter range worth the hunt... varietal wines all spot on, and rarities are modern classics.

Valdivieso Cur, San A ★→★★★ S America's 1st major sparkling producer. Mostly everyday, but Caballo Loco range is playful, age-worthy.

Vascos, Los Rap ★★ Largely classic portfolio from Lafite Rothschild's (*see* Bordeaux) Col winery, although now with ALBARIÑO.

Ventisquero, Viña Casa, Col, Mai ★→★★★ Felipe Tosso heads up large Col producer. Highlights: GARNACHA blend, Atacama SAUV BL in Grey range. (Try more Atacama in natural-wine offshoot Tara.)

Veramonte Casa, Col ★★ Organic CASA, Col everyday wines, owned by González Byass (*see* Spain).

Vigno Mau 16 wineries unite to celebrate Chile's old-vine, dry-farmed CARIGNAN in collective brand. Powerful social impact; age-worthy wines.

Vik Cach ★★→★★★ One of Chile's most stunning wineries and luxury hotels, with luxurious Bx blends. Also own cooperage, using fallen oak from estate.

Villard Casa, Mai ★★→★★★ Family dedicated to coastal wines from CASA. Brilliant value and quality PINOT N; playful JCB range for adventurous.

Viñedo Chadwick Mai ★★★★ Stunning CAB SAUV from MAI's Puente Alto. Now under hand of Emily Faulconer of ERRÁZURIZ.

Viu Manent Casa, Col ★★ In heart of Col making rich reds, plus fresh CASA whites.

von Siebenthal, Viña Aco ★★→★★★ Swiss banker Mauro von S moved to chase dream in ACO in 1998 – a vision of warming Bx blends and unctuous VIOGNIER.

ARGENTINA

It's been a rocky ride for Argentina in recent years with annual inflation pushing 185%, but the wine industry is surviving and pushing ahead. Malbec is still king, but the quality of the top whites is booming, with Chardonnay and Semillon at the forefront, while lighter styles of Grenache, Pinot Noir and native Criolla varieties are steadily on the rise. That isn't to say Argentina has slowed down with its big red steak wines; on the contrary. This is the land of steak. But you'll now find Cabernet Franc, Cabernet Sauvignon and Petit Verdot joining Malbec on the top tables.

Achaval Ferrer Men ★★→★★★ Single-vyd MALBEC still calling card, but now with a world of blends (Quimera), CARMENÈRE and more.

Alandes Men ★★★ Karim Mussi traverses the Andes for expressive blends: SEM/SAUV BL blend is Argentina's best.

Aleanna Men ★★ →★★★★ Ale Vigil, Adrianna Catena combine for eccentric El Enemigo range. Known for top CAB FR, MALBEC, but TORRONTÉS is hidden gem.

Alpasión Men ★★ Eno-tourism project; hearty but balanced reds, mostly organic.

Alta Vista Men ★→★★★ Franco-Argentine adventure making single-vyd Malbec since 1997. Smart reds, aromatic whites, and fab Atemporal bubbly.

Altocedro Men ★★→★★★ Karim Mussi helped put La Consulta and TEMPRANILLO on map with elegant Altocedro. Old-vine MALBEC v.gd too.

Altos las Hormigas Men ★★★ →★★★★ One of best for MALBEC; strong terroir focus (world-class Jardín De Hormigas). Also fab SEM, BONARDA, CAB FR.

Argento Men ★★→★★★ Stunning value, organic. Top Single Vyd CAB FR, MALBEC.

Atamisque Men ★→★★★ The 1st winery as you enter Uco, excellent value, fresh. Brilliant MERLOT, red blends, CHARD. Nice hotel too.

Bemberg Estate Wines ★★★ Luxury wines by Daniel Pi for owner of PEÑAFLOR. Single-vyd CHARD, CAB SAUV, MALBEC, PINOT N all delicious.

Benegas Men ★★→★★★ Wine royalty, 100-yr-old+ vines; CAB FR, SANGIOVESE, MALBEC.

Bianchi, Bodegas Men ★→★★ Leader in San Rafael, growing status in new 'hood, Los Chacayes. IV Generación is top stuff, lots of bubbly too.

Bosca, Luigi Men ★★→★★★ Over 120 yrs and still a leading name. La Linda is everyday, while Finca Las Nobles is age-worthy; v.gd RIES and white blend.

Bressia Men ★★→★★★ Son joins Walter B to continue family trad of complex reds.

Cadus Men ★★ Santiago Mayorga breathes new energy into premium winery of Nieto Senetiner. Single Vyd range v.gd: Criolla Chica, orange VIOGNIER.

Callia San J ★→★★★ Prolific producer, everyday, easy-drinking; SYRAH (asado match).

Canale, Bodegas Humberto Río N ★→★★★ Flying flag since 1909; v.gd Old Vyd range (RIES, SEM, MALBEC).

Caro Men ★★★ Opulent red Bx blend, offspring of Rothschild/CATENA investment, sibling to second label Amancaya and 3rd-tier Aruma.

Casarena Men ★★→★★★ Championing single vyds in Luján with smart MALBEC, spicy CAB SAUV, peppery CAB FR. Fab hotel too.

Catena Zapata, Bodega Men ★★→★★★★ Family winery ruling the premium roost since late 90s. Adrianna vyd is top for ethereal MALBEC, world-class CHARD. Elsewhere: silky Bx blends and more. Alamos is everyday pour. (*See also* CARO.)

Chacra Río N ★★★→★★★★ Burgundian enclave in RÍO N with old-vine PINOT N, newly grafted CHARD. Italian Piero Incisa della Rocchetta's Argentine playground.

Chandon Men ★→★★ The 1st serious sparkling producer, still one of biggest. Lots of everyday, but Baron B offers more serious pour. *See* TERRAZAS DE LOS ANDES.

Cheval des Andes Men ★★★★ Cheval Blanc team (*see* Bordeaux) visit 4x/yr to ensure luxurious Bx blend from Uco. Luján keeps rising the ranks. It is working.

Clos de los Siete Men ★★ Collective red from estates of Bx vignerons, Michel Rolland invited to join in, creating clos in heart of Uco (*see* BODEGA ROLLAND, CUVELIER LOS ANDES, DIAMANDES, MONTEVIEJO).

Cobos, Viña Men ★★★→★★★★ Paul Hobbs 25 yrs here. Rich Bx reds, opulent CHARD.

Colomé, Bodega Sal ★★→★★★ Founder Donald Hess RIP 2023, but estate continues: daringly high-altitude, thrillingly remote and characterful, impressive wines.

Cruzat Men ★★★ Premier premium sparkling producer. Lees ageing from 1–8 yrs.

Cuvelier Los Andes Men ★★→★★★ Classy producer of Bx-style reds in Uco. Usually structured, firm, except gluggable maceration Cuvée Nature.

Decero, Finca Men ★★ One of 1st to market varietal PETIT VERDOT. Still highlight in portfolio of structured reds.

DiamAndes Men ★★ Stunning winery, smart restaurant, Bonnie family's (Malartic Lagravière, *see* Bordeaux) well-matured Uco reds. Top CHARD increasingly fresh.

Doña Paula Men ★★→★★★ Martin Kaiser leads SANTA RITA's winery here with gd-value range. Altitude blends v.gd.

Durigutti Men ★★→★★★★ Rescuing old vines in Las Compuertas from real estate, Durigutti bros wave flag for this exciting – if disappearing – subregion of Luján. Fresh, bright, nuanced. Superb restaurant too.

Estancia Uspallata Men ★★→★★★ At 2000m (6560ft), MEN's highest-altitude vyd, making vibrant mtn wines with punchy acidity. MALBEC, PINOT N and fab fizz by Colo Sejanovich.

Esteco, El Sal ★★→★★★ PEÑAFLOR's n outpost; old vines, characterful wines at heights of Cafayate. Excellent, ever-so-spicy CAB SAUV, oily TORRONTÉS highlights.

Etchart Sal ★→★★★ Household brand in n; gd-value TORRONTÉS, bold Cafayate reds.

Fabre Montmayou Men, Río N ★★→★★★ Making polished reds in Luján, RÍO N since 90s. Particularly gd for MERLOT, rare in MEN.

Fin del Mundo, Bodega Del Neu ★→★★ No longer winery at end of world, but still quite far s. Rich reds: try CAB FR.

Flichman, Finca Men ★★ Making wines in historic Maipú since 1910; owned by Sogrape (*see* Portugal). Mainly everyday, although Paisaje Bx blend is age-worthy.

Kaikén Men ★★→★★★★ MONTES-owned (*see* Chile), but with Argentine personality: structured mtn reds, Obertura CAB FR, terroir-led Aventura MALBECS highlights.

La Anita, Finca Men ★★ Manual Mas's Luján winery; full-bodied reds and whites; v.gd PETIT VERDOT.

Posh pinks

Posh pinks are on the rise... with prices that could top Provence. All sorts of grapes get drafted in, incl GARNACHA, MALBEC, PINOT N, and prices go up to nr US$50 on official exchange rate. Priciest are SUSANA BALBO, RUTINI, CHACRA, CATENA, Otronia, LURTON: for big beach wallets only.

La Celia, Finca Men ★★ Uco pioneer, v.gd CAB SAUV, increasingly bright MALBEC. New Pioneer PINOT N v.gd.

Manos Negras / Tinto Negro / TeHo / ZaHa / Buscado Vivo o Muerto Men ★★→★★★ Fab CAB FR, MALBEC, MARSANNE and more from one of Argentina's best, Colo Sejanovich.

Masi Tupungato Men ★★ At entrance of Uco, gateway between Argentina and Italy, with *ripasso*-style MALBEC/CORVINA.

Winery road trip? Take snacks. Expect hrs of dirt roads, maybe rivers to drive through.

Mendel Men ★★★ Legendary Roberto de la Motta, seasoned winemaker, plays his cards effortlessly with top Bx reds, steely SEM.

Mendoza Heart of Argentine wine, home to two-thirds of industry. Maipú is closest to city: old vines galore. Luján is cradle of CAB SAUV, MALBEC; Uco is highest altitude and refreshingly contemporary.

Monteviejo Men ★★→★★★★ Classic Bx in Uco portfolio made in gd taste. Top for age-worthy MALBEC (try Lindaflor).

Moras, Finca Las San J ★→★★★ Large; everyday wine. Sagrado Pedernal step above.

Neuquén Pat Region: bigger, bolder neighbour of RÍO N. Bold, ripe reds are forte.

Nieto Senetiner, Bodegas Men ★→★★★ Large producer (sp and still), from entry-level Benjamín to sophisticated NS.

Noemia Pat ★★★→★★★★ RÍO N royalty. Finest Bx reds of region: elegant, nuanced.

Norton, Bodega Men ★→★★★ David Bonomi is brains behind smart portfolio. Plenty of classic reds; now also elegant pink MALBEC, GRÜNER V.

Otronia Pat ★★★→★★★★ Pioneer of steppes, and still world's most s commercial winery, at 45°S. Sublime CHARD, etherial MALBEC, intense Alsace blend (w).

Passionate Wine Men ★★→★★★ Matías Michelini is still wild child – natural, bio and laser-sharp whites. Also in Spain.

Pelleriti, Marcelo Men ★★→★★★ Eponymous line of top winemaker. Classy reds with penchant for CAB FR, MALBEC.

Peñaflor Men ★→★★★ Largest wine group: EL ESTECO, FINCA LAS MORAS, Mascota, Navarro Correas, Santa Ana, Suter, TRAPICHE.

Piatelli Sal ★★ One family, two wineries (MEN, Cafayate): bold reds, aromatic whites.

Piedra Negra Men ★→★★★ Pioneer of Los Chacayes in Uco, still a leader in quality. Excellent reds (try Chacayes) and some of MEN's best white blends.

Porvenir de Cafayate, El Sal ★★→★★★ Increasingly innovative family winery in Calchaquis. Elegant TORRONTÉS, fragrant GARNACHA, MALBEC.

Pulenta Estate Men ★★→★★★ Local wine dynasty. Bros Eduardo and Hugo founded premium brand 2002. Making waves with Bx reds (esp CAB FR) ever since.

Renacer Men ★★ MALBEC specialist but with v.gd CABS SAUV/FR. Young team continues to innovate with special releases.

Riccitelli, Matias Men ★★→★★★★ Electric high-altitude whites, juicy Criolla, sophisticated MERLOT, MALBEC: diverse yet boutique portfolio.

Riglos Men ★★ One of 1st in Gualtallary, continuing single-estate story of rich reds.

Riojana, La La R ★→★★ Over 400 growers part of this 85-year-old co-op making floral TORRONTÉS and more.

Río Negro Old vines, milder climate here are back in fashion; winemakers migrating to these historic riverbanks. Best for MALBEC, PINOT N, RIES, SEM.

Rolland, Bodega Men ★★★ Michel R (*see* France) put his stamp on Uco with rich reds, silky PINOT N, punchy SAUV BL.

Rutini Men ★★→★★★ Historic and important brand, now in Uco. Top wines show Mariano di Paolo's great mastery for blends.

Salentein, Bodegas Men ★★→★★★ Stunning winery, v.gd range, top value from San Pablo, Uco. Portillo is everyday drinking; Single Vyd range is special.

Salta Main region of Calchaquí valleys where TORRONTÉS reigns. All high altitude, also renowned for meaty MALBEC, TANNAT.

San Juan Little brother to MEN and less known, but still a big player with 30,000 ha+. Mainly table wines, MALBEC, SYRAH, TORRONTÉS best, but Pedernal and Calingasta subregions are cut above.

San Pedro de Yacochuya Sal ★★★ Michel ROLLAND/ETCHART collaboration. Some vines 100-yrs-old+, and all at 2000m (6560ft)+: gd concentration/intensity.

Schroeder, Familia Neu ★★ A dinosaur species was named after Schroeder (*Panamericansaurus schroederi*) after fossils found in the cellar. Replica lies there next to younger bottles of PINOT N, MALBEC and more.

Sophenia, Finca Men ★★→★★★ Consistent range, precision in reds, whites (SAUV BL) from long-standing bottling in Gualtallary. *Antisynthesis Field Blend* v.gd.

Susana Balbo Wines Men ★★→★★★★ Crios is flagship range, but Signature, Brios and BenMarco are where the excitement lies. Susana remains queen of complex red blends.

Tapiz Men ★★→★★★ Often excellent value from this large family business with vines in Luján, Uco and now RÍO N. Alta CAB FR a gem.

Terrazas de los Andes Men ★★→★★★ Pioneer of high-altitude Uco: El Espinillo, 1650m (5413ft), highest in Gualtallary; v.gd Parcel range, mouthwatering Grand CHARD.

Tikal / Alma Negra / Animal / Stella Crintina Men ★★→★★★ Diverse family of wines from Ernesto Catena and wife Joanna in Uco, but all focused on vibrant, fresh styles, bio vyds.

Toso, Pascual Men ★★→★★★ Classic lineup of mainly Bx-style reds and opulent CHARD, as well as bubbles, from historic producer in Maipú.

Trapiche Men ★→★★★ Long-running, wide-reaching winery, extensive portfolio: opulent Terroir Series mtn MALBECS, zesty Costa y Pampa ALBARIÑO on coast in Buenos Aires. Iscay is delicious line of blends.

Trivento Men ★→★★ Powerhouse winery owned by CONCHA Y TORO. Large portfolio: everyday varietals to old-vine Eolo MALBEC. New highlight is SEM.

Vines of Mendoza / Winemaker's Village Men ★★ Luxury resort, vines set in 600 ha. 248 owners, 330 wines. Winemaker's Village incl Corazon del Sol, Gimenez Riili, Super Uco.

Zorzal Men ★★→★★★ Gualtallary giant: fresh, vibrant, with penchant for steely SAUV BL, spicy CAB FR, nervy PINOT N.

Zuccardi Men ★★→★★★★ Continuing to move the dial, Sebastian Z is at top of his game. Stylish, modern, often somewhat austere wines focused on single-vyd MALBEC. Top: Finca, Alluvional, Concreto, Piedra Infinita. Sister brand Santa Julia for everyday pours.

BRAZIL

Change is brewing in Brazil. A growing movement of smaller, independent wineries and winemakers is beginning to take on the Goliath-sized wineries and is making its mark. Rio Grande do Sul is still the most important region, but vignerons are taking stakes further north in Santa Catarina, Minas Gerais and São Paulo too. While Merlot and Chardonnay are still at the top, Italian varieties are on the rise with fascinating wines from Paverella and Teroldego. Bubbles are still Brazil's best, especially traditional method.

Aurora ★→★★ One of Brazil's biggest, with hundreds of families in co-op. Mainly everyday vinho.

Casa Valduga ★→★★★ Top for fizz, but also strong portfolio of rich Bx-style blends. Winery is popular visit in heart of Vale dos Vinhedos.

Cave Geisse ★★★ Leader in premium, trad-method bubbly, and put Pinto Bandeira on map. Delicious Nature range.

Era dos Ventos ★★★ Niche, natural wines from older vines and one of most exciting visions for Brazil today. Delicious orange.

Guaspari ★★→★★★ Leading winery in Serra da Mantiqueira, making top SYRAH.

Lidio Carraro ★★ Promising family winery making supple reds and aromatic whites around Rio Grande do Sul.

Miolo ★→★★★ One of Brazil's best big brands with wines from all over. Lote 43 is a top pour.

Pizzato ★→★★★ Flavio continues to drive change and innovation in Brazil. Great bubbly, bright SEM and juicy reds.

Salton ★→★★ Historic, large family winery big in fizz and still. Domenico terroir range an appealing new addition.

URUGUAY

"Good things come in small packages" rings true for this S American gem. It's the second-smallest country on the continent, but it punches above its weight in wine. Just under 6000 ha, but diverse varieties and regions make Uruguay one to watch. Thrilling Albariño, stylish Tannat, poignant Chardonnay and spicy Cabernet Franc are among its highlights. Wineries are almost all exclusively family-run; most are based in Canelones, but Maldonado towards the east continues to expand.

Alto de la Ballena ★→★★★ Family winery on schist outcrop of Maldonado, making juicy CAB FR, SYRAH and fab TANNAT/VIOGNIER blend.

Bouza ★★→★★★ One of Uruguay's best. Canelones reds are age-worthy, dense, while more extreme Maldonado wines are spicy, fresh. Also standout producer for ALBARIÑO, RIES.

Cerro del Toro ★★→★★★ Contemporary wines from stunning Maldonado estate. Fósiles de Mar CHARD and Sobre Lias ALBARIÑO particularly gd.

Deicas, Familia ★→★★★★ Now in capable hands of 3rd-generation winemaker Santiago D, this large winery continues to set bar for quality and value. Extreme Vyds range is exciting, and new Cru ALBARIÑO exceptional.

Garzón, Bodega ★★→★★★★ Big and beautiful estate in Maldonado, with precise, focused portfolio of stylish reds and refreshing whites. Balasto is top, but all are age-worthy.

Pablo Fallabrino Wines ★★ Pablo offers B-side to Canelones with vibrant, refreshing lo-fi wines, incl niche Italian varieties ARNEIS, BARBERA, NEBBIOLO.

Pisano ★→★★★ Charming Pisano bros make characterful portfolio of structured reds, incl sparkling TANNAT.

OTHER SOUTH AMERICAN WINES

Bolivia Landlocked country, and landlocked wines. But if you venture into Bolivia, the wines are worth a try: seriously high altitude and with big personality. Tarija is the wine capital, with mainly bold reds (Aranjuez, Kohlberg and Kuhlmann); Cinti is filled with ancient vines and fragrant Criolla vines (Cepa de Oro and Jardin Oculto); Santa Cruz valleys are a hidden discovery high in sierras (Vinos 1750).

Peru Historically 1st of S America's wine countries, but trailing behind today. A revival in artisanal wines from old vines of Pisco varieties is brilliant new direction (Bodega Murga, Mimo), while adventures into Andes show promise (Apu). But most are more trad Bx-style reds in Ica (Intipalka, Tacama, Vista Alegre).

Australia

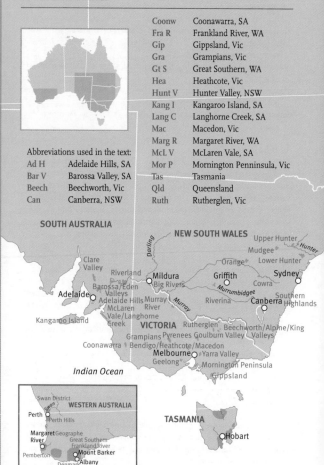

Coonw	Coonawarra, SA
Fra R	Frankland River, WA
Gip	Gippsland, Vic
Gra	Grampians, Vic
Gt S	Great Southern, WA
Hea	Heathcote, Vic
Hunt V	Hunter Valley, NSW
Kang I	Kangaroo Island, SA
Lang C	Langhorne Creek, SA
Mac	Macedon, Vic
Marg R	Margaret River, WA
McL V	McLaren Vale, SA
Mor P	Mornington Penninsula, Vic
Tas	Tasmania
Qld	Queensland
Ruth	Rutherglen, Vic

Abbreviations used in the text:

Ad H	Adelaide Hills, SA
Bar V	Barossa Valley, SA
Beech	Beechworth, Vic
Can	Canberra, NSW

While the news came as no surprise, it is, nonetheless, shocking: 2023 went down as the hottest year on record, so far. Given Australia is the world's driest inhabited continent, the impact is acute. But all is not lost. Grape-growers and winemakers are adapting. The notion of Oz wine as "sunshine in a bottle", ie. cheap and cheerful, must be buried. Those wines largely came off heavily irrigated land in the Murray-Darling Basin. That is not sustainable farming, so producers are getting better at reducing water usage, not least by planting appropriate grape varieties, especially Mediterranean ones, more able to cope with warmer temperatures and less water. Regenerative farming – which is about restoring degraded land back to health – is ultimately the key to producing quality wine, not more wine. There's hope, and value, with that outcome.

Recent vintages

New South Wales (NSW)

2023 Cool, wet, disease pressure, low yields, yet Hunter V has excellent Shiraz.
2022 La Niña strikes. Heavy rain, not much heat. Difficult vintage.
2021 Heavy rain, some disease pressure. Whites generally gd, choose wisely.
2020 Hot, fire-affected yr with all manner of challenges.
2019 Hot, with just enough rain for generous whites/reds.
2018 Big ripe reds for long haul. Hot/tough yr for whites.

Victoria (Vic)

2023 Challenging, flooding ne. Some fine (r/w). Yields down in Yarra V, Mor P.
2022 Cool, often wet, low yields. High acidity, v.gd whites, esp Yarra V.
2021 Stark contrast to 20. Many calling it season of elegance, balance; gd yields.
2020 Fire-affected in ne and generally challenging. Yields down.
2019 Compressed season, but wines (r/w) look vibrant.
2018 Overshadowed by 17. Slow evolving.

South Australia (SA)

2023 La Niña in force; wet, cool, lower yields. Clare V v.gd Ries.
2022 Cool, long ripening; v.gd overall. McLaren V solid (r/w).
2021 Said to be nr perfect. Bar V outstanding, Clare V exceptional (r/w).
2020 Hard/tragic yr, but Ries and reds look promising. Seriously low yields.
2019 Exceptionally low yields should produce concentrated wines.
2018 Gutsy reds with yrs up their sleeve. Whites gd but not in same class.

Western Australia (WA)

2023 Cool spring, mild conditions. Marg R, Gt S v.gd (r/w).
2022 Excellent in Marg R but low yields, esp Chard.
2021 Challenging due to late-season rain but ultimately rewarding.
2020 Early, low-yield, high-concentration yr.
2019 Cool vintage, the kind to sort the wheat from the chaff.
2018 Reds will outlive most of us; whites will do medium term in a canter.

Accolade Wines Owned by global investment firm Carlyle Group. Hardys, HOUGHTON, KATNOOK, PETALUMA, ST HALLETT. Selling assets: in 2023, off-loaded Bay of Fires winery/cellar door (not brand) and fizz enterprise House of Arras.

Adams, Tim Clare V ★★ Solid performer with RIES esp; robust CAB/MALBEC, SHIRAZ.

Adelaide Hills SA Diverse region in the Mt Lofty ranges, 70 km long, cool: up to 650m (2132ft). Two official subregions: Lenswood, Piccadilly V. CHARD, SAUV BL, GRÜNER V; SHIRAZ over PINOT N, sparkling. Try ASHTON HILLS, DEVIATION ROAD, HAHNDORF HILL, HENSCHKE, JERICHO, SHAW & SMITH, SIDEWOOD ESTATE.

Adelina Clare V ★★★ Reds (SHIRAZ, GRENACHE, MATARO, NEBBIOLO); outstanding RIES. Great vyds, skilled winemaking.

Alkina Wine Estate Bar V ★★ Argentinian-owned. No expense spared; est 50s site, now bio; concrete tanks, eggs, *qvevri*, older oak. Compelling GRENACHE, SHIRAZ.

Alkoomi Fra R ★★ Large, family-owned estate; gd RIES; regionally expressive CABS SAUV/FR, SHIRAZ

All Saints Estate Ruth ★★★ Rating for exceptional fortifieds, esp Museum MUSCAT, MUSCADELLE, average-age 100-yrs+ solera. Table wines solid.

Alpine Valleys Vic Foothills of Victorian Alps. Many growers of cool-climate red/white, esp Italian varieties (v.gd TEMPRANILLO). Stars: BILLY BUTTON, MAYFORD.

Angove's SA ★★→★★★ Family business, founded 1886. Keenly priced across range; MCL V site organic with a focus on premium and single-vyd GRENACHE, SHIRAZ.

Arenberg, d' McL V ★★ Some kooky names (eg. The Cenosilicaphobic Cat SAGRANTINO), but wines solid, incl v.gd GRENACHE, SHIRAZ.

Ashton Hills Ad H ★★ (PINOT N) 20' 21 22 Distinctive Pinot N from 30-yr-old+ vyds CHARD, RIES v.gd.

Baileys of Glenrowan Glenrowan ★★ Rich Durif, SHIRAZ, fabulous fortified MUSCAT (★★★★), TOPAQUE; vyds all organic. Owned by CASELLA.

Balnaves of Coonawarra SA ★★ Family-owned COONW champion. Rich CHARD, v.gd spicy SHIRAZ, full-bodied Tally CAB SAUV flagship. "Joven-style" Cab gd.

Bannockburn Vic ★★★ (CHARD) 19 20' 21' 22 (23) (PINOT N) 18' 19' 20 21 22 (23) Structured, detailed Chard, complex Pinot N, RIES always a delight. Advocate of high-density vyds; quality stamped all over.

Barossa Valley SA Bastion of v.-old-vine CAB SAUV, GRENACHE, MOURVÈDRE, SHIRAZ. Expect richness but more restraint latterly. ELDERTON, GRANT BURGE, HENTLEY FARM, JOHN DUVAL, LANGMEIL, PETER LEHMANN, ROCKFORD, RUGGABELLUS, ST HALLETT, SALTRAM, SEPPELTSFIELD, SPINIFEX, TEUSNER, WOLF BLASS, YALUMBA.

Barry, Jim Clare V ★★★ RIES rules thanks to top vyds and lots of them. LoosenBarry Wolta Wolta a collaboration with Mosel mogul Ernst Loosen (*see* Germany). Reds solid: age-worthy Armagh SHIRAZ. Also Oz's only ASSYRTIKO.

Basket Range Wine Ad H ★★ Lead player in avant-garde: CAB SAUV, PINOT N, pét-nat.

Bass Phillip Gip ★★★→★★★★ (PINOT N) 20' 21' 22' Tiny amounts of distinctive Pinot, exceptional Res off high-density vyds; CHARD equally gd; delightful GEWURZ, GAMAY. Burgundian vigneron J-M Fourrier (*see* France) leads winemaking.

Beechworth NE Vic Spectacular rocky region in highlands. CHARD, SHIRAZ best-performing, but NEBBIOLO making a statement. A RODDA, DOMENICA, FIGHTING GULLY ROAD, GIACONDA, SAVATERRE, SCHMÖLZER & BROWN, SORRENBERG.

Bekkers McL V ★★★ Emmanuelle and Toby B, top GRENACHE, SYRAH, organic focus.

Bellwether Coonw ★★ Love of CAB SAUV kept winemaker Sue Bell in COONW, turning Glen Roy 1868 shearing shed into boutique winery, cellar door and more. CHARD from TAS v.gd, sources Italian varieties too.

Bendigo Vic Hot central Vic region. Balgownie Estate, PASSING CLOUDS, SUTTON GRANGE. Home of rich CAB SAUV, SHIRAZ.

Best's Great Western Gra ★★★ (SHIRAZ) 17' 19' 20' 21 22 Shiraz superstar, in best yrs flagship Thomson Family Shiraz from 120-yr-old vines; *v.gd mid-weight reds*; old-vine PINOT M exceptional; RIES excellent.

Pinot Noir rules cool

PINOT N is the darling of Oz's cooler regions and arguably its most revered variety. All credit to the fanatical, fastidious producers, because some of the finest world-class renditions fall into the still-affordable range, around A$100 (£52). Vine cuttings arrived in the 1800s, but Pinot's renaissance began in the 80s, as it found the areas best suited to it. So please don't call it generic Oz Pinot N; it's Gip, MAC, MOR P, YARRA V, or TAS, the regional leaders. Also, gd wines from AD H, GEELONG, Henty, PEMBERTON. To appreciate the diversity of styles/quality, try ASHTON HILLS, BASS PHILLIP, BANNOCKBURN, BINDI, Delamere Vyds, DR EDGE, GARAGISTE, GIANT STEPS, HODDLES CREEK ESTATE, KOOYONG, OAKRIDGE, PLACE OF CHANGING WINDS, POOLEY, SCORPO, TOLPUDDLE, WILLIAM DOWNIE, YABBY LAKE.

Billy Button Alpine V ★★ Umpteen varieties, styles – alas, small quantities. Italian varietals incl rare SCHIOPPETTINO; also CHARD, SAPERAVI, SHIRAZ, more. Delicious.

Bindi Mac ★★★★ (PINOT N) 20' 21' 22' (23) Outstanding single-block Pinot N, CHARD. Small production, high-density vyds: Block 8 jewel in crown.

Bleasdale Lang C ★★→★★★ Historic winery est 1850. Fabulous fortifieds and top CAB SAUV, MALBEC, SHIRAZ, plus gd-value range. Ever reliable.

AI algorithms uploaded to smartphones quickly detect trunk disease in Oz vineyards.

Bondar McL V ★★ GRENACHE, SHIRAZ stars. Dabbling in Italian varieties, plus v.gd AD H CHARD.

Bortoli, De Griffith, Yarra V ★→★★★ (Noble SEM) Sauternes-style from irrigated region Griffith; YARRA v for cool-climate, quality CHARD, PINOT N, SHIRAZ. Loads of styles, range of prices yet serious player.

Brave New Wine Marg R ★★ Natural-wine producer capable of v. high highs, so to speak; CHARD, GEWURZ, SHIRAZ can all be excellent.

Bremerton Lang C ★★ Family-owned/run; richly flavoured CAB SAUV, MALBEC, SHIRAZ. Red stars, but CHARD, FIANO no slouches.

Brokenwood Beech, Hun V ★★★ (ILR Res SEM) 11' 14' 15 17' (Graveyard SHIRAZ) 14' 17' 18' 19' 21 both HUN v classics. *Cricket Pitch* Sem/SAUV BL gd value, quality high. And suite of excellent CHARD, SHIRAZ, TEMPRANILLO from BEECH.

Brown Brothers King V, Tas, Yarra V ★→★★ Crowd-pleaser and no. 1 producer by volume of PROSECCO variety; premium Patricia range, fizz esp excellent. Innocent Bystander (YARRA v), Devil's Corner/Tamar Ridge (TAS) savvy acquisitions.

Burge, Grant Bar V ★★ Smooth red/white from best grapes of large vyd holdings. Owned by ACCOLADE.

Campbells Ruth ★★ Rich, ripe reds (esp Bobbie Burns SHIRAZ); extraordinary Merchant Prince Rare *Muscat*, Isabella Rare TOPAQUE (★★★★).

Canberra District NSW High-end, cool-climate, quality-driven. CLONAKILLA top; also MOUNT MAJURA, Nick O'Leary, RAVENSWORTH and Collector.

Cape Mentelle Marg R ★★ Renewed vigour of late CAB SAUV can be a highlight, CHARD promising and SAUV BL/SEM ever appealing.

Casella Riverina ★ Yellow Tail budget range became an empire. Now owns heritage brands BAILEYS OF GLENROWAN, Brand's of Coonawarra, MORRIS, PETER LEHMANN.

Chalmers Hea, Murray D ★ Grower, vine-nursery specialist, focus on Italian varieties. Range of diverse wines: gd FIANO, VERMENTINO.

Chambers Rosewood NE Vic With MORRIS, greatest maker of fortified TOPAQUE (★★★★), *Muscat*.

Chandon, Dom Yarra V ★★ Cool-climate fizz and table wine. Owned by LVMH. Known in UK as Green Point. NV cuvées in best-ever shape.

Chapel Hill McL V ★★ High-profile McL V producer. CAB SAUV, SHIRAZ the bread and butter, but TEMPRANILLO and esp GRENACHE make statements.

Charlotte Dalton Wines Ad H ★★ Breath of fresh air. Classic varieties CHARD, SHIRAZ, but also v.gd Lang C FIANO.

Chatto Tas ★★★ Young vyd, yet some v. fine PINOT N. Fragrance, layers of flavours, beautiful tannins, delicious.

Clarendon Hills McL V ★★ Full Monty reds (high alc, intense fruit) from grapes grown on hills above McL V. Cigar wines.

Clare Valley SA Bucolic, high-quality region 160 km n of Adelaide. Top RIES. Unique CAB SAUV, gumleaf-scented SHIRAZ. JIM BARRY, GROSSET, KILIKANOON, MOUNT HORROCKS, PIKES, and WENDOUREE jewel in crown.

Clonakilla Can ★★★★ (SHIRAZ/VIOGNIER) 15' 16' 18' 19' 21' 22' Regional legend and superstar. RIES, Viognier outstanding, Shiraz/Viognier famous, elegant SYRAH.

Clyde Park Vic ★★ Single-vyd CHARD, PINOT N v.gd form. SHIRAZ turning heads.

Cobaw Ridge Mac ★★★ Cool-climate, compelling CHARD, SYRAH; bio, some *qvevri*, amphorae used; super-fine PINOT N, finest LAGREIN in Oz.

Coldstream Hills Yarra V ★★→★★★ Excellent CHARD, PINOT N to drink young with *Res and single-vyd to age*. Part of TWE.

Coonawarra SA Home to some of Australia's finest, most distinctive CAB SAUV, and certainly to its richest red soil (on limestone). WYNNS, leader of the pack. BALNAVES, BELLWETHER, KATNOOK, Lindeman's, MAJELLA, YALUMBA all solid.

Coonwawarra is one of 13 old seashores, exposed as land lifted. But only 1m years old.

Coriole McL V ★★ (Lloyd Res SHIRAZ) 15' **16'** 18' 19 20 21 from 100-yr-old+ vines. Pioneer of FIANO, SANGIOVESE. PIQUEPOUL, NEGROAMARO, NERO D'AVOLA also v.gd.

Corymbia Marg R, Swan V ★★★ Textural CHENIN BL, elegant CAB SAUV, impressive TEMP/MALBEC. Superstar owners/winemakers Rob and Genevieve Mann.

Craiglee Sunbury ★★★ (SHIRAZ) **16'** 17' 18' 19 20' Salt-of-the-earth producer on historic farm. Rich CHARD, distinctive, fragrant, peppery Shiraz.

Crawford River Henty ★★★ Outstanding RIES producer. Cool, cold, scintillatingly dry, intense. Highly age-worthy.

Crittenden Estate Mor P ★★→★★★ Focus on v.gd CHARD, PINOTS GR/N; Cri de Coeur Sous Voile SAVAGNIN excellent *vin jaune*-style.

Cullen Wines Marg R ★★★★ (CHARD) **20'** 21' 22 (CAB SAUV) 18' 19' 20' 21' 22' A bio advocate. Best CHARD, CAB SAUV expressing place.

Curly Flat Mac ★★★ (PINOT N) **19'** 20' 21 22 Distinctive cool-climate Pinot N off single blocks; rich, textural CHARD.

Dal Zotto King V ★★ "Prosecco" pioneer, many styles today, incl excellent Col Fondo. Italian lineup morphs into fresh and lively or structured, detailed wines.

Dappled Yarra V ★★★ Top-flight/value, elegant-but-complex CHARD, PINOT N.

Deep Woods Estate Marg R ★★★ CHARD, CAB SAUV steal limelight, yet styles/varieties range from frisky rosé to succulent SHIRAZ. Star of FOGARTY GROUP juggernaut.

Devil's Lair Marg R ★★ Opulent CHARD, CAB/MERLOT is this estate at its best. Solid performer. Owned and therefore largely hidden by TWE.

Dirty Three Wines Gip ★★→★★★ Name relates to vyds where Marcus Satchell, aka Mr Gip, sources fruit; new plantings of MENCÍA, REFOSCO, TEROLDEGO; cracking CHARD, PINOT N (All The Dirts and Magic Dirt, 100% whole-bunch fermented).

Domenica Beech ★★★ Excellent BEECH producer with est vyds. Textural MARSANNE. Exuberant, spicy SHIRAZ, but NEBBIOLO shines.

Downie, William Gip ★★★ Whip-smart farmer, leader of local avant-garde, dedicated to PINOT N. Bull Swamp, Camp Hill Pinot N, farmed organically, minuscule quantities. Always compelling, always thoughtful, cool labels.

Dr Edge Tas ★★★ Leading light of Oz wine, Peter Dredge has inveigled his way into TAS from mainland, making compelling CHARD, PINOT N. Major contract winemaker too, and Pinot N from Oregon.

Eden Valley SA Climatically cooler cousin of neighbour BAR v. Hilly region. Stars: RIES, SHIRAZ, from HENSCHKE, Max & Me, PEWSEY VALE, TORZI MATTHEWS, more.

Elderton Bar V ★★★ Old vines; opulent CAB SAUV, SHIRAZ built to last. Something for everyone, incl v.gd RIES. Family-owned/run.

Eldorado Road Beech ★★ Small, family-owned; old-vine SHIRAZ planted 1890s, plus powerful reds (Durif, blends). Surprise is NERO D'AVOLA, arguably finest in Oz.

Eldridge Mor P ★★→★★★ Owned by enthusiasts who appointed ex-GIANT STEPS Steve Flamsteed to help. Expect CHARD, GAMAY, PINOT N to stay strong.

Entropy Wine Gip ★★→★★★ New name already turning heads with thoughtful winemaking, sourcing v.gd fruit with wonderfully expressive PINOT N, textural SAUV BL/SEM, peppery SYRAH and more, crafted by Ryan Ponsford.

Eperosa Bar V ★★★ Organic off-grid winery, 6th-generation BAR V vigneron.

Magnolia and Krondorf vyds, former incl 1896 SHIRAZ, latter GRENACHE from 1903. Respectful of past with nod to future; flavoursome, detailed wines.

Faber Vineyards Swan V ★★ John Griffiths is a guru of WA winemaking. Home estate redefines what's possible for SWAN V SHIRAZ. Polished power.

Fighting Gully Road Beech ★★★ Lauded producer in BEECH, plus sourcing fruit from ALPINE V. Outstanding CHARD, AGLIANICO, SANGIOVESE, SYRAH, TEMPRANILLO. New plantings of VERDICCHIO, GRENACHE V. promising.

Flametree Marg R ★★→★★★ No vyds but sources excellent CHARD, CAB SAUV, esp for SRS (subregional series), Wallcliffe and Wilyabrup respectively; v.gd SHIRAZ surprise late entry.

Forest Hill Vineyard Gt S ★★★ Regional pioneer est 1965; RIES the hero, Block 1 the star; v.gd MALBEC, SHIRAZ.

Frankland Estate Fra R ★★★ (RIES) 20' 21' 22' 23 Oz Ries royalty, outstanding organic vyd, Isolation Ridge (most remote in WA), range of styles. Plus medium-bodied CAB SAUV, SYRAH and mighty impressive GRÜNER V, MOURVÈDRE.

Fraser Gallop Estate Marg R ★★ Rich yet stylish CHARD, SEM/SAUV BL, CAB SAUV. Reliable on all levels.

Freycinet Tas ★★★ (PINOT N) 18' 19' 20' 21' 22 Pioneer family winery on TAS e coast; v.gd CHARD, outstanding RIES, fragrant Pinot N, Radenti (sp) too.

Garagiste Mor P ★★★ Tiny producer, outstanding CHARD, PINOTS GR/N. Quality from vyd care, run but not owned by winemaker Barnaby Flanders. Impressive.

Geelong Vic Region w of Melbourne, maritime, dry climate. Leaders: BANNOCKBURN, By Farr, LETHBRIDGE, PROVENANCE.

Gembrook Hill Yarra V ★★★ Cool site on upper reaches of Yarra River: CHARD par excellence, fine-boned PINOT N. Excellent gin a sideline.

Gemtree Vineyards McL V ★★ Rich SHIRAZ, TEMPRANILLO and other exotica, linked by quality; bio/organic.

Gentle Folk Ad H ★★ Marine scientists turned vignerons, part of AD H natural-wine scene; excellent CHARD, PINOT N, SYRAH. Viti- and regenerative-farming expert Dr Dylan Grigg advises.

Giaconda Beech ★★★★ (CHARD) 18' 19' 21' 22' Stellar producer comprising NEBBIOLO, PINOT N, SHIRAZ, but CHARD the star.

Giant Steps Yarra V ★★★ 18' 19' 20' 21' 22' Top single-vyd CHARD, PINOT N, SHIRAZ. Owned by Jackson Family Wines (*see* California, US).

Glaetzer-Dixon Tas ★★→★★★ Nick G turned his S Oz wine family history on its head by relocating to cool TAS. Euro-style RIES, autumnal PINOT N, Rhône syrah.

Goulburn Valley Vic Warm region in mid-Vic taking in Nagambie Lakes. Full-bodied reds, distinct whites: MARSANNE, CAB SAUV, SHIRAZ the pick. MITCHELTON, TAHBILK perpetual flag-bearers.

Grampians Vic Temperate region in NW Vic with RIES, excellent, distinct peppery SHIRAZ (and sp). MOUNT LANGI GHIRAN head and shoulders above all.

Granite Belt Qld High-altitude, (relatively) cool, improbable region just n of Qld/ NSW border. Spicy SHIRAZ, rich SEM (Boireann, Golden Grove, Ridgemill Estate). Plus Italian varieties.

Trailblazing Fighting Gully Road has Oz's 1st Petite Arvine and Cornalin.

Great Southern WA Remote cool area at bottom left corner of Oz; Albany, Denmark, Fra R, Mount Barker, Porongurup are official subregions; 1st-class RIES, CAB SAUV, SHIRAZ. *Style, quality, value here.*

Grosset Clare V ★★→★★★ (RIES) 21' 22 23 (Gaia) 19' 20 21' Nervy, acid-driven Ries in youth, many styles incl high-end G110 from one clone, organic site. *Gaia*, mainly CAB SAUV, is distinctive, FIANO appealing.

Gundog Estate Hun V ★ Aspirational SEM, SHIRAZ from CAN, HUN V.

Hahndorf Hill Ad H ★★★ Made GRÜNER V its own, consistently richly spiced, textured; interest, experimentation across range.

Hardys SA ★★ Historic company, but glory days gone, part of ACCOLADE; CHARD, SHIRAZ often excellent despite lack of company direction.

Heathcote Vic 500-million-yr-old Cambrian geology, calcium-rich, red soils can produce compelling reds, esp SHIRAZ, but Italian varieties flourishing. JASPER HILL, PAUL OSICKA, TAR & ROSES, Whistling Eagle, WILD DUCK CREEK.

Henschke Eden V ★★★★ (SHIRAZ) 05' 09' 10' 14' **15'** 16' 17 18' (CAB SAUV) 12' 15' 16' 17 18 Oz wine royalty, 150-yr-old family business; jewel is Hill of Grace, site and wine (Shiraz), but v.gd single-vyd Cab Sauv Cyril Henschke. Red blends gd, whites also from AD H, incl GRÜNER V.

Hentley Farm Bar V ★★★ Consistent SHIRAZ of immense power, concentration – wall-of-flavour territory – though in a (generally) fresh, almost frisky context.

Hewitson Bar V ★★ (*Old Garden Mourvèdre*) 17' 18' 19 20 Old Garden planted 1853, making it the world's oldest MOURVÈDRE; v.gd SHIRAZ, range of prices.

Hoddles Creek Estate Yarra V ★★★ Outstanding cool-climate varieties. Quality high, value too. Top-tier wines are single-block CHARD, PINOT N.

Hoosegg Orange ★★→★★★ Veteran Philip Shaw made Rosemount a roaring success in Southcorp days, now TWE. His eponymous label run by his sons, this the nest egg – boutique compilation of excellent CHARD, CABS SAUV/FR, more.

Houghton Marg R Brand with ACCOLADE, shadow of former self. Fruit from GT s and MARG R, wines made in latter. ★★★ for Jack Mann CAB SAUV.

House of Arras Tas ★★★★ Most prestigious sparkling house in Oz, all credit to winemaker Ed Carr. Key is magic confluence of tannins, ageing on lees and acidity. In a word: stunning. Sold to Handpicked Wines 2023.

Howard Park WA ★★→★★★ With v.gd RIES from GT s, plus MARG R CHARD, CAB. *MadFish* can be gd value. Marchand & Burch, family collaboration with Burgundian vigneron Pascal Marchand.

Hugh Hamilton Wines McL V ★★ All-rounder, quirky names: The Larrikin CAB/SHIRAZ, The Mongrel SANGIOVESE; SAPERAVI a speciality, several styles incl powerful Oddball the Great.

Hunter Valley NSW Historic region 250 km n of Sydney. Unique SEM can be battery acid in youth, elixir with age; mid-weight, earthy SHIRAZ. ANDREW THOMAS, BROKENWOOD, MOUNT PLEASANT, *Tyrrell's*.

Inkwell McL V ★★ Diverse styles, late-harvest to fortified; GRENACHE, SHIRAZ, ZIN.

Jacob's Creek Bar V ★ Owned by Pernod Ricard. Mostly focused on tiers of uninspiring but reliable wines; RIES solid though.

Jasper Hill Hea ★★ Emily's Paddock SHIRAZ/CAB FR blend, Georgia's Paddock Shiraz intense. Much-needed vyd work on-going. Now run by 2nd generation, Emily McNally with husband Nick.

Jericho Ad H, McL V ★★ Careful fruit selection, skilled winemaking, modern, tasty wines, esp FIANO, GRENACHE, SHIRAZ, TEMPRANILLO.

John Duval Wines Bar V ★★★ John D (ex-PENFOLDS Grange) makes *delicious Rhôney reds* of great intensity and character.

Joshua Cooper Wines Mac ★★★ Son of COBAW RIDGE founders, uber-talented with love of Oz wine history. Site in MAC, sources fruit within and outside region. Outstanding CHARD, PINOT N, teases best from BENDIGO CAB SAUV 1970 plantings.

Kalleske Bar V ★★ Old family farm makes captivating single-vyd SHIRAZ; all intensely flavoured; bio/organic.

Katnook Estate Coonw ★→★★ (Odyssey CAB SAUV) **14' 15'** 19 Pricey icons Odyssey, Prodigy SHIRAZ. Big wines in need of restrained love. ACCOLADE-owned.

Kilikanoon Clare V ★★ RIES, SHIRAZ excellent performers. Luscious, generous, beautifully made. Owned by Chinese investment group.

King Valley Vic Altitude range 155–860m (509–2821ft) has big impact stylistically. Noted for Italian varieties. Quality from BROWN BROTHERS, Chrismont, DAL ZOTTO, PIZZINI (esp).

Kirrihill Clare V ★★ RIES, CAB SAUV, SHIRAZ v.gd, often at excellent prices.

Knappstein Wines Clare V ★ Reliable RIES, SHIRAZ, CAB SAUV; gd value.

Kooyong Mor P ★★★ PINOT N, *excellent Chard* of detail, structure. PINOT GR of charm. High-quality single vyds.

Lake Breeze Lang C ★★★ Succulently smooth, gutsy, value CAB SAUV, SHIRAZ; few producers do mid-level so consistently well.

Lake's Folly Hun V ★★ (CHARD) **20' 21' 22** (Cab blend) **18' 19' 20 21** Pioneer of HUN V CAB SAUV, now part of FOGARTY GROUP. Still a beacon of quality, character.

Lambert, Luke Yarra V ★★ Focus only on NEBBIOLO at new estate vyd, yet to produce. Until then, v.gd cool CHARD, PINOT N, SYRAH.

Langmeil Bar V ★★ Custodian of some of world's oldest SHIRAZ vines (planted mid-1800s), and other ancient vyds, producing big CAB SAUV, GRENACHE, Shiraz.

Larry Cherubino Wines Fra R, Marg R ★★★ Outstanding CHARD, RIES, SAUV BL, SHIRAZ, plus classy CAB SAUV. Lots of labels, lots of polish.

LAS Vino Marg R ★★★ Wine in his blood, Nic Peterkin is grandson of Kevin and Diana CULLEN, and son of PIERRO founder Mike. Now a trailblazer, experimenter, yet fastidious producer of outstanding CHARD, CHENIN BL, CAB SAUV.

Leeuwin Estate Marg R ★★★★ (CHARD) **18' 19' 20' 21'** Iconic producer. All about age-worthy Art Series Chard; RIES, SAUV BL solid; *Cab Sauv* v.gd.

Leo Buring Bar V ★★ All about RIES; Leonay top label *ages superbly*. Gets lost in TWE empire, still v.gd.

Lethbridge Vic ★★ Estate wines v.gd; CHARD, PINOT N, with regional RIES, SHIRAZ. Dabbles in Italian (r/w). Always interesting.

Limestone Coast Zone SA Important and increasingly diverse region, incl COONW, Mt Benson, Mt Gambier, PADTHAWAY, Robe, WRATTONBULLY.

Living Roots Ad H ★★ Sebastian Hardy and wife Colleen also make wine in Finger Lakes (*see* US), with focus on mid-weight reds: AD H SHIRAZ, MCL V GRENACHE.

Lowestoft Tas ★★★ New addition to burgeoning FOGARTY GROUP; est vyd nr Hobart, excellent CHARD, PINOT N, terrific fizz.

Macedon and Sunbury Vic Adjacent regions: Macedon high elevation, cold; CHARD, PINOT N the stars; Sunbury, nr Melbourne airport, for SHIRAZ. Quality from BINDI, COWBAW RIDGE, CRAIGLEE, CURLY FLAT.

Mac Forbes Yarra V ★★★ Smart operator. Obsessed by wines of place, ie. single-site CHARD, PINOT N from YARRA V.

McHenry Hohnen Marg R ★★→★★★ More detail and class in past few yrs with CHARD, CAB SAUV, plus the surprise, SHIRAZ.

McLaren Vale SA Outstanding, diverse region nr Adelaide. Centre of Italian varieties FIANO, VERMENTINO to NERO D'AVOLA and SANGIOVESE, plus weighty, rich or elegant reds, esp SHIRAZ, but dry-grown, old-bush-vine GRENACHE today's hero. Stars: BEKKERS, BONDAR, CORIOLE, Hither & Yon, JERICHO, SAMUEL'S GORGE, SC PANNELL, WIRRA WIRRA, YANGARRA.

Salt of the sea

Could salt be an alternative to sulphur in winemaking? And does it affect fermentation? The ancient Greeks used to immerse grapes in the sea to get the waxy bloom off their skins, before sun-drying: maybe they knew something. Nic Peterkin from LAS VINO in MAR R tried it with VERMENTINO to see if sea water might change the flavour and microbes in winemaking. Results: sea-water immersion reduced acidity, but salt probably can't replace sulphur. And as for flavour: some salt = gd, lots of salt = horrible.

McWilliam's SE Aus ★★ Historic producer, owned by Calabria Family Wines since 2021, quality focus guaranteed (*see* MOUNT PLEASANT).

Main Ridge Estate Mor P ★★★ Pioneer of region, newish owner (2015) respecting its history. Full-bodied, rich CHARD, distinctive PINOT N. Small quantities.

Majella Coonw ★★ Rich, archetypal CAB SAUV, SHIRAZ. Value at every level.

Margaret River WA Maritime region s of Perth. Arguably finest CHARD, CAB SAUV in country. CAPE MENTELLE, CORYMBIA, CULLEN, DEEP WOODS ESTATE, FLAMETREE, FRASER GALLOP, LAS VINO, LEEUWIN ESTATE, MOSS WOOD, PIERRO, TRIPE ISCARIOT, VASSE FELIX, VOYAGER ESTATE, WOODLANDS and more. Premium location of bush, beaches and surfing.

Mayford NE Vic ★★★ Tiny vyd in hidden valley. Put ALPINE V region on map. CHARD, SHIRAZ and Oz's finest TEMPRANILLO.

Meerea Park Hun V ★★ Age-worthy SEM, SHIRAZ often as single-vyd expressions.

Mike Press Wines Ad H ★ Reliable and affordable: SAUV BL, CAB SAUV, SHIRAZ.

Mitchelton Goulburn V ★★ Stalwart producer: RIES, CAB SAUV, SHIRAZ, plus speciality *Marsanne*, ROUSSANNE. Fancy new hotel set among fabulous river red gums.

Montalto Mor P ★★→★★★ Focus on single-vyd CHARD, PINOT N highlighting best of MORN P. Fab cellar door, restaurant, sculptures dotted through vyd.

Moorilla Estate Tas ★★ Pioneer nr Hobart on Derwent River; CHARD, RIES, PINOT N; v.gd restaurant, extraordinary art gallery (MONA). Owner also of nearby Dom A.

Moorooduc Estate Mor P ★★→★★★ Solid performer of region's best varieties: CHARD, PINOTS N/GR.

Moppity Vineyards Hilltops ★ CAB SAUV, SHIRAZ (Hilltops) gd. CHARD (TUMBARUMBA) elegant. Best known for value offerings.

Mornington Peninsula Vic Stunning coastal area se of Melbourne; cool, maritime climate noted for CHARD, PINOTS GR/N. Wine/surf/beach/food and playground for wealthy. ELDRIDGE, GARAGISTE, KOOYONG, MAIN RIDGE ESTATE, MONTALTO, MOOROODUC ESTATE, PARINGA ESTATE, RARE HARE WINES, STONIER, TEN MINUTES BY TRACTOR, YABBY LAKE and more.

Morris NE Vic ★★★★ Producer of arguably the finest fortifieds, *Muscats*, TOPAQUES. In RUTH with 5th-generation David Morris at helm; owned by CASELLA.

Moss Wood Marg R ★★★ (CAB SAUV) 18' 19' 20 21 Most opulent (r) wines of MARG R. Star is Cab Sauv; gd CHARD, SEM.

Mount Horrocks Clare V ★★ Racy RIES, SEM, CAB SAUV, SHIRAZ in gd shape. Note NERO D'AVOLA.

Mount Langi Ghiran Gra ★★★ (SHIRAZ) 14' 15' 17' 18' 19' Peppery, *Rhône-like Shiraz*. Excellent Cliff Edge Shiraz. Estate-grown on special patch of dirt.

Mount Majura Can ★★ Leading TEMPRANILLO producer plus other Iberian varieties; CHARD, SHIRAZ gd; excellent RIES.

Mount Mary Yarra V ★★★★ (Quintet) 19' 20' 21' 22' YARRA V pioneer goes from

---

Orange or orange?

The word "orange" cannot be used to describe an Oz skin-contact white. Why? ORANGE, NSW, is a geographical indication or GI, akin to an appellation, and protected. Ironically, an orange wine, as in a skin-contact white, made in Orange can be described as an orange wine and an Orange wine. Don't worry. No one will be locked up for describing a wine as, well, orange in style; it's about context. "Amber" is a much better descriptor anyway. Even Josko Gravner, the Italian winemaker credited with popularizing the style, calls it amber wine. So does winemaker Tom Ward from Orange with Swinging Bridge #003 Amber. Other fab egs: Arfion Fever, HODDLES CREEK Skins, RAVENSWORTH Seven Months, plus one of the finest, YANGARRA Roux Beauté.

strength to strength. Best known for Bx-blend Quintet and Triolet (w), yet CHARD, PINOT N outstanding. Rhône-variety latest additions, all made by Sam Middleton, grandson of founder, late Dr. John M.

Mount Pleasant Hun V ★★★★ Owned by Medich. One of most important names in Oz wine thanks to its history, single-vyd SEM (esp *Lovedale*) and Maurice O'Shea SHIRAZ. Old vyds, great sites, sensational wines.

Mudgee NSW Region nw of Sydney. Full CHARD, textural RIES, fine SEM, earthy reds. Quality gd but needs a hero.

Mulline Geelong ★★→★★★ Exciting new name, rhymes with divine; collaboration between friends. Fruit sourced from Geelong, top single-vyd CHARD, PINOT N, SYRAH. Focus on org, eco business. Winner all round.

Ngeringa Ad H ★★ Perfumed NEBBIOLO, PINOT N, SHIRAZ; savoury rosé; bio.

Oakridge Yarra V ★★★★ Leading producer of CHARD in Oz, plus excellent PINOT N, SHIRAZ, and CAB SAUV. Multiple single-vyd releases.

O'Leary Walker Clare V ★★ Pure CLARE V RIES, solid CAB SAUV, big, bolshie MCL V SHIRAZ. Value all round.

Oliver's Taranga Vineyards McL V ★★ A 6th-generation grower supplying high-end producers (eg. PENFOLDS); GRENACHE, SHIRAZ v.gd. Trailblazer Corrina Wright 1st family winemaker, esp Italian, Spanish vines: FIANO, MENCÍA highlights.

Orange NSW Cool-climate, high-elevation region. Lively SHIRAZ (when ripe), but best suited to (intense) aromatic whites esp RIES, also CHARD.

Osicka, Paul Hea ★★★ Family-owned/run. Vines dating back to 50s. Both character and flavour writ large. Small-scale, low-profile, high-impact and quality CAB SAUV and SHIRAZ.

Ossa Wines Tas ★★ New, exciting player: CHARD, GRÜNER V, PINOT N and fizz. Watch.

Padthaway SA Rarely mentioned these days but important region: CHARD, CAB SAUV, SHIRAZ v.gd. Soil salinity on-going issue.

Pannell, SC McL V ★★★★ Trailblazer. Intuitive winemaking, gd vyds. Midas touch with GRENACHE, SHIRAZ, plus AGLIANICO. Dabbles with Spanish varieties.

Paringa Estate Mor P ★★ Big, rich PINOT N, SHIRAZ; same with CHARD.

Parker Coonawarra Estate Coonw ★★ In gd yrs full-bodied, age-worthy, tannic CAB SAUV of authority, distinction.

Passing Clouds Bendigo ★★ Down-to-earth folk producing reliable, robust reds, esp CAB SAUV (often a showstopper) and SHIRAZ. Mac CHARD has verve.

Patrick Sullivan Wines Gip ★★★ Smart winemaker obsessed with CHARD. New planting will be highest-density Chard in Oz. Farms other sites (with WILLIAM DOWNIE); Ada River and Bullswamp Chards outstanding, plus PINOT N.

Paxton McL V ★ Prominent organic/bio grower-producer: note GRENACHE, SHIRAZ.

Pemberton WA Region between MARG R and GT S; initial enthusiasm for PINOT N replaced by CHARD, RIES, SHIRAZ and v.gd fizz.

Penfolds ★★★★ (Grange) 96 06' 08' 10' 14' 17' 18' 19' (CAB SAUV Bin 707) 15 18 19 21 Oz's most famous (r) brand. So many Bins, so many wines: now incl Bx, Champagne, California. Outstanding CHARD Bin A and *Yattarna*.

Penley Estate Coonw ★★→★★★ Owned by sisters Ang and Bec Tolley; star winemaker Kate Goodman. Cellar door in MCL V, but CAB SAUV rules; diverse styles, all excellent from experimental Project wines, ie. whole-bunch CAB SAUV (it works), to high-end, structured Helios.

Petaluma Ad H ★→★★ RIES, SHIRAZ (AD H); CAB SAUV (COONW); gd wines, Croser (sp) can be v.gd.

Peter Lehmann Wines Bar V ★★ Well priced overall, incl easy RIES. Rich, structured Stonewell SHIRAZ among many others. Part of CASELLA.

Pewsey Vale Eden V ★★ Most recognizable RIES brand and done well. Value with several styles, incl Museum release The Contours grown on beautiful tiered vyd.

Pierro Marg R ★★★ (CHARD) 20' 21 22 Rich, distinct Chard with loyal fanbase; gd SEM/SAUV BL and tiptop Bx blend.

Pipers Brook Tas ★★ (RIES) 21' 22 23 Cool-area pioneer; gd RIES; PINOT N variable; *restrained Chard and sparkling* from Tamar V. Second label: Ninth Island. Owned by Belgian Kreglinger family.

Pizzini King V ★★ Pioneer of Italian varieties in KING V and Oz generally: NEBBIOLO, SANGIOVESE (all styles, authentic). Wonderful family.

Place of Changing Winds Mac ★★★ Powerful, rich CHARD, PINOT N, grown on high-density vyds. Also Rhône-style SHIRAZ from HEA fruit.

Pooley Tas ★★★→★★★★ Historic, impressive property c.1832 in Coal River V. Some of TAS's nay, Oz's finest RIES; CHARD, PINOT N. All stamped with sense of place.

Primo Estate SA ★★★ Joe Grilli's many successes: rich MCL V SHIRAZ, tangy COLOMBARD, potent Joseph CAB SAUV/MERLOT, complex sparkling Shiraz, NEBBIOLO.

Provenance Geelong ★★★ Top CHARD from GEELONG and surrounding regions; SHIRAZ the red star.

Punch Yarra V ★★★ Lance family ran Diamond Valley for decades. Retained close-planted PINOT N vyd when it sold: can make beautiful, age-worthy wines.

Pyrenees Vic Central Vic region; rich, often minty reds. Blue Pyrenees, Dog Rock, Mitchell Harris, Summerfield, TALTARNI leading players; happy hunting ground for assorted small producers.

Rare Hare Wines Mor P ★★ Known as Willow Creek until 2022. Impressive CHARD, PINOT N esp. Power and poise.

Ravensworth Can ★★★ Innovative producer, brilliant classic styles, eg. SHIRAZ/VIOGNIER, plus skin-contact whites and Italian varieties too, outstanding RIES. Texture a big part, no surprise as winemaker Bryan Martin is an ex-chef.

Rieslingfreak Clare V, Eden V ★★→★★★ Apt name as John Hughes only makes RIES. Winemaker is wife Belinda (ex-GRANT BURGE).

Riverina NSW Large-volume irrigated zone centred on Griffith.

Robert Oatley Wines Mudgee ★★→★★★ Three brands: everyday Signature Series, single vyds with Finisterre, best barrels for The Pennant. Fruit from MARG R, GT S, MCL V. Reliable, gd value, can be excellent.

Rochford Yarra V ★★→★★★ Main outdoor entertainment venue in YARRA V makes complex CHARD, CAB SAUV, PINOT N of note.

Rockford Bar V ★★★ Various old low-yielding vyds; reds best; iconic Basket Press SHIRAZ and noted *sparkling Black Shiraz*.

Rodda, A Beech ★★ Excellent CHARDs from est vyds; *Tempranillo* grown at high altitude can be a beauty.

Ruggabellus Bar V ★★★ Modern iteration of BAR V, savoury, even lighter-framed. Old oak, wild yeast, whole bunches/stems. Blends of CINSAULT/GRENACHE/MATARO/SHIRAZ. Compelling.

Rutherglen and Glenrowan NE Vic Two regions in warm NE Vic, both offer rich

---

Only in Oz

Whether in a hipster Sydney wine bar or a chic mood-lit basement venue in Melbourne, there are loads of cool, eclectic wines that don't travel further than the border between each city. Visit the Emerald City to drink Vinden, Renzalglia or the range from Frankly, This Wine Was Made by Bob, or more mainstream but v.gd Gilbert Family Wines (RIES). If in the culture capital, Melbourne, check out Moon Wine, Little Frances (slinky SYRAH), newcomer Fleet Wines (CHARD, PINOT N), or The Wine Farm, committed bio producer from Gip. If in Perth or MARG R, seek out Sam Vinciullo's no-added-sulphur wines and the wonderful Vino Volta (GRENACHE from 65-yr-old bush vines).

reds, outstanding fortifieds. ALL SAINTS, BAILEYS OF GLENROWAN, CAMPBELLS, MORRIS, SCION, TAMINICK CELLARS.

St Hallett Bar V ★★ (Old Block) 18' 19' 20 Star: SHIRAZ; rest of range is smooth, sound, stylish. ACCOLADE-owned.

Saltram Bar V ★★ Value Mamre Brook (CAB SAUV, SHIRAZ) and No. 1 Shiraz leaders. Main claim to fame is ubiquitous Pepperjack Shiraz.

Samuel's Gorge McL V ★★ Justin McNamee makes (at times) stunning GRENACHE, SHIRAZ, TEMPRANILLO of character, place.

Savaterre Beech ★★★ (CHARD) 19' 21' 22 (PINOT N) 18' 19' 21 Star: full-bodied Chard; meaty Pinot N, close-planted SAGRANTINO, SHIRAZ.

Schmolzer & Brown Beech ★★ Estate vyd, Thorley, highest in BEECH. Scintillating CHARD, perfumed PINOT N, spicy SYRAH, excellent RIES, NEBBIOLO to watch.

Scion Ruth ★★ Fresh, vibrant approach to region's stalwarts SHIRAZ and Durif.

Sentio Beech ★★★ Picks the eyes out of various cool-climate regions to produce compelling CHARD, PINOT N, SHIRAZ.

Seppelt Gra ★★★ (St Peter's SHIRAZ) 18' 19' 20 21 22 Historic name owned by TWE. Excellent CHARD, RIES. Lost its way when business gutted; some love now with new winemaker Clare Dry. Here's hoping.

Seppeltsfield Bar V ★★★→★★★★ National Trust Heritage Winery owned by Warren Randall. Fortified wine stocks back to 1878. A must-visit.

Serrat Yarra V ★★ Micro-vyd of noted winemaker Tom Carson (YABBY LAKE) and wife Nadège. CHARD, PINOT N, SHIRAZ/VIOGNIER and Rhône varieties.

Seville Estate Yarra V ★★★ (CHARD) 20' 21' 22' YARRA V pioneer, still on song. Excellent Chard, SHIRAZ, structured PINOT N. Founders' grandson now winemaker.

Shaw & Smith Ad H ★★★ Savvy outfit: complex CHARD; crisp, *harmonious Sauv Bl*; and, surpassing both, *Shiraz*. PINOT N v.gd.

Sidewood Estate Ad H ★★ Cidery, winery, snazzy restaurant, cellar door with v.gd wines in tow. Fizz a feature, cool CHARD, SHIRAZ too.

Sorrenberg Beech ★★★★ No fuss, but highest quality. CHARD, SAUV BL/SEM, Oz's finest GAMAY, Bx blend. Ultimate "in the know" winery.

Southern NSW Zone NSW Cool-climate zone incl CAN, Gundagai, Hilltops, TUMBARUMBA. Scintillating CHARD, pure RIES, savoury SHIRAZ.

Spinifex Bar V ★★★ Reds dominate, attention to detail in winemaking. Spicy GRENACHE, rich SHIRAZ, MATARO. Single vyds of note.

Stefano Lubiana S Tas ★★★ Beautiful bio vyds on banks of Derwent River, nr Hobart. Stamped with quality from sparkling to outstanding CHARD, PINOT N, plus Italian, Austrian varieties making a statement. Osteria Vista restaurant Italian to core.

Stella Bella Marg R ★★→★★★ Solid performer across range of styles, prices. Top CHARD, CAB SAUV called Luminosa often illuminating.

Stoney Rise Tas ★★ Cricket champ-turned-winemaker Joe Holyman crafts compelling CHARD, PINOT N; also v.gd GRÜNER V, RIES.

Stonier Wines Mor P Pioneering producer of CHARD, PINOT N. Re-energized with new owners 2022; winemaker Julian Grounds (ex-Craggy Range, NZ) from 2024.

Sunbury Vic *See* MACEDON AND SUNBURY.

Sutton Grange Bendigo ★★ Noteworthy SYRAH; Rosé rocks; FIANO, Aglianico, SANGIOVESE more than a sideshow.

Swan Valley WA Vines 1st planted 1829, 25 mins n of Perth. CHENIN BL still a star; also SHIRAZ, GRENACHE, plus fortifieds.

Swinney Fra R ★★★ Grower for decades, now excellent own-label RIES, GRENACHE, SHIRAZ, TEMPRANILLO. Top-tier Farvie; by WA winemaking royalty Rob Mann.

Tahbilk Nagambie ★★ (1927 Vines MARSANNE) 08' **12'** 13' 15' 16 17 Oldest family-owned winery in Vic, original 1860s estate/cellar door still going strong. Best: old-vine *Marsanne*. Res CAB SAUV, SHIRAZ can be v.gd. Rare 1860 Vines Shiraz.

Taltarni Pyrenees ★★ CAB SAUV, SHIRAZ in gd shape. Long-haul wines, now less scary.

Taminick Cellars Glenrowan ★★ Booth family has farmed this tough, dry patch since 1914. Fair amount of character accumulated along way.

Tapanappa SA ★★→★★★ WRATTONBULLY collaboration between Brian Croser, Bollinger and J-M Cazes of Pauillac (*see* France). Splendid CHARD, CAB SAUV blend, MERLOT, SHIRAZ. Surprising *Pinot N* from Fleurieu Peninsula.

Tar & Roses Hea ★★ Inspired by Med varieties and others. SANGIOVESE, SHIRAZ to NEBBIOLO all gd. Modern success story.

Greatest no. of Cornish descendents outside Cornwall are in S Oz. Incl Brian Croser.

TarraWarra Estate Yarra V ★★ (Res CHARD) 20' 21' 22' (Res PINOT N) 18' 19 21 Great Chard, Pinot N, plus Rhône and Italian varieties: BARBERA a delight. Sarah Fagan (ex-DE BORTOLI) joined 2023. Home to TarraWarra Museum of Art.

Tasmania Cold island region with hot reputation. Outstanding sparkling, CHARD, PINOT GR, RIES, SAUV BL, PINOT N. Mainland producer interest.

Taylors Wines Clare V ★→★★ Large scale, family-owned. RIES, CAB SAUV, SHIRAZ solid; umpteen labels, keen to enter luxury market with flagship The Legacy CAB SAUV, v.gd but eye-watering A$1000 (£521), matching PENFOLDS Grange price without its history. Ambitious. Exports as Wakefield Wines.

Ten Minutes by Tractor Mor P ★★→★★★ Top-notch wines, top-notch restaurant. Focus on single-vyd CHARD, PINOT N.

Teusner Bar V ★★ Old vines, clever winemaking, pure fruit flavours. Leads a BAR V trend towards "more wood, no good".

Thomas, Andrew Hun V ★★ Old-vine SEM; SHIRAZ. A HUN V game-changer, esp with more elegant expressions of SHIRAZ.

Tolpuddle Tas ★★★ SHAW & SMITH owns this outstanding 1988-planted vyd in Coal River V: CHARD powerful, PINOT N superb.

Topaque Vic Ho-hum replacement name for iconic RUTH fortified "Tokay", directive of EU.

Torbreck Bar V ★★→★★★ Dedicated to (often old-vine) Rhône varieties led by GRENACHE, SHIRAZ. Ultimate expression of rich, sweet, high-alc style.

Torzi Matthews Eden V ★★→★★★ Aromatic, stylish, big-hearted SHIRAZ. Value RIES, SANGIOVESE. Incredible consistency yr-on-yr.

Tripe Iscariot Marg R ★★ Kooky name, compelling wines. Highlights greatness of CHENIN BL, yet excels in region's finest grapes, CHARD, CAB SAUV.

Tumbarumba NSW Cool-climate region tucked into Australian Alps. Sites 500–800m (1640–2625ft); CHARD the out-and-out star; v.gd sparkling base.

Turkey Flat Bar V ★★★ Top producer of rich rosé, GRENACHE, SHIRAZ from 150-yr-old vyd. Controlled alc/oak. Single-vyd wines. Old but modern.

TWE (Treasury Wine Estates) Aussie wine behemoth. COLDSTREAM HILLS, DEVIL'S LAIR, Lindeman's, PENFOLDS, Rosemount, SALTRAM, WOLF BLASS, WYNNS COONAWARRA ESTATE among them.

Two Hands Bar V ★★★ Big reds, lots of them. They've turned volume down a fraction; glory of fruit seems all the clearer.

Tyrrell's Hun V ★★→★★★★ (Vat 1 SEM) 16' 17' 18' 19' 21 22' 23 (Vat 47 CHARD) 15' 17' 18' 22 23 Benchmark Sem Vat 1 plus individual vyd or subregional renditions. *Vat 47*, Oz's 1st Chard, continues to defy climatic odds. Outstanding old-vine 4 Acres SHIRAZ, Vat 9 Shiraz. Family-owned/run, a gem.

Vasse Felix Marg R ★★★→★★★★ (Heytesbury CHARD) 19' 20' 21' 22' (CAB SAUV) 18' 19' 20' 21 Pioneer of MARG R. Excellent, flinty Chard. Elegant Cab Sauv, top-tier Tom Cullity exceptional. Diversity throughout, incl Idée Fixe sparkling.

Voyager Estate Marg R ★★★ Organic viticulture; range of styles/prices from value Coastal to top-tier MJW CHARD, CAB SAUV.

Wanderer, The Yarra V ★★★ Exceptionally fine-boned PINOT N, equally fine CHARD. Excellent gin, too, more than a side-project.

Wantirna Estate Yarra V ★★★ Flies under radar for a regional pioneer. Worth seeking out. Lovely wines from Bx blend, PINOT N to CHARD, and cute labels via renowned Oz cartoonist and artist Michael Leunig.

Wendouree Clare V ★★★★ DRC of Australia (*see* France). Old vines, commitment to quality, history. Long-lived reds now veering towards more refined, elegant CAB SAUV, MALBEC, MATARO, SHIRAZ. Demand outstrips supply.

West Cape Howe Mt Barker ★→★★ Affordable, flavoursome reds, yet RIES the star. Can often shine, surprise.

Wild Duck Creek Hea ★★ Super-concentrated, high-octane reds, mostly CAB SAUV, MALBEC, SHIRAZ. Yet vigour, freshness somehow kept intact.

Wirra Wirra McL V ★★ High-quality, concentrated, in flashy livery. The Angelus CAB SAUV named Dead Ringer outside Australia.

Wolf Blass Bar V ★★ Owned by TWE. Not the shouty player it once was, but still churns through an enormous volume of clean, inoffensive wines.

Woodlands Marg R ★★★ With 7 ha of 40-yr-old+ CAB SAUV among top vyds in region, plus younger but v.gd plantings of other Bx reds. Brooding impact.

Wrattonbully SA Important growing region in LIMESTONE COAST ZONE; profile lifted by activity of TAPANAPPA, Terre à Terre, Peppertree.

Wynns Coonawarra Estate Coonw ★★→★★★★ (SHIRAZ) 17' 18' 19' 20' 21 (CAB SAUV) 15' 16' 18' 19' 20' 21 Legendary yet largest producer in region; excellent vyds; TWE-owned. Fair CHARD, RIES, but reds star with Cab Sauv, Shiraz, esp Black Label and pinnacle *John Riddoch*, plus single-vyd. Long-lived propositions.

Xanadu Wines Marg R ★★★→★★★★ 18' 19' 20' 21' (22) Single-vyd and Res CAB SAUV shining light, diverse styles; super-fine CHARD. Excellent at all price points. Top winemaking with fruit from top sites.

Yabby Lake Mor P ★★★ Made name with CHARD, PINOT N and boosted with single-site releases; spice-shot SYRAH adds to reputation. Now TAS vyd too.

Yalumba Bar V, SA ★★★ Oldest family-owned winery in Oz, with eye on quality as much as affordability. Powerhouse of reds: The Caley, benchmark CAB/SHIRAZ. Flies flag for country's finest VIOGNIER, The Virgilius.

Yangarra Estate McL V ★★★★ Exquisite GRENACHE thanks to superb vyds incl old bush vines planted 1946; bio. Respectful winemaking, pushing boundaries with long-skin-contact ROUSSANNE of such beauty. Excellent SHIRAZ, blends and more. Dress-circle producer.

Yarra Valley Vic Cool, high-end region ne of Melbourne. Emphasis on CHARD, PINOT N, SHIRAZ, elegant CAB SAUV. COLDSTREAM HILLS, DE BORTOLI, DOM CHANDON, GEMBROOK HILL, GIANT STEPS, HODDLES CREEK ESTATE, MAC FORBES, MOUNT MARY, OAKRIDGE, PUNCH, ROCHFORD, SERRAT, SEVILLE ESTATE, TARRAWARRA, WANTIRNA ESTATE, YARRA YERING, YERINGBERG, YERING STATION a formidable lineup.

Oldest block of Hunter V Semillon for Tyrrell's Vat 1 turned 100, 2023. Happy b'day.

Yarra Yering Yarra V ★★★★ (Dry Reds) 19' 20' 21' 22' One-of-a-kind YARRA V pioneer. Powerful PINOT N; deep, refined CAB SAUV (Dry Red Nº 1); SHIRAZ (Dry Red Nº 2); CHARD morphed into magnificence of late. Absolute upper echelon (r/w). Winemaker Sarah Crowe winning many accolades.

Yeringberg Yarra V ★★★★ (MARSANNE/ROUSSANNE) 20' 21' 22' (CAB SAUV) 18' 19' 20' 21 22' Historic estate (1862) still with founding Swiss family. Small quantities of v. high-quality CHARD, Marsanne, Roussanne, Cab Sauv, PINOT N.

Yering Station / Yarrabank Yarra V ★★ Site of Vic's 1st vyd; replanted after 80-yr gap. Snazzy table wines (Res CHARD, VIOGNIER, PINOT N, SHIRAZ). Yarrabank (sp), joint venture with Champagne Devaux (*see* France).

AUSTRALIA

New Zealand

Abbreviations used
in the text:

Auck	Auckland
B of P	Bay of Plenty
Cant	Canterbury
Gis	Gisborne
Hawk	Hawke's Bay
Hend	Henderson
Marl	Marlborough
Mart	Martinborough
Nel	Nelson
N/C Ot	North/Central Otago
Waih	Waiheke Island
Waip	Waipara Valley
Wair	Wairarapa

The international thirst (especially in the US) for Marlborough's strikingly aromatic, explosively flavoured Sauvignon Blanc shows no sign of waning. It means that New Zealand exports nearly all its wine. Over the past decade, Sauvignon Blanc has increased its plantings by 35%. Pinot Gris has expanded by 14%. Pinot Noir, sadly, has barely risen, and Chardonnay and Merlot are down. Quality overall is improving as the country's vineyards – and wine-growers – mature, and more and more single-vineyard – even single-block – wines are emerging, vividly expressing their origins in their flavours.

Recent vintages

2023 North I: record, cyclone-related rain; some top Hawk reds not made.
      Marl: cool, drier; intense Sauv Bl. C Ot: favourably warm, dry.
2022 Record crop. Marl/Hawk: wet/cold, hit quality. C Ot: clean, ripe Pinot N.
2021 Marl: small, frost-affected, but vigorous, flavour-packed. Hawk: warmer,
      drier than usual, esp gd Chard, Syrah.
2020 Marl: crisp, intense. Hawk: outstanding Chard, reds.

Akarua C Ot ★★★ Owned by Edmond de Rothschild Heritage (France). Plans for organic and new super-premium PINOT N. Complex Bannockburn Pinot N, from mature vines. Top red: sturdy, lush The Siren Pinot N.

Allan Scott Marl ★★ Family-owned, est 1990. Atmospheric, rammed-earth winery, extensive vyds in heart of WAIRAU v. Fresh, easy-drinking. Top range: black labels. With Steytler family "Stellenbosch + Marlborough" SAUV BL: rare, gd-value blend of S African and NZ wine.

Alpha Domus Hawk ★★→★★★ Family winery in Bridge Pa Triangle. MERLOT, CAB SAUV-based reds (classy The Aviator); SYRAH, CHARD, VIOGNIER, honey-sweet SEM.

Amisfield C Ot ★★★ Tourist drawcard, with cellar door, bistro, spectacular views. Classy RIES (dr/s/sw); rich PINOT N (esp RKV Res), floral rosé.

Astrolabe Marl ★★→★★★ Impressive range: refined CHARD, vibrant CHENIN BL, punchy SAUV BL (AWATERE V), scented PINOT N; 2nd-tier Durvillea range top value.

Ata Rangi Mart ★★★→★★★★ Esteemed PINOT N producer, founded 1980. Age-worthy: 14′ 15′ 16′ 17 18 19′ 20′ 21′ NZ classic. Refined Craighall CHARD; oak-aged Lismore PINOT GR; lush, sweet Kahu RIES.

Auckland Largest city (n, warm, cloudy) in NZ; 0.7% vyd area (not expanding), but 12% of producers. Nearby districts with clay soils: W Auckland, incl Henderson, Huapai, Kumeu, Waimauku (long est, pioneered by Croatians); newer (since 80s): Clevedon, Matakana, WAIH (island vyds with restaurants, helipads, touristy). Rich, ripe, underrated CHARD, sturdy, savoury Bx blends in dry seasons, bold SYRAH rivals HAWK for quality.

Auntsfield Marl ★★★ Characterful wines from site of region's 1st (1873) vyd (replanted 1999). Derelict, original underground cellar rebuilt as museum. Weighty SAUV BL, citrus CHARD, deep PINOT N.

NZ increasingly known as Aotearoa. Next: Te Tauihu-o-te-waka (Marl) Sauv Bl?

Awatere Valley Marl Key subregion (pronounced "Awa-terry", meaning fast-flowing river); silt-loam soils, few wineries, but huge vyd area (more than HAWK). Major component in many regional blends of MARL SAUV BL. Cooler, drier, less fertile than WAIRAU V, with highly aromatic, racy ("tomato stalk") Sauv Bl (style more popular in UK than US). Also fresh, crisp PINOT GR; vibrant RIES; flavour-packed GRÜNER V, often slightly herbal PINOT N.

Babich Hend ★★→★★★ NZ's oldest family-owned winery, est 1916, now 3rd gen. Biggest seller: Marl SAUV BL. Age-worthy single-vyd Irongate from GIMBLETT GRAVELS. Top red: The Patriarch (Bx style).

Bilancia Hawk ★★★→★★★★ Owned by Warren Gibson (TRINITY HILL) and Lorraine Leheny. Classy CHARD, VIOGNIER, SYRAH. Majestic La Collina SYRAH, from steep, early ripening site overlooking GIMBLETT GRAVELS, one of NZ's greatest.

Blackenbrook Nel ★★ Sloping, coastal vyd. Swiss owners. Richly scented whites. Rich PINOT N, exuberantly fruity MONTEPULCIANO.

Black Estate Cant ★★→★★★ Small organic WAIP producer with popular eatery, serving locally foraged food (incl truffles in winter). Three vyds on dense clay-limestone soils. Characterful CHARD, CHENIN BL, dry RIES, CAB FR, PINOT N.

Blank Canvas Marl ★★★ Focus on alternative styles and unusual techniques, eg. co-fermenting HAWK SYRAH with GRÜNER V skins. Impressive MARL Holdaway Vyd SAUV BL, Escaroth Vyd CHARD, McKee Vyd Grüner V, Settlement Vyd PINOT N.

Borthwick Wair ★★→★★★ Stony vyd at Gladstone. Two brands: Paddy Borthwick, Paper Road. Incisive style.

Brancott Estate Marl ★→★★★ Owned by PERNOD RICARD. Long known as Montana, but brand caused export problems in US. Huge-selling SAUV BL. Icon range: Chosen Rows Sauv Bl, PINOT N. Letter Series: high quality. Living Land: organic. Identity: subregional styles. Res range: v.gd value.

Brightwater Nel ★★ Impressive whites grown on edge of river terrace. Top range: Lord Rutherford, named after illustrious scientist, born "just down the road", SAUV BL from mature vines, fleshy CHARD, bold PINOT N.

Brookfields Hawk ★★→★★★ Smallish, with atmospheric winery from 1937. Typically great value. Reputation for sturdy CHARD, VIOGNIER, CAB/MERLOT, SYRAH; MALBEC from sun-dried grapes promoted as "Malbec on steroids".

Burn Cottage C Ot ★★★ Organic; vyds at Pisa and Bannockburn. Owned by Sauvage family (Nevada-based). PINOT N specialist, incl refined Burn Cottage Vyd, compelling Sauvage Vyd. Intense RIES/GRÜNER V.

Canterbury 64 producers, most in relatively warm WAIP district. Greatest success with aromatic RIES, savoury PINOT N. SAUV BL heavily planted, but often minor component in other regions' wines.

Carrick C Ot ★★★ Bannockburn winery on n-facing slopes with gravel and sand glistening with silica. Organic focus. Powerful PINOT N, esp The Magnetic, drink-young Unravelled, characterful, organic Pot De Fleur made in flowerpots.

Catalina Sounds Marl ★★→★★★ Australian-owned, regional blends incl weighty PINOT GR, top estate-grown CHARD, SAUV BL, PINOT N from Sound of White vyd.

Central Otago High-altitude, dry inland region in s of S Island. Sunny, hot days, v. cold nights. Most vines in Cromwell Basin. Fast-improving, vibrant CHARD, PINOT GR, RIES; famous PINOT N has drink-young charm, with older vines now yielding more savoury, complex wine. Much Pinot N sold to producers in other regions. Top Pinot N rosé and trad-method fizz.

Chard Farm C Ot ★★ Pioneer in precipitous gorge, famous for bungee-jumping. Floral, graceful, mid-weight PINOT N. Most vyds now in Cromwell Basin. Second label: Rabbit Ranch.

Church Road Hawk ★★→★★★★ PERNOD RICARD NZ winery with historic (1896) HAWK roots. Powerful, complex wines. Popular CHARD, Alsace-style PINOT GR, MERLOT/CAB, SYRAH. Grand Res range impressive, esp showstopping Chard. Intense "1 Single Vineyard" selection aimed at duty-free market. Prestige range: Tom, named after founder Tom McDonald.

Churton Marl ★★ Elevated Waihopai V site. Organic, 1st in modern NZ to replace tractors with horses. SAUV BL, PINOT N, esp The Abyss: oldest vines, greater depth. Honey-sweet PETIT MANSENG.

Clearview Hawk ★★→★★★★ Coastal, shingly vyd at Te Awanga, plus grapes from inland. Powerful, complex, often hedonistic CHARD, incl White Caps, designed to "go back to the excesses of the 1980s", with "loads of oak and buttery toast".

Clos Henri Marl ★★→★★★ Organic; est by Henri Bourgeois (*see* France). SAUV BL from stony soils, one of NZ's best; savoury PINOT N (clay). Second label: Bel Echo (reverses variety/soil match). Strikingly gd Chapel Block Blanc de Noirs.

Cloudy Bay Marl ★★★ Large-volume, still-classy SAUV BL is NZ's most famous wine. Wines serious, stylish rather than pungent. Te Wahi C OT PINOT N since 2010. Stylish Pelorus NV (sp). LVMH-owned.

Coal Pit C Ot ★★→★★★★ Finely crafted, mostly estate-grown PINOT N in GIBBSTON.

Constellation New Zealand Auck ★→★★ Owned by NY-based Constellation Brands. Focus on solid, modestly priced supermarket labels, incl Monkey Bay, SELAKS.

Craggy Range Hawk ★★★→★★★★ Founded 1999 by Peabody family, Australians with background in liquid waste, wanting a more exciting investment. High-profile winery restaurant, Terroir. Sturdy, rich, refined.

Deep Down Marl ★★→★★★★ Organic, single-vyd wines; sulphur-free, fruity PINOT N.

Delegat Auck ★★ Croatian origin, est 1947, still mostly family-owned. Consistently attractive, mid-priced, v.gd value. Hugely successful OYSTER BAY. Instantly likeable CHARD, MERLOT. Owns Barossa Valley Estates (Australia).

Mapping Marlborough
Are MARL's SAUV BL almost identical, in terms of their aromas and flavours? No way, insist members of Appellation Marlborough Wine, who have produced a beautiful, detailed Wine Map of Marlborough (appellationwine.co.nz/store). The region's "hugely diverse soils, microclimates and, ultimately, terroirs, mean producers can craft wildly different expressions of Sauvignon Blanc here", observes Matt Thomson, of Blank Canvas. The idea is that wine enthusiasts can use the map to pinpoint the subregional style they prefer.

Delta Marl ★★→★★★ Owned by SAINT CLAIR; gd-quality/value. Hatters Hill: richer.

Destiny Bay Waih ★★→★★★ Small, n-facing amphitheatre; expat Americans make distinguished, pricey CAB SAUV-based blends, French and American oak-aged. Magna Praemia, flagship. Lush Mystae, mid-tier. Destinae, earlier drinking.

Deutz Auck ★★★ Champagne house (*see* France) gives name to great-value fizz from MARL by PERNOD RICARD NZ. Lively Brut NV, min 2 yrs on lees; gd Vintage Blanc de Blancs. Vivacious Rosé NV; outstanding Prestige (disgorged after 3 yrs).

Dog Point Marl ★★★ Organic; est 2004 by prominent grape-grower Ivan Sutherland and winemaker James Healy (ex-Cloudy Bay). Elegant, intense, tight structure.

Domaine-Thomson C Ot ★★→★★★ Small, organic PINOT N vyds in two hemispheres: Gevrey-Chambertin and Lowburn. Elevated, sloping site, deep gravels. Highly fragrant, rich, harmonious reds.

Dry River Mart ★★★ Small, acclaimed producer, flat, shingly terrain, est 1979. Alsace-style PINOT GR, NZ's 1st outstanding eg. and still one of greatest. Classy CHARD, GEWURZ, RIES, PINOT N, sweet whites.

Elephant Hill Hawk ★★→★★★ Stylish, German-owned winery on Pacific coastline, also grapes from inland. Soils vary from shingle to clay. Serious wines with depth, never flashy, esp CHARD, CAB SAUV, SYRAH.

Escarpment Mart ★★★ Organic, owned by Torbreck (*see* Australia). Named after a km-long escarpment that falls sharply from the vyd (alluvial loams over gravels) to Huangarua River. Top label: Kupe PINOT N. Single-vyd, old-vine reds esp gd.

Esk Valley Hawk ★★ →★★★★ Brand retained by VILLA MARIA. Characterful, gd quality, value. Innovative Artisanal Collection: excellent ALBARIÑO, CHENIN BL, GAMAY N, GRENACHE, TEMPRANILLO. Flagship, MALBEC-influenced Heipipi The Terraces.

Felton Road C Ot ★★★★ Owned by Englishman Nigel Greening, former rock guitarist. Best known for savoury PINOT N, but deep CHARD and RIES classy too. Famous Bannockburn Pinot N is estate-grown, four-vyd blend, native yeasts, barrel-aged, unfined, unfiltered.

Forrest Marl ★★→★★★ Family-owned, 2nd generation; latest releases best yet. Big success with The Doctors' SAUV BL, low abv (9.5%). Wide range, gd value, finely crafted whites. Rich, fruit-packed LAGREIN.

Framingham Marl ★★→★★★ Lovely walled gardens, subterranean cellar. Owned by Sogrape (*see* Portugal). Best known for scented Classic RIES (s/sw) from mature vines. Top: F-Series.

Fromm Marl ★★★ Swiss-owned; organic, focus on intense, long-lived wines. Estate vyd, close-planted 1992, has clay and shingle subsoils. Distinguished PINOT N, incl multi-site Cuvée H. Bold Fromm Vyd MALBEC.

Gibbston Valley C Ot ★★→★★★★ One of NZ's most-visited wineries. Now US-owned; most vyds at Bendigo. Strong name for PINOT N, esp fragrant GV Collection; old-vine, organic Le Maitre; powerful Res; gd Blanc de Blancs.

Giesen Cant ★★→★★★ Large winery, multiple vyds in MARL, family-owned. Huge-selling Marl SAUV BL, alc-free Sauv Bl bland. Popular RIES (s/sw), plus attractive single-vyd Gemstone, partly fermented in granite. Memorable Clayvin SYRAH.

Gimblett Gravels Hawk Defined area of shingly, arid, former riverbed long avoided by farmers, but popular for drag racing. Rich Bx-style reds (mostly MERLOT-led, but stony soils also suit CAB SAUV – recent renewed interest). Super SYRAH. Best reds world-class 13' 14' 15' 18 19' 20' 21'. Age-worthy CHARD from siltier soils.

Gisborne 5th-largest region. Declining planted area. Abundant sunshine but often rainy; highly fertile alluvial soils. CHARD key (often for fizz). CHENIN BL, GEWURZ, VIOGNIER gd; PINOT GR, MERLOT variable. Interest in rain-resistant ALBARIÑO.

Gladstone Vineyard Wair ★★ One of larger producers in N WAIR. SAUV BL, PINOT GR, VIOGNIER. Generous PINOT N; single-vyd reds since 18 best yet.

Grasshopper Rock C Ot ★★→★★★ Single label, PINOT N specialist, estate-grown on n-facing slope with diverse soils, surrounded by rock shelves. One of Alexandra subregion's top reds: perfumed, age-worthy, great value.

Greenhough Nel ★★ →★★★ One of region's leading boutiques; 1st vines 1979, deep river-stones over clay. Top label: Hope Vyd; rich CHARD; NZ's finest PINOT BL; mushroomy PINOT N.

Greystone Waip ★★★ Star organic producer, on slopes and flats with high limestone content. Fleshy whites. Graceful PINOT N, esp Thomas Brothers. Pétillant Naturel: slightly austere, dry fizz, from RIES, closed with a crown cap.

Greywacke Marl ★★★ Distinguished CHARD, SAUV BL, powerful PINOT GR, RIES, PINOT N. Named after NZ's most abundant bedrock (pronounced *greywacky*). Wild Sauv, handled in old French barriques, full of personality.

Grove Mill Marl ★★ Attractive, gd-value whites, WAIRAU V subregional focus.

Haha Hawk, Marl ★→★★ Fast-growing producer; lively, easy-drinking, gd value.

Hans Herzog Marl ★★★ Powerful, characterful, organic; estate-grown at stony, warm, early ripening site. Many varieties, incl NZ's 1st BLAUFRÄNKISCH (exuberantly fruity). Notably refined Grandezza 19 (r). Hans brand in EU, US.

Hawke's Bay Large region, sunny, dryish climate, extreme soil diversity. Distinguished CAB SAUV and MERLOT-based Bx-style reds in favourable yrs 19' 20' 21'; spicy SYRAH; weighty CHARD; SAUV BL; NZ's best VIOGNIER. Promising PINOT N from cooler, elevated, inland districts. *See also* GIMBLETT GRAVELS.

Hunter's Marl ★★ →★★★ Owned by Jane H, MD since 1987. Famous for vibrant, tropical-fruit SAUV BL. Rich RIES. Excellent fizz Miru Miru NV, esp late-disgorged Res. Home Block: top Sauv Bl, CHARD from mature vines.

Invivo Auck ★★ Young, entrepreneurial producer. Vibrantly fruity whites, rosé and reds from various regions, often with celebrity labels (Graham Norton in UK, Sarah Jessica Parker in US).

Jackson Estate Marl ★★→★★★ Best known for fleshy, ripe Stich SAUV BL, named after founding Stichbury family. Rich PINOT N from vyds on s side of WAIRAU V. Ownership link to PASK.

Johanneshof Marl ★★ Small winery with candle-lit tunnel 50m (164ft) into hillside, full of maturing wine (Emmi sp lees-aged 5–10 yrs). GEWURZ one of NZ's finest.

Jules Taylor Wines Marl ★★ →★★★ Stylish, gd value, named after MARL-born winemaker. SAUV BL, GRÜNER V, complex top OTQ ("On The Quiet").

Kim Crawford Wines Hawk ★ →★★ Owned by CONSTELLATION NZ. Punchy MARL SAUV BL, in bottles and cans, is huge seller in US.

Kumeu River Auck ★★★★ Celebrated CHARD producer, Croatian origin, best known for weighty, savoury "village wine", labelled Estate Chard: clay soils, indigenous yeasts, barrel-fermented. Single-vyd bottlings incl opulent flagship Mate's (pronounced *ma-teh*) Vyd, from original site. Newish Rays Road CHARD and PINOT N from elevated site in HAWK.

Kiwi Pinot Noir – instant style guide

Far more PINOT NS than SAUV BLS are made in NZ. Cheaper wines typically display light, raspberry flavours, but the finest have substance, suppleness and a gorgeous spread of cherry, plum, fruit-cake and spice. Distinct regional styles range from the sturdy, warm, savoury, earthinesss of MART (1st CAB off the rank in the 80s), to C OT's seductively perfumed, buoyant fruit; with advancing vine age becoming more complex and age-worthy. The top labels of MARL are widely underrated, at their most floral and graceful from elevated, clay-based sites; N CANT (WAIP) and NELSON are also gd. Look also for Alexander and Nga Waka (Mart); TWO RIVERS Tributary (Marl); Q (WAITAKI V); Domain Road, Maori Point, ROCK FERRY Trig Hill, Wild Earth (C Ot).

Lawson's Dry Hills Marl ★★→★★★ World's 1st winery to use screwcaps for all. Consistent quality, value. Top range: The Pioneer (lush, old-vine GEWURZ).

Lindauer Auck ★→★★ Hugely popular (in NZ) low-priced fizz, esp bottle-fermented Lindauer Brut Cuvée NV, but Australian grapes now part of recipe.

Loveblock Marl ★★→★★★ Estate vyd in AWATERE V, partly organic, owned by Kim and Erica Crawford (ex-owners KIM CRAWFORD). Vibrantly fruity, ripe SAUV BL – some handled without sulphur, using green tea powder as a natural antioxidant.

Most leading rugby nations are also important wine producers. Not Fiji.

Mahi Marl ★★→★★★ Small winery, owner Brian Bicknell (ex-SERESIN) not after "fruit-bombs; we want texture, wines that give real palate satisfaction". Characterful CHARD, SAUV BL (partly oak-aged), PINOT N. Top range: Single Vyd.

Man O' War Auck ★★→★★★ Largest vyd on WAIH (plus grapes from adjacent Ponui Island). Owned by Spencer family, one of NZ's richest. High, windy sites, loam-clay soils. Often suits PINOT GR. Powerful Valhalla CHARD; Gravestone SAUV BL/SEM, Dreadnought SYRAH, red Bx blends (Ironclad).

Marisco Marl ★★ Large Waihopai V producer. Several brands: Leefield Station, The Craft Series, The Kings Series, The Ned. Best known for lively The Ned SAUV BL; more concentrated The King's Favour.

Marlborough Biggest region, at top of S Island. Best land now in short supply; SAUV BL 1st planted 1975. Both gravelly and silty soils on valley floors. Hot, sunny days, cold nights give aromatic, crisp whites and PINOT N-based rosés. Intense Sauv Bl in a familiar style; some top wines oak-influenced. Some of NZ's best GEWURZ, PINOT GR, RIES; CHARD slightly leaner than HAWK, more vibrant, can age well. High-quality, gd-value fizz and classy botrytized Ries. Pinot N underrated; top examples from n-facing clay hillsides among NZ's finest. Interest stirring in ALBARIÑO, GRÜNER V. (*See also* AWATERE V, WAIRAU V.)

Martinborough Wair Small, prestigious subregion in S WAIR (foot of N Island), popular playground for Wellington city. Cold s winds reduce yields, warm summers, usually dry autumns, free-draining soils (esp on Martinborough Terrace). Success with several whites (CHARD, GEWURZ, PINOT GR, RIES, SAUV BL), but renowned for weighty PINOT N: higher % of mature vines than elsewhere.

Martinborough Vineyard Mart ★★★ Famous for PINOT N since 1984 (old-vine Home Block). CHARD, RIES (s/sw). Te Tera ("The Other") value, earlier-drinking range.

Matawhero Gis ★★ Former star GEWURZ producer of 80s, now different ownership. Easy drinking: generous, ripe, rounded.

Maude C Ot ★★→★★★ Mature vines on steep, terraced Mt Maude Vyd, at Wanaka: CHARD, RIES (dr/s/sw), PINOT N. Stylish regional blends: dry PINOT GR, ROSÉ.

Mills Reef B of P ★★→★★★ Easy-drinking Estate selection: gd-value MERLOT/CAB. Top Elspeth range from HAWK (CHARD, CABS SAUV/FR, MERLOT, SYRAH and blends); Bespoke: 2nd tier. Res: 3rd tier.

Millton Gis ★★→★★★ NZ's 1st organic producer, despite warm, moist climate. Hill-grown, single-vyd Clos de Ste Anne range in gd seasons, incl VIOGNIER, SYRAH. Fleshy CHARD, lemony RIES, long-lived CHENIN BL honeyed in wetter vintages.

Misha's Vineyard C Ot ★★→★★★ Gently sloping terraces and one steep face ("the ski slope"). Scented GEWURZ, PINOT GR, RIES; lovely rosé; graceful PINOT N.

Mission Hawk ★★→★★★★ NZ's oldest producer, 1st vines 1851, still owned by Catholic Society of Mary. Popular cellar door and restaurant. Large vyd in AWATERE V. Fine-value Estate range. Quality, value Res. Rich, complex Jewelstone and (esp) Huchet labels.

Mondillo C Ot ★★→★★★ Rising star at Bendigo: intense, dryish RIES (lovely sw Nina Late Harvest); lush PINOT N (esp Bella Res); off-dry rosé.

Mount Edward C Ot ★★→★★★ Small, organic, innovative. Crafted and harmonious.

Mount Riley Marl ★★ Medium-sized family firm, named after peak on n side of WAIRAU V. Great-value regional selection (incl ALBARIÑO, GEWURZ, SYRAH). Top range is Seventeen V. Ripe, supple style.

Mt Beautiful Cant ★★ Large vyd in Cheviot hills, n of WAIP, silt-loam soils over alluvial gravels, with mudstone base. Fragrant, weighty, strongly varietal wines.

Mt Difficulty C Ot ★★★ Sloping vyds and popular restaurant with sweeping views, owned by US billionaire Bill Foley. Expanding range of single vyds. Best known for powerful PINOT N Roaring Meg, named after legendary barmaid: drink young. CHARD, RIES, rich, peppery SYRAH.

Next big NZ thing: Albariño. Suits a warming climate. Likes rain too.

Mud House Cant ★★→★★★ Large, Australian-owned, MARL-based; also vyds in C OT, WAIP. Impressive Waipara Hills brand; gd-value subregional, regional, Marl/N CANT blends. Excellent Single Vyd collection, esp rich, dry PINOT GR.

Nautilus Marl ★★→★★★ Medium-sized, owned by S Smith & Sons (*see* Yalumba, Australia). Yeasty NV sparkler one of NZ's best; min 3 yrs lees. Wines finely balanced, gd vigour, complexity.

Nelson Small region w of MARL; climate markedly wetter but equally sunny. Clay soils of Upper Moutere hills (CHARD, PINOT N) and silty WAIMEA plains (strength in aromatic whites). Over half of all plantings SAUV BL (some sold for multi-region blends), but also v.gd GEWURZ, PINOT GR, RIES.

Neudorf Nel ★★★→★★★★ Pronounced "Noy-dorf". Smallish; big reputation. Hillside, clay-gravel vyds. Refined, organic Home Block Moutere CHARD, mature vines, one of NZ's greatest. Savoury Home Block Moutere PINOT N (Tom's Block: gd 2nd-tier), off-dry PINOT GR, ALBARIÑO. Tiritiri: recent "grower series".

Nº 1 Family Estate Marl ★★→★★★ Specialist in v.gd fizz; no longer controls Daniel le Brun brand. Best known for citrus CHARD-based NV, 2 yrs on lees. Res Blanc de Blancs (5 yrs+ on lees): rich, toasty.

Nobilo Marl ★→★★ Owned by E&J Gallo (*see* US). Known for SAUV BL: top Icon label grown in AWATERE V. Gallo's goal: make Nobilo biggest-selling Sauv Bl in US.

Novum Marl ★★★ Identifies small vyd pockets of top grapes, from "sites within sites"; sells via mail order. Weighty CHARD; graceful PINOT N.

Oyster Bay Marl ★★ From DELEGAT. Named after a bay in MARL Sounds. Marketing triumph: huge sales in UK, US, Australia. Attractive, easy-drinking, mid-priced.

Palliser Mart ★★→★★★ One of district's largest. Many small shareholders. Finely textured single-vyd Om Santi CHARD, Hua Nui PINOT N. SAUV BL, PINOT GR, RIES, rosé, intense fizz (3 yrs+ on lees). Mid-tier: Pencarrow (gd value). Bottom tier: The Luminary.

Pask Hawk ★★→★★★ Key pioneer of GIMBLETT GRAVELS, now with ownership link to JACKSON ESTATE. Vibrant CHARD, MERLOT, SYRAH; Declaration range is best.

Passage Rock Waih ★★→★★★ Star performer on show circuit, based on warm site on island's se coast. Powerful, dark SYRAHS; complex, rich CAB SAUV blends; robust, ripe CHARD, VIOGNIER.

Pegasus Bay Waip ★★ →★★★★ Family firm best known for RIES (dr/s/sw/sw), PINOT N, but classy CHARD, SAUV BL, GEWURZ, MERLOT/CAB, CAB FR. Second label: Main Divide, top value. Aged Release: 10 yrs old.

Peregrine C Ot ★★ Architecturally inspired winery, "blade of light" roof. Vibrant whites, esp PINOT GR; smooth-flowing PINOT N; 2nd tier, Saddleback, gd value.

Pernod Ricard NZ Auck ★→★★★★ Wineries in HAWK, MARL. Huge-selling BRANCOTT ESTATE SAUV BL. Major strength in fizz, esp big-selling DEUTZ Marl Cuvée. Recent collaboration with MUMM (C OT Blanc de Noirs NV). Wonderful-value CHURCH ROAD CHARD and reds. Other key brand: STONELEIGH.

Prophet's Rock C Ot ★★★ Small, top producer. Alsace-style PINOT GR, Dry RIES,

CHARD. Savoury PINOT N; Home Vyd: high-altitude site, long barrel-ageing. Top: authoritative Cuvée Aux Antipodes Pinot N, 3rd-tier Rocky Point.

Puriri Hills Auck ★★★→★★★★ Distinguished, Bx-style MERLOT-based blends from small vyd. Estate, ripe, earthy; reserve Harmonie Du Soir, more new oak. Top: Pope has wow factor.

Pyramid Valley Cant ★★★ Classy, distinctive. Originally flinty CHARD, perfumed PINOT N from inland, elevated site in N CANT. Now other single-vyd and regional wines, incl MARL SAUV BL, C OT Pinot N. *See also* SMITH & SHETH CRU.

Quartz Reef C Ot ★★★ Pioneer of elevated, warm Bendigo district; n-facing slope, sandy clay soils. Small, bio. Perfumed, deep PINOT N, v. stylish fizz. Also rich CHARD, GRÜNER V, PINOT GR, rosé (all dry).

Rapaura Springs Marl ★★→★★★ Finely crafted, gd-value CHARD, PINOT N, SAUV BL. Revealing Rohe subregional range, esp Blind River Sauv Bl.

Rippon Vineyard C Ot ★★★→★★★★ Pioneer vyd on gentle schist slope, on shores of Lake Wanaka – much-published view, incl rabbits. Fragrant, savoury style. Mature Vine PINOT N is "the farm voice". Majestic Tinker's Field Pinot N: oldest vines, age-worthy. Striking GAMAY. Wanaka Village: drink-young Pinot N.

Rockburn C Ot ★★→★★★★ Refined estate-grown PINOT N, off-dry PINOT GR, vibrant CHARD. Silky Gibbston Vyd and Parkburn Vyd reds, barrel-selected. Scented, lively wines, enjoyable young, but age-worthy.

Rock Ferry Marl ★★★ Highly individual; organic estate vyds in C OT, MARL. Weighty, dry, concentrated. Graceful NEBBIOLO. Powerful, C Ot PINOT N, esp Mid Hill.

Sacred Hill Hawk ★★→★★★ Acclaimed Riflemans CHARD from mature vines on spectacular elevated site, cool, low fertility. Rich Brokenstone MERLOT, Helmsman CAB/Merlot, Deerstalkers SYRAH from GIMBLETT GRAVELS; gd-value MARL SAUV BL, PINOT GR.

Saint Clair Marl ★★→★★★ Best known for pungent SAUV BL, esp Dillons Point district in lower WAIRAU V (hints of sea salt). Large range of single-vyd Pioneer Block. Top: Res. James Sinclair: subregional focus. Origin: large-volume regional blends. Vicar's Choice, everyday. Also owns DELTA, Lake Chalice.

Seifried Estate Nel ★★ Region's biggest winery, family-owned. Perfumed GEWURZ, medium-dry RIES, punchy SAUV BL all gd value; 3rd-tier Old Coach Road. Top: Winemakers Collection. NZ's only Wurzer, ZWEIGELT.

Selaks Marl ★→★★ Croatian pioneer winery, now supermarket brand of CONSTELLATION NZ. Origins (regional): solid, easy-drinking. Mid-tier: The Taste Collection. Top: Founders. Some wines now from Australian grapes (cheaper).

Seresin Marl ★★→★★★ Organic; owned by film-maker Michael S. Grown on n-facing clay soils in Raupo Creek Vyd, Omaka V. Sophisticated SAUV BL one of NZ's finest. Intense RIES (dr/s/sw/sw); complex CHARD Res, single-vyd PINOT N; v.gd-value Momo range, esp dry rosé.

Sileni Hawk ★★ Estate vyds in warm Bridge Pa Triangle and on inland, cooler sites. Strong Grand Res range, incl complex Lodge CHARD, dark, rich Triangle MERLOT, spicy Peak SYRAH. Cellar Selection (rosé, MARL SAUV BL) gd value.

50 years since NZ's first Sauvignon Blanc, Matua Valley 1974, hit the shelves.

Smith & Sheth Cru Hawk ★★→★★★ Partnership of US billionaire Brian Sheth and viticulturist Steve Smith. Single-vyd range, mature vines. Fleshy ALBARIÑO, complex CHARD, delicious, SYRAH-based rosé, rich Syrah, CAB FR. Lush Cantera (CABS SAUV/FR, TEMPRANILLO). (*See also* PYRAMID V.)

Spy Valley Marl ★★→★★★ Waihopai V was used for monitoring satellite comms, hence name. Whites gd value: esp fragrant, fleshy PINOT GR, rich GEWURZ, part-oak-aged SAUV BL. Easy Tiger: gd, low-alc Sauv Bl. Generous, harmonious PINOT N. Envoy, top selection (esp RIES).

Starborough Family Estates Marl ★★ Family-owned vyds in AWATERE V, WAIRAU V. Full CHARD, dryish PINOT GR, racy SAUV BL (top value), generous PINOT N.

Stonecroft Hawk, Marl ★★ Small, organic GIMBLETT GRAVELS winery with NZ's oldest SYRAH vines, planted 1984. Dense, age-worthy Res, fruity Undressed (no sulphur added), drink-young Serine. Excellent CHARD, GEWURZ, VIOGNIER, CAB SAUV. NZ's only ZIN.

NZ's coastline is c.15,000 km; but only 1600 km north to south as the albatross flies.

Stoneleigh Marl ★★ Owned by PERNOD RICARD NZ. Based on relatively warm, stony Rapaura vyds. Huge-selling SAUV BL. Top: Rapaura Series. Wild Valley: native yeasts. Organic range (gd rosé, CHARD); Latitude range designed to be full-on.

Stonyridge Waih ★★★→★★★★ Boutique winery; poor, free-draining clay, threaded with decomposed rock. Popular vyd restaurant. Famous for CAB SAUV blend Larose. Dense SYRAH-based Pilgrim, bold Luna Negra MALBEC ("like going on an energetic dance with a Cuban beauty queen").

Te Kairanga Mart ★★→★★★ One of district's oldest, largest. New hospitality centre. Attractive CHARD, PINOT GR, RIES, gd-value PINOT N; 3rd-tier Runholder; 2nd-tier John Martin Pinot N. Luxury WPF (William Patrick Foley) Pinot N.

Te Mata Hawk ★★★→★★★★ CAB SAUV flourishes in Havelock North Hills, sheltered by Te Mata Peak. Coleraine 13' 14' 15' 16 17 18 19' 20' 21', Bx style, breed, longevity. Lower-priced Awatea Cabs/Merlot also classy. Bullnose SYRAH among NZ's finest. Powerful Alma HAWK PINOT N. Weighty Elston CHARD; soft Zara VIOGNIER, oak-aged Cape Crest SAUV BL. Estate Vyds for gd-value early drinking.

Te Pa Marl ★★→★★★ Home vyd on Wairau Bar, archaeological site with ancient *pa* (fortified settlements). Vibrantly fruity CHARD, off-dry RIES, SAUV BL, PINOT N, rosé all gd value. Top: Res Collection, incl intense Seaside Sauv Bl.

Terra Sancta C Ot ★★→★★★ Bannockburn's 1st vyd, at end of Felton Road. Fragrant Mysterious Diggings PINOT N, early drinking; generous, mid-tier Bannockburn Pinot N; Slapjack Block Pinot N from district's oldest vines (1991). Pinot N Rosé one of NZ's finest. Special Release First Vines, NZ's highest-priced rosé.

Te Whare Ra Marl ★★ Label: TWR. Region's 1st boutique winery, still small. Perfumed GEWURZ, punchy RIES, SAUV BL, Toru ("three"): Gewurz/Ries/PINOT GR.

Tiki Marl ★★ McKean family owns extensive vyds in MARL, WAIP. Fresh, fruit-focused. Single-vyds, esp generous N CANT SAUV BL, PINOT N. Hariata NV: complex fizz. Second label: Maui.

Tohu Marl, Nel ★★ Maori-owned venture. Tight-knit Rewa Blanc de Blancs. Incisive AWATERE V SAUV BL, lively PINOT GR. Top: Whenua Awa Single Vyd CHARD, PINOT N.

Trinity Hill Hawk ★★→★★★★ Quality, value. Extensive vyds in GIMBLETT GRAVELS. Stylish CHARD, fleshy MARSANNE/VIOGNIER, spicy SYRAH, refined The Gimblett (Bx r blend). Majestic Homage Syrah 14' 15' 16 17 18' 19' 20' 21'. Weighty TEMPRANILLO. Lower-tier white-label range gd value.

Two Paddocks C Ot ★★ Actor Sir Sam Neill makes several PINOT N. Vibrant main label; also single-vyd Prop Res: herbal First Paddock (Gibbston), riper Last Chance (Alexandra), earthy The Fusilier (Bannockburn). Drink-young Picnic. Au Naturel Pinot N: organic, no added preservatives, silky-textured, delicious.

Two Rivers Marl ★★→★★★ Vibrant, penetrating wines. Vivacious Convergence SAUV BL, striking Saint Maur Sauv Bl (aged in concrete egg, clay amphora). Excellent CHARD, RIES, Isle of Beauty Rose (dr), PINOT N (esp Brookby Hill). Second label: Black Cottage v.gd value.

Valli C Ot ★★★ Grant Taylor, ex-GIBBSTON V winemaker, makes impressive single-vyd PINOT N. WAITAKI V PINOT GR, rich, ripe in favourable vintages.

Vavasour Marl ★★→★★★ Original pioneer of AWATERE V. Now owned by US billionaire Bill Foley. Rich CHARD, off-dry PINOT GR; punchy SAUV BL. Generous

PINOT N; classy dry rosé. New, generous, complex Papa ("mudstone") CHARD, Sauv Bl: home block, mature vines.

Vidal Hawk ★★ Founded 1905. Owned by VILLA MARIA. Top Legacy, Soler selections dropped, leaving standard and Res ranges. Both have top-value HAWK CHARD and MERLOT/CAB, MARL SAUV BL.

Villa Maria Auck ★★→★★★ Owned by MARI-based Indevin, promises to "protect brand value". Also owns ESK V, VIDAL. Distinguished top ranges: Single Vyd (individual sites) and Res (regional character). Cellar Selection (less oak) excellent, superb value (esp HAWK CHARD, MERLOT). Huge-volume Private Bin range can also be v.gd. Three icon wines: oak-aged Woven Marl SAUV BL, dense CAB SAUV-based Ngakirikiri; superb Attorney Marl PINOT N.

Waiheke Island Helipad heaven at lovely, sprawling, touristy island. Hilly sites, handpicking, sea transport, high prices. Acclaim since 80s for stylish CAB SAUV/MERLOT blends, esp from warm Onetangi district (clay soils); more recently for bold SYRAH. Rare, classy MONTEPULCIANO. Sturdy CHARD, VIOGNIER.

Waimea Nel ★★ One of region's largest, owned by investment fund. Reputation for gd-value, aromatic whites; 2nd-tier Spinyback.

Waipara Valley Cant Dominant CANT subregion, n of Christchurch. Gravelly soils on flats, and richer, clay-based soils on e hills. Hot, dry nor'westerlies devigorate vines. (Trees, even power poles, lean with the winds.) High profile for complex PINOT N, intense RIES (also heavy plantings of PINOT GR, SAUV BL). Rising organic output. Increasingly calling itself "North Canterbury".

Wairarapa NZ's 7th-largest wine region (not to be confused with WAIP). *See* MART. Also incl Gladstone subregion in n (slightly higher, cooler, wetter). Driest, coolest region in N Island, but exposed to cold s winds, reducing crops. Strength in whites: SAUV BL esp widely planted, CHARD, PINOT GR, RIES. Acclaimed since mid-80s for sturdy, warm, savoury PINOT N. Starting to promote itself as "Wellington Wine Country".

Wairau Valley Marl Largest MARL subregion. Wairau means "many waters". Biggest town Blenheim gateway to 30+ cellar doors, but many producers don't own wineries, using large contract-winemaking facilities. Three important side valleys to s (Southern V): Brancott, Omaka, Waihopai. SAUV BL thrives on pancake-flat plains, shingly soils speed-ripening, giving riper, more tropical-fruit notes. PINOT N on clay-based, n-facing slopes. Much recent planting in wetter, more frost-prone upper Wairau V.

Waitaki Valley Small subregion in N Ot, limestone, frost-prone. Much hyped by wealthy land speculators in 2000, but just three producers. Promising PINOT N, can be leafy; scented PINOT GR, RIES superb in top vintages.

Whitehaven Marl ★★ Part-owned by Gallo. Flavour-packed SAUV BL, RIES (s/sw), CHARD, PINOT GR (dr). Generous PINOT N. Top range: Greg.

Wither Hills Marl ★★ Big producer owned by Lion brewery. Best known for vibrant SAUV BL, but harmonious PINOT N also gd value. Intense Single Vyd Rarangi Sauv Bl from coastal site.

Kiwi-designed, biodegradable vine clips to replace 30m plastic clips used/year to hold nets/keep pests at bay.

Yealands Marl ★★ NZ's biggest "single vyd" (about 1000 ha), at coastal AWATERE V site, owned by utility firm Marlborough Lines. Partly estate-grown, mostly MARL. High profile for sustainability, but most not certified organic. Best known for pungent green-capsicum Marl SAUV BL, zesty Res Awatere Sauv Bl. Supple Res PINOT N; drink young. Other key brands: Babydoll, The Crossings.

Zephyr Marl ★★→★★★ Family vyd in lower WAIRAU V, bounded by Opawa River. Impressive whites: Alsace-style PINOT GR, generous PINOT N.

South Africa

Abbreviations used in the text:

Bre	Breedekloof		Oli R	Olifants River
Cdorp	Calitzdorp		Pie	Piekenierskloof
Cape SC	Cape South Coast		Pri	Prieska
Ced	Cederberg		Rob	Robertson
Coast	Coastal Region		Sim-P	Simonsberg-Paarl
Const	Constantia		Stell	Stellenbosch
Ela	Elandskloof		Swa	Swartland
Elg	Elgin		Tul	Tulbagh
Fran	Franschhoek		V Pa	Voor Paardeberg
Hem	Hemel-en-Aarde		Wlk B	Walker Bay
Rdg/Up/V	Ridge/Upper/Valley		Well	Wellington
Kl K	Klein Karoo			

South Africa, obviously, is not one place. It encompasses not just many climates and terroirs, but many traditions too. For Cabernet-lovers, South Africa means Stellenbosch; for Pinot-lovers, Hemel-en-Aarde; for Chardonnay-lovers, perhaps Elgin. Sauvignon-lovers know Elim, and Chenin Blanc-lovers know Swartland and its many-faceted and sometimes mysterious blends. But while these neat pigeonholes are easy to remember, it's worth bearing in mind that soil diversity and adventurous growers also mean that you might find aromatic Syrah from Elim and Cabernet from Hemel-en-Aarde. Even that home of perfumed Muscat, Constantia, makes some chewy Nebbiolo. In Breedekloof, there are multiple expressions of Chenin Blanc, from fruit-sweet to savoury-dry, and varying levels of, say, Pinotage, including an innovative blend with Carignan. In Stellenbosch, you can also find Assyrtiko, that charismatic Greek white that, with other exotics like Viura and Albariño, is being planted across the winelands potentially to help with the climate challenge. For the same reason, there is increased interest in cooler areas like Lower Duivenhoks River on the Cape South Coast, and development of new, high, inland sites such as Karoo-Hoogland near Sutherland, South Africa's coldest town. Common to many areas are old vines (defined as 35 years plus, though many are properly old); Stellenbosch has the most. And heirloom grapes like Pontac (Teinturier du Cher) are clawing their way back from near-extinction with recent plantings in Swartland and Paarl, inter alia.

Recent vintages
2023 Cool kick-off for whites and early reds, wet 2nd half needed steady nerves.
2022 Smaller crop, but slow ripening built flavour while preserving freshness.
2021 Late but bountiful, gd early rains, cool conditions. Much excitement (r/w).
2020 A humdinger: exceptional structure, intensity, verve, with moderate alc.
2019 Another arid yr, but milder temps balance concentrated fruit/freshness.

AA Badenhorst Family Wines Swa ★★→★★★★ From mid-2000s, prime-mover Adi B helped revolutionize SA's wine aesthetic, approach, with subtle, savoury-edged bottlings from Med and trad varieties like CHENIN BL – accenting site, old vines, wild yeasts et al. Secateurs label "second" only in price.

Alheit Vineyards W Cape ★★★★ Chris and Suzaan A brought novelty to the avant-garde in 2010s: an explorer's approach, seeking out individual CHENIN BL pockets on Cape coast to vinify alongside sublime multi-site Cartology. Latterly also SEM. Mostly old vines, but younger field blend (w) from HEM home farm as exciting.

Anthonij Rupert Wyne W Cape ★→★★★★ Wide, impressive portfolio honours owner Johann R's late brother. Some exceptional 3rd-party vyds in acclaimed Cape of Good Hope collection but mostly own vines, incl old CHENIN BL transplanted lock, stock and tendril from SWA to FRAN home estate. Upcyclable Protea range an eye- and pocket-pleaser.

Anysbos Bot R ★★★ Heyns family's pair of blends, GRENACHE N- and CHENIN BL-led, aromas hinting at the anise in brand name. Winemaker Marelise Niemann also crafts her praised Momento label (mostly GRENACHE BL and N, rare solo Tinta Barocca) on-site.

Babylonstoren Sim-P ★★→★★★ Media tycoon Koos Bekker and wife Karen Roos's reinvigorated C17 wine-and-lifestyle farm nr PAARL with every imaginable amenity, incl awarded wine museum. Lineup led by plush, long-haul-styled Bx-style blend Nebukadnesar. The Newt in Somerset is sibling property in UK.

Bartho Eksteen Estate Wine W Cape ★★★→★★★★ Eksteen clan's boutique in HEM V, Bartho (CWG member) and son Pieter Willem make elegant SAUV BL, SYRAH. Also run academy ("Wijnskool", with own namesake label) for aspiring vintners, hence pedagogy-themed wine names. Pieter and Argentinian wife Sol make steak-friendly MALBEC from STELL under Yerden Eksteen brand.

Bartinney Private Cellar W Cape ★★→★★★★ Rose and Michael Jordaan's boutique winery and panorama on steep Simonsberg slopes; classic CHARD, CAB SAUV; recently acquired Plaisir estate on warmer side of mtn hitting its straps; lifestyle range Noble Savage and newly relaunched mid-tier Montegray.

South Africa's per capita wine consumption: 7 litres. Uber-thirsty Portugal: 50 litres.

Beaumont Family Wines Cape SC ★★★→★★★★ Excellent Bot R estate with old-time ambience and suitably gnarled vines. Handmade wines incl superlative CHENIN BL and newer (w) blend New Baby. Matriarch Jayne B's CHARD and PINOT N worthy complements.

Beck, Graham W Cape ★★→★★★★ A-list CAP CLASSIQUE house nr ROB with portfolio that ticks the consumer boxes: vintage-dated and NV, Brut to Demi-Sec, water-white to salmon-hued. (Delicious) surprises in Artisan Collection, eg. Extra Brut on lees 157 mths.

BEE (Black Economic Empowerment) Initiative aimed at increasing wine-industry ownership and participation by previously disadvantaged groups. Now with fillip from new non-profit company South Africa Wine, helping industry "to become more robust, transformed, agile and competitive".

Heritage vyds (35 years and older) recognized by Old Vine Project now c.4300 ha.

Beeslaar Wines W Cape ★★★★ Masterclass in refined PINOTAGE by outgoing KANONKOP winemaker Abrie B. Thrilling eg. of trad styling taken to next level.

Bellingham W Cape ★★→★★★ Enduring DGB brand with v.gd fruit-driven limited releases The Bernard and newer The Founders, homage to World War Two-era couple, Pod and Freda Podlashuk.

Benguela Cove Lagoon Wine Estate Wlk B ★★★ Penny Streeter OBE's cellar, vyds and destination on Bot R lagoon. Top wine is SEM named Catalina for flying boat based on estuary in World War Two. Johann Fourie also crafts Penny's UK wines (Leonardslee and Mannings Heath), plus those of now US-owned SA-wine brand Brew Cru.

Beyerskloof W Cape ★★→★★★★ PINOTAGE champion nr STELL: 11 fruit-forward versions (12, incl spirit for "port"), soloists, blends, blush. Equally fine CAB SAUV from 1st vines planted 1988/9 by co-founder Beyers Truter.

Boekenhoutskloof Winery W Cape ★→★★★★ Among SA's most important producers, for quality and volume, based in FRAN. Enviable consistency 40 yrs+ under Boekenhoutskloof and Porcupine Ridge labels, later Wolftrap range and stand-alone ventures in HEM, SWA (*see* CAP MARITIME, PORSELEINBERG). New CAB SAUV/CINSAULT Helderberg Winery Res a homage to trad STELL blends.

Bon Courage Estate W Cape ★→★★★ Bruwer family nr ROB with stylish Brut CAP CLASSIQUE trio, aromatic desserts (MUSCAT, RIES) in broad range.

Boplaas Family Vineyards W Cape ★→★★★ Carel Nel and family at CDORP, known for "port" and deep-flavoured table wines of Portuguese grapes (r/w).

Boschendal Wines W Cape ★→★★★ Evergreen DGB brand on hospitable C17 estate nr FRAN. Fruit-forward Bx/Rhône (r/w) blends, CHARD, SAUV BL, SHIRAZ, CAP CLASSIQUE in various tiers.

Boschkloof Wines W Cape ★★★→★★★★ Reenen Borman in STELL with, eg., stellar SYRAH under Boschkloof (home farm's name), Kottabos labels. With partners, notable Saga Vyds (was Patatsfontein) bottlings (w) from unsung area Montagu.

Botanica Wines Stell ★★→★★★ Superlative CHENIN BL from old w-coast bush vines and newer ALBARIÑO from wine- and flower-growing home farm nr STELL, owned/made by American Ginny Povall.

Bouchard Finlayson Cape SC ★★★→★★★★ Family-owned HEM pioneer, with v. fine expressions of PINOT N, CHARD, latter incl unoaked version, among SA's best.

Breedekloof Breede River V DISTRICT (c.12,700 ha) previously bulk- and entry-level-focused, lately lifted by new generation, often working with heritage vines.

Brookdale Estate Paarl ★→★★★ Dynamic UK-owned mtn-side winery advised by eminent Duncan SAVAGE, with refined old-vine CHENIN BL and field blend (w).

Bruce Jack Wines W Cape ★★→★★★ From home base nr Napier, multi-tasking Bruce J makes varietals, blends, fizz from unusual grapes for estate label The Drift; collaborates with others for namesake international brand; produces Mary Le Bow (r blend) and VIOGNIER, both US-oak scented, and newer range Ghost In The Machine, incl lemony version of heirloom grape CLAIRETTE BL. Now owns boutique brand The Berrio, starring racy SAUV BL from Africa's windblown tip.

Buitenverwachting W Cape ★★→★★★ Family farm in CONST with lovely trad feel yet modern, forthright wines CHARD, SAUV BL, Bx-style reds and varying mix of Ltd Releases. "Bayten" for export.

Calitzdorp KL K DISTRICT (c.270 ha) with similar climate to Douro V (*see* Portugal), known for "port" and lately unfortified Port-grape wines (r/w).

Cap classique Bottle-fermented sparkling still officially known as "méthode cap classique" but producers urging use of shortened version. Major success: labels have more than doubled the past decade, to 400+.

Cape Blend Usually red with a significant PINOTAGE component; occasionally a CHENIN BL blend, or simply wine with "Cape character".

Cape Coast Umbrella appellation ("OVERARCHING REGION" in officialese) for Coast (w and central) and CAPE SC regions.

Capensis W Cape ★★★→★★★★ Starry venture in STELL specializing in sophisticated CHARD, multi-site and single-vyd, now wholly owned by US Jackson Family's Barbara Banke. *See also* DALKEITH.

Cape Point Vineyards W Cape ★→★★★★ Family winery nr tip of CAPE TOWN peninsula. Cellarable Bx-style (w), CHARD, SAUV BL. Sibling to Cape Town Wine Co.

Cape Rock Wines W Cape ★★→★★★ Oli R's leading boutique grower. Characterful, strikingly packaged Rhône- and Port-grape varietals and blends (r/w).

Cape South Coast Cool-climate REGION (c.2610 ha) comprising DISTRICTS of Cape Agulhas, ELG, Lower Duivenhoks River, Overberg, Plettenberg Bay, Swellendam, WLK B, plus stand-alone WARDS Herbertsdale, Napier, Stilbaai E. *See also* CAPE COAST.

Cape Town Coast DISTRICT (c.2600 ha) covering namesake city, its peninsula WARDS, CONST and Hout B, plus nearby wards DURBANVILLE and Philadelphia.

Cape West Coast Only subregion; incl Darling and Lutzville V DISTRICTS, plus Bamboes Bay, Lamberts B and part of St Helena B WARDS. *See also* CAPE COAST.

Cap Maritime Cape SC ★★★ Classy CHARD, PINOT N specialist in UP HEM owned by BOEKENHOUTSKLOOF. Great success with bought-in grapes while own young vyds mature.

Catherine Marshall Wines W Cape ★★★ Cool-climate (chiefly ELG) specialist Cathy M focused on CHENIN BL, SAUV BL, PINOT N and dry, mineral RIES.

Cederberg Tiny (c.100 ha), high-altitude, free-standing WARD in the Cederberg Mtns. Mostly CHENIN BL and SHIRAZ. CEDERBERG PRIVATE CELLAR and Driehoek the main producers.

Cederberg Private Cellar W Cape ★★→★★★★ Nieuwoudt family with among highest (CED) and most s (ELIM) vyds. Make mostly varietals and bubbly, incl exceptional CWG SHIRAZ. David N shareholder in exciting new Escape Wines overlooking Bot R lagoon.

Central Orange River DISTRICT (c.7500 ha) in N CAPE GU. Hot, dry, irrigated; trad white (most is Sultana for dried/table grapes) and fortified, but major producer ORANGE RIVER CELLARS pushing envelope with eg. SHIRAZ.

Certified Heritage Vineyard *See* OLD VINE PROJECT.

Chamonix Wine Farm Fran, Stell ★★→★★★ Top cellar and vyds overlooking FRAN, also sourcing grapes from STELL. Age-worthy CHARD, PINOT N, Bx varietals and blends (r/w).

Need exercise? Try padel tennis, now at Avontuur and Lourensford cellar doors.

Charles Fox Cap Classique Wines Elg ★★★ A trad-method bubbly house co-founded by 1964 Olympics swimmer, with eight classic, delicious Bruts.

Coastal Region Largest REGION (c.43,900 ha); incl sea-influenced CAPE TOWN, DARLING, Lutzville V, STELL and SWA DISTRICTS, plus Bamboes Bay WARD. Also incl non-maritime FRAN, PAARL, TUL, WELL DISTRICTS.

Colmant Cap Classique & Champagne W Cape ★★★→★★★★ Sparkling house in FRAN, owned by a Belgian family. Brut Nature, Brut, Sec and Nectar, all NV and excellent.

Constantia CAPE TOWN WARD (c.420 ha), est 1685 on cool Constantiaberg slopes; SA's 1st and most historically famous growing area, still a pace-setter.

Constantia Glen Const ★★★ Waibel family-owned model of consistency and quality on upper Constantiaberg. Trio of Bx blends (r/w), solo SAUV BL.

Constantia Uitsig W Cape ★★→★★★ Prime vyds, cellar and multi-faceted cellar door in CONST. Makes mostly still white, incl new aromatic sweet MUSCAT DE FRONTIGNAN named Gravitas.

Creation Wines W Cape ★★★→★★★★ Buzzy, inventive cellar door and bold flavours vie for attention/awards at scenic estate in HEM RDG, part-owned by Martin family. Standouts: CHARD, PINOT N, incl versions by daughter and son.

Crystallum W Cape ★★★→★★★★ Always impressive and satisfying CHARD and PINOT N from cool sites, mostly ELA, HEM, vinified at GABRIËLSKLOOF by Peter-Allan Finlayson, brand co-owner with brother Andrew.

CWG (Cape Winemakers Guild) Independent, invitation-only association of 41 top growers. Stages benchmarking annual auction of limited premium bottlings.

Dalkeith Stell, Swa ★★★ Pair of fine, textured CHENIN BL, siblings to CAPENSIS CHARD trio in Cape portfolio of California's Jackson Family.

Darling DISTRICT (c.2500 ha) around this w-coast town. Best vyds in hilly Groenekloof WARD. Most fruit goes into 3rd-party brands, some spectacular.

David & Nadia Swa ★★★★ Quietly arresting sextet of CHENIN BL (single- and multi-site, latter incl new CWG bottling), blends (r/w), GRENACHE N, PINOTAGE, mostly from heritage vyds, by Sadie husband and wife on Paardeberg Mtn-side.

David Finlayson Wines Coast ★★→★★★ Expressive, fruit-forward, incl mostly old-vine Camino Africana series, by 3rd-generation vintner David F nr STELL.

De Grendel Wines W Cape ★★★ Sir De Villiers Graaff's Table Mtn-facing venture in DURBANVILLE draws on own and far-flung contracted vyds. Showy lineup led by Op Die Berg SYRAH from elevated Ceres Plateau and magnum-only ELIM SHIRAZ from SA's most s vines.

De Krans Wines W Cape ★→★★★ Nel family at CDORP noted for Port styles and fortified MUSCAT. Success with robust unfortified (r/w) from Portuguese grapes.

Delaire Graff Estate W Cape ★★→★★★★ UK diamond merchant Laurence Graff's eyrie vyds, winery and visitor venue nr STELL. Glittering portfolio headed by age-worthy CAB SAUV Laurence Graff Res.

Delheim Wines Coast ★→★★★ Eco-minded family venture nr STELL. PINOTAGE (powerful single-block, charming rosé), cellar-worthy CAB SAUV Grand Res, ever-scintillating botrytis RIES.

DeMorgenzon W Cape ★★→★★★★ Gorgeous music-themed family winery on

---

You can, but should you?

Wine in aluminium cans – approved by regulators in 2019 and touted with a panoply of benefits, from ready recyclability to take-anywhere light weight and compactness – was slow off the mark but is now accelerating nicely. The latest (revised) official figures suggest that volume doubled, to 1.4m litres, between 2021 and 2022. That's just 0.3% of all still wine, but a vindication and boost for, eg., Renegade Wines, which pioneered the format with its CanCan brand and wines named for late C19 French cabaret stars. Other labels worth trying: Black Elephant Vintners' Yes, You Can range, incl a PINOT N; Perdeberg Winery's Soft Smooth Can, with dab of sugar for extra crowd appeal; Vinette Wine, with inter alia a perlé Rosé.

STELL hilltop hits high notes with Res CHARD, CHENIN BL (incl vine-selected The Divas), Maestro Bx and Rhône blends (r/w), DMZ stylish early drinkers.

De Trafford Wines Elg, Stell ★★★→★★★★ Trafford family's boutique venture on saddle between STELL and Helderberg mtns, reputed for unabashedly bold wines, eg. Bx-style/SHIRAZ Elevation 393, CAB SAUV (incl new version from Belfield vyd in ELG), SYRAH, CHENIN BL (dr/sw). *See* SIJNN.

First commercial bottling of Lledoner Pelut, hairy Grenache, by Swa's Kloovenburg.

DGB W Cape Long-est producer/wholesaler in WELL/FRAN. Owns/controls high-end brands Backsberg, BELLINGHAM, BOSCHENDAL, Fryer's Cove, Old Road. Also easy-drinking labels, eg. newer Vineyard Friends, some export-only.

Diemersdal Estate W Cape ★→★★★ DURBANVILLE Louw family excelling with confident, full-fruited site-, row-, style-specific CAB SAUV, PINOTAGE, CHARD, SAUV BL and SA's only commercial GRÜNER V.

Distell *See* Heineken Beverages.

District *See* GU.

Dorrance Wines W Cape ★→★★★★ French family boutique, with cellar in CAPE TOWN city heritage building. Delicate, consistently excellent CHARD, CHENIN BL, SYRAH. Newer PINOT N Cuvée Monrache La Culotte.

Durbanville Cool, hilly WARD (c.1370 ha) in CAPE TOWN DISTRICT, best known for SAUV BL and whites generally.

Durbanville Hills Dur ★→★★★ Area pioneer, owned by HEINEKEN BEVERAGES, local growers and staff, noted for generous, fruit-focused styling and fair prices. Excellent pinnacle Bx blends, Tangram (r/w); entry-level SAUV BL appears on every wine list.

Eagles' Nest Const ★★★ Constantiaberg mtn-side winery, now German-owned, with reliably superior VIOGNIER, MERLOT, SHIRAZ. Also vibrant SAUV BL.

Elgin Cool-climate DISTRICT (c.720 ha) recognized for CHARD, SAUV BL, PINOT N. Exciting CHENIN BL, RIES, SYRAH, CAP CLASSIQUE. Mostly family boutiques.

Elim Windswept WARD (c.150 ha) in most S DISTRICT, Cape Agulhas, producing aromatic white blends, SAUV BL, SYRAH. Grape source for majors and boutiques.

Ernie Els Wines W Cape ★→★★★★ Star golfer's wine venture nr STELL, centred on CAB SAUV: four cellar-worthy labels, earlier-ready Big Easy tier. Co-proprietor Baron Hans von Staff-Reitzenstein also owns eminent STELLENZICHT and Alto nearby.

Estate wine Grown, made and bottled on "units registered for the production of estate wine". Not a quality designation.

Fairview W Cape ★→★★★ Back family's caprine-themed wine and cheese venture on panoramic Paarl Mtn farm, sourcing on-site and more widely for cornucopia of varietal, blended, single-vyd and fizzy bottlings under Fairview, Goats do Roam, La Capra, Spice Route and Klein Amoskuil labels. Bustling, multi-faceted cellar-door experience, incl famous goat herd and tower.

FirstCape Vineyards W Cape ★→★★ Huge export venture involving four Breede River V cellars. Mostly entry-level wines in multiple ranges.

Flagstone Winery W Cape ★→★★★ Accolade Wines' high-end winery, housed in a former glycerine refinery at Somerset W, sourcing widely for plush-fruited PINOTAGE, Bx-style (w), SAUV BL et al. Mid-tier Fish Hoek, entry-level KUMALA sibling brands.

Fleur du Cap W Cape ★→★★★ HEINEKEN BEVERAGES premium label, with opulent headliner Laszlo (Bx r blend) and v.gd Series Privée Unfiltered CHARD, MERLOT.

Foundry, The Stell, V Pa ★★★→★★★★ Among 1st to focus on the Rhône (r/w) in 2000. Cellar and more source vyds in PAARL's V Pa but still mostly STELL grapes for elegantly crafted original and newer Geographica varietal bottlings.

Franschhoek Huguenot-founded DISTRICT (c.1150 ha) known for CHARD, SEM, CAB SAUV and CAP CLASSIQUE. Home to some of SA's oldest farms and vines.

Free State Province and GU. Mile High Vyds sole producer (under The Bald Ibis label) in viticulturally challenging e highlands.

Gabriëlskloof W Cape ★→★★★ CWG member and CRYSTALLUM co-owner Peter-Allan Finlayson makes this lauded range in family cellar nr Bot R. Emphasis on CHENIN BL, CAB FR and site/technique-based expressions of SYRAH.

Glenelly Estate Stell ★★★→★★★★ May-Eliane de Lencquesaing's (Bx eminence) "retirement" venture in STELL. Glossy flagships Lady May (Bx-style r), Res CHARD and Bx-style/SHIRAZ. Remarkable glass collection at cellar door.

Groot Constantia Estate Const ★★★ Magnet attracting 450,000 visitors to beautifully preserved farmstead and SA's longest-producing cellar. Suitably eminent wines, esp MUSCAT DE FRONTIGNAN Grand Constance helping restore CONST dessert to C18 glory.

GU (geographical unit) Largest of the wo demarcations: FREE STATE, KWAZULU-NATAL and LIMPOPO, plus E, N, W Cape – last three constitute the OVERARCHING GU known as Greater Cape. Other WO appellations (in descending size): overarching region, REGION, subregion, DISTRICT and WARD.

Hamilton Russell Vineyards Hem V ★★★→★★★★ The 1st to succeed with Burgundy grapes in cool S Cape in early 80s at Hermanus. Long-lived CHARD, elegant PINOT N under HRV banner. Same varieties in stand-alone employee brand Tesselaarsdal. Super SAUV BL, PINOTAGE in Southern Right and Ashbourne labels.

Hartenberg Estate W Cape ★★→★★★ Hospitality- and eco-minded family farm nr STELL with tiers of SHIRAZ/SYRAH; also fine CHARD, RIES (dr/s/sw/botrytis), Bx-style red.

Heineken Beverages SA's biggest drinks company, a 2023 merger of Distell,

---

The "impossibility" of Pinot Noir

Though closely associated with the Cape's s coast, specifically ELG, HEM and Overberg, the roots of SA PINOT N lie elsewhere: on the mtns around STELL in the early 20s, where, it is thought, Alto Estate saw the v. 1st plantings, followed some yrs later by Muratie Estate on Simonsberg Mtn. The latter provided a more conducive and longer-lived home, and Muratie's remained the sole varietal bottling until the 70s, when a handful of enthusiasts, notably Tim HAMILTON RUSSELL, began pursuing their ideal (a pipe dream, most said at the time) of growing Burgundy's great red grape in local soil. Availability of alternative (French) clones to the ubiquitous Swiss "sparkling wine" BK5 was the turning point. In terms of footprint, Stell remains important, with 244 of the total 1171 ha under vine thanks to the CAP CLASSIQUE industry, as well as quality, with, eg., DAVID FINLAYSON, MEERLUST and now MULDERBOSCH producing exceptional wines. But, most top-league producers are in, or source from, cooler areas: pioneers BOUCHARD FINLAYSON, Hamilton Russell, OAK VALLEY; longer-est ventures like CAP MARITIME, CATHERINE MARSHALL, CREATION, CRYSTALLUM, IONA, KERSHAW, PAUL CLÜVER, SHANNON, STORM; and more recent top performers like Hasher, KARA-TARA and Saurwein. With just 1% of SA's vines, and 12th place on the list of national plantings, Pinot N remains a niche variety yet enjoys disproportionate cachet and a passionate following, plus a cottage industry dedicated to uncovering the ultimate gem: an affordable bottle. Value-seekers will find their grail in Iona's Mr P, THORNE & DAUGHTERS' Copper Pot and MULLINEUX employee brand Great Heart.

Namibia Breweries and Heineken SA, headquartered in upcountry Sandton. Owns or has interests in many wine brands, spanning styles/quality scales. *See* DURBANVILLE HILLS, FLEUR DU CAP, JC LE ROUX, NEDERBURG WINES.

Hemel-en-Aarde Trio of cool-climate WARDS (Hem V, Up Hem, Hem Rdg) in WLK B DISTRICT, producing outstanding CHARD, SAUV BL, PINOT N.

Chenin Blanc African style? Serve with crocodile, à la L'Avenir Vyds.

Iona Vineyards Cape SC ★★→★★★ Family winery in ELG co-owned by staff; excels with taut, mineral expressions of CHARD, SAUV BL, PINOT N. Also v. fine SYRAH under Wines of Brocha label. Well-priced lifestyle brand Sophie.

JC le Roux, The House of W Cape ★→★★ The 1st specialist fizz producer in 80s, now HEINEKEN BEVERAGES-owned with must-visit brand home nr STELL. CAP CLASSIQUE named Scintilla and carbonated, sugar-dabbed Nectar and Sélection Vivante sparklers, some trendily de-alcoholized.

Joostenberg Wines W Cape ★★→★★★ Organic family business nr PAARL with flavoursome SYRAH, CHENIN BL (incl sw botrytis) et al. Honours forebears via Myburgh Bros lineup. Also partners with STARK-CONDÉ in revitalized STELL estate Lievland, and in volume, value brand MAN Family Wines.

Jordan Wine Estate W Cape ★★→★★★★ Family venture nr STELL, admired for consistency, quality, value, from entry Chameleon to stellar CWG bottlings.

Kaapzicht Wine Estate Stell ★→★★★ Steytler family with charmingly packaged portfolio of boldly fruited wines, featuring, inter alia, SA's 2nd-oldest CHENIN BL.

Kanonkop Estate Coast ★★★→★★★★★ "First Growth" status since early 70s, mainly with (Bx-style r) Paul Sauer, CAB SAUV, PINOTAGE (regular and old-vine Black Label). Insatiable demand for 2nd-tier Kadette. Owns organic STELL neighbour Ladybird Vyds.

Kara-Tara W Cape ★★★ Former STARK-CONDÉ winemaker Rüdger van Wyk's young brand, featuring knockout Res PINOT N ex-Overberg. Also wider-sourced CHARD.

Keermont Vineyards Stell ★★★ Family estate on terraced slopes with intense CHENIN BL, SHIRAZ and more by recent CWG inductee Alex Starey. Neighbour and a grape supplier to A-league DE TRAFFORD.

Keet Wines Stell ★★★★ Owner-winemaker Chris K with single, beautifully crafted, classic Bx-blend First Verse.

Ken Forrester Wines W Cape ★→★★★ With French AdVini partners, STELL vintner Ken F sets a high bar for Med grapes and CHENIN BL (dr/sp/off-dry/ botrytis). Tasty trolley-fillers under Petit label. New range The Misfits gives co-winemaker Shawn Mathyse's creativity free rein.

Kershaw Wines W Cape ★★★→★★★★ UK-born MW Richard K's refined CHARD, PINOT N, SYRAH from ELG; constituent sites showcased in separate Deconstructed bottlings. GPS, Smuggler's Boot ranges spotlight other areas, new techniques, respectively.

Klein Constantia Estate W Cape ★★→★★★★ Iconic mtn-side property focused on SAUV BL and luscious, cellar-worthy non-botrytis MUSCAT DE FRONTIGNAN Vin de Constance, convincing re-creation of legendary C18 CONST. Sibling winery Anwilka (r) in STELL.

Kleine Zalze Wines W Cape ★→★★★★ A STELL star, majority-owned by France's AdVini. Family Res and Vyd Selection shine brightest; lab range Project Z tinkers spectacularly; Cellar Selection overachieves. Stand-alone BEE venture Visio Vintners uplifts staff.

Klein Karoo Region (c.2000 ha), mostly semi-arid and known for fortified, esp Port style in CDORP. Revived old vines feature in some premium terroir bottlings.

Krone W Cape ★★★ Made at Twee Jonge Gezellen estate in TUL. Krone label houses expanding collection of elegant, vintage-dated CAP CLASSIQUE (dr/off-dr) inspired by French grower-Champagne movement; tweaked sibling range TJG changes from pair of varietal wines to aromatic blends with CHENIN BL, GRENACHE N.

Kumala W Cape ★ Major entry-level export label, and sibling to premium Flagstone and mid-tier Fish Hoek. Owned by Accolade Wines (*see* Australia).

KwaZulu-Natal Province and GU on e coast; not-ideal tropical climate nr ocean; central plateau and, further n, Drakensberg foothills more propitious but no cakewalk. Abingdon Estate, Cathedral Peak, Highgate only producers.

Hail King Cardboard: bag-in-box now within whisker of half of all still wine sold.

KWV W Cape ★→★★★ Formerly national wine co-op and controlling body; today one of largest producers/exporters, based in PAARL. Close to a dozen labels, headed by serially decorated The Mentors.

Leeu Passant *See* MULLINEUX.

Le Lude Cap Classique W Cape ★★★→★★★★ Celebrated family-owned sparkling house in FRAN. Elegant offering incl CHARD/PINOT N Agrafe, 1st locally to undergo 2nd ferment under cork.

Le Riche Wines Stell ★★★→★★★★ Fine, modern-classic boutique CAB SAUV (varietal and "heritage" blend with CINSAULT) by Christo LR and siblings.

Limpopo Most n province and GU in wo system.

Lowerland Pri ★★★ Meaning "Verdant Land", part of family agribusiness in Prieska WARD beside Orange R. Area's most exciting winery, exuberant (r/w), unusual CAP CLASSIQUE from COLOMBARD vinified in w CAPE by top names.

Meerlust Estate Stell ★★★ Myburgh family-owned vyds, cellar since 1756. French-inspired classics led by elegant Rubicon, among SA's 1st Bx-style reds.

Méthode cap classique *See* CAP CLASSIQUE.

Miles Mossop Wines Coast ★★★→★★★★ CWG member Miles M's polished bottlings, most named after his family. Latterly wider sourcing, same top quality.

Morgenster Estate Stell ★★★ Historic farm nr Somerset W developed into prime wine and olive estate in early 90s by late Italian industrialist Giulio Bertrand, advised by Pierre Lurton (Cheval Blanc, Bx). Bertrand children continue Old World varieties, styling for red/white/rosé.

Motte, La W Cape ★★→★★★ Elegant estate, winery and cellar door at FRAN owned by Koegelenberg-Rupert family. Classically constructed varietals and blends. Neighbour and sibling Leopard's Leap emphasizes food side of wine match.

Mulderbosch Vineyards W Cape ★→★★★ Reputed US-owned STELL winery and welcoming cellar door with modern, amply fruited CHENIN BL, CAB FR, pair of Bx-style reds, new cherry-earthy PINOT N.

Mullineux & Leeu Passant W Cape ★★★→★★★★ Chris M and US-born wife Andrea transform SWA CHENIN BL, SYRAH and handful of compatible varieties into ambrosial soil-specific varietals, blends, CWG bottlings and *vin de paille*. Leeu Passant portfolio (FRAN-based), incl new own-vine CAB FR plus wider-sourced wines, as sublime. Also v.gd Great Heart (r/w, recently expanded) owned and made by staff.

Mvemve Raats Stell ★★★★ Mzokhona Mvemve, 1st qualified Black winemaker, and Bruwer Raats (RAATS FAMILY) select barrels for forthright, best-of-vintage Bx blend MR de Compostella.

Nederburg Wines W Cape ★→★★★★ One of SA's biggest (2m cases) and best-loved brands, PAARL-based, HEINEKEN BEVERAGES-owned. Top ranges: Two Centuries, Heritage Heroes, Manor House, many purse-pleasers and wine-list fixtures.

Neil Ellis Wines W Cape ★★→★★★★ Pioneer STELL négociant sourcing mostly cooler-grown parcels locally and around w CAPE for masterly site expressions.

Newton Johnson Vineyards Cape SC ★★★→★★★★ Family cellar in UP HEM with acclaimed CHARD, PINOT N. SA's 1st commercial ALBARIÑO also superb.

Northern Cape (N Cape) Largest province and GU in WO scheme. Semi-arid to arid, with temp extremes. *See* SUTHERLAND-KAROO.

Oak Valley Estate Cape SC ★★★→★★★★ Extensive family agribusiness in ELG. Exceptional, fine-boned, single-clone bottlings of CHARD, PINOT N in Tabula Rasa range.

Old Vine Project Groundbreaking initiative aided by businessman/vintner Johann Rupert (ANTHONIJ RUPERT) to locate, catalogue and preserve SA's old vyd blocks (35 yrs+). Certified Heritage Vyd seal on bottle shows planting date.

Olifantsberg Family Vineyards Bre ★★→★★★ Dutch-owned rising star draws on own and area vines for restrained Rhône-style (r/w), CHENIN BL, PINOTAGE.

Olifants River REGION on w coast (c.5750 ha). Warm valley floors gd for organics; cooler sites for fine wine in vaunted Citrusdal Mtn DISTRICT and its WARD, Pie.

Opstal Estate W Cape ★→★★★ One of BRE's quality leaders, family-owned, in mtn amphitheatre. Old-vine CHENIN BL, SEM; new v. fine, floral VERDELHO.

Orange River Cellars N Cape ★→★★★ Vast operation with c.140 grower-owners and 1100-ha vyd on Orange R banks. Increasingly impressive Res bottlings complement the trad speciality, sweet fortified MUSCAT, led by spectacular, spicy 10-yr-old Omstaan XO.

Overarching GU / region *See* GU.

Paarl DISTRICT (c.8500 ha) around historic namesake town with WARDS Agter Paarl, Sim-P, V Pa. Diverse styles, approaches; best results from Med vines (r/w), CHENIN BL, CAB SAUV, PINOTAGE.

Paul Clüver Family Wines Elg ★★→★★★ Area pioneer, family-owned/run estate. Elegant CHARD and PINOT N; also convincing RIES (wood-touched semi-dr and unoaked botrytis).

Porseleinberg Swa ★★★★ BOEKENHOUTSKLOOF's organic vyds/cellar, with superb SYRAH. Handcrafted, incl front label printed on-site by winemaker.

Raats Family Wines Stell ★★★→★★★★ Exquisite CHENIN BL (oaked and not), CAB FR, esp CWG and single-vyd Eden High Density bottlings. Bruwer R and cousin Gavin Bruwer Slabbert also join forces to unearth vinous gems as Bruwer Vintners Vine Exploration Co. *See* MVEMVE RAATS.

Radford Dale Coast ★★→★★★ Thoughtful and dynamic STELL venture with Australian, French, SA and UK shareholders. Land of Hope, Radford Dale, Thirst, Vinum, Winery of Good Hope brands, restrainedly New World in style. Also owns bio vyd/cellar in ELG. Viticulturist Edouard Labeye has own, eponymous GRENACHE BL and N.

Rall Wines Coast ★★★→★★★★ Owner-winemaker and consultant Donovan R has outstanding track record since late 2000s. Initial SWA blends (r/w) since joined by Med varietals (r/w) and CHENIN BL showing same flavoursome understatement. Also vinifies Callender Peak wines (w) from vines (some ungrafted, v. rare) on snowy Ceres Plateau.

Bring on the mutants
Everybody needs to be different. Why grow plain SEM when you could grow mutation Sem Gr? MULLINEUX's The Gris Old Vines Sem is made by Andrea M for the CWG auction (vines also propagated and planted on their Roundstone farm in SWA). Other bottlings of Sem Gr: THORNE & DAUGHTERS' Tin Soldier, JC Wickens' Rooi-Groen Sem, with recent plantings at Ashbourne in HEM, among others. Then there are pink-skinned variants of another white grape, SAUV BL, by CAPE POINT VYDS and CEDERBERG PRIVATE CELLAR, inter alia. Also mutations of black-skinned grapes, such as RALL WINES Cinsault Bl and ArtiSons' The White Cinsault, an intra-block selection.

Region *See* GU.

Restless River Wines U Hem ★★★→★★★★ Wessels and Fourie families' small, thoughtfully run vyd/cellar, as successful with area calling cards CHARD, PINOT N as scarcely planted CAB SAUV, all showing cool-climate minerality.

Reyneke Wines W Cape ★→★★★★ Leading certified bio producer nr STELL. Pure, beguiling CHENIN BL, SAUV BL, CAB SAUV, SYRAH; characterful Vinehugger easy-sippers (r/w, new rosé).

Proposed Karoo-Hoogland region sign of (climate) times: bone-dry, cool, 1000m (3281ft) up.

Robertson Valley Low-rainfall inland DISTRICT with 14 WARDS; c.12,800 ha; lime soils; historically gd CAP CLASSIQUE, CHARD, desserts; more recently SAUV BL, CAB SAUV and SHIRAZ.

Robertson Winery Rob ★→★★★ Consistency, value throughout extended portfolio. Best: Constitution Rd CHARD, SHIRAZ.

Roodekrantz Wines Swa, Paarl, Stell ★★→★★★★ Subtly thrilling collection of mostly CHENIN BL from old-vine grapes rescued from big-brand anonymity. Equally satisfying sibling lineup named Fuselage inspired by cellar's location on family owners' private airfield nr WELL.

Rustenberg Wines Stell ★→★★★★ Barlow family on Simonsberg Mtn nr STELL; gracefulness of cellar complex, gardens and vyds reflected in portfolio based on French classics.

Rust en Vrede Wine Estate W Cape ★→★★★★ Historic STELL farm and winery making powerful, polished reds. Sibling brands owned by Jean Engelbrecht: Afrikaans (trendy CAB SAUV/CINSAULT heritage blend et al); Cirrus (PINOT N expressing elevated Ceres Plateau terroir); Donkiesbaai (all ex-Pie, CHENIN BL v.gd); Guardian Peak (range, plus cellar door for non-estate wines); Stell Res (mostly varietals). Visitor facilities.

Sadie Family Wines, The Oli R, Piek, Stell, Swa ★★★★ Iconic portfolio by revered Eben S. Signature Series: SYRAH blend Columella, multi-variety Palladius (w), both Cape benchmarks. Magnificent Old Vine Series, pure, detailed wines celebrating heritage, incl new mineral Rotsbank from c.40-year-old CHENIN BL on granite.

Saronsberg Cellar W Cape ★★→★★★ Family estate in TUL. Awarded SHIRAZ and Bx/Rhône blends/varietals, incl rare solo ROUSSANNE, bracing CHARD CAP CLASSIQUE.

Savage Wines W Cape ★★★→★★★★ CWG member Duncan S ranges far and wide from CAPE TOWN city base for thrilling, understated wines from mostly Med varieties, CHENIN BL. Assistant Banele Vakele's own label Tembela (r/w) also finely crafted.

Shannon Vineyards Elg ★★★→★★★★ Top MERLOT, also v.gd PINOT N, SAUV BL, SEM, Bx-style white showing area's elegance, freshness. Grown by siblings James and Stuart Downes, vinified by NEWTON JOHNSON.

Sijnn Mal ★★★→★★★★ Pronounced "Sane", DE TRAFFORD co-owner David T and partners' pioneer maritime venture on stony promontory overlooking the Breede River. Distinctive, aromatic blends and Varietal Series with new lush ROUSSANNE.

Silverthorn Wines Rob ★★★→★★★★ Distinguished collection of special-occasions CAP CLASSIQUE (w/rosé) crafted in ROB by CWG member John Loubser. All Brut, mostly CHARD, some PINOT N and, unusually, SHIRAZ and area speciality COLOMBARD.

Simonsig Wine Estate W Cape ★→★★★★ Malan family nr STELL admired for unwavering quality; 1st with CAP CLASSIQUE in 70s, original Brut since joined by sweeter, equally delicious celebrators. Boundary-pushing Med white blends under stand-alone label The Grapesmith now have red sibling, featuring rare-variety MARSELAN.

Solms-Delta W Cape ★★★ Ambitious early 2000s wine-growing, land restitution and community upliftment venture nr FRAN, dormant since 2018, now revitalized by US national Tommy Hall and family. Wine reboot begins brilliantly with serious-yet-swiggable Rhône blends Hiervandaan (r) and Amalie (w).

Spier W Cape ★→★★★★ Major winery and tourist magnet nr STELL. Flagship ranges: 21 Gables, Creative Block, Frans K Smit (honouring cellarmaster, a CWG member); expanding organic lines; pocket-pleasing Signature with new, locally rare ALBARIÑO. All fruit-focused, carefully made, mostly vegan.

Stark-Condé Wines Stell ★★★→★★★★ US-born boutique vintner José Condé in postcard Jonkershoek. Intensity, freshness in CAB SAUV, SYRAH; differentiation/excitement via rarities: field blend (w) and terraced vyd (CHENIN BL).

Steenberg Vineyards W Cape ★★→★★★ GRAHAM BECK'S CONST winery, vyds, chic cellar door; glossy SAUV BL/SEM blend, SAUV BL (still/sp), CAP CLASSIQUE and rare NEBBIOLO.

Stellenbosch University town, demarcated wine DISTRICT (c.12,200 ha) and heart of wine industry – the Napa of SA. Many top estates, esp for reds, tucked into mtn valleys and foothills. All tourist facilities.

Stellenbosch Vineyards Stell ★→★★★ Big-volume winery with impressive, fruit-centred limited releases incl only bottling of SA-developed white grape Therona.

Stellenrust Stell ★→★★★★ Family winery with wide portfolio from trio of own prime STELL sites. Headliner range of magnificent barrel-fermented old-vine CHENIN BL. Partly wider-sourced ArtiSons lineup pushes envelope with, eg., new whole-bunch fermented CINSAULT.

Stellenzicht Wines Coast ★★→★★★ Famous Helderberg Mtn cellar and vyds rejuvenated by Baron Hans von Staff-Reitzenstein, also owner of neighbour Alto Estate and long-time partner in nearby ERNIE ELS. Powerful but not blockbusting CHARD and CAB SAUV, SYRAH (solo, blended).

Storm Wines Hem Rdg, Hem V, U Hem ★★★→★★★★ PINOT N and CHARD specialist Hannes S uniquely expresses three HEM wards in one portfolio with precision and sensitivity. Free-standing label Wild Air spotlights HEM V SAUV BL on shale soil.

Sutherland-Karoo DISTRICT in challenging N CAPE, not to be confused with separate, distant KL K. Only 5 ha under vine, chiefly PINOT N, SHIRAZ, CHARD, nr SA's coldest town, Sutherland.

Swartland COASTAL DISTRICT, c.9600 ha of mostly shy-bearing, unirrigated bush vines producing concentrated, distinctive, fresh wines. Profound influence on winemaking since early 2000s through innovators, eg. SADIE FAMILY.

Testalonga Swa ★★→★★★ Range name El Bandito says it all: Craig Hawkins's natural vinifications defy convention; much respected and loved nonetheless. Earlier/easier Baby Bandito label for hipsters-in-training.

Farewell "Demi-Sec", hello "Nectar". Same sugar-sprinkled bubbly, sounds better.

Thelema Mountain Vineyards W Cape ★★→★★★★ STELL pioneer of SA's modern wine revival, still beacon of quality, consistency (and touch of hedonism, per Rabelais-inspired brand name). Complementary flavours from ELG vyds.

Thorne & Daughters Wines W Cape ★★★→★★★★ Bot R vintners John Thorne Seccombe and wife Tasha's wines, some from v. old vines and heirloom grapes, cerebral yet sensual, expressed with marvellous clarity and refinement.

Tokara W Cape ★★→★★★★ Wine, food, art showcase nr STELL; vyds also in ELG. Gorgeous, elegant Director's Res blends (r/w); Res CHARD, SAUV BL, CAB SAUV.

Trizanne Signature Wines Cape SC ★→★★★★ Female soloists like Trizanne

Barnard still rare. Avid surfer sources from mostly COAST vyds for seriously gd boutique CHARD, SAUV BL (solo/blend), SYRAH. Dawn Patrol brand mostly for export.

Tulbagh Inland DISTRICT (c.860 ha) historically associated with white and CAP CLASSIQUE, latterly also red, esp PINOTAGE, SHIRAZ, some sweet styles.

Tulbagh Mountain Vineyards Tul ★★★ Lately producing single Rhône-style Estate Red from mostly SYRAH planted on extensive Witzenberg Mtn property.

Uva Mira Mountain Vineyards Stell ★★★ Helderberg Mtn eyrie vyds and cellar owned by Toby Venter, CEO of Porsche, Bentley and Lamborghini SA. Leashed power in SYRAH, CHARD, SAUV BL et al.

Van Loggerenberg Wines W Cape ★★→★★★★ PAARL-based Lukas VL star of light-styled, new-wave scene. Top: CHENIN BL, CAB FR; affordable range Break a Leg features v.gd pink CINSAULT. Vinifies most of also-excellent Carinus Family portfolio of mainly Chenin Bl.

Vergelegen Wines Stell ★★★→★★★★ Resources company Anglo-American's historic mansion and gardens, with stylish cellar door at Somerset W. Leashed power in wines from classic French varieties. Deserved WWF-SA Conservation Champion.

Vilafonté W Cape ★★★ Founded by California's Zelma Long and Phil Freese, and local eminence Mike Ratcliffe. Trio of luxurious red blends, vinified in STELL.

Vetkoek ("fat cake", traditional fried bread) paired with wine at Bemind cellar door.

Villiera Wines Over, Stell ★★→★★★★ Respected STELL winery and eco leader founded by Grier family, now in French hands. Exceptional quality/value ratio, esp in famed CAP CLASSIQUE range, featuring new apple-scented demi-sec Pearls of Nectar from CHARD.

Vondeling V Pa ★→★★★ UK-owned, sustainability-focused estate nr PAARL. Eclectic offering covers everything from Bx-style red to pét-nat to vine-dried MUSCAT (sw).

Walker Bay Highly regarded maritime district (c.1000 ha) with standout CHARD, SAUV BL, PINOT N, SHIRAZ in Bot R, HEM, Springfontein Rim, Stanford Foothills, Sunday's Glen wards.

Ward *See* GU.

Warwick Wine Estate W Cape ★→★★★★ US-owned tourist drawcard on STELL fringe. Classic French varieties plus PINOTAGE yield rich yet harmonious and fresh wines.

Waterford Estate W Cape ★→★★★ Ord family's Tuscany-inspired winery nr STELL, with suave, multi-faceted flagship red blend The Jem, one of several themed winetasting options at stylish courtyard cellar door. Winemaker Mark le Roux's freewheeling namesake brand worth a try.

Waterkloof W Cape ★→★★★ British wine merchant Paul Boutinot's organic vyds, cellar on exposed hilltop nr Somerset W. Flurry of recent additions to single-vyd apex range Waterkloof continues with new perfumed Bx-style red, aptly named after wind god Boreas.

Wellington Warm-climate DISTRICT (c.3800 ha) bordering PAARL and SWA. Growing reputation for CHENIN BL, PINOTAGE, SHIRAZ, red blends.

Western Cape (W Cape) Most s province and dominant GU in WO system, with 120 of 140 official appellations.

Worcester Sibling DISTRICT (c.6300 ha) to ROB and BRE in Breede R basin. Largely bulk produce for export, but some fine wines by mostly family estates and a dynamic joint venture named Stettyn Family Vyds, owned by local growers and an empowerment company.

WO (Wine of Origin) "AOP" but without French restrictions. Certifies vintage, variety, area of origin and, on opt-in basis, sustainable production.

The lure and allure of Pinot Noir

Is Pinot Noir now the world's favourite red wine style?

I'm choosing my words carefully. It may or may not be the world's favourite red wine. But that style is infusing nearly all reds now. A couple of decades ago, we saw the Cabernetization (good word?) of reds, including burgundy. That meant more extraction of tannins and colour from the grapes, more oak, more structure. Now we're seeing the Pinotization of everything. Look at Garnacha/Grenache: what used to be powerful and tannic, often overripe, has now lightened and become aromatic, fresh and balanced. Weight for its own sake is no longer fashionable; and Pinot Noir has come into its own. It is, for many drinkers, the epitome of elegance. It has complexity and elusive, indefinable perfumes; it unwinds sinuously and silkily on the palate and lingers seductively. It can also be maddeningly disappointing.

It took far longer for winemakers around the world to make really good Pinot than it did for them to make really good Cabernet. For years, Pinot was the holy grail: legendary and demanding. But one by one they got there. There are now lovely Pinots being made across the globe – from the Sonoma Coast to the Adelaide Hills, by way of the Crouch Valley.

That's in Essex, eastern England, by the way. Which brings me to my next point: climate change has brought Pinot into its comfort zone everywhere. And it is in danger of taking it out the other side: Burgundy is having to find ways to row back on ripeness, in order to keep producing the sort of flavours we recognize as burgundian. It's not as forgiving a grape as Chardonnay or Cabernet.

Nor, as those who lay it down for years know, is it as reliable. It can disappoint; perhaps never live up to its early promise. It can be unrewardingly closed if you open it too young, and annoyingly tired if you leave it too late.

And yet we love it. The next pages will seek to explore the essence of this fascinating grape, starting with a look at what exactly it is.

Is Pinot Noir just one grape?

"Exactly" is a word to be used with care when Pinot Noir is involved. It is one of the oldest grapes we have: its morphology is said to be similar to that of wild vines, but no specific genetic link to local wild vines in its supposed birthplace, the Île-de-France, has been established.

It first appears in records in the 13th century but is quite likely 2000 years old, that estimate being based on the enormous number of mutations it has produced. Pinot Gris and Pinot Blanc are colour mutations of Pinot Noir: according to the standard DNA markers that are used, they are genetically the same variety as Pinot Noir. Pinot Meunier, Pinot Noir Précoce and Pinot Noir Teinturier are all mutations of Pinot Noir.

And that's before you get into the many commercially available clones of Pinot Noir – a clone being a cutting of a single chosen vine, propagated thereafter in a nursery – or the hundreds of chance mutations to be found in Burgundy vineyards. Such mutations, such clones, can be earlier or later budding and ripening; smaller or larger berried, more or less prone to this or that disease, more or less upright in growing habit, more or less tannic, or aromatic, or with higher or lower sugar levels: most Burgundy growers like to have a mix. Nursery-grown clones are more predictable but more limited in their variety; besides, they cost money. So growers take cuttings themselves of favoured vines where they have noted one characteristic or another – a method of propagation called massal selection. In newer growing countries, this might be more difficult: importing vine cuttings, even those from the most distinguished vineyards, is difficult or impossible, and nursery-grown clones with a nice tidy identification number attached are the only way of planting a vineyard.

But if Pinot can be so varied, and if some high-yielding, big-berried vine giving lots of watery juice can be just as much Pinot Noir as a small-berried vine yielding small quantities of intensely perfumed juice, and if Pinot Blanc is the same vine as Pinot Noir even though it might not look like it, you might well ask this: what does a mutation have to do to be acknowledged as a separate variety?

It's a fair question. The answer – from ampelographers who study grape varieties – is always this: when you look at plant DNA, you look at particular markers. If these are the same, it's the same variety. If enough of them are different, it's a different variety. How many is enough is something they tend to be vague about. I could sum up their replies over the years as, "Well, we take a view."

You see what I mean about the word "exactly"? We are dealing with shifting sands here. These shifting sands are part of the elusiveness of Pinot, part of the reason why it took so long to make good Pinot in different regions of the world. Those DNA markers might be key to an ampelographer, but to a grower, all the other differences in DNA between this Pinot vine and that can be the difference between complexity and simplicity, between great wine and good-enough wine. The choice of clone isn't everything in wine-growing – and some growers say that the vine adapts to its surroundings so much that, after a couple of decades or more, it's not very important at all. But in a new country, a better clone can be a stepping stone to better Pinot. It was in Australia, to name but one.

But how did it happen? How did growers learn how to handle this most fickle of grapes? And why did they bother? That's next.

The struggle for style

You can find good, very good and sometimes great Pinot Noir in many countries now. A couple of decades ago, you'd have been hard put to find real excitement in many places outside Burgundy. Why? How difficult can be it be?

And here's another question: how many Pinots from around the world, even now, would make people fall in love with Pinot Noir if burgundy didn't exist?

I'm not saying that burgundy is the only Pinot worth drinking – far from it. I'm saying that this was a winemaker-led movement, not a consumer-driven movement. Not-terribly-good Pinot, learning-curve Pinot, is not a lesser, lighter version of great Pinot. Usually it's dull, or earthy, or jammy, or green. It would not make you fall in love with Pinot.

Even now, a lot of Pinot settles for being inoffensive: soft, fairly aromatic, quite pretty, anonymous.

The makers of those learning-curve Pinots had to be determined; they had to believe that if they persevered for long enough, they would succeed in making something of which a Pinot-lover – a burgundy-lover – would approve.

Burgundy was always the target. Chardonnay could succeed with a fat, buttery style that was resolutely not burgundian, even if its starting points were burgundian techniques – but nobody gave

Pinot that leeway. Why not? Because few of those learning-curve Pinots were good enough to offer an alternative style. Burgundy continued to be the gold standard.

Not only does Burgundy offer very particular conditions, but it can be surprisingly hard to pin down exactly what matters, if you are trying to replicate those conditions elsewhere. It has chalk, but it also has clay. Clay comes in different kinds: some have water-holding ability and some don't. Some shrink in droughts and swell in rain, and some don't. Clay can be fertile or infertile; it can be a hero, or it can be a villain. And much depends on the local climate. Imitating the conditions of the Côte d'Or, which is itself a geological mosaic, is tricky.

If you start from climate, it's not much easier. Yes, the Côte d'Or is certainly cool, and it was a challenge to find spots in the New World that were cool enough and ticked enough of the other boxes without being too frost-prone. Growers tended to be a bit nervous of replicating the Côte d'Or's susceptibility to frost, or indeed hail. Carneros was an early leader; Chile's Casablanca, Australia's Adelaide Hills and Mornington Peninsula, NZ's Central Otago and Martinborough, and Oregon's Dundee Hills and Willamette Valley followed. Germany had been growing Pinot, under the name of Spätburgunder, for aeons, but it had to move from its early pale sweetness to something more substantial.

The key, in the end, was who you learned from. In the 80s, the internationally influential University of California, Davis, and Australia's Roseworthy College knew about warm climates but knew less about cool climates. The advice on clones was often wrong. The official view was that Pinot could never work in Australia. So Pinot became relegated to determined eccentrics – who ignored the "experts" and looked directly to Burgundy.

And that was how they learned how to make Pinot: by drinking a lot of great burgundy, by working their socks off in Burgundy domaines, by picking it apart and putting it back together. Only by ignoring the expert advice, and going straight to the source, did they understand how to handle Pinot in their own, often rather different conditions.

Are there now different styles of Pinot from different places? Insofar as Pinot is very good at transmitting its terroir into the glass, yes. Marlborough has a different style to Central Otago; Santa Rita is different to Sonoma Coast. Pfalz Pinot is way better than Alsace Pinot, although it's really just an extension of the same vineyard area. They are Pinot with different accents. But they all look towards burgundy.

But then burgundy itself is not just one thing. And we'll look into that next.

The weight question

Should Pinot Noir be rich or light? If your answer to that is "It depends," then you're right. It depends, most of all, on fashion.

Terroir? Yes, of course that matters. Some crus in Burgundy give lighter, more delicate wines than others: Chambolle-Musigny is naturally more delicate than Pommard. But back in the bad old days when burgundies reflected not so much their terroir as consumer expectations, Pommard would be beefed up to taste like "proper" Pommard, Chambolle adjusted in a different way. The chunky, bone-setter wines of the Rhône and North Africa found a ready market in the merchants' cellars of Burgundy. And when all that changed, in the 80s, burgundy-lovers were often outraged to discover that their much-adored wines were suddenly lighter in colour and weight and more aromatic – and they didn't taste or look like "proper" burgundy at all.

A little later, when weight and extraction were what everybody seemed to want from red wine, techniques changed again. Back in the 90s, Burgundy had a 200%-new-oak moment (racking from new oak into more new oak). That fashion faded quickly. New-oak aromas and flavours are seldom sought in Pinot now. Oak is more subtle, and used more subtly. Whole-cluster fermentation has lasted rather longer.

This is what it sounds like: whole bunches in the fermentation vat, stalks and all. Of course, the stems have to be ripe; adding unripe tannins would be disastrous. It adds spice notes and slightly reduces acidity, but it adds freshness. The beauty of whole-cluster is that, yes, it can add weight and tannin if you want your wine to be more imposing; but it can also be used to frame a delicate wine and keep all that delicacy at the forefront. All depends on how you use it: with lots of extraction or with minimal extraction; 100% whole-cluster or just a bit; whole bunches in the top of the vat or the bottom, or layered like a lasagne – all have different effects.

You might think that this reflects an instinctive desire on the part of winemakers to turn what we now think of as an intrinsically light wine into a bigger, heftier one. There can be an element of that sometimes. But generally, I think it comes from seeing that a vineyard can make serious wines, and trying to encourage that – without swamping the very lightness that appeals in the first place. Pinot can be swamped, quite easily. Too much structure – be that from extraction, oak, or whatever – can give the impression of all work and not much fun. To my mind, Pinot should never feel heavy. Even the most serious Pinot should wear its weight effortlessly, with ease and charm. It should be fresh and lively, singing and dancing.

It might, in the case of the greatest wines, be a rather stately dance, but it should not – ever – tread on your toes.

And that's not always a matter of ripeness. Riper wines are not necessarily bigger. It's to do with the way flavour develops in the grapes: with a shorter growing season you tend to get red-fruit flavours, because those are what Pinot gets first. Then, after ripeness of around 12.5–13% potential alcohol, later in the season, the black-fruit flavours start to kick in. That last point seems to be when the vine starts to go into dormancy, so you need a long growing season to get those savoury, dark-fruited flavours. Simple wines have juicy immediateness; more serious wines are less about simple fruitiness and more about layered detail. Weightier, yes, but not that much more.

Climate is another matter, and a very topical one. We'll look at that next.

Terroir and climate change

Even on France's Côte d'Or, that sweet spot for Pinot, there is a super-sweet spot, a place where climate, slope and soil come together in as near to ideal balance as you will find. It's the mid-slope – and with climate change, it has moved slightly further up the slope than it was.

It wasn't so long ago that red burgundy was moving into its comfort zone, climate-wise; now it seems in danger of moving out of it, the other side. The search for ripeness has become a search for freshness.

This is affecting all aspects of wine-growing. Until quite recently, viticulture was focused on achieving maximum ripeness. It follows that there are lots of adjustments – many of them small in themselves – that can be made in the quest for freshness. Different rootstocks, different massal selections and clones, greater shading, ploughing at different times, pruning at different times – all these can help.

The current obsession in Burgundy is berry size: if you let the vine grow shoots as it wants, instead of trimming them, you get more open clusters and smaller berries, and thus less disease and more concentrated flavours. Whole-cluster fermentation (*see* p.326) has gone from being a fashion to being a widely used and subtle tool, though it can reduce acidity so is used with care.

In Champagne, you'll see houses choosing Pinots from the north of the Montagne de Reims rather than the traditional Grands Crus like Aÿ, Bouzy, or Ambonnay, for greater freshness. And while still red Coteaux Champenois is still a rarity, it's less rare than it was.

In the rest of the world, where growers are still identifying their best Pinot sites, they have to balance climate and soil. Limestone will give leaner, brisker wines; clay, more weight and opulence. Hamilton Russell says that, in its newish Oregon vineyards, it gets purity of fruit

effortlessly, but that it has to work for structure; in South Africa, at Hermanus, it's the opposite. In Australia's Mornington Peninsula, there is ocean on three sides, so it's naturally cool and growers don't need to look for altitude. In the Yarra Valley and Adelaide Hills, there's a bit more warming from climate change, and they are having to pick slightly earlier. But in Australia generally, it's difficult to get the pH and acidity right without "adjustment". (That's acidification to you and me. Done gently it can be fine. Overdone, acidification can taste like razor blades.) Germany's finest often come from warm Pfalz, sheltered by the Haardt mountains. Chile's newest Pinots come from the far south, in Bío-Bío, where it's properly cool, and the wines can have real precision.

What this adds up to is partly an adjustment in how we see Pinot and perhaps an adjustment in where we get it from. Pinot Noir is not elastic in terms of climate. Red burgundy is, more years than not now, opulent rather than crunchy. You might like that style, or you might not. But most drinkers would view 14.5% abv in Pinot as too high – and that level can be reached now on the Côte d'Or.

Not surprisingly, Burgundians are starting to sniff around Essex's Crouch Valley. Many other places too. But the (tiny) Crouch Valley has clay, gravel, good exposure and plenty of light since it's so near the sea. It's not going to take over the world, but it's a small example of the sort of spots that will come to the fore in future years.

In the past, the availability of good Pinot was limited by the difficulty of growing it and making it outside Burgundy – lack of the right expertise, you might say. Now there's far greater understanding of it. There's less learning-curve Pinot about and more highly enjoyable Pinot. But inexpensive Pinot – that's another matter. We'll take a look at that next.

Can there be good cheap Pinot?

A colleague of mine, many years ago, was perpetually on the edge of writing a book titled *Affordable Burgundy*. He never wrote it, partly perhaps because so little of what was affordable then was good. Nowadays you couldn't write it because while much more burgundy is good, so little could be considered affordable.

Pinot just isn't cheap. Burgundy prices have rocketed in the past few years and show no sign of stopping, and that's because of demand. The Côte d'Or is a small area, and the top vineyards can be tiny, and divided between numerous owners. There might be just one barrel of Grand Cru Clos de Prix Énorme from Domaine Très Célèbre. That's 288 bottles, for which consumers and collectors worldwide are competing: it will sell. (In Bordeaux, where quantities are much bigger, it became clear with the 2022 vintage that price does matter, and there is a limit to what collectors think is reasonable.)

There's a knock-on effect: if Grands Crus go up, so do Premiers Crus, and so do village wines and basic Bourgogne Rouge. But demand is softer at this level, and if you fancy going to a wine merchant and saying, I want to drink red burgundy, they will always have stocks of village wines and some Premiers Crus to get you going. They won't be cheap, but they will be available. And they will be very good. Burgundy is being made and grown better now than probably at any time in its history.

But what about the rest of the world? Other regions don't have the same constraints; surely there should be affordable Pinot elsewhere? Only up to a point. Yes, you can find very cheap Pinot in California, but it will not make you fall in love with Pinot. It will probably be jammy and sweetish, perhaps with some oak chips as a stiffener. If you want those aristocratic perfumes and that graceful precision, you have to pay for it – in California or anywhere else.

Chile has some inexpensive and good Pinots, especially from Cono Sur, which has put a great deal of research and effort into this grape. But here, too, you'll see a noticeable improvement in quality if you move up the scale.

The reason is that Pinot is a very finicky grape. It's inelastic in climate, as we've seen, and it requires particular conditions in the vineyard. It's prone to disease. It needs a lot of care in the vineyard. There are lots of different clones, and those that give high yields do not give the best wine. It also needs care in the cellar: fermentation temperatures, the amount of oak, the choice of individual barrel. That precision, those aromas, don't happen by accident. To get the best out of wonderful Pinot grapes, you have to know exactly what you're doing.

Making great Pinot is a mix of detailed craftsmanship and intuition. It just isn't suited to mass production.

When you're buying Pinot, look for the producer first. Don't ever say, Oh, Mornington Peninsula (or Santa Rita, or wherever) is famous for Pinot, therefore anything from there will be good. That doesn't apply anywhere. A good producer's basic Pinot might include young vines from higher-status vineyards, or odds and ends that don't make the cut elsewhere; such wines can be great value. And you will always get a better wine from a producer who knows what they're doing than from one planting Pinot because it's become a cash cow but who doesn't know or care what to do next.

Paying more doesn't guarantee more complexity or more fascination. Only the producer, on a great terroir, can do that. One reason why Pinot becomes so expensive is because of all the slightly disappointing bottles you buy in your search for perfection – but it has always been like that. A pessimist would say there are now more ways of being faintly disappointed; but Pinot leads one on and fills one's cellar.

Which brings us to the question of when to drink it, and that's where we are going next.

How does Pinot age?

To taste Pinot Noir young – at the Burgundy primeur tastings, perhaps, where a lot of the wines are cask samples – is to fall in love. The aromas, the spice, the cherry fruit, the incense notes, the touches of flowers, of earth, of stones: there is hardly anything in a bottle that is more wonderful.

A Premier Cru wine from a top producer can bowl you over. But you then look at the possibly astonishing figure that is quoted on the list for a case of six bottles (ex-cellars) and start totting up the additions of tax and shipping, and then swallow hard and think, Well...

Fast-forward a few months. Your wine has arrived! The doorbell rang this morning, and there it is: a neat box of pristine bottles. But do they say "drink me", or do they say "keep me"?

This is where Pinot can get really annoying. There never was a more disobliging grape. It can close up when it's first bottled – well, that's reasonable, and expected. But does it ever again express that first fine careless rapture of the cask sample?

No, it doesn't. That early exuberance is the flush of youth, and by the time it's been bottled and shipped, it's not quite as young anymore. It will change – it changes all the time. Add to that the differences between vintages, terroirs and producers, and you have a grape for which peak drinking is almost impossible to predict. This is tricky if you only have six bottles of it. The usual advice for wine available in larger quantities – open a bottle at the beginning of the expected drinking window, and then open another a year later, and so on until you reckon it's as good as it's going to get – is profoundly unhelpful when you don't have much of it.

So here are some suggestions. First, second and always, talk to your merchant. They have tasted other vintages and probably been to the property, and they will have a pretty good idea.

The simpler the wine, the earlier you can and should drink it, of course. For the simplest wines – Bourgogne Rouge or the equivalent from elsewhere – I would give the wine maybe six months, maybe a year from bottling, and then try.

If a Pinot is not intended to be aged, you should probably drink it within four to five years max – usually. With Pinot, there are exceptions to every generalization, so bear that in mind for the following generalizations. Village burgundy? Give it five years, and then more according to the producer and site. Premiers Crus will probably need eight or more; some Premiers Crus are pretty substantial, others less so. And it's worth pointing out that we don't really understand yet whether the very solar vintages of recent years will come around faster or take longer. It's a moving target.

Grands Crus should be given plenty of time – at least ten years. Given how much you've paid for them, you want to taste them at their peak; and this is where you can really nag your merchant for up-to-date information. How is this Grand Cru from this grower tasting at the moment?

If you thought Burgundy was complicated, what about the picture elsewhere? Trying to decide the burgundian equivalent of a Central Otago or Sonoma Coast Pinot will only take you so far. The vast majority of Pinots from elsewhere can be drunk young – it's worth remembering that. But a producer's top crus may well blossom with ten years or more in bottle, becoming silky and perfumed with undergrowth and spices, mushrooms and scented leather. You lose those incense and cherry notes of youth, and you gain layers and layers of complexity. Ideally.

And for Pinot in fizz, the picture is different again.

Pinot Noir in fizz

In a sense, this is hidden Pinot. It's not visibly red and it's seldom bottled as a single variety. Usually it seems a bit mad to blend Pinot – why go to all that trouble and then blend it away? – but this is the acceptable face of Pinot blends. It's more than the sum of its parts.

As an aside, why would you not then make still blends of Pinot and Chardonnay? Because it wouldn't be the same. If you want a still version, buy a sparkling one and let it go flat. Much of the character of good fizz comes from the second fermentation in the bottle and the ageing on the lees, which produce many, many flavours that would not otherwise be there.

The Pinot flavours are transformed by the process, but they come through as weight and red-fruit flavours – how pronounced these are depends on how much Pinot there is in the blend. The classic blend is Chardonnay, Pinot Noir and Pinot Meunier, in different proportions according to the wish of the blender and the available base wines. Chardonnay gives elegance, energy and drive, and Pinot Noir gives weight on the mid-palate and finish. Pinot Meunier – which we are otherwise ignoring here for reasons of space – gives immediate fruit and lushness. Sparkling wines made only from Pinot are weightier, sometimes a bit chunky; they need a light hand and the right base wines if they are to have elegance. And in pink sparkling, Pinot has

a double role to play, because it gives the colour too. Usually that's done via blending: a small percentage of red wine is added to the blend. The alternative – macerating the juice on the red skins until the colour is right – is fiddly and makes it more difficult to have consistency of colour from year to year.

What has happened in Champagne, which means that other regions have followed or will follow, is that Pinot Noir intended for red blending wine is not just from grapes that happened to get riper. It is planted and grown specifically for red wine, using different clones in selected sites, and picked and vinified with particular flavours in mind. It's that sort of detail that has created the current golden age for Champagne. It has to be the right vines in the right spot, even for the roughly 10% of the blend that is red. Pinot destined to be pressed off its skins and made as white has to be at optimum ripeness; so does Pinot destined to be made red. And they are not interchangeable.

You might think, especially in a cool climate like southern England, that it would be easy: if you want to make still red Pinot but it doesn't get ripe enough, press it for white and make it into sparkling. But it can have too much flavour for sparkling. The wine will be clumsy, unbalanced. Pinot for sparkling must be grown as carefully as Pinot for still: the right clone in the right place, picked at the right moment. That means wines of precision and poise that can age for years and years.

Pinot Noir with food

This is the fun bit, with few complications. Suddenly, Pinot becomes thoroughly easy and obliging. About time, you might say.

Pinot as it is today – with silky tannins, subtle fruit and that lovely fresh ripeness – goes with almost anything. Not desserts. Not oysters. But just about any meat is good, up to and including game; cheese is a natural; even fish, especially salmon (though not smoked or cured), if the tannins in the wine are light enough and the other flavours on the plate permit.

So we can afford to be picky. How would you show off your probably pricey bottles? Game birds like partridge, pheasant, or grouse, in ascending order of flavour, are ideal. Venison will suit bigger wines, though with a really flavoursome venison casserole, perhaps one should edge more towards Syrah. Otherwise, casseroles are a natural match for Pinot, the texture of the wine matching that of the sauce. Pork in all its manifestations is terrific with Pinot: pulled pork, slow-cooked and juicy; ham or gammon, straightforward or with cheese – tartiflette is very good with Pinot; charcuterie too. And then chicken, turkey, or goose. A Christmas goose with a good bottle of Pinot is wonderful, but only if your guests appreciate what they're getting.

Take the meat away, and Pinot is still happy. Root vegetables work well, especially beetroot; you'll often find a beetroot note in the wine, as well. Potato dishes, mushrooms too; but I would draw the line at tomatoes. Mediterranean-type vegetable dishes probably won't flatter Pinot, but lentils and beans will. In the food section at the start of the book, you'll find specific ideas, but it's the silky tannins of Pinot that make it so versatile. The lowish acidity that is the result of warm summers is the only thing to watch: anything that needs acidity in wine might not go as well with Pinot now as it might have in the past.

And if anything in this supplement has encouraged you to try more Pinot – enjoy it.